CHINA

LINKING MARKETS FOR GROWTH

CHINA

LINKING MARKETS FOR GROWTH

Ross Garnaut and Ligang Song (eds)

E PRESS

Asia Pacific Press
The Australian National University

SOCIAL SCIENCES ACADEMIC PRESS (CHINA)

Co-published by ANU E Press and Asia Pacific Press
The Australian National University
Canberra ACT 0200 Australia
Email: anuepress@anu.edu.au
This title available online at http://epress.anu.edu.au/chinalink_citation.html

Asia Pacific Press
Crawford School of Economics and Government
ANU College of Asia and the Pacific
The Australian National University
Canberra ACT 0200 Australia
Ph: 61-2-6125 0178 Fax: 61-2-6125 0767
Website: www.asiapacificpress.com

Co-published with SOCIAL SCIENCES ACADEMIC PRESS (CHINA) under the China Book International scheme. This scheme supports co-publication of works with international publishers.

National Library of Australia Cataloguing in Publication entry

China linking markets for growth.

Bibliography.
Includes index.
ISBN 9780731538133 (pbk.).
ISBN 9781921313387 (online)

1. Free enterprise - China. 2. International business enterprises - China. 3. Labour market - China. 4. Energy consumption - China. 5. China - Economic conditions. 6. China - Commercial policy. I. Garnaut, Ross. II. Song, Ligang.

338.900951

Cover design: Annie Di Nallo Design

Contents

Tables

Figures

Symbols used in tables

..	not available
n.a.	not applicable
-	zero
.	insignificant

Abbreviations

ADB	Asian Development Bank
ADF	augmented Dickey-Fuller test
APEC	Asia Pacific Economic Cooperation
ASEAN	Association of Southeast Asian Nations
BBA	British Bankers Association
BECZ	Bordered Economic Cooperative Zones
BIS	Bank for International Settlements
BP	British Petroleum Global Limited
CAAC	Civil Aviation Administration of China
CAD	comparative advantage-defying
CAF	comparative advantage-following
CASS	Chinese Academy of Social Sciences
CFETS	China Foreign Exchange Trading System
CHIBOR	China inter-bank offer rate
CNY	Chinese yuan
CPI	consumer price index
CSEZ	China Special Economic Zone
CSIS	Centre for Strategic and International Studies
CSRC	China Securities Regulatory Commission
DFID	Department for International Development (UK)
EDZ	Economic Development Zone
EIU	Economist Intelligence Unit
EPZ	Export Processing Zone
ETDZ	Economic and Technological Development Zone
FDI	foreign direct investment
FTA	Free Trade Agreement
FTZ	Free Tariff/Trade Zone
GATS	General Agreement on Trade in Services
GDP	gross domestic product
GLS	generalised least squares
GTAP	Global Trade Analysis Project
Hibor	Hong Kong inter-bank offer rate
HRS	Household Registration System
HSBC	Hong Kong and Shanghai Banking Corporation
HTDZ	High and New Technology Development Zone
HRS	Household Registration System (*hukou*)
ICBC	Industrial and Commercial Bank of China

IRF impulse response functions
IMF International Monetary Fund
IPO initial public offering
Libor London inter-bank offer rate
MII Ministry of Electronic Industries
MW Maddala-Wu test
NBS National Bureau of Statistics
NDF non-delivarable forward
NGO non-government organisation
NAFTA North American Free Trade Agreement
NDRC National Development and Reform Commission
NERI National Economic Research Institute
NIE newly industrialised economy
NPL non-performing loans
NRA nominal rates of assistance
OECD Organisation for Economic Co-operation and Development
OLG overlapping generation model
PBC People's Bank of China
PCAM Principal Component Analysis Method
PPP purchasing power parity
PRC People's Republic of China
QFII Qualified Foreign Insitutional Investor
REER real effective exchange rates
RMB renminbi
RPI retail price index
SCE state-controlled enterprise
SEZ special economic zone
SHIBOR Shanghai inter-bank offer rate
SIC former Soviet Union, India and China
SITC Standard International Trade Classification
SME small and medium enterprise
SOE state-owned enterprise
TAA Trade Adjustment Assistance program
TRIMs Trade-Related Investment Measures
UNCTAD United Nations Conference on Trade and Development
USTR United States Trade Representative
VAR vector autoregression
VAT value added tax
WTO World Trade Organization

Contributors

Chunlai Chen — Crawford School of Economics and Government, The Australian National University, Canberra.

Min Chen — State University of New York at Albany, New York.

Zhao Chen — China Center for Economic Studies, Fudan University, Shanghai.

Yang Du — Division of Labour and Human Capital Institute of Population and Labour Economics, Chinese Academy of Social Sciences, Beijing.

Fang Cai — Division of Labour and Human Capital Institute of Population and Labour Economics, Chinese Academy of Social Sciences, Beijing.

Christopher Findlay — School of Economics, University of Adelaide, Adelaide.

Gang Fan — National Economic Research Institute, China Reform Foundation (NERI-China), Beijing.

Ross Garnaut — Division of Economics, Research School of Pacific and Asian Studies and the China Economy and Business Program, Crawford School of Economics and Government, The Australian National University, Canberra.

Jane Golley — School of Economics, College of Business and Economics, The Australian National University, Canberra.

Nicolaas Groenewold — Department of Economics, The University of Western Australia, Perth.

Qihan Gui — Employment and Social Security Research Center, Fudan University, Shanghai.

Jikun Huang — Center for Chinese Agricultural Policy of the Chinese Academy of Sciences, Beijing.

Yiping Huang — Citigroup Global Markets Asia Limited, based in Hong Kong, and The Australian National University.

Roy Chun Lee — Taiwan WTO Centre, Chung Hua Institution for Economic Research, Taipei, Taiwan.

Kunwang Li — School of Economics, Nankai University, Tianjin.

Justin Yifu Lin — China Center for Economic Research, Peking University, Beijing.

Yu Liu — Center for Chinese Agricultural Policy of the Chinese Academy of Sciences, Beijing.

Ming Lu — School of Economics, Fudan University, Shanghai.

Guonan Ma — Representative Office for Asia and the Pacific of the Bank for International Settlements, Hong Kong.

Will Martin — World Bank, Washington, DC.

Robert N. McCauley — Representative Office for Asia and the Pacific of the Bank for International Settlements, Hong Kong.

Huw McKay — Westpac Institutional Bank, based in Sydney.

Xin Meng — Division of Economics, Research School of Pacific and Asian Studies, The Australian National University, Canberra.

Mari Pangestu — Centre for Strategic and International Studies (CSIS), Jakarta.

Scott Rozelle is with Stanford University, California.

Ted Rule — Da Zheng Yuan International Capital Limited, based in Shenzhen.

Ligang Song — Crawford School of Economics and Government and the China Economy and Business Program, The Australian National University, Canberra.

Rod Tyers — School of Economics, College of Business and Economics, The Australian National University, Canberra.

Xiaolu Wang — National Economic Research Institute, China Reform Foundation, Beijing.

Wei Zhang— School of Economics, Cambridge University, Cambridge.

Wing Thye Woo — Brookings Institution, Washington, DC, University of California–Davis and Central University of Finance and Economics, Beijing.

Geng Xiao — Brookings Institution, Washington, DC, Brookings-Tsinghua Centre in the School of Public Policy and Management, Tsinghua University, Beijing, and the University of Hong Kong, Hong Kong.

Hengpeng Zhu — Economic Research Institute of the Chinese Academy of Social Sciences, Beijing.

Xingjun Zhao — School of Economics, Nankai University, Tianjin.

Changbao Zhao — Research Center of Rural Economy, Ministry of Agriculture, Beijing.

Nansheng Bai — School of Agricultural Economy and Rural Development, Renmin University, Beijing.

Yu Sheng — Crawford School of Economics, The Australian National University, Canberra.

Lijian Sun — School of Economics, Fudan University, Shanghai.

Shengxing Zhang — School of Economics, Fudan University, Shanghai.

Acknowledgments

The China Economy and Business Program gratefully acknowledges the financial support for China Update 2007 from the Australian government's development agency, AusAID, and the assistance provided by Rio Tinto through the Rio Tinto-ANU China Partnership.

1

Linking markets for Chinese growth

Ross Garnaut

The world is in its fifth year of extraordinarily strong economic growth and Chinese economic growth is at its centre. Strong growth with low to moderate inflation and historically low real interest rates is the global norm in 2007.

The linking of markets has been a key to accelerated and sustained growth in China and its transmission to the global economy. The beginnings of the use of markets at the dawn of Chinese reform 29 years ago triggered what turned out to be a long-term lift in the rate of economic growth. The span of time joining the present to the decisive political events that set reform and opening to the outside world in motion in December 1978 is now as long as the whole life of Maoist central planning. Since the late 1970s, Chinese domestic markets for goods, services, capital and labour have been linked more and more closely, under the pressures of market opportunity that have been created by expanded reform. Chinese economic interaction with the global community proceeded alongside the expansion of domestic markets, helping to drive the domestic processes. Chinese entry into the World Trade Organization (WTO) in November 2001 helped—most importantly through the changes in domestic policies and attitudes that accompanied it—to maintain momentum in international integration.

Chinese international trade and capital flows have grown more rapidly than domestic output or expenditure throughout the reform era. This has had large effects on economic development far beyond China's borders. Driven by relentless expansion of Chinese demand, global commodity prices—the export mainstays of the poorer developing economies—have reached and remained at levels in real terms that are higher than they have ever been for comparably long periods, without upsetting the strong trajectory of non-inflationary growth in China or the rest of the world (Garnaut and Song 2006). The flow of capital from China has helped to hold real interest rates at historically low levels all over the world, despite unprecedentedly high budget deficits in the United States. This has been important in reconciling high levels of investment and growth with moderate inflation through a period of exceptionally strong global expansion.

Within China—supported by the beneficent international environment, and driving it—growth in the past year has lifted a notch, and with it investment, real incomes of most workers and most people, and domestic asset values.

The widening reach of markets and the associated rapid growth has forced structural change in established institutions and patterns of production, resource allocation and income distribution throughout the Chinese economy. Inevitably, this has been associated with political tensions; however, the sustained strong growth so far has been less and less problematic as the years have passed.

Wise observers continue to note that China will face challenges in adapting its political superstructure to the changes in society that accompany sustained rapid growth. The wisest note that for the time being the growth in incomes and wealth is a salve for many wounds, and that eventual change might not necessarily take forms that are familiar in detail to citizens of industrialised countries.

The most challenging questions about the sustainability of growth today come from China's relations with the international economy. The combination of the emergence of China as a large economy on a world scale and deepening market linkages to the global economy means that change in China is felt as pressure on resources and pressure for structural change in the rest of the world. This has made the institutions and policies through which China interacts with the global economy a matter of intense interest for people everywhere.

The sharpest point of contention in China's external economic relations at present is the foreign exchange value of the renminbi.[1] Exchange rate appreciation accelerated in early 2007 against the US dollar, but remained gradual to the point of exasperation to those who looked for this to be the mechanism for correction of payments surpluses. Exports continue to grow strongly—and imports moderately—as productivity growth outweighs the effects on international competitiveness of rising labour costs and currency appreciation. This raised tensions with the United States. Less obvious to those in the international community who regret the scale of Chinese current surpluses are the massive purchases of Western financial instruments, especially US official securities, which underpin contemporary global stability and growth by keeping real interest rates well below what they would otherwise be. Woo and Xiao (Chapter 4) caution about the consequences of US policymakers getting what they wish for in the way of large reductions in the Chinese trade and current account surpluses. Any fracture in China's trade or payments relations with the international system that emerged from industrialised countries' political responses to Chinese surpluses would threaten prosperity through this financial as well as real economy mechanisms.

A rapidly emerging point of contention is China's contribution to the global warming problem. China is still a relatively small contributor to the accumulation of greenhouse gases in the atmosphere, which began with the acceleration of human use of fossil fuels accompanying the emergence of modern industrial activity 200 years ago. The problem has crept up on the world—without market processes automatically generating a corrective response—because the costs of greenhouse gas emissions are external to the calculations of any firm or household undertaking activities that release them into the atmosphere. Stern (2007) has commented that this represents the most important market failure in human history. The international nature of the greenhouse gas externalities makes this a particularly daunting challenge.

China is not a major part of the reason why the world faces large problems of anthropogenic warming at this time. The arrival of sustained rapid growth in China, however, fuelled to an unusual extent by coal—the most emissions-intensive of major energy sources—is accelerating the world's movement towards critical points. In 2006, China overtook the United States as the largest current emitter of greenhouse gases (Song and Sheng, Chapter 12). This coincided with increasing awareness throughout the international community—including in China and the United States, following Europe and Japan some time ago—that anthropogenic global warming is a problem of large dimension, requiring a strong response from the international community.

The contribution of Chinese growth to global warming raises the most critical and difficult questions about the sustainability of the contemporary pattern of Chinese economic growth. This potential threat to future global prosperity is in some ways the other side of the coin to the exceptional prosperity that Chinese growth has conferred on the world, and especially to resource-rich countries such as Australia and some of its developing-country neighbours. The answers lie in creating new markets—inside China and internationally—to enhance the social and economic efficiency of all of the other markets whose deepening and improvement have generated the current Chinese and global prosperity.

The chapters in this book discuss recent developments in international markets in China, in ways that illuminate the main contemporary challenges to Chinese growth: the linkages that shape the terms of capital flows in China and with the international economy; the linkages that frame the national labour market during the historic transition, which was described last year and since as the 'turning point in China's economic development' (Garnaut and Huang 2006); the quality of markets for goods and services within China and their connections with the rest of the world; and the global market failures associated with the global warming problem. The Chinese exchange rate issue is important in discussion of capital flows and trade, and is covered in greatest detail when it first arises in relation to capital movements.

Linking capital markets and the role of the exchange rate

The deepening integration of domestic capital markets and increasing international capital flows are discussed in almost half of the chapters in this volume. Garnaut and Huang (Chapter 2) show that the rapid expansion of Chinese foreign trade continued in 2006 and early 2007. The increase in the trade surplus has accelerated, as have the current account surplus and growth in foreign reserves. The accumulated depreciation of the renminbi exchange rate since the loosening of the tie to the US dollar in 2005 has been too small to affect significantly either real economic transactions or the politics of external economic relations.

Woo and Xiao (Chapter 4) delve further into these issues, and analyse the debate in the United States on the deficit with China. It makes sense for China to contribute to reduction of the payments surplus, but effective adjustment would require use of a wider range of Chinese policy instruments than those that feature in the American discussion, and also policy adjustment in the United States. There are risks that misjudgement on two sides of the Pacific could be damaging to both.

Ma and McCauley (Chapter 14) note the extraordinary intensification of links with global capital markets reflected in growth of gross capital flows to the extent that they now exceed annual gross domestic product (GDP). This has widened opportunities for avoiding official controls. Nevertheless, interest rates continue to move with global rates only partially (adjusted for expected exchange rate movements), indicating that controls continue to have noticeable effects. McKay (Chapter 15) notes the consequences of the payments surplus and increasing international financial integration for monetary policy. He observes that the Chinese authorities have been able to sterilise much of the domestic monetary consequences of foreign exchange reserves recently growing at a rate that has no precedent anywhere. Domestic policy will need support from exchange rate flexibility, but successful liberalisation will require careful management—and McKay suggests a process for effective change.

Golley and Tyers (Chapter 16) look over the current powerful tendencies to payments surplus, and examine long-term influences on the exchange rate. They argue that not all the long-term pressures will be supportive of appreciation.

Sun and Zhang (Chapter 17) point out links between the payments surplus and the appreciation of real estate asset values that were recently a powerful factor in Chinese development. The moderation of risks associated with real estate bubbles will require action across a wide range of instruments, including in exchange rate and fiscal policy. Rule (Chapter 13) tells a fascinating story of the growth and internationalisation of Chinese equity markets—to the point where market influence now goes from China to the world's major markets, as well as in the opposite direction.

Zhang (Chapter 19) describes how, from 1984, the Special Economic Zones played a major but transitional role in China's integration into the international economy. They were a place for experimentation with reform, and their success encouraged more general opening of the economy. Since about 2003, their proportionate role has declined.

Chen (Chapter 11) describes the broader history of direct foreign investment. The early years of reform involved slow progress in changing the regulatory, institutional and policy frameworks for direct foreign investment. Maturation of this process led to a high tide of investment from 1991 to 2001, with the proportionate role of new direct foreign investment peaking at the end of this period. Far-reaching liberalisation of direct foreign investment after WTO entry has nevertheless been important.

Linking labour markets and the turning point in economic development

Since the publication of *The Turning Point in China's Economic Development* a year ago (Garnaut and Song 2006), there has been much discussion and new research within China on the rising cost of labour in China and the implications of this for the national economy.

Wu (2007) recently reviewed some of the material. He records the results of research for the Development Research Center of the State Council, based on a survey of almost 3,000 villages in 17 provinces. The results of the survey indicate that 74 per cent of the villages no longer have any surplus labour available for employment in distant cities. The 'labour shortage' began in coastal areas but has now spread through the inland.

Wu also draws attention to the *Green Paper on Population and Labour* published by the Chinese Academy of Social Sciences (CASS) in June 2007. The paper argues that China is now approaching a 'Lewisian turning point' (compare this with the similar analytical framework applied in Garnaut 2006 and Garnaut and Huang 2006). It notes that labour will be 'short' throughout China by 2009—in rural as well as urban areas. It describes an acceleration in rates of increase in wages of rural migrant workers—from 2.8 per cent in 2004 to 6.5 per cent in 2005 and 11.5 per cent in 2006. Wu notes the conclusion drawn by CASS scholar Wu Yaowu that reforms of the *hukou* system to reduce barriers to internal labour migration are necessary in response to these large changes in the labour market.

Garnaut and Huang (Chapter 2) present evidence of continuing strong wage growth, particularly in relatively poor inland and western provinces.

Cai, Du and Zhao (Chapter 8) focus on the increasing integration of the national labour market. They note that more than 100 million rural labourers have migrated to urban jobs (and 132 million people from rural areas are working in urban areas), alongside the re-employment of laid-off workers from state-owned enterprises. The restructuring of employment within a strongly growing economy has moved China towards a historical Lewisian turning point, at which surplus labour is no longer available to support rapid expansion of labour-intensive industry. The looming labour shortage is generating pressure for more efficient integration of labour markets. Reform of the *hukou* system—with its systematic discrimination against migrants from rural areas—has begun, but so far with a strong bias in favour of migrants with relatively high education and skills. In any case, competition for labour in a post-Lewisian world will force deeper labour market integration. It will be accompanied by reduction in regional and other wage differentials, and an adjustment of labour relations legislation to reduce discrimination against labour—or else risk labour unrest. They note that a tendency for wages to rise more strongly in poorer than in richer regions can already be observed.

Meng and Bai (Chapter 9) offer a different perspective, based on detailed payroll data from seven labour-intensive factories operating in Guangdong Province between 2001 and 2004. The data have the advantage that they relate specifically to migrant workers. Meng and Bai found no evidence of a substantial tendency for incomes of migrant workers to rise in these factories in Guangdong in the early years of the twenty-first century.

Linking goods and services in China and abroad

A number of chapters document and analyse the effects of deepening domestic market integration, and analyse the relationship between domestic and international linkages.

Wang, Fan and Zhu (Chapter 3) apply a new index to measure the expanding role of markets in the Chinese economy. The role of markets in domestic and international economic relations has become large by any standards, with the process of change having been accelerated by WTO entry. Findlay, Pangestu and Lee (Chapter 6) apply innovative and productive approaches to analysis of liberalisation in the services sector. The parallel analysis of agricultural exchange by Huang, Liu, Martin and Rozelle (Chapter 7) demonstrates that the Chinese farm economy is more open to the international market than this sector in most industrialised countries, and that openness has been assisted by WTO entry. Li, Song and Zhao (Chapter 5) describe another dimension of the internationalisation of the Chinese economy in recent years: expansion of exports has been accompanied by huge growth in components imports from other East Asian companies, allowing China and its neighbours to specialise more and more finely in production and trade according to comparative advantage.

Two chapters look more broadly at the relationship between domestic and international market integration. Golley and Groenewold (Chapter 10) note that linkages across markets in China are less impressive than links to the international economy. The better-developed economies are more closely linked to overseas than internal markets. Chen, Gui, Lu and Chen (Chapter 18) conclude that deeper international integration tends to weaken domestic market linkages for a while, but to strengthen them at a later stage of development.

The need for new markets for environmental amenity

Chinese economic growth—like sustained economic growth in many countries—has been associated with pressure on the local environment. Chinese economic growth is now on such a prodigious scale that it is placing pressure on global environmental amenity through its contribution to current and prospective global warming.

A recent report from the Netherlands Environment Assessment Agency (2007) on global emissions of greenhouse gases recorded that China overtook the United States in 2006 as the country with the highest levels of greenhouse gas emissions—by a margin of 8 per cent. China contributed two-fifths of the 2.6 per cent growth in global emissions last year.

International market reform, embodying internalisation of global environmental externalities, is needed if the continuation of strong growth is to be reconciled with the conservation of aspects of the biosphere on which all human activity depends. These difficult but fundamentally important issues are discussed briefly in the concluding section of Garnaut and Huang (Chapter 2).

The Chinese dimension of the global warming issue has its origin in the extent and character of Chinese energy use in the process of rapid economic growth. Song and Sheng (Chapter 12) assess in detail the relationship between growth and energy consumption in China. They introduce recent official discussion of climate change in China to provide important insights into Chinese thinking and possible future contributions to management of this international issue.

Integrating ideas about economics

This volume concludes with reflections by Lin (Chapter 20) on the adequacy of ideas from modern neoclassical economics in understanding growth in China and other transitional economies in the reform period.

One of the impressive and influential processes of linking Chinese to international markets in the reform era has involved the market for ideas about economics. The modern economics profession has grown prodigiously, so that the received economic wisdom of the West is understood and taught widely in the best universities and social science research institutions. Lin, and the China Center of Economic Research at Peking University, which he was instrumental in establishing, is the prime locus of this new knowledge.

One of the strengths of modern economics as professed in China is that it has been capable of critical rigour in application of ideas developed elsewhere to the Chinese situation. Lin analyses the sources of modern economics' failure to comprehend the failure of simple application of received doctrine in the former Soviet Union, and the success of departures from it in China. He draws attention to the importance of retaining a critical mass of 'viable' enterprises, which can maintain economic activity through disruptive structural change.

Note

1 Throughout the following chapters, the terms 'renminbi' and 'yuan' are used interchangeably.

References

Garnaut, R., 2006. 'The turning point in China's economic development', in R. Garnaut and L. Song (eds), *The Turning Point in China's Economic Development*, Asia Pacific Press, The Australian National University, Canberra:1–11.

Garnaut, R. and Huang, Y., 2006. 'Continued rapid growth and the turning point in China's development', in R. Garnaut and L. Song (eds), *The Turning Point in China's Economic Development*, Asia Pacific Press, The Australian National University, Canberra:12–34.

Garnaut, R. and Song, L. (eds), 2006. *The Turning Point in China's Economic Development*, Asia Pacific Press, The Australian National University, Canberra.

Netherlands Environmental Assessment Agency (MNP), 2007. China now no.1 in CO_2 emissions; USA in second position, Press release, Netherlands Environmental Assessment Agency. Available from www.mnp.nl/en/service/pressreleases/2007/20070619Chinanowno1inCO2emissionsUSAinsecondposition.html

Stern, N., 2007. *Stern Review Report on the Economics of Climate Change*, Cambridge University Press, Cambridge. Available from www.hm-treasury.gov.uk/independent_reviews/stern_review_economics_climate_change/sternreview_index.cfm

Wu, Z., 2007. 'China's cheap labour pool drying up', *China Business*, 17 June, Hong Kong.

2

Mature Chinese growth leads the global Platinum Age

Ross Garnaut and Yiping Huang

China's strong and accelerating growth, with low inflation and growing external payments surpluses, continued in 2007. The longer that strong growth in China continues, the greater is China's influence on global outcomes. Global growth looks set to exceed 5 per cent in 2007 for the fourth successive year—higher than the 4.9 per cent average of the 'Golden Age' from 1950 to 1973. China is now at the centre of what could turn out to be the strongest period of global economic growth the world has seen—a 'Platinum Age'.

Investment as a share of Chinese output rose again in 2007, from levels that many had said could go no higher. Our conclusion in the 2005 China Update volume (Garnaut and Song 2005)—that there was no sound basis for external and Chinese assessments that growth based on the high investment shares of the early twentieth century was unsustainable—seems so far to have been validated by subsequent experience. The continued rapid increase in nominal and real wages alongside some (albeit small) currency appreciation confirms that 'turning-point' adjustments—the focus of last year's China Update volume (Garnaut and Song 2006)—have begun without dislocation of the growth process. Chinese officials talk privately of the economic system functioning better than at any time for 5,000 years, and an economist with historical interests can see where they are coming from.

The two most difficult challenges to the sustainability of current Chinese and global prosperity come from China's relations with the international economy. The external payments surpluses—the trade surplus, the current account surplus and the capital account surplus, adding up to an extraordinary rate of increase in foreign exchange reserves—are straining relations with the United States in particular as never before. And sustained, super-charged growth is placing unprecedented stress on the global biosphere.

An overview of macroeconomic performance

China's growth reached 10.7 per cent in 2006, taking the average of the past three years to 10.4 per cent—almost a full percentage point above the average of the first quarter-century of the reform era. Gross domestic product (GDP) growth accelerated further—to 11.1 per cent for the year to the first quarter of 2007 (Figure 2.1). Inflation also rose—to more than 3 per cent for the first time in the recent period of exceptionally strong growth.

Investment and net exports led growth, but consumption, while growing strongly by the standards of other countries, lagged behind. External account surpluses surged, causing concerns at home and abroad. In 2006, investment contributed 55 per cent and net exports 29 per cent to GDP growth (Figure 2.2).

The investment share of GDP rose from 35.3 per cent in 2000 to 42.7 per cent in 2006, and the net exports share rose from 2.4 per cent to 7.3 per cent in the same period (Figure 2.3). Meanwhile, household consumption as a share of GDP dropped by 10 percentage points in the six years, from 46.4 per cent to 36.4 per cent.

Figure 2.1 **Quarterly real GDP growth and CPI inflation in China, 2000–2007** (per cent, year on year)

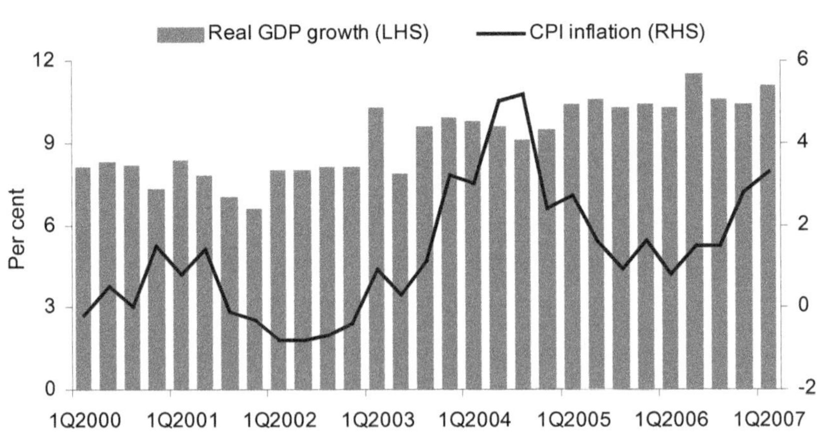

Source: CEIC Data Company and National Statistics Bureau of China.

Figure 2.2 **Contribution of various components to GDP growth, 1979–2006**

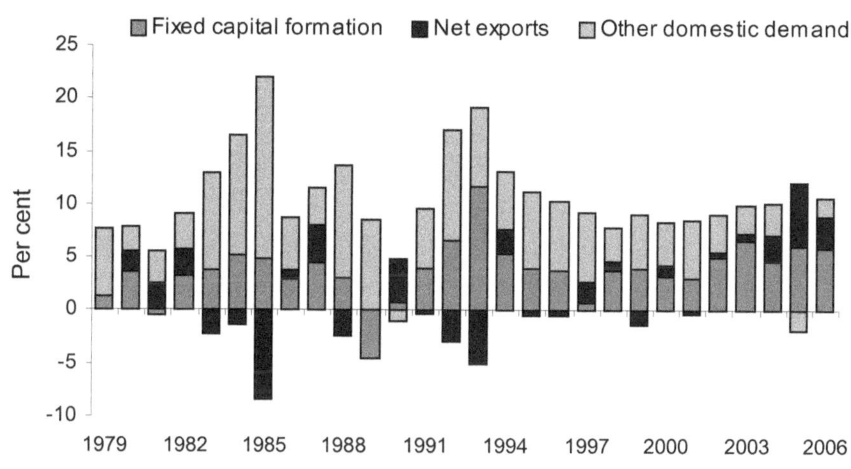

Source: CEIC Data Company and National Statistics Bureau of China.

Figure 2.3 **Shares of main components of GDP in China, 2000–2006**

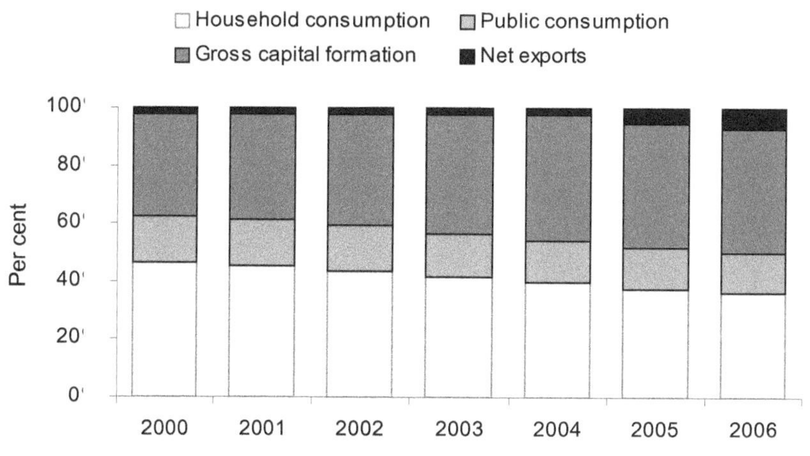

Source: CEIC Data Company and National Statistics Bureau of China.

While we have challenged for several years the conventional wisdom of the early twentieth century that the investment share of Chinese production was already unsustainable and had to fall, we have acknowledged the arithmetic reality that the share could not increase without limit (Garnaut and Huang 2005). There was, therefore, comfort in the signs of falling rates of growth in investment and rising consumption growth rates through 2006. Fixed-asset investment growth moderated to about 25 per cent from close to 30 per cent. Retail sales growth picked up from 13–14 per cent early in 2006 to more than 15 per cent through the first half of 2007 (Figure 2.4). Fixed-asset investment has, however, re-accelerated through the early months of 2007. The overall result has been an acceleration in growth momentum without significant rebalancing of the sources of growth so far in 2007.

The near consensus two years ago that the investment rate was too high and that its reduction would require a fall in the rate of growth is now less widely held. Weakening, too, are some analysts' expectations of a hard landing for the Chinese economy on the basis that input prices—wages and costs of materials—are growing much faster than output prices in most Chinese industries. This had been expected by some to lead to narrowing profit margins, declining investment and increasing non-performing assets in the financial system. None of these events have occurred. Strong productivity growth helped Chinese industry to absorb the cost pressure and supported profit growth. According to growth accounting analysis by Bosworth and Collins (2007), total factor productivity growth contributed about 55 per cent of output growth in the manufacturing sector in China in 1995–2004. Total profits of the industrial sector have continued to grow at about 30 per cent annually in recent years. Earnings of listed Chinese companies increased by 46 per cent in 2006.

Inflation rates for non-food prices were generally well behaved. Energy prices have given way to food prices as the main driver of headline inflation. Between March and May, headline consumer price index (CPI) increases rose above 3 per cent, breaching an informal target set by the People's Bank of China. Food prices, which account for about one-third of the basket, increased significantly, affected by bad weather across the country.

In the first half of 2006, pork prices jumped by close to 50 per cent year-on-year, exacerbated by a number of pig disease incidents in southern China. Purchasers from southern China, including Hong Kong, went as far away as northeast China to buy pork, pushing up national prices.

While food prices could remain volatile—especially with recent floods in parts of the country—the fact that non-food inflation has been stable at about 1 per cent (Figure 2.5) suggests that headline inflation could stabilise at about 3 per cent relatively soon.

Figure 2.4 **Growth of retail sales and fixed asset investment in China, 2005–2007** (per cent, year on year)

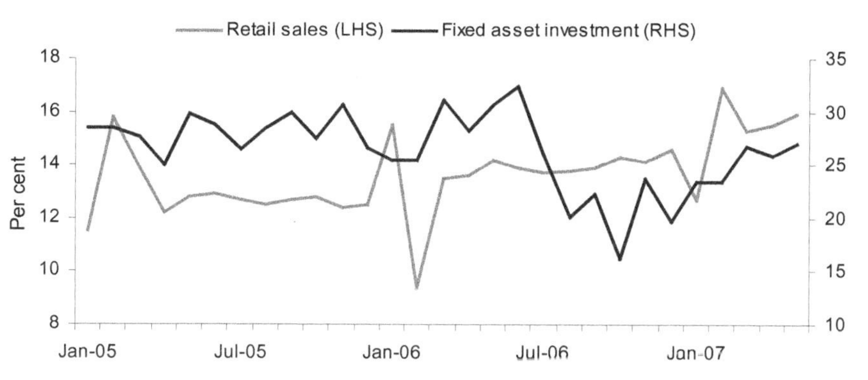

Source: CEIC Data Company and National Statistics Bureau of China.

Figure 2.5 **Some components of CPI, 2001–2007** (per cent, year on year)

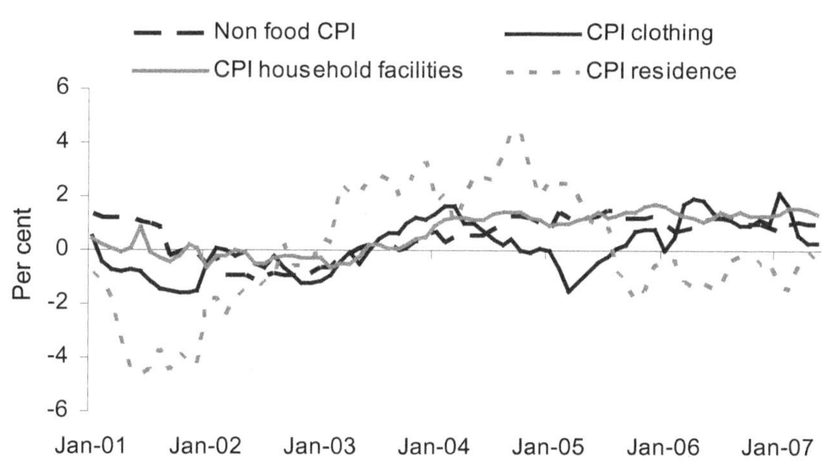

Source: CEIC Data Company and National Statistics Bureau of China.

Recent spikes in CPI inflation have already invited the concern of monetary policymakers. The People's Bank of China has related its general goal of holding CPI increases within 3 per cent specifically to the outcome for 2007. Since the beginning of 2007, the central bank has raised the reserve requirement three times and hiked deposit and lending rates three times. On 18 May, the People's Bank of China announced three policy measures at once: it increased the reserve requirement ratio by half a percentage point; it raised base deposit rates by 27 basis points and lending rates by 18 basis points; and it widened the trading band of the exchange rate to 0.5 per cent from 0.3 per cent.

These were modest adjustments. The current official reserve requirement ratio—11.5 per cent—remains way below the real reserves that commercial banks deposit with the central bank, which are close to 13 per cent of total commercial banks' deposits. While deposit and lending rates increased by 81 and 72 basis points respectively in the first half of 2006, this was significantly less than the increase in the CPI. Real interest rates, from this perspective, declined. Citigroup's monetary conditions index—which is a weighted average of real interest rates, real effective exchange rates and real credit growth—suggests that monetary conditions in China showed little tightening (Figure 2.6).

Figure 2.6 **Monetary conditions index of China, 2001–2007**

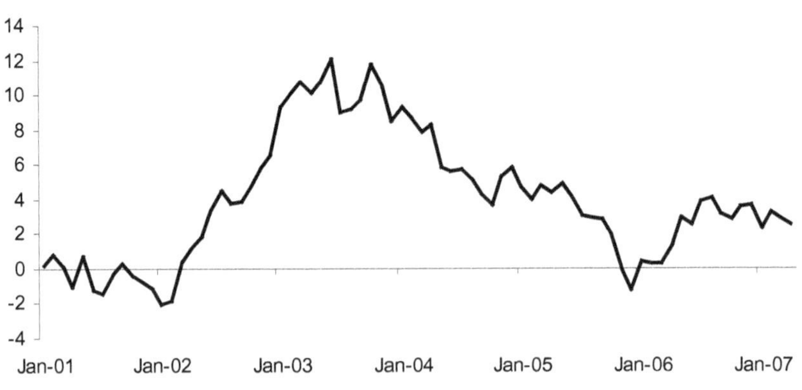

Note: The MCI is a weighted average of real interest rate, real effective exchange rate and real credit growth.
Source: Citigroup estimates.

Policymakers have not tightened monetary policy much because they think that overall macroeconomic conditions remain healthy. With GDP growth more than 10 per cent and CPI inflation well below 5 per cent, some officials argue privately that the Chinese economy is probably in its best state for 5,000 years. They also recognise limits on the extent to which monetary tightening can be effective with a fixed exchange rate.

Increasing income inequality

Unequal income distribution affects consumer spending, especially spending of low-income households. What focuses the minds of officials is that it can lead to social and political tension. There has been a rapid increase in incidents of social unrest. Most of these problems have been caused by local issues, such as corruption of local officials, land compensation for property development projects and uncivilised implementation of family planning policies. Unrest would be harder to manage if local concerns were joined by tensions over systemic increases in inequality.

Asset price bubbles

With regard to asset price bubbles, a few years back the authorities were worried about the housing market. In Shanghai and Beijing, prices of luxurious properties doubled every three to four years, and there was a strong increase in property prices more generally. This raised two types of concerns among policymakers: damage to housing affordability of ordinary households and potential implications for quality of financial assets if the bubble were to burst.

From 2004, the national government started to introduce a number of measures to cool the property markets around the country, including a higher requirement of equity for property development loans, tighter controls on land supply, higher interest rates for second mortgage loans and regulated proportions of small apartments in new housing developments. Local governments in most areas were initially resistant to the restrictive measures. Some local authorities, however, later supplemented the national policies with specific measures, such as banning construction of villas, prohibiting sales off the plan and levying capital taxes. After implementation of these policies, property markets in large cities such as Shanghai and Beijing showed signs of stabilisation; however, housing prices in many second-tier cities continued to show double-digit growth.

From early 2006, concerns about asset bubbles shifted to the stockmarkets. By the end of 2005, China's domestic A-shares had experienced a multi-year bear market. The domestic stockmarkets, however, experienced a significant turn around in 2006. By early 2007, A-share prices had risen by 180 per cent year-on-year (Figure 2.7). Some security market participants and regulators argue that the fundamentals support a long bull market in China. China in recent years has implemented a number of equity-market reforms, including reform of non-tradable shares (98 per cent completed), the establishment of incentive structures for listed companies, the development of institutional investors, the introduction of the Qualified Foreign Institutional Investor (QFII) plan and reform of the initial public offering (IPO) process. Many government officials argue that today's stockmarkets are already fundamentally different from those of a few years ago, justifying higher values.

Corporate earnings and liquidity conditions also support a strong market. Earnings were strong even in labour-intensive sectors such as clothing (see Figure 2.8). Domestic liquidity remains abundant. Bank deposits, for instance, are almost 200 per cent of GDP and more than double the stockmarket capitalisation.

So why do so many government officials worry about the risk of stockmarket bubbles? Mainly because of the increasing role played by retail investors, and the resulting political sensitivity of any crash. The amount of retail investment is already double that of institutional funds. The number of investment accounts was growing by one million every three days in the second quarter of 2007.

The market has continuously ignored policy messages during the past years—share prices kept rising after the various tightening announcements by the People's Bank of China. What eventually caused a short-lived correction was the increase in stamp duty on stock trading from 0.1 per cent to 0.3 per cent in the night of 29 May. On 30 May, the A-share index declined by 6.5 per cent. This caused widespread market shudders, including in Indonesia, Hong Kong, India, Taiwan and Australia and on the major world exchanges. International markets quickly stabilised, as they refocused on the fundamental strengths of the Chinese economy. The domestic market remained volatile in the following weeks, but then recovered its losses and stabilised.

While the stockmarket seems likely to lift further after a period of stabilisation, it is worth analysing, by way of risk analysis, what would follow if there were, say, a 30 per cent decline in A-share prices. The first point to note is that the market has risen by more than 100 per cent during the 12 months to mid 2007, so the hypothetical correction would leave prices way above the levels of a few months earlier. High-level inspection of the historical data reveals no clear general relationship between A-share prices and GDP. During the past 15 years, stockmarkets had roller-coaster variability, while GDP growth was strong and stable. Any effects of a major correction would be in three main

Figure 2.7 **Growth of property prices and Shanghai A-share prices, 2005–2007** (per cent)

Source: CEIC Data Company and National Statistics Bureau of China.

Figure 2.8 **Profit/asset ratios of selected industries in China, 2000–2006** (per cent)

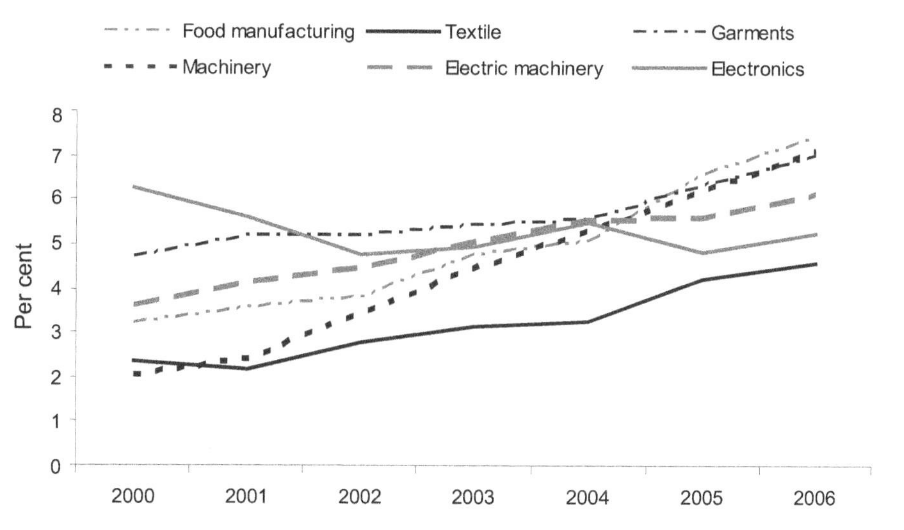

Source: CEIC Data Company and National Statistics Bureau of China.

areas—consumption through the wealth effect, non-performing loans in the banking sector and social instability.

In 2002, stocks accounted for only 10 per cent of households' total financial assets. This proportion has increased, but it would still be low. Total stockmarket capitalisation still accounts for only 20 per cent of China's financial assets. Applying the historical monthly share price and retail sales data between 1994 and 2006, we estimate the elasticity of retail sales with regard to share prices at 0.1. In other words, a 10 per cent decline in the A-share index tended to be associated with a 1 per cent slow-down in retail sales.

This means that if the A-share index declined by 30 per cent, retail sales growth could fall by 3 percentage points below what it would otherwise have been. A hypothetical sustained fall by 30 per cent could bring down retail sales growth from a recent 15 per cent to about 12 per cent. This would be noticeable, but not devastating. It might translate into a single percentage point slow-down in GDP growth, in the absence of countervailing adjustments in fiscal or monetary policy.

Given that most investors do not borrow from banks for stockmarket investment and there are no margin accounts, the impact of a potential equity-market correction on loan quality should be limited. In fact, a significant fall in the stockmarket could result in the withdrawal of funds from that market and flows into the property markets and bank deposits. A rebound of property prices could result. This would modify the wealth effect on consumption.

The authorities would seek especially to avoid a major stockmarket fall in the year of a new round of leadership change, with the five-yearly Party Congress late this year. Many investors would blame the government for a large correction—as they have done many times during the past 10 years. The political reaction would be more significant this time, with the number of active investment accounts rapidly approaching 30 million. This is an important constraint on any aggressive policy actions to prick the bubble.

Growing external imbalances and conflict with the United States

Exports now account for 36 per cent of GDP (national accounts measure) and are still growing at a rate of more than 20 per cent. Export growth has helped to absorb the increase in productive capacity each year. This is one reason why the National Development and Reform Commission's consistent warnings in the past 10 years about an over-investment problem have not been reflected in developments in the real economy.

The expansion of China's external account surpluses has accelerated since its accession to the World Trade Organization (WTO) in late 2001 (Figure 2.9).

China's imports grew rapidly, but its exports grew more rapidly still. China's trade surplus surged from US$23.1 billion in 2001 to US$177.5 billion in 2006, and its current account surplus jumped from 1.5 per cent of GDP to 9 per cent of GDP during the same period. The largest increases in the trade surplus occurred during 2005 (211 per cent) and 2006 (74 per cent). During the first five months of 2007, the surplus rose again by 87 per cent from the same period in the previous year. Part of this increase has come from slower growth in China's deficit with—or, in the case of the Association of Southeast Asian Nations (ASEAN), a real decline in—bilateral trade deficits with these countries. This reflects the shift of more and more components supply into China (Figure 2.9), driven by increasing Chinese competitiveness with the world as a whole. Increasing self-sufficiency in components strengthens Chinese enterprises' position to meet rules of origin of bilateral preferential trade agreements as they become more important through the Asia Pacific region.

The bilateral trade imbalances with the United States and the euro area have been contentious. Until 2006, China's bilateral trade surpluses with the United States were often significantly greater than its overall surpluses. China had trade deficits with other trading partners considered together. Athukorala

Figure 2.9 **China's trade surpluses, 2001–2006** (US$ billion)

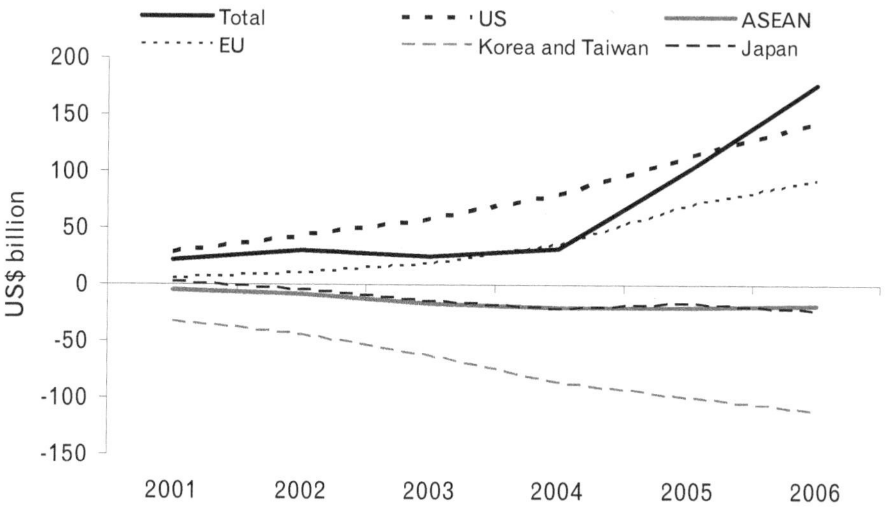

Source: CEIC Data Company.

(2005) has described how this has reflected the movement of final assembly of many manufactured goods into China for supply to North America and Europe, by firms that drew components from a range of Asian economies according to comparative advantage. Between 2001 and 2004, China's overall trade surpluses were relatively stable at about US$30 billion a year, despite changes in bilateral imbalances.

This pattern, however, started to change in 2005. China's trade deficits with Japan and ASEAN economies have recently stagnated or fallen, while its surpluses with the United States and Europe have continued to rise rapidly. In fact, the only major trading partners that still enjoy rapidly growing bilateral trade surpluses are Korea and Taiwan. Such developments reduce the benefit of China's rapid growth to the rest of Asia, and are likely to make China's imbalances more widely contentious.

Current account surpluses have also increased rapidly (Figure 2.10). The sum of gross domestic investment and net exports—that is, China's national savings rate—is now more than half of GDP. This is high by the standards of other East Asian economies through their periods of strongest growth.

Large and increasing external surpluses pose two types of risks for China. First, there is international resistance to absorption of increasing values of

Figure 2.10 **China's current account and trade balances, 1989–2008** (per cent of GDP, US$ billion)

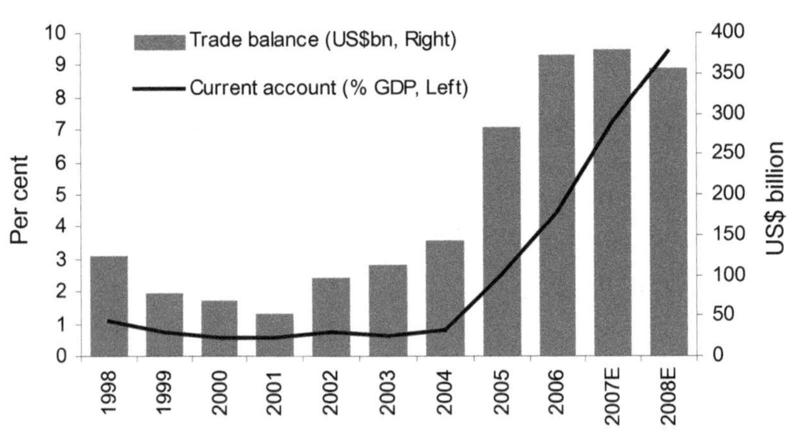

[E] **estimate**
Source: CEIC Data Company and Citigroup estimates.

Chinese exports, especially when external payments are in large surplus. Second, escalating external surpluses threaten monetary stability.

Chinese growth has become more susceptible to fluctuations in the global economy. Exports already account for 36 per cent of GDP, of which about 22 per cent goes to the United States. This implies that exports to the United States are equivalent to 8 per cent of GDP. Analyses applying the Oxford macroeconomic forecasting model suggest that a decline of the US economy by 1 per cent slows Chinese growth by 1.3 percentage points. China could maintain 10 per cent growth if external demand softens temporarily through domestic demand expansion, especially through fiscal policy. Any serious slow-down in external demand would, however, challenge the momentum of Chinese growth. No such general slow-down is currently within sight.

International politics also set important constraints for China's export-led growth. China already accounts for 8 per cent of world exports. Growth in Chinese exports above 20 per cent year after year requires significant structural adjustment in the rest of the world. While expansion of Chinese exports is a result of market forces and benefits consumers world-wide, the adjustment costs caused by this expansion generate political tensions in some other countries. This is most obvious in the United States and Europe, where bilateral trade deficits with China have been largest. Already, the United States has imposed countervailing duties on imports of Chinese coated paper and lodged three complaints with the WTO about intellectual property rights and income tax subsidies. If China does not respond quickly, new waves of trade protectionism could swell in and beyond the United States.

Policymakers in both countries recognise the importance of maintaining smooth trade and economic relations. The semi-annual China–US Strategic Economic Dialogue is fundamentally important to mature political and economic relations between two of the world's largest economies. With little demonstrable change in the exchange rate or the overall trade surplus, however, calls for more substantial policy changes are rising within the US Congress. The International Monetary Fund's Multilateral Consultation on Global Imbalances has not generated immediate economic effects.

The risks of trade protectionism in the United States have increased significantly since November 2006, when the Democrats won control of Congress. Recently, two new bills were put forward in Congress: one by Senators Dodd and Shelby and another by Senators Baucus, Grassley, Schumer and Graham. Both aim to limit the scope for executive discretion in judging exchange rates and to prescribe explicit sanctions if manipulation or fundamental misalignment is found. The upcoming presidential election could push the policy debate further in that direction, especially in relation to China.

As a matter of domestic policy, large current account surpluses and capital inflows on the back of a rigid exchange rate regime also hurt domestic monetary policy autonomy. Massive foreign reserves and excess domestic liquidity are two obvious outcomes (Figure 2.11). The central bank is forced to buy as much foreign exchange as the market offers at the controlled rate, in order to maintain exchange rate stability. This injects local currency liquidity into the domestic system. In order to reduce the inflationary consequences, the central bank engages in sterilisation. For the past years, however, the People's Bank of China has found sterilisation increasingly difficult. Domestic commercial banks have become increasingly reluctant to purchase central bank paper given the very low returns on these assets. The scale of the outstanding central bank paper makes rollover pressure heavy. In response, during the past year, the central bank has focused more on reserve requirements as a way to tighten liquidity.

In March 2007, the National People's Congress approved the establishment of a new National Foreign Exchange Investment Corporation, which is mandated initially to manage about US$200 billion of the foreign reserves. The Ministry of Finance will issue special T-bonds to commercial banks and exchange the revenue for foreign reserves from the central bank. Meanwhile, by issuing longer-term bonds to the financial sector, the Ministry of Finance will share responsibility for sterilisation. Given that US$200 billion will be about 10 per cent of Chinese GDP and one third of the existing stock of treasury bonds, this

Figure 2.11 **China's monthly increase in foreign reserves and sum of FDI and trade surplus, 2005–2007** (US$ billion)

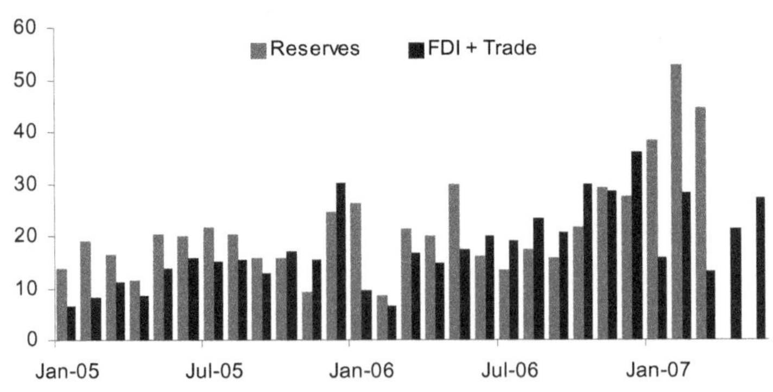

Source: CEIC Data Company.

is likely to increase yields significantly. Indeed, domestic bond yields jumped by between 25 and 50 basis points in late June 2007.

The Chinese government has identified containing the trade surplus as a top policy priority in 2007. It has recently taken a number of policy decisions that could have some modest effect on the growth in exports and the trade surplus.

First, it announced the unification of the corporate income tax, effective January 2008. Previously, corporate income tax rates were 15 per cent for foreign-invested firms and 33 per cent for domestic enterprises. As foreign-funded companies contribute 60 per cent of Chinese exports, this preferential tax treatment has been seen as effectively boosting the export sector. In March of this year, the National People's Congress approved unification of corporate income tax rates to 25 per cent for all types of enterprises. This measure was also required by China's WTO entry commitment to treat national and foreign enterprises in similar ways, but it could have some dampening effect on export growth.

Second, the government has cut export tax rebates. The Ministry of Finance adjusted value-added tax (VAT) rebates on export goods in the steel industry on 10 April. Of 159 tax categories for steel products, 83 will enjoy no VAT rebates and 76 will have rebates cut from 8 per cent to 5 per cent. Since April 2005, China has nullified a 13 per cent export tax rebate on steel billets. On 20 June, the Ministry of Finance announced another package of massive reduction of export tax rebates, especially for resource-based products and goods with low margins but associated with high trade friction.

Third, the government has imposed new export taxes. On 21 May, the Ministry of Finance decided to impose export tariffs on 142 goods, effective 1 June. Approximately 80 steel products (including steel wire, rods and plates) will face 5–10 per cent export tariffs.

Fourth, it has widened the daily trading band of the exchange rate. The People's Bank of China decided to widen the daily trading band for the yuan–US dollar rate to 0.5 per cent from 0.3 per cent, effective 21 May. This might not affect near-term currency appreciation, but it has been interpreted by some as raising the potential for future revaluation.

Fifth, the government has introduced and increased a number of taxes and controls to improve energy efficiency and promote environmentally friendly technology, which are likely to have a dampening effect on the export of some manufactured goods.

At the centre of the international policy dialogue is the renminbi exchange rate policy. On 21 July 2005, China abandoned its *de facto* peg of the renminbi to the US dollar and introduced a 'managed float' system with reference to a basket of currencies. Since then, the renminbi has risen by 7.6 per cent against the dollar, but by only 4.3 per cent in real effective exchange terms (REER) (see Figure 2.12). This appreciation has been small compared with the demands of prominent US analysts. What matters economically is China's international competitiveness, taking account of Chinese—relative to international—cost and productivity increases, as well as the nominal exchange rate. The appreciation in this wider context has been too small so far to reduce significantly Chinese export or increase import growth.

Rational economic analyses suggest that even a large appreciation of the renminbi would do little to increase manufacturing employment in the United States or to solve America's current deficit problem. Nevertheless, the reality is that China's current expansion of external account surpluses cannot continue for long. While currency appreciation alone would not remove current tensions between China and its major trading partners, exchange rate policy needs to be a part of any effective adjustment package.

Recent evidence about the turning point in the labour market

Last year's book in this series, *The Turning Point in China's Economic Development*, triggered considerable discussion in China about whether China was indeed approaching the point in economic development at which labour supply to modern sector activities becomes scarce and increasingly expensive, forcing structural changes of many kinds (Garnaut and Song 2006; Garnaut and Huang 2006). Among other things, it was followed by substantial research efforts on this subject for the Chinese Academy of Social Sciences and the Development Research Centre of the State Council (see Chapter 1, this volume, for reference to these studies).

The labour market data at a national level reveal that wages and related costs have been rising strongly (Figure 2.13). Regional (Table 2.1) and sectoral (Table 2.2) wage data indicate acceleration in wage increases in recent times.

The lift in real wage growth in 2006 coincided with a rise in the rates of domestic inflation and nominal appreciation against the US dollar. It therefore understates the labour cost adjustment relative to other countries. The rate of wage increase remains well behind the prodigious increase in labour productivity, a fact that goes a long way towards explaining the absence of general inflationary pressures, and the strength of the continuing momentum in the growth of exports and the trade and payments surpluses. Rising labour costs will have been placing pressure on the profitability of labour-intensive activities using standard technologies. These parts of the economy—having

Figure 2.12 **Renminbi exchange rates: bilateral rates and real effective exchange rate, 2005–2007**

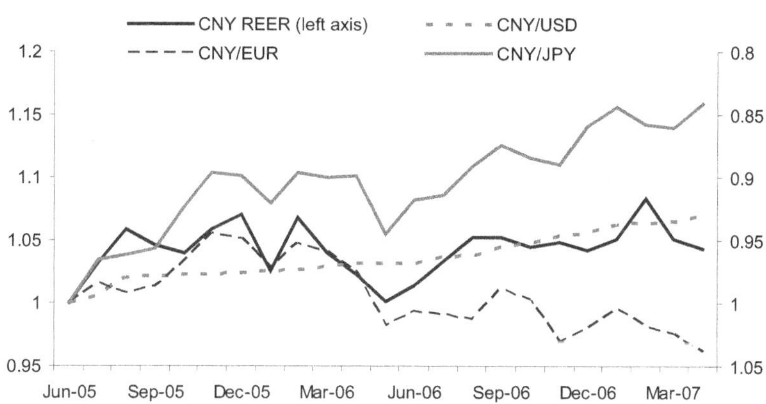

Source: Citigroup estimates.

Figure 2.13 **Increases in national real wages and labour productivity, 1999–2006** (per cent)

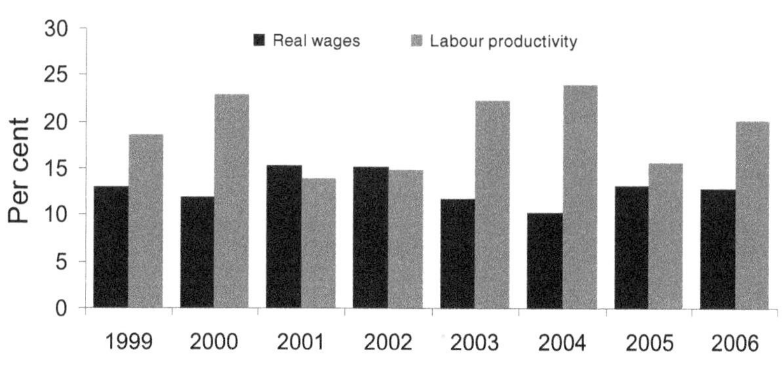

Source: CEIC Data Company and National Statistics Bureau of China.

Table 2.1 **Wages by province, 1999–2006** (yuan constant 1999 prices and per cent per annum increase)

	Beijing	Liaoning	Shanghai	Zhejiang	Hubei	Guangdong	Sichuan	Ningxia
1999	14,572	7,780	16,588	11,074	6,766	12,108	7,134	7,226
2000	16,994	8,738	18,298	12,931	7,304	13,701	8,267	8,541
2001	20,011	10,233	21,098	16,279	8,524	15,828	9,936	10,250
2002	23,666	11,662	23,363	19,008	9,522	18,167	11,152	11,515
2003	25,626	13,226	25,614	22,065	10,696	20,618	12,580	13,741
2004	29,400	15,128	27,756	25,987	11,818	23,179	14,003	14,265
2005	33,764	17,231	31,875	28,723	13,766	25,183	15,968	16,924
2006[e]	39,597	19,496	37,649	30,563	15,948	26,831	17,888	20,187
Growth								
1999–2006	15.4	14.0	12.4	15.6	13.0	12.0	14.0	15.8
2005–2006	17.3	13.2	18.1	6.4	15.9	6.5	12.0	19.3

Note: Beijing, Shanghai, Guangdong and Zhejiang are from the dynamic coastal region; Liaoning from the old industrial Northeast; Hubei from central China; and Sichuan and Ningxia from the Southwest and West respectively.
Source: CEIC Data Company.

played useful roles in past growth—are being forced to change into new types of specialisation or to shrink rapidly.

One interesting feature of the regional data is the marked acceleration of wage increases in a number of poorer provinces: Hubei in the central region and Ningxia in the west. There was a deceleration in the high-income coastal provinces of Zhejiang and Guangdong which have long been the locus of the strongest internationally oriented growth. The opportunity cost of labour from backward inland areas has been rising rapidly.

Unsurprisingly, wages have been rising more rapidly in mining than in other sectors. Chinese mining has been participating in the global resources boom and mining-related skills are in high demand. The rate of wage increases has been high in all sectors, including wholesale and retail trade, with their intensive utilisation of less-skilled labour. The rate of increase in wages in agriculture remains below that in other industries.

China and global environmental problems

Local environmental problems have been accumulating through the years of market reforms and rapid growth. Government commitment to action has been strengthening in response to them, although real policy measures so far have been small in their effects. Awareness of the external environmental costs of established growth patterns has been heightened in the past year by growing appreciation that China is at once a victim and an increasingly important cause of human-induced global warming.

The environmental costs of established growth patterns were recognised first as dark skies and air that was unpleasant to breathe, and in the obvious health problems associated with these conditions; as poisoned water in rivers and lakes that humans had used for centuries; and as soils that required increasing applications of chemical fertilisers to maintain yields. In recent

Table 2.2 **Average annual wage rates for agriculture, manufacturing, construction and finance, 1978–2005** (yuan, constant 1999 prices and per cent per annum increase)

	Agriculture	Mining	Manufacture	Construction	Wholesale and retail	Finance
1985	878	1,324	1,112	1,362	1,007	1,154
1986	1,048	1,569	1,275	1,536	1,148	1,353
1987	1,143	1,663	1,418	1,684	1,270	1,458
1988	1,280	1,964	1,710	1,959	1,556	1,739
1989	1,389	2,378	1,900	2,166	1,660	1,867
1990	1,541	2,718	2,073	2,384	1,818	2,097
1991	1,652	2,942	2,289	2,649	1,981	2,255
1992	1,828	3,209	2,635	3,066	2,204	2,829
1993	2,042	3,711	3,348	3,779	2,679	3,740
1994	2,819	4,679	4,283	4,894	3,537	6,712
1995	3,522	5,757	5,169	5,785	4,248	7,376
1996	4,050	6,482	5,642	6,249	4,661	8,406
1997	4,311	6,833	5,933	6,655	4,845	9,734
1998	4,528	7,242	7,064	7,456	5,865	10,633
1999	4,832	7,521	7,794	7,982	6,417	12,046
2000	5,184	8,340	8,750	8,735	7,190	13,478
2001	5,741	9,586	9,774	9,484	8,192	16,277
2002	6,398	11,017	11,001	10,279	9,398	19,135
2003	6,969	13,682	12,496	11,478	10,939	22,457
2004	7,611	16,874	14,033	12,770	12,923	26,982
2005	8,309	20,626	15,757	14,338	15,241	32,228
Average growth (per cent)						
2000–2005	9.9	19.9	12.5	10.4	16.2	19.1
2004–2005	9.2	22.2	12.3	12.3	17.9	19.4

Source: CEIC Data Company.

years, attention has been drawn more dramatically to the links between health and exposure to the atmosphere of China's most vibrant cities; Chinese media attracted the attention of citizens with reports that the life expectancy of traffic police in major cities—exposed constantly to extremes of atmospheric pollution—was 49 years, compared with a national average of 73 years.

An incomplete estimate by the National Bureau of Statistics and the National Environmental Protection Agency put environmental costs not measured in the national accounts at 3.5 per cent of GDP in 2004.

For some time, commentators have drawn comfort from the 'environmental Kuznets curve': the observed tendency for countries to make environmental amenity a major objective when average incomes exceed a threshold level—above those in China today. Public concern and official policy action have begun in China at an income level below that suggested by the experience of other countries.

There are important reasons why China needs to take decisive action now, in advance of its environmental Kuznets position. The concentration of economic activity on an immense scale in small areas in coastal China creates risks beyond those seen in other countries at comparable stages of development. And the scale and timing of China's extraordinary growth is coinciding with the crystallisation of the long-heralded problem of global warming.

The interaction of local environmental pressures with global warming has the potential to be severely disruptive. Chinese scientists are drawing attention to the likelihood that this interaction is behind the severe water problems in northern China and the floods in the south. One response to water shortages in the north has been the launching of three massive projects to transport water by pipeline from the south. Scientists are, however, noting the vulnerability of the sources of these southern rivers to global warming, as evidence mounts of shrinking ice coverage and changing patterns of melting on the Tibetan Plateau—source of the Yangtse, Yellow and other rivers.

These were all matters of increasingly common discussion when news came through in June 2007 that China had overtaken the United States as the world's largest source of greenhouse gas emissions (see Song and Sheng, Chapter 12).

China's prosperity is at the core of the emerging Platinum Age of global economic growth. But the economic growth that makes up the Platinum Age—first of all but not only in China—if left unmodified by major action to change radically the relationship between economic growth and the emission of greenhouse gases, could be so disruptive to economic and political arrangements everywhere that it gradually introduces problems for international development that severely damage growth opportunities in China and elsewhere.

Chinese officials and private citizens have now entered the search for a means of reconciling continued strong growth with avoidance of macroeconomic disruption on a massive scale. A satisfactory outcome will require effective cooperation across national borders, which has so far eluded the international community in other spheres.

References

Athukorala, P.C., 2005. 'Components trade and implications for Asian structural adjustment', in R. Garnaut and L. Song (eds), *The China Boom and Its Discontents*, Asia Pacific Press, The Australian National University, Canberra:215–39.

Bosworth, B. and Collins, S.M., 2007. *Accounting for growth: comparing China and India*, Working Paper 12943, National Bureau of Economic Research, Cambridge, MA. Available from http://www.nber.org/papers/w12943

Garnaut, R., and Song, L. (eds), 2005. *The China Boom and its Discontents*, Asia Pacific Press, The Australian National University, Canberra.

Garnaut, R., and Song, L. (eds), 2006. *The Turning Point in China's Economic Development*, Asia Pacific Press, The Australian National University, Canberra.

Garnaut, R. and Huang, Y., 2006. 'Continued rapid growth and the turning point in China's development', in R. Garnaut and L. Song (eds), *The Turning Point in China's Economic Development*, Asia Pacific Press, The Australian National University, Canberra:12–34.

3

Marketisation in China

Progress and contribution to growth

Xiaolu Wang, Gang Fan and Hengpeng Zhu

China has persevered in its market-oriented economic reform for nearly 30 years. Guided by a reform strategy of 'groping for stones to cross the river', China managed to avoid major economic decline and the crises that occurred in other transitional economies such as Russia and Eastern European countries. It successfully transformed the previously centrally planned economy into a mainly market-oriented economy with continued rapid growth, although there are still many conflicts between the new and the old systems.

Progress in marketisation

As indicated in the *NERI Index of Marketisation for China's Provinces*, newly published by the National Economic Research Institute (NERI) (Fan et al. 2007), China has achieved significant marketisation since its WTO accession in 2001. Measured by a zero to 10 score system for the base year (2001), the average score for marketisation of China's 31 provinces (including five autonomous minority ethnic regions and three municipalities directly under the control of the central administration) increased 1.88 in the four years from 2002–05, to reach 6.52 in 2005. Thirty provinces out of the total of 31 made positive progress (Figure 3.1). In comparison, the average score of marketisation increased only 0.61 in the previous four years from 1998–2001.

The NERI index is an assessment system for relative progress in marketisation for China's provinces using a comparative method. Marketisation is assessed in five fields by a total of 23 basic indicators. Data are either from statistics or enterprise and household surveys. The NERI index is now available for the

Figure 3.1 **NERI index for progress in marketisation in China's provinces, 2001 and 2005**

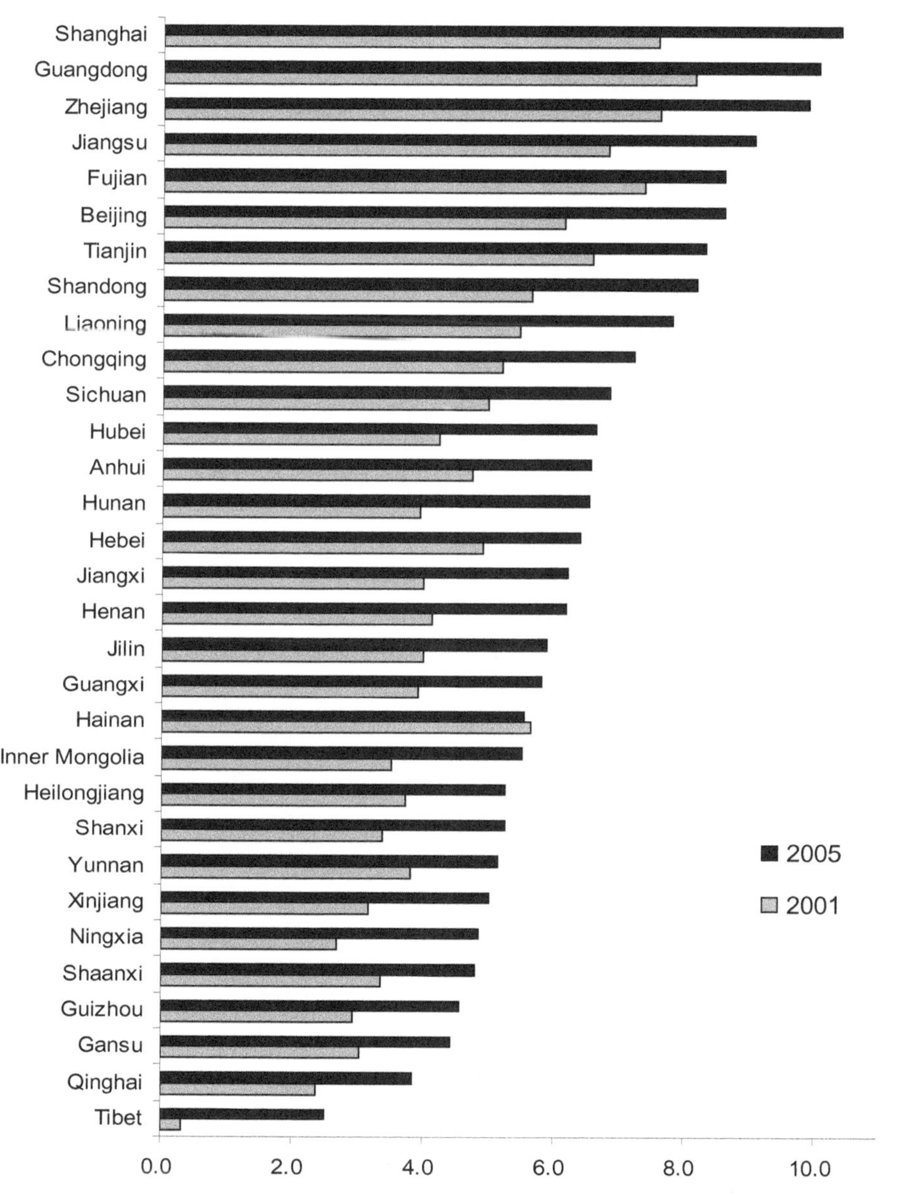

Source: Fan, G., Wang, X. and Zhu, H., 2007. *NERI Index of Marketisation for China's Provinces: 2006 report* (in Chinese), Economic Science Press, Beijing.

years from 1997 to 2005. Four reports have been published (Fan and Wang 2001; Fan et al. 2003, 2004, 2007). A map of China shows the relative achievements of China's provinces in marketisation in 2005 (Figure 3.2).

In this index system, each of the 23 indicators is normalised into a basic index with a zero–10 relative score system at the base year. For data shown in Figure 3.1, the base year is 2001. The best and worst performing provinces in a particular indicator receive scores of 10 and zero, respectively. Other provinces receive scores in between, according to their performance in this indicator relative to the best and worst performing provinces. For a positively related

Figure 3.2 **Marketisation in China, 2005**

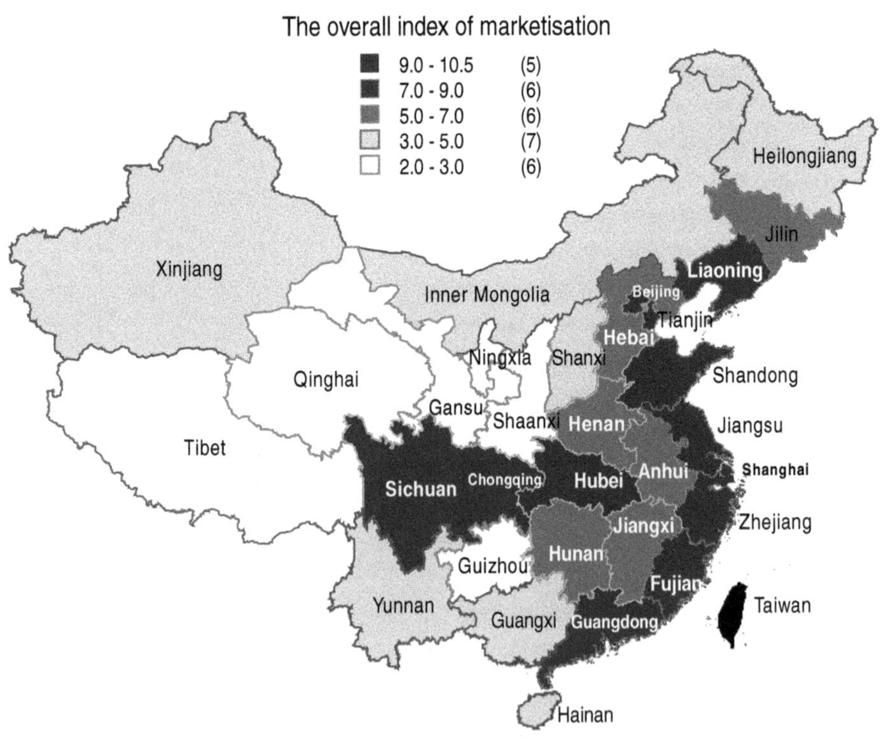

Source: Fan, G., Wang, X. and Zhu, H., 2007. *NERI Index of Marketisation for China's Provinces: 2006 report* (in Chinese), Economic Science Press, Beijing.

indicator, for instance, the score of a basic index j for province i, noted as S_{ij}, is calculated with the following equation

$$S_{ij} = \frac{V_i - V_{min}}{V_{max} - V_{min}} \times 10$$

After positive or negative variations over years, a basic index allows a province to have scores above 10 or below zero, so that its progress over time can be measured.

For a certain field—for instance, development of the non-state enterprise sector—a field index is constituted using a few basic indices. A total of five field indices constitute the overall marketisation index. All the field indices are weighted equally in the overall index, as are the basic indices in each field index.[1]

The next section reviews progress in marketisation in China in the five fields as classified in the NERI Index of Marketisation using mainly direct statistical and survey data other than the scores of the index.

Government and market relations

We measure the level of resource allocation by governments and the market using the share of government budgetary expenses in gross domestic product (GDP). In this measure, the government share was lowered significantly during the reform period, while the market played increasingly important roles in resource allocation. At the national level, the share was 30.8 per cent in 1978 (the first year of economic reform), decreasing to 18.5 per cent in 2005 (the lowest ratio during this period was 11.2 per cent in 1995 and 1996) (National Bureau of Statistics various years). There were slight decreases in this share during the period 2001–05. The budgetary share in GDP is certainly not a linear indicator for marketisation; it will become stable at a certain level after the transitional period. We have found, however, that changes in this share in the past generally related to market-oriented institutional reforms, and provinces with relatively low shares were generally more marketised in different aspects. It is, therefore, still a good indicator, for the time being, to reflect relative changes in the role of governments and the market in resource allocation.

Nevertheless, this is not a full picture for resource allocation between governments and the market, because there is a large amount of non-tax financial collection by different levels of government, which is used outside the budget. Two additional indicators are helpful for these issues. One is the non-tax financial burden of enterprises as a proportion of their total sales (data are from enterprise surveys covering about 4,000 enterprises). As a provincial average, the burden fell from 2.8 per cent in 2001 to 1.6 per cent in 2005. Another indicator is farmers' tax and non-tax burdens as a proportion of their per capita income. This fell from 3.6 per cent in 2001 to 0.4 per cent in 2005. Both indicators show improvement in the past four years. In particular, the reduction in the latter share is remarkable, and it resulted mainly from abolition of the agricultural tax and non-tax collections in rural areas.

It is also important to examine the level of government intervention in enterprises. This can be indicated by the survey data on the proportion of entrepreneurs' working time spent dealing with various government departments and their officials (survey data from more than 4,000 enterprises, by NERI). It fell slightly from an average of 18 per cent to 17.2 per cent in the four years covered, but the level of government intervention remains high (Fan et al. 2007).

One indicator shows a worsening situation: the size of government (number of employees) as a share of the total population. At the national level, it increased from 0.86 per cent in 2001 to 0.95 per cent in 2005 (National Bureau of Statistics various years).[2]

The above indicators generally show progress in government–market relations, although they also show that further reform of the government sector is needed, especially to reduce the size of government and to reduce unnecessary government intervention in enterprises.

Development of the non-state enterprise sector

The non-state enterprise sector is basically the private enterprise sector, which consists mainly of private enterprises, foreign-funded enterprises, shareholding companies and a small number of collectively owned enterprises (in the pre-reform period, it consisted entirely of collectively owned enterprises).

Development of non-state enterprises made the most remarkable progress among the five fields of marketisation. In the industrial sector in the pre-reform period, state-owned enterprises held a dominant position. The non-state share in gross output value was only 22.4 per cent in 1978, the first year of economic reform. This share increased to 69.2 per cent in 2005. The share of state-owned enterprises shrank from 77.6 per cent to 30.8 per cent during this period (National Bureau of Statistics various years).

In the four years between 2001 and 2005, the non-state share in the industrial sector increased by five percentage points. Meanwhile, the non-state share in total investment in fixed assets increased by 13 percentage points, from 52.6 to 65.6 per cent; and the share of the urban non-state sector in urban employment increased by eight percentage points, from 68.1 to 76.3 per cent (Fan et al. 2007).

Data for the non-state share in the services sector are unavailable. The share could be lower than the share in industry, because a few sectors in services are state dominated, including banking, insurance, telecommunications, railways and aviation. Nevertheless, some other services—such as retail sales, catering, road transport and various personal/residential services—are nearly fully privatised. The non-state shares in total investment and urban employment indicate a general situation of non-state domination of the economy.

Development of the commodity market

In the pre-reform period, prices of most products were controlled by the state. In 2001, the share of prices determined in commodity markets achieved 92 per cent, rising to 92.8 per cent in 2004 (Fan et al. 2007).

During the reform period, most non-tariff trade barriers were removed. The general tariff level reduced substantially before and after WTO accession, from 16.4 per cent in 2000 to 9.8 per cent in 2007 (*China Securities Newspaper*, 27 December 2006).

Local trade protection was also reduced. The NERI index uses enterprise survey data to show that the score for reducing local trade protection—as an average of the 31 provinces—increased from 6.5 to 9.7 in the 2001–05 period, meaning there was a remarkable reduction in local trade barriers (Fan et al. 2007).

Development of factor markets

Although the development of factor markets lagged behind that of the commodity market, various indicators show improvement in factor markets in recent years.

For labour market development, the share of rural workers in total urban employment, as a provincial average, increased from 8.1 per cent in 2001 to 11.9 per cent in 2004 (National Bureau of Statistics various years), which indicates increases in labour mobility and reductions in institutional barriers in the labour market. These statistics are likely to be understated due to incomplete data. Some widely accepted estimates suggest that about 100–120 million rural workers work in cities and towns, and possibly 60–100 million work in rural non-agricultural sectors. The next thing to be done is policy restructuring to enable rural migrants to settle in cities and to be treated equally by the urban social welfare systems.

For development of the financial market, two indicators are important. One is the level of deposits in non-state financial institutions as a share of total deposits in the banking sector, which increased gradually from 32.2 to 36.4 per cent in the four years until 2005. This indicates reductions in the share of state-owned banks, although they remain in a dominant position. Another indicator is the share of bank loans credited to non-state enterprises, which increased from 55.7 to 70.2 per cent during the same period—the latter basically consistent with non-state shares in the industrial sector. This shows significant progress in the commercialisation of the banking sector. State-owned enterprises no longer enjoy the favourable position in obtaining bank loans that they did in the earlier period (Fan et al. 2007).

To indicate development of the technology market, the market transaction value of technologies increased from 2,566 yuan to 4,848 yuan per capita technical personnel during the period from 2001 to 2005. Nevertheless, the latter figure is still low in its absolute value (Fan et al. 2007).

One worsening indicator in this field is foreign direct investment (FDI) as a ratio of GDP. As a provincial average, this ratio decreased from 30.7 to 20.5 (million US dollars per billion yuan of GDP, both in current prices) during the period from 2001 to 2005. This is because GDP is growing faster than FDI, although total FDI is still large. In 2005, FDI was US$60 billion, but there have been large regional variations. While FDI in the traditional major recipient region, Guangdong Province, is declining, it increased rapidly in the Yangzi River Delta region—that is, in Jiangsu, Zhejiang and Shanghai—and a few other provinces in the coastal and central areas (Fan et al. 2007).

Market intermediaries and the legal environment for the market

To measure development of market intermediaries, one should consider numbers of independent accountants, lawyers, consultants, chambers of commerce, and other professionals. However, data are available only for independent accountants and lawyers. These two indicators, together as a share in total population, increased slightly during 2001–05. This reflects market development in the current stage because there were no lawyers in the pre-reform period, and accountants were not independent.

To measure the legal environment for businesses, an available indicator is 4,000 company leaders' judgments collected from enterprise surveys. The average score at the provincial level in the NERI index is generally low, and shows slight deterioration in the legal environment in 2005 from that in 2001 (2.85 for 2005 and 2.88 for 2001).

To measure protection of intellectual property rights, the only available information is patent applications and grants per technical personnel. These data nearly doubled during the period, showing a rapid improvement.

A general assessment of marketisation in China

A basic market framework has been established in China. Marketisation has made progress in nearly all fields in recent years. The most remarkable achievement is development of the non-state enterprise sector, which has held the dominant position in the Chinese economy. Development of the commodity market has been relatively rapid, and market competition is now playing a dominant role in industry and trade. Factor markets developed more slowly in general, although they have been making significant progress in recent years.

There are also bottlenecks in market-oriented transformation. Most importantly, institutional and legal frameworks are incomplete and, to some extent, conflict with the market mechanism. There are still unnecessary government interventions, unregulated financial collections and low transparency in administration. The size of government is inflating. The legal environment for the market is still undesirable. These all indicate a need for further institutional change and public sector reform.

At the sector level, the manufacturing sector is now nearly fully market-oriented, whereas marketisation in the financial sector is lagging. A few service sectors are still low in efficiency and lack market competition. Market intermediaries are underdeveloped.

In terms of regional development, the process of marketisation is uneven. While the eastern coastal areas are more marketised than other regions, the achievement of marketisation in some central and western provinces is relatively low. The non-state enterprise sector is underdeveloped in these provinces, and the business climate there is less desirable than elsewhere. In spite of this, the encouraging news is that most provinces made remarkable progress in marketisation in recent years (see Figure 3.1).

Does marketisation contribute to economic growth?

In this section, we test empirically whether marketisation contributes to China's economic growth at the provincial level, using the NERI Index of Marketisation and a panel data growth model. The NERI index was first established in 2001, and has been updated four times (Fan and Wang 2001; Fan et al. 2003, 2004, 2007). It aims to assess relative achievements in marketisation in China's 31 provinces. It has so far covered nine years, from 1997 to 2005. Within each of four sub-periods, the scores for each province are comparable not only with other provinces, but over years, so progress in marketisation in each province can be traced. Due to changes in some statistical indicators, however, and modification of the index system, scores were not comparable between different sub-periods.

In this chapter, we convert all the indices into a consistent style: that is, we make all the scores comparable for the whole period from 1997 to 2005 (see Table A3.1 for a consistent version of the NERI Index of Marketisation and Table A3.2 for the whole structure of the NERI index system). This enables us to carry out a panel data analysis to test the contribution of marketisation to China's economic growth. A Solow-type growth model with modification to include a human capital variable (see Solow 1956; Lucas 1988) and a few structural variables—that is, the marketisation index, trade dependency ratio and a regional dummy—is specified as follows

$$lnY_{it}=C+a_1lnK_{it}+a_2lnL_{it}+a_3E_{it}+a_4M_{it}+a_5R_{it}+a_6D_{it} \quad (1)$$

where Y is provincial GDP in constant prices for year 1990; K is provincial capital stock in 1990 prices; L is provincial employment; E is the average year of schooling of the provincial population; M is the marketisation index; R is the trade dependency ratio (sum of the import and export value as a proportion of GDP) for possible growth effects of economic openness; D is a dummy variable for the coastal areas to catch the geographic differences in initial levels of log GDP (D=1 for coastal provinces and zero otherwise); and C is the intercept term. The subscripts $_i$ ($_i$= 1...31) and $_t$ ($_t$=1997...2005) represent provinces and years, respectively.

An earlier version of the model also includes a variable for urbanisation, which is represented by urban share in total employment. A non-positive and insignificant result was derived, probably due to low accuracy of the data (statistical data for rural–urban migrant workers are incomplete). It is therefore omitted from the model.

Data are calculated mainly from provincial statistics from 1997 to 2005 (National Bureau of Statistics 2005b), except the marketisation index. GDP is deflated using the implied GDP deflators from the National Bureau of Statistics. Capital stock is calculated from provincial investment in fixed assets during the 1952–2005 period, using a perpetual inventory method, and is deflated using the price index for investment in fixed assets.[3] The average year of schooling is calculated from the grouped data for the population at six years old and above with the following assumptions: six years of schooling for primary education, nine years for junior secondary education, 12 years for senior secondary education and 16 years for tertiary and postgraduate education. Export and import values are converted into yuan using average exchange rates for the corresponding year. The dummy variable for coastal areas covers the following provinces: Liaoning, Beijing, Tianjin, Hebei, Shandong, Shanghai, Jiangsu, Zhejiang, Fujian, Guangdong and Hainan. Guangxi is excluded because it does not have a major port, and it is customarily not classified as a coastal province.

The model is estimated using fixed-effect and random-effect generalised least squares GLS regressions. The two results are very similar, and the Hausman Test accepts the random-effect regression. The results of the unrestricted model show a nearly perfect nature of constant returns to capital and labour—very close to that of the restricted model. With inclusion of the education variable, the economy shows an increasing return to scale technology, thus indicating a significant contribution of human capital to economic growth (Table 3.1). This could include its direct contribution to growth and possibly a spillover effect.

The marketisation index is positive and significant, indicating an important effect on economic growth (Table 3.1). The trade dependency ratio has a positive, although insignificant, estimate. The growth effect of economic openness is therefore unconfirmed.

In Table 3.2, the contribution of factors to economic growth is calculated based on the estimates of the unrestricted model in Table 3.1. Statistical data for inputs and output are of provincial averages, divided into two sub-periods—that is, 1998–2001 and 2002–05. The table shows that capital growth made a major contribution to economic growth. Education made a 1.3 percentage point contribution to the economic growth rate in the first sub-period, but contributed only 0.4 percentage points in the second sub-period. Marketisation contributed 0.8 percentage point to growth in the first sub-period, but 2.4 percentage points in the second sub-period. This is clear evidence that marketisation has made an important contribution to China's economic growth. The marketisation process was accelerated after China's WTO accession, and has led to significant increases in its contribution to economic growth.

Conclusions

We have shown that marketisation in China accelerated during the period from 2001 to 2005—that is, the period after China's WTO accession. The basic framework of a market economy has been established, although there are still

Table 3.1 **Estimation results**

	Restricted model (fixed effect)	Restricted model (random effect)	Unrestricted model (random effect)
lnK	0.5790	0.5843	0.5900
	(20.33*)	(25.70*)	(21.49*)
lnL	0.4210	0.4157	0.4195
			(16.70*)
E (year of schooling)	0.0819	0.0798	0.0782
	(5.31*)	(6.26*)	(5.80*)
M (marketisation)	0.0529	0.0518	0.0501
	(6.54*)	(7.61*)	(6.08*)
R (trade/GDP)	0.0153	0.0229	0.0263
	(0.34)	(0.57)	(0.64)
D (coastal dummy)	(dropped)	0.1193	0.1179
		(2.58*)	(2.58*)
C (constant)	–1.1942	–1.2199	–1.2716
	(10.70*)	(–13.06*)	(–7.40*)
R2: within	0.9593	0.9498	0.9590
Between	0.9882	0.9624	0.9899
Overall	0.9850	0.9602	0.9878

Notes: The numbers in parentheses are 'z' ratios. Those with * are significant at the 1 per cent level.
Source: Authors' calculations.

Table 3.2 **Growth accounting: factor contribution to economic growth**

	GDP	Capital	Labour	Education	Marketisation
Coefficient		0.590	0.419	0.078	0.050
Annual input–output growth					
1998–2001 (per cent)	9.8	11.3	–0.2	0.161	0.153
2002–05 (per cent)	12.5	14.5	1.9	0.048	0.471
Contribution to growth rate (percentage points)					
1998–2001		6.7	–0.1	1.3	0.8
2002–05		8.6	0.8	0.4	2.4
Share of contribution (growth rate=100 per cent)					
1998–2001 (per cent)		67.8	–1.0	12.8	7.8
2002–05 (per cent)		68.5	6.2	3.0	18.9

Notes: Education is measured by annual changes in years of schooling, and marketisation is measured by annual changes in the scores of the NERI Index of Marketisation. Statistics for the GDP growth rate at the provincial level, on average, are higher than at the national level.
Sources: Table 3.1 and Table A3.1; National Bureau of Statistics (NBS), various years. *China Statistical Yearbook*, China Statistical Press, Beijing.

bottlenecks in further development of market mechanisms, due mainly to lack of government sector reform and an undesirable legal environment for a market economy. This indicates a need for further institutional reforms.

Using the NERI Index of Marketisation as a basis for empirical study, this chapter finds that marketisation made a significant contribution to economic growth during the period from 1997 to 2005, especially in recent years.

Notes

1 In our earlier reports, we used the Principal Component Analysis Method (PCAM) for weight determination. We found, however, that the PCAM and an equal-weighting method produce very similar results. In addition, the PCAM leads to incomparability of scores over time due to changes in weights, whereas an equal-weighting method has an advantage in providing consistent scores over time.

2 The size of government is indicated approximately by employment in public management and social organisations, which includes employment in political parties and other social organisations, however, employment in the government and the ruling party accounted for the greatest part.

3 The initial national total capital stock in 1952 is assumed to be 69 billion yuan in 1952 prices, based on the estimate of Chow (1993); also see Wang (2006). With an assumption of equal capital–output ratio, the initial capital stock is distributed to each province based on the provincial share in GDP in 1952. The depreciation rate is set at 5 per cent for the pre-reform period, and gradually increased to 9.2 per cent from 1979 to 1992.

References

China Securities Newspaper, 2006. 'The general tariff level of China will reduce to 9.8%', *China Securities Newspaper,* 27 December.

Chow, G.C., 1993. 'Capital formation and economic growth in China', *The Quarterly Journal of Economics*, 58(3):809–42.

Fan, G. and Wang, X., 2001. *NERI Index of Marketisation for China's Provinces: 2000 report* (in Chinese), Economic Science Press, Beijing.

Fan, G., Wang, X. and Zhu, H., 2003. *NERI Index of Marketisation for China's Provinces: 2001 report* (in Chinese), Economic Science Press, Beijing.

——, 2004. *NERI Index of Marketisation for China's Provinces: 2004 report* (in Chinese), Economic Science Press, Beijing.

——, 2007. *NERI Index of Marketisation for China's Provinces: 2006 report* (in Chinese), Economic Science Press, Beijing.

Lucas, R.E., 1988. 'On the mechanics of economic development', *Journal of Monetary Economics*, 22:3–42.

National Bureau of Statistics (NBS), various years. *China Statistical Yearbook* (in Chinese), China Statistical Press, Beijing.

——, 2005b. *China Compendium of Statistics: 1949–2004* (in Chinese), China Statistical Press, Beijing.

Solow, R.M., 1956. 'A contribution to the theory of economic growth', *Quarterly Journal of Economics*, 70:65–94.

Wang, X., 2006. 'Growth accounting after statistical revisions', in R. Garnaut and L. Song (eds), *The Turning Point in China's Economic Development*, Asia Pacific Press, The Australian National University, Canberra:35–52.

Table A3.1 **NERI index of marketisation for China's provinces, 1997–2005**

	1997	1998	1999	2000	2001	2002	2003	2004	2005
Beijing	4.786	4.550	4.567	4.886	6.171	6.917	7.498	8.188	8.619
Tianjin	4.795	5.204	5.432	5.846	6.589	6.732	7.027	7.863	8.342
Hebei	4.507	4.714	4.733	4.777	4.926	5.288	5.585	6.048	6.405
Shanxi	2.855	3.078	3.044	3.058	3.402	3.928	4.626	5.130	5.262
Inner Mongolia	3.048	3.499	3.223	3.318	3.531	3.998	4.389	5.119	5.521
Liaoning	4.941	5.002	4.708	4.956	5.473	6.064	6.605	7.365	7.835
Jilin	3.665	3.728	3.672	3.752	3.999	4.579	4.691	5.493	5.890
Heilongjiang	2.876	3.486	3.266	3.472	3.734	4.089	4.451	5.046	5.263
Shanghai	5.847	5.897	6.011	6.627	7.616	8.344	9.355	9.808	10.407
Jiangsu	6.227	6.385	6.516	6.611	6.829	7.396	7.966	8.625	9.065
Zhejiang	6.619	6.879	6.904	7.203	7.643	8.373	9.100	9.772	9.896
Anhui	4.734	4.698	4.509	4.554	4.750	4.951	5.370	5.992	6.556
Fujian	6.642	6.973	6.943	7.156	7.393	7.632	7.972	8.330	8.624
Jiangxi	3.733	4.189	3.800	3.914	4.003	4.634	5.059	5.758	6.225
Shandong	5.182	5.597	5.237	5.355	5.661	6.229	6.812	7.522	8.210
Henan	4.025	4.254	3.893	3.986	4.136	4.300	4.889	5.638	6.198
Hubei	3.718	4.107	3.783	3.892	4.248	4.654	5.468	6.105	6.652
Hunan	3.709	3.991	3.658	3.703	3.939	4.407	5.032	6.113	6.546
Guangdong	7.255	7.456	7.491	7.774	8.183	8.627	8.992	9.361	10.057
Guangxi	3.960	4.021	3.862	3.854	3.934	4.750	5.000	5.415	5.818
Hainan	5.423	5.311	5.192	5.215	5.664	5.094	5.032	5.411	5.542
Chongqing	4.616	4.741	4.693	4.789	5.202	5.706	6.469	7.196	7.234
Sichuan	4.525	4.670	4.406	4.542	4.999	5.346	5.855	6.383	6.860
Guizhou	2.740	3.032	2.855	2.954	2.947	3.044	3.667	4.171	4.572
Yunnan	3.636	3.894	3.561	3.688	3.823	3.797	4.231	4.813	5.153
Tibet	0.100	0.150	0.200	0.250	0.325	0.625	0.792	1.555	2.500
Shaanxi	2.792	3.179	3.220	3.347	3.369	3.905	4.109	4.457	4.797
Gansu	2.832	3.160	2.951	2.920	3.044	3.054	3.323	3.949	4.445
Qinghai	1.547	1.785	1.866	2.168	2.375	2.446	2.596	3.099	3.838
Ningxia	1.990	2.367	2.473	2.558	2.696	3.238	4.238	4.564	4.850
Xinjiang	1.474	1.662	1.879	2.526	3.183	3.409	4.264	4.762	5.024
Average	4.026	4.247	4.147	4.311	4.638	5.018	5.499	6.098	6.523

Note: The original data are comparable only within each of the four sub-periods (that is, 1997–99, 1999–2000, 2000–02, 2001–05), due to changes in statistical definition, modification of the index system and changes in base years. Because each sub-period's first year overlaps with the last year of the previous sub-period, this enables us to calculate the conversion factors for scores in every adjacent two sub-periods, and then recalculate the scores in all the earlier sub-periods using a nesting method. Data in this table are therefore comparable over the entire period from 1997 to 2005.

Source: Calculated from the NERI Index of Marketisation: Fan, G. and Wang, X., 2001. *NERI Index of Marketisation for China's Provinces: 2000 report* (in Chinese), Economic Science Press, Beijing; Fan, G., Wang, X. and Zhu, H., 2003. *NERI Index of Marketisation for China's Provinces: 2001 report* (in Chinese), Economic Science Press, Beijing; Fan, G., Wang, X. and Zhu, H., 2004. *NERI Index of Marketisation for China's Provinces: 2004 report* (in Chinese), Economic Science Press, Beijing; Fan, G., Wang, X. and Zhu, H., 2007. *NERI Index of Marketisation for China's Provinces: 2006 report* (in Chinese), Economic Science Press, Beijing.

Table A3.2 **The structure of the NERI Index of Marketisation**

Title of the indices	Sequence number of basic indices
The overall index of marketisation	
I Government–market relations	
I-1 Government allocation of resources in GDP	1
I-2 Tax and non-tax burden of farmers	2
I-3 Government intervention in enterprises	3
I-4 Non-tax burden on enterprises	4
I-5 Size of government	5
II Development of the non-state enterprise sector	
II-1 Non-state share in industrial output	6
II-2 Non-state share in total investment in fixed assets	7
II-3 Non-state share in total urban employment	8
III Development of the commodity market	
III-1 Market pricing	
III-1-1 Market pricing in retail sales of consumer goods	9
III-1-2 Market pricing in capital goods	10
III-1-3 Market pricing in farm products	11
III-2 Local trade protection	12
IV Development of factor markets	
IV-1 Marketisation of the financial sector	
IV-1-1 Share of non-state financial institutions in total deposits	13
IV-1-2 Share of bank loans credited to non-state enterprises	14
IV-2 Foreign investment	15
IV-3 Labour mobility	16
IV-4 Development of the technology market	17
V Intermediate/legal framework	
V-1 Development of market intermediaries	
V-1-1 Share of lawyers in local population	18
V-1-2 Share of independent accountants in local population	19
V-2 Legal environment for businesses	20
V-3 Protection of intellectual property rights	
V-3-1 Patent applications per research and development personnel	21
V-3-2 Patents granted per research and development personnel	22
V-4 Protection of consumers' rights	23

Source: Fan, G., Wang, X. and Zhu, H., 2007. *NERI Index of Marketisation for China's Provinces: 2006 report* (in Chinese), Economic Science Press, Beijing.

4

Facing protectionism generated by trade disputes

China's post WTO blues

Wing Thye Woo and Geng Xiao

The escalation of friction between China and its trading partners

China's current account in the balance of payments has been in surplus since 1994 and it has shown a clear upward trend, reaching US$184 billion in 2006, or 9 per cent of gross domestic product (GDP). As China's capital account is also in persistent surplus because of the large inflows of foreign direct investment (FDI) and capital controls on outflows, its foreign exchange reserves reached US$1.07 trillion in 2006—the largest in the world. China also became the second-largest holder of US Treasury securities, holding as much as US$353.6 billion, trailing only Japan, which holds US$648.8 billion.

At the time of writing (June 2007), China's overall trade surplus, the China–US trade surplus and the China–EU trade surplus continued to soar,[1] causing a marked escalation in concern about China's unfair trading practices and the gross undervaluation of the renminbi. In February 2007, the US Trade Representative (USTR) had filed a case with the World Trade Organization (WTO) against prohibited subsidies in China. This action was followed by two more WTO cases against China in April 2007—challenging market access restrictions on products of copyright-intensive industries and challenging weaknesses in the legal regime for protection and enforcement of copyrights and trademarks.[2]

In order to appreciate adequately the high intensity of the sound and the fury of the anti-China rhetoric—and the global character of these criticisms—it is worthwhile to quote a number of news reports from the barrage of press articles on the trade imbalance issue that appeared on 13 June 2007.[3]

The *Financial Times* (2007a) reported

> Peter Mandelson, the EU trade commissioner...called various aspects of China's trade policy 'illogical, indefensible' and 'unacceptable and accused [China] of doing nothing to rein in rampant counterfeiting...Mr Mandelson also refused to grant China market economy status...[because it had] fulfilled [only] one of five criteria.[4]

The Straits Times (2007) of Singapore reported

> Peter Mandelson proclaimed that the...[EU] trade deficit with China was no longer 'tolerable' and warned that relations with Beijing were now at a 'cross-roads'...[Trade is] so skewed that the EU now exports more to Switzerland... than to the entire Chinese market.

USA Today (2007) reported that

> [a]fter years of inconclusive skirmishing, trade tensions between the United States and China are about to intensify. 'We are competing not only with a country with low wages but with very high and heavy subsidies and a rigging of their currency,' says Rep. Sander Levin, D-Mich., chairman of the House trade subcommittee. 'I hate the term trade war because it is always used when you try to get a fair break...Sometimes pressure works.'

In confirmation of the growing perception of—and deepening dissatisfaction about—unfair Chinese trading practices, the media on 13 June 2007 also contained reports on the actions being undertaken by the Bush administration and the Chinese government to forestall protectionism.

The *Standard* (2007) of Hong Kong reported

> US lawmakers plan to introduce legislation today seeking to pressure China to raise the value of the yuan to stem a ballooning trade imbalance... Sponsored by Democratic senator Charles Schumer, the bill will lay out the US response whenever countries 'unfairly undervalue their currency'. Currently, there are half a dozen measures before the US Congress aimed at China, including proposals to apply sanctions unless it allows the yuan to appreciate by at least 10 per cent.

The *Wall Street Journal* (2007b) reported

> [t]urning aside growing congressional anger over the US trade deficit with China, President George Bush's administration today will reject demands that it formally accuse Beijing of 'manipulating' its currency to give Chinese companies an edge over American businesses. 'There might be an initial sigh of relief in the markets that the Treasury has not taken a more confrontational line, but protectionist pressures are only likely to build', Julian Jessop, chief

> international economist at Capital Economics in London, warned clients in a note yesterday. Meanwhile Beijing took steps yesterday apparently aimed, at least in part, at defusing US concerns. Chinese authorities permitted an unusually large rise in its tightly controlled currency.

The *International Herald Tribune* (2007) reported that 'the yuan had the biggest gain since the end of a dollar link in July 2005. The yuan rose 0.26 per cent to 7.6436 against the dollar...[yielding a cumulative gain of] 8.3 per cent since...July 2005.'

Events then moved quickly. On 14 June 2007, Senators Max Baucus (Democrat from Montana), Charles E. Grassley (Republican from Iowa), Charles E. Schumer (Democrat from New York) and Lindsey Graham (Republican from South Carolina) introduced legislation 'to punish China if it did not change its policy of intervening in currency markets to keep the exchange value of the currency, the yuan, low' (*New York Times* 2007).

On 19 June 2007, the International Monetary Fund (IMF) adopted a new country surveillance framework that set out

> ...a catch-all obligation on countries not to adopt policies that undermine the stability of the international system, and lists a set of objective criteria that will be used to indicate whether a country is complying with its commitments. Warning lights will include large-scale currency intervention, the accumulation of reserves and 'fundamental exchange rate misalignment'—a term that mirrors language in a bill before the US Congress that would impose penalties on nations that fail to correct such misalignments. Rodrigo Rato, managing director of the IMF, said: 'This decision is good news for the IMF reform programme and good news for the cause of multilateralism... [because this new framework] gives clear guidance to our members on how they should run their exchange rate policies, on what is acceptable to the international community and what is not' (*Financial Times* 2007b).

The above developments were warnings that China, Europe and the United States could be marching towards a trade war. In this chapter, we examine the reasons for the trade friction with China and propose policies to reduce that friction. Our discussion will focus on four questions

1. What are the problems caused by trade imbalances?
2. What are the problems revealed by the appearance of trade imbalances?
3. Is a large yuan appreciation the best cure for trade friction?
4. What is to be done?

What are the problems caused by trade imbalances?

It is not uncommon to encounter allegations that the US–China trade deficit represents the export of unemployment from China to the United States. A recent study by Robert Scott (2007), of the Economic Policy Institute, used an input–output model to arrive at the claim that the bilateral trade deficit of US$49.5 billion in 1997 caused the loss of 597,300 jobs that year and the 2006 bilateral trade deficit of US$235.4 billion caused the loss of 2,763,400 jobs—and that every state had suffered a net loss of jobs from the rise in the bilateral trade deficit during 1997–2006. The alleged job losses in 2006 from the bilateral trade deficit implied that the 2006 unemployment rate was 1.21 percentage points higher than if the bilateral trade balance had been zero.[5]

There are two major problems with the Scott (2007) study. First, the overall unemployment rate in the United States did not grow in line either with the widening overall US trade deficit or with the widening US–China trade deficit. The average unemployment rate of 4.9 per cent in the 1998–2006 period was lower than the average unemployment rates in the previous periods of 1980–88 and 1989–97, which were 7.5 per cent and 6 per cent respectively. In reality, the US economy was a highly successful job-creation machine in the 1997–2006 period.

Second, in the face of the strong demand for labour in the US economy during the period of growing trade deficit, a substantial amount of the so-called job losses could have been voluntary departures by workers—rather than involuntary displacement of workers—from import-competing industries that paid low wages or had potentially low wage growth in the future.

The more sophisticated complaint against the growing trade deficit is that the displacement of workers adds to the downward pressure on US wages created by globalisation. This downward wage pressure comes from the post 1990 integration of the labour force in the former Soviet Union, India and China into the international division of labour. The number of workers already engaged in the international division of labour was 1.08 billion in 1990, and the combined labour force of the former Soviet Union, India and China was 1.23 billion (Table 1). The division of labour in 1990 was certainly an unnatural one because half of the world's workforce had been kept out of it voluntarily by the autarkic policies of the former Soviet Union, India and China.

The economic isolation of the Soviet bloc started crumbling when the new non-communist Solidarity government of Poland began marketisation and internationalisation of its economy on 1 January 1990. The economic transition and political disintegration of the Soviet bloc became irreversible when President Boris Yeltsin replaced Mikhail Gorbachev as the unambiguous leader of Russia in August 1991 and implemented market-oriented reforms in January 1992.[6]

For the Chinese élite, the events in the Soviet Union confirmed that there did not exist a third way in the capitalism versus socialism debate. In early 1992, Deng Xiaoping led a successful campaign to put China firmly on the path of convergence to a private market economy (Sachs and Woo 2000, 2003). Today, under the heading of a socialist market economy with Chinese characteristics, the Chinese constitution gives private property the same legal status as public property, and the Chinese Communist Party accepts capitalists as members.

In 1991, India faced a balance-of-payments crisis, and it responded by going well beyond administration of the standard corrective macroeconomic medicine of fiscal monetary tightening and exchange-rate devaluation into comprehensive adjustments of microeconomic incentives. The trade regime was deregulated significantly, restrictions on foreign investment were relaxed, reform of the banking sector and the capital markets was initiated, and divestment of public enterprises and tax reforms were announced (Acharya 2004).

A decade after the start of internationalisation, the number of workers involved in the international economic system had increased to 2.67 billion in 2000 (with 1.36 billion workers from the former Soviet Union, India and China) (Table 4.1). The Heckscher-Ohlin model would predict that this doubling of world labour—achieved by bringing in cheaper labour from the former Soviet Union, India and China—would lower the relative price of labour-intensive goods and hence reduce real wages in industrialised economies.[7]

The fact that US capital could now move abroad to set up production facilities in the economies of the former Soviet Union, India and China to service the

Table 4.1 **The distribution of the global labour force, 1990 and 2000** (million persons)

		Non-SIC[a] countries		SIC countries		
	Total	Industrialised economies	Developing economies	China	India	Soviet bloc
1990	2,315	403	680	687	332	213
2000	2,672	438	851	764	405	214

[a] SIC— former Soviet Union, India and China.
Source: Freeman, R., 2004. Doubling the global work force: the challenge of integrating China, India, and the former Soviet Bloc into the world economy, Harvard University, 8 November (unpublished). Our figure for 'total' in 2002 is different from that in Freeman (2004).

US market provided another channel (besides the cross-border movement of goods) for globalisation to depress US wage rates. It is important to note that the imposition of a very high US tariff would not only drastically curb imports from the former Soviet Union, India and China, it would also radically reduce this type of FDI flow from the United States to the former Soviet Union, India and China.

The inconvenient fact is, however, that the US real wage has not fallen. One possible explanation to reconcile the theoretical prediction with the real outcome is the remarkably high US productivity growth since the late 1980s, perhaps enabled in large part by the information and communications technology revolution. This productivity growth was high enough to prevent the real wage from declining but not enough to keep it growing at the same rate as GDP growth—and the economic impact of globalisation is manifested in a diminished labour share of GDP.

While the Heckscher-Ohlin model does provide a coherent mechanism for globalisation to lower the labour share of US income and to widen the distribution of US wages, the inconvenient truth is that China cannot be blamed as the most influential factor in these two wage outcomes, even though China accounted for 764 million of the combined labour force of the former Soviet Union, India and China of 1.38 billion in 2000. China is not the main culprit because there have been three other, independent developments that have had important consequences for US wages.

First, there have been technological innovations that have substituted capital for labour—for example, fewer secretaries are needed because answering machines can now convert messages into voice files and email them to the travelling professionals. Technological innovations have also transformed many of what were traditionally non-tradable services into tradable services, allowing jobs to be outsourced to foreign service providers. For example, the information and communications technology revolution has allowed offshore call centres to handle questions from US customers, offshore accountants to process US-based transactions and offshore medical technicians to read the X-rays of US patients.[8]

Second, there have been institutional changes that attenuated the labour share of income. Union membership has declined, reducing the bargaining power of labour. There has also been an upward shift in the compensation norms for high-level executives, often using vehicles such as stock options, which in effect make them co-owners of the company. This could reflect a combination of a shift in social attitudinal norms and more collusion between managers and their boards.[9]

Third, there was increased immigration into the United States (before 2001), especially a disproportionate inward immigration of low-skilled labour.[10]

Based on a partial review of the literature, our assessment is that the pressure that is preventing US wages (especially of unskilled labour) from rising in line with GDP growth can be roughly decomposed among the various factors as follows

- 70–80 per cent of the downward wage pressure is from labour-substituting technological innovations, and wage-weakening institutional changes
- 5–10 per cent of the downward wage pressure is from inward immigration
- 15–20 per cent of the downward pressure is from import competition and the relocation of manufacturing activities abroad.

In short, the popular outcry in the United States and the European Union against China's trade surpluses is misplaced. Even if China's trade balance were zero, the pains of structural adjustment and income redistribution caused by technological innovations, institutional changes, globalisation and immigration would still be there. The additional pain from the incremental structural adjustment caused by the widening trade deficit is minor in comparison.

What are the problems revealed by the appearance of trade imbalances?

Before discussing the economic problems in China and the United States that generated the trade imbalances, we should mention a troubling basic data issue: there is strong disagreement about the size of the US–China trade deficit. Figure 4.1 shows that the Chinese figure for the bilateral deficit in 2006 (US$145 billion) was only 57.7 per cent of the US figure (US$251 billion).[11] The huge gap between these two estimates in 2006 was a huge improvement in accuracy from the past in two ways. First, the gap was usually much larger in previous years: for example, the 1993 Chinese estimate of the trade deficit was only 25.6 per cent of the US estimate. Second, the recent period is one in which the two countries could agree whether the bilateral balance was in surplus or in deficit! Throughout the 1983–92 period, the Chinese data showed China to be running a deficit in its trade with the US but the US data showed a surplus.

Given these wildly different measures of the size of the bilateral trade imbalance, it is only to be expected that each side would regard the bilateral trade imbalance with a different degree of concern. The primary reason for the discrepancy between the Chinese and US estimates is the different national treatment of US–China trade that goes through Hong Kong.[12] Drawing on the work of Feenstra et al. (1999) for the analysis in this chapter, we will measure the US–China trade balance as the simple average between the US estimate and the Chinese estimate, as reported in the IMF's *Direction of Trade Statistics* database.[13]

Figure 4.2 displays three items: China's overall trade balance, the China–US trade balance and the China–EU trade balance. China has been running a surplus on its US trade since 1986, a surplus on its EU trade since 1997 and a surplus on its overall trade since 1994. Since 1986—except for the four years associated with an economic downturn in China (1990, 1991, 1997 and 1998)—the bilateral surplus with the United States exceeded China's overall trade surplus, meaning that China was running massive deficits in its trade with some of its other trading partners.

The changing configuration of China's bilateral trade balances reflects mainly the steady expansion of production networks into China. In this new geographical division of the production of components and of the production stages in manufacturing, China usually makes the cheaper components and assembles the final products by combining the domestically produced components with imported components. The fast transfer of manufacturing and assembly operations to China from Japan, Taiwan and South Korea translates directly into high growth in the China–US trade surplus because this transfer reduces the Japan–US trade surplus and the South Korean–US trade surplus correspondingly. In short, the China–US trade deficit could be reduced by transferring the assembly operations of Korean, Taiwanese, Japanese and European production networks to Vietnam, but the Vietnam–US trade deficit would then increase, leaving the overall US trade balance unchanged.

China's chronic and growing overall trade surplus reveals a deep-seated problem in its economy: its dysfunctional financial system. This problem is revealed by the aggregate-level accounting identity that the overall current account balance (of which, in China, the overall trade account is the biggest part) is determined by the fiscal position of the government, and by the savings-investment decisions of the state-controlled enterprise (SCE) sector and the private sector.[14] Specifically,

$$CA = (T - G) + (S_{SCE} - I_{SCE}) + (S_{private} - I_{private}) \tag{1}$$

where CA is the current account in the balance of payments.

$$CA = (X - M) + R \tag{2}$$

Figure 4.1 **US–China trade deficit: discrepancy between US and Chinese data, 1980–2006** (US$ million)

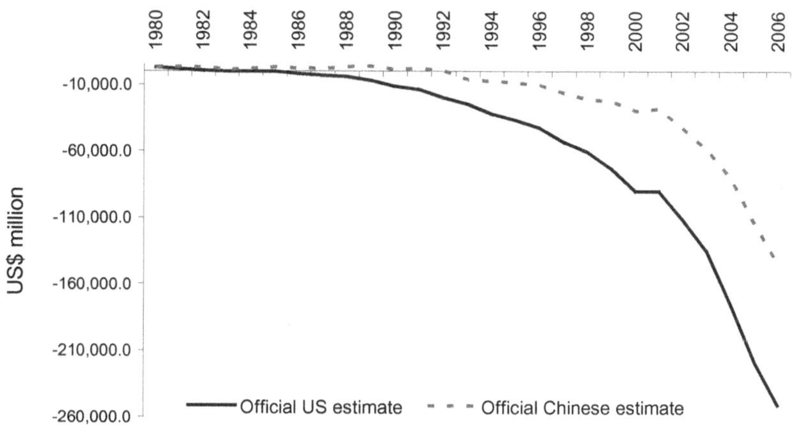

Source: International Monetary Fund (IMF), 2007. *Direction of Trade Statistics*, 9 May, Statistics Department, International Monetary Fund, Washington, DC.

Figure 4.2 **China trade account balance, 1980–2006** (US$ million)

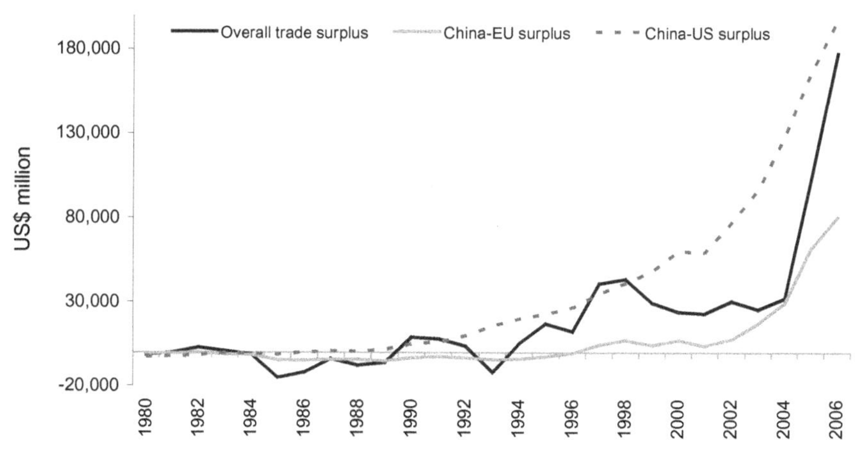

Source: International Monetary Fund (IMF), 2007. *Direction of Trade Statistics*, 9 May, Statistics Department, International Monetary Fund, Washington, DC.

where X is the export of goods and non-factor services, M is the import of goods and non-factor services, R is the net factor earnings from abroad (that is, export of factor services), T is state revenue, G is state expenditure (including state investment), S_{SCE} are the savings of the SCEs, I_{SCE} is investment of the SCEs, $S_{private}$ is savings of the private sector and $I_{private}$ is private-sector investment.

The Chinese fiscal position $(T–G)$ has for the past decade been a small deficit, so it was not the cause for the swelling current account surpluses in the 2000s. The current account surplus exists because the sum of savings by SCEs and the private sector exceeds the sum of their investment expenditures. The current account surplus has expanded steadily because the non-government savings rate has been rising steadily. We will argue later that there is a link between the existence of the current account surplus and the growth of the surplus.

Why has China's financial system failed to translate the savings into investments? Such an outcome was not always the case. Before 1994, the voracious absorption of bank loans by SCEs to invest recklessly kept the current account mostly negative and the creation of non-performing loans high. When the government implemented stricter controls on the state-owned banks from 1994 onwards (for example, by removing top bank officials whenever their bank lent more than its credit quota or allowed the non-performing loan ratio to increase too rapidly), the state-owned banks slowed the growth of loans to SCEs. This cut-back created an excess of savings because the state-owned bank-dominated financial sector did not then channel the released savings (which were also increasing) to finance the investment of the private sector. This failure in financial intermediation by the state-owned banks is quite understandable. Firstly, the legal status of private enterprises was, until recently, lower than that of state-owned enterprises; and, secondly, there was no reliable way to assess the balance sheets of the private enterprises, which were naturally eager to escape taxation. The upshot was that the residual excess savings leaked abroad in the form of the current account surplus. Inadequate financial intermediation has made developing China a capital-exporting country!

This perverse current account outcome is not new. Taiwan had exactly this problem until the mid 1980s when all Taiwanese banks were state owned and were operated according to the civil service regulation that the loan officer had to repay any bad loan that he had approved. The result was a massive failure in financial intermediation, which caused Taiwan's current account surplus to be 21 per cent of GDP in 1986. The reason why China has not been producing the gargantuan current account surpluses seen in Taiwan in the mid 1980s is because of the large amount of SCE investments.

Why is the savings rate of the non-government sector rising? The combined savings of the state-owned enterprise and non-state-owned enterprise sector rose from 20 per cent in 1978 to 30 per cent in 1987, and then went above 45 per cent after 2004. In discussions on the rise of the savings rate, a common view is that the rise reflects the uncertainty about the future that many state-owned enterprise workers feel in the face of widespread privatisation of loss-making state-owned enterprises. We find this explanation incomplete because it seems that there has also been a rise in the rural savings rate even though rural residents have little to fear about the loss of jobs in the state-owned enterprise sector because none of them are employed there.[15]

We see two general changes that have caused urban and rural savings rates to rise significantly. The first is increased worries about the future. The steady decline in state subsidies to medical care, housing, loss-making enterprises and education, and mismanagement of pension funds by the state, have led people to save more to insure against future bad luck (for example, sickness, job loss), to buy their own lodging, build up nest eggs for retirement and invest in their children.

The second change is the secular improvement in the official Chinese attitude towards market capitalism. Given the high rate of return to capital, this increasingly business-friendly attitude of the Communist Party of China has no doubt encouraged rural and urban residents to save for investment: that is, greater optimism about the future has spawned investment-motivated saving.[16] Our investment-motivated savings hypothesis is not new. According to Jeffrey Williamson (1988), the historical record of Western Europe and North America shows that 'investment demand seems to have been the driving force behind private saving and accumulation, past and present'.

In our explanations for the existence and the growth of the current account surpluses, there is a common element: China's financial system. The fact is that savings behaviour is not independent of the sophistication of the financial system. An advanced financial system will have a variety of financial institutions that enable pooling of risks by providing medical insurance, pension insurance and unemployment insurance; and transform savings into education loans, housing loans and other types of investment loans to the private sector. *Ceteris paribus*, the more sophisticated a financial system, the lower the savings rate—a proposition that finds formal statistical support in Liu and Woo (1994) and Woo and Liu (1995). China generates the current account surplus because of inadequate financial intermediation, and the surplus grows over time because the dysfunctional financial system fails to pool risks to reduce uncertainty-induced savings and fails to provide loans to reduce investment-motivated saving (Figure 4.2).

The overall US trade balance has been in deficit at least since 1980, and it has always been much bigger than the US–China trade balance (Figure 4.3). This pattern of imbalances suggests three conclusions. First, the US–China trade deficit is only 22.4 per cent of the overall US trade deficit, so even if the bilateral trade balance were brought to zero by tariffs aimed at China, the overall trade deficit would still be large. Second, the bilateral trade deficit surplus is created by the same factors that are causing the overall trade deficit: the large annual budget deficit created by the tax cuts enacted by the Bush administration in 2001 and the post 2001 growth in defence expenditure. Third, the highly sophisticated US financial system (which pioneered the sub-prime mortgage market and corporate junk bonds to enable consumption and investment) has lowered the US private savings rate.

Clearly, the sustained nature of the overall US trade deficit was possible only because foreign lenders had faith in the growth prospects of the US economy, and because the East Asian central banks were willing to hold an increasing amount of US financial instruments. The paradox is why the US Congress is so concerned about trade deficits when foreigners have such confidence in the economic future of the United States. Both groups cannot be right.

Figure 4.3 **US trade imbalance, 1980–2006** (US$ million)

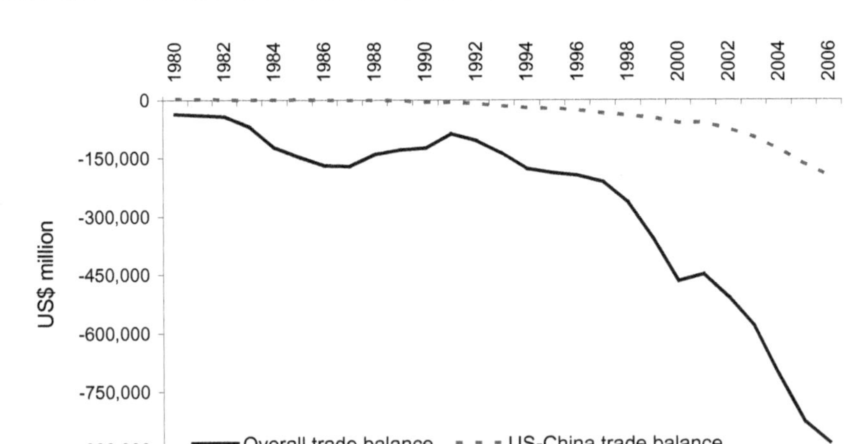

Source: International Monetary Fund (IMF), 2007. *Direction of Trade Statistics*, 9 May, Statistics Department, International Monetary Fund, Washington, DC.

Is a large yuan appreciation the cure for trade friction?

China has been under foreign pressure at least since 2002 to appreciate the yuan significantly. In December 2002, Haruhiko Kuroda and Masahiro Kawai (2002) from Japan's Ministry of Finance called for a yuan appreciation in order to stop China exporting its price deflation to the rest of the world. In September 2003, US Treasury Secretary, John Snow, declared that China should appreciate the yuan as part of its international responsibility to eliminate imbalances in the global balance of payments.[17] In September 2003, Morris Goldstein and Nicholas Lardy (2003) of the Institute for International Economics in Washington, DC, claimed that an immediate yuan appreciation of 15–25 per cent would benefit China because it would remove 'the incentive for further speculative capital inflow and reserve accumulation. No longer would the foreign component of the money supply be working at cross-purposes with the needs of domestic stabilization.'

In March 2007, Goldstein (2007) offered the opinion to the US Congress that the

> ...renminbi (RMB) is now grossly undervalued—on the order of 30 percent or more against an average of China's trading partners and 40 percent or more against the US dollar...[The] US Treasury has refused to label China as a 'currency manipulator' despite overwhelming evidence to the contrary and the managing director of the International Monetary Fund continues to reject the role of global umpire for exchange rate policies that was laid out for the Fund in its charter. China should deliver right away a meaningful 'down payment' of a 10–15 per cent appreciation of the RMB from its current level. Failure by China to drastically reduce its large-scale, one-way intervention in the exchange market should result in a finding of 'currency manipulation' in the Treasury's May 2007 report to the US Congress...Finally, the IMF should return to its roots by taking up in earnest the role that its founders set out for it as the global umpire for exchange rate policies.

We will use the format of question and answer to analyse the question posed in the title of this part of the paper and to assess the validity of the above assertions.

Did China export deflation, as Kuroda and Kawai (2003) claimed?

The fundamental problem with Kuroda and Kawai's claim is that it is impossible to blame Japan's deflation on China's deflation because the timing is wrong. Japan's deflation started with the bursting of the stock market cum real estate bubble in 1992, which was well before China's trade account surpluses started to soar in the 2000s. If anything, trade with China since 2003 has been an important stimulus to Japanese economic recovery. Sustained high Chinese investment spending has sucked in large amounts of intermediate inputs, machinery and capital equipment from Japan.

Would a yuan appreciation reduce global imbalances, as Bergsten (2007) claimed?

There is little doubt that a large appreciation of the yuan against the US dollar—say, 40 per cent, as suggested by Goldstein (2007)—could eliminate the US–China trade deficit as well as China's overall trade surplus. But this move would only hurt China and would not 'save' the world. *Ceteris paribus*, in the aftermath of a 40 per cent yuan appreciation, foreign companies producing in China for the G7 markets would move their operations to other Asian economies (such as Vietnam and Thailand) and export from there, and G7 importers would start importing the same goods from other Asian countries instead. In the absence of a collective appreciation of all Asian currencies, a yuan appreciation would only reconfigure the geographical distribution of the global imbalances, not eliminate them.

How could a collective regional appreciation against the US dollar be achieved?

It would be naive to assume that Asian currencies tend to move closely together when one of them moves a large amount, such as 40 per cent. The last time the Asian currencies moved together by a large amount was during the Asian financial crisis of 1997–98, and China did not join in despite many predictions to the contrary. Should the US government now expand its currency appreciation campaign serially to other East Asian countries and undertake a 'surge' in exchange rate activism on any country that pushes back? For many reasons, this would not be a desirable international economic strategy for the United States.[18]

Would a large, simultaneous collective appreciation of the Asian currencies be an unambiguous gain for the United States?

We are not sure. Immediate cessation of the foreign financing of the US savings gap would translate into an immediate zero current account balance, and this would require an immediate increase in US exports and/or an immediate decrease in US imports. Exports would increase quickly only if there were substantial excess production capacity or if there were a substantial drop in domestic demand that freed up the domestic goods for sale abroad. Imports would decrease quickly only if there were excess production capacity (to enable replacement of imports) or if there were a substantial drop in domestic demand that reduced the use of consumer goods and inputs. Since there is no substantial excess production capacity in the US economy today, the immediate elimination of the current account deficit would require a huge drop in domestic demand, which would have its origin in a large negative wealth shock, possibly in the form of a stock market collapse or an inflationary spike.[19]

Would the absence of a yuan appreciation cause high inflation in China, as Goldstein and Lardy (2003) claimed?

The growth of Chinese money supply has not slowed drastically despite the heightening of anti-inflation rhetoric by the Chinese government in response to the continued high growth of investment expenditure. Has the Chinese government lost control of its money supply, as a number of analysts have warned? Not at all. The speculative inflows and growth in foreign exchange reserves cannot expand the money supply without the agreement of the People's Bank of China (PBC). As well as sterilisation through open-market operations, China has the use of credit quotas on bank lending. The fact is that all Chinese banks are state controlled, and their high-ranking executives are appointed by the state. Given the choice between maximising bank profits or heeding orders from the prime minister's office, the bank chiefs can always be counted on to choose the latter. There is no question about the Communist Party of China losing control of the money supply since 2002.

Money supply growth in 2005–07 did not slow markedly because China chose not to enforce the credit quotas stringently. First, the inflation rate, although rising, is still low. Second, it is good politics to have a booming economy in the period leading up to the important seventeenth Party Congress in November 2007, which will ratify important personnel appointments for the next five years.

What is the correct level for the exchange rate?

The *Economist* magazine constructs a purchasing power parity (PPP) exchange rate based on the prices of Big Mac hamburgers sold in different countries. In 2006, it cost 10.4 yuan to buy a Big Mac in China and US$3.15 in the United States, so the PPP exchange rate was 3.3 yuan per US dollar in 2006, compared with the actual (nominal) exchange rate of 8 yuan per US dollar. Is it, therefore, meaningful to say that the Chinese exchange rate was undervalued by almost 60 per cent in 2006? The answer is no, because the prices of the hamburgers included non-tradable inputs, and the prices of non-tradables were lower in China than in the United States. In general, the prices of non-tradables are lower in developing economies than in industrialised economies because labour costs are lower in the former. With economic development, the prices of non-tradables in the developing economies will rise to bring the price ratio of non-tradables to tradables closer to the price ratio in the industrialised economy.

To see that the gap between the usual PPP exchange rate and the actual exchange rate reflects the development gap between the two countries, we first make the following definitions

a) Defining the consumer price index in China and the United States

$$\text{CPI of China, } CPI^C = (1\text{-}a)\ P^C_T + a\ P^C_N$$
$$\text{CPI of the United States, } CPI^U = (1\text{-}a)\ P^U_T + a\ P^U_N \qquad (3)$$

where CPI is the consumer price index, C is China, U is the United States, P^i_T is the price of the tradable good in country 'i', P^i_N is the price of the non-tradable good in country 'i', and 'a' is the weight of non-tradable goods in the price index.

b) Defining the PPP exchange rate

$$e^{PPP} = CPI^C / CPI^U \qquad (4)$$

We next state the equilibrium conditions.

a) Goods arbitrage

$$P^C_T = e^{actual}\ P^U_T \qquad (5)$$

where e^{actual} is the actual (nominal) exchange rate expressed as the number of yuan per US dollar.

b) Relationship between prices of tradables and non-tradables within each country

$$\text{for developing China, } P^C_T = d\ P^C_N$$

$$\text{for industrialised United States, } P^U_T = f\ P^U_N \qquad (6)$$

c) The difference between the industrialised and the developing economy is that the relative price of non-tradables is higher in the former.

$$d > f > 0 \qquad (7)$$

We can now derive the following relationship between the PPP exchange rate and the actual exchange rate

$$e^{PPP} = CPI^{C} / CPI^{U}$$

$$e^{PPP} = [(1\text{-}a+af)/(1\text{-}a+ad)]\ e^{actual}$$

$$e^{PPP} < e^{actual} \qquad (8)$$

The above exercise shows that it is conceptually difficult to determine the 'correctness' of a country's exchange rate on the basis of PPP exchange rates. The actual (nominal) exchange rate of a developing economy will always be undervalued in relation to the PPP exchange rate, and it is ludicrous to demand that the government of the developing economy set its exchange rate equal to the PPP exchange rate (because this is not a sustainable policy).

One meaningful definition of the 'correct exchange rate' is that it is the 'market-clearing exchange rate': the exchange rate that is generated by the foreign exchange markets in the absence of intervention by any central bank. The fact that the People's Bank of China has been accumulating foreign reserves during every period means that the yuan is undervalued according to this definition. What would happen, however, if China were to go further in its marketisation of foreign exchange transactions by removing its capital controls? Diversification of asset portfolios by private Chinese agents would surely result in a great outflow of funds, possibly causing the yuan to depreciate. In such a case, the present exchange rate of 8 yuan per US dollar would be overvalued compared with the 'complete free-market exchange rate'. Of course, no one knows whether the complete free-market exchange rate would be higher or lower than 8 yuan per US dollar.

Suppose the value of the complete free-market exchange rate was 6.5 yuan per US dollar and the market-clearing exchange rate with controls on capital outflows was 4.5 yuan per US dollar—and suppose the government stops intervention immediately and then removes capital controls a few years later, after it has strengthened the supervision, management and technical capability of the domestic financial institutions. One plausible result of this particular two-step market liberalisation (which we call Option A) would be appreciation to 4.5 yuan per dollar on cessation of foreign exchange market intervention followed by depreciation to 6.5 yuan per dollar on removal of the capital controls.

Suppose China adopts another form of two-step liberalisation (Option B), incremental appreciation of the yuan and removal of the capital controls after a few years. Option B is better than Option A because the exchange rate overshooting in Option A creates an unnecessary to-and-fro movement in resources. As mentioned, the removal of capital controls could very well cause the yuan to depreciate past 8 yuan per dollar, say, to 9.5 yuan per dollar, meaning that Option A would result in very severe exchange rate overshooting compared to Option B.

In effect, the Chinese government has been implementing a form of Option B since July 2005. In our opinion, the Chinese government has chosen a speed of exchange rate adjustment that is too slow, causing the yuan to depreciate significantly against the euro. We recommend that the Chinese government increases the speed of the yuan appreciation, but not in the form of an immediate discrete 10–15 per cent appreciation as advocated by Goldstein (2007).[20]

In our opinion, the instinctive calls by some economists for the use of the exchange-rate mechanism to solve China's external imbalance is only partially correct. Given China's capital controls, a freely floating currency regime could mean a value for the yuan that would be greatly over-appreciated compared with what its value would be under free capital flows, and could therefore reduce economic growth significantly.[21] Freeing capital flows is not, however, an option at this time. Given the weakness of the balance sheets of China's state-owned banks and the considerable embezzlement of state assets that has occurred—and the experience of the East Asian financial crisis—we advise against allowing the free movement of capital in the short term.

The correct way to think about exchange-rate management is to analyse the issue within the context of overall macroeconomic management and not just in regard to its impact on the balance of payments. It is likely that there are alternative combinations of macroeconomic policies that would produce results superior to the one generated by appreciating the yuan alone. The general point is that because the balance of payments is only one of the main outcomes of concern[22] and the exchange rate is only one of the ways to affect the balance of payments,[23] it is seldom the optimum to concentrate exclusively on one policy target (which does not dominate the other policy targets in importance) and then to employ only one policy tool (which is chosen idiosyncratically) to achieve that target.

What is to be done?

The real source of the anxieties that have given rise to the present US obsession with yuan appreciation is not the large trade imbalances but the large amount of structural adjustment necessitated by the acceleration of globalisation and of labour-saving technological progress. Dollar depreciation and trade barriers will slow the process of structural adjustment but will not stop it because the main driver of structural adjustment in the United States is technological progress. The optimal solution is a policy package that emphasises multilateral action to achieve several important objectives. It is bad economics and bad politics to dwell on just one region (China alone must change), to dwell on just one instrument (yuan appreciation alone) and to dwell entirely on one target (external imbalance).

We start by stating what should be done in the United States. Congress should quicken the reduction in fiscal imbalance, and expand trade adjustment programs, especially those that upgrade the skills of younger workers. The Trade Adjustment Assistance (TAA) program still functions inadequately after its overhaul in 2002. Lael Brainard (2007) reported that

> [p]articipation has remained surprisingly low, thanks in part to confusing Department of Labor interpretations and practices that ultimately deny benefits to roughly three-quarters of workers who are certified as eligible for them. TAA has helped fewer than 75,000 new workers per year, while denying more than 40 per cent of all employers' petitions. And remarkably, the Department of Labor has interpreted the TAA statute as excluding the growing number of services workers displaced by trade. Between 2001 and 2004, an average of only 64 per cent of participants found jobs while they participated in TAA. And earnings on the new job were more than 20 per cent below those prior to displacement.

The TAA program is in clear need of further improvement. Brainard's (2007) proposal for the establishment of wage insurance is an excellent way to bring the US social safety net more in line with the type of structural adjustments driven by globalisation and technological changes.

What is to be done in China? The obvious short-term policy package has three components. First, the steady process of yuan appreciation begun in July 2005 should be quickened—and should be used more aggressively as an anti-inflation instrument. Second, import liberalisation should be accelerated (for example, commitments made in negotiations for WTO membership, such as intellectual property rights protection, should be implemented) and expanded beyond WTO specifications.

The third component of the short-term policy package is to have an expansionary fiscal policy (such as rural infrastructure investments) to soak up excess savings, with an emphasis on import-intensive investments (for example, buying aeroplanes and sending students abroad). There must be time limits put on the expanded public works and SCE investments because, in the long term, increased public investments could follow an increasingly rent-seeking path that is wasteful (for example, building a second big bridge to a low-populated island to benefit a politically connected construction company, as happened in Japan), and the increased SCE investments could convert themselves into non-performing loans at the state-owned banks.

It is now common to hear calls for China to rebalance its growth path by reducing savings to increase consumption. This advice on increasing consumption cannot be wrong, however, consumption in China today is largely under the control of individual families and firms. They have probably already tried their best to optimise their consumption given all the constraints they face, and are unlikely to welcome the government telling them how to spend their money.

Since the health insurance and social security networks in China are in their infancy, many Chinese people are choosing to save a great deal of money as a hedge against severe illness. In the absence of student-loan programs, families are also choosing to save a great deal for their children's education. Many middle-class Chinese families have bought property in anticipation of capital gains but have refrained from moving into the new property because roads, subways and schools for many newly developed residential communities are underdeveloped. These are their best choices given the structural and economic constraints on Chinese society. As a result, the consumption of Chinese households remains low and savings rates remain high. All of these factors beg the question, 'how can China increase domestic consumption?'.

In the context of the above examples, the answers are quite straightforward: build an integrated health insurance system; create student-loan and scholarship programs; and build more roads, subways and schools.[24] The optimal solution to the problem of excess saving is not, however, for the government to absorb it by increasing its budget deficit but to establish an improved mechanism for coordinating private savings and private investments. Establishment of a modern financial system will not only achieve this objective, it will enhance welfare and lower the savings rate by pooling risks through vehicles such as medical and pension insurance. In a nutshell, China's main challenge today is to develop smoothly functioning financial, planning and regulatory systems that can employ the remaining rural surplus labour (as indicated by an average wage of about US$120 per month for 480 million rural and migrant workers) and surplus capital, which now shows up in China's sustained current account surplus and rising foreign exchange reserves.

The most important priority for financial-sector development is the appearance and growth of competitive domestic private banks. As China is required by its WTO accession agreement to allow foreign banks to compete against its state-owned banks on an equal basis by 2007, it would be akin to self-loathing not to allow the formation of truly private banks of domestic origin. There is no reason to favour foreign private banks over domestic private banks, and there is no reason why China should not allow its best financial minds to compete with—and achieve the same glorious success as—the best foreign financial minds.

We therefore recommend that after the recapitalisation of the big four state banks, at least two of them should be broken into several regional banks, and the majority of these regional banks should be privatised. At the same time, laws on the establishment of new banks should be loosened, and interest rates deregulated. It is crucial, however, that financial-sector liberalisation proceeds no faster than the development of the financial regulatory ability of the state. Even then, the danger of substituting a financial crash for financial repression is real. A modern financial system requires a modern system of supervision and prudential regulation for its proper functioning.

It would be a good idea to sell a few of the regional state banks to foreign banks. This would facilitate the transfer of modern banking technology to Chinese banks. The more local staff the foreign bankers train, the larger is the pool of future managers for Chinese-owned banks. An accelerated process of promoting the growth of sound domestic private financial institutions and allowing the entry of foreign financial institutions would shorten the time needed for Shanghai to assume its rightful place among the major international financial centres, and to contribute to more efficient intermediation of the world's savings.

An important part of financial reform should be promotion of the development of sound rural financial institutions. The government can usefully draw on the wealth of international experience with various schemes in developing economies to direct investment credit to rural areas. In particular, we wish to draw attention to the successful Indonesian experience of establishing a self-sustaining and profitable banking system (the 'Unit Desa' system) in the countryside to provide a starting point for discussing how to accelerate financial development in rural China.[25] China should allow the appearance of new small-scale rural financial institutions that will mobilise local savings to finance local investments as quickly as adequate prudential supervision can be put into place.

The widespread international attention on the value of the yuan is possibly the first time in international monetary history that the value of the currency of a developing economy has so greatly exercised the finance ministries and central banks of the largest industrialised economies for such a sustained period. This anomalous situation reveals two noteworthy points about China's return to the international stage: it shows the significant economic impact that China is already having on the world; and it portends that the anticipated continued fast growth of China in the next two decades will not only force more structural adjustments in other countries, it will require China to assume a broader 'global system' perspective in resolving disputes caused by cross-border spillovers from its policies. The most important and obvious area for collaboration between China and industrialised economies at this point is working together to further liberalise the multilateral free-trade system, and, at the minimum, to prevent it being eroded.

As China continues to grow rapidly, there is the unfortunate possibility that the range of international disputes could expand—possibly in the medium term—to include international concerns about China's public health readiness and environmental protection. Hopefully, the world will be more multilateral in its approach to the solution of these issues rather than insisting on a unilateral solution by China, as in the present case of the yuan.

Notes

1 At the end of May, the National Development and Reform Commission predicted that 'China's trade surplus will swell to between US$250 billion to US$300 billion this year, driven by price competitiveness and strong external demand. The surplus for the first four months of this year totaled US$63.3 billion, up 88% from the same period of last year' (*Wall Street Journal* 2007a). In mid June, it was revealed that China's overall trade surplus had widened to US$22.45 billion in May 2007, which was a 33 per cent gain on April's figure (*Standard* 2007).

2 Details of these three WTO cases are found in USTR 2007a, 2007b and 2007c.

3 Neither the date nor the sample of newspapers was selected randomly. These were the newspapers that were on the Singapore Airlines flight from Singapore to San Francisco (via Hong Kong) on the day of our travel.

4 The article also reported that Peter Mandelson 'wants greater access for European companies to China and a crackdown on piracy—threatening extra tariffs or import quotas if not. He also wants the renminbi pegged to a basket of currencies.'

5 The US civilian labour force in 2006 was 151.4 million (United States President 2007:Table B-35).

6 For details and analysis of the economic transition in the former Soviet bloc and China, see the papers in Woo et al. 1997.

7 More accurately, the wage of the formerly isolated worker in the former Soviet Union, India and China would rise while the wage for the worker in the industrialised economy would fall.

8 There is a large empirical literature on the relative impact of technological changes and globalisation on the US wage rate; notable contributions include Sachs and Shatz (1994) and Feenstra and Hanson (1996 and 1998).
9 Akerlof (2007) is a recent discussion on 'norms' and their economic consequences.
10 Borjas (1994) and Ottaviano and Peri (2005) are good discussions of this topic.
11 The data are from the *Direction of Trade Statistics* database maintained by the International Monetary Fund (IMF 2007).
12 See Feenstra et al. 1999 for the details of the different national treatments. This study re-estimated the export and import data of China–US trade, and reduced the gap between the two estimates: for example, the US$29 billion gap between the two official figures in 1996 was reduced to US$5 billion after revision of the data.
13 The simple average of the *Direction of Trade Statistics* data was closer than the simple average of the official data to the simple average of the revised data of Feenstra et al. (1999); the latter two are reported in Feenstra et al. (1999:Table 1).
14 The SCE category covers companies that are classified as state-owned companies and joint ventures and joint-stock companies that are controlled by third parties (for example, legal persons), who are answerable to the state.
15 The Economist Intelligence Unit (2004:23) reported that 'farmers' propensity to save seems to have increased'.
16 Liu and Woo (1994) and Woo and Liu (1995) contain formal modelling and econometric support for the investment-motivated saving hypothesis.
17 See, for example, *Financial Times* (2003).
18 For one thing, serial exchange-rate activism and the surge of it are unlikely to be more successful than the expansion of the war from Afghanistan to Iraq and the surge of US military effort in Iraq in 2007.
19 Considerations like this might be the reason why Goldstein and Lardy (2003) and Goldstein (2007) advocated a two-step strategy of yuan appreciation: a modest appreciation followed by incremental appreciation.
20 Our analysis therefore leads us to agree with the three recent policy positions of the US Treasury: that China must increase the pace of reform in financial services market (Paulson 2007), that China has not engaged in currency manipulation, and that China should increase the rate of yuan appreciation.
21 In Robert Mundell's opinion, 'China's growth rate could fall by half and foreign direct investment (FDI) could slow to a crawl if the country were to abandon its long-standing support of pegging the currency' (quoted in *South China Morning Post* 2003).
22 The inflation rate and unemployment would be among the other key concerns.
23 Other ways include monetary and fiscal policies.
24 Xiao (forthcoming) discusses this issue more fully and emphasises the problem of distinguishing productive investments from non-productive investments.
25 Indonesia is similar to China in key economic and institutional features: a geographically vast and heavily populated economy, and a rural financial system dominated by branches of a state bank (Bank Rakyat Indonesia and Agricultural Bank of China respectively). See Woo (2005).

References

Acharya, S., 2004. 'Why did India reform?', *Business Standard*, 24 February. Available from http://www.rediff.com/money/2004/feb/24guest1.htm

Akerlof, G.A., 2007. 'The missing motivation in macroeconomics', *Presidential Address to the American Economic Association Meeting in Chicago*, University of California at Berkeley.

Bergsten, C.F., 2007. The dollar and the renminbi, Statement to the Hearing on US Economic Relations with China: strategies and options on exchange rates and market access, Subcommittee on Security and International Trade and Finance, Committee on Banking, Housing and Urban Affairs, United States Senate, Washington, DC, 23 May.

Borjas, G.J., 1994. 'The economics of immigration', *Journal of Economic Literature*, 32(4):1,667–717.

Brainard, L., 2007. Meeting the challenge of income instability, Testimony to Joint Economic Committee Hearing, 28 February, Washington, DC. Available from http://jec.senate.gov/Documents/Hearings/02.28.07%20Income%20Instability/Testimony%20-%20Brainard.pdf

Feenstra, R.C. and Hanson, G.H., 1996. 'Globalization, outsourcing, and wage inequality', *American Economic Review*, LXXXVI:240–5.

——, 1998. The impact of outsourcing and high-technology capital on wages: estimates for the United States, 1979–1990, Department of Economics, University of California, Davis (unpublished).

Feenstra, R.C., Hai, W., Woo, W.T. and Yao, S., 1999. 'Discrepancies in international data: an application to China–Hong Kong entrepot trade', *American Economic Review*, 89(2):338–43.

Financial Times, 2003. 'Snow calls on Beijing to let currency float', *Financial Times*, 2 September.

——, 2007a. 'Surplus fuels EU–China war of words', *Financial Times*, 13 June.

——, 2007b. 'IMF set to scrutinise exchange rate policies', *Financial Times*, 19 June.

Freeman, R., 2004. Doubling the global work force: the challenge of integrating China, India, and the former Soviet Bloc into the world economy, Harvard University (unpublished).

Goldstein, M., 2007. Assessing progress on China's exchange rate policies, Testimony to the Hearing on Risks and Reform: the role of currency in the US–China relationship, Committee on Finance, US Senate, 28 March, Washington, DC.

Goldstein, M. and Lardy, N., 2003. 'Two-stage currency reform in China', *Asian Wall Street Journal*, 12 September.

International Herald Tribune, 2007. 'Yuan gain is biggest since end of peg', *International Herald Tribune*, 13 June.

International Monetary Fund (IMF), 2007. *Direction of Trade Statistics*, 9 May, Statistics Department, International Monetary Fund, Washington, DC. Available from http://www.imf.org/external/pubs/cat/longres.cfm?sk=20954

Kuroda, H. and Kawai, M., 2002. 'Time for a switch to global reflation', *Financial Times*, 1 December.

Liu, L.Y. and Woo, W.T., 1994. 'Saving behavior under imperfect financial markets and the current account consequences', *Economic Journal*, May.

New York Times, 2007. '4 in Senate seek penalty for China', *New York Times*, 14 June.

Ottaviano, G.I.P. and Peri, G., 2005. *Rethinking the gains from immigration: theory and evidence from the US*, NBER Working Papers 11672, National Bureau of Economic Research, Cambridge, MA.

Paulson, H.M., 2007. 'Prepared remarks by Treasury Secretary Henry M. Paulson, Jr. on the growth and future of China's financial markets', HP-301, 7 March, The Department of the Treasury, Washington, DC. Available from http://www.treas.gov/press/releases/hp301.htm

Sachs, J.D. and Shatz, H.J., 1994. 'Trade and jobs in US manufacturing', *Brookings Papers on Economic Activity*, 1:1–84.

Sachs, J.D. and Woo, W.T., 2000. 'Understanding China's economic performance', *Journal of Policy Reform*, 4(1):1–50.

——, 2003. 'China's growth after WTO membership', *Journal of Chinese Economics and Business Studies*, 1(1):1–31.

Scott, R.E., 2007. *Costly trade with China: millions of US jobs displaced with net job loss in every state*, EPI Briefing Paper, No. 188, 2 May, Economic Policy Institute, Washington, DC.

South China Morning Post, 2003. 'Abandoning peg will slash growth 50 pc in China', *South China Morning Post*, 15 September.

Standard, 2007. 'US lawmakers turn up yuan heat', *Standard* (Hong Kong), 13 June.

Economist Intelligence Unit, 2004. *Country Report: China*, December, Economist Intelligence Unit, Paris.

The Straits Times, 2007. 'EU's ties with China at crucial crossroads', *The Straits Times*, 13 June.

United States, Office of the President, 2007. *Economic Report of the President*, Washignton, DC. Available from http://www.gpoaccess.gov/eop/index.html

United States Trade Representative (USTR), 2007a. *WTO Case Challenging Chinese Subsidies*, 2 February. Available from http://www.ustr.gov/assets/Document_Library/Fact_Sheets/2007/asset_upload_file143_10465.pdf

——, 2007b. *WTO Case Challenging Market Access Restrictions in China on Products of Copyright-Intensive Industries*, 9 April. Available from http://www.ustr.gov/assets/Document_Library/Fact_Sheets/2007/asset_upload_file971_11063.pdf

——, 2007c. *WTO Case Challenging Weaknesses in China's Legal Regime for Protection and Enforcement of Copyrights and Trademarks*, 9 April. Available from http://www.ustr.gov/assets/Document_Library/Fact_Sheets/2007/asset_upload_file908_11061.pdf

USA Today, 2007. 'Tensions push US to get even with China', *USA Today*, 13 June.

Wall Street Journal, 2007a. 'China says trade surplus isn't likely to shrink soon', *Wall Street Journal*, 30 May.

——, 2007b. 'Bush, resisting Congress, won't slap China on yuan', *The Wall Street Journal* (Asia edition), 13 June.

Williamson, J., 1988. 'Comments on *Reflections on Development*', in G. Ranis and T.P. Schultz (eds), *The State of Development Economics: progress and perspectives*, Basil Blackwell, New York:24–30.

Woo, W.T., 2005. 'China's rural enterprises in crisis: the role of inadequate financial intermediation', in Y. Huang, A. Saich and E. Steinfeld (eds), *Financial Sector Reform in China*, Harvard University Asia Centre, Cambridge, MA.:67–91.

——, 2006, 'The structural nature of internal and external imbalances in China', *Journal of Chinese Economic and Business Studies*, 4(1):1–20.

Woo, W.T. and Liu, L.Y., 1995. 'Investment-motivated saving and current account malaise', *Asia-Pacific Economic Review*, 1(2):55–68.

Woo, W.T., Sachs, J. and Parker, S. (eds), 1997. *Economies in Transition: Asia and Europe*, Massachusetts Institute of Technology Press, Cambridge, MA.

Xiao, G., (forthcoming). 'What is special about China's exchange rate and external imbalance? A structural and institutional perspective', *Asian Economic Papers*.

5

Component trade and China's global economic integration

Kunwang Li, Ligang Song and Xingjun Zhao

A symbol of China's economic integration into the global economy is its progressive engagement in international commodity trade, with an increasing scale and intensity. From 1992 to 2005, the average growth rate of China's total trade was 18.5 per cent per annum—twice as high as the growth of gross domestic product (GDP) in the same period. China's total trade reached US$1.76 trillion in 2006, with a trade dependency ratio (defined as the ratio of total trade over its GDP) rising to about 68 per cent by the national account measures (UNCTAD 2006). Among this increasing trade, China's engagement in the so-called international fragmentation of production—namely, 'cross-border dispersion of component production/assembly within vertically integrated manufacturing industries' (Feenstra 1998; Jones and Kierzkowski 2005)—has become an increasingly important form of its economic integration into the regional as well as the global economy.

The development of component trade is significant for the following reasons (Jones, Kierzkowski and Chen 2005). First, it has exhibited a dynamism exceeding that of trade in final goods, as breaking down the integrated process into separate stages of production opens up new possibilities for exploiting gains from specialisation (Jones and Kierzkowski 2001). Second, despite it being a type of trade increasingly paramount in advanced stages of globalisation, it opens up an important role for developing economies (unlike intra-industry trade, which has been conducted mainly among industrialised countries). Third, it is more closely related to the development and liberalisation of the services sector than final good trade is particularly with respect to transportation, communication, banking and insurance, and other connecting service links. This is because increasing returns to scales tend to be associated with the development of these service sectors, which could in turn reduce the costs associated with the fragmentation process.

The global total trade in parts and components increased from US$400 billion in 1992 to US$1.25 trillion in 2005. The share of components trade in the total trade of manufacturing goods increased from 21 per cent to 26 per cent. Such a trend is especially pronounced in the East Asian region, which has accounted for more than half of the trade in parts and components. East Asia is progressively replacing the United States and the European Union as the world's largest region for trade in parts and components, forming a large integrated network for production (Athukorala 2006). China has been playing an increasingly important role in this development.

This chapter presents the recent trend of trade in parts and components between China and its main trading partners. It explores how China's pattern of trade in parts and components is being determined in terms of the shares of this trade in its total exports and imports, and their respective shares in total manufacturing trade. The analytical approach adopted is an adjusted gravity modelling method incorporating relative labour costs, foreign direct investment (FDI) and telecommunications in estimating the regression models. Policy implications with respect to the role of technology, labour productivity, further development and liberalisation of the services sectors are then discussed.

China's increasing trade in parts and components

The rise of China's trade has been an important part of the changing pattern of international production segmentation in East Asia. On the import side, the share of parts and components had already accounted for more than two-thirds of the total imports in China in 2002. Among the intermediate goods trade, imports of parts and components increased more significantly than any other intermediate goods and the share of parts and components in total imports increased from 19 per cent in 1997 to 27 per cent in 2002. On the exportation side, final goods played a dominant part in total exports—accounting for more than 60 per cent of the total in 2002. Meanwhile, China's intermediate goods trade has been concentrated mainly in Asia: more than 80 per cent comes from Asia and more than 60 per cent of exports of parts and components goes to other Asian economies (Gaulier et al. 2005). In general, importing intermediate goods, then processing and exporting the final goods characterises China's trading relations with its main trading partners.

To analyse China's trade in parts and components with its main trading partners, we select 219 kinds of parts and components taken from the United Nations' Standard International Trade Classification (SITC Version 3) numbers SITC-7 and SITC-8, consisting of 2,800 commodities, following Yeats (2001) and Athukorala (2006).[1] Altogether, there are 25 trading partners: the United States, Canada, Mexico, the United Kingdom, France, Germany, Italy, Australia, Japan, Korea, Hong Kong, Singapore, Malaysia, the Philippines, Thailand, Indonesia, Vietnam, Myanmar, Cambodia, Brunei, Laos, India, Brazil, Pakistan and South Africa.[2]

Since the early 1990s, trade in parts and components between China and its trading partners has been increasing rapidly. In 1992, China's imports and exports of parts and components were worth US$12.1 billion and US$4.3 billion respectively (Figures 5.1 and 5.2). By 2005, China's imports and exports of parts and components increased to US$176 billion and US$110 billion—15 times and 26 times those in 1992 respectively (Figure 5.1). Growth of imports of parts and components is continuing to outpace that of exports.

At the same time, the share of imports of parts and components in total manufacturing imports increased dramatically from 16 per cent in 1992 to 35 per cent in 2005 (Figure 5.2). The fact that component trade accounted for more than one-third of total manufacturing imports illustrates China's increasing role in international fragmentation of production.

To further analyse the increasing trend of trade in parts and components, one needs to look at the distribution of component trade by sector as well as by destination. The former tells how component trade concentrates on certain sectors and the latter shows with whom China has engaged in developing component trade.

The pattern of component trade by sectors

In 1992, China's exports of parts and components for machinery and transportation (SITC-7) were worth US$3.4 billion, which accounted for 80 per cent of the total exports of parts and components and 5.1 per cent of manufacturing exports (Table 5.1). In the same year, its exports of parts and components for other manufacturing goods were worth US$800 million, accounting for 19 per cent of total exports of parts and components and 1.2 per cent of manufacturing exports. Exports of parts and components accounted for 6.3 per cent of total manufacturing exports.

In 2004, China's exports of parts and components for machinery and transportation were worth US$87.5 billion, accounting for 94 per cent of the

Figure 5.1 **China's imports and exports of parts and components: 1992–2005** (US$ billion)

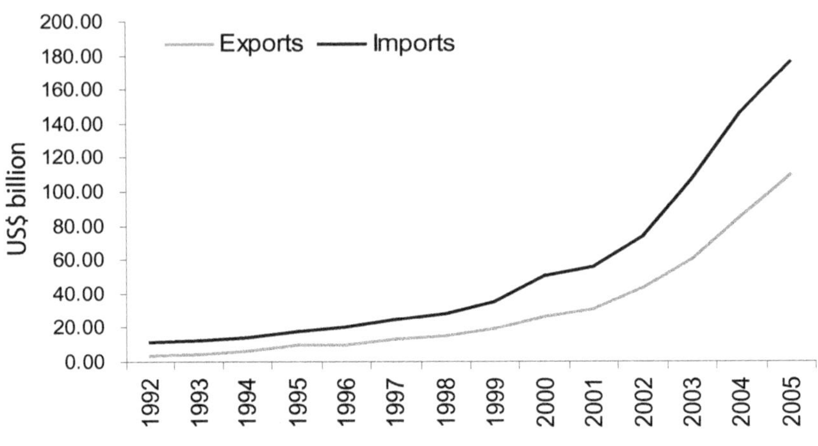

Source: Calculated using the data from UN COMTRADE, 2006.

Figure 5.2 **Share of parts and components trade in manufacturing trade, 1992–2005** (per cent)

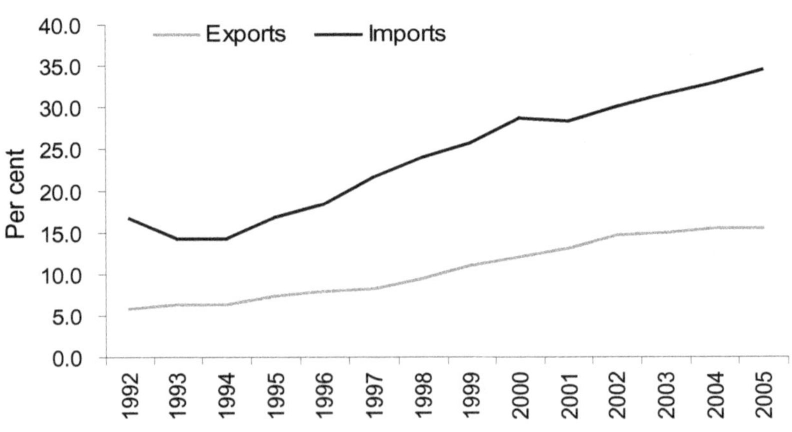

Source: Calculated using the data from UN COMTRADE, 2006.

total exports of parts and components and 15.9 per cent of total manufacturing exports. Its exports of parts and components for other manufacturing goods were worth US$5.5 billion, accounting for 5.8 per cent of the total exports of parts and components and 1 per cent of manufacturing exports. Total exports of parts and components accounted for 16.9 per cent of total manufacturing exports. The annual growth rate of exports of parts and components for machinery and transport in this period was 31 per cent, while that of other manufacturing was 17.1 per cent. The annual growth rate of total exports of parts and components was 29.3 per cent.

China's imports of parts and components for machinery and transportation were worth US$10 billion in 1992, accounting for 87 per cent of total imports of parts and components and 15.8 per cent of total manufacturing imports (Table 5.1). China's imports of parts and components for other manufacturing goods were worth US$1.6 billion, accounting for 13 per cent of total imports of parts and components and 2.4 per cent of total manufacturing imports in the same year. Total imports of parts and components accounted for 18.2 per cent of total imports of manufactured products.

In 2004, China's imports of parts and components for machinery and transportation increased to US$148 billion, accounting for 97 per cent of total

Table 5.1 **China's trade in parts and components, 1992–2004**

	SITC-7			SITC-8		
	Value (US$ billion)	Share in P&C (per cent)	Share in manufacturing (per cent)	Value (US$ billion)	Share in P&C (per cent)	Share in manufacturing (per cent)
Exports						
1992	3.4	80	5.1	0.8	19.1	1.2
1996	10	87	7.8	1.5	13.2	1.2
2000	28	92	12.4	2.4	8.0	1.1
2004	87	94	15.9	5.5	5.8	1.0
Imports						
1992	10	87	15.8	1.6	13.1	2.4
1996	20	92	17.7	1.7	8.1	1.1
2000	51	96	29.1	2.1	4.0	1.2
2004	148	97	33.4	4.1	2.7	1.0

Note: SITC-7 denotes parts and components for machinery and transport equipment, and SITC-8 represents miscellaneous manufacturing commodities.
Source: Authors' calculations based on United Nations Conference on Trade and Development (UNCTAD), 2006. *Trade and Development Report*, United Nations, New York and Geneva.

imports of parts and components and 33.4 per cent of total manufacturing imports. China's imports of other parts and components climbed to US$4.1 billion, accounting for 2.7 per cent of total imports of parts and components and 1 per cent of total manufacturing imports. Total imports of parts and components accounted for 34.3 per cent of manufacturing product imports. The annual growth rate of imports of machinery and transportation products was, on average, 24.7 per cent and that of imports in other parts and components was 8.2 per cent in this period. The annual growth rate of total imports in parts and components was 23.4 per cent, on average, in this period.

Machinery and transportation products increased more quickly than other products in component trade. In particular, office machinery and equipment (SITC-75), telecommunications and recording equipment (SITC-76) and electrical machinery and parts (SITC-77) played dominant roles, accounting for nearly 80 per cent of the total component trade. As a result, the share of machinery and transportation in the total trade of parts and components is increasing while that of other manufacturing products is decreasing over time. This finding is consistent with the fact that the composition of China's exports has been moving quickly towards those capital and technology-intensive products in recent years.

China has been running component-trade deficits, caused mainly by rapid increases in its importation of parts and components for machinery and transportation products. This trade gap tends to increase further as China's capacity for producing these products increases, so China will continue to rely heavily on imported parts and components. On the other hand, China has become a net exporter of parts and components relating to labour-intensive manufacturing products since 2000.

The growth rates of China's component trade have been higher than the growth rates of manufacturing sectors as well as the growth rates of total trade. This suggests that the pattern of the international division of labour in which China has participated has been deepened to cover finer international fragmentation of production. The further development of such patterns means that countries involved will gain from trade in parts and components rather than from trade in final goods. Such development will cement even closer trading relationships among countries involved in such a network of production. This point can be illustrated by looking at China's trade in parts and components by partners.

China's trade in parts and components by partners

Although the regional distribution of China's imports of parts and components varies over time, the main sources of China's imports of parts and components seem to concentrate in Northeast Asia, which accounted for more than 50 per cent of China's total imports of components (Table 5.2). Japan's share was increasing between 1992 and 1997, but started to fall after 1998, due possibly to the impact of the East Asian financial crisis. Japan, however, together with Korea (whose share increased rapidly throughout the period), ranked the highest in terms of their shares of China's imports of components. The shares of the United States and Canada reached their peak about 2000 and started to decline thereafter. Hong Kong's share decreased from 38.7 per cent to 2.15

Table 5.2 **Shares of component imports trade in China, by region, 1992–2005** (per cent)

Region/country	1992	1993	1996	1997	2000	2001	2004	2005
World	100	100	100	100	100	100	100	100
NAFTA[a] members	10.1	10.7	10.7	11.9	10.7	11.4	7.0	6.5
United States	9.6	10.3	9.8	10.9	8.5	9.4	5.8	5.5
Canada	0.6	0.4	0.9	0.9	1.6	1.2	0.5	0.4
Mexico	-	-	-	0.1	0.6	0.8	0.6	0.6
European Union (4)	13.9	13.7	10.2	10.8	10.9	11.2	7.6	6.1
Germany	8.2	8.7	6.4	6.3	5.7	6.4	5.2	3.7
France	2.4	1.6	1.4	1.8	2.7	2.3	1.2	1.2
United Kingdom	1.3	1.7	1.3	1.7	1.7	1.5	0.6	0.6
Italy	2.1	1.6	1.2	0.9	0.9	0.9	0.6	0.5
Northeast Asia	61.5	54.5	58.8	57.6	52.7	51.1	52.9	53.4
Hong Kong	38.7	16.2	9.5	7.6	5.4	5.1	2.6	2.1
Japan	20.2	32.1	35.1	32.3	25.9	24.2	20.8	17.9
Korea	1.8	3.9	7.5	8.4	9.3	8.4	12.6	15.3
ASEAN (5)	0.8	2.2	6.7	9.3	12.1	13.4	16.8	18.0
Indonesia	-	-	0.1	0.2	0.4	0.5	0.5	0.4
Malaysia	0.1	0.3	1.5	2.1	4.5	5.4	6.6	6.9
Philippines	-	-	0.3	0.2	1.9	2.2	4.4	5.2
Singapore	0.6	1.6	3.7	5.4	2.8	2.7	3.1	3.4
Thailand	0.1	0.1	1.1	1.4	2.4	2.6	2.2	2.1
Australia	0.1	0.2	0.2	0.2	0.1	0.1	0.1	0.1
Other	14.2	20.9	19.3	19.4	25.3	25.8	32.1	33.7

[a] North American Free Trade Agreement

Source: Authors' calculations based on United Nations Conference on Trade and Development (UNCTAD), 2006. *Trade and Development Report*, United Nations, New York and Geneva.

per cent, reflecting the fact that it was no longer a major supplier of parts and components to China. The shares from four EU countries (Germany, France, the United Kingdom and Italy) also decreased to low levels in 2005. Imports of parts and components from five Association of South-East Asian Nations (ASEAN) countries (Malaysia, the Philippines, Indonesia, Singapore and Thailand) increased rapidly from less than 1 per cent in 1992 to 18 per cent in 2005.

The data show that China has been relying less and less on the major industrialised countries in Europe and North America to provide parts and components for its part in the international fragmentation of production. In contrast, the newly industrialised economies and ASEAN countries have become important sources of China's imports of parts and components. There is also a strong tendency for Korea and large ASEAN countries to replace Japan and Hong Kong in providing China with parts and components. The rapid development of component trade between China and its neighbouring economies in East and Southeast Asia indicates that these regional economies have become increasingly integrated through the international fragmentation of production.

Total exports of parts and components from China to industrialised countries have been increasing steadily, while those to East Asia—in particular, to Hong Kong and Japan—have been falling (Table 5.3). Despite this trend, East Asia's average share of China's exports to the world was about 55 per cent compared with 17 per cent for the North American Free Trade Agreement (NAFTA) countries and 7 per cent for the European Union in 2005. Exports to Korea have increased from 1.3 per cent to 5 per cent and those to six ASEAN countries (Singapore, Philippines, Indonesia, Malaysia, Thailand and Vietnam) have also increased—from 4.1 per cent in 1992 to 12 per cent in 2005.

Korea, Japan and the six ASEAN countries have become important sources of China's imports of parts and components, accounting for more than 50 per cent of China's total imports of these products (Table 5.3). As those of Japan and Hong Kong are decreasing, the shares of Korea and ASEAN countries have been increasing. This implies that there have been some substitution effects between Japan, Hong Kong and other Asian countries in providing parts and components to China. Despite this substitution effect, China's continuing strong demand for parts and components from the region will be conducive to the economic growth of regional economies.

About 55 per cent of China's exports of parts and components have been to Northeast and Southeast Asia, with China's major exporting markets being Hong Kong, Japan, Korea, Singapore, Malaysia and Thailand. This trend is likely to be strengthened further. At the same time, China's export shares to North America and Europe have been steadily increasing over time. Overall,

China's relatively high export and import shares of parts and components to East Asia supports the view that China has engaged more deeply with East Asian economies in forging this new type of international specialisation in production. China's export shares of parts and components to Australia have been generally higher than its import shares, but both shares have been relatively low compared with East Asian economies.

Determinants of China's component trade

In explaining the phenomenon of component trade or international fragmentation of production, Jones (2007) postulates the following theories. The first is a Ricardian one, which says that workers have different skills across

Table 5.3 **Share of exports of parts and components from China, by region, 1992–2005** (per cent)

Region/country	1992	1993	1996	1997	2000	2001	2004	2005
World	100	100	100	100	100	100	100	100
NAFTA members	7.2	17.2	16.0	16.0	16.1	16.6	17.2	17.2
United States	6.8	16.1	15.2	15.0	14.4	14.9	15.5	15.4
Canada	0.3	0.9	0.7	0.7	1.0	0.7	0.6	0.7
Mexico	0.1	0.2	0.1	0.3	0.6	1.0	1.0	1.0
European Union (4)	2.2	9.1	5.8	6.2	7.4	6.6	7.1	7.1
Germany	1.0	4.6	2.6	2.6	3.1	2.6	3.2	3.7
France	0.3	1.8	0.9	1.1	1.2	0.9	1.1	0.9
United Kingdom	0.7	2.1	1.7	1.9	2.3	2.2	2.0	1.9
Italy	0.2	0.7	0.6	0.5	0.8	0.8	0.7	0.7
Northeast Asia	77.1	56.7	63.6	62.5	59.5	59.6	57.4	55.7
Hong Kong	62.3	30.1	26.7	26.4	26.6	27.0	28.0	28.4
Japan	9.1	17.4	20.5	19.6	15.4	15.0	11.7	10.5
Korea	1.2	2.4	5.5	4.9	4.8	4.6	5.3	4.9
ASEAN (5)	4.1	6.4	10.7	11.2	12.4	12.7	12.3	11.8
Indonesia	0.6	1.2	1.4	1.6	1.1	1.1	0.9	0.9
Malaysia	0.8	1.2	2.3	2.2	2.0	3.4	3.3	3.2
Philippines	0.3	0.3	0.7	1.3	1.3	0.7	1.4	1.2
Singapore	1.9	2.6	5.1	4.9	5.7	5.1	4.8	4.8
Thailand	0.5	0.8	0.8	1.0	2.0	2.1	1.4	1.4
Australia	0.2	0.3	0.4	0.4	0.5	0.5	0.5	0.5
Other	14.2	20.9	19.3	19.4	25.3	25.8	32.1	33.7

Source: Authors' calculations based on United Nations Conference on Trade and Development (UNCTAD), 2006. *Trade and Development Report*, United Nations, New York and Geneva.

different areas of a country, and when the skills required in each production block (fragments) differ, then a dispersion of activity according to comparative advantage could lower marginal production costs. The second theory is a Heckscher-Ohlin type of difference, namely the production blocks differ from each other in the proportions of different factors that are required. This suggests that labour-intensive production blocks would better be located in regions in which labour is relatively inexpensive compared with productivity.

The third theory is that fragmentation introduces new costs, namely the costs of connecting the two or more production blocks by service links such as transportation and communication. Therefore, 'the movement towards deregulation, especially of services, and the technological changes that have drastically reduced the costs of communication as well as making transportation less expensive have all encouraged a fragmentation of previously vertically integrated production processes' (Jones and Marjit 2001:365). Furthermore, it is argued that the optimal degree of fragmentation depends on the size of the market, so economic growth in general encourages fragmentation and trade in parts and components (Jone, Kierzkowski and Chen 2005). We examine in this section the main determinants of China's trade in parts and components based on these theories.

The theory of comparative advantage has been consistent with China's trading pattern: China produces and exports a large range of mainly labour-intensive goods, such as textiles and clothing, shoes, toys, travel goods and furniture.

The question is whether the theory of comparative advantage can be applied also in analysing intra-product trade based on vertical specialisation of production such as component trade. China tends to focus on producing parts and components relating to labour-intensive products due to its abundant supply of labour. For example, the production of personal computers requires a lot of components, including central processing units, mainboards, sound cards, display cards, screens and so on. Although China has no comparative advantage in producing some of the key components, it can assemble and export a large quantity of personal computers since it has low-cost production for the assembly of those components.

One way to examine the relationship between comparative advantage and the production and trade of parts and components is to compare labour-cost differences across different countries. Wages are a good index as they reflect the supply and demand of the labour market as well as the quality of labour. When a country's wage levels are relatively low, it could indicate that the country has comparative advantage in producing labour-intensive products, including parts and components.

In the period 1992–2004, labour costs in China were far lower than those in most industrialised countries, including the United States, Japan, Canada, Germany and the United Kingdom (Table 5.4). They were also relatively lower than many developing economies in Asia such as Korea, Hong Kong, Singapore, Malaysia and Thailand.

With respect to the impact of economy of scale on component trade, it is usually the case that rapid economic growth requires a large market to accommodate the products being produced. The process of trade liberalisation in the past few decades—enhanced through multilateral, bilateral or unilateral means—provides China with an external environment in which rising trade from China has been accommodated rather smoothly. The enlarged markets for products made in China have created an enormous economy of scale in production. It is known that the degree of specialisation of production tends to be intensified when there are economies of scale in production. As economy of scale is enlarged, the production and trade of parts and components within and across different countries tend to be enhanced.

On the other hand, China has a large domestic market, implying that there is a relative thickness in the market in those competitive sectors (meaning that there are relatively more suppliers of intermediate goods for a given sector). This is especially true in those sectors such as textiles and clothing, shoes, computers and automobiles. As Grossman and Helpman (2003) note, this characteristic reduces the search costs for multinational companies investing in overseas markets. At the same time, continuing domestic reforms in China provided an improved legal and regulatory environment in which foreign investments have flourished, deepening the process of international specialisation in production.

China's transportation and telecommunications industries have experienced rapid growth since the 1990s, providing the necessary infrastructure for China's participation in international specialisation. Figures 5.3 and 5.4 show the recent development of China's transportation industry. The number of civil aviation airline routes increased from 287 in 1986 to 1,257 in 2005—increasing by 3.4 times—and international airline routes also increased, from 108,000 kilometres to 856,000 kilometres. The capacity of seaports also increased—from 300 million tonnes in 1985 to 2.9 billion tonnes in 2005.

China's telecommunications industry has developed rapidly. The number of fixed lines per 1,000 people increased from less than 10, on average, in 1992 to 241 in 2004 (Figure 5.5). Along with the development of the telecommunications industry, call fees are declining. For example, in 1997, the average cost of calling the United States was US$6.70, but this reduced to US$2.90 in 2004. Meanwhile, the number of mobile phones in China has reached 480 million by March

Table 5.4 **Unit labour costs across different countries, 1992–2004** (US$ of unit labour per hour)

Country	1992	1993	1994	1995	1996	1997	1998	1999	2000	2001	2002	2003	2004
United States	16.0	16.4	16.8	17.2	17.8	18.2	18.6	18.9	19.7	20.6	21.4	22.3	22.9
Canada	17.6	16.9	16.3	16.5	17.0	16.8	15.9	16.1	16.5	16.2	16.7	19.4	21.4
Mexico	..	..	..	1.1	1.0	1.1	1.2	1.3	1.6	1.9	1.9	1.9	1.9
Germany	25.2	23.9	25.3	30.1	29.6	26.0	25.2	24.6	22.7	22.5	24.2	29.6	32.5
France	17.3	16.5	17.1	19.3	19.0	17.1	17.3	17.0	15.5	15.6	17.1	21.1	23.9
United Kingdom	14.3	12.5	13.0	13.8	14.1	15.7	17.0	17.3	16.7	16.7	18.2	21.2	24.7
Italy	18.9	15.4	15.4	15.7	17.1	16.1	15.8	15.5	13.8	13.6	14.7	18.1	20.5
Australia	13.2	12.6	14.1	15.4	17.0	16.7	15.1	15.9	14.4	13.3	15.4	19.8	23.1
Japan	16.2	18.9	21.0	23.6	20.5	19.1	17.7	20.5	22.0	19.4	18.6	20.3	21.9
Korea	5.2	5.6	6.4	7.3	8.2	7.8	5.7	7.4	8.2	7.7	8.8	10.0	11.5
Hong Kong	3.9	4.3	4.6	4.8	5.1	5.4	5.4	5.4	5.4	5.7	5.7	5.5	5.5
Singapore	4.9	5.2	6.2	7.6	8.2	8.0	7.4	7.0	7.2	7.0	6.7	7.2	7.4
Philippines	0.6	0.7	0.7	0.8	0.8	0.8	0.7	0.7	0.7	0.7	0.7	0.7	0.7
Indonesia	0.3	0.3	0.4	0.4	0.5	0.4	0.1	0.2	0.3	0.3	0.4	0.5	0.5
Thailand	1.2	1.3	1.2	1.4	1.5	1.3	1.1	1.2	1.1	1.0	1.1	1.1	1.2
Malaysia	1.9	2.0	2.2	2.5	2.7	2.6	1.9	2.0	2.1	2.1	2.2	2.2	2.2
Brazil	n.a.	n.a.	n.a.	n.a.	5.8	5.8	5.6	3.5	3.6	3.0	2.7	2.8	3.4
India	0.5	0.4	0.5	0.5	0.5	0.5	0.5	0.6	0.6	0.6	0.7	0.8	0.9
China	0.2	0.3	0.3	0.3	0.4	0.5	0.5	0.5	0.6	0.7	0.8	0.9	1.0

Source: Economist Intelligence Unit (EIU).

2007—making it the largest mobile-phone market in the world—and the number of people accessing the internet reached 144 million by March 2007, making China the second largest internet-using country after the United States.[3] These facts suggest that the rapid development of China's transportation and telecommunication industries could be another factor influencing the pace and depth of China's participation in international fragmentation of production. This is mainly because the developments in these service links tend to reduce the costs of transactions with considerable benefits from the economies of scale associated with such developments.

FDI has been considered an important determinant of trade in parts and components in the literature because multinational corporations are an important channel for conducting trade in intermediate goods through intra-firm trade. Multinational firms can choose to invest in host countries and make use of the local comparative advantage to produce their intermediate goods. For example, Kaminski and Smarzynska (2001) studied the impact of FDI on Poland's internationalisation process and found that the large FDI inflow helped Poland access international specialisation and increased the country's trade. Cheng et al. (2001) studied the relationship between FDI and international specialisation by using a partial equilibrium model to examine trade between Hong Kong and Guangdong Province, incorporating FDI. They found that FDI was an important factor for production specialisation and trade in parts and components in China.

China has absorbed a large amount of FDI since the 1990s and has now become the leading country in the world for the receipt of FDI inflows (Figure 5.6). The rapid increase of FDI inflows into China promotes the development of processing trades (Spencer 2005). The share of the FDI-related manufacturing sector in the total manufacturing sector has been increasing rapidly, and the share of total processing trade increased from 35 per cent in 1988 to 57 per cent in 2003, surpassing the share of ordinary trade.

Based on the theories surveyed and the background information, we adopted an adjusted gravity model to examine the determinants of trade in parts and components between China and its trading partners. The basic formula is introduced by Egger and Egger (2005) as follows

$$\begin{aligned} LnPC_{j.China.t} &= C_0 + \alpha_1 LnAGDP_{j.China.t} + \alpha_2 LnDIST_{j.China.t} \\ &\cdots\cdots\cdots + \alpha_3 LnRWAGE_{j.China.t} + \alpha_4 LnFDI_{j.china.t} + LnTeleline_{j.China.t} \end{aligned} \quad (1)$$

where *PC* represents either the exportation or importation of parts and components between China and its trading partners, *AGDP* is the average real

Figure 5.3 **Number of civil aviation airline routes in China, 1986–2005**

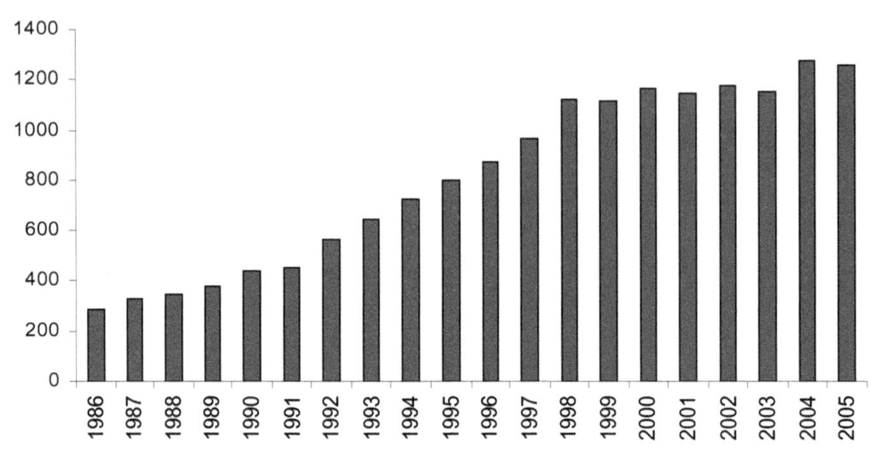

Source: China Economic Information Network. Available from http://www.cei.gov.cn

Figure 5.4 **Scale of seaport trade in China, 1985–2005** (10,000 tonnes)

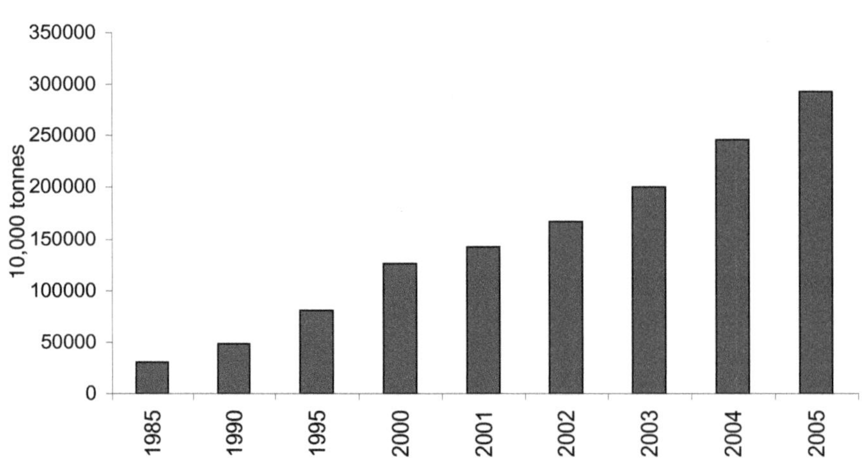

Source: National Bureau of Statistics (NBS), 2006. *China Statistical Yearbook*, China Statistical Press, Beijing.

Figure 5.5 **Number of telephones per 1,000 people in China, 1992–2004**

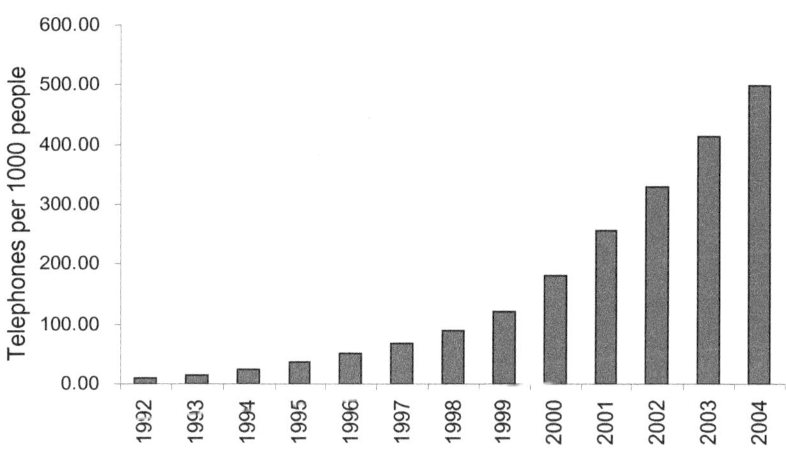

Source: World Bank, 2006. *World Development Indicators*, World Bank, Washington, DC.

Figure 5.6 **China's utilised FDI, 1983–2005** (US$100 million)

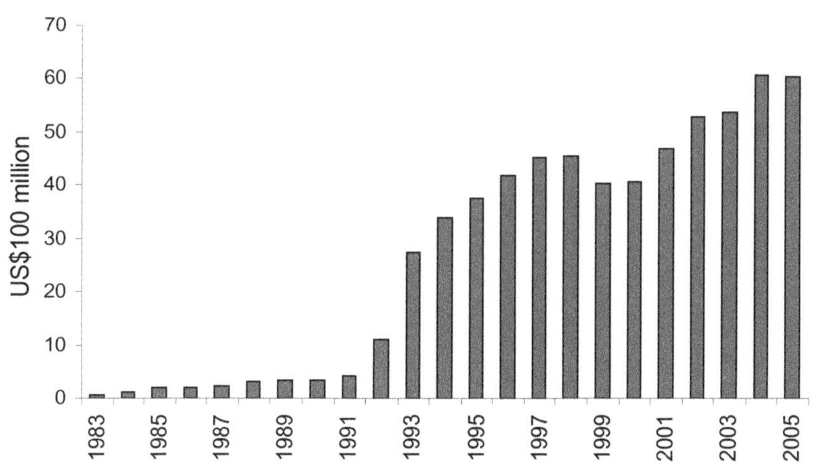

Source: China Economic Information Network, 2007. Available from http://www.cei.gov.cn

GDP of China and its trading partners, *DIST* is the economic distance between China and its trading partners, *RWAGE* is the relative labour cost of China and its trading partners, *FDI* is the foreign direct investment, and *Teleline* is the average number of fixed telephones in China and its trading partners.

According to Jones and Kierzkowski (2005), these factors can affect the trade in parts and components as well as the final goods. Thus, Equation 1 can be revised as follows

$$LnSPC_{j.China.t} = C_0 + \alpha_1 LnAGDP_{j.China.t} + \alpha_2 LnDIST_{j.China.t} \cdots\cdots\cdots + \alpha_3 LnRWAGE_{j.China.t} + \alpha_4 LnFDI_{j.china.t} + LnTeleline_{j.China.t} \quad (2)$$

where *SPC* is the share of exports of parts and components in the total trade in manufactured products. A fixed effect is introduced in both equations while conducting the panel data regressions.

The variables used in the regressions are defined as follows: to capture the impact of economy of scale, we use the average GDP of China and its trading partners.

$$AGDP_{j.China} = \frac{GDP_j + GDP_{China}}{2} \quad (3)$$

For the distance variable, we use the weighted-average economic distance to represent the transportation costs in which $DIST_f$ is the physical distance between countries.

$$DIST_{China.f} = \frac{DIST_f * GDP_f}{\sum_{f=1}^{20} GDP_f} \quad (4)$$

To reflect the impact of comparative advantage, we use the relative wage (*RWAGE*) to represent the unit costs of China and its trading partners.

$$RWAGE_{j.China} = \frac{Average\ cost\ of\ unit\ labour\ per\ hour_j}{Average\ cost\ of\ unit\ labour\ per\ hour_{China}} \quad (5)$$

In order to examine the impact of FDI on trade in parts and components, we simply use the share of FDI over that of GDP. To capture the impact of telecommunications, we use the number of telephone lines per 1,000 people to represent the index for telephone lines.

The data on trade in parts and components between China and its trading partners are taken from UNCTAD (2006), covering 219 products. The time period runs from 1992 to 2004 and the sample comprises 20 countries, as introduced in the last section. GDP for each country is taken from the Penn World Table 6.2. The indexes we have chosen are 'CGDP' and 'POP' and their products are used as the GDP variable. The data of FDI are taken from the *China Statistical Yearbooks* for 1993–2005 (NBS various issues). The data for economic distance are taken from Haveman (2004). The data of telephone lines per 1,000 people are taken from the *World Development Indicators* (World Bank 2006). The data of average labour unit costs per hour are taken from *EIU Country Data* (Economist Intelligence Unit 2007).

The empirical results are reported in Tables 5.5 and 5.6, showing the determinants of China's imports and exports of parts and components respectively. In each table, there are two groups of results: one contains no variable of *LNTELELINE* and the other contains this variable . Both results show good fitness of our model specification, since the R-squares for the two model estimations are 0.7 and 0.8 respectively.

The results show that the coefficients of *LNAGDP* in all regressions are positive and statistically significant at the 1 per cent level, implying that China's size and economies of scale and its trading partners has a positive impact on China's imports of parts and components. That is, the larger the economies of scale, the greater trade in parts and components will be. Furthermore, comparing this result with that from the regression using Equation 2, we found that the impact of economies of scale on trade in parts and components was larger than that of final goods. This is consistent with findings obtained in Jones and Kierzkowski (2005).

The coefficients of *LNDIST*—as the measurement of the impact of transport and other costs on bilateral trade flows—are negative and statistically significant, as expected. Despite the fact that the rapid development of telecommunications techniques leads to the 'death of distance' (Cairncross 1997), the estimated coefficient of economic distance is still negative and statistically significant. This implies that trade in parts and components in China relative to its trading partners is still sensitive to the changes in transportation costs and the physical distance between them.

As expected, FDI has a positive impact on China's imports and exports of parts and components and it is statistically significant at the 1 per cent level. The regression results show that the impact of FDI on exports of parts and components is similar to that of imports and the magnitudes of the estimated coefficient are within the range of 0.2–0.3. This finding implies that a 1 per cent increase in FDI could lead to a 0.2–0.3 per cent increase in China's exports of parts and components. The purpose of FDI is twofold: one is to sell products to China's domestic market and the other is to make use of China's comparative advantage of low-cost labour. Both motives could lead to increased trade in parts and components.

Tables 5.5 and 5.6 also show the results when *LNTELELINE* is incorporated as the measurement to capture the impact of telecommunications on component trade. As is expected, the telecommunications service and its coverage have a significant positive impact on international specialisation through trade in parts and components.

The results of *LNRWAGE* show significant differences between the regressions of imports of parts and components, which is consistent with what the theory of comparative advantage would predict. For China's imports of parts and components, The coefficients of foreign countries' labour costs are positive and statistically significant at the 5 per cent level (Table 5.5). The results imply that the relatively low cost of labour in China is one of the most important determinants of the rapid development of trade in parts and components between China and its trading partners—since China's comparative advantage in labour costs attracts greater imports of parts and components for assembly.

The estimated results show, however, that there is no significant difference for the variable of *LNRWAGE* (Table 5.6) in determining China's exports of parts and components. The insensitivity of wage differentials in determining China's exports of parts and components remains a puzzle, which requires further study.

Since all the factors included in the regressions would have similar effects on trade in final products, we can also run the regression with the share of trade in parts and components in total manufacturing trade as the dependent variable in both equations. The estimation results are reported in Table 5.7. Comparison with the previous results shows that economies of scale have a significantly positive impact on trade in parts and components, while transportation costs have a significantly negative impact. The findings are consistent with those reported in Tables 5.5 and 5.6. Furthermore, the impact of FDI on exports in parts and components is not statistically significant compared with the results in Table 5.6.

The impact of labour costs is significantly negative in the export shares in total manufacturing exports, which is in contrast with the finding of positive correlation in China's imports of parts and component (Table 5.5). This suggests that the theory of comparative labour cost applies more to China's

Table 5.5 **Estimation results of Equation 1: imports**

	LNIMPORT			
Variable	(1)		(2)	
C	−83.84***	−57.32***	−85.10***	−43.69***
	(−14.27)	(−12.51)	(−15.45)	(−5.72)
LNAGDP	4.83***	3.53***	4.70***	2.76***
	(16.42)	(15.51)	(16.31)	(6.59)
LNDIST	−0.96***	−0.74***	−0.90***	−0.58***
	(−11.75)	(−11.12)	(−10.69)	(−5.84)
LNFDI	0.19***	0.26***	0.16***	0.28***
	(3.85)	6.60	(3.43)	(7.16)
LNRWAGE	0.71***	0.64***	0.31**	0.32**
	(5.39)	4.98	(2.36)	(2.17)
LNTELELINE			0.99***	0.55*
			(3.88)	(2.40)
Fixed effect	Yes	No	Yes	No
Adjusted R^2	0.74	0.73	0.76	0.74
SE	1.14	1.13	1.10	1.12
F-statistic	36.73	147.32	38.15	122.31
Number of observations	221	221	221	221

Note: *** 1 per cent significant level, ** 5 per cent significant level, * 10 per cent significant level. T-statistics are in parentheses.

Source: Authors' calculations.

Table 5.6 **Estimation results of Equation 1: exports**

	LNEXPORT			
Variable	(1)		(2)	
C	−70.70***	−47.49***	−71.42***	−41.76***
	(−9.79)	(−15.42)	(−8.54)	(−7.45)
LNAGDP	4.19***	3.05***	4.12***	2.73***
	(11.37)	(18.54)	(9.63)	(8.71)
LNDIST	−0.68***	−0.48***	−0.65***	−0.41***
	(−8.08)	(−9.65)	(−6.90)	(−5.29)
LNFDI	0.24***	0.30***	0.22***	0.31***
	(4.32)	(7.19)	(3.72)	(6.66)
LNRWAGE	0.13	0.05	−0.16*	−0.09
	(1.63)	(0.89)	(−1.71)	(−0.78)
LNTELELINE			0.56***	0.23*
			(7.56)	(1.72)
Fixed effect	Yes	No	Yes	No
Adjusted R^2	0.86	0.85	0.87	0.85
SE	0.64	0.65	0.62	0.65
F-statistic	81.32	311.78	83.35	253.01
Number of observations	221	221	221	221

Notes: *** 1 per cent significant level, ** 5 per cent significant level, * 10 per cent significant level. T-statistics are in parentheses.

Source: Authors' calculations.

Table 5.7 **Estimation results of Equation 2: export shares in total manufacturing exports**

	LNSEXPORT			
Variable	(1)		(2)	
C	–19.37***	–19.00***	–19.46***	–17.14***
	(–5.97)	(–10.30)	(–6.16)	(–9.88)
LNAGDP	1.09***	1.07***	1.09***	0.97***
	(6.87)	(11.93)	(7.06)	(11.33)
LNDIST	–0.34***	–0.33***	–0.34***	–0.31***
	(–12.25)	(–16.43)	(–12.94)	(–16.76)
LNFDI	–0.02	–0.01	–0.02	0.00
	(–1.04)	(–0.54)	(–1.15)	(–0.33)
LNRWAGE	–0.12***	–0.14***	–0.15***	–0.18***
	(–4.46)	(–5.11)	(–6.24)	(–5.85)
LNTELELINE			0.07*	0.08**
			(1.77)	(2.54)
Fixed effect	Yes	No	Yes	No
Adjusted R2	0.70	0.67	0.70	0.67
S.E.	0.39	0.40	0.40	0.40
F-statistic	29.44	110.79	27.69	88.81
Number of observations	221	221	221	221

Note: *** 1 per cent significant level, ** 5 per cent significant level,* 10 per cent significant level, T-statistic in parentheses.
Source: Authors' calculations.

imports of parts and components than to its exports of them. Since China's imports of parts and components concentrate more on capital and technology intensive goods such as machinery and transportation (Table 5.1), the finding of positive correlation of labour cost differentials may suggest that foreign firms investing in China are more sensitive to labour cost differences between China and elsewhere in those more sophisticated parts and components. It is understandable as labour costs in producing these kinds of intermediate goods in developed countries are much higher than that in China (Table 5.4), whereas the labour cost differentials between industrialised and developing economies in producing less sophisticated intermediate goods tend to be narrower. Since China's exports of parts and components concentrate more on those less sophisticated labour intensive products, both foreign firms and domestic firms producing such intermediates goods tend to become less sensitive to labour cost differentials. Under this circumstance, market size, economies of scale and service links rather than FDI and labour cost differentials will play more important roles in determining the pattern of exports of parts and components. Finally, consistent with the findings reported in Tables 5.5 and 5.6, the development in telecommunications is also correlated positively with the shares of exports of parts and components in total manufacturing exports.

Conclusion

The empirical results reveal the following points. First, China's rapid economic growth, increasing market size and economies of scale are important factors in explaining the rapid increase of bilateral trade in parts and components with its trading partners. Second, the spatial distance and transportation costs have significant negative impacts on China's trade of parts and components. This suggests that the reduction in transportation costs by technological innovation and investment could enhance trade in parts and components, and thereby deepen the process of international specialisation involving China and its main trading partners. Third, FDI has a positive impact on China's participation in international fragmentation of production, taking advantage of China's comparative advantage in low labour costs in assembly of intermediate goods and producing final goods for domestic sales and exports. Finally, the development of the telecommunications and related services sector helps intensify the degree of international specialisation by reducing transaction costs, which will encourage more domestic and foreign firms to be involved in international fragmentation of production.

Along with the trend of globalisation, China has become an important player in the international production chain through its increasing share of trade in parts and components with its main trading partners. China has now been incorporated into the regional production network consisting of Korea, Japan, Hong Kong, Taiwan and six ASEAN countries and is engaged in trading relationships with North American and European economies for parts and components. China has achieved tremendous dynamic gains from engaging in trade in parts and components especially with respect to its industrial upgrading through technological learning associated with processing trade (Amighini 2004). For the East Asian economies, the accession of China into such a regional production network has not only encouraged the further development of regional trade liberalisation including service trade liberalisaion, it has also provided an enlarged market for all the regional economies. As a result, all parties involved will gain from participating in this dynamic process. Given the prospects of the rapid growth of the Chinese economy, its current and planned massive investments in research and development and in infrastructure including transportation and telecommunications, its continual policies in attracting FDI and its rapid move towards liberalising its services sectors, the scope for China and its trading partners to benefit from the process of international fragmentation of production is tremendous.

Notes

1 SITC Version 3 was adopted in 1992 so the data series used in this chapter began in that year.

2 In selecting partnering countries, consideration includes country representation and availability of data.

3 See 'Internet in the People's Republic of China' on Wikipedia (available online at http://www.wikipedia.com).

References

Amighini, A., 2004. 'China in the international fragmentation of production: evidence from the ICT industry', *The European Journal of Comparative Economics*, 2(2):203–19.

Athukorala, P.C., 2005. 'Component trade and China's regional economic integration', in R. Garnaut and L. Song (eds), *The China Boom and Its Discontents*, Asia Pacific Press, The Australian National University, Canberra:215–39.

——, 2006. Multinational production networks and the new geo-economic division of labour in the Pacific Rim, Paper for the thirty-first Pacific Trade and Development Conference, Guadalajara, Mexico.

Cairncross, F., 1997. *The Death of Distance*, Harvard Business Press, Boston.

Cheng, L., Qiu, L.D. and Tan, G., 2001. 'Foreign direct investment and international fragmentation of production', in S. Arndt and H. Kierzkowski (eds), *Fragmentation: new production patterns in the world economy*, Oxford University Press, New York:165–86.

China Economic Information Network, 2007. Available from http://www.cei.gov.cn

Economist Intelligence Unit (EIU). *Country Data*. Available from http://www.eiu.com

Egger, H. and Egger, P., 2005. 'The determinants of EU processing trade', *The World Economy*, 28(2):147–68.

Feenstra, R., 1998. 'Integration of trade and disintegration of production in the global economy', *Journal of Economic Perspectives*, 12(4):31–50.

Gaulier, G., Lemoine, F. and Unal-Kesenci, D., 2005. *China's integration in East Asia: production sharing, FDI and high-tech trade*, Working Paper, No.2005-09, CEPII.

Grossman, G.M. and Helpman, E., 2003. 'Outsourcing vs FDI in industry equilibrium', *Journal of the European Economic Association*, 1:317–27.

Hanson, G.H., Mataloni, R.J. and Slaughter, M.J., 2004. *Vertical production networks in multinational firms*, Working Paper 9723, National Bureau of Economic Research, Cambridge, MA.

Haveman, J., 2004. Industry Concordances available from http://www.macalester.edu/research/economics/PAGE/HAVEMAN/Trade.Resources/TradeConcordances.html#gravity

Hummels, D.L., Ishii, J. and Yi, K.-M., 2001. 'The nature and growth of vertical specialization in world trade', *Journal of International Economics*, 54(1):75–96.

Jones, R.W. and Kierzkowski, H., 2001. 'A framework for fragmentation', in S. Arndt and H. Kierzkowski (eds), *Fragmentation: New Production Patterns in the World Economy*, Oxford University Press, Oxford:17–34.

——, 2005. 'International fragmentation and the new economic geography', *North American Journal of Economics and Finance*, 16(1):1–10

Jones, R.W., Kierzkowski, H. and Chen, L., 2005. 'What does evidence tell us about fragmentation and outsourcing?', *International Review of Economics and Finance*, 14:305–16.

Jones, R.W. and Marjit, S. 2001. 'The role of international fragmentation in the development process', *American Economic Review*, 91(2):363–6.

Jones, R.W., 2007. Production fragmentation and outsourcing: general concerns, University of Rochester, unpublished article.

Kaminski, B. and Smarzynska, B.K., 2001. *Foreign direct investment and integration into global production and distribution networks: the case of Poland*, World Bank Policy Research Working Paper, No. 2646, Washington, DC.

Kimura, F. and Ando, M., 2005. 'Two-dimensional fragmentation in East Asia: conceptual framework and empirics', *International Review of Economics and Finance*, 14:317–48.

Lemoine, F. and Unal-Kesenci, D., 2004. 'Assembly trade and technology transfer: the case of China', *World Development*, 32(5):829–50.

National Bureau of Statistics (NBS), 2006. *China Statistical Yearbook*, China Statistical Press, Beijing.

——, various issues. *China Statistical Yearbook*, China Statistical Press, Beijing.

Ng, F. and Yeats, A., 2001. 'Production sharing in East Asia: who does what for whom, and why?', in L.K. Cheng and H. Kierzkowski (eds), *Global Production and Trade in East Asia*, Kluwer Academic Publishers, Boston:63–109.

Penn World Tables, Centre for International Comparisons at the University of Pennsylvania, Philadelphia.

Spencer, B.J., 2005. *International outsourcing and incomplete contracts*, National Bureau of Economic Research Working Paper, No.11418.

United Nations Conference on Trade and Development (UNCTAD), 2006. *Trade and Development Report*, United Nations, New York and Geneva.

Yeats, A.J., 2001. 'How big is global production sharing?', in S. Arndt and H. Kierzkowski (eds), *Fragmentation: new production patterns in the world economy*, Oxford University Press, Oxford.

World Bank, 2006. *World Development Indicators*, World Bank, Washington, DC.

6

Service sector reform options

The experience of China

Christopher Findlay, Mari Pangestu and Roy Chun Lee

The gains from reform and liberalisation of services have attracted a growing literature. Messerlin and Zedillo (2004), for example, note the effect of service sector reform on competition, market scale, diversity, lower prices and higher quality, as well as the capacity to remove bottlenecks to growth in the infrastructure sector. They remark on the contribution of services to export performance, and they stress the interests of developing economies in market access for services exports.

Policy reform in services that delivers these benefits has a wider scope than reform programs in the goods sectors. There are services policy measures that apply only to foreigners: for example, rules on the form in which they can enter local markets. Services markets are also regulated by measures such as licensing, which affect all suppliers, wherever they come from. As Whalley (2004) observes in his review of empirical work on the effects of services liberalisation in developing economies, 'one is talking of domestic regulation, entry barriers, portability of providers, competition policy regimes more so than barriers at national borders, as with tariffs' (Whalley 2004:1,250). The connections between regulatory reform and services trade liberalisation are examined in detail in Mattoo and Sauve (2003).

The scope of the services agenda also differs from that of goods because of the substitutability between the modes of supply: that is, delivery of the service through establishment in the customer country, through the movement of people (either consumers or providers) or through the cross-border modes of supply—options for which are expanding through technological change. Cross-border supply is the mode most similar to trade in goods.

The architects of the GATS recognised the value of considering all the modes of supply and all the impediments that applied to those modes. They sought commitments in the GATS to open up sectors and modes of supply and to eliminate measures that limit entry by all suppliers and those which discriminate against foreign suppliers.

Studies of services reform have examined these various dimensions. Some concentrate on the removal of discriminatory policy in a limited range of modes of supply, such as that across borders (Francois and Spinanger 2001). Others stress the value of coverage of other modes of supply (Whalley 2004; Walmsley and Winters 2003). Some examine the different impacts of the removal of discriminatory policy (that is, implementation of the principle of national treatment) compared with reform of policy affecting entry to markets by all services suppliers (in GATS language, matters of market access) (Dee and Hanslow 2000a, 2000b).

Services sector policymakers are confronted by questions of which sectors are the priorities for reform, which modes of supply should be included and to what extent should commitments refer to national treatment and market access questions? More specifically, they must decide whether domestic markets should be deregulated before foreign suppliers are allowed to enter, whether these reforms should be carried out simultaneously or whether foreign firms should be able to enter while impediments remain to domestic entry.

The first step in this chapter is to characterise options for services sector policy change in broad terms, and to discuss what factors determine the direction of change. Some of the points derived from the framework are illustrated by reference to China's experience in services, which offers many lessons. China made substantial commitments to reform its services sector, as part of its WTO accession. Mattoo (2004) reviews the significance of these reforms and notes how extensive they are compared with the experience of even industrialised economy commitments in the WTO (see also WTO 2006:Table AIV.2, for a summary of China's accession commitments). The commitments made are now being implemented. The construction of the original commitments and the pattern of their implementation are a source of insight for other policymakers contending with a similar task.

Options for services sector reform are presented in the next section. One is to free up entry to domestic suppliers. Another is to open markets to all suppliers. These are referred to below as 'domestic deregulation' and 'liberalisation' respectively. There are other outcomes, called 'foreign rent seeking' and 'back-sliding'. Some comment is offered on the welfare implications of each of these.

China's experience of services sector reform is then reconsidered. Some comments are offered on the relative importance of various aspects of the policy and political economy frameworks. That discussion includes reference to reform in the financial services, transport, distribution and telecommunications sectors. The chapter concludes with some key points and a suggestion for further empirical work that is relevant to these questions.

Options for reform

Many impediments to entry into services markets apply to domestic and foreign producers, and in some cases foreign producers face extra requirements. An index of policy restrictiveness has been developed to assess the importance of both types of restrictions, following the work of Warren (2000), Findlay et al. (2002) and McGuire and Findlay (2005). The index is a frequency measure that estimates the restrictiveness of an economy's trading regime based on the trade barrier framework developed for the GATS.

Under the GATS framework, trade impediments are classified into two primary categories.

1. Market access. The GATS identified four modes of supply for trade in services: that is, cross-border, consumption abroad, commercial presence and presence of natural person. Market access represents the restrictions on market entry by either of the four supply modes on national and foreign new entrants (Warren 2000).
2. National treatment. National treatment obligations require GATS members to identify all measures that discriminate against foreign services suppliers in terms of advantages given to domestic suppliers or extra regulatory requirements imposed on foreign suppliers.

Following the GATS framework, the first step is to classify trade restrictions into two primary categories.

- Establishment. The ability of services suppliers to establish a physical outlet in a territory and supply services through those outlets, which includes market entry via foreign investment. This runs parallel with the mode of commercial presence in the GATS.
- Continuing. The operations of a services supplier after it has entered the market, including an interconnection regime, or its equivalent, and cross-border supplies. Regulatory measures that foster and enhance competition would also be captured under this category.

The second step is to reclassify trade restrictions into discriminatory and non-discriminatory categories to capture the degree of compliance with national treatment obligations.

- Non-discriminatory. Restriction applied to domestic and foreign services suppliers equally.
- Discriminatory. Restricting only foreign or only domestic services suppliers.

Table 6.1 provides an example of how restrictions in telecommunications are classified under the index.

The index value is then calculated for each economy using a methodology of scores and weights. Scores are assigned for each liberalisation index on the basis of a judgment about its stringency. The more stringent the restriction, the higher is the score. For example, a country that restricts the number of fixed-line licences is assigned a higher score than an economy that issues several new licences.

The restriction categories are then weighted together according to a judgment about their relative economic cost. For example, in telecommunications, restrictions on the issuance of licences are weighted more heavily than restrictions on leased-line operations. The weights are chosen so that the total restrictiveness index score ranges from zero to one.

An index score is calculated separately for domestic and foreign services suppliers (Figure 6.1). A foreign index (F) is calculated to measure all the restrictions that hinder foreign firms from entering and operating in an economy. It covers discriminatory and non-discriminatory restrictions. A domestic index (D) represents restrictions that are applied to domestic firms and it generally

Table 6.1 **Examples of restriction categories of trade in telecommunications services**

	Establishment	Continuing operations
Non-discriminatory	The number of fixed-line local service licences is restricted	Voice resale is prohibited
Discriminatory	Foreign investment in fixed-line local service is restricted	Voice resale is permitted only to domestic operators

Source: McGuire, G. and Findlay, C., 2005. 'Restrictions on trade in services: trade liberalisation strategies for APEC member economies', *Asian-Pacific Economic Literature*, 19(1):18–41.

covers only non-discriminatory restrictions. The difference between the foreign and domestic index scores is a measure of discrimination against foreigners. This classification of the restrictions suggests a number of paths for reform, which can be specified. For example, F and D could be reduced at the same rate, or by the same amounts in absolute terms, or one could be reduced faster than the other.

These options are illustrated in Figure 6.2. The horizontal axis represents the size of the domestic index (D). The vertical axis shows the size of the gap between F and D—that is, the extent of discrimination. The maximum value of the D axis is shown as one.[1] At point O, the value of D is zero, and the maximum value of (F-D) is one. There is an additional constraint since the value of F is also, at most, equal to one. Given any value of D, the value of (F-D) must therefore lie on or below the line XY: for any value of D, a point along XY implies an index value for F of one.

Figure 6.1 **An illustration of the results from the trade restrictiveness index**

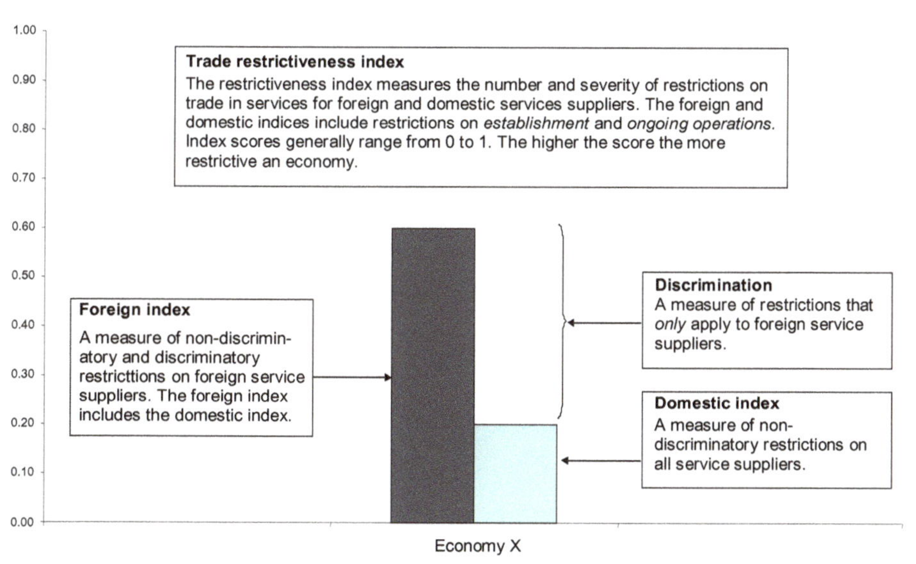

Source: McGuire, G., 2003. 'Methodologies for measuring restrictions on trade in services', in Organisation for Economic Co-operation and Development (ed.), *Quantifying the Benefits of Liberalising Trade in Services*, Organisation for Economic Co-operation and Development, Paris.

Suppose the current policy leads to a situation in which the index values of F-D and D lie at point A. In that case, there are four main options for policy change (noting that movement into the area XYZ is not possible).

One option (or liberalisation) is reform in which D and the margin of discrimination are reduced and point A moves into the space OCAB. If the ratio of (F-D) to D is maintained, the reduction would take place along the line OA, while above that line the proportionate reduction in D exceeds that in (F-D).

Another option is domestic deregulation, in which D is reduced but F-D increases. In this case, A moves into the area ACXE. The value of F does not necessarily increase but will do so if point A moves into the space AHXE.

Another option is that point A moves into the space BAJY, in which the extent of discrimination falls but the restrictions on domestic entry rise (when D moves to the right of BA). This case could be called foreign rent seeking, since foreign suppliers emerge with a relatively less restricted position compared with domestic suppliers. The effect of the policy change could, however, also be to increase the value of F (the total value of the index confronting foreigners), when the point A moves into the space AJYG.

Figure 6.2 **Options for policy reform**

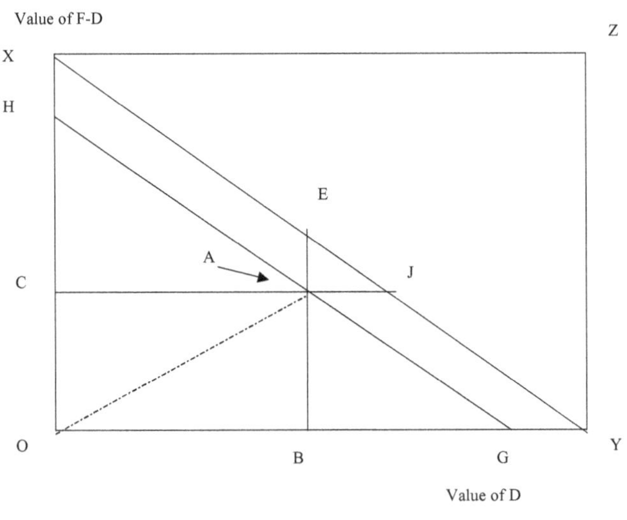

One other less likely option is back-sliding, in which A shifts into the region AEJ, in which domestic restrictions and the margin of discrimination increase—along the extremes of which D is constant (along AE) or the extent of discrimination is constant (along AJ).

There are some other important special cases.

- Along the line AC, the extent of discrimination remains constant while restrictions on domestic entry fall. This could be called market access reform, in terms of the language of the GATS, since restrictions to foreign and domestic entry are being decreased by the same amount (although F-D—that is, the margin of discrimination—is constant).
- Along the line AB, the extent of restrictions on domestic entry remains constant but there is a reduction in the extent of discrimination. In terms of the language of the GATS, this could be referred to as reform in the direction of national treatment, since (F-D) is being reduced, while other universally applied impediments to entry stay the same.

The empirical work on the benefits of services reform tends to focus on the impact of removal of discrimination against foreigners. Francois and Spinanger (2001), for example, examined the effects of China's WTO accession. Their model included a number of services sectors. China's services policy was characterised by implicit tariff rates derived from gravity equations in which Hong Kong's relationships were used as the benchmarks. The gap between real and expected imports, according to this benchmark, was used with an estimate of an import demand elasticity, to estimate a price effect of the policy (akin to a tariff that would have the same effect of reducing imports relative to their free trade level). The data were therefore based on services that were traded across borders (not including those delivered through commercial presence). Further, the measures they assessed included policy that affected foreign relative to domestic supply, that is, the (F-D) margin. The modelling results, therefore, in terms of Figure 6.2, refer to a movement along the AB line, but with respect only to operations, not to establishment. The results, therefore, capture only part of the reforms made by China in the context of its GATS commitments.[2]

Empirical work on the effects of services reform can isolate the contribution of reform in these different directions, though so far at the expense of a narrower sectoral coverage. For example, Dee and Hanslow (2000b) provide some modelling results that classify policy measures in the manner illustrated in Table 6.1. They find that removing restrictions on market access causes much larger gains than reductions in discrimination—partly, this is because of the size of the reductions in restrictions on market access.

The experience in China

China had already made substantial changes to policy in many services sectors before 2001 and its accession to the WTO led to further development of that policy. Our interest here is whether these two steps were in the same or different directions, and how the negotiating process has affected the direction of change. China's services reform commitments are reviewed also by Mattoo (2004) and Whalley (2003).

As observed in the cases to follow, China had in many cases already embarked on a reform program before the WTO accession negotiations had been resolved—but were those changes in the form of liberalisation, as defined in Figure 6.2, or were they a form of domestic deregulation? To see this, we examine the situation in banking, insurance, transport, distribution and telecommunications.

Telecommunications

Dramatic changes have occurred in the telecommunications market, but the main drivers appear to have been the consequences of technological change.

Pangestu and Mrongowius (2004) review China's experience in the telecommunications sector. They report significant price reductions and increases in tele-density since 1998. These changes obviously occurred in advance of WTO accession. Pangestu and Mrongowius attribute these changes to competition in telecommunications markets, but they stress that the government orchestrated this competition and price reduction. In addition, there were instances of the influence of technological advancement that overcame government control, such as the use of the Internet for telephone calls.

While China's rate of reform in telecommunications has been rapid, it remains an outlier. Findlay et al. (2002), in a sub-sample of Asia-Pacific Economic Cooperation (APEC) countries, find that the extent of liberalisation in China exceeds that in all other countries reviewed. But they also note that despite the rapid change, China's degree of openness remains less than the sample average.

According to the WTO accession commitments (reviewed by Pangestu and Mrongowius 2004), foreign investment was allowed to enter but initially at a lower ownership level and with geographical restrictions. In a certain period—two years for value-added services, five years for mobile telephony and six years for domestic and international services—the geographical restrictions were to be removed. Foreign ownership caps were to be removed gradually according to a schedule running through the next few years: the removal of this restriction has been accelerated, although the 50 per cent ceiling still applies. The Chinese authorities reaffirmed in 2006 their decision to increase the foreign participation cap in joint ventures for basic services (fixed-lined and mobile) to 49 per cent by 2007, in line with China's WTO commitments (WTO 2006).

Even after accession, foreign investment is not intended to hold a majority in the sector, although the treatment of foreign entry is more liberal in value-added services than for the other two sub-sectors. Geographical restrictions also continue to apply, including to some extent to domestic firms. In May 2002, China Telecom—the former monopoly in fixed-line operations—was split into two entities along provincial lines, with China Telecom serving 21 provinces in the south and the newly created China Netcom serving 10 northern provinces. Both operators enjoy the right to compete in each other's territories. These two share about 95 per cent of the market (WTO 2006). Two minor domestic suppliers—China Unicom and China TieTong—have also entered the fixed-line market with a limited presence.[3]

The major operators in basic telecommunications in China are state owned, and this situation is unlikely to change even in the short term. The main issue, however, is not the presence of government ownership but whether the few and predominantly state-owned players will be operating in a competitive environment. This increases the importance of China meeting its commitments to establish an independent regulatory body. Instead of having a separate regulatory agency, the Ministry of Electronic Industries (MII) remains as the policymaking body as well as the sectoral regulator. While according to China's own statement, the MII will act as an impartial and independent regulator (WTO 2006:232), the United States Trade Representative (USTR 2004) makes clear its concerns about the agency's regulatory practices, including the licensing process. Other issues have been the reclassification (in April 2003) of some services from the value-added category to basic services, in which the latter are on a slower schedule of liberalisation and with higher capitalisation requirements. China still has no central piece of telecommunications legislation, although a draft Telecommunications Law was circulated among ministries in 2004.

The progress of reform can be summarised in Figure 6.3. China moves into the area OCAB after WTO accession in late 2001, and has been progressively reducing its restrictions on foreigners. This is captured by the change in score between 2004 and 2007. This refinement is consistent with China's WTO commitments. On the other hand, not much improvement was observed after

1998 for the elimination of non-discriminatory restrictions on market access. This is demonstrated in the movement of scores along a straight line between 2004 and 2007, which reflects the fact that while discriminatory treatment against foreigners is reducing, domestic reforms that would benefit domestic and foreign suppliers have been relatively slack. Details of the scoring methods are in Table A6.1.

China's experience can be compared with that of Taiwan. Taiwan's experience is a movement into OCAB, that is, liberalisation—and this is the more common case, which is observed also in Hong Kong, Japan and Korea, for example (Figure 6.4). While discriminatory measures persist, Taiwan's liberalisation pattern is highlighted by the non-discriminatory and simultaneous liberalisation approach. Specifically, Figure 6.4 shows that the index value for Taiwan migrates from point A—which is the original value in the base year—into the space OCAB. It also demonstrates that the level of discrimination between domestic and foreign suppliers remains when restrictions for domestic firms are removed completely by 2007.

Banking

In banking, foreign banks continued until recently to be restricted in their forms of entry and operations compared with their locally owned competitors. Interestingly, one of the most important remaining issues is of equal significance to local and foreign banks.

In early 2006, business interests in the United States (Overmyer 2006) remained concerned about geographical restrictions on operations, restrictions

Figure 6.3 **China's telecommunications reform**

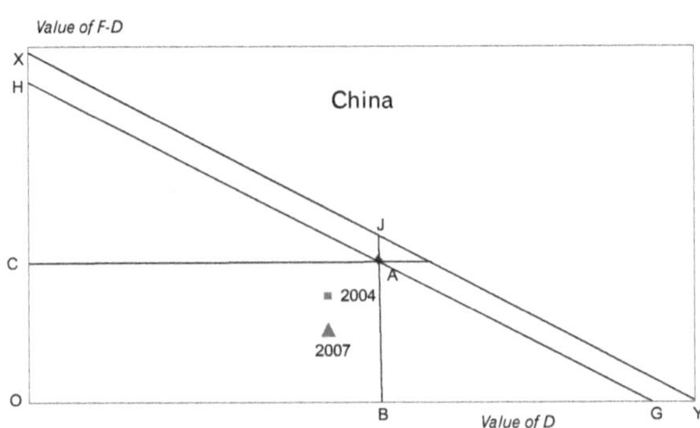

Source: Table A6.2.

Figure 6.4 **Taiwan's telecommunications reform**

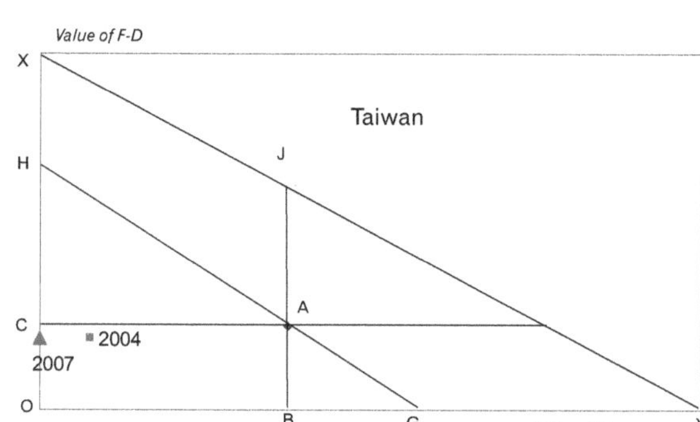

Source: Table A6.2.

on doing business in local currency for local citizens and limits on foreign investment in Chinese banks (25 per cent in total and 20 per cent for any one investor). These restrictions were consistent with the staging process laid out in the GATS commitments, but it was pointed out that domestic banks did not face the geographical and customer restrictions that were faced by wholly foreign-owned banks. Many of these restrictions were, however, to be removed in 2006. Other issues are 'exorbitant capital requirements and slow licence-approval processes' that limit the growth of branch networks (delays of up to one year are reported and biases are evident in the allocation of licences for interior cities).

On 11 December 2006, China did indeed announce that foreign banks could offer renminbi services to local consumers (China 2006). Regional restrictions were also removed. Foreign-owned banks would be treated the same as domestic banks. Foreign banks could also incorporate a local legal entity from this time, however, the caps on ownership in domestic banks remain: the issue then becomes the rate at which foreign entrants can establish a branch network.

More important in the near future is likely to be the debate about foreign bank access to electronic payment systems, although this is an issue for local and foreign banks. The US Coalition of Services Industries (USCSI 2007) reports that foreign electronic payment cards cannot be issued by any bank, local or foreign, unless they are branded with China UnionPay, the monopoly domestic electronic payments processor. There is debate about whether or not this requirement is consistent with the December 2006 GATS commitments.

Insurance

Changes in insurance policies in China are compared with those in other countries for the period 1997–2004 in Figure 6.5, which shows the changes in (rather than the levels of) (F-D) and D. This figure was reported by Dee and Dinh (2007), who pointed out that, for many countries, the policy change in this period was relatively small. China, however, is one of the outliers, along with India. China's reform was driven by its WTO accession, but India's was driven by unilateral action. In China's case, significant contributors to reform were the removal of economic needs tests and quantitative restrictions on the issuance of licences for foreign firms, a widening of the scope of business that foreign insurers could undertake and a gradual reduction in the proportion of business that had to be reinsured with a nominated domestic reinsurer.

The USCSI (2007) points out that a number of impediments remain in the insurance sector, including a differential approach to approving branches for foreign and domestic companies, delays in approval of applications to convert foreign-owned branches to subsidiaries, excessive capitalisation requirements for new branches or subsidiaries, a high qualifying threshold for companies to invest their foreign exchange capital in overseas funds or equities (applies also to domestic firms), a rule that says providers that have held licences for more than eight years (which rules out foreign companies entering the market since WTO accession) can set up insurance asset management companies, protection for domestic reinsurers and differential treatment of companies that invested in China before or after its WTO accession.

Transport

In many cases, the domestic markets for road transport, inland water transport, forwarding, storage and warehousing and courier services had already been deregulated. WTO commitments then extended that policy to foreign entry, though the policy change was not usually applied immediately (for details see Luo and Findlay 2004). It was instead according to a schedule and with restrictions on the form of foreign entry. With the exceptions of air transport (which is discussed in more detail below) and internal water transport, the impact of the commitments at the time of accession and in the medium term—as commitments to higher levels of foreign ownership are phased in—will be significant. Even the relatively closed rail sector will be open to foreign entry under China's WTO commitments. The strategy in logistics, in other words, has been first a movement to domestic deregulation followed by a reduction in the discrimination against foreigners.

Figure 6.5 **Reform of barriers to trade in insurance services, 1997–2004**

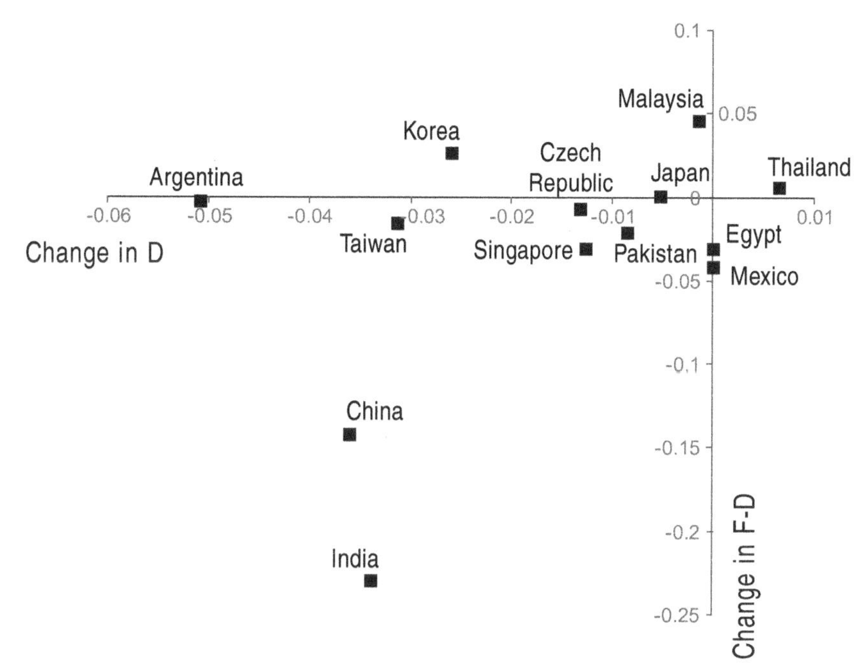

Source: Dee, P. and Dinh, H., 2007. Regulatory barriers to trade in insurance services, The Australian National University, Canberra (unpublished).

Luo and Findlay (2004) stress the effect of liberalisation on process innovation. They note that the demand for integrated logistics services—that is, those provided by so-called third-party logistics firms—is increasing. These firms try to provide and control the whole chain of services. They need to have access to all the relevant licences, which could include international freight forwarding, different modes of transportation (air, international shipping, domestic shipping, road, rail), storage and warehousing, container station and depot services, as well as courier services. The opening up of the different sectors in logistics, Luo and Findlay argue, would have a significant impact on the ability of third-party logistics firms to provide the whole chain of services. Some foreign and domestic firms that originally had restricted access to some links of the services (for example, international freight forwarding) will develop integrated services after the restrictions are lifted.

The commitment to allow fully foreign-owned international freight forwarding operations was implemented in rules issued in December 2005. According to the USCSI, a problem remains in the application of the regulations: it says that its experience has been that wholly foreign-owned firms have been unable to obtain a licence that allows then to book cargo space on airlines within China or operating internationally.

The airline sector provides an example of domestic deregulation: the policy on foreign entry has remained restrictive while restrictions on entry to domestic routes have been relaxed (Zhang and Chen 2003).

The first steps in reform of the air transport sector in China involved the separation of commercial operations from government. This process began in 1987, when six key state-owned airlines were separated from regional administration bureaux, while the entry of new operators was encouraged. The main carriers tended, however, to have a regional specialisation.

The only source of capital for these airlines initially was government funding, but this constraint was relaxed in 1993 and the sector was opened to foreign investment with some remaining restrictions on foreign control (still at a maximum of 49 per cent) (WTO 2006:236). Prices on major routes charged by these businesses remained under government control, until that regulation was relaxed in 1997.

A process of reorganisation of the sector under government leadership began in 2001. The airlines then under the regulatory control of the Civil Aviation Administration of China (CAAC)—a total of 10—were consolidated into three groups. Policy had shifted, in other words, from a position encouraging entry to one of a process of managed consolidation. An important driver was the financial losses earned in the industry. Non-CAAC airlines were not affected by the plans for consolidation and a number continued to operate.

While domestic policy moved through a cycle from state monopoly to free entry to managed consolidation, international policy remained conservative. Chinese policymakers—in the bilateral negotiations on market access that operate in international aviation—aimed to balance market shares, sought commercial arrangements between carriers from both ends of a route, limited the number of Chinese and foreign airlines designated to operate on a route and attempted to limit entry by third-country carriers.

In July 2004, the United States and China signed a new bilateral agreement, however, it was not the form of 'open-skies' agreement promoted by the United States. The agreement added substantial capacity to the routes, opened up more cities for services and increased the number of operators. In a speech on 2 December 2004, US Under-Secretary of Transportation, Jeffrey Shane, said that the agreement 'was a huge step forward but did not remove all constraints and left "a lot to be desired"'—mainly because of the processes used to regulate access to the routes by carriers from each country.[4]

Zhang and Chen (2003) attribute this conservative stance on international policy to a perception of a lack of competitiveness of Chinese airlines, including lack of management experience in competing in international markets, an expected imbalance between foreign arrivals (likely to prefer their own home-country carriers) and Chinese tourist departures, and inadequate airport capacity (although this constraint is being relaxed).

Distribution

Distribution of trade services is composed of four main sub-sectors: commission agents' services, wholesaling, retailing and franchising. Principal activities include reselling merchandise, accompanied by a variety of related subordinated services, such as: inventory management; assembly, sorting and grading of bulk lots; breaking bulk lots and redistributing into smaller lots; delivery services; refrigeration, storage, warehousing and garage services; sales promotion, marketing and advertising, installation and after-sales services, including maintenance and repair and training services. Chul et al. (2003) review China's experience in reform in this sector.

Before the reform that began in 1978, state-owned firms or government bureaucracies dominated the retail and wholesale distribution system and nearly all prices were government controlled. By 2000, in the consumer goods sector, state-owned firms accounted for 18.2 per cent of sales, collectively owned firms for 15.6 per cent and the balance was in the hands of private firms or foreign-owned firms from Hong Kong, Macau or Taiwan (the last group accounting for 1.7 per cent).

Until 1992, foreign investors were prohibited from operating joint ventures or wholly owned enterprises in retailing or wholesaling. In that year, however, new regulations permitted joint ventures (in which the Chinese partners were dominant and with some limitations on operations) in retailing in selected cities. After that time, local governments also took the initiative to approve a number of joint ventures, but most were not mandated by the central government and were set up without permanent establishments—for example, through management contracts or leasing arrangements. A new regulation in 1998 prohibited local governments from offering approvals in this sector. Further regulatory change in 1999 removed the geographical restrictions on the location of joint ventures that the central government had previously imposed.

Wholesaling was opened to foreign firms (operating as minority foreign ownership joint ventures) within a year of China's WTO accession. Longer time limits applied to books, pharmaceutical products, pesticides and films (all three years after accession) and fertilisers and oil products (five years), although salt and tobacco remained exceptions. Majority foreign-owned joint ventures were permitted after two years. All geographical restrictions on wholesaling and all restrictions on ownership were to be removed within three years—that is, by 11 December 2004. In retailing, caps were retained on the number of joint ventures in some larger cities and special economic zones. Geographical restrictions were removed in the case of provincial capitals. The same time limits applied in retailing to the groups of products to which schedules applied in wholesaling. Otherwise there was no constraint on the types of products that could be sold. All market access limitations were to be removed within three years (various restrictions remained for longer on operations and ownership of some types of chain stores and very large department stores).

China fell behind schedule in the implementation of these commitments (USTR 2004). For example, in wholesaling, participation was limited to minority-owned joint ventures beyond the December 2003 deadline for a further relaxation of that rule. Also a number of qualification requirements were imposed (for example, rules on sales volumes and asset values). The schedule was reinstated by mid 2004, when a commitment was made to also meet the next milestone of 11 December 2004. This commitment was embodied in new regulations, which continued to require approval from the Ministry of Commerce before services could be provided. The USTR (2004) remained concerned, however, that there was no guidance on how the process of approving applications would operate (the USTR report is dated 11 December 2004). The same experience occurred in retail services. By 2006, US businesses were referring to distribution as a 'success story' (United States-China Business Council 2006). The Ministry of Commerce devolved the right to grant licences to provincial authorities and 'the problem largely disappeared' (p.2). In some parts of distribution, however, devolution does not necessarily solve the problem. As the United States-China Business Council also points out (p.10), municipal authorities can reject applications for new retail outlets on the grounds that otherwise local commerce would be 'disrupted'. Strictly, this concern applies to domestic and foreign entrants.

WTO accession shifted the direction of reform to removing discrimination against foreigners. The assessment by Chul et al. (2003) is that the deregulation of the 1990s had larger impacts on distribution than those expected from WTO accession, at least within the first couple of years. Many large foreign retailers had already entered China and their geographical spread was widening. Foreign participation in this period had the advantage of providing new methods (including those related to information technology) and different retail formats, which were examples of process innovation similar to those observed in logistics. Reform had also contributed to competition, which was associated with a fall in sales margins.

Conclusions

China's experience to date in financial services, transport, distribution and telecommunications services shows the importance of distinguishing between key elements of the reform process.

The first step in China has usually been to deregulate the domestic market. In some cases, restrictions on foreign participation have not changed and, if they did, the extent of discrimination against foreigners increased. In other cases, foreign participation has been permitted, but usually with restrictions on the form of establishment and the nature of operations.

The second stage—implemented in most cases after WTO accession—has been to reduce the extent of discrimination against foreigners. This stage also involves a schedule of steps, not an immediate movement to full liberalisation.

Services reform tends to be partial, for good public policy reasons. It involves a series of steps, and in that respect China's experience is not unique. But the problem is that different sequences can be followed. In one of these—more likely when a process of international negotiations drives reform—foreign entry receives priority while entry by domestic firms remains regulated. This approach risks welfare losses from rent seeking by foreign providers, who form a new set of political interests affecting the next steps in the reform process.

In another sequence, evident in China's approach, the priority in the first stages is given to domestic deregulation instead of foreign entry. This avoids the risk of foreign rent seeking, but there are trade-offs. A focus on domestic deregulation delays the receipt of the benefits of foreign participation (and, in the short term, discrimination against foreign suppliers could even increase). There is also a risk that reform could stall, as this sequence creates a new set of domestic interests who oppose further reform.

The choice among these options hinges on the ease of management of the various interests created as a consequence of the sequencing problem—domestic and foreign. China's choice clearly has been to prioritise domestic deregulation before a wider opening. This process has been effective in the sectors studied here, though with substantial progress remaining to be achieved in some sectors, particularly telecommunications and aviation.

WTO commitments play a key role in either approach. Even as in China's case, with a schedule of implementation, they help deal with the risk that partial reform could be captured and stalled. They set up a credible set of policy commitments, which trading partners can monitor and influence, as illustrated by the annual reporting of the USTR. Further application of WTO principles avoids a situation in which putative foreign entrants seek a share of the market and then argue to hold out further entry, as might happen as a consequence. This argument is explained in more detail by Dee and Findlay (2007).

Our interests in this chapter are China's commitments under the GATS and their implementation. China has, however, become an active participant in bilateral negotiations and in some of these agreements services are included. Antkiewicz and Whalley (2005) review China's negotiations in preferential trading arrangements. They point out that, at least for the negotiations with Hong Kong and Macao in 2003, eligible suppliers 'gain improved access to Chinese markets and sooner than those from other countries' (p.1544). In this case, the continuing implementation of China's WTO commitments could limit the impact of the preferential elements of these agreements, although firms from Hong Kong and Macao have important 'first-mover' advantages. Antkiewicz and Whalley (2005:1,544) also note the possibility that the effect of local regulations could prove to be the 'binding restriction' and, in that case, commitments under the preferential agreements would be of little importance.

The China material here is illustrative, but further empirical work on the nature of services sector policy reform is valuable, including work on the modelling of options for reform. The calculation of a set of indices of services policy restrictiveness in China for a time period beginning as early after the start of reforms as possible and continuing through to the present could be used to 1) confirm the impressions of the path of reform, in particular, its two-step structure; 2) test hypotheses about the differences between sectors in the degrees of restriction and the trajectories of their removal, including the rate at which the WTO commitments are implemented; 3) extend the options for the design of experiments in policy modelling; and 4) identify the factors that add to or ameliorate the risks of stalling reform. A further application of this material is to relate the changes in the index values to outcomes in services markets and to various performance indicators, such as productivity improvements, price falls, quality increments, innovation and so on, and thereby to assess the contribution of policy reform to these changes.

Notes

1 Generally, the value of D will be less than one, since some restrictions that apply to foreign entry do not apply to domestic firms. For more discussion of the calculation of the indices, see the papers in Findlay and Warren (2000).

2 Kox and Lejour (2004) review a number of other studies that examine the effect of reform of cross-border trade. Whalley (2004), in his review of the empirical work, highlights the complementarity of openness in factor markets with liberalisation of cross-border transactions but pays less attention to the sequencing questions examined here. Walmsley and Winters (2003) estimate the benefits of more open markets for labour.

3 For example, China Unicom has fixed-line operations only in the city of Tianjin and part of the province of Sichung.

4 From US Department of State (2004). Available online at http://usinfo.state.gov/eap/Archive/2004/Dec/06-984604.html

References

Anderson, K., 1995. 'Lobbying incentives and the pattern of protection in rich and poor countries', *Economic Development and Cultural Change*, 43(2):401–23.

Antkiewicz, A. and Whalley, J., 2005. 'China's new regional trade agreements', *The World Economy*, 28(10):1,539–57.

Bhattasali, D., Li, S. and Martin, W.J., 2004. *China and the WTO: accession, policy r*eform, and poverty reduction strategies, World Bank, Washington, DC.

China, 2006. 'China fully opens up its banking industry from Monday', Embassy of the People's Republic of China in the United States of America, Washington, DC, 12 November. Available online at http://www.china-embassy.org/eng/gyzg/t283169.htm

Chul, K.H., Itoh, M., Luo, W., McGuire, G., Moon, W. and Shimoi, N., 2003. The costs and benefits of distribution services trade liberalization, University of Tokyo, Tokyo (unpublished).

Dee, P. and Findlay, C., 2007. Services in PTAs—donuts or holes?, The Australian National University, Canberra (unpublished).

Dee, P. and Hanslow, K., 2000a. *Multilateral liberalisation of services trade*, Staff Research Paper, March, Productivity Commission, Canberra.

——, 2000b. 'Modelling the liberalisation of services', in *Achieving Better Regulation of Services*, Conference Proceedings, AusInfo, November, Productivity Commission and The Australian National University, Canberra.

Dee, P. and Dinh, H., 2007. Regulatory barriers to trade in insurance services, The Australian National University, Canberra (unpublished).

Dee, P. and Sidorenko, A., 2003. The rise of services trade: regional initiatives and challenges for the WTO, Paper prepared for the twenty-ninth PAFTAD Conference, 'Reshaping the Asia Pacific Economic Order', Jakarta, December.

Domah, P., Pollitt, M.G. and Stern, J., 2002. *Modelling the costs of electricity regulation: evidence of human resource constraints in developing countries*, DAE Working Paper, No. 0229, Department of Economics, University of Cambridge, Cambridge.

Findlay, C. and Warren, T. (eds), 2000. *Impediments to Trade in Services: measurement and policy implications*, Routledge, London.

Findlay, C., Chun Lee, R., Sidorenko, A. and Pangestu, M., 2002. Telecommunications, Paper presented to the twenty-eighth Pacific Trade and Development Conference, 'Competition Policy in the New Millennium', Philippine Institute for Development Studies, Manila, 16–18 September.

Francois, J. and Spinanger, D., 2001. Greater China's accession to the WTO: implications for international trade/product and for Hong Kong, Paper prepared for the Hong Kong Development Council, December.

Hoekman, B., 1999. The next round of services negotiations: identifying priorities and options, Paper presented at the Federal Reserve Bank of St Louis conference, 'Multilateral Trade Negotiations: issues for the millennium round', 21–22 October (revised 4 November 1999).

Kox, H. and Lejour, A., 2004. *A different approach to WTO negotiations in services*, CPB Discussion Paper, No. 36, July.

Luo, W. and Findlay, C., 2004. 'Logistics in China: accession to the WTO and its implications', in D. Bhattasali, S. Li and W.J. Martin, *China and the WTO: accession, policy reform, and poverty reduction strategies*, World Bank, Washington, DC.

Mattoo, A., 2004. 'China's accession to the WTO: the services dimension', in D. Bhattasali, S. Li and W.J. Martin, *China and the WTO: accession, policy reform, and poverty reduction strategies*, World Bank, Washington, DC.

Mattoo, A. and Sauve, P., 2003. *Domestic Regulation and Service Trade*, World Bank, Washington, DC.

McGuire, G., 2003. 'Methodologies for measuring restrictions on trade in services', in Organisation for Economic Co-operation and Development (ed.), *Quantifying the Benefits of Liberalising Trade in Services*, Organisation for Economic Co-operation and Development, Paris.

McGuire, G. and Findlay, C., 2005. 'Restrictions on trade in services: trade liberalisation strategies for APEC member economies', *Asian-Pacific Economic Literature*, 19(1):18–41.

Messerlin, P. and Zedillo, E., 2004. *Trade, Development and the WTO: an action agenda beyond the Cancun Ministerial*, Interim report, 20 April. Available from http://www.unmillenniumproject.org/html/tf9docs.shtm

Overmyer, M., 2006. 'WTO: year five—with China's WTO entry requirements winding down, will 2006 become China's "Year of the bank"?', *China Business*

Review Online. Available from http://www.adelaide.edu.au/news/news19001.html (accessed 21 May 2007).

Pangestu, M. and Mrongowius, D., 2004. 'Telecommunications services in China: facing the challenges of WTO accession', in D. Bhattasali, S. Li and W.J. Martin, *China and the WTO: accession, policy reform, and poverty reduction strategies*, World Bank, Washington, DC.

United States-China Business Council (US-CBC), 2006. China's implementation of World Trade Organization commitments, Written testimony, 28 September.

United States Coalition of Services Industries (USCSI), 2007. Statement by the Coalition of Service Industries for Senate Finance Committee Hearing on Challenges in US–China Economic Relations, 27 March.

United States Trade Representative (USTR), 2004. *2004 Report to Congress on China's WTO Compliance*, Washington, DC, 11 December. Available from http://www.ustr.gov/assets/Document_Library/Reports_Publications/2004/asset_upload_file281_6986.pdf

Walmsley, T.L. and Winters, L.A., 2003. *Relaxing the restrictions on the temporary movement of natural persons: a simulation analysis*, CEPR Discussion Paper, No. 3719, CEPR, London.

Warren, T., 2000. 'The impact on output of impediments to trade and investment in telecommunications services', in C. Findlay and T. Warren (eds), *Impediments to Trade in Services: measurement and policy implications*, Routledge, London and New York:85–100.

Whalley, J., 2003. *Liberalization in China's key service sectors following WTO accession: some scenarios and issues of management*, NBER Working Paper 10143, National Bureau of Economic Research, Cambridge, MA.

——, 2004. 'Assessing the benefits to developing countries of liberalisation in services trade', *The World Economy*, 27(8):1,223–53.

World Trade Organization (WTO), 2006. *Trade Policy Review, Report by the Secretariat—People's Republic of China—Revision*, WT/TPR/S/161/Rev.1, 26 June, World Trade Organization, Washington, DC.

Zhang, A. and Chen, H., 2003. 'Evolution of China's air transport development and policy towards international liberalization', *Transportation Journal*, 42:31–49.

Acknowledgments

Thanks to Will Martin and Aaditya Mattoo for comments on earlier versions of this chapter. Thanks to Philippa Dee for providing the insurance sector diagram and commentary on that figure. Errors are the authors'. Work on this chapter was supported by a grant from the Australian Research Council.

Table A6.1 **Telecommunications index components**

Category weight	Score	Policy categories
0.3		Licensing of new fixed-network operation licences
	1.00	Issues no new licences
	0.75	Issues 1 new licence
	0.50	Issues up to 3 new licences
	0.25	Issues more than 3 new licences
	0.00	No limitation on the number of new licences
0.3		Licensing of new mobile network operation licences
	1.00	Issues no new licences
	0.75	Issues 1 new licence
	0.50	Issues up to 3 new licences
	0.25	Issues more than 3 new licences
	0.00	No limitation on the number of new licences except for technical reasons
0.3		Investment restrictions—general
		The score is inversely proportional to the maximum direct equity participation permitted in an existing telecom operator. For example, equity participation to a maximum of 75 per cent would be given a score of 0.25[a]
0.1		Investment restrictions—incumbent
		The score is inversely proportional to the maximum direct equity participation permitted in a specific domestic telecom operator. If there is no operator-specific restriction, the score will be the same as the score for general restriction.[a]

[a] In circumstances where no new operator is allowed, a score of one is recorded for domestic and foreign indices, whereas in circumstances where new licences are issued only to domestic new entrants, a score of one is recorded for the foreign index only.

Table A6.2 **Telecom index, 1998, 2004 and 2007**

		China		Taiwan	
		Domestic	Foreign	Domestic	Foreign
1998					
Restrictions on establishment	Weight				
Licensing of new fixed-line operator	0.3	1	1	1	1
Licensing of new mobile operator	0.3	0.75	1	0.25	0.25
Direct investments					
— General	0.3	-	1	-	0.51
— Incumbents	0.1	-	1	-	0.80
Total		0.525	1	0.375	0.608
2004					
Restrictions on establishment	Weight				
Licensing of new fixed-line operator	0.3	0.5	0.5	0.25	0.25
Licensing of new mobile operator	0.3	0.75	0.75	-	-
Direct investments					
— General	0.3	-	0.75	-	0.4
— Incumbents	0.1	-	0.75	-	0.8
Total		0.375	0.675	0.075	0.275
2007					
Restrictions on establishment	Weight				
Licensing of new fixed-line operator	0.3	0.5	0.5	-	-
Licensing of new mobile operator	0.3	0.75	0.75	-	-
Direct investments					
— General	0.3	-	0.51	-	0.4
— Incumbents	0.1	-	0.51	-	0.8
Total		0.375	0.579	-	0.2

7

Integrating China's agricultural economy into the global market

Measuring distortions in China's agricultural sector

Jikun Huang, Yu Liu, Will Martin and Scott Rozelle

Although there has long been an interest in the agricultural economy, it is quite surprising to many observers that China's agricultural sector has a record that is impressive in many dimensions. Growth rates of gross domestic product (GDP), agricultural gross value added and food per capita increased substantially since the early 1980s. Indeed, agricultural performance in the past two to three decades was more impressive than in any other country in Asia. Markets have boomed and the structure of agriculture has shifted fundamentally. Despite having the largest population in the world and high income growth (which has had a wrenching change on the nation's consumption bundle), China has, since the early 1980s, been a net exporter of food in all but one year.

While the performance of the economy is well documented, there is less understanding about the environment within which this growth occurred. In particular, there have not been many studies of the economic environment that created some of the incentives for producers. In the past, there has been work on the nature of the distortions of China's agricultural economy (for example, Huang et al. 2004; OECD 2005; Orden et al. 2007). Unfortunately, previous studies have been only partial. For example, Huang et al. (2004) looked only at the distortions in a single year; Orden et al. (2007) examined only six years between 1995 and 2001. The OECD (2005) examined only a small set of commodities and made a number of simplifying assumptions about some of the most important commodities, such as pork meat and poultry. Perhaps because of the partial nature of these studies, they reached a number of different conclusions.

The purpose of this chapter is to examine the extent of the Chinese agricultural sector's integration into the world market by estimations of indicators of direct and indirect interventions by the Chinese government in agriculture from 1981 to 2005. The main part of our analysis examines the differences between international prices and domestic wholesale prices at the border (nominal rates of assistance or NRA). We also consider distortions in the domestic economy by examining the differences between farm-gate and border prices (NRAf).

The wide scope of the objectives, as with other studies, necessitates certain limitations. First, the absence of data precludes us from examining the entire agricultural sector. Instead, we examine commodities that account for nearly two-thirds of the gross value output in all of the study years. Second, although we are able to judge from the price trends and from an understanding of domestic marketing and pricing and trade policy reforms the source of the shifts in the distortions of the agricultural economy, we cannot identify the exact source of changes. Also, although we use our revised exchange rate series to calculate what we believe to be the correct values at which we convert international values into currency—which is useful for making comparisons with prices in China's domestic economy—we do not analyse the effect of these assumptions. This is done elsewhere (Martin et al. 2006).

In the next section, we discuss our quantitative approach and sources of data. The results of the distortion analysis are presented in the third section, while the final section offers conclusions.

Methodology and data sources

We have utilised the approach specified in Anderson et al. (2006), which is based broadly on comparisons between domestic and international prices. During the reform era, these price comparisons provided indicators of the incentives for production, consumption and trade, and the income transfers associated with interventions.

Our approach creates essentially two measures of distortions for each major commodity in the agricultural economy. The first measures in our analysis are the NRA, which are used to compare the prices of commodities in the domestic economy (at the port) with the international prices of commodities at the border (that is, 'c.i.f.' in the port for importable goods; 'f.o.b.' in the port for exportable ones). The quality adjustments on the border prices were made before we estimated the NRA. Conceptually, with the NRA, we are trying to measure the extent of the distortions due to tariffs, exchange rate distortions and other non-tariff barriers—at the border.

Because of barriers within the domestic economy, the extent of protection (or lack of protection) that is afforded by trade policies might not be the same as the real rate of protection to farmers. Since we have independent observations on the prices obtained by farmers in local markets, we are able to estimate the nominal rate of assistance at the farm level, taking into account border distortions and distortions affecting farmer returns (NRAf). NRAf are calculated after allowing for quality adjustment, tax or subsidies, transport, storage and handling costs in moving commodities from the farm to the wholesale level. Differences between NRA and NRAf arise from subsidy or transfer payments that cause the prices received by farmers to differ from what they would receive under competitive internal market conditions.

While NRA (and NRAf) measure only differences in output prices, there could also be distortions on the input side. To capture these, it is possible to provide measures to take into account direct subsidies and differences between the international prices of inputs and the prices that farmers pay for these inputs. While these forms of protection (or taxation) are important in many countries—and particularly in Organisation for Economic Co-operation and Development (OECD) countries—we find that they are generally relatively small, so we focus on the NRA and NRAf measures when examining distortions to producers.

Exchange rate distortions present particular measurement problems and require detailed analysis if price comparison-based measures are not to be misleading. The assumption and methods that were used to generate our exchange rate series are in Table A7.1. For documentation of our complete domestic and international price series, see Martin et al. (2006).

In compiling our data, we had to make choices on the coverage of the commodities. We have included 11 commodities: rice, wheat, maize, soybeans, cotton, pork, milk, poultry, fruit (using apples as a representative product), vegetables (using tomatoes as a representative product) and sugar (sugar-beet and sugar-cane). During the study period, these commodities accounted for between 75 per cent (in the late 1980s) and 60 per cent (during the early 2000s) of the total value of agricultural output in China. Because decisions on production and consumption in China's domestic market prices were being allowed to respond to domestic prices only gradually, and because we do not have access to reliable data on the secondary market exchange rates before 1988, we focus on data for the period beginning in 1980.

The data used in our study come from a number of sources, depending on the time period of analysis and the commodity. Commodity balance data (production, utilisation, trade and others) are from the Centre for Chinese Agricultural Policy's CAPSiM database, which are mainly from the Ministry of

Agriculture (production), National Bureau of Statistics of China (consumption and others) and the Ministry of Commerce (trade). Domestic prices are from several different ministries. Specifically, farm-gate output prices come from the cost-of-production surveys conducted by the National Development and Reform Commission (NDRC). Wholesale and retail prices for most products are from the Center for Price Monitoring, the NDRC, the Ministry of Agriculture (various years [b]) and the Department of Rural Survey under the National Bureau of Statistics of China. Where wholesale and retail prices for some commodities in some years were not available, price margins from farm-gate to wholesale and retail were estimated. Much of the data on margins, transportation costs and other transaction costs are from an extensive set of surveys by Huang and Rozelle during the 1990s and the early 2000s, which served also to establish which commodity price series provided appropriate bases for price comparisons. Some of this was reported previously in Rozelle et al. (2000) and Huang et al. (2004), which provided information on substantial quality differences between some imported and domestic commodities and resulting biases in price comparisons as a measure of protection. For more recent years, survey teams from the Center for Chinese Agricultural Policy interviewed traders in 10 cities throughout China in 2006. The complete data series are in the appendices of Huang et al. (2007).

The international price data ('f.o.b.' and 'c.i.f.') for all commodities except milk are the unit values of the exports or imports with adjustments for quality. These data are from the Ministry of Commerce and China's Customs Administration. For the border price of milk, because no import prices for milk are available, we use the farm-gate price of milk in New Zealand, adjusted by international transportation and insurance rates, to create a series for the international price of milk (c.i.f.), which we refer to as the 'reference price'.

Results

The role of domestic price and marketing policies

Before examining the role of distortions at the border, it is useful to examine the relationship between the available domestic price series for farm and retail prices for the major grain crops (Table 7.1). The importance (and role) of China's domestic price and marketing policy for rice and wheat (two of the three largest crops in China) can be seen by comparing the state-set urban retail price and the state-set rural farm-gate procurement price with the rural retail price (a free-market price) before 1993, when the urban grain rationing system was formally abolished. Until 1993, urban retail grain prices were generally substantially below the price on the free market in rural areas, despite the costs

Table 7.1 **Rural retail, urban retail and farm-gate sales prices of rice and wheat in China, 1980–2005** (yuan per tonne in real 2005 prices)

	1980–93	1994–2001	2002–05
Rice (in milled rice equivalent)			
Farm-gate price	1,375	1,889	1,939
Rural retail price	2,069	2,145	2,112
Urban retail price	989	2,144	2,112
Wheat			
Farm-gate price	1,126	1,305	1,268
Rural retail price	1,700	1,433	1,325
Urban retail price	920	1,433	1,325

Note: We use the years of 1993 and 2001 as time-division points because the former is the year the grain ration policy ended in urban areas and the latter is the year before China joined the World Trade Organization.

Sources: Calculated by the authors based on various sources.

associated with transferring grain to urban areas. This was a consequence of a procurement price system designed to provide urban residents with relatively inexpensive food. Only urban residents could buy grain at these low prices and only with ration coupons that were available in limited quantities.

The marketing and procurement system could have been the source of additional distortions. The relatively low selling price of grain at the farm-gate shows that China's food system in the 1980s was set up to transfer income from rural to urban areas (Table 7.1, Column 1). The amount that farmers received for the mandatory deliveries was far below the free-market price. There is, however, some question about the effects on incentives for production and consumption given the infra-marginal nature of many of these transfers (Sicular 1988). This is because after the mid 1980s, farmers were able to sell additional amounts at higher market prices once they had met their obligation to deliver a fixed-quota quantity at the low purchasing price. If a farmer sold more grain than was required by his or her delivery quota—and the above-quota price was determined by market forces—there could have been less of a distortion. Ultimately, however, even such policies are not fully decoupled from incentives, with seemingly infra-marginal transfers away from rural households, for instance, giving their members an incentive to move out of agriculture. These linkages have been shown by Wang et al. (1999). Therefore, the distortions created by domestic marketing and procurement systems could have affected incentives relative to international prices.

From 1994, however, changes to China's domestic marketing and procurement system appear to have eliminated this additional layer of regulation for producers of rice and wheat (Table 7.1, Columns 2 and 3). In the early 1990s, the urban price began to rise above the farm-gate price; urban and rural retail prices also came much closer together (Huang et al. 2007). This reflects the phasing out of the implicit taxation of farmers through the grain procurement system. The gap between urban and rural retail prices essentially disappeared after 1994 (Table 7.1), and the gap between the rural retail price and the farm price declined—possibly suggesting an improvement in marketing efficiency (Park et al. 2002). With the disappearance of the distortions from the marketing and procurement system, the remaining distortions after the mid 1990s reflect only trade policies and not trade and domestic policies.

Nominal rates of assistance for China's main agricultural commodities

All NRA and NRAf are computed at adjusted exchange rates (the estimated equilibrium exchange rates; Table A7.1), since we believe this measure is the right one to use to calculate the true rate of protection. In Martin et al. (2006), we report how the measures of distortions vary when using official and adjusted exchange rates.

Distortions to the grain economy before the mid 1990s. The distortions to the rice economy of China in the 1980s and early 1990s were characterised by two important features (Table 7.2, Row 1). First, the NRA of rice—an exportable commodity—was negative between 1980 and 1993. Averaging –23 per cent, the negative NRA show that China was highly competitive in international rice markets during these years. Trade policy, however, kept exporters from shipping large quantities of rice onto world markets and kept the free-market price of rice in China's port cities below the world price. This demonstrates clearly China's commitment to keeping domestic prices low. Even if there had been no other distortions in the rice economy, producers would have faced prices below world market prices.

The second feature demonstrates how domestic marketing and procurement placed a greater tax on farmers and insulated the domestic price of rice from the world market price even if trade policy had been liberalised (Table 7.2, Rows 1 and 4). Because of China's marketing policy, which lasted through the mid 1990s, the state's artificially low procurement price kept the price received by farmers systematically below the free-market price of rice, as seen by the NRAf. Because of this, the tax on rice farmers averaged –42 per cent. Rice producers

Table 7.2 **Nominal rates of assistance (NRA) and nominal rates of assistance for farmers (NRAf) in the cereal sector in China, 1980–2005** (per cent)

	1980–93	1994–2001	2002–05
NRA			
Rice	–23	–4	–6
Wheat	47	25	-
Maize	–1	7	16
NRAf			
Rice	–42	–8	–9
Wheat	10	24	1
Maize	–28	6	11

Source: Authors' estimations.

were among the most heavily taxed farmers in China, given the large share of the crop's sown area and large negative rates of protection. Importantly, our analysis shows how the state used trade and procurement policy to tax its rice farmers.

The NRA measures show that trade policy offered high rates of protection for wheat farmers in China between 1980 and the mid 1990s (Table 7.1, Rows 2 and 5). Between 1980 and 1993, the free-market price of wheat in China's port cities was 47 per cent higher than the international price (c.i.f., China's port cities). Unlike rice, which China produced competitively during the 1980s, wheat producers—who have been shown to produce at a higher cost than many producers in other countries (Huang and Ma 2000)—received strong protection from trade policy. This policy on its own, unlike that for rice, would not be consistent with providing inexpensive food for consumers. It would, however, be consistent with a policy of food self-sufficiency, since it would encourage greater production by keeping out imports and keeping domestic prices high.

Domestic marketing policies, however, were working in the opposite direction to trade policies. The trends of the NRAf show how the forced deliveries of wheat quotas insulated farmers from the high rates of protection (Table 7.2, Row 5). Although there was still positive protection for wheat farmers in most years between 1980 and 1994, the rates were lower (averaging about 10 per cent). These figures—along with those for rice—show that at least for China's staple food crops, the government was not trying to use prices to encourage food security.

The story of maize is a mixture of those for rice and wheat (Table 7.2, Rows 3 and 6). Considering Row 3, trade policy was providing very little protection for maize in the period 1980–93, with an average of –1 per cent. Procurement policy, as in the case of rice and wheat, depressed the price of maize for China's farmers. Measured at the farm-gate level, maize farmers were taxed by 28 per cent in the period 1980–93.

Distortions to the grain economy after the mid 1990s. Our distortions analysis shows that, after 1994, China's international trade and domestic marketing policies changed strikingly (Table 7.2, Columns 2 and 3). It is apparent from the way the differences in the estimates of NRA and NRAf narrow that China's reformers were able to eliminate the procurement policies that had been taxing rice, wheat and maize farmers (either by reducing the tax imposed by trade policy, as in the case of rice, or reducing protection, as in the case of wheat). In another work, Huang et al. (2006) show that the elimination of the procurement quota contributed significantly to a reduction in the implicit tax burden shouldered by farmers.

The liberalisation of domestic markets in the mid 1990s was accompanied by a liberalisation of trade policy—at least in the case of China's major food grains such as rice and wheat. After the mid 1990s, the taxation and subsidisation of rice and wheat clearly were being phased out, as the NRA for rice rose steadily (became less negative) and those for wheat fell. Likely in part in preparation for accession to the WTO, China's leaders liberalised trade for the main food grains to such an extent that between 1995 and 2001 most of the protection for crops was eliminated. Since 2001, the NRA for rice and wheat have been close to zero.

Interestingly, the case of maize is a little different than that for other crops (Table 7.2, Row 3). While NRA moved towards zero in the case of maize, in a number of years after 2000, the NRA for maize were positive (not shown by the average figures in Table 7.2). This indicates that at least in some years national leaders have been protecting maize producers. In part, as discussed in Rozelle and Huang (2004), this could be due to lobbying from Jilin Province, which has been successful in gaining protection for the producers of its most important crop.

Edible oils and cotton. The biggest difference between the analysis of distortions of grain crops and cash crops (at least for soybean and cotton) is that domestic marketing policy has historically played less of a role in incentive distortion. Although in some counties in China there was a procurement delivery quota for soybean producers, it was not as widespread as that for grain (in many counties, soybeans were not procured by the state system). In addition, the implicit tax on soybeans in places in which soybean quotas were collected was lower than that for the staple grain crops; there is little difference between the graphs for NRA and NRAf (Huang et al. 2007). The same is true for cotton: except in the mid 1990s, free-market procurement of cotton by private traders was not allowed. When reform finally came to the cotton industry in the mid 1990s, leaders did not move to a two-tier pricing system, but instead allowed for private and commercialised government cotton procurement stations. As a result, the measures of distortion for the NRA and NRAf of cotton are nearly the same (Huang et al. 2007). In fact, the same is true for all the other commodities (livestock, horticulture, milk and sugar). As a result, the discussion in the rest of this section—for all three periods—focuses on trade policy.

The trends in the NRA after 1995 show the strong commitment to trade liberalisation for soybeans (Table 7.3, Row 1). Beginning in the late 1990s and continuing through to 2005, protection for soybeans fell from about 25 per cent to about 10 per cent. This decreasing protection should not, in fact, be surprising given the integration of China into world soybean markets and the monotonic rise in imports (which exceeded 25 million tonnes in 2005). The story of soybeans—and the fall in protection and almost full liberalisation—stands in sharp contrast with that of maize, which enjoyed increasing protection.

The distortion analysis for cotton, in some senses, produces results similar to that for rice (Table 7.2, Row 2). The combination of trade and monopoly procurement policies kept domestic cotton prices lower than world market prices in the 1980s and early 1990s. It appears that China's planners were taxing cotton farmers to supply emerging textile industries with relatively inexpensive raw materials. It is no wonder—with such high implicit taxes on cotton—that

Table 7.3 **Nominal rates of assistance for farmers (NRAf) for soybean, cotton and sugar crops in China, 1980–2005** (per cent)

	1980–93	1994–2001	2002–05
Soybean	n.a.	24	12
Cotton	–31	–6	–1
Sugar crops	33	28	23

Note: The figures for sugar crops are the sugar output weighted average of sugar-cane and sugar-beet.
Source: Authors' estimations.

the lack interest from many suppliers, and serious insect problems, led to stagnation and even decreases in the number of areas sown with cotton in many regions (National Bureau of Statistics various years (a)).

After 1994, however, with the liberalisation of most domestic markets and somewhat increased trade liberalisation, there clearly was a shift in the level of distortions faced by cotton producers (Table 7.2, Row 2). Although there were years in which there was fluctuations, since the mid 1990s, the NRAf have been falling gradually to nearly zero. In recent years, despite the fact that national leaders could impose tariff-rate quotas on cotton after a certain volume had been imported, trade officials essentially left the level of imports in most years to be determined by the market.

Livestock and horticultural commodities. With the exception of milk, the patterns of distortions to China's livestock and horticultural sectors are quite similar (Table 7.4). Between 1980 and 1993, there was heavy implicit taxation on pork and vegetables. In part, as noted by Huang et al. (2004), this situation was created by China's grain-first policy. Although China can produce livestock and horticultural products competitively, producers were encouraged neither to produce nor to export these commodities on a large scale. This was due, in part, to China's own barriers, such as quotas on exports into Hong Kong. Another part of the price gap shown in these figures reflects trade barriers facing China in export markets. While there were possibly grounds for some of the barriers (for example, foot and mouth disease is widespread in China), even if a claim was blatantly false it could not be adjudicated effectively since China was not then part of the WTO. As a consequence, China's livestock and horticultural producers produced commodities far below the world market price and were neither inclined nor able to increase exports into global markets.

Since the mid 1990s, the gap between domestic and world prices for livestock products has lessened, but the trends are not clear for the horticultural sector. Emerging markets and relaxation of grain-first policies (often called agricultural structural adjustment policies inside China) allowed producers to greatly expand livestock and horticultural production in large part to meet the rising demand inside China (Rosen et al. 2004). At the same time, China's accession to the WTO and the appearance of an export-oriented segment of the livestock and horticultural industries has increased the interest in and feasibility of participating in international markets. In response, the price gap measures have been falling. It should be noted, however, that the NRAf are all still negative. If anything, China's presence in global food markets has given rise to more stringent rules and regulations on the importation of livestock and horticultural commodities from China.

Table 7.4 **Nominal rates of assistance for farmers (NRAf) for livestock and horticultural sectors in China, 1980–2005** (per cent)

	1980–93	1994–2001	2002–05
Milk	73	17	24
Poultry	–11	–28	–19
Pork	–57	–19	–8
Vegetables	–50	–22	–23
Fruit	–19	–29	–28

Source: Authors' estimations.

Milk and sugar. The story for milk and sugar is in some senses the opposite of that for livestock and horticultural commodities. During the 1980s and early 1990s, the NRAf for milk and sugar were positive and large (Table 7.3, Row 3 and Table 7.4, Row 1). Those for milk averaged 70 per cent in the period 1980–93. Those for sugar were above 33 per cent in the same period. After the mid 1990s, protection was lowered, and NRAf for milk and sugar fell (to about 20–25 per cent in 2002–05).

Conclusions and implications

The main finding of our chapter is that the nature of policy intervention in China's agriculture has changed dramatically in the past 25 years, transforming the agricultural sector from one characterised by high distortions to one that is relatively liberal and more integrated into the world market. In the 1980s and early 1990s (or the early reform period), there were distortions in external and domestic policies that isolated domestic producers and consumers from international markets. Importantly, during the early reform period, domestic marketing and pricing policies served to make the prices that domestic producers and consumers faced almost independent of the effects of trade policy. Because of this—even in the case of an exportable commodity, such as rice, a commodity that enjoyed little protection at the border from tariffs (meaning that the international and the free-market prices of rice were nearly identical)—domestic pricing and marketing policies did not allow producers to reap the profits from international-level prices and instead forced farmers to sell much of their surplus to the state at an artificially low price. Hence, domestic policies levied a tax on farmers even though there was little protection at the border. Similar dynamics characterised importable commodities such as wheat and soybeans where, despite fairly high rates of protection from trade policies, producers were receiving much less protection than they would have had there been a free domestic market for the importable commodities—while consumers were being taxed implicitly.

In contrast, since the early 1990s (the late reform period), the liberalisation of domestic markets has reduced the distortions from domestic policies (as the market has gradually replaced the state as the primary mechanism for allocating resources and has become the basis of farmer production and marketing decisions). At the same time—especially in the case of importable commodities—trade policy has become more liberalised, with distortions from border measures falling substantially. As a result, we find that in recent years (that is, since China jointed the WTO at the end of 2001), China's agriculture is much less distorted in two ways. First, the differences between international and domestic market prices have narrowed considerably for many commodities due to trade policy liberalisation. Second, the elimination of domestic policy distortions means that when trade liberalisation allows for the increased import or export of agricultural commodities, prices in China's domestic market change, directly affecting farmers.

Despite the finding that considerable liberalisation had occurred due to reforms in domestic and external policies, distortions to agriculture remained in the mid 2000s—25 years after the beginning of reforms. In some cases, these remaining distortions arise from tariffs on importable commodities and the non-tariff trade barriers of other countries on China's exportable commodities. While low in international comparisons, China is still providing a degree of protection for a number of importable commodities (for example, maize, sugar and milk).

With this analysis, we have shown that China's agricultural economy has become one of the least distorted in the world. Clearly, the combination of domestic marketing reforms and international trade liberalisation has greatly freed up the decision-making environment for producers. In such an environment, phenomena such as rapid structural change from grain to more labour-intensive commodities and the rise of a horticultural and livestock-based export economy become more understandable. When farmers face less distortion they tend to move into those commodities in which they have a comparative advantage.

References

Anderson, K., Martin, W., Sandri, D. and Valenzuela, E., 2006. *Methodology for measuring distortions to agricultural incentives*, Working Paper, Development Research Group, World Bank, Washington, DC.

Huang, J. and David, C.C., 1995. 'China's agricultural policy', report submitted to Food and Agricultural Organization of the United Nations, Rome (unpublished).

Huang, J. and Ma, H., 2000. 'International comparison of agricultural prices', *International Trade*, 10:20–4.

Huang, J., Liu, Y., Martin, W. and Rozelle, S., 2007. *Distortions to agricultural incentives in China, 1981 to 2005*, Working Paper, World Bank, Washington, DC.

Huang, J., Rozelle, S. and Chang, M., 2004. 'The nature of distortions to agricultural incentives in China and implications of WTO accession', *World Bank Economic Review*, 18(1):59–84.

Huang, J., Rozelle, S. and Wang, H., 2006. 'Fostering or stripping rural China: modernizing agriculture and rural to urban capital flows', *The Developing Economies*, XLIV-1:1–26.

Martin, W., Huang, J. and Rozelle, S., 2006. *Exchange rates and agricultural distortions in China's agriculture, 1981 to 2004*, Working Paper, World Bank, Washington, DC.

Ministry of Agriculture, various years (a). *China's Agricultural Yearbook*, various issues, China Agricultural Press, Beijing.

——, various years (b). *China Agricultural Development Report*, China Agricultural Press, Beijing.

Ministry of Commerce, various years. *China Foreign Trade Yearbook*, various issues, China Foreign Economic and Trade Press, Beijing.

National Bureau of Statistics of China (NBS), various years (a). *Statistical Yearbook of China*, China Statistical Press, Beijing.

——, various years (b). *China Yearbook of Agricultural Price Survey*, China Statistics Press, Beijing.

National Development and Reform Commission (NDRC), various years. *Agricultural production cost and revenue materials compilation*, Price Department, China Statistics Press, Beijing.

——, (various years) National major commodity (service) price monitoring data compilation, Center for Price Monitoring, National Development and Reform Commission, Beijing (unpublished).

Office of Tariff Regulation, State Council, 1996–98. *Import and Export Tariff Regulation of the People's Republic of China, 1996, 1997 and 1998*, Law Press, Beijing.

——, 2005. *Import Tariff and Export Tariff Rebate Compilation, 2005*, Economic and Scientific Press, Beijing.

Orden, D., Cheng, F., Nguyen, H., Grote, U., Thomas, M., Mullen, K. and Sun, D., 2007. *Agricultural producer support estimates for developing countries: measurement issues and evidence from India, Indonesia, China, and Vietnam*, Research Report, No. 152, International Food Policy Research Institute, Washington, DC.

Organisation for Economic Co-operation and Development (OECD). OECD PSE/CSE database.

——, 2005. *OECD Review of Agricultural Policies: China*, Organisation for Economic Co-operation and Development, Paris.

Park, A., Jin, H., Rozelle, S. and Huang, J., 2002. 'Market emergence and transition: arbitrage, transition costs, and autarky in China's grain market', *American Journal of Agricultural Economics*, 84(1):67–82.

Rosen, D., Huang, J. and Rozelle, S., 2004. 'Roots of competitiveness: China's evolving agriculture interests', *Policy Analysis in International Economics*, Vol.72, June 2004, Institute for International Economics, Washington, DC.

Rozelle, S. and Huang, J., 2004. China's maize economy: supply, demand and trade, Report for the United States Grains Council, Beijing.

——, 2005. China's soybean economy: supply, demand and trade, Report for the American Soybean Association, Beijing.

Rozelle, S., Park, A., Huang, J. and Jin, H., 2000. 'Bureaucrat to entrepreneur: the changing role of the State in China's transitional commodity economy', *Economic Development and Cultural Change*, 48(2):227–52.

Sicular, T., 1988. 'Plan and market in China's agricultural commerce', *Journal of Political Economy*, 96(2):283–307.

Wang, D., Rozelle, S. and Huang, J., 1999. *The impact of procurement quota on agricultural production in China's agriculture*, Working Paper, Center for Chinese Agricultural Policy, Chinese Academy of Agricultural Sciences, Beijing.

Acknowledgments

The authors are grateful for helpful comments from workshop participants and for funding from the World Bank Trust Funds provided by the governments of Ireland, Japan, the Netherlands (BNPP) and the United Kingdom (DFID), and the Chinese Academy of Agricultural Sciences (KSCX2-YW-N-039).

Table A7.1 **Raw numbers for exchange rate analysis, China, 1980–2005**

Year	Official rate	Secondary market rate	Retention rate[a]	Discount to secondary market rate	Estimated equilibrium exchange rate
1980	1.50	1.95	0.20	1.95	1.95
1981	1.71	2.05	0.20	2.05	2.80
1982	1.89	2.27	0.20	2.27	2.80
1983	1.98	2.39	0.20	2.39	2.80
1984	2.33	2.69	0.20	2.69	2.80
1985	2.94	3.05	0.25	3.05	2.95
1986	3.45	4.03	0.25	4.03	3.81
1987	3.72	4.40	0.44	4.40	5.29
1988	3.72	6.50	0.44	6.50	5.79
1989	3.77	6.60	0.44	6.60	4.94
1990	4.78	6.60	0.44	6.60	5.44
1991	5.32	6.60	0.80	6.60	5.84
1992	5.52	6.92	0.80	6.92	7.12
1993	5.76	8.28	0.80	8.28	8.41
1994	8.62	8.70	0.80	8.70	8.69
1995	8.35	n.a.	n.a.	n.a.	8.35
1996	8.31	n.a.	n.a.	n.a.	8.31
1997	8.29	n.a.	n.a.	n.a.	8.29
1998	8.28	n.a.	n.a.	n.a.	8.28
1999	8.28	n.a.	n.a.	n.a.	8.28
2000	8.28	n.a.	n.a.	n.a.	8.28
2001	8.28	n.a.	n.a.	n.a.	8.28
2002	8.28	n.a.	n.a.	n.a.	8.28
2003	8.28	n.a.	n.a.	n.a.	8.28
2004	8.28	n.a.	n.a.	n.a.	8.28
2005	8.19	n.a.	n.a.	n.a.	8.19

[a] The proportion of foreign currency sold by all exporters at the parallel market rate.
Sources: For the official rates, National Bureau of Statistics of China, various years (a). *Statistical Yearbook of China*, various issues from 1981 to 2006, China Statistical Press, Beijing. National Bureau of Statistics of China, various years (b). *China Yearbook of Agricultural Price Survey*, various issues, China Statistics Press, Beijing; For the secondary market rates, Huang and David 1995. For the estimated equilibrium exchange rates, on the exchange rate methodology, see Anderson, K., Martin, W., Sandri, D. and Valenzuela, E., 2006. *Methodology for measuring distortions to agricultural incentives*, Working Paper, Development Research Group, World Bank, Washington, DC; Huang, J., Liu, Y., Martin, W. and Rozelle, S., 2007. *Distortions to agricultural incentives in China, 1981 to 2005*, Working Paper, World Bank, Washington, DC.

8

Regional labour market integration since China's WTO entry

Evidence from household-level data

Fang Cai, Yang Du and Changbao Zhao

For an economy in transition, development of the market is a sign of a successful transition and a premise for a sustainable form of economic growth. Development and integration of labour markets are key components that indicate the move towards a market system. Despite wide acknowledgment of success in China's market-oriented reform, there is disagreement about the effects of marketisation, especially in regard to the level of regional market integration. Reforms of production factor markets, for instance—especially in the labour and capital markets—have been considered less far reaching than the reform efforts made in commodity markets (Lardy 1994:8–14). There are also scholars who believe that segmentation of the market has become severe as a result of decentralisation in the reform process. Such scholars argue that although decentralisation rectified the concentration of decision making and resource allocation, it has also generated a 'border effect'—something present in independent economies and in administratively divided regions—thus preventing the labour markets of separate regions from integrating into a national market (Poncet 2002, 2003a, 2003b; Young 2000). Others suggest that the deepening of the Chinese reform process will increase the degree of marketisation in the country, including the regional integration of production factor markets (Fan and Wang 2001; Wang and Fan 2004; Fan et al. 2003).

Labour market integration is a historical concept. Studies in economic history show that during the era of pre-industrialisation, even in now-industrialised countries, labour markets were not integrated due to limited regional mobility.

The process of labour market integration through industrialisation begins in the local labour market and then widens to regional labour markets and, finally, to the national labour market (Rosenbloom 1990, 1997). This process is integral to improving the market mechanism.

In addition to spontaneous forces of marketisation, outside shocks can be sources of encouragement for labour market integration. For example, the common market in Europe promotes labour market integration between member countries of the European Union. Another example is the impact that the North American Free Trade Agreement (NAFTA) has had on integration, bringing labour markets closer in border areas of the United States and Mexico (Robertson 2000).

China's transition from an administered labour system to a labour market is unique—not only because it is the largest economy in the world to experience such a process, but because it has adopted a typically Chinese style of gradual change. Three elements of China's labour market integration are important. First, it has been carried out with an emphasis on incremental reforms, while not entirely negating the importance of shock reform. Second, economic globalisation has stimulated the process of labour market integration. Finally, the move towards a labour market parallels the transformation from a dual economy to one that is integrated.

As China's demographics change and the country approaches a turning point that will lead to a labour shortage, the speed of labour market integration has increased. Through integration into the global division of labour, China has increased its production of labour-intensive exports and accepted world-wide employment opportunities. As a result, more than 100 million rural labourers have migrated to urban jobs, and laid-off and unemployed workers have been re-employed in an economy with high growth rates. With economic development, the pattern of resource endowment in China is being restructured, implying the coming of a historical turning point.

According to population predictions, the desirable population structure that has brought about a demographic dividend in the past three decades will disappear within the next 10 years. At this point, the dependant population ratio (the ratio of the population aged younger than 16 and older than 64 with respect to those aged between 16 and 64) will stop decreasing and begin increasing. When comparing the growth rates of labour forces in other countries, it becomes clear that China will have no advantage in labour supply within two decades. While the population shift will not occur overnight, it will be necessary to drink from the river while the water levels are high: labour abundance must be taken advantage of while it still exists. In fact, the outcome of demographic changes has already appeared in the labour market. The spread of labour shortages from coastal areas to the rest of the country not only indicates the end of an era of unlimited labour supply, it marks the coming of a 'Lewisian turning point'. This is also a driving force behind labour market integration, given that the competition for skilled and unskilled workers has intensified the level of labour mobility.

This chapter seeks to demonstrate that economic reform, opening up and the transition from a dual economy have all encouraged integration of the labour market. First, we explain how the labour market has developed and integrated with respect to three distinct changes in the economic order: the move from a planned labour system to market-based labour allocation; the move from a closed economy to one that is increasingly globalised; and, finally, the move from a dual economy characterised by unlimited labour supply to a Lewisian turning point. Second, we introduce briefly the effects on the urban labour market of migrant labour. The third section demonstrates empirically that the wages of migrant workers have converged, which is evidence of labour market integration.

The labour market in China has developed in two ways. First, the expansion of the private sector has absorbed labourers made redundant as the planned system came to an end. Second, there has been competition from the private sector to force state-owned enterprises to reform their employment system and the state to deregulate the labour market. These aspects of reform tend to promote labour market integration, with an additional incentive provided by the pressures of a coming labour shortage. By employing a statistical method to household-level data, we are able to test the points made above. The final section concludes with some suggestions for further reform to the labour market.

Labour market integration as reform, opening up and growth move on

Like related institutional arrangements in China, labour policy under the planned system resulted in two kinds of inefficiencies. First, the inherent lack of labour supervision and lack of an incentive mechanism in the micro-management system led to low technical efficiency. Second, the distorted allocation of labour, capital and other resources between regions and sectors led to low allocative efficiency. Accordingly, the subsequent incentive mechanism and allocation system reforms have improved technical and allocative efficiencies, and have become dominant drivers of the high economic growth that has occurred during the post-reform period in China. Changes in labour policy have played an important role during the whole process of reform—contributing directly and indirectly to efficiency improvements.

China's gradual institutional changes embodied two initiatives: a 'bottom-up' initiative and one that is 'top-down'. In the first case, once the political climate at large began to change, producers who had previously suffered under the strict constraints of the old system and who could see the potential gains from the new system actively encouraged reform. In the second case, the government perceived the way in which the old institutions constrained productivity, and the potential efficiency gains of a new institution, and after comparing the costs and benefits of an institutional change, it implemented the policy reform on its own initiative. The formation of labour markets in China came about this same way: the implementation of the Household Responsibility System meant that rural labourers were released from their engagement in only the agricultural sector, and began migrating between villages and towns and even provinces. When a large number of migrant workers found jobs in urban sectors, competition began between the state-owned sector and the non-state sector, forcing the former to consider reform of the labour recruitment and hiring system. Partly as a response to this—and partly because of the problem of low productivity—the government gradually relaxed its labour policy. Since policymaking is, after all, a function of government and since it is a decisive force in the liberalisation of a labour market, the intention and the extent of reforms of government labour allocation policies will determine the pace of labour market formation.

In the process of institutional change, playing the role of supplier of the institution, government is also a rational agent, taking into consideration economic and political aspects in its decision making. Whether or not to abolish an old policy while adopting a new one depends not only on the revealed efficiency gains, it must be restrained by the costs and benefits of this change. The terms 'cost' and 'benefit' here can refer to economic and political effects. Increasingly deepened reform brings about an expansion in the market as a principle force of allocating resources. To avert conflict between traditional government methods and market forces, the Chinese government has duly adjusted its policies in response to market development. Labour policy reforms have depended directly on the overall extent of market maturity. While on the one hand, the development of the labour market makes up a key part of the economic reform as a whole, on the other, it goes only as far as the reach of the overall reform.

During the process of labour policy reform, the Chinese government and other players interacted with one another by following the rationale of political economy. As part of marketisation, the reform of labour policy and the implementation of other related reforms are pre-conditional on each other. Following this framework, the deregulation of labour mobility has been embodied mainly in rural–urban migration, characterised as gradual abolition of the *hukou* (household registration) system.

The gradual reform of *hukou* can be characterised by a bottom-up process since the beginning of the twenty-first century: that is, relaxation of *hukou* control began in small towns and gradually extended to medium-sized towns and big cities. *Hukou* reform in more than 20,000 small towns was characterised by 'minimum criteria and complete opening-up'. After years of experimentation in some regions, in 2001, the Ministry of Public Security initiated action to reform the *hukou* system in small towns. In most small towns, the minimum requirement for receiving local *hukou* is that the applicants must have a permanent source of legal housing in the locality. This was considered one of the greatest and most complete steps in *hukou* reform since the system was formed in 1958. Relaxation of the *hukou* system in some medium-sized cities (even in some larger cities and provincial capitals) is characterised by 'abolishing quota and conditioned entry'. The threshold for settling in those cities with *hukou* status has been lowered substantially. This approach to reforming the *hukou* system meets the needs of maturing labour markets and corresponds with gradualism. *Hukou* relaxation in especially large cities such as Beijing and Shanghai is characterised by 'lifting up the threshold and opening the gate'. Those cities have actively encouraged the arrival of intellectuals and professionals, while imposing strict criteria of entry on ordinary migrant workers. In short, lifting the threshold means narrowing the doorway. Comparatively, *hukou* reform in those cities has not made progress.

The reforms in urban employment, social security and welfare provision have created an institutional climate for rural–urban migration. Such reforms include the expansion of urban non-state sectors, the removal of rationing, the privatisation of the housing distribution system and changes in employment policies and the social security system. These reforms have reduced the costs of migrating to, working and living in cities. In the late 1990s, while the urban employment 'iron rice bowl' was broken, rural workers began to enter the urban labour market on a massive scale. It is becoming more common and much easier for rural labourers to seek work and live in cities, even though the *hukou* system still functions. In short, labour mobility motivated by reforms of the *hukou* system and other institutions deterring migration is not only an important part of economic development, it is a significant process of the economic transition towards market forces. This transition has been pre-conditioned by the reforms in a much wider sphere. As the result of the reform in this respect, the allocation of the labour force across sectors and among regions is based increasingly on market forces. The characteristics of migration in transitional China reflect that of marketisation as a whole.

In the process of demographic transition characterised by a shift from a pattern of high death rates, high birth rates and high growth rates in the population to a pattern of low death rates, low birth rates and low growth rates, the time difference between the declines of birth and death rates leads to three phases of age structure characterised by a high dependency ratio of children, a high proportion of working population and a high dependency ratio of the elderly, respectively (Williamson 1997). During the period between the earlier decline in death rates and the lagging decline of birth rates, the natural growth rate of the population climbed persistently and the share of dependant youth in the total population increased accordingly. As the fertility rate begins to fall, the share of working-age population increases in a lagging pace of about 20 years. The further drop in fertility rates will lead to a slower growth in population and the population will age. Therefore, two sequential inversely U-shaped curves, for the natural growth rate of the population and for the growth rate of the working-age population, can be expected if one tries to outline the experience of demographic transition by time series. In the entire period of reform, China has witnessed a continuing increase in the share of the working-age population and gained a demographic dividend from the productive population structure.

This demographic dividend, translated from success in demographic transition, has been capitalised on through reform of the resource-allocation mechanism. Furthermore, the comparative advantage of labour-intensive products has been realised by China's integration into economic globalisation, and thus, the phenomenon of diminishing returns to capital has been deterred by the extra sources of growth. While the total volume of global international trade has expanded rapidly, in just more than one-quarter of a century of reform in China's economy, the country's trade volume has increased at a much faster rate. China's share of commodity imports and exports as a proportion of the world total has been enhanced from only slightly more than 1 per cent in the early 1980s to more than 6 per cent in 2004. The high revealed comparative advantage in labour-intensive commodities clearly links trade expansion to China's advantageous population structure (Yue 2001; Batra and Khan 2005). The world-wide allocation and flows of international capital make it possible for China to utilise more efficient capabilities of resource allocation from outside investors and to fill up its twin gaps in domestic savings and foreign exchange at the early stage of reform and opening up. Taking the total dependency ratio as a proxy of the advantageous population structure in the period between 1982 and 2000, each 1 per cent decrease in the dependency ratio led to 0.115 per cent of growth in per capita gross domestic product (GDP); that is, the decline in total dependency rates contributed to more than one-quarter of the per capita GDP growth in the reform period (Cai and Wang 2005).

Under a dual economy, wage rates will persist at a subsistence level until the expanding modern sector exhausts the surplus labour. As a consequence of the emerging labour shortage, competition for the labour force will inevitably lead to wage rises in the modern sector and, in turn, in agriculture, and the relationship between wage rates and productivity in agriculture will become close to economists' expectations (Watanabe 1994). In other words, once the demographic transition occurs, the Lewisian turning point—characterised as a transition from an unlimited labour supply to labour scarcity—will lead to an increase in wage rates and hence labour costs. The result of higher wages and the Lewisian turning point is an increase in competition for unskilled workers. Employers, sectors and regions will compete for labour and this will lead to a more integrated labour market.

Migrant workers in the urban labour market

Due to the dual economic system implemented in China, there is significant segmentation between the rural and urban labour markets. The two markets have different levels of regulation—leading to migrant and local workers being employed in two separate labour markets within the same city. Governments tend to have less regulation for migrant workers, protecting them less than local workers. For this reason, employment and wage formation for migrant workers are determined mainly by market forces. Since the mid 1980s, migrant workers have been the major components of labour flows between urban and rural areas and across regions. We can take this group of workers as those whose behaviour was the first to be marketised in China. The following features of migrant workers could reflect the mechanism of labour market integration across regions.

Migrant workers have already been the major component of the urban labour market. Rural–urban migration began in the 1980s, and since then migration has continued to increase. On the one hand, this has been because a fast-growing economy creates increasing labour demands in non-agricultural sectors; on the other hand, the urban labour market tends to be friendlier to migrant workers. Since China's entry into the World Trade Organization (WTO), the labour-intensive industries in which China possesses international competitiveness have grown, intensifying the demand for the agricultural labour force. Migrant workers in the urban labour market provide an important human resource that supports rapid economic growth. In 2006, migrant workers accounted for 46.7 per cent of total employment in urban areas (Table 8.1). Therefore, it makes sense to understand regional labour market integration through the examination of employment and wage levels for migrant workers.

The wage rates of migrant workers are a good indicator of the relation between the supply of and demand for labour. Despite informal employment, the market mechanism plays an active role in migrant workers' employment determination and wage formation. Relative to that for urban residents, the market for migrant workers is more flexible. In particular, institutional factors intervene less in wage formation. Therefore, it is useful to analyse labour market integration across different regions from the perspective of the wage inequality of migrant workers.

Finally, migrant workers mobilise across regions frequently. In the beginning of the reform period, society was sensitive to migration from the country to the city, and disputes arose about how best to judge migration. Labour mobility across regions did, however, reflect the fact that migrant workers were responsive to market signals while the most concentrated areas of migrant workers had always been the ones with fast growth rates and strong labour demands. Meanwhile, migrants moving back and forth between their place of work and their home towns pass market information to one another, which helps to inform new entrants into the labour market. Labour mobility across regions is the premise for labour market integration. It is migration that makes labour market integration possible.

Convergence of wages among regions

As one of the key outcomes of the labour market, the wage rate is the most important indicator available to observe the interaction between labour markets of different regions. Similarities and differences are evident in research on labour market integration and on the product market or the capital market. If wages converge between regions, the trend implies a process of labour market integration that is similar to the integration of the product market, reflected by the law of one price. There is, however, a certain degree of uniqueness in each labour market, particularly when discussing integration. Hiring or firing is often an issue of political economy, which means that changes in the price of labour tend not to be reflected immediately in the market. The market for migrant workers undergoes dramatic shifts about the time of Chinese New Year, when it is often considered important to adjust labour allocation for the coming year. For this reason, annual data on product markets, rather than quarterly, monthly

Table 8.1 **Migrant workers in China's urban labour market, 2000–2006** ('000 persons)

	Migrant workers ('000)	Urban employment ('000)	Share of migrant workers in urban employment (per cent)
2000	78,490	212,740	36.9
2001	83,990	239,400	35.1
2002	104,700	247,800	42.3
2003	113,900	256,390	44.4
2004	118,230	264,760	44.7
2005	125,780	273,310	46.0
2006	132,120	283,100	46.7

Sources: The size of the migrant workforce from National Bureau of Statistics, various years (a). *Yearbook of Rural Household Survey*, China Statistical Press, Beijing. Data on urban employment are from National Bureau of Statistics, various years (b). *Yearbook of Labour Statistics in China*, China Statistical Press, Beijing.

or even weekly data, could be more helpful for understanding why there are regional movements of migrant workers.

Depending on the availability of data, two possible methods are employed when exploring wage changes and labour market integration. First of all, analysis on long time series among various labour markets explores whether the link exists between markets. When price changes in one market are reflected in another market, the two markets are regarded as integrated. Based on this idea, Robertson (2000) studied the impact of NAFTA on labour market integration between the United States and Mexico in border areas. Second, we can also take advantage of data that reflect long-term trends in labour markets and apply the law of one price. Since the migration flow between markets eliminates the wage difference, the convergence of wages between markets will eventually reflect market integration when controlling the disparity caused by individual characteristics.

There are advantages and disadvantages when applying the two methods above. The time-series analysis is useful for observing the dynamics of the labour market, although long time-series data are not usually rich in individual information. As is the case with China, the long time-series data between various markets are not currently available and won't be in the near future. Therefore, it is all but impossible to analyse regional labour market integration in China based on such an idea. The disadvantage of cross-sectional data with short time series is obvious: it is hard to observe long-term trends in short periods. When, however, the individual characteristics are controlled in the wage equation, we can exclude the impact of individual factors on wage inequality and observe the role of regional factors more precisely.

In our previous study, we used aggregated wage data on sub-sectors in manufacturing to analyse the deviation of average wages by province and found that markets were integrated between regions (Cai and Du 2004). Although industrial factors that affect wages are controlled, the study cannot reflect the impact of purely regional effects since, with aggregated data, it is impossible to control individual characteristics. Hence, we take advantage of data at a micro level and expect to observe impacts of regional factors on labour market integration since China's WTO entry.

Data

Data in this chapter were collected by the Research Center of Rural Economy, in the Ministry of Agriculture. In the past decade, the centre has fixedly surveyed 20,000 households distributed through 300 villages. In each household, a basic form was filled in that included information such as level of education, age, gender and health status. Since 2003, a complementary labour survey has been done in order to gain more information about labour migration. From the individuals surveyed, we can gain information about the destinations in which migrants go to work. Combining the household and individual data, we can gain information on individual characteristics, wages and working places so we can begin to understand the impacts that geographic factors have on wage inequality.

Inequality measures and decomposition: regional effects

In general, the disparities of individual earnings can be attributed to factors in three categories. The first is individual characteristics, including human capital, and demographic characteristics such as age and gender. The second is industrial and occupational features. Even in industrialised countries, where labour markets functions very well, earning disparities between industries exist persistently: that is, workers in different industries with similar individual characteristics can earn different incomes. The last factor is regional. Regional disparities do not easily disappear when labour mobility between regions does not occur. As we saw before, the market mechanism plays an active role in the market for migrant workers and the industrial and occupational distribution of migrant workers concentrates in a few industries and occupations. It is therefore plausible to explore the role of regional effects of market integration when individual features of particular markets are controlled.

The wages of migrant workers have converged in recent years. No matter which inequality measure was applied, wages were more equal in 2006 than in 2003 (Table 8.2). Theil entropy went down from 0.27 to 0.196 and the Gini coefficient went from 0.374 to 0.332; the other general entropy and Atkinson indices also decreased. Percentage ratios showed that the gap between the top 10 per cent and the bottom 10 per cent was slightly smaller in 2006 than in 2003, which could be a result of more protection for migrant workers in recent years. Despite the decreasing trend in income inequality indices, there is a need to look further into the role of geographic factors in inequality, which should be found by inequality decomposition.

The data used here include information on distribution of destination provinces, so we can simply decompose those decomposable inequality measures as inequality within provinces and inequality between provinces. In general, inequality within provinces dominates inequality between provinces, regardless of which index of general entropy is considered (Table 8.3). For example, about 90 per cent of Theil entropy came from within provincial factors nd 10 per cent was between province factors in 2003; and the shares were 93.4 per cent and 6.6 per cent respectively in 2006. The table also indicates that

Table 8.2 **Income inequality measures, 2003–2006**

	2003	2004	2005	2006
Percentile ratios				
p90/p10	4.469	4.444	4.436	4.232
p90/p50	2.083	2.222	2.096	2.081
p10/p50	0.466	0.500	0.472	0.492
p75/p25	2.143	2.143	2.013	2.083
General entropy				
GE(-1)	0.299	0.285	0.236	0.232
GE(0)	0.240	0.226	0.192	0.189
Theil	0.270	0.246	0.204	0.196
GE(2)	0.436	0.377	0.282	0.258
Gini	0.374	0.360	0.334	0.332
Atkinson indices				
A(0.5)	0.119	0.110	0.093	0.091
A(1)	0.214	0.202	0.175	0.172
A(2)	0.374	0.363	0.321	0.317

Source: Authors' calculations.

Table 8.3 **Inequality decomposition by provinces: general entropy, 2003–2006**

	2003	2004	2005	2006
GE(-1)	0.299	0.285	0.236	0.232
Within	0.275	0.258	0.223	0.219
Between	0.024	0.027	0.012	0.013
GE(0)	0.240	0.226	0.192	0.189
Within	0.215	0.197	0.180	0.176
Between	0.025	0.029	0.012	0.013
Theil	0.270	0.246	0.204	0.196
Within	0.244	0.215	0.191	0.183
Between	0.027	0.031	0.013	0.013
GE(2)	0.436	0.377	0.279	0.258
Within	0.407	0.342	0.268	0.245
Between	0.029	0.035	0.011	0.013

Source: Authors' calculations.

the share of regional factors fluctuates instead of monotonically decreasing. Therefore, we cannot infer that the labour market is more integrated based simply on such decomposed results, because it is possible to correlate some regional factors with individual characteristics—for example, more-able people are more capable of migrating to a place with high wage rates.

To further explicate the components of income inequality, we will decompose those decomposable indices based on regression of earnings of income determinants. According to Shorrocks (1982), the inequality indices can be expressed as a sum of weighted incomes

$$I(\mathbf{y}) = \sum a_i(\mathbf{y}) y_i \tag{1}$$

In this equation, $I(\mathbf{y})$ is the total inequality index—such as Theil entropy, Gini coefficients and coefficients of variation—and y_i is the income of individual i and $a_i(\mathbf{y})$ is the weight applied to every individual, which varies with choice of indices. In the regression equation, every regressor contributes to inequality. The symbol s^k is the contribution of factor k, which is an explanatory variable or is residual to the total income inequality.

$$s^k = \frac{\sum_{i=1}^{n} a_i(\mathbf{y}) y_i^k}{I(\mathbf{y})} \tag{2}$$

Since y_i^k in Equation 2 is determined by coefficients of the explanatory variables and the magnitude of x_i^k, the income inequality based on regression can be decomposed as:

$$s^k = \hat{\beta}_k \left(\frac{\sum_{i=1}^{n} a_i(\mathbf{y}) x_i^k}{I(\mathbf{y})} \right) \tag{3}$$

Following Morduch and Sicular (2002) we decompose Theil entropy and the index can be decomposed by sources based on regression results presented in Table 8.4.

$$I_T(\mathbf{y}) = \frac{1}{n} \sum_{i=1}^{n} \frac{y_i}{\mu} \ln\left(\frac{y_i}{\mu}\right) \tag{4}$$

Therefore, the component of each source of inequality is expressed as

$$s_T^k = \frac{\frac{1}{n} \sum_{i=1}^{n} y_i^k \ln\left(\frac{y_i}{\mu}\right)}{\frac{1}{n} \sum_{i=1}^{n} y_i \ln\left(\frac{y_i}{\mu}\right)} \tag{5}$$

Regression-based decomposition

A linear earning regression model is used to facilitate decomposition of inequality measures.

$$E_i^t = \alpha_0^t + \alpha_1^t edu_i^t + \alpha_2^t sex_i^t + \alpha_3^t age_i^t + \alpha_4^t health_i^t + \sum_{j=1}^{9} \beta_j^t d_j^t + \varepsilon_i^t \tag{6}$$

where the left-hand side variable is monthly earnings of a migrant, and the first four right-hand side variables are individual characteristics, including years of schooling, gender, age and self-reported health status. Except for an error term, the last two terms include the sum of provincial dummies. Unlike typical earnings equations using a log of wages as a dependent variable, for the purpose of decomposing the inequality index—such as Theil entropy—we sacrifice the advantage of a semi-log equation since the main goal in this research is to look at the role of geographic factors in wage inequality, instead of returns to human capital. Table 8.4 presents some of the regression results on individual characteristics; the provincial dummies are not included in order to save space, while the effects of specific provinces are not of interest here. The regression results are generally consistent with traditional predictions: that is, educated, healthy, male and aged labour have a relatively better economic performance in the labour market.

Table 8.4 provides the basis for wage inequality decomposition. According to Equation 4 and Equation 5, combining the information in the right-hand side variables, it is possible to decompose Theil entropy into regional effects, which are the sum of provincial effects, individual effects, constants and residuals. The results are presented in Table 8.5. Our main interest in this chapter is to look at the contribution of regional factors to general inequality measures when individual characteristics are controlled. In 2003, 28 per cent of wage inequality could be explained through regional factors, while the share was 20.3 per cent in 2006 (Table 8.5). A monotonic decreasing trend of regional inequality is also found during the years since China's WTO entry. Although only a few observations are available due to a very short time series, the first row of the table tells us that regional labour markets have been integrated, at least for migrant workers.

The results of inequality decomposition are also consistent with some other observations. The shortage of unskilled workers, for example, was first reported

Table 8.4 **Regression results of linear wage equation, 2003–2006**

	2003	2004	2005	2006
Years of schooling	37.63	29.66	20.11	34.94
	(3.08)	(3.17)	(3.27)	(2.71)
Gender (1 = male)	197.44	197. 86	54.33	231.78
	(15.96)	(15.56)	(15.81)	(13.84)
Age	10.41	10.02	6.93	9.35
	(0.71)	(0.69)	(0.69)	(0.60)
Self-reported health status	–59.97	–74.94	–17.37	–108.19
	(12.72)	(12.70)	(13.30)	(11.21)
Provincial dummies	yes	yes	yes	yes
R2 (adj-R2)	0.13	0.15	0.061	0.12
	(0.12)	(0.15)	(0.056)	(0.12)
No. of observations	8,372	7,986	6,040	10,094

Notes: Standard errors in parentheses. Health status is self-reported in five ranks, where one is more healthy than five.
Source: Authors' calculations.

Table 8.5 **Theil decomposition based on regression**

Components of inequality	2003	2004	2005	2006
Theil entropy	0.270	0.246	0.204	0.196
Regional factors (per cent)	28.08	26.10	22.84	20.31
Individual factors (per cent)	–63.88	–52.92	–33.03	–44.49
Constant (per cent)	–11.16	–26.22	–60.89	–41.06
Residual (per cent)	146.96	153.04	171.08	165.24
Total (per cent)	100.00	100.00	100.00	100.00

Source: Authors' calculations.

in coastal areas and then passed on to other parts of the country. The same pattern was found in changes of wage rates, which increased significantly in coastal areas first and then transmitted to the interior (Cai and Du 2007). Those stylised facts indicate that employment and wage information are passed on across provinces through migration flows, which is the basis of an integrated labour market.

Conclusions

China's employment expansion has kept pace with its unprecedented economic growth in the reform period. After accession to the WTO, China's reform and opening up has not only continued, it has intensified in a way that is consistent with globalisation. By breaking up the iron rice-bowl in urban employment policy and eliminating a series of *hukou*-related institutional barriers deterring labour mobility, more jobs have been created and more labourers now migrate from rural to urban sectors. Furthermore, as a result of substantial increases in employment in rural and urban China and a decline in the working-age population, labour shortage is becoming an issue for the labour market. All those changes have created necessary institutional and structural conditions for labour market integration and the analysis of wage convergence of migrant workers has proven that the Chinese labour market has in fact moved towards integration.

Labour market reform is, however, far from complete. In addition, the coming Lewisian turning point further challenges institutional reforms. Abolition of the various institutional obstacles that hinder the development of a labour market will not only enhance migration flows, they will make it a rational movement, by helping to create the developmental climate and job opportunities for labour mobility, which in turn matures the conditions for abolition of the *hukou* system.

The Chinese government, which has specific development goals for the next 10–20 years, should grasp every opportunity to push institutional reforms and to encourage labour migration once its importance is further realised.

In the course of China's dual-economy development, modern urban economic sectors expand rapidly and attract mass labour migration from rural to urban areas, supplying an inexhaustible labour force to urban sectors at a low cost. Thanks to the unlimited supply of labour, migrant workers in urban sectors have neither collective bargaining power for their wage determination, nor can they influence the labour market policies of local governments. At the development stage, therefore, rural–urban migrants confront a host of institutional obstacles, among which is the *hukou* system, dividing the rural and urban labour market. Legitimised by the *hukou* system and its resulting discriminatory institutions, local governments often blame urban employment pressure on competition from migrant workers and hence form a policy orientated towards discriminating against migrants, cycling in accordance with the fluctuation of the employment situation in urban labour markets (Cai et al. 2003). Every time labour mobility from rural to urban areas experiences systematic obstruction by government policy, migrant workers have no choice but to return to contracted land or other family businesses in their home villages, which serve as a pool that cyclically absorbs the rural surplus of labour.

This Chinese-style wage-sharing system causes labour migration to be temporary, instability of off-farm income for rural households and persistence of a rural–urban income gap. Only when the relationship between supply of and demand for labour changes in an inverse direction against the long-standing figures can these problems be solved. In the histories of most industrialised countries, the moment when systematic labour shortages occurred became a turning point in which the employer–employee relationship improved. Furthermore, at this point, income inequality tends to decline and government policymakers and legislators tend to favour ordinary workers. As international experience suggests, however, if governments are incapable of making sound policy choices, even when they understand the requirements of the next phase of economic development, it is likely that the discriminatory institutions of the dual economy will continue. If such discrimination against ordinary workers continues, it will leave the working class severely disgruntled and could lead to fierce social conflict.[1]

Notes

1 Korea in the late 1980s is an example that a majority of the conditions necessary for institutional changes satisfying ordinary workers matured, but the changes were not made, so the society experienced severe conflict between the government and the working classes (Freeman 1993).

References

Batra, A. and Khan, Z., 2005. *Revealed comparative advantage: an analysis for India and China*, Working Paper No. 168, August, Indian Council for Research on International Economic Relations, New Delhi.

Cai, F. and Du, Y., 2004. 'Labour market integration: evidence from wage convergence in manufacturing', *China: is rapid growth sustainable?*, Asia Pacific Press, The Australian National University, Canberra:137–55.

—— (eds), 2007. *The Coming Lewisian Turning Point and Its Policy Implications*, Social Sciences Academic Press, Beijing.

Cai, F., Du, Y. and Wang, M., 2003. *The Political Economy of Labor Migration in China*, Sanlian Press, Shanghai.

Cai, F. and Wang, D., 2005. 'China's demographic transition: implications for growth', in R. Garnaut and L. Song (eds), *The China Boom and its Discontents*, Asia Pacific Press, The Australian National University, Canberra:34–52.

Fan, G. and Wang, X., 2001. *Indices of Marketisation in China: 2000*, Economic Science Press, Beijing.

Fan, G., Wang, X. and Zhu, H., 2003. *Indices of Marketisation in China: 2001*, Economic Science Press, Beijing.

Freeman, R.B., 1993. 'Labor markets and institutions in economic development', *American Economic Review*, 83(2):403–8.

Lardy, N.R., 1994. *China in the World Economy*, Institute for International Studies, Washington, DC.

Morduch, J. and Sicular, T., 2002. 'Rethinking inequality decomposition, with evidence from rural China', *Economic Journal*, 112(476):93–106.

National Bureau of Statistics (NBS), various years (a). *Yearbook of Rural Household Survey*, China Statistical Press, Beijing.

——, various years (b). *Yearbook of Labour Statistics in China*, China Statistical Press, Beijing.

Poncet, S., 2002. 'A fragmented China: measure and determinants of Chinese domestic market integration', *CERDI Etudes et Documents*, 21:38.

——, 2003a. 'Domestic market fragmentation and economic growth in China', paper presented at the 43rd European Congress of the Regional Science Association, Jyvsky, Finland, 27–30 August.

——, 2003b. 'Measuring Chinese domestic and international integration', *China Economic Review*, 14:1–21.

Robertson, R., 2000. 'Wage shocks and North American labour-market integration', *The American Economic Review*, 90(4):742–64.

Rosenbloom, J., 1990. 'Was there a national labour market at the end of the nineteenth century? New evidence on earnings in manufacturing', *The Journal of Economic History*, 56:626–56.

——, 1997. 'One market or many? Labour market integration in the late nineteenth-century United States', *The Journal of Economic History*, 50:85–107.

Shorrocks, A.F., 1982. 'Inequality decomposition by factor components', *Econometrica*, 50(1):193–211.

Wang, X. and Fan, G., 2004. *Regional Disparity in China: tendency and the influential factors in 20 years*, Economic Science Press, Beijing.

Watanabe, S., 1994. 'The Lewisian turning point and international migration: the case of Japan', *Asian and Pacific Migration Journal*, 3(1):119–47.

Williamson, J., 1997. *Growth, distribution and demography: some lessons from history*, Working Paper Series 6244, National Bureau of Economic Research, Cambridge, MA.

Young, A., 2000. 'The razor's edge: distortions and incremental reform in the People's Republic of China', *The Quarterly Journal of Economics*, 115(4):1,091–135.

Yue, C., 2001. 'Comparative advantage, exchange rate and exports in China', paper prepared for the conference Has China Become a Market Economy?, CERDI, Clermont-Ferrand, 17–18 May.

Acknowledgments

The authors would like to thank Wu Zhigang for assistance in processing data.

9

How much have the wages of unskilled workers in China increased?

Data from seven factories in Guangdong

Xin Meng and Nansheng Bai

China has experienced strong economic growth for a long time. The sustainability and character of that growth depends, to a large extent, on whether China has exhausted its rural surplus labour. In this chapter, we use unique payroll data from seven large manufacturing factories to show that wages of unskilled labour in these factories have not increased significantly, if at all. These findings could shed some light on whether China has reached a 'Lewisian turning point' and the extent to which Chinese economic growth could be sustainable.

China has had 15 years of unprecedented economic growth, which, to a significant extent, is related to a large-scale movement of surplus labour from the low-productivity rural sector to the high-productivity urban sector. Rural–urban migration provided Chinese industries with cheap labour and facilitated the rapid growth of labour-intensive manufacturing exports. Those who are interested in the issue of the sustainability of Chinese economic growth would be eager to learn the extent to which rural–urban migration can continue to drive the fast pace of economic growth.

Many recent studies have predicted that China has exhausted its surplus labour and reached the point whereby labour shortages (the Lewisian turning point) are occurring (Garnaut and Huang 2006; Cai and Wang 2006; Cai and Wang 2007a, 2007b). The most effective way to measure whether China has reached the Lewisian turning point is to examine the wage trend of unskilled labour. The idea is that if surplus labour is approaching exhaustion, the wages of unskilled workers will start to rise significantly. Unfortunately, Chinese official statistics do not provide data on the wages of migrant workers, who make up the majority of non-agricultural unskilled labour. Survey data of migrant workers are often based on non-random sampling of migrants and are cross-sectional in nature. A few studies that indicate the possible exhaustion of surplus labour use mainly wage data of urban residents as indicators (see, for example, Garnaut and Huang 2006; Cai and Wang 2007a). This could be misleading, as the Chinese urban labour market still operates under a two-tier system whereby urban-resident workers are paid a premium wage and are hired mainly in high-status jobs, while their rural-migrant counterparts are employed mostly in unskilled jobs and are paid a wage below the marginal productivity level (Meng and Zhang 2001; Knight et al. 1999; Meng 2001). To date, no study has examined how the wages of unskilled migrant workers have changed in recent years—due mainly to the lack of available data.

Here we employ a unique payroll data set for seven labour-intensive manufacturing factories in Guangdong Province for the period from 2000 to 2004 to examine how the wages of migrant workers in these factories have changed in that period. Hopefully, our findings will shed some light on the bigger issue of whether China has reached the Lewisian turning point.

Data

In 2004–05, we participated in a wage and working condition study of some labour-intensive factories in Guangdong Province, contracted by an outsourcing company. The project was designed to investigate whether factories in China, which work for the outsourcing company, are fulfilling their fair-wage commitments and following the outsourcing company's code of conduct.

The outsourcing company provided a list of 82 contracting factories in Guangdong Province. Based on this list, a group of 20 factories was selected randomly based on the stratification of region (Guanzhao, Dongguan, Shenzhen, Zhongshan and others), products (footwear, apparel and accessories and gears) and size (firms with more than 1,000 workers and with 1,000 or less workers). Nine of the 20 firms either refused or did not respond to the request from the outsourcing company. The remaining 11 firms represent Guangzhou and Shenzhen cities, the footwear industry and large firms. To correct for this bias, five additional factories were added to the list and two of them were selected. The final list comprised 13 factories, and each was then interviewed.

Although the factories were given assurances that the study would not reveal any identifying information about individual factories, many were nevertheless apprehensive about participating.

During interviews, the general situation regarding wages, employment and benefits was discussed and the requirements of payroll data collection were presented, stressing that original data collected would not be provided to the outsourcing company. Among the 13 factories visited, six refused to participate. Seven factories agreed to provide payroll and personnel data, of which one factory agreed to provide data only for one of its many production lines.

Participating factories provided personnel and monthly records of payroll data for the period from 2000 onwards. Of the seven factories involved, two were footwear factories, two were apparel factories and three were accessories and gear factories. Most of the factories were large; three were in Dongguan, two in Guangzhou, one in Shenzhen and one in Zhongshan. The valid data consisted of 1,163,857 wage records. In August 2004 (the last month for which all sample firms had wage records), the largest factory in the sample had 12,032 workers, while the smallest had 651 workers. In that month, three of the sample factories had more than 1,000 workers and the remaining four had less than 1,000 workers (Table 9.1).

The purpose of the data collection and the voluntary nature of data provision could indicate that the seven factories that provided data were the best performers (law abiding) in the area of fair wages and living conditions. The results obtained from these data, therefore, might not be representative of China in general; however, they are likely to be an overestimate in terms of wages, wage growth and other conditions, and hence, are likely to be biased in favour of the conjecture that China has reached the Lewisian turning point.

Table 9.1 **Industry, region, and size distribution of the sample factories**

Firm code	City	Reported number of workers	Factory type	Number of workers in August 2004	Data period
1	Dongguan	5,553	Footwear	12,032	2000–2004
2	Guangzhou	7,326	Footwear	7,641	2000–2004
3	Dongguan	1,200	Apparel	837	2001–2004
4	Dongguan	900	Apparel	669	2002–2004
5	Shenzhen	550	Accessories and gears	651	2002–2004
6[a]	Zhongshan	6,900	Accessories and gears	701	2000–2004
7	Guangzhou	917	Accessories and gears	1,119	2002–2004

[a] data provided for only one production line.

Table 9.2 presents summary statistics of the data. The first panel shows the sample distribution by year and industry. Figures from this panel indicate that in each of the five years the sample is dominated by the footwear industry, which accounted for a minimum of 83 per cent of the sample (2003) and a maximum of 99 per cent of the sample (2000) when investigating annual data. This important feature of the data should be kept in mind when interpreting the results presented below. Note that among the three types of industry, footwear has the most labour-intensive and unskilled jobs. Most workers work on production lines. Apparel workers, although working on individual machines, require a fairly low level of skill. The accessories and gear industry, on the other hand, requires higher skill levels. These factories were producing mainly golf clubs, in which the major job involved metal polishing, which had a high skill content.

The second panel of Table 9.2 shows the gender distribution of workers in the sample. On average, the sample is female dominated, with women accounting for 75 per cent of workers. The distributions vary considerably, however, across different industries. For example, while the footwear industry is mainly female dominated, accessories and gear is dominated by male workers.

The third panel presents the distribution of rural migrant workers relative to urban workers. The footwear industry has the largest percentage of rural migrants, the proportion for all industries has increased to more than 80 per cent since 2003 and, by 2004, the proportion of rural workers accounted for 90 per cent of the total sample.

The fourth panel summarises the average age of the sample population. The mean age of the sample in 2000 was 23.4 years, while in 2004 it increased to 25.5 years. Anecdotal evidence provided to support the idea that China has reached the Lewisian turning point is that many factories are unable to find young workers (aged 15–25), who are more energetic and more suited to these factory jobs. Does the increase in the average age of our sample over time support such a conjecture? One of the reasons for a two-year increase in average age could be related to the panel nature of the data. As workers stay longer, they become older. To understand the extent to which this increase in average age of the sample is due to the panel nature, we also examine the age of the newly hired workers to see if factories are hiring older workers. The data show that for the new workers, the average age increased from 22.5 in 2000 to 23.3 in 2004—an increase of less than one year. Although this is consistent with the anecdotal evidence, the change is not significant.

The educational distribution of the workers is presented in the bottom panel of the table. As indicated, the majority of workers are junior high school graduates: about 81–86 per cent. A substantially higher proportion of male workers have senior high or technical high school qualifications relative to female workers. Just less than 1 per cent of the total workers have a college or university degree. Here again, there is a larger proportion of male workers than female workers. For the newly hired workers, the proportion of junior high school graduates increased from 81 per cent in 2000 to 87 per cent in 2004. At the same time, the proportion of people who held primary school qualifications and those held senior high school qualifications decreased.

Wages and wage growth: first glance

The most important data for this chapter are wages and hourly wage rates. Before presenting data on wages it is important to understand the wage structure in these factories. Table 9.3 presents the different reporting methods regarding wages used in each of the seven factories.

Table 9.3 shows that the sample factories record wages in very different ways, and some records are much more complicated than others. Although many factories use piece rates to calculate the wages of production workers—especially in the apparel and accessories and gear industries—when it comes to accounting, all the wage data are converted to some type of time-rate wages (based mostly on the new rules set by the outsourcing company with differential normal time and overtime pay for Monday to Friday, weekends and public holidays).[1] The general format of the payroll data is to record the amount workers earned (A), the amount of deductions (B) and the final (net) payment, which equals (A)-(B).

Wages reported in the payroll data are at a monthly rate, including a basic wage and other components. Payroll data also provide workers' working days and hours. In some cases, however, working days and hour data are not directly available. Formulae provided by the factories are used to calculate workers' monthly working hours. Based on this information, hourly wage rates can be calculated. In addition, as the data present the five years of wage changes, a city-specific consumer price index (CPI) series is used to calculate real wages based on the price level in 2000.[2]

Table 9.4 presents summary statistics for wages and hours worked. The left panel of the table presents the average real total monthly wages, working hours and hourly wage rates for the total sample for the five-year period by gender and product types,[3] while the right panel presents the data for migrant production workers only.

The data from the left panel show that, on average, real monthly total earnings increased by 3.3 per cent per annum (Column 1). Male workers earn, on

Table 9.2 **Industry distribution of the data, 2000–2004**

Annual industrial share of workers	2000	2001	2002	2003	2004	Total
Footwear	98.57	94.90	85.15	82.82	83.81	87.72
Apparel		1.75	6.33	6.99	6.53	4.91
Accessories and gears	1.43	3.35	8.52	10.18	9.66	7.36
Total number of records	167211	182864	259881	293031	260870	1163857
September share of workers						
Footwear	97.94	97.07	83.03	82.72	83.18	87.11
Apparel		0.00	6.02	7.05	6.37	4.64
Accessories and gears	2.06	2.93	10.95	10.23	10.45	8.25
Total number of records	12846	16786	21943	23027	23916	98518
Annual proportion of male workers						
Footwear	27.53	23.62	20.34	20.24	22.29	22.18
Apparel		22.54	42.25	39.28	38.57	39.17
Accessories and gears	71.39	75.42	59.52	62.79	67.02	64.00
Total	28.05	25.02	24.27	24.93	26.93	25.66
The share of rural migrants in the sample						
Footwear	59.88	71.12	81.43	85.03	90.91	79.08
Apparel		16.40	31.93	60.71	84.65	57.08
Accessories and gears	51.72	56.26	82.22	76.11	82.76	77.55
Total	59.76	69.67	78.36	82.42	89.72	77.89
Average age of the sample						
Footwear	23.38	23.76	24.11	25.00	25.54	24.57
Apparel			28.59	27.86	27.35	27.71
Accessories and gears	23.12	23.17	25.48	25.89	26.14	25.67
Total	23.38	23.74	24.35	25.21	25.69	24.75

Average age for the new entrance						
Footwear	22.49	22.02	22.32	23.17	23.11	22.74
Apparel			27.58	24.88	25.66	25.52
Accessories and gears	21.59	20.33	23.40	22.47	23.65	23.13
Total	22.48	21.98	22.48	23.19	23.32	22.88
Education distribution (total)						
Primary	4.86	3.81	2.52	2.08	2.05	2.69
Junior high	81.72	82.82	84.88	85.76	84.87	84.51
Senior high	10.2	9.41	8.56	8.37	8.74	8.85
Technical high	2.71	3.35	3.36	3.02	3.52	3.25
College	0.44	0.56	0.54	0.59	0.65	0.57
University	0.06	0.05	0.14	0.17	0.17	0.14
Education distribution (males)						
Primary	1.27	1.54	1.7	1.61	1.53	1.56
Junior high	73.07	70.74	70.76	71.03	71.16	71.2
Senior high	20.71	21.34	20.6	20.37	19.46	20.31
Technical high	3.69	4.66	5.05	5.1	6.03	5.15
College	1.03	1.54	1.38	1.32	1.3	1.32
University	0.22	0.18	0.51	0.58	0.52	0.46
Education distribution of the new entrance						
Primary	3.40	2.54	0.14	0.46	1.16	1.11
Junior high	80.97	85.25	90.86	87.73	87.15	87.47
Senior high	9.47	6.82	4.22	6.84	6.69	6.34
Technical high	5.51	5.02	3.60	4.03	4.20	4.22
College	0.64	0.37	0.70	0.63	0.66	0.63
University	0.00	0.00	0.49	0.32	0.14	0.23

Table 9.3 **Wage structures of the sample factories**

Factory 1
Total wage=Time rate+Bonus+Customer reward+Other reward+Position pay+Seniority pay+efficiency reward
Total deductions =Meal charge+Accom. Charge+Medical insurance+Income tax+Other deduction
Net wage=Total wage-Total deduction-balance
End of year bonus (not included in the wages)

Factory 2
Total wage=basic pay+weekday overtime pay+weekend overtime pay+holiday overtime pay+Other pay
Total deductions=Penalty deduction+accom. charge+social security+unemployment insurance+Income tax
Net wage=Total wage-Total deduction
End of year bonus

Factory 3 (2001.09-2003.06)
Total wage =Transport subsidy+Other subsidy+pay back bond for borrowed tools+basic wage+night work pay+bonus+pieace rate
Total deductions =deduction of no excuse leave+accom. charge+penalty+social security+Medical charge+electricity charge+temporary registration charge+Factory ID charge
Net wage = Total wage-Total deduction
End of year bonus

Factory 3 (2003.07-2004.09)
Total wage =basic wage+weekday overtime pay+weekend overtime pay+holiday overtime pay+bonus+other subsidy
Total deductions =accom charge and electricity charge+social security charge+Medical expenditure+temporary registration charge+meal charge+Other charge+no excuse leave penalty
Net wage = Total wage-Total deduction
End of year bonus

Factory 4
Total wage =Basic wage+Subsidy+Bonus
Total deductions =Accom. Charge+Government adm. Charge
Net wage = Total wage-Total deduction
End of year bonus plus paid holiday (Not included in the wages)

Factory 5

Total wage =basic wage100%+overtime pay150%+weekend overtime pay 200% +holiday overtime pay 300%+bonus+extra production bonus+piece rate+Holiday pay +subsidy for night time work meal

Total deductions =Income tax+superannuation+medical insurance+meal charge+other charge

Net wage = Total wage-Total deduction

End of year bonus

Factory 6

Total wage=piece rate+basic wage+special subsidy+living subsidy+night work subsidy+bonus+No leave bonus+New year subsidy+Managerial subsidy+work subsidy+transport subsidy+medical subsidy+meal subsidy+Other subsidy+overtime pay+overtime subsidy+wages paid when waiting for material

Total deductions =Meal charge+Contract charge+Supperannuation+Other social security payment+Income tax+pay beck borrowing+Other deduction

Net wage+Total wage-Total deduction

End of year bonus

Factory 7 (before Oct. 2004)

Total wage =Basic wage+Overtime wage+No leave bonus+efficiency bonus+subsidy+Other bonus

Total deductions =Social security payment

Net wage = Total wage-Total deduction

End of year bonus

Factory 7(since Oct. 2004)

Total wage =Basic wage+overtime1.5+Overtime2+Overtime3+bonus+Other subsidy+piece rate

Total deductions =Social security payment

Net wage = Total wage-Total deduction

End of year bonus

Table 9.4 **Monthly and hourly real wages and hours worked, 2000–2004** (yuan)

	Total sample				Migrant production workers			
	(1)	(2)	(3)	(4)	(5)	(6)	(7)	(8)
Total monthly earnings	Total[a]	Females (F)	Males (M)	F/M	Total	Females (F)	Males (M)	F/M
2000	838.96	806.07	923.34	87.30	829.22	794.72	941.90	84.37
2001	847.35	794.35	1006.35	78.93	812.19	766.79	972.99	78.81
2002	942.85	875.66	1153.65	75.90	912.83	851.75	1143.16	74.51
2003	929.67	872.42	1103.79	79.04	896.09	847.43	1073.20	78.96
2004	988.82	930.46	1148.34	81.03	952.51	904.41	1110.35	81.45
Average annual growth (%)	3.34	2.91	4.46		2.81	2.62	3.35	
Monthly hours worked								
2000	200.08	200.35	199.36	100.49	200.80	200.66	201.23	99.72
2001	192.35	190.91	196.65	97.08	191.66	190.12	197.09	96.46
2002	210.75	210.45	211.72	99.40	210.32	210.10	211.20	99.48
2003	199.67	200.36	197.59	101.40	198.87	199.95	194.94	102.57
2004	206.82	207.12	205.99	100.55	206.44	207.09	204.29	101.37
Average annual growth (%)	0.66	0.67	0.66		0.56	0.63	0.30	
Total hourly earnings[b]								
2000	4.34	4.15	4.88	85.11	4.21	4.05	4.75	85.34
2001	4.47	4.24	5.14	82.50	4.30	4.12	4.95	83.17
2002	4.59	4.23	5.76	73.45	4.46	4.12	5.77	71.36
2003	4.89	4.42	6.34	69.73	4.75	4.29	6.42	66.79
2004	5.06	4.60	6.36	72.34	4.94	4.48	6.46	69.37
Average annual growth (%)	3.11	2.08	5.45		3.23	2.03	6.34	

Notes: [a] The sample for the total differs from that by gender as around 20 per cent of the sample has no personnel records.
[b] The sample for hourly earnings is slightly different from that for total earnings as around 2 per cent of the sample has no record of working hours.

average, 13–25 per cent more than female workers (Column 5) and the annual growth of monthly real earnings is much faster for men than for women, with a difference of 1.5 percentage points per annum.[4]

Turning to monthly hours worked, the total hours worked are about 197 to 212 a month, which amounts to 46 to 50 hours a week. This is about 8–8.3 hours a day, with six working days a week. This seems to be on the low side relative to common perceptions and common findings of hours worked for migrant workers from other survey data sources. For example, Meng and Zhang (2001) found that in Shanghai in 1995 migrant workers worked an average of 56 hours a week. A recent survey of income distribution for migrant workers in 11 provinces (including Guangdong) showed that the sample migrant workers worked, on average, 61 hours a week in 2002, whereas the number for Guangdong Province was 65 hours weekly.[5] Interestingly, the average weekly hours worked was also much lower than the maximum 60 hours a week required by the outsourcing company. One possible reason for this is that the pattern of production is seasonal, with peaks and troughs. When calculating annual monthly averages, they could appear lower than the maximum hours required by the outsourcing company. The other possible reason is that firms could have misreported information about hours worked to satisfy the outsourcing company's code of conduct. The total monthly hours worked varies only slightly across different years: on average, they increased by 0.2 per cent per annum, and did not differ between men and women. The number of monthly hours worked, however, is often higher for female than for male workers.

Combining the information on monthly earnings and hours worked, hourly earnings data are then calculated. Note that as information on hours worked could be biased downwards, hourly earnings data could be biased upwards accordingly. The major difference observed between data on hourly earnings and monthly earnings is that the annual growth of hourly earnings for male workers is much higher than the annual growth of their monthly earnings. This further prompts one to wonder if the information provided for hours worked is accurate.

The above descriptions are based on the total sample, including service workers, managerial and technical staff. The right panel of Table 9.4 presents the same information for migrant production workers, which indicates the wages for unskilled workers. The most important difference between the total sample and the sample of production workers is that the rate of wage growth is much slower for the latter, with an annual monthly wage increase of 2.8 per cent—about 0.5 percentage points lower than that for the total sample. In particular, for female production workers—the most unskilled group—the real hourly wage increased by only 2 per cent per annum.

Monthly and hourly earnings data for the migrant production workers is shown in Figure 9.1. While male monthly earnings increased significantly between 2001 and 2002, they flattened out after 2002. For the total and female samples, the monthly wage increase has been limited. For example, female monthly earnings were about 800 yuan and, by 2004 (five years later), had increased to only 900 yuan—an annual increase of 2.6 per cent—whereas for males the increase was faster, at an annual rate of 3.4 per cent. The hourly earnings data indicate a much larger difference in the wage growth rate, with 2 per cent for women and 6.3 per cent for men.

Having described average levels and changes of wages in these factories, we wonder how they compare with the average minimum wages for the regions covered and with average urban wage changes in Guangdong Province. More importantly, how do they compare with the income levels of the migrant workers' respective rural home towns? Since about 90 per cent of the sample workers are from Jiangxi, Henan, Hubei, Hunan and Sichuan provinces, aggregated data for these five provinces are presented.

Table 9.5 compares average minimum wages for the four regions covered in this study, urban manufacturing workers' wages for Guangdong Province and average per capita rural net income for the five provinces listed above, with the

Figure 9.1 **Monthly and hourly earnings by gender, 2000–2004** (yuan)

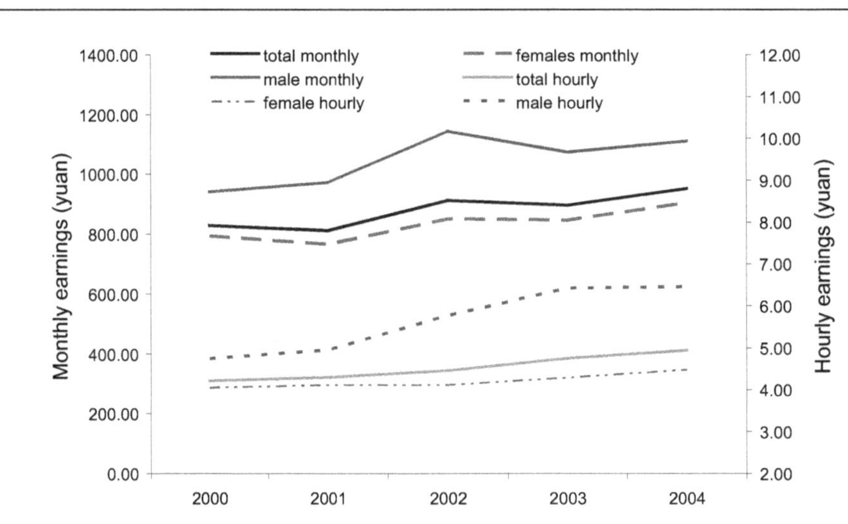

Source: Authors' calculations.

average basic monthly pay and the average monthly wages for the sample of migrant production workers in the period 2000–04. The first two rows present the average minimum wages for the four regions in Guangdong—the average nominal monthly basic pay for our sample of production workers. They show that while the minimum wages increased by 2.62 per cent per annum between 2000 and 2003, the basic pay for the sample of production workers increased by 4.2 per cent per annum in the same period. When comparing the level of average minimum wages with the average basic pay, the basic pay for the production workers in every single year is higher than the official minimum wages. In 2002 and 2003, it is about 9–10 per cent higher. This finding suggests that the sample firms have been paying their workers in line with local government labour legislation. It is important to keep in mind that all seven firms studied in this chapter are large and volunteered their payroll data. This finding might not be representative of the large number of factories that refused to participate in the study. In fact, anecdotal evidence and many newspaper articles have revealed problems regarding firms' violation of the minimum wage law.[6]

Rows (4) and (5) present the average monthly total earnings for the sample of migrant production workers and the urban manufacturing sector in Guangdong.[7] It is found that migrant workers earned about 67–80 per cent of the urban manufacturing average wage during the whole period and the gap has been enlarged.

Table 9.5 also compares average monthly wages of the sample firms with the rural average net monthly income[8] per labourer for Hunan Province, where almost 40 per cent of the sample workers come from. We find that although the average annual growth rate of rural-per-labourer income amounted to 4.2 per cent during this period, it was driven mainly by the 2004 government policy to cut the rural tax to zero. Before that, the average annual growth rate of rural income per labourer between 2000 and 2003 was only 2.6 per cent. Most importantly, we find that, on average, migrant workers in the sample factories earned 2.7 to 2.9 times the income they would have earned had they stayed in rural Hunan. This difference is, perhaps, the best explanation as to why migrant workers are willing to work in these factories. It is also a good indication of whether China has reached the Lewisian turning point: when rural surplus labour is exhausted, rural and urban wages will start to equalise. This is certainly not happening in China—if anything, the rural–urban income gap has increased over time (Figure 9.2).

The above comparison, however, has one crucial weakness. The *China Statistical Yearbooks* do not provide data on hourly wage rates. It is likely that urban Guangdong workers work fewer hours and hence have much higher

Table 9.5 **Comparison of wages and incomes, 2004–2004**

		2000	2001	2002	2003	2004	Annual growth rate
Sample production workers average monthly basic wage	(1)	433	458	497	511	524	4.22
Guangdong four regions average minimum monthly wage[a]	(2)	422	448	453	468		2.62
(1) as proportion of (2)	(3)	102.64	102.25	109.82	109.19		
Sample production workers average monthly total wages	(4)	829	812	913	896	953	2.81
Guangdong urban manufacturing average wages[b]	(5)	1043	1126	1225	1258	1417	6.32
(4) as proportion of (5)	(6)	79.48	72.13	74.51	71.25	67.21	
Hunan rural per household net monthly income[c]	(7)	822	847	879	922	1026	4.54
Hunan rural net monthly income per labourer[d]	(8)	291	300	312	323	356	4.17
(4) as proportion of (8)	(9)	285.45	270.43	292.81	277.86	267.25	

Notes: [a] Guangdong four regions' (Guandzhou, Dongguan, Shenzhen, Zhongshan) average mimimum monthly wages are provided by Adidas Guangdong office.

[b] Guangdong urban manufactory average wages are reported in Tables 5–22 of *China Statistical Yearbook*, 2001, 2002 and 2003 and Table 5–25 of *China Statistical Yearbook*, 2004. The data presented here are annual figures divided by 12.

[c] Per capita net income per households is generated by multiply per capita income and average households size for western China reported in Table 10–18 on page 380 of *China Statistical Yearbook*, 2004. The figures presented here are annual figures divided by 12.

[d] Per household labourer net income is generated by dividing per household net income by average number of labourer for western China reported in Table 10–18 on page 380 of *China Statistical Yearbook*, 2004. The figures presented here are annual figures divided by 12.

Figure 9.2 **Income gap among urban workers, migrant workers and rural workers, 2000–2004**

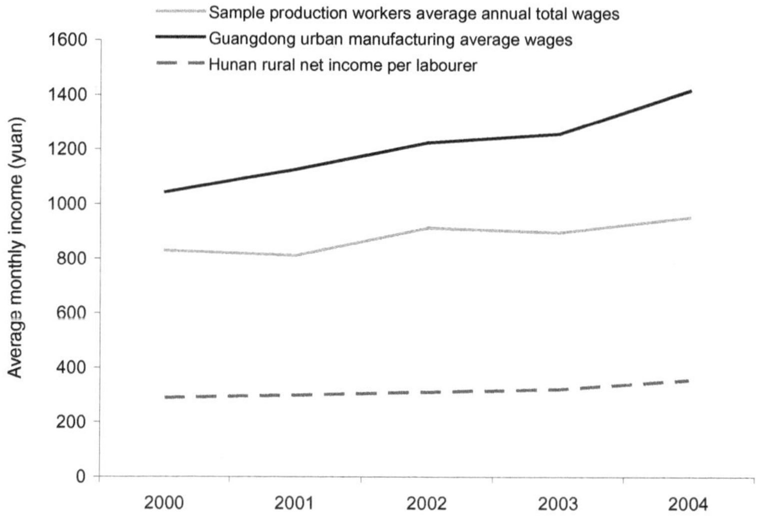

Sample production workers average annual total wages
Guangdong urban manufacturing average wages
Hunan rural net income per labourer

Average monthly income (yuan)

1600
1400
1200
1000
800
600
400
200
0

2000 2001 2002 2003 2004

Source: Authors' calculations.

hourly wage rates than the sample workers. Du et al. (2006) show that, on average, migrant workers work 55 per cent more hours a week than their urban-resident counterparts. It can be imagined that the hourly earnings gap between urban workers and migrant workers should be much more prominent than the gap between the annual wages shown in Figure 9.2.

Wage growth: more in-depth analysis

The above analyses present the raw data on wage levels and changes for migrant workers. Raw data could, however, be misleading, as many different factors could contribute to the level and change of wages. For example, the longer a worker stays with a factory, the higher his/her earnings will be. Given that our data trace individuals over five years, at the end of the data period, the average firm tenure of the worker is longer than at the beginning of the period (19 months versus 26 months), and this could contribute to the higher average earnings at the end of the period. In addition, factories could hire more better-educated workers at the end of the period than at the beginning. This could also contribute to a seeming increase of earnings by looking at only the raw data. To examine the wage changes due purely to supply shortage, all these factors have to be controlled for. We estimate the following earnings equation for this purpose

$$ln(Y_{ijt}) = \alpha + \beta X_{ijt} + \delta_t + \theta_j + \varepsilon_{ijt} \qquad (1)$$

where Y_{ijt} is hourly earnings of individual i in firm j at time t; X_{ijt} is a vector of control variables that could affect earnings, including age and its squared term, firm tenure as measured in months and its squared term, education level, occupation and industry dummy variables, dummy variables for each month to capture seasonality effects, a dummy variable for urban workers and a gender dummy variable. θ is factory fixed effect, δ is year fixed effect and ε is a random error term. While education measures the formal training, firm tenure indicates on-the-job training. Age, on the other hand, proxies for general labour market experience and some possible age-related physical conditions, such as eyesight and physical strength, which could affect labour productivity. Gender and migrant status could to some extent capture labour-market discrimination. To investigate wage changes over time, the most important coefficients for this study are the year fixed effects, δ. If, over the period we studied, there is a significant labour shortage, we should observe a significant increase in δ.

The earnings model is estimated for the total sample and a sample of migrant production workers only. The results are presented in Table 9.6 (the left panel for the total sample and the right panel for the migrant production workers). The first and fourth columns of each panel report the results for the total sample, while the rest of the columns present the results for male and female workers separately. Results from the total sample reveal that about 21–27 per cent of the wage variations are explained by the variables included in the regression. All human capital related variables have the right signs and are statistically significant. In particular, firm tenure and general labour market experience have a normal relationship with earnings. Education contributes positively to earnings and managerial staff earn more than production workers, while women earn about 10–12 per cent less than men. Note that in Table 9.4 much larger gender raw wage differentials are observed (about 15–32 per cent); the lower results indicated here suggest that part of the gender earnings differential can be explained by the difference in human capital possessions and other firm and individual characteristics controlled for in the regression. The seasonal variables play an important role in earnings determination. In particular, earnings in January are much higher than the rest of the year and this is due mainly to the fact that most factories pay an extra bonus before the Chinese New Year (the results are available on request from the authors).

More interesting results are revealed when the earnings equations are estimated separately by gender. In particular, on-the-job training (firm tenure) plays a more significant role in earnings determination for men than for women. Figure 9.3 shows the relationship between the number of months a worker works in a firm and his/her earnings (tenure–earnings profile) and it indicates that after one year a male worker earns about 5 per cent more than when he first entered the factory; this rate doubles in two years to 10 per cent, all other things being equal. In contrast, the wages of female workers increase by only 4.2 per cent after two years in the factories. Note that in the less-skilled footwear and apparel industries, more than 77 per cent of workers are women, while in the more skill-intensive accessories and gear industry, 63 per cent of workers are men.

The observed difference by gender could, to a large extent, reflect structural wage differences across different industries. The types of skills required in different jobs and industries differ significantly. For example, during interviews, accessories and gear factories indicated that it required two years for a worker to become skilled. Consequently, workers in this industry are more likely to be paid piece rates. In this kind of environment, the longer you work, the more skilled you become, the more pieces you make and the higher pay you receive. On the other hand, workers in footwear and apparel factories—where most female workers in our sample work—tend to be unskilled and operate in

Figure 9.3 **Tenure earnings profile for migrant production workers**

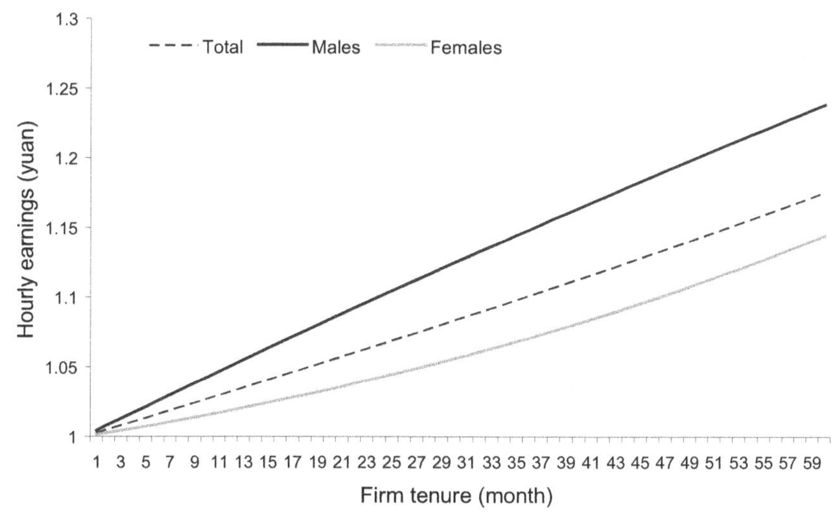

Source: Authors' calculations.

Table 9.6 **Earnings equations for the total sample and the sample of production workers**

	Total sample			Migrant workers' sample		
	Total	Males	Females	Total	Males	Females
Constant	0.942	0.526	1.028	0.976	0.291	1.067
	(0.006)***	(0.017)***	(0.006)***	(0.008)***	(0.023)***	(0.007)***
Age	0.035	0.067	0.030	0.033	0.087	0.028
	(0.000)***	(0.001)***	(0.000)***	(0.001)***	(0.002)***	(0.001)***
Age^2	–0.001	–0.001	–0.001	–0.001	–0.001	–0.001
	(0.000)***	(0.000)***	(0.000)***	(0.000)***	(0.000)***	(0.000)***
Firm tenure/10	0.024	0.039	0.010	0.027	0.043	0.014
	(0.000)***	(0.000)***	(0.000)***	(0.000)***	(0.000)***	(0.000)***
Firm $tenure^2/10^4$	0.089	–0.047	0.237	0.007	–0.120	0.143
	(0.000)***	(0.000)***	(0.000)***	(0.000)**	(0.000)***	(0.000)***
Senior and technical high	0.063	0.024	0.112	0.034	–0.013	0.109
	(0.001)***	(0.002)***	(0.001)***	(0.001)***	(0.003)***	(0.001)***
College and university	0.379	0.360	0.386	0.259	0.230	0.259
	(0.004)***	(0.007)***	(0.005)***	(0.007)***	(0.012)***	(0.012)***
Service workers	0.000	0.030	–0.029			
	–0.002	(0.004)***	(0.003)***			
Managerial/technical	0.165	0.105	0.202			
	(0.001)***	(0.002)***	(0.001)***			
Dummy urban workers	–0.041	–0.043	–0.032			
	(0.002)***	(0.005)***	(0.002)***			
Dummy for males	0.101			0.120		
	(0.001)***			(0.001)***		

2001	−0.028	−0.028	−0.030	−0.038	−0.052	−0.038
	(0.001)***	(0.004)***	(0.001)***	(0.001)***	(0.004)***	(0.001)***
2002	−0.064	−0.070	−0.070	−0.070	−0.082	−0.075
	(0.001)***	(0.003)***	(0.001)***	(0.001)***	(0.004)***	(0.001)***
2003	−0.029	−0.024	−0.037	−0.034	−0.038	−0.042
	(0.001)***	(0.003)***	(0.001)***	(0.001)***	(0.004)***	(0.001)***
2004	0.019	0.011	0.012	0.015	−0.003	0.009
	(0.001)***	(0.003)***	(0.001)***	(0.001)***	−0.004	(0.001)***
Observations	769598	193709	575889	660247	143313	516934
R-squared	0.27	0.24	0.28	0.21	0.25	0.19

Notes: Standard errors in parentheses
* significant at 10 per cent; ** significant at 5 per cent; *** significant at 1 per cent
Source: Authors' calculations.

production lines. By and large, they are paid time-rate wages. In this kind of job, the extent to which experience on the job can increase productivity is limited. Thus, job tenure does not seem to affect wages as much as in the other industries.

Another interesting result is the difference of formal education levels on earnings between men and women. While formal education plays an important role in earnings for women, male workers with senior high school qualification earn less than their counterparts who have only junior high school qualification. One of the reasons why formal education plays an important role for women—who work mainly in the unskilled footwear and apparel industries—is, perhaps, due to the inability of the current study to control for detailed types of work performed by individuals. The data used here identify only whether a worker is involved directly in production and do not reveal the exact type of work they do. Perhaps more educated workers are more likely to be a foreman or supervisor and hence earn more. Another reason could be that when workers work on production lines, productivity and quality cannot be monitored individually. Thus, education is used as a screening device.

The results showing that male workers with more education (those working mainly in the accessories and gear industry) are receiving lower pay are abnormal. One possible conjecture is that for these types of jobs, experience at a younger age might be important. Younger people could learn quickly and be more dexterous than older people. People who have only junior high school qualifications could start working earlier than people who have higher education and hence be more skilful than those with higher qualifications, other things being equal. This could not be tested empirically as the data we use have information only about current employment: earlier similar experience cannot be investigated.

The most important result for this chapter is the year effect. We find that controlling for all the other variables, wages barely increased in the five years studied. Almost all the year dummy variables have negative signs, indicating that, relative to the year 2000, earnings of other years have reduced. Figure 9.4 presents the results on δ for the migrant production worker sample. It uses the coefficients obtained from the estimation of Equation 1 to simulate wages for a 20-year-old, with a junior high or primary school qualification and zero months of firm tenure, in January for each of the five years. The figure shows that a newly hired 20-year-old with junior high school qualification earned almost the same amount in 2004 as his/her counterparts in 2000. For a woman, her hourly earnings were 4.12 yuan in 2000, which declined to 3.8 yuan in 2002, and then increased gradually to 4.16 yuan in 2004—an average annual growth of less

Figure 9.4 **Wage growth simulation, hourly earnings, 2000–2004**

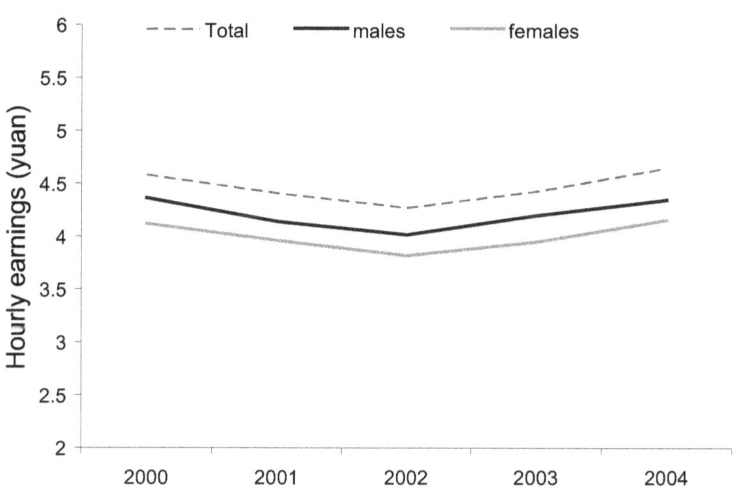

Figure 9.5 **Wage growth simulation, monthly earnings, 2000–2004**

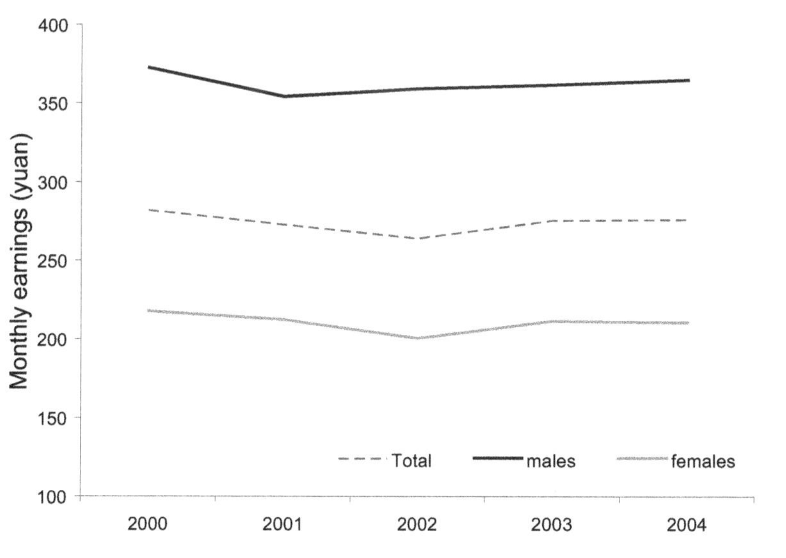

Source: Authors' calculations.

than 0.2 per cent. For a man, the 2000 hourly earnings were 4.36 yuan, dropping to 4 yuan in 2002, and increasing to 4.35 yuan in 2004—barely catching up with the 2000 level. If, however, we ignore the first two years, when there was a reduction in earnings, and compare the lowest earnings in 2002 with those of the final year, we observe a slight wage increase of about 2.5 per cent per annum for men and women.

Recall that factories could have misreported the data for hours worked. If so, it could bias the estimated earnings growth. To test this, we also estimated Equation 1 using log monthly earnings as the dependent variable.[9] The simulation using these results is presented in Figure 9.5, which shows that the monthly earnings growth for men and women is zero to negative for the entire period and 0.5–1.5 per cent for the last three years.

Based on the data available, wage growth in the sample factories between 2000 and 2004 has been very slow, in particular for migrant production workers.

Conclusions

The empirical results indicate three main findings.

1. Of the seven sample factories, average hourly wages increased by about 6 per cent per annum between 2000 and 2004 for the total sample of workers, but for production workers the annual average growth rate was much lower, at 3.5 per cent.
2. The major wage growth comes from wage growth for male workers. For female workers—who accounted for more than 70 per cent of the total sample—the average annual wage growth was about 2.4 per cent.
3. Once we control for education, firm tenure and other variables that could affect wage levels, the observed wage growth for the total sample and male and female samples are all very low. For the five years, average annual wage growth has been negative or near zero. For the last three years, the growth rate was about 0.5–1.5 per cent. With such small wage increases, one could hardly argue that China has reached the Lewisian turning point.

The main finding, although important, could suffer from the following caveats. First, the current study could suffer significantly from a sample selection bias. Although effort was made to make sure that the sample was selected randomly, due to the unwillingness to participate among the listed firms, the final sample is not a randomly selected one. It is possible that the factories that were willing to participate in the study were those that followed the outsourcing company's code of conduct and the official minimum wage increases better than those that refused to participate. Thus, the general picture of wage levels and wage growth might not be as optimistic as we find in this chapter.

Second, the main data used in this study are from payroll records. It is not clear whether these records are genuine. It is commonly known that many factories in China adopt a double accounting practice. There is evidence that the payroll data provided by some factories are based on some kind of conversion rules required by the outsourcing company. In addition, the data on hours worked seem to be low. Although it is not clear to what extent this kind of behaviour could affect the accuracy of the earnings and hours-worked data, the direction of the effect is clear. Factories that volunteered to participate would want to present higher earnings and earnings growth (keeping up with the increase in minimum wages). If there is any systematic bias of the data, it should be biased upwards.

Finally, the data used in this study end in 2004. It is possible that since 2004 wages have been growing at a much faster pace than what we found for the period between 2000 and 2004. The lack of a systematic study of migrants, however, and their wage changes have prevented us from finding out this information. The current studies that argue that China has reached the Lewisian turning point do not seem to be based on unskilled workers' wage data. We hope that the current study can shed limited light on the issue, at least up to 2004.

Notes

1 Based on the interview record, the Monday–Friday normal time pay is set at one; Monday–Friday overtime pay is 50 per cent higher (1.5 times normal pay); weekend pay is 100 per cent higher (two times normal pay); while public holiday pay is 200 per cent higher (three times normal pay).

2 The city-level CPIs provided by the Guangdong Bureau of Statistics are presented in Table A1.

3 The data calculated by region are not presented for confidentiality reasons, as two of the four regions have only one factory.

4 Note that as the data used for the total sample differ significantly from those used for males and females separately—due to a 20 per cent sample without personnel records—the figures presented using the total sample are not directly comparable with those for the gender groups. Nevertheless, the trends are comparable.

5 This survey was conducted by the Institute of Economics at the Chinese Academy of Social Sciences in 2003. The total sample of workers was 5,327 and the sample for Guangdong Province was 368 migrant workers.

6 See, for example, http://finance.dayoo.com/gb/content/2006-07/14/content_2566970.htm

7 Manufacturing comprises about 23 different industry types. Ideally, the average annual

earnings of the footwear, apparel and accessories and gear industries for Guangdong Province should be used for this comparison. The *China Statistical Yearbook*, however, does not provide detailed information for these industries separately, nor does it indicate the employment and earnings distribution among these different industry types. The comparison presented here, therefore, should be read with caution.

8 This is calculated by dividing annual data by 12.

9 The results are not presented, but are available on request from the authors.

References

Cai, F. and Wang, D., 2006. 'Employment growth, labour scarcity and the nature of China's trade expansion', in R. Garnaut and L. Song (eds), *The Turning Point in China's Economic Development*, Asia Pacific Press, The Australian National University, Canberra.

Cai, F. and Wang, M., 2007a. Growth and structural changes in employment in transitional China, Institute of Labour and Population Economics, CASS, Beijing (unpublished).

——, 2007b. Labor cost increase and growth pattern transition, Institute of Labour and Population Economics, CASS, Beijing (unpublished).

Du, Y., Gregory, R.G. and Meng, X., 2006. 'Impact of the guest-worker system on poverty and the well-being of migrant workers in urban China', in R. Garnaut and L. Song (eds), *The Turning Point in China's Economic Development*, Asia Pacific Press, Canberra:172–202.

Garnaut, R. and Huang, Y., 2006. 'Continued rapid growth and the turning point in China's development', in R. Garnaut and L. Song (eds), *The Turning Point in China's Economic Development*, Asia Pacific Press, The Australian National University, Canberra:12–34.

Knight, J., Song, L. and Jia, H., 1999. 'Chinese rural migrants in urban enterprises: three perspectives,' *Journal of Development Studies*, 35(3):73–104.

Meng, X. and Zhang, J., 2001. 'Two-tier labour markets in urban China: occupational segregation and wage differentials between urban residents and rural migrants in Shanghai', *Journal of Comparative Economics*, 29:485–504.

Meng, X., 2001. Profit sharing and the earnings gap between urban and rural-migrant workers in Chinese enterprises, The Australian National University, Canberra (unpublished).

National Bureau of Statistics, various issues. *China Statistical Yearbook*, China Statistical Press, Beijing.

Table A9.1 **City level CPI 2000=100**

	2000	2001	2002	2003	2004
Guangzhou	100.00	98.90	96.53	96.62	98.27
Shenzhen	100.00	97.80	98.97	99.67	100.96
Dongguan	100.00	98.20	96.33	97.01	99.92
Zhongshan	100.00	99.80	99.10	100.29	103.40

Source: Data provided by National Bureau of Statistics of China

10

Domestic market integration and inter-regional growth spillovers

Jane Golley and Nicolaas Groenewold

While China's integration into the global economy during the past three decades has been extremely impressive, the integration among regions within China has been much less so. Domestic market integration has a critical role to play in binding together a country that has suffered from disintegrative tendencies throughout its history. As such, the importance of integration cannot be overstated, particularly in light of recent research that seems 'to confirm the pertinence of alarming forecasts concerning the danger of China's move towards internal disintegration' (Poncet 2003:17). Numerous other researchers have reached similar—if not quite as dramatic—conclusions in their analyses of China throughout the Communist era (Donnithorne 1967; Lyons 1987; Young 2000; World Bank 2005).

This chapter contributes to a growing literature that addresses the extent of domestic market integration in the Chinese economy. The next section defines integration and discusses the costs and benefits associated with it. This alone reveals that answering two of the most relevant questions—how integrated are China's provinces and how integrated should they be—is far from straightforward. A brief discussion of the numerous methodologies available for assessing the degree of integration further demonstrates this point and implies that our own method of empirical analysis—measuring inter-regional output spillovers—is only one part of a highly complicated picture.

The next section reviews the changing nature of Chinese domestic market integration during the Communist era. Regardless of the methodology employed, a salient feature of the discussion is the almost universal recognition that China's regions are less integrated than might be expected of regions in a unified nation-state. Our empirical results lend further support to this claim. A vector autoregressive (VAR) framework is introduced to assess the extent of output spillovers between six regions in China during the period from 1953 to 2003. The results suggest that while China's better-developed regions are relatively well interconnected with each other, spillovers between these regions are neither pervasive nor strong. Meanwhile, the least-developed regions—that is, those most in need of positive growth spillovers from elsewhere—are connected only weakly, if at all, with the rest of the country. Policy implications and recommendations are offered in the concluding section.

Regional integration: theory and measurement

Integration can be defined broadly as the increasing interdependence of regions, either within or across countries, as reflected in the flow of goods, services and/or factors of production. The process of integration requires the gradual elimination of economic frontiers and trade-restricting instruments between regions so that the mobility of goods, services and factors is not constrained. This process of 'integration from below' can be reinforced by 'integration from above', which entails the active promotion of economic cooperation between territories through appropriate policies or institutions (Tinbergen 1965).

The expansion of trade that arises due to falling trade barriers underpins one of the major benefits of integration. According to the standard neoclassical analysis, a reduction in trade barriers leads to welfare gains through the exploitation of comparative advantage and the consequent increase in productivity. Higher gross domestic product (GDP) growth rates occur during the transitional period—or the short term—in which resources are reallocated and capital accumulation takes place, as the economy approaches its new steady-state levels of capital and output per worker. Theories relating the gains from trade to long-term growth are based typically on models of endogenous technological change.[1]

Trade can increase the rate of technological progress—and hence productivity growth—either through an expansion of output markets enabling domestic producers to exploit economies of scale, or through an expansion of input markets resulting in lower production costs (for example, by giving domestic producers access to a wider variety of capital goods, effectively enlarging the base of productive knowledge, as described by Romer 1990). The gains from trade can be dynamic rather than static if specialisation stimulates productivity growth through learning by doing, as in Lucas (1988). On the flip side of these benefits, while trade can act as a conduit for technology transfer, theories of technological diffusion stress the importance of the host country (or region) having a sufficiently high level of 'social capability' in order to be able to successfully implement technologies developed in more advanced economies, while regions below a threshold level of development could be unable to make effective use of technology spillovers (see, for example, Abramovitz 1986 and Howitt 2000). That is, it is not guaranteed that all regions will be able to benefit equally from the trade that takes place between them, while some regions could miss out altogether.[2]

Beyond the trade-related benefits, integration should also improve the inter-regional transmission of growth from faster growing regions to lagging ones, through a variety of connections that are presumably stronger between highly integrated regions. These include the increase in imports from and investments in lagging regions, the diffusion of innovations originating in more rapidly growing regions and the ability of a more rapidly growing region to absorb some of the unemployed or underemployed labour from elsewhere. These effects all contribute to the equalisation of regional incomes, which is beneficial in itself from political and socioeconomic perspectives. With the hope that faster growing regions will exert a beneficial influence on other regions, however, comes the likelihood that more highly integrated markets will cause each other to suffer more when economic growth falters in any one region. Marshall (1920:241) describes how 'integration, that is, the growing intimacy and firmness of connections between separate parts of the industrial organism' enables each part of that organism 'to be less and less self-sufficient, to depend for its wellbeing more and more on other parts, so that any disorder in any part...will affect other parts also'. Moreover, while trickle-down effects are likely to be stronger across highly integrated regional markets, so too are their counterparts: 'polarisation' effects, which describe the adverse effects that rapid growth in better-developed regions can have on economic progress elsewhere (Hirschman 1958). These effects include the inability of comparatively inefficient, yet income-creating, industries in lagging regions to compete, 'brain drain' and capital depletion as savings are redirected towards more profitable investments in the rapidly growing regions.

While most arguments point to the long-term benefits of integration outweighing the costs, the same cannot necessarily be said of the short term. For example, in a developing economy, the freeing of restrictions on labour movements is likely to result in migrants moving to wealthier regions in search of higher wages. Meanwhile, the spread of innovation could remain tardy because of poor communication and transport links between the integrating regions. This combination would benefit the more rapidly growing regions to the detriment of poorer ones—an issue that resonates with the current Chinese situation. Thus, while integration is regarded generally as desirable, unless it proceeds far enough and in the right ways, a negative consequence of improved integration could be the worsening of regional disparities, in turn threatening the social stability and national unity that policymakers are trying to achieve.

Measuring the extent of integration in its various guises, let alone its costs and benefits, is fraught with difficulties. If the definition of regional integration was simplified to the removal of inter-regional trade barriers, the most direct way to measure the extent of integration would be to examine the prevalence of these barriers. The lack of tariffs, however, and other well-defined barriers to trade within a single nation make this simple approach inappropriate for our analysis here. Another direct approach examines inter-regional trade flows, based on the assumption that integration will result in rising trade flows. This method is problematic in China, given the paucity of inter-provincial trade data, although some attempts have been made (Naughton 2003; Poncet 2003, 2005). It is also problematic to distinguish the impact of integration from other factors influencing inter-regional trade, including transport costs and regional endowments.

The production approach assumes that the more integrated the regions, the more specialised the industry at the regional level, with changes in specialisation taken as evidence of changes in integration over time (Young 2000; Bai et al. 2004). One obvious shortcoming here is that much trade between regions can be intra-industry trade, which is consistent with similar industrial structures, not different ones. Alternatively, the marginal returns approach assesses factor returns in different regions, based on the assumption that these should converge in an integrated market (Tan and Zhang 2005), while similar methodologies can be used to assess price equality across regions, based on the law of one price (Parsley and Wei 1996; Fan and Wei 2003). The business cycle approach assumes that more closely integrated economies will exhibit strongly correlated business cycles (Xu 2002; Xu and Voon 2003; Tang 1998), and therefore focuses on the similarity of shocks across regions.

Of greater interest here, however, is the way in which shocks in one region are transmitted to others, based on the idea that more integrated regions will show stronger transmission of shocks. This brings us to the inter-regional growth spillover approach, which is described and adopted below, and which, simply speaking, seeks to identify how shocks to GDP in one region impact on GDP in that region and on GDP elsewhere, and how those impacts are transmitted over time. While this approach does not make it possible to draw strong conclusions regarding the precise transmission mechanisms between regions—that is, which trickle-down or polarisation effects are dominant—it does provide a useful starting point for further investigation into the issue. Before attempting this, however, the next section reviews the literature on regional integration in China during the Communist period.

Regional integration in Communist China[3]

Integration has been a central theme in explanations of economic development in the United States and other countries. In each case, the relationship between integration and development is complex and circular. Indeed, 'integration is perhaps best viewed not as a cause or result of development, but simply as an aspect of development itself' (Lyons 1987:14). This is the starting observation made by Lyons—in his seminal work on China's domestic market integration—who describes how the particular nature of China's planning system during the command era (1953–78) caused 'economic fragmentation' (or disintegration) along regional lines. Unlike the standard Soviet plan, China's plan was formulated and implemented primarily along provincial, rather than sectoral lines. The relative importance of regional units in the planning process meant that if inter-regional coordination was deficient—which it was—the disintegrative tendencies associated with compartmentalised planning would be felt largely along regional lines.

Various policies pursued by central and local governments reinforced the disintegrative nature of China's provincially focused planning mechanism. Donnithorne (1967) described how Mao Zedong's principle of self-reliance within administrative units created the incentive for self-sufficiency within those units. This strengthened the tendency towards a 'cellular economy' in which independent, comprehensive and relatively autarkic sub-systems at each and every geographic and sectoral unit were designed to operate independently. One negative consequence of this was increasing regional inequality, since '[i]n an administrative unit where economic drive and entrepreneurship is [sic] plentiful, the policy of self-reliance and self-sufficiency may give added encouragement to local initiative. Where these qualities are scarce, the likelihood of repairing this lack from elsewhere will be diminished' (Donnithorne 1972:612). The cellular economic structure and fragmentation that emerged during the period of command planning left a strong and lasting mark on inter-provincial relations. During the reform period, while the sources (and the wording) of the problem have changed, 'provincialism', local protectionism and the consequent lack of domestic market integration remain key policy issues.

The World Bank (1994) conducted the first major study of China's internal market developments during the reform period. Evidence of significant regional price differentials across a broad range of producer and consumer goods, combined with declining inter-provincial trade and investment flows, limited inter-provincial labour and capital mobility and bottlenecks in transport, led the bank to conclude that China was far from realising the benefits of its potentially large internal market. It called for the harmonisation of fees and fines levied on inter-provincial trade, the prohibition of inter-provincial trade barriers, changes in regulations affecting factor mobility and the removal of residual price controls.

While some of these issues have since been resolved, the essence of the problem remains, according to the World Bank's (2005) extensive report on the degree of integration in China's product and factor markets. In product markets, converging prices and increasing specialisation indicate increased integration, but new forms of protectionism—in local government procurement practices, for example—combined with the slow pace of institutional and transport infrastructure development, continue to impede the spread of growth across regions. Labour markets, while improving in recent years, still show significant fragmentation across regions and sectors. The bank's analysis of capital markets shows not only large misallocations across regions and sectors, it indicates that the degree of fragmentation has deteriorated over time. Key problems that remain include underdeveloped capital markets and large differences in the regulations and institutional and infrastructure environments that affect the relative attractiveness of different localities.

Young (2000) blames the lack of internal integration on the incompleteness of China's economic reforms. He begins with a story of the 'silkworm cocoon war' of the late 1980s, during which Zhejiang Province began to restrict the sale of silk cocoons to other parts of China, and silk factories in neighbouring Shanghai found it necessary to import raw silk from abroad. He then describes more generally how incremental economic reforms that devolved power to local governments resulted in competitive local industrial policies and the imposition of a variety of barriers to inter-provincial trade. Evidence of converging provincial industrial structures combined with fluctuating periods of converging and diverging provincial prices leads Young to conclude that 'the reform process led to the fragmentation of the domestic market and the distortion of regional production patterns away from comparative advantage' (2000:1,091). Replace 'reform' with 'planning' and the phrase could just as well be in Lyons' (1987) seminal work on fragmentation during the planning period.

Naughton (2003) presents the most optimistic analysis to date, disputing Young's analysis in particular but also going against the tide in arguing that China is a relatively well-integrated nation-state and is becoming more so over time. He makes the point that regional integration cannot be separated from an understanding of enterprise reform, privatisation and marketisation, noting, for example, that organisational changes at the enterprise level—such as conversions of state firms to joint stock companies—are making it more costly for local governments to intervene in market operations. While challenging the views of most other authors, Naughton agrees that further efforts to integrate the domestic market are called for, and he sees China's challenge as consisting of two types of integration.

> The first consists of building adequate infrastructure to permit adequate transport of bulky, energy-intensive commodities and fuels at reasonable cost. The second consists of creating a unified competitive marketplace in which enterprises can exploit productivity differentials and comparative advantage so that the economy as a whole can reap gains from trade. Progress has been made in these areas, but much more needs to be done (Naughton 2003:205).

There have inevitably been comparisons drawn between China's—or, more aptly, coastal China's—exceptional integration into the global economy and the perceived lack of progress internally. About the same time as the first World Bank study, Ash and Kueh (1993) noted that increasing integration of southern China (Guangdong and Fujian) with Hong Kong and Taiwan contrasted with—and could indeed have contributed to—poor internal integration in the sense that backward and forward linkages between the south and the rest of China remained weak. Poncet (2003) uses data on provincial trade flows to compare the magnitude and evolution of Chinese provinces' engagement in domestic and international trade, and confirms Ash and Kueh's findings on a bigger scale one decade later. She shows that China's increasing openness in international markets has gone hand in hand with internal fragmentation between 1987 and 1997, and concludes that while reforms obviously succeeded in promoting the former, they have failed to reduce impediments to the latter.

Fu (2004) argues that the emphasis on foreign direct investment (FDI) driven labour-intensive processing industries in the rapidly developing southeastern coastal provinces has attracted relatively mobile and efficient resources from the inland regions, but it has generated only limited linkages and weak spillovers in return—thereby describing a situation in which polarisation effects are dominating trickle down. Yao and Zhang (2001) confirm this, and attribute the divergence in regional incomes to the slow process of spillovers from the coastal region inwards. Hu and Jefferson (2002), drawing on evidence from China's electronic and textile industries, take this point a step further in establishing that FDI enhances the productivity of the recipient firm, but it depresses that of non-FDI firms, whether located nearby or not. While their findings suggest that non-FDI firms will eventually catch up in terms of productivity in the longer term, the short-term implications are that trickle down is limited even within coastal cities where FDI is concentrated, let alone across to other areas. In sum, there seems to be ample evidence that the better-developed coastal region is becoming better integrated with the rest of the world than it is with the rest of China.

That is not to say that transmissions of inter-regional growth are completely absent within China. Ying (2000) uses provincial output data and finds the strongest significant influence being exerted by Guangdong, which has significant GDP growth correlations with four of its five contiguous provinces, although, notably, two of those correlations are negative, not positive. Brun et al. (2002) and Zhang and Felmingham (2002) find evidence of spillovers from the coastal region to the central region and, in the latter, to the western region as well. Groenewold et al. (2006) use annual GDP data for three regions (coastal, central and western) and find strong spillovers from the coast to the other regions and from the central to the western region, but none from the western region to anywhere else. Groenewold et al. (forthcoming) extend the analysis to six regions and conclude that the three core regions forming China's industrial heartland—the southeast, the Changjiang River region and the Yellow River region—are relatively well interconnected. Even across these regions, however, they find that the spillover effects are neither pervasive nor strong, while effects are even weaker or entirely absent elsewhere.[4] Thus, while there is some evidence that some growth is being transmitted from the better-developed regions to the rest of the country, none of the results are indicative of a highly integrated national economy in which the regions depend increasingly on each other for their prosperity rather than on themselves alone.

China's inter-regional growth spillovers

As the preceding section demonstrates, a wide range of approaches has been used for assessing the strength of regional integration in China and researchers are far from agreed on the extent of integration implied by their results. Despite this diversity, one common theme appears to be that the regions making up China's industrial core are becoming more integrated with each other (and with the rest of the world) than they are with the rest of the country. This section provides the results of a spillover analysis to directly address the inter-regional transmission of growth among China's regions. The limited extent of transmissions—as one of the key components of the integration issue—lends further support to this developing consensus.

The model used to generate the estimates of inter-regional spillovers is a VAR model estimated using data for six Chinese regions, given as follows:

southeast, SE (Guangdong [including Hainan], Fujian and Guangxi); Changjiang River, CR (Shanghai and Jiangsu, Zhejiang, Hubei, Hunan, Jiangxi and Anhui); Yellow River, YR (Inner Mongolia, Henan, Shanxi, Beijing, Tianjin, Shandong and Hebei); northeast, NE (Heilongjiang, Jilin and Liaoning); southwest, SW (Yunnan, Guizhou, Sichuan and Chongqing); and northwest, NW (Xinjiang, Gansu, Qinghai, Ningxia and Shaanxi).[5] A map of the regions is provided in Figure 10.1.

The results are based on the estimated VAR model in Groenewold et al. 2006. As argued there, the VAR model is well suited to our application: it does not require a prior theoretical specification (an advantage when there are so many competing theories) and it is parsimonious in its data requirements (a decided advantage when working with Chinese data). The absence of a theoretical framework does, however, have a cost in terms of interpretation, which is necessarily more speculative than it would be had we estimated a more complex structural model.

Figure 10.1 **The six regions of mainland China**

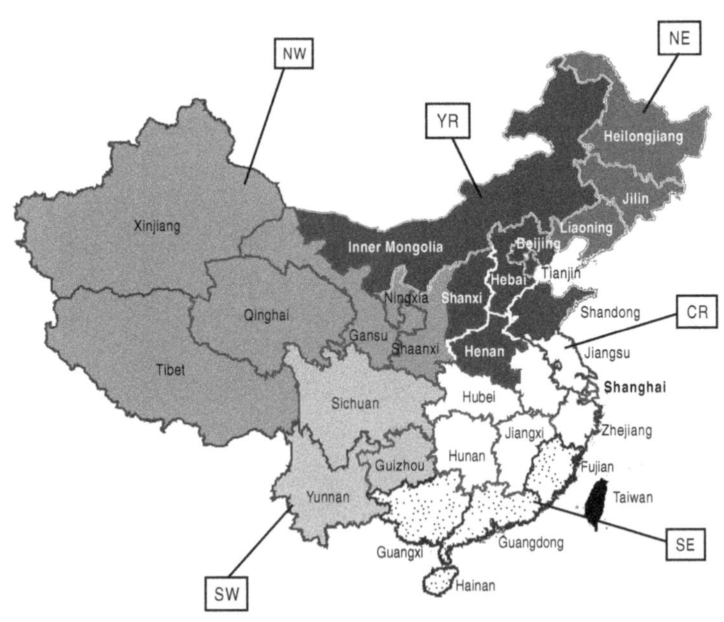

The VAR model consists of a set of dynamic equations of the form

$$Y_{it} = \beta_{i0} + \beta_{i1}Y_{1t\text{-}1} + \beta_{i2}Y_{2t\text{-}1} + \ldots + \beta_{in}Y_{nt\text{-}1} + \varepsilon_{it}, \quad i = 1, 2, .., n \qquad (1)$$

where the βs are constants to be estimated, Y_{it} is log output for region i in period t and ε_{it} is the error term for the ith region. More lags of each Y can be added to the right-hand side without affecting the argument that follows.

The model parameters can be estimated from time-series data for regional outputs. The estimated model is then used to analyse spillovers by shocking one of the error terms (say, ε_j) for one period and following through the effects on all regional outputs in the current and subsequent periods. The effects of a shock in period t to ε_j on regional outputs from time t to some future time (t+15 in our analysis) are captured by impulse response functions (IRFs). There will be n^2 IRFs associated with the model, one for each Y_i and ε_j combination; the value of the ij^{th} IRF for period τ is the effect of a shock to ε_j on Y_i, τ periods after the shock occurred. We use the IRFs as measures of spillovers from the shocked region to the other regions.

There is one complication in what follows. The above explanation assumes that it is reasonable to shock one ε_j independently of the others. In practice, however, the error terms can be correlated with each other and this correlation needs to be taken into account in the simulation exercise. The most common way to do this is to transform the error terms to make them independent, using a Choleski procedure and then to shock the transformed errors.[6] Unfortunately, the resulting IRFs are not independent of the order in which the variables are entered into the model—an order that could be arbitrary to some extent. This dependence on order is particularly pronounced when the residuals derived from the estimation of (1) are strongly correlated with each other. This is the case in our application to regional spillovers in China.

There are various ways of addressing this ordering problem. One—not uncommon in the application of VARs—is to ignore it and assume that the errors are independent or, at least, that it makes sense to shock them independently. Another is to argue that a particular ordering is more appropriate than others. A further alternative, which we follow, is to conjecture about the source of the residual correlation and base the resolution on this conjecture. We argue that the strong residual correlation is due to an important common component to regional shocks, which is caused by national shocks that have an impact on all regions. If this is the case, we ought to be able to resolve the ordering problem by accounting for the common national shock. At least two methods can achieve this: 1) purge the regional output series of the common national component by a preliminary regression of each regional output on national output, and 2) include the national output variable in the VAR together with the regional outputs and order national output first. The second method works because IRFs based on the Choleski decomposition assign any common component of the shocks to the first variable, so if the correlation is due to a national shock and the first variable is national output, the procedure based on the Choleski decomposition will correctly assign the common component to national output. In this application, we use the second method. It turns out that the resulting IRFs are not sensitive to ordering as long as national output is ordered first, lending some support to our conjecture that national shocks are the source of the common correlations.

The data we use are based on provincial real GDP for the period 1953–2003. The sources of the data are twofold: the early data come from Wu (2004), who obtained the 1953–95 series from *The Gross Domestic Product of China, 1952–95* (National Bureau of Statistics 1997). Data for 1996–2003 come from the *Statistical Yearbook of China* (National Bureau of Statistics various years).

The data are in log form and all series are tested for stationarity before specifying the model. The (log) regional outputs (and national output) are all stationary about trend as long as a break in trend at 1978 and level breaks at 1966 and 1978 are allowed for. We therefore specify the model in log levels with these breaks. Two lags are sufficient to remove autocorrelation from the residuals.

We estimate the model using data for the entire 1953–2003 period, despite the dramatic changes in economic organisation and structure during this period, which will almost certainly have affected the nature of spillovers. In particular, the opening up of the economy since 1978 after a long period of central planning and a policy of regional self-sufficiency led to a strong presumption of structural change in our model. We would have liked to estimate the model separately over the pre and post-1978 periods—to improve parameter stability and to test hypotheses about the nature of changes in spillovers during our sample. Limited experimentation with sub-period estimates made it clear, however, that there were not enough data points in the two sub-periods to adequately estimate the model and we had to base our results on the model estimated over the entire 1953–2003 period (but allowing for trend and intercept breaks at 1978).

The VAR results show a high explanatory power for all the equations—not surprisingly given that they are specified in log levels and all include a trend as well as break variables. The national output variable (NAT) is significant in all equations at one lag (at least) with the exception of the southwest region, where it is only marginally significant, suggesting that this region could be related only weakly to the national economy.

The estimated VARs can be used to generate 49 IRFs associated with this seven-equation model (six regions plus the national equation) and we use the 36 IRFs associated with the regional output equations to assess regional spillovers. Space constraints make it impossible to report them all and we report one set (for a shock to SE region output) and summarise the implications of the remainder in Table 10.1. The IRFs that capture the effects of a unit shock to SE output on each of the regions are pictured in Figures 10.2 and 10.3.[7] We compute the IRFs and the cumulative IRFs, the latter being the accumulation over time of the IRFs.

Figures 10.2 and 10.3 show that in the short term the strongest effect of a shock to SE is on SE itself. Over time, there is also a substantial effect on CR and YR and these effects overshadow that on SE itself after seven or eight years. There are effectively no spillovers to NE and SW, and the overall effects on NW are negative.

The model is specified in terms of logs so that the values of the IRFs have the dimension of elasticities of output in one region with respect to a shock

Table 10.1 **Summary of spillover effects**

	Shock to					
Effect on	SE (8)	CR (9)	YR (13)	NE (10)	SW (12)	NW (7)
SE: SR	0.7546	0.0716	0.0733	0.0858	0.0825	0.0801
Max	1.2634	−0.2056	−0.5986	−0.1009	−0.5868	−0.3982
CR: SR	0.2834	0.6163	0.2520	0.2948	0.2836	0.2752
Max	5.0284	0.0261	0.5655	0.5541	−0.8673	0.0852
YR: SR	0.2198	0.3298	0.5359	0.3624	0.3486	0.3383
Max	2.9103	−0.1907	0.5365	0.3330	−0.0836	0.4044
NE: SR	0.1788	0.3107	0.3411	0.5287	0.2564	0.2488
Max	0.4696	−0.1057	0.3253	0.2673	0.7172	−0.1115
SW: SR	0.1016	0.0135	0.0517	−0.0526	0.5436	0.0758
Max	0.1071	0.0113	0.0004	−0.1385	0.569	0.4946
NW: SR	0.0549	0.0559	0.0705	0.0887	0.1337	0.3062
Max	−0.3357	−0.0282	−0.1013	−0.0864	0.2288	0.2157
Mean GDP	93	252	210	97	54	42

Note: Numbers measure the effect on the row region of a one-unit shock to the output of the column region. The numbers in the 'SR' rows represent short-term (first-period) effects and the numbers in the 'Max' rows measure the effect when the cumulative effect is at its maximum. The numbers in parentheses in the column headings are the number of years after the shock when the maximum occurs. The mean GDP figures in the last row are in terms of billions of yuan in 1953 prices.
Source: Authors' calculations.

Figure 10.2 **IRFs for a shock to SE**

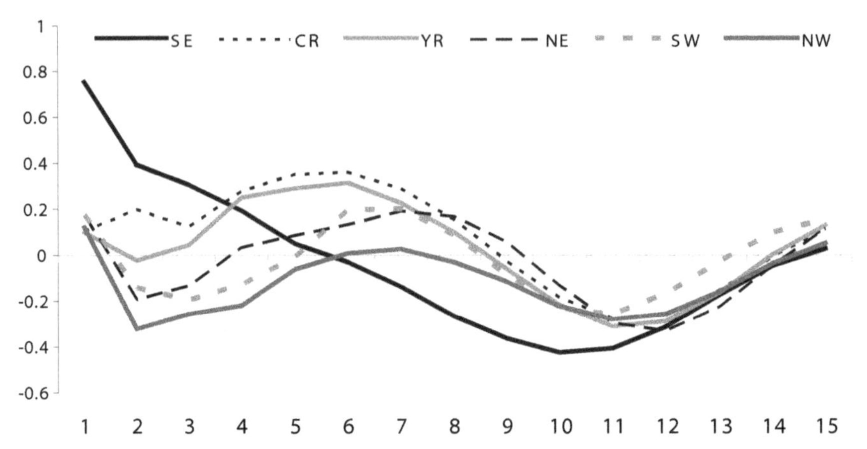

Source: Authors' calculations.

Figure 10.3 **Cumulative IRFs for a shock to SE**

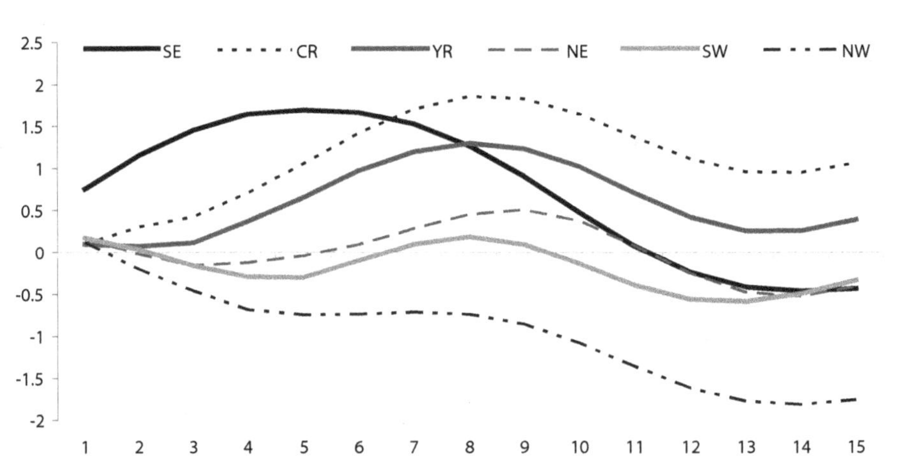

Source: Authors' calculations.

to output in another region. Since the regions are of very different sizes, the elasticities are difficult to compare across regions, so we convert them to levels at the sample means and report summary measures in Table 10.1. The table gives results for the impact (that is, within-the-year) effect and the cumulative effect at its maximum. The date of the maximum cumulative effect for the shock to SE output pictured in Figure 10.3 was chosen to be eight years. Table 10.1 shows, for example, that the effect of a one-yuan shock to SE output was to increase CR output by 0.2834 yuan in the year of the shock and by a cumulative amount of 5.0284 yuan at its maximum effect after nine years. The first column of figures therefore summarises all the cumulative IRFs in Figure 10.3.

The effects of a shock to the SE region seem plausible. The strongest positive spillovers by far are on the CR and YR regions, which is not surprising given the contiguity of the SE and CR regions and also the dominance of these three regions in China's industrial output (producing, for example, close to 80 per cent of all manufacturing output in the early 1990s). It is *prima facie* surprising that there seems little evidence of a spillover to the other adjoining region, SW—although the lack of a connection here could simply reflect the quite different structure of the two regions as well as the lack of backward linkages from the SE to the SW region. It shows that contiguity does not guarantee spillovers. The lack of effect on the NE region could be explained by the large distance between the regions and the fact that the NE region has a relatively obsolete industrial structure and few resources. An overall negative spillover might normally be explained as evidence that a boost to one region attracts resources that would otherwise have gone to the other region and therefore shows a decline in the output of the second region. In the case of the relationship between the SE and NW regions, it could reflect the reallocation of public investment resources away from the coastal regions to the inland regions and vice versa at times during the sample period.

The second column of Table 10.1 summarises the effects of a shock to the Changjiang River region and shows that the initial effects are dominated by those on the CR region itself, although there are also marked effects on the YR and NE regions. Over time, all spillovers are relatively small, with negative effects on the SE, YR and NE regions. Thus, it appears that, in the short term, the NE region is related more closely to the CR region than to the SE region, which is not unexpected. The subsequent effects, however, show that shocks to the CR region have at best short-term positive spillovers, particularly on the NE and YR regions.

A shock to the Yellow River region shows that the initial effects are dominated by those on the region itself, although there are also substantial short-term effects on the CR and NE regions. It is interesting that the spillover to NE is larger than spillovers to NE from CR and SE, which suggests that geographic proximity matters in this case. This is borne out by the negligible spillovers to the SE, SW and NW regions. In the longer term, the spillovers are very modest: the largest are to YR itself and to CR, but these are small compared with the long-term effects of spillovers from SE. The combination of positive growth spillovers from SE to YR and CR, combined with limited spillovers in the opposite direction, suggests that upstream industries in the latter two regions could benefit from growth of downstream industries in the former, while the reverse does not seem to be true.

The IRFs showing the effects of a shock to the NE region show that the short-term effect of a shock to this region is dominated by the effect on the region itself, although there are small spillovers to the CR and YR regions. There are no short-term spillovers to the SE, SW and NW regions. In the longer term, the results of a NE shock are small, the largest being on CR, while spillovers to the SE, SW and NW regions are negative (but small absolutely). Thus, we can conclude that the linkages from the NE region to the rest of the country are weak in the short and the long term, which suggests that it is relatively isolated economically from the rest of the country—perhaps handicapped by its increasingly outmoded industrial base, as recognised by the recent policy to 'revitalise the northeast' (Geng and Weiss 2005).

A shock to the southwest region has small positive short-term spillovers to all other regions except the SE region, suggesting again that contiguity is not sufficient for strong linkages. Over time, many of these are reversed so that the cumulative effects are negative, although there is a substantial continuing effect on NE and a smaller one on NW. The latter can be explained by its close proximity but this cannot explain the effect on the NE region, which is at the opposite corner of the country.

Finally, the initial effects of a shock to the NW region are similar to those for the SW region except that now there is effectively no spillover to the SW region, whereas there was from SW to NW. Over time, the largest spillover is to SW (despite the absence of a short-term effect between these regions), and there is also a modest effect on YR. Long-term spillovers to other regions are negligible or negative. This supports the notion that the northwest's dominance in coal, natural gas and oil production has resulted in an energy-industry enclave, which offers little in terms of transmitting growth towards the rest of the country.

To sum up the implication of the IRFs, overall spillovers are relatively weak. Not unexpectedly in light of earlier literature, the SE region has the largest sustained spillovers but these are limited to the CR and YR regions. The CR and

YR regions have modest spillover effects and these are limited to the CR, YR and NE regions, with (surprisingly) little effect on SE. The NW and SW regions have weak linkages—they are little affected by shocks to other regions and, in turn, have little effect on the rest of the country. Thus, these core industrial regions of China (SE, CR and YR) appear to be relatively well integrated (although this is uni-directional in SE's case), the western regions are connected only loosely and the NE receives small spillovers from most other regions but has positive effects only on the core CR and YR regions.

Conclusions

Regional integration has been a major policy challenge throughout China's history, and remains so today. Broadly defined as the increasing interdependence of regions as reflected in the flow of goods, services and/or factors of production, integration, so we have seen, can be promoted from 'below', by the removal of impediments to trade and factor mobility, and from 'above', by the active promotion of economic cooperation through appropriate policies or institutions. The transition away from the former system of command planning—in which planning was deliberately compartmentalised along provincial lines and in which the policy of self-sufficiency encouraged provincial independence—should in itself have spurred improvements in inter-provincial relations, with integration following as a natural consequence of development in an increasingly market-based economy. Yet the bulk of the evidence suggests that China's regions do not appear to be as highly integrated as they should be. Given the wide range of definitions and methodologies available for assessing the extent and dynamic pattern of integration, it is unlikely that any one piece of research will provide a definitive assessment of China's integration issue. Instead, this chapter has contributed a small piece to what is quite clearly a large and complex puzzle.

Our own empirical results contribute to a developing consensus indicating that integration among China's industrial core regions has proceeded further than their integration with the rest of the country. In particular, the positive transmission of growth from the southeast towards the Yellow River and Changjiang River regions implies that when the first region performs well, the last two regions benefit, while the rest of the country receives little impetus to their own regional rates of growth. With these three regions containing the country's eight richest provinces and only two of the country's eight poorest, a major cause of concern is that China is becoming polarised into a set of relatively well-integrated and developed regions and a set of isolated and underdeveloped outsiders—hardly an optimal scenario for national unity, economic and social stability and, perhaps most crucially, preserving political power. Furthermore, the one-way street of spillovers from the southeast region to the Yellow River and Changjiang River regions, but not in return, suggests that China is heavily reliant on the former region—and on Guangdong in particular—for sustaining its rapid rate of GDP growth. Although this 'engine of growth' has served China well to date, a slow-down in the southeast region will impact negatively on the main industrial centres, while receiving little offset in terms of positive growth spillovers from elsewhere in the country. A key challenge for the government, then, is to improve the positive transmissions of growth among China's regions.

One of the major limitations of the VAR model is that it says nothing about the channels by which spillovers are transmitted, so we can only conjecture as to why certain regions appear to be more integrated than others. Still, it provides a useful take-off point for further investigation of this issue. Why, for example, are the benefits of growth in the southeast region failing to reach the contiguous southwest, and what could be done to improve this situation? How important are transport linkages between these regions, and what about the attitudes of local governments towards promoting inter-regional trade? Are the southeast, Yellow River and Changjiang River regions more highly integrated because of common industrial structures or because of complementary industrial structures (that is, underpinned by intra-industry or inter-industry trade, respectively)? Are the northeast and northwest isolated because of failures to promote integration from above or below? Answers to these questions—and many more—will help to identify the appropriate role of the central and local governments in improving integration in the future.

One thing, however, is clear: a comprehensive approach towards domestic market integration is essential, since partial reforms run the risk that the costs of integration will outweigh the benefits. For example, the government needs to ensure not only that impediments to inter-regional trade are minimal, but that less-developed regions have the capacity to benefit from technological transfers embodied in that trade. Perfectly mobile labour in the absence of fully developed capital markets could result in excessive migration out of less-developed areas (with the consequent brain drain there and rising congestion pressures in industrial centres), without investments flowing in or innovations trickling down. If the recent findings of the World Bank (2005) are accurate, much remains to be done to reduce the misallocations of capital across regions and to prevent further fragmentation of regional capital markets, thereby enabling investment funds to be channelled to those regions most in need. Nationally uniform regulations and institutions designed to minimise inter-regional barriers to trade and transaction costs also have an important role to play.

A further limitation in the application of the VAR model to China is that data constraints make it necessary to use the entire period from 1953 to 2003, while ideally the command and reform periods would have been analysed separately. The analysis is undeniably a little clouded by the fact that integration was deliberately discouraged in the command era, and also by the fact that during this time the transmission of growth from one region to another presumably had more to do with central government decisions than with the market-based transmissions of growth described above. To the extent that integration has improved over time, our results will understate the strength of inter-regional linkages today. However understated they might be, they do not indicate the need for an alarmist view of potential internal disintegration within China, but rather that more research remains to be done.

Notes

1 Winters 2004 reviews the mechanisms by which trade could impact on growth.

2 Dowrick and Golley (2004) provide empirical evidence that, since the 1980s, the benefits of trade have accrued mainly to richer countries, with little benefit for less-developed ones.

3 This section draws on Golley (2007).

4 This finding confirms state media reports that 'administrative disintegration' has resulted in redundant industrial construction within the Yangtze (Changjiang) River Delta, with 11 of the 15 major cities concentrating on spare auto parts manufacturing, and 12 on telecommunications. Meanwhile, vicious competition is hurting the overall prosperity of the region. Calls are being made to improve financial cooperation and to standardise qualifications, taxes and regulations within the area. Similarly, the Pearl River Delta's market accession restrictions—'the area's most pressing problem'—need to be eliminated (*Beijing Review* 2003:35).

5 For greater detail on the reasons for the definition of the regions and a general description of their characteristics, see Groenewold et al. (forthcoming).

6 For a recent textbook treatment of this procedure, see Enders (2004:Chapter 5).

7 While it is common to compute IRFs based on one-standard-deviation shocks, we use unit shocks. This allows for easier comparison of results across regions and implies that the IRFs have the dimension of elasticities. For each simulation, we shock the region in question as well as national output in order to incorporate the constraint that, in terms of levels, the regional outputs add to national output so that it is not possible to shock one region's output—holding all other regional outputs constant—without allowing for the consequent contemporaneous effect on national output. In log terms, we shock the national log output by the same as the shock to regional output multiplied by its share in national output. The order of the variables/regions underlying these IRFs is NAT, SE, CR, YR, NE, SW and NW. Experimentation with alternative ordering of the regional outputs shows that our overall conclusions are not affected.

References

Abramovitz, M., 1986. 'Catching up, forging ahead, and falling behind', *Journal of Economic History*, 46:385–406.

Ash, R. and Kueh, Y.Y., 1993. 'Economic integration within Greater China: trade and investment flows between China, Hong Kong and Taiwan', *China Quarterly*, 136:711–45.

Bai, C.-E., Du, Y., Tao, Z. and Tong, S.Y., 2004. 'Local protectionism and regional specialization: evidence from China's industries', *Journal of International Economics*, 63:397–417.

Beijing Review, 2003. 'Tale of two deltas', *Beijing Review*, 31 July:34–5.

Boyreau-Debray, G. and Wei, S.-J., 2004. *Can China grow faster? A diagnosis of the function of its domestic capital market*, IMF Policy Discussion Papers 04/76, International Monetary Fund, Washington, DC.

Brun, J.F, Combes, J.L. and Renard, M.F., 2002. 'Are there spillover effects between coastal and non-coastal regions in China?', *China Economic Review*, 109:1–9.

Donnithorne, A., 1967. *China's Economic System*, George Allen and Unwin, London.

——, 1972. 'China's cellular economy: some economic trends since the Cultural Revolution', *China Quarterly*, 52:605–91.

Dowrick, S. and Golley, J., 2004. 'Trade openness and growth', *Oxford Review of Economic Policy*, 20(1):38–56.

Enders, W., 2004. *Applied Econometric Time Series*, Second edition, Wiley, Hoboken, NJ.

Fan, C.S. and Wei, X., 2003. 'The law of one price: evidence from the transitional economy of China.' Available from www.hiebs.hku.hk/events_updates/pdf/weixiangdong.pdf

Fu, X., 2004. 'Limited linkages from growth engines and regional disparities in China', *Journal of Comparative Economics*, 32:148–64.

Geng, X. and Weiss, J., 2005. *Development in North East People's Republic of China: an analysis of enterprise performance, 1995–2002*, Asian Development Bank Institute Discussion Paper, No. 34, Asian Development Bank, Manila.

Golley, J., 2007. *The Dynamics of Chinese Regional Development: market nature, state nurture*, Edward Elgar, Cheltenham.

Groenewold, N., Lee, G. and Chen, A., 2006. *Inter-regional output spillovers in China: disentangling national from regional shocks*, Economics Discussion Paper 06-25, University of Western Australia, Perth.

——— (forthcoming). 'Inter-regional spillovers in China: the importance of common shocks and the definition of the regions', *China Economic Review.*

Hirschman, A., 1958. *The Strategy of Economic Development*, Yale University Press, New Haven, Conn.

Howitt, P., 2000. 'Endogenous growth and cross-country income differences', *American Economic Review*, 90(4):111–30.

Hu, A. and Jefferson, G., 2002. 'FDI impact and spillover: evidence from China's electronic and textile industries', *World Economy*, 38(4):1,063–76.

Lucas, R.E., 1988. 'On the mechanics of economic development', *Journal of Monetary Economics*, 22(1):3–42.

Lyons, T., 1987. *Economic Integration and Planning in Maoist China*, Columbia University Press, New York.

Marshall, A., 1920. *Principles of Economics*, Macmillan Press, London.

Naughton, B., 2003. 'How much can regional integration do to unify China's markets?', in N. Hope, D.T. Yang and M.Y. Li (eds), *How Far Across the River? Chinese Policy Reform at the Millennium*, Stanford University Press, California:204–32.

National Bureau of Statistics, various years. *Statistical Yearbook of China*, China China Statistical Press, Beijing.

———, 1997. *The Gross Domestic Product of China, 1952–95*, Dongbei University of Finance and Economics Press, Dongbei.

———, 2006. *China Statistical Abstract 2006*, China Statistical Press, Beijing.

Parsley, D.C. and Wei, S.J., 1996. 'Convergence to the law of one price without trade barriers or currency fluctuations', *Quarterly Journal of Economics*, 111(4):1,211–36.

Poncet, S., 2003. 'Measuring Chinese domestic and international integration', *China Economic Review*, 14:1–21.

———, 2005. 'A fragmented China: measure and determinants of Chinese domestic market disintegration', *Review of International Economics*, 13(3):409–30.

Romer, P.M., 1990. 'Endogenous technological change', *Journal of Political Economy*, 98(5):S71–102.

Tan, K. and Zhang, X., 2005. Incremental reform and distortions in the product and factor market in China, Paper prepared for the Stanford Center for International Development annual conference, China's Policy Reforms: progress and challenges, 29 September–1 October, Stanford University.

Tang, K.K., 1998. 'Economic integration of the Chinese provinces: a business cycle approach', *Journal of Economic Integration*, 13:549–70.

Tinbergen, J., 1965. *International Economic Integration*, Elsevier Publishing Company, Amsterdam.

Winters, L.A., 2004. 'Trade liberalisation and economic performance: an overview', *Economic Journal*, 114(493):F4–21.

World Bank, 1994. *China: internal market development and regulation*, World Bank Report, No. 12291-CHA, Washington, DC.

——, 2005. *China: integration of national product and factor markets: economic benefits and policy recommendations*, Report, No. 31973-CHA, 13 June, Washington, DC.

Wu, Y., 2004. *China's Economic Growth: a miracle with Chinese characteristics*, Routledge Curzon, London.

Xu, X., 2002. 'Have the Chinese provinces become integrated under reform?', *China Economic Review*, 13:116–33.

Xu, X. and Voon, J.P., 2003. 'Regional integration in China: a statistical model', *Economics Letters*, 79:35–42.

Yao, S. and Zhang, Z., 2001. 'On regional inequality and diverging clubs: a case study of contemporary China', *Journal of Comparative Economics*, 29:466–84.

Ying, L.G., 2000. 'Measuring spill-over effects: some Chinese evidence', *Papers in Regional Science*, 79:75–89.

Young, A., 2000. 'The razor's edge: distortions and incremental reform in the People's Republic of China', *Quarterly Journal of Economics*, 15(4):1,091–135.

Zhang, Q. and Felmingham, B., 2002. 'The role of FDI, exports and spillover effects in the regional development of China', *Journal of Development Studies*, 38:157–78.

11

Foreign direct investment in China

Trends and characteristics after WTO accession

Chunlai Chen

Foreign direct investment (FDI) in China has been one of the most significant features of the country's economic reform and opening up to the outside world. The gradual liberalisation of restrictions on FDI since 1979 and the government's commitment to further opening up have greatly improved the investment environment. Foreign firms have been attracted by the huge domestic market and pool of relatively well-educated, low-cost labour, which has made China one of the most attractive destinations for FDI in the world.

China became a member of the World Trade Organization (WTO) in December 2001, after 15 years of negotiations in which China agreed to reduce tariff and non-tariff barriers to trade in agriculture and manufactured goods, to liberalise and open trade in services to foreign participation, remove restrictions on FDI—particularly in services—and improve protection of intellectual property rights. In terms of FDI, China has made substantial commitments in investment liberalisation, especially in the services sector, and has agreed to comprehensively implement the Trade-Related Investment Measures (TRIMs) agreement. Undoubtedly, the reduction in foreign investment barriers and the liberalisation of the FDI regime will provide great opportunities for foreign investors to operate in China.

There have been many studies on the impact of China's entry into the WTO on FDI inflows into the country (for example, McKibbin and Wilcoxen 1998; Hu 1999; Walmsley and Hertel 2000; UNCTAD 2000; Chen 2002). The most common findings are that China's WTO accession will have a positive impact on its gross domestic product (GDP) growth—mainly through efficiency gains resulting from trade and investment liberalisation—and it will accelerate FDI inflows into China and increase the share of foreign ownership in China's assets.

What, however, has really happened with FDI inflows since China's WTO accession? This chapter intends to provide a brief overview of the trends and characteristics of FDI inflows into China since its WTO accession by analysing aspects of the general trend of FDI inflows, the composition of FDI sources, the sectoral and regional distribution of FDI inflows and the structure of FDI in China's manufacturing.

The general trend of FDI inflows into China

FDI inflows into China presented three distinct phases (see Figure 11.1): the experimental phase from 1979 to 1991, the boom phase from 1992 to 2001, and the post-WTO phase from 2002 to 2006.

During the experimental phase, FDI inflows were low, but they grew steadily. The period was characterised by small investment projects, high investment costs, restrictive price controls, poor infrastructure and lack of legal frameworks.

In the second phase, FDI inflows initially increased very rapidly, however, they slowed after 1997 and declined in 1999 and 2000, followed by a moderate recovery in 2001. The slow-down from 1997 to 2000 could be explained by several factors. First, there has been a slow-down from the surge in transfers of labour-intensive activities from neighbouring Asian economies. In addition, the East Asian financial crisis weakened substantially the outward investment abilities of East and Southeast Asian economies. As a result, FDI flows into China from East and Southeast Asia declined substantially since 1997. Second, market rates of return to investment in China have not been as high as foreign investors expected. Informal relationships and corruption still hinder many business transactions by foreigners. In addition, inefficient state-owned enterprises continue to dominate many key sectors of the economy, especially the services sector. Third, there still are restrictions on FDI, such as on ownership shares, modes of FDI entry, business operations and regional and sectoral restrictions.

Therefore, China's accession to the WTO came at a critical time, when the country was facing difficulties sustaining a high level of FDI inflows. Could China's WTO accession revive the trend of increasing high levels of FDI inflows?

After entry into the WTO—with the implementation of its commitments and broader and deeper liberalisation in trade and investment—China's economy has been growing rapidly. The average annual growth rate of China's GDP was

Figure 11.1 **FDI inflows into China, 1980–2006** (US$ billion at current prices)

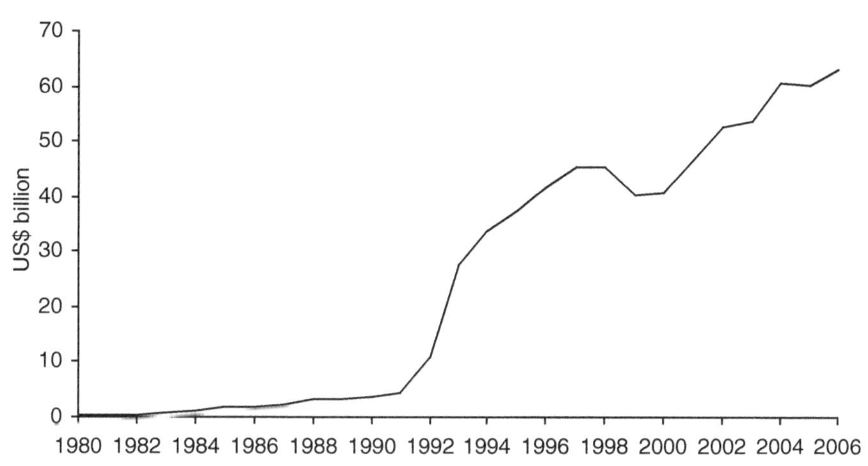

Source: National Bureau of Statistics, various issues (a). *China Statistical Yearbook*, China Statistical Press, Beijing.

10 per cent during 2002–06.[1] China's foreign trade has been expanding even more rapidly than its overall economic growth. The total value of China's foreign trade increased from US$509.65 billion in 2001 to US$1,760.4 billion in 2006, with an annual growth rate of 28.2 per cent. Undoubtedly, China's economy has benefitted from entry into the WTO, especially from a more open and liberalised international trade and FDI regime.

After China's accession to the WTO, FDI inflows presented an increasing trend. FDI inflows increased from US$46.9 billion in 2001 to US$63 billion in 2006,[2] with an annual growth rate of 6.1 per cent (Figure 11.1). This has demonstrated that with trade and investment liberalisation and reduction in foreign investment barriers, China's WTO accession has accelerated FDI inflows.

There has, however, long been an issue of 'round-tripping' of investment in China. Round-tripping is driven by differences in the treatment of foreign and domestic investors, which can motivate investors to channel funds out of, and subsequently into, an economy in the form of FDI. Because the funds originate in the host economy itself, round-tripping inflates FDI inflows. In China, because of the preferential treatment offered to foreign investors (mainly through tax incentives), a significant share of FDI inflows are round-tripped, mainly via Hong Kong (UNCTAD 2007) and, more recently and increasingly, via tax havens such as the Virgin, Cayman and Samoan islands (He 2006). Official estimates from the Chinese government are not available, but one estimate, made by Harrold and Lall (1993), suggested that round-tripping inward FDI accounted for 25 per cent of China's FDI inflows in 1992. Some experts estimate that round-tripping FDI currently accounts for 33 per cent of China's total FDI inflows (He 2006).

On 16 March 2007, Chinese lawmakers passed the much talked about corporate income tax law, unifying tax rates for foreign and domestic enterprises. The new tax rate for domestic and foreign enterprises will be 25 per cent. The law is due to take effect on 1 January 2008 (Xinhua News Agency 2007). The new law has unified the two existing tax codes—one for domestic enterprises, the other for foreign-invested enterprises—and represents a fundamental change in China's tax policy. Many of the tax incentives and tax holidays that existed in the old code for foreign investors have been changed or eliminated.

Undoubtedly, the new law and the unification of the tax rate will substantially reduce the incentive for round-tripping. What, however, are the impacts of the new tax law on domestic and foreign-invested companies and on FDI inflows into China?

Although the current nominal income tax rate is set at 33 per cent, the real average income tax burden on China's domestic companies is 25 per cent (Xinhua News Agency 2007), so on average the new tax law will not reduce the real tax burden on domestic companies.

The current real income tax burden on foreign-invested companies is 15 per cent (Xinhua News Agency 2007). On average, the new law will increase the tax burden on foreign-invested companies by 10 percentage points. It seems that the new law will have a negative impact on foreign-invested companies—especially in the short term on small-scale, labour-intensive, quick profit-earning enterprises from developing economies.

I would argue, however, that China's proposed unified corporate income tax rate of 25 per cent for domestic and foreign-invested companies will have little effect on foreign investment in China, especially from large multinational enterprises.

First, the average corporate income tax rate for the 159 countries and regions that levy corporate income tax is 28.6 per cent, and the average corporate income tax rate for China's 18 neighbouring countries and regions is 26.7 per cent (Xinwen Shishi 2007). China's proposed unified tax rate of 25 per cent is below the global average, so it is quite competitive for attracting foreign and domestic investment, therefore, there is little reason to believe that the new law will have a significant effect on foreign investment.

Second, in the past few decades, time-series econometric analyses and numerous surveys of international investors have shown that tax incentives are not the most influential factor for multinationals when selecting investment locations (Morisset 2003). Foreign investors are, of course, interested in tax rates, but they are more interested in factors such as a broad investment climate and domestic market, the cost and availability of labour, basic infrastructure, economic and political stability, and the like.

Third, China's overall investment environment is quite competitive, with relatively efficient public services, good infrastructure, a large and fast-growing domestic market, abundant and well-educated human resources, low labour costs and macroeconomic and political stability—making China one of the most attractive locations for FDI. According to the *2005 Foreign Direct Investment Confidence Index* (A.T. Kearney Inc. 2007), in 2005 China was the world's most attractive FDI location in the world. China has maintained its lead in the index for the fourth consecutive year. Once again, China is the top FDI location for first-time investors, with more than half (55 per cent) of investors expected to make first-time investments there in the next three years. One in five FDI dollars for first-time investments will be committed to the Chinese market. China has successfully overcome the perceived risk associated with first-time market entry, which is typically the biggest barrier to generating new FDI.

Fourth, the new tax law still has preferential stipulations: China will continue to offer tax incentives to investment in projects relating to environmental protection, agricultural development, water conservation, energy saving, production safety, high-technology development and public welfare. High-technology enterprises can still enjoy a 15 per cent income tax rate, and small and medium-sized enterprises with slim profits are required to pay income tax at only 20 per cent. Certain tax breaks will also be granted to enterprises in special economic zones and in the less-developed western areas of the country (Xinhua News Agency 2007).

Finally, the new tax law also provides five-year transitional periods to offset the impact on foreign companies. The income tax rate will be increased gradually to 25 per cent during this period, and existing foreign enterprises can still enjoy tax breaks within a regulated time limit (Xinhua News Agency 2007).

Therefore, the new law will bring China's tax laws more in line with international standards. It is the fulfilment of a commitment to the WTO for equal treatment for domestic and overseas investors. The change in the law not only proves that the Chinese government is determined to continue its reform and opening up policies—and to work hard to improve the investment climate—it will help to create a sound investment environment and promote China's industrial restructuring and upgrading.

The composition of FDI sources

By the end of 2001, FDI in China was dominated overwhelmingly by developing economies, which accounted for 73.8 per cent of the total accumulated FDI inflows, while industrialised economies accounted for only 26.2 per cent. In terms of individual investors, FDI was dominated by four investors: Hong Kong, the United States, Japan and Taiwan, accounting for 48 per cent, 8.7 per cent, 8.2 per cent and 7.3 per cent of the total accumulated FDI inflows respectively.

After China's accession into the WTO, developing and industrialised economies increased investments in China. FDI inflows from developing economies increased from US$32.2 billion in 2001 to US$39.8 billion in 2005, with an annual growth rate of 5.4 per cent. FDI inflows from industrialised economies also increased but at a much slower pace, rising from US$13.6 billion in 2001 to US$14.4 billion in 2005, with an annual growth rate of 1.5 per cent (Figure 11.2).

Among the major investors from developing economies, Hong Kong is still the largest; however, its FDI inflows into China stagnated at about US$16–17 billion from 2001 to 2005 (Table 11.1). As a result, its share in total FDI inflows into China declined from 48.1 per cent at the end of 2001 to 32 per cent in the period 2002–05. FDI inflows from Taiwan and Singapore increased in 2002 and then declined continuously. Consequently, their shares also declined in the period 2002–05. In contrast, FDI inflows from South Korea increased dramatically from US$2.1 billion in 2001 to US$4.6 billion in 2005. As a result, its share increased from 3.1 per cent at the end of 2001 to 8.2 per cent in the period 2002–05.

The most notable feature is the large increase in FDI inflows from three tax-haven economies—the Virgin, Cayman and Samoan islands. FDI inflows from the Virgin Islands increased dramatically from US$4.9 billion in 2001 to US$8.1 billion in 2005, an increase of 64.8 per cent. As a result, its share in total FDI inflows increased from 4.4 per cent at the end of 2001 to 12.1 per cent in the period 2002–05, making it the second largest investor in China during this period. Investments from the Cayman and Samoan islands also increased, as did their shares in total FDI inflows into China in the period 2002–05.

The large increase in FDI inflows into China from the three tax-haven island economies might involve 'round-tripping', as discussed above, in which domestic Chinese investors invest in the tax-haven economies (often through a shell company) and then reinvest in China to take advantage of the preferential treatment offered to foreign investors.

Another explanation for the rise in FDI into China from the Virgin, Cayman and Samoan islands is the 'transit' investment in China from other economies—notably Hong Kong and Taiwan—via the island economies in order to lower (or

Figure 11.2 **FDI inflows into China, by source, 1983–2005** (US$ billion at constant 2000 prices)

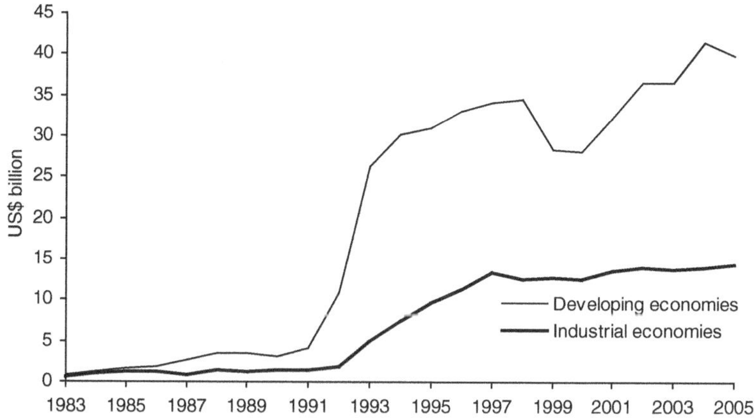

Source: National Bureau of Statistics, various issues (a). *China Statistical Yearbook*, China Statistical Press, Beijing.

eliminate) their fiscal commitments. For example, the number of companies in Hong Kong that are incorporated in Bermuda and the Cayman Islands jumped 5.2 times from 178 in 1990 to 924 in 2000 (Wu et al. 2002). As for Taiwanese companies, partly to take advantage of the tax regime, but also to bypass the Taiwanese government's restrictions on investment in the mainland, the Virgin Islands and the Cayman Islands rank second and third respectively after China as the biggest recipients of Taiwan's outward investment (Breslin 2003). This suggests that FDI in China from Hong Kong and Taiwan is more significant than the official data reveal. The data also reflect use of tax havens by investors from industrialised economies.

In terms of the major investors from industrialised economies, FDI inflows from the United States increased from US$4.3 billion in 2001 to US$5.2 billion in 2002, then declined continuously to US$2.7 billion in 2005. As a result, its share in total FDI inflows into China declined from 8.7 per cent (making it the second largest investor) at the end of 2001 to 7.4 per cent (ranking it in fourth place) in the period 2002–05. Investment from the United Kingdom dropped from US$1 billion in 2001 to about US$0.8 billion during 2002 and 2005, while investment from France increased marginally during the period 2001–05. In

Table 11.1 **FDI inflows into China, 2001–2005** (US$ at constant 2000 prices)

	FDI inflows (US$ billion)					Share of accumulated FDI inflows (1983–2001)	Share of accumulated FDI inflows (2002–05)	Share of accumulated FDI inflows (1983–2005)
	2001	2002	2003	2004	2005	Per cent	Per cent	Per cent
Major investors from developing economies								
Hong Kong	16.3	17.1	16.7	17.4	16.1	48.1	32.0	42.7
Taiwan	2.9	3.8	3.2	2.9	1.9	7.3	5.6	6.7
Singapore	2.1	2.2	1.9	1.8	2.0	4.7	3.8	4.4
South Korea	2.1	2.6	4.2	5.7	4.7	3.1	8.2	4.8
Virgin Islands	4.9	5.9	5.4	6.2	8.1	4.4	12.1	7.0
Cayman Islands	1.0	1.1	0.8	1.9	1.8	0.6	2.6	1.3
Samoa	0.5	0.8	0.9	1.0	1.2	0.4	1.9	0.9
Major investors from industrialised economies								
Japan	4.3	4.0	4.8	5.0	5.9	8.2	9.3	8.6
United States	4.3	5.2	4.0	3.6	2.8	8.7	7.4	8.3
United Kingdom	1.0	0.7	0.7	0.7	0.9	2.5	1.5	2.1
Germany	1.2	0.9	0.8	1.0	1.4	1.8	1.9	1.8
France	0.5	0.6	0.6	0.6	0.6	1.2	1.1	1.2
Netherlands	0.8	0.6	0.7	0.7	0.9	0.9	1.4	1.1
Others	3.8	4.9	5.7	7.0	6.1	8.2	11.3	9.3
Developing economies	32.2	36.6	36.6	41.6	39.8	73.8	73.4	73.7
Industrialised economies	13.6	14.0	13.7	14.0	14.4	26.2	26.6	26.3
Total	45.8	50.6	50.3	55.6	54.2	100.0	100.0	100.0

Source: National Bureau of Statistics, various issues (a). *China Statistical Yearbook*, China Statistical Press, Beijing.

contrast, FDI inflows from Japan increased from US$4.25 billion in 2001 to US$5.9 billion in 2005, maintaining its position as the third largest investor in China in the period 2002–05. Investments from Germany and the Netherlands also increased in 2005.

FDI inflows from other countries presented an increasing trend, rising from US$3.8 billion in 2001 to US$6.1 billion in 2005. As a result, their combined share in total FDI inflows into China increased from 8.2 per cent at the end of 2001 to 11.25 per cent in the period 2002–05. The increasing share of FDI inflows from other countries is an indication of the diversification of FDI sources.

In general, since China's WTO accession, developing and industrialised economies have increased their investments in the China because of the overall improvement of the investment environment and the reduction of trade and investment barriers. The growth rate of FDI inflows from developing economies is, however, much faster than that of industrialised economies. As a result, developing economies still dominate FDI inflows into China, and the composition of FDI sources in terms of developing and industrialised economies has barely changed.

The domination of developing economies in FDI in China could be attributed to their economic development level and the nature and characteristics of their firms. Because developing economies have moderate technological and innovative capabilities and are at the mid-level of economic development, the ownership advantages possessed by their firms are concentrated in the forms of labour-intensive production technology, standardised product manufacturing and well-established export market networks. Obviously, China—having relatively abundant labour resources and a comparative advantage in labour-intensive activities—is an attractive location for developing-economy investors to explore overseas investment opportunities, particularly for export-oriented FDI. Since its accession to the WTO, China has, on the one hand, reduced trade and investment barriers and improved the investment environment, while, on the other, its export markets have been greatly enlarged as WTO member countries—particularly industrialised economies—have opened domestic markets for China's exports. Therefore, there are great incentives for developing-country investors to increase FDI in China in general and to increase export-oriented FDI in particular. It is expected that China will remain an important host country for investments from developing economies well into the future.

In general, enterprises from industralised economies with high technological and innovative capabilities and high overall economic development levels will possess greater ownership advantages in the form of high technology, product differentiation, managerial and entrepreneurial skills and intangible knowledge-based assets than those from developing economies. Because of these enterprise-specific ownership advantages, FDI from industrialised economies is more market-oriented than that from developing economies. The general implication is that host countries with larger markets, faster economic growth and a higher degree of economic development will attract more market-oriented FDI. China's huge domestic market, fast economic growth and increasing per capita income are very attractive to industrialised-country investors, particularly to market-oriented FDI. Therefore, China's accession to the WTO has provided great opportunities for industrialised-country investors to explore China's huge domestic markets. It is expected that with fulfilment of China's commitments to the WTO in trade and investment liberalisation, China will become an increasingly important host country for FDI from industrialised economies, which will not only increase the total FDI inflows from industrialised economies, it will increase their quality.

Regional distribution of FDI inflows

Since China started to attract FDI, the regional distribution of FDI inflows has been very uneven. FDI inflows into China are concentrated overwhelmingly in the east of the country. Although there have been some small fluctuations, the gap between the eastern and the central and western regions has been increasing, especially since the early 1990s. By the end of 2001, the eastern region attracted 87.8 per cent of the total FDI inflows into China, while the central and western regions received only 9 per cent and 3.3 per cent of the total respectively.

Trade and investment liberalisation are expected to bring more benefits to the eastern region than to the rest of the country, especially the western region. Therefore, economic growth in the east will be higher and faster than in the west. Consequently, it is expected that more FDI will flow into the eastern region and the uneven regional distribution of FDI inflows into China—especially between the eastern and the western regions—might be reinforced in the short term.

After China's WTO entry, FDI inflows continued to concentrate in the eastern region—increasing rapidly from US$39.8 billion in 2001 to US$48 billion in 2004, with an annual growth rate of 6.5 per cent (Figure 11.3 and Table 11.2). From 2002 to 2004, the eastern region attracted US$135.2 billion in FDI inflows, accounting for 86.8 per cent of the total during that period. Among the provinces in the eastern region, Jiangsu's performance was the most outstanding. During the period 2002–04, Jiangsu attracted US$27.9 billion in FDI inflows, accounting for 17.9 per cent of the total. As a result, Jiangsu surpassed Guangdong in attracting FDI inflows and became the largest FDI recipient in China during the period. Although its share has been declining, Guangdong is still one of the most attractive locations for foreign investment. It attracted US$27.4 billion in FDI inflows, accounting for 17.6 per cent of the total during the period 2002–04. Liaoning, Shanghai and Zhejiang also witnessed a large increase in FDI inflows and their shares in the total have increased. In contrast, FDI inflows into Fujian, Guangxi and Hainan have declined.

The central region has witnessed a large increase in FDI inflows since 2001: from US$4.1 billion in 2001 to US$6.4 billion in 2004, with an annual growth rate of 16.2 per cent. As a result, its share in total FDI inflows into China increased from 9 per cent at the end of 2001 to 10.9 per cent in the period 2002–04. In the central region, the increasingly attractive provinces for FDI are Jiangxi, Hubei and Hunan. These three provinces contributed to the majority of the increase in FDI inflows into the central region.

The western region has experienced a declining trend in FDI inflows since 2001: from US$1.4 billion in 2001 to US$1 billion in 2004, with an annual declining rate of 10.3 per cent. Provinces with a large decline in FDI inflows were Sichuan, Shaanxi and Gansu.

Figure 11.3 **FDI inflows into China by region, 1983–2004** (US$ billion at constant 2000 prices)

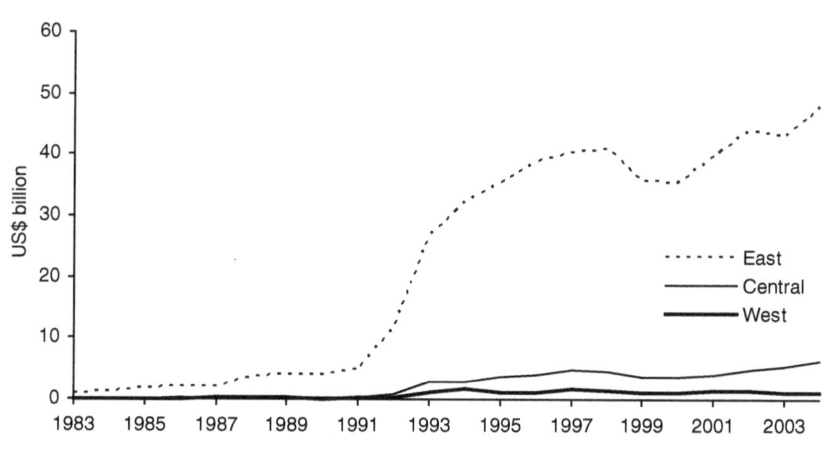

Sources: National Bureau of Statistics, various issues (a). *China Statistical Yearbook*, China Statistical Press, Beijing.

Table 11.2 **FDI inflows into China by province, 1983–2004** (US$ at constant 2000 prices)

	FDI inflows (US$ billion)				Share of accumulated FDI inflows (1983–2001) (per cent)	Share of accumulated FDI inflows (2002–04) (per cent)	Share of accumulated FDI inflows (1983–2004) (per cent)
	2001	2002	2003	2004			
Eastern region	39.77	44.03	43.09	48.03	87.76	86.83	87.50
Beijing	1.73	1.66	2.06	2.35	4.17	3.90	4.10
Tianjin	2.08	1.52	1.44	1.58	3.92	2.92	3.65
Hebei	0.65	0.75	0.91	0.64	1.92	1.48	1.80
Liaoning	2.46	3.27	2.66	4.96	4.49	7.00	5.18
Shanghai	4.19	4.10	5.14	5.79	8.39	9.66	8.74
Jiangsu	6.75	9.78	9.94	8.20	12.90	17.94	14.28
Zhejiang	2.16	2.95	4.69	5.25	3.42	8.28	4.75
Fujian	3.83	3.68	2.44	1.76	9.67	5.07	8.41
Shandong	3.44	4.54	5.66	7.94	6.41	11.66	7.85
Guangdong	11.65	10.88	7.36	9.18	28.78	17.61	25.72
Guangxi	0.38	0.40	0.39	0.27	1.78	0.68	1.48
Hainan	0.46	0.49	0.40	0.11	1.89	0.64	1.55
Central region	4.11	4.98	5.57	6.44	8.98	10.91	9.51
Shanxi	0.23	0.20	0.20	0.08	0.44	0.31	0.41
Inner Mongolia	0.10	0.17	0.08	0.31	0.19	0.36	0.24
Jilin	0.33	0.23	0.18	0.18	0.86	0.38	0.72
Heilongjiang	0.33	0.34	0.30	0.31	1.08	0.61	0.95
Anhui	0.33	0.37	0.35	0.39	0.88	0.71	0.83
Jiangxi	0.39	1.04	1.52	1.87	0.80	2.85	1.36
Henan	0.45	0.39	0.51	0.39	1.23	0.82	1.12
Hubei	1.16	1.37	1.48	1.60	1.94	2.86	2.19
Hunan	0.79	0.86	0.96	1.30	1.56	2.01	1.68

Western region	1.40	1.35	1.14	1.01	3.26	2.26	2.99
Chongqing	0.25	0.19	0.25	0.23	0.70	0.43	0.62
Sichuan	0.57	0.53	0.39	0.33	0.98	0.81	0.93
Guizhou	0.03	0.04	0.04	0.06	0.13	0.09	0.12
Yunnan	0.06	0.11	0.08	0.13	0.27	0.20	0.25
Tibet	-	-	-	-	-	-	-
Shaanxi	0.34	0.35	0.31	0.13	0.89	0.51	0.79
Gansu	0.07	0.06	0.02	0.03	0.14	0.07	0.12
Qinghai	0.04	0.05	0.02	0.00	0.01	0.04	0.02
Ningxia	0.02	0.02	0.02	0.06	0.04	0.06	0.04
Xinjiang	0.02	0.02	0.01	0.04	0.10	0.04	0.09
Total	45.28	50.36	49.80	55.48	100	100	100

Source: National Bureau of Statistics, various issues (a). *China Statistical Yearbook*, China Statistical Press, Beijing.

It was hoped that China's accession to the WTO would help to improve the uneven regional distribution of FDI inflows, however, evidence has shown that since accession, the pattern of regional distribution has been essentially maintained. The eastern region is still the most attractive for FDI, the central region is increasing its attractiveness and the western region still has a long way to go to improve its overall investment environment.

The attractiveness of the eastern region to FDI is its relatively more open and developed economy, closer connections with the outside world, better infrastructure, higher levels of scientific research and technical innovation and the higher quality of its labour forces. Therefore, it is expected that with further liberalisation in trade and investment, the region will attract more FDI inflows.

The poor performance of the western region is attributed mainly to its poor overall investment environment. To boost economic growth and thereby reduce the gap between the eastern and the central and western regions, the Chinese government launched the West Development Strategy in 1998.[3] The strategy emphasises infrastructure development, environmental protection, industrial structural readjustment, development of sciences and education and economic reform and openness. To improve the investment environment and accelerate economic growth in the western region, China has invested heavily in infrastructure development. According to the western development strategy, major infrastructure projects include, for example: investing 120 billion yuan in highway and road construction between 2000 and 2020; investing 100 billion yuan in large and medium-sized railway projects between 2000 and 2005; creating a hydroelectricity generation base in the western region and constructing a national electricity supply network to transport electricity from the west to the east, between 2000 and 2015; investing 300 billion yuan in gas pipeline construction to transport natural gas from the west to the east, between 2000 and 2007; and constructing more airports in the western region (Office of the West Development Leading Group of the State Council 2000).

Undoubtedly, the western development strategy and the further opening up of the central and western regions have provided great opportunities for foreign investors. The comparative advantages of the central and western regions are rich natural resources, low labour costs and growing markets. In addition, there are many state-owned enterprises in these regions with huge amounts of idle capital stock. China is stipulating relevant laws and regulations on cross-border mergers and acquisitions and foreign investors are being encouraged to participate in state-owned enterprise reform and transformation through mergers and acquisitions. Such measures are aimed at increasing the flow of foreign capital into the central and western regions in the medium and long term. However, this had not been manifested in direct foreign investment flows into the west up to 2004.

Sectoral distribution of FDI inflows

By the end of 2001, the sectoral distribution of FDI in China was characterised by its concentration in the manufacturing sector, which attracted 61 per cent of the total FDI inflows into China during the period 1997–2001; the services sector attracted 36 per cent, while the primary sector attracted only 3 per cent.[4]

After WTO accession FDI inflows continued to concentrate in the manufacturing sector, increasing from US$30.2 billion in 2001 to US$38.2 billion in 2005, with an annual growth of 6 per cent (Table 11.3). As a result, the share of FDI inflows into the manufacturing sector increased from 66 per cent in 2001 to 70 per cent in 2005.

Studies of the impacts of China's WTO accession predict that, after accession, China's labour-intensive manufacturing industries—especially textiles and clothing—will grow rapidly, led by the expansion of exports as a result of the reduction of import tariffs and the elimination of import quotas from industrialised economies on China's labour-intensive manufactured goods. To realise this potential, however, China needs to introduce foreign capital, technology and advanced equipment to help upgrade its relatively backward labour-intensive industries in order to compete in global markets. Therefore, WTO accession provides great opportunities for foreign investors to invest in China's labour-intensive and export-oriented manufacturing industries. It is expected that more FDI will flow into these industries.

China's accession also provides great opportunities for foreign companies to invest in China's capital-intensive and technology-intensive manufacturing industries. Foreign companies in these industries have advantages over China's domestic enterprises. With further implementation of its WTO commitments, China will further relax controls on foreign ownership, allow direct transactions of cross-border mergers and acquisitions by foreign companies of its enterprises—especially state-owned enterprises—and improve the protection of intellectual property rights. As a result, it is expected that increasing amounts of FDI—especially from large industrialised-country multinationals—will flow into China's capital-intensive and technology-intensive manufacturing industries.

FDI inflows into the primary sector continued to decline after 2001: their share declined from 4 per cent in 2001 to only 2 per cent in 2005. This is not surprising given the declining share of the agricultural sector in China's national economy

Table 11.3 **FDI inflows into China by sector, 2001–2005** (US$ billion at constant 2000 prices)

	2001		2002		2003		2004		2005	
Sector	Value	(per cent)	Value	(per cent)	Value	(per cent)	Value	(per cent)	Value	(per cent)
Primary	1.67	3.65	1.54	3.05	1.26	2.50	1.51	2.73	0.96	1.78
Manufacturing	30.18	65.93	35.32	69.77	34.75	69.03	39.43	70.95	38.16	70.37
Services[a]	13.93	30.42	13.76	27.18	14.33	28.47	14.63	26.32	15.10	27.85
Total	45.78	100.00	50.62	100.00	50.33	100.00	55.58	100.00	54.22	100.00

[a] excluding financial services.

Sources: Calculated from National Bureau of Statistics, various issues (a). *China Statistical Yearbook*, China Statistical Press, Beijing; National Bureau of Statistics, various issues (b). *China Foreign Economic Statistical Yearbook*, China Statistical Press, Beijing.

and the rapid loss of overall comparative advantage in agricultural production in China (Chen 2006). In addition, China's agricultural land tenure system and the traditional small-scale, family-based agricultural production pattern have greatly limited the inflows of agricultural FDI with large-scale production and advanced technology. Therefore, China will not attract large amounts of FDI inflows into its agricultural sector without fundamentally changing its land tenure system and dramatically reforming the traditional farming pattern.

It is expected that after accession, more FDI will flow into the services sector, however, such inflows have been increasing at a slow pace—from US$13.9 billion in 2001 to US$15.1 billion in 2005, with an annual growth rate of only 2 per cent. Because of the slow growth rate, the share of FDI inflows into the services sector declined from 30 per cent in 2001 to 28 per cent in 2005.

In the services sector, in 2005, FDI inflows concentrated mainly in the following industries: real estate (32 per cent); leasing and business services (22 per cent); transport, storage and postal services (11 per cent); electricity, gas and water production and supply (8 per cent); wholesale and retail trade (6 per cent); and information, computer services and software (6 per cent). Together, the above industries received 86 per cent of total FDI inflows into the services sector.

In 2005, China for the first time published the data for FDI inflows into its financial sector: they were US$12.1 billion in 2005 and US$6.5 billion in 2006. By the end of 2005, 72 foreign banks from 12 countries and regions had established 254 operational institutions; 117 foreign banks from 40 countries and regions had established 240 representative offices in China, and the total assets of foreign banks increased to US$87.7 billion. There were 40 foreign-invested insurance companies, and their business accounted for 7 per cent of China's insurance market (Zhang 2006).

China made substantial commitments to the WTO to open its services sector to international trade and FDI. However, it has taken a step-by-step approach to implementing these commitments. In most of the services sectors—especially in telecommunications, banking and insurance, wholesale and retail, storage and transportation—China will fulfil its commitments in three to five years after accession.

China's services sector has been underdeveloped in the national economy. The share of the services sector in China's GDP has been about 30 per cent, while the global average is about 40 per cent. Obviously, the slow development of this sector will have a serious bottleneck effect on the overall development of China's economy.

There are many reasons for the slow development of China's services sector—two of the most important are the closed nature of the sector and monopoly. Before China's WTO accession, its services sector was relatively closed to foreign direct participation, which effectively protected the state monopoly. At present, many of China's service industries are still monopolised by state-owned enterprises, especially in finance and telecommunications.

Opening the services sector has been one of the most important issues in the bilateral negotiations for China's WTO accession. China has made some important and concrete commitments in opening the sector to foreign investors and it is expected that with full implementation, it will attract more FDI inflows.

Changes in FDI in the manufacturing sector

FDI inflows into China have been directed overwhelmingly to the manufacturing sector, and foreign-invested firms have become a major part of this sector. In 2005, foreign-invested firms made up 22 per cent of manufacturing enterprises, held 32 per cent of manufacturing assets, employed 32 per cent of the manufacturing labour force and contributed 33 per cent of manufacturing value-added.

Since China's accession to the WTO, foreign-invested firms in the manufacturing sector have undergone rapid expansion and structural changes.

Rapid expansion of foreign-invested firms in the manufacturing sector

From 2001 to 2005, foreign-invested firms in the manufacturing sector expanded dramatically. The total assets of these firms grew from 1,386 billion yuan in 2001 to 2,952 billion yuan in 2005—an increase of 113 per cent. Compared with domestic firms—whose total assets increased by 50 per cent between 2001 and 2005—the growth of foreign-invested firms was more than two times higher (Table 11.4).

Among the three industry groups, from 2001 to 2005, the growth in total assets of foreign-invested firms was the highest in technology-intensive industries[5]—increasing 137 per cent—followed closely by capital-intensive industries,[6] which increased 125 per cent. Foreign-invested firms' total assets in labour-intensive industries[7] increased by 81 per cent.

From 2001 to 2005, the expansion of foreign-invested firms was particularly significant in furniture manufacturing (183 per cent), chemical materials and products (128 per cent), ferrous metal smelting (297 per cent), non-ferrous metal smelting (193 per cent), general machinery (145 per cent), special machinery (206 per cent), transport equipment (134 per cent), electronics and

Table 11.4 **Total assets of foreign-invested and domestic firms in the manufacturing sector, 2001 and 2005** (billion yuan in constant 1991 prices)

Industry	2001	2005	Change (per cent)
Foreign-invested firms			
Food processing	40.3	85.3	112.0
Food manufacturing	38.1	59.4	56.1
Beverage manufacturing	42.7	54.5	27.5
Tobacco processing	1.0	0.8	-20.0
Textiles	73.8	145.9	97.7
Clothing and other fibre products	46.0	74.3	61.6
Leather and fur products	29.2	57.2	96.3
Timber processing	15.0	19.7	31.2
Furniture manufacturing	10.5	29.7	182.7
Paper and paper products	52.8	104.6	98.0
Printing	21.3	28.6	34.1
Cultural, educational and sports goods	18.6	32.4	74.2
Petroleum refining and coking	22.4	38.0	69.6
Chemical materials and products	85.3	194.3	127.9
Medical and pharmaceutical products	31.9	59.4	86.5
Chemical fibres	18.3	36.9	101.8
Rubber products	24.1	44.4	83.9
Plastic products	57.4	108.9	89.7
Non-metal mineral products	71.0	112.0	57.8
Ferrous metal smelting	27.8	110.3	297.3
Non-ferrous metal smelting	16.9	49.7	193.4
Metal products	61.3	89.3	45.5
General machinery	56.8	139.4	145.5
Special machinery	25.3	77.2	205.6
Transport equipment	117.5	274.9	133.9
Electrical machinery and equipment	96.7	191.8	98.4
Electronics and telecommunications equipment	263.8	649.3	146.2
Instruments and meters	20.6	55.4	169.3
By industry group			
Labour intensive	506.6	915.6	80.7
Capital intensive	384.6	863.8	124.6
Technology intensive	494.9	1,172.6	136.9
Total	1,386.2	2,951.9	113.0
Domestic firms			
Labour intensive	1,104.9	1,713.7	55.1
Capital intensive	2,052.2	2,997.7	46.1
Technology intensive	985.3	1,487.7	51.0
Total	4,142.3	6,199.2	49.7

Source: National Bureau of Statistics, various issues (a). *China Statistical Yearbook*, China Statistical Press, Beijing.

telecommunications equipment (146 per cent), and instruments and meters (169 per cent), which had an above-average rate of increase in total assets (Table 11.4). It is interesting to note that in the above nine industries, only one (furniture manufacturing) is a labour-intensive industry, while the others are capital and technology intensive.

The relative importance of foreign-invested firms in the manufacturing sector

Because of the high growth rate in investment, foreign-invested firms have become increasingly important in the manufacturing sector. In terms of total assets, the share of foreign-invested firms in the manufacturing sector increased from 25 per cent in 2001 to 32.3 per cent in 2005. In other words, one-third of the total assets of China's manufacturing sector were held by foreign-invested firms in 2005.

Among the three industry groups, foreign-invested firms in technology-intensive industries gained a greater share, and therefore, more importance than those in labour-intensive and capital-intensive industries in the manufacturing sector. By 2005 the share of foreign-invested firms in technology-intensive industries reached 44 per cent—increasing 11 percentage points over 2001 (Figure 11.4). The share in labour-intensive industries increased to 35 per cent in 2005—rising by 3 percentage points compared with 2001. The share in capital-intensive industries is still relatively low compared with those in technology-intensive and labour-intensive industries; however, it also increased—to 22 per cent in 2005, rising by 6.6 percentage points from 2001.

With such rapid growth, foreign-invested firms in some industries have already gained dominant or significant positions in the manufacturing sector. Foreign-invested firms have gained a dominant position in: leather and fur products (58.5 per cent); furniture manufacturing (57.5 per cent); cultural, educational and sports goods (63.7 per cent); and electronics and telecommunications equipment (71.9 per cent). The shares of foreign-invested firms have reached between 40 and 50 per cent of the industries' total assets in: clothing and other fibre products (46.6 per cent); paper and paper products (44.9 per cent); rubber products (45.4 per cent); plastic products (49.1 per cent); and instruments and meters (49.7 per cent).

The structure of foreign-invested firms in the manufacturing sector

Empirical studies have revealed that multinational enterprises, relative to indigenous firms, tend to concentrate their activities in sectors in which the

Figure 11.4 **Share of foreign-invested firms in manufacturing, 2001 and 2005** (per cent)

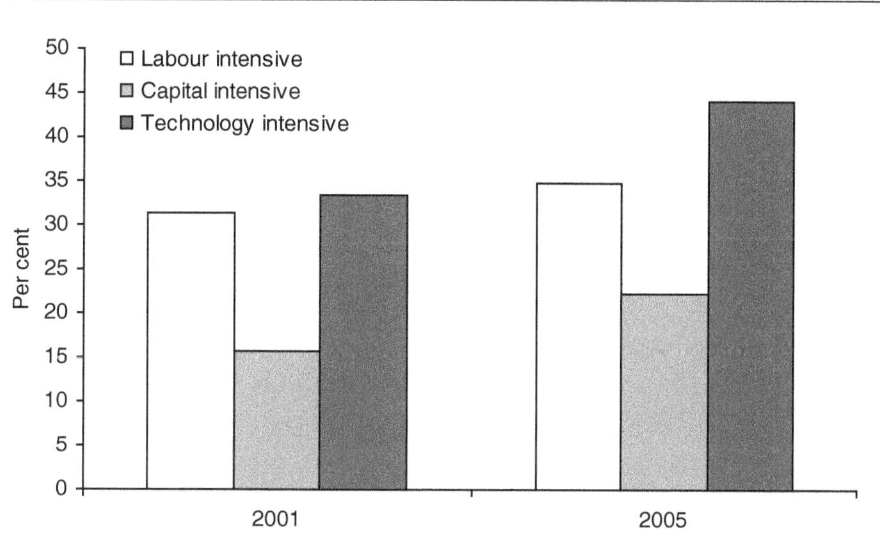

Source: National Bureau of Statistics, various issues (a). *China Statistical Yearbook*, China Statistical Press, Beijing.

revealed comparative advantage index is greater than one, or is increasing over time (Dunning 1993)—in other words, in the industries in which the country has a comparative advantage or the comparative advantage is increasing.

For developing economies, because they have a comparative advantage in labour-intensive activities, inward FDI flows usually concentrate in labour-intensive industries. In the case of China, in the early stage of FDI inflows into the manufacturing sector, foreign-invested firms were concentrated overwhelmingly in labour-intensive industries. By the end of 1995, in terms of the total assets of foreign-invested firms in the manufacturing sector, 47 per cent were in labour-intensive industries, while only 25 per cent and 27 per cent were in capital-intensive and technology-intensive industries respectively.

With rapid economic growth, a high level of capital accumulation, improvements in human capital development and technology progress, China's comparative advantage has changed rapidly. Though it still has a strong comparative advantage in labour-intensive activities due to its huge population and abundant labour supply, China has greatly increased its comparative advantages in capital-intensive and technology-intensive activities. As a result, FDI flows into China's manufacturing sector have shifted gradually from a high concentration in labour-intensive industries towards increasing investment in capital-intensive and technology-intensive industries.

By the end of 2001, the structure of foreign-invested firms in the manufacturing sector had changed. In terms of the total assets of such firms, the share in labour-intensive industries had fallen to 36 per cent, while shares in capital-intensive and technology-intensive industries had risen to 28 per cent and 36 per cent respectively.

Since China's accession to the WTO, FDI in its manufacturing sector has made even further and larger structural changes. Although a large amount of FDI still flows into labour-intensive industries, the share of such industries in the total assets of foreign-invested firms has continued to fall, while shares of capital-intensive and technology-intensive industries in the total assets have been increasing. By the end of 2005, the investment structure of foreign-invested firms in China's manufacturing sector had changed fundamentally (Figure 11.5). Technology-intensive industries have surpassed labour-intensive industries and become the most important and the largest sector in receiving FDI. In terms of the total assets of foreign-invested firms, the share of technology-intensive industries has increased to 40 per cent, while the share of labour-intensive industries has fallen to 31.02 per cent. Capital-intensive industries have also increased their importance in receiving FDI: the share has increased to 29.26 per cent of the total assets of foreign-invested firms.

In 2005, electronics and telecommunications equipment industries attracted the largest amount of FDI, accounting for 22 per cent of the total assets of foreign-invested firms, followed by transport equipment (9 per cent); chemical materials and products (7 per cent); electrical machinery and equipment (7 per cent); and textiles (5 per cent). Together, the above five industries held nearly 50 per cent of the total assets of foreign-invested firms. It is worth noting that, except for the textiles industry, the other four industries are all capital and technology intensive.

The above analysis reveals three important characteristics of FDI inflows into the manufacturing sector since China's accession to the WTO. First, such inflows have increased significantly. The growth rate of investment in the total assets of foreign-invested firms was more than twice as high as that of domestic firms.

Second, although FDI inflows into all three industry groups in the manufacturing sector increased dramatically, the growth rates of FDI inflows into technology-intensive and capital-intensive industries were much higher

Figure 11.5 **Structural changes of foreign-invested firms in manufacturing, 1995, 2001 and 2005** (per cent)

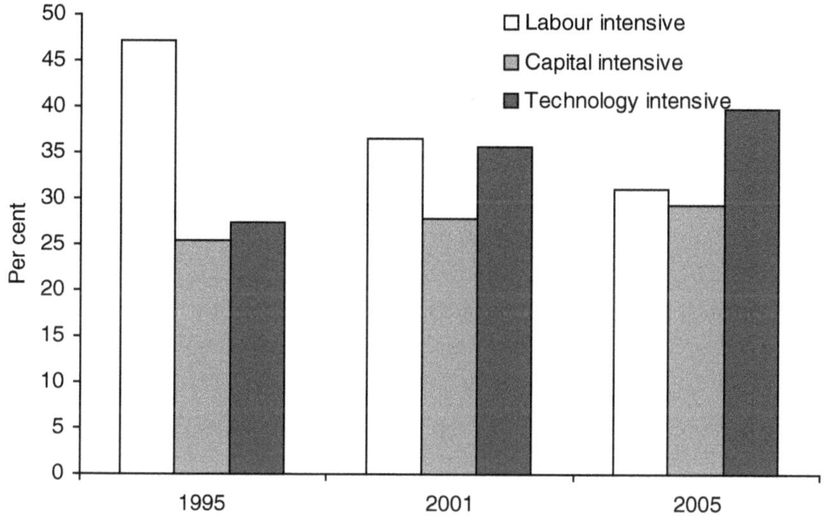

Source: National Bureau of Statistics, various issues (a). *China Statistical Yearbook*, China Statistical Press, Beijing.

than that into labour-intensive industries. As a result, the relative importance of foreign-invested firms in the three industry groups has changed: technology-intensive industries have surpassed labour-intensive industries. In 2005, foreign-invested firms in technology-intensive industries held 44 per cent of the total assets, while those in labour-intensive industries held 35 per cent of the total assets.

Third, FDI inflows into the manufacturing sector have gradually changed investment structures, shifting from a high concentration in labour-intensive industries towards increasing investment in technology-intensive and capital-intensive industries. As a result, the last two have become increasingly important to FDI, and, in 2005, their combined share reached 69 per cent of the total assets of foreign-invested firms in the manufacturing sector.

Several factors could be attributed to the changing structure of FDI in the manufacturing sector. First, China's changing pattern of comparative advantage in its economy has influenced the investment pattern. Although China still has a strong comparative advantage in labour-intensive activities, it has greatly increased its comparative advantages in capital-intensive and technology-intensive activities. As foreign-invested firms tend to invest in the industries in which the host country has a comparative advantage or in which the advantage is increasing, it is expected that China's increasing comparative advantage in capital-intensive and technology-intensive activities will attract increasing FDI inflows into these industries.

Second, through enterprise reform and intense competition, China's domestic firms have greatly improved their competitiveness. In 2005, the labour productivity of domestic firms in labour-intensive industries had surpassed that of foreign-invested firms in the manufacturing sector.[8] The increasing, fierce competition from domestic firms in labour-intensive industries has seen foreign-invested firms gradually losing competitiveness in such industries, pushing FDI towards capital-intensive and technology-intensive industries, in which foreign-invested firms have relatively strong competitiveness compared with domestic firms.[9]

Third, China has greatly improved its business environment and strengthened intellectual property protection, which has increased the confidence of foreign investors, encouraging them to bring more capital and technology through their investments.

Fourth, increasing per capita income and the enlargement of China's domestic market demand for high-quality goods attract increasing numbers of capital-intensive and technology-intensive multinational enterprises to China.

Conclusion

Since China's accession to the WTO, with the implementation of its WTO commitments and broader and deeper liberalisation in trade and investment, FDI inflows into China have resumed an upward trend.

Developing and industrialised economies have increased their investments in China. The growth rate of FDI inflows from developing economies is, however, much faster than that from industrialised economies. As a result, FDI inflows into China are still dominated by developing economies and the composition of FDI sources has barely changed. The increasing share of FDI inflows into China from other countries is, however, a positive indication of the diversification of FDI sources.

It is expected that China will remain an important host country for investments from developing economies into the future. It is also expected that with further implementation of its commitments to trade and investment liberalisation—particularly in strengthening intellectual property rights protection and opening more economic sectors, especially the services sector, to FDI—China will become an increasingly important host country for FDI from industrialised economies, which will increase the total and the quality of FDI inflows.

Since China's accession to the WTO FDI inflows are still concentrated overwhelmingly in the eastern region. Although there is an increasing trend of FDI inflows into the central region, inflows into the western region declined. The poor performance of the western region in attracting FDI inflows is attributed mainly to its poor investment environment. Although the Chinese government has undertaken massive investment projects to improve the overall investment environment in the west, the full effects will take a long time to materialise.

It was expected that with WTO accession and the opening up of the services sector, more FDI would flow into this sector. However, inflows have been increasing at a very slow pace. China made substantial commitments to the WTO to open its services sector to international trade and FDI, and has taken a step-by-step approach to implementation. In most of the services sectors, China will fulfil its commitments in three to five years after WTO accession. Therefore, it is unrealistic to expect that there will be a large immediate increase in FDI inflows into China's services sector. With further and full implementation of its commitments to the WTO, however, China will attract more FDI inflows into the services sector.

After China's accession into the WTO, FDI inflows continued to concentrate in the manufacturing sector. China's manufacturing is very competitive in attracting FDI inflows. It maintained its position as the number one destination for manufacturing and assembly in 2005 (A.T. Kearney Inc. 2007), and this sector will continue to attract large FDI inflows.

With the rapid increase in FDI inflows into manufacturing, foreign-invested firms in the sector have undergone some structural changes. Two changes are most important. First, the growth rate of FDI inflows into technology-intensive and capital-intensive industries was much higher than that of FDI inflows into labour-intensive industries. As a result, the relative importance of foreign-invested firms in technology-intensive industries has surpassed their relative importance in labour-intensive industries in the manufacturing sector. Second, the investment pattern of foreign-invested firms in manufacturing has been changing gradually. FDI inflows into the manufacturing sector have shifted from concentrating in labour-intensive industries towards increasing investment in technology-intensive and capital-intensive industries. As a result, the last two have become increasingly important to FDI.

In 2007, China passed the new corporate income tax law, which will take effect on 1 January 2008. The new law unified the tax rates for foreign and domestic enterprises at 25 per cent. It will bring China's tax laws closer to international standards and is a fulfilment of commitments to the WTO for equal treatment for domestic and overseas investors. Although meeting the WTO commitments will raise rates of taxation on foreign enterprises, it is not generally expected to have a significant effect on FDI in China. Its most important effect will be to reduce substantially the incentives for round-tripping, improving the quantity and quality of FDI inflows into the country.

Notes

1 China revised its GDP growth rate for the period 1979–2004 in January 2006. The revised rates for 2002, 2003 and 2004 were 9.1 per cent, 10 per cent and 10.1 per cent, respectively, and the GDP growth rates in 2005 and 2006 were 9.9 per cent and 10.7 per cent respectively.

2 The data are FDI inflows into non-financial sectors only. In 2005, China for the first time published the data for FDI inflows into its financial sector: they were US$12.1 billion in 2005 and US$6.5 billion in 2006.

3 According to this strategy, western areas include 12 provinces, municipalities and autonomous regions—Sichuan, Chongqing, Guizhou, Yunnan, Gansu, Shaanxi, Qinghai, Ningxia, Xinjiang, Tibet, Guangxi and Inner Mongolia—as well as two prefectures—Enshi of Hubei Province and Xiangxi of Hunan Province.

4 Data for real FDI inflows by sector are not available before 1997.

5 Technology-intensive industries include medical and pharmaceutical products; general machinery; special machinery; electrical machinery and equipment; electronics and telecommunications equipment; and instruments and meters.

6 Capital-intensive industries include beverage manufacturing; tobacco processing; paper and paper products; petroleum refining and coking; chemical materials and products; chemical fibres; ferrous metal smelting; non-ferrous metal smelting; and transport equipment.

7 Labour-intensive industries include food processing; food manufacturing; textiles; clothing and other fibre products; leather and fur products; timber processing; furniture manufacturing; printing; cultural, educational and sports goods; rubber products; plastic products; non-metal mineral products; and metal products.

8 The ratio of labour productivity of foreign-invested firms to domestic firms in labour-intensive industries in the manufacturing sector in 2005 was 0.93. Calculated from *China Statistical Yearbook 2006* (National Bureau of Statistics, various issues [a]).

9 The ratio of labour productivity of foreign-invested firms to domestic firms in capital-intensive and technology-intensive industries in the manufacturing sector in 2005 was 1.58 and 1.43 respectively. Calculated from *China Statistical Yearbook 2006* (National Bureau of Statistics, various issues [a]).

References

A.T. Kearney Inc., 2007. *2005 Foreign Direct Investment Confidence Index*. Available from www.atkearney.com

Breslin, S., 2003. Foreign direct investment in China: what the figures don't tell us, Paper presented at Asia-Link Conference, 'Regional governance: greater China in the 21st century', 24–25 October, University of Durham.

Chen, C., 2002. 'Foreign direct investment: prospects and policies', in *China in the World Economy: the domestic policy challenges*, Organisation for Economic Co-operation and Development, Paris:321–58.

——, 2006. 'Changing patterns in China's agricultural trade after WTO accession', in R. Garnaut and L. Song (eds), *The Turning Point in China's Economic Development*, Asia Pacific Press, The Australian National University, Canberra:227–55.

Dunning, J., 1993. *Multinational Enterprises and the Global Economy*, Addison-Wesley, Wokingham.

Harrold, P. and Lall, R., 1993. *China reform and development in 1992–93*, World Bank Discussion Paper, No.215, World Bank, Washington, DC.

He, Q., 2006. 'China's FDI policy is undergoing important changes' (in Chinese), *My China News Digest*, 12 November.

Hu, F., 1999. *Global economics*, Paper No. 14, 26 April, Goldman Sachs, New York.

McKibbin, W. and Wilcoxen, P., 1998. *The global impacts of trade and financial reform in China*, Working Paper 98-3, Asia Pacific School of Economics and Management, The Australian National University, Canberra.

Morisset, J., 2003. *Tax incentives: using tax incentives to attract foreign direct investment*, Note No. 253, Public Policy for the Private Sector, World Bank Group, Private Sector and Infrastructure Network. Available from http://rru.worldbank.org/Viewpoint/index.asp

National Bureau of Statistics (NBS), various issues (a). *China Statistical Yearbook*, China Statistical Press, Beijing.

——, various issues (b). *China Foreign Economic Statistical Yearbook*, China Statistical Press, Beijing.

Office of the West Development Leading Group of the State Council, 2000. *Guojia Zhichi Xibu Dakaifa de Youguan Zhengce Cuoshi (State's Relevant Policies and Measures on Supporting the Development of West Areas)*.

United Nations Conference on Trade and Development (UNCTAD), 2000. *World Investment Report: cross-border mergers and acquisitions and development*, United Nations, New York and Geneva.

——, 2007. *Rising FDI into China: the facts behind the numbers*, United Nations

Conference on Trade and Development Investment Brief No. 2, Investment Issues Analysis Branch, New York and Geneva. Available from http://www.unctad.org/

Walmsley, T. and Hertel, T., 2000. *China's Accession to the WTO: timing is everything*, Centre for Global Trade Analysis, Purdue University.

Wu, F., Siaw, P.T., Sia, Y.H. and Keong, P.K., 2002. 'Foreign direct investments to China and Southeast Asia: has ASEAN been losing out?', *Economic Survey of Singapore*, Third Quarter:102.

Xinhua News Agency, 2007. 'Parliament adopts corporate income tax', 16 March.

Xinwen Shishi, 2007. 'China's corporate income tax will be unified to 25%' (in Chinese), 8 March.

Zhang, Y., 2006. China's economic progress and its role in strengthening cooperation between East and South Asia, Paper prepared for the Asian Development Bank Research Project on Strengthening East and South Asia Economic Relations, Asia Development Bank, Manila.

12

China's demand for energy

A global perspective

Ligang Song and Yu Sheng

The surge in China's demand for energy in recent years raises some questions about the possible causes for the significant shift in the energy intensity of the Chinese economy at this stage of its industrialisation, as well as its long-term implications for future global supply of and demand for energy, and its potential impact on the environment. What has been the overall trend of world energy consumption in the past few decades? How does China's pattern of demand for energy fit into the normal pattern experienced by some other East Asian economies in the periods during which these economies were going through a similar stage of development? Has the increased energy intensity been driven primarily by China's ever increasing level of investment, which has reached an unprecedented scale in recent years? Or has it been caused by increases in domestic demand by households, resulting largely from rising per capita income propelled by reform and structural changes, including the unprecedented pace and scale of urbanisation?

Will China's pattern of energy consumption, which concentrates on coal, need to be changed radically in order for it to deal with its environmental issues while sustaining its economic growth in the long term? What kind of energy strategy does China need to adopt now in order to effectively reduce its current and future energy intensity to mitigate its impact on supply of world energy and prices as well as on the environment?[1] This chapter discusses these issues from a global perspective.

World demands for energy: the long-term trend and structural change

With steady economic and population growth in most countries and regions, the global demand for energy has maintained a rapidly increasing trend during the past four decades. It increased from a total world demand of 3.9 billion tonnes of oil equivalent in 1965 to 10.6 billion tonnes of oil equivalent in 2005—an increase of 2.7 times for the period (Figure 12.1). The average annual growth rate of world energy demand climbed to 2.6 per cent over the last 5 years, and is likely to continue to grow strongly for at least the next 25 years (IEA 2006).

This firm increase in demand for energy has helped fuel global economic growth but has also placed considerable pressure on many issues of public concern such as sustainable energy supply, national development security in importing countries and global environmental protection. In particular, how to reduce the dependency of economic growth on energy usage and especially on carbon emission-intensive energy usage, has become the focus of public debate and government policies in industrialised and developing economies.

Current world energy consumption exhibits two significant patterns of change. One is that fossil fuels (including crude oil, natural gas and coal) continue to dominate world energy consumption, meeting about 88 per cent of total consumption (Figure 12.2). For example, crude oil, natural gas and coal accounted for 37, 23 and 28 per cent respectively of total world energy consumption in 2005, while other energy products—such as hydropower, nuclear power, biomass, geothermal, solar, wind and other renewable energy products—accounted for only 12 per cent.

The second feature is that energy demand in industrialised countries including the United States, the European Union, Japan, Australia, New Zealand and Russia still accounted for more than half of the total energy demand (54 per cent of total consumption). The United States was the largest (22 per cent), followed by the European Union (16 per cent), Russia (10 per cent), Japan (5 per cent) and Australia and New Zealand (1 per cent). The energy demand from developing economies—including South Korea, Association of South-East Asian Nations (ASEAN) members, China and India—has taken the remaining 46 per cent share. Among these, China ranked top (15 per cent), followed by India (4 per cent), ASEAN members (3 per cent), South Korea (2 per cent) and the rest of the world (21 per cent). China has become the second largest energy consuming country in the world (Figure 12.3).

The rapid increase of energy demand and its increasing trend means the world faces two energy-related challenges: finding adequate and secure supplies of energy at prices that are consistent with economic stability; and environmental degradation caused by excessive fossil-fuel consumption.

Figure 12.1 **World primary energy consumption, 1965–2005** (billion tonnes of oil equivalent)

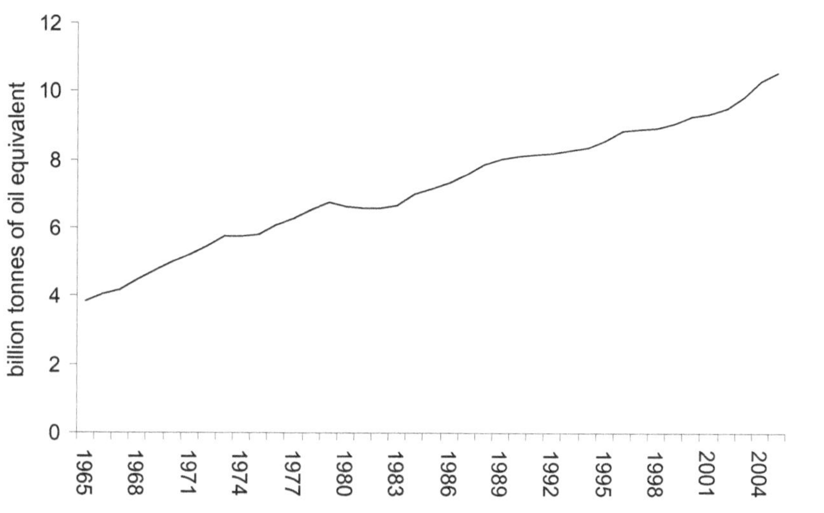

Note: Primary energy comprises commercially traded fuels only—excluded, therefore, are fuels such as wood, peat and animal waste.
Source: British Petroleum Global Limited (BP), 2006. *BP Statistical Review of World Energy*, 2006, British Petroleum Global Limited, London.

Figure 12.2 **World primary energy consumption structure, by product, 2005** (per cent)

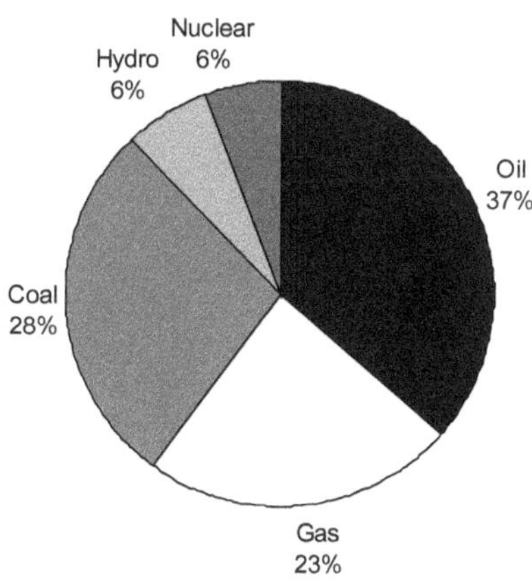

Note: Primary energy comprises commercially traded fuels only—excluded, therefore, are fuels such as wood, peat and animal waste.
Source: British Petroleum Global Limited (BP), 2006. *BP Statistical Review of World Energy*, 2006, British Petroleum Global Limited, London.

Against this background, the following characteristics of world energy demands can be observed.

First, global demand for cleaner energy products has been increasing more rapidly than that for traditional fossil-fuel products, suggesting that the pattern of global energy consumption is undergoing some environmentally favourable structural change. For example, in the period 1965–2005, the average annual growth rates of demand for natural gas, hydropower and nuclear power were 3.9, 3.2 and 108.1 per cent respectively (Figure 12.4). These growth rates were not only much higher than that of the average primary energy demand (2.7 per cent), they were higher than those for traditional fossil fuels such as crude oil and coal (2.5 per cent and 1.9 per cent respectively). In particular, the United States, the European Union, Japan and Russia have all significantly increased their use of natural gas and nuclear power while reducing their demand for coal. The structural change in favour of the use of cleaner energy products has been taking place mainly in industrialised countries.

Figure 12.3 **World primary energy consumption structure, by country, 2005** (per cent)

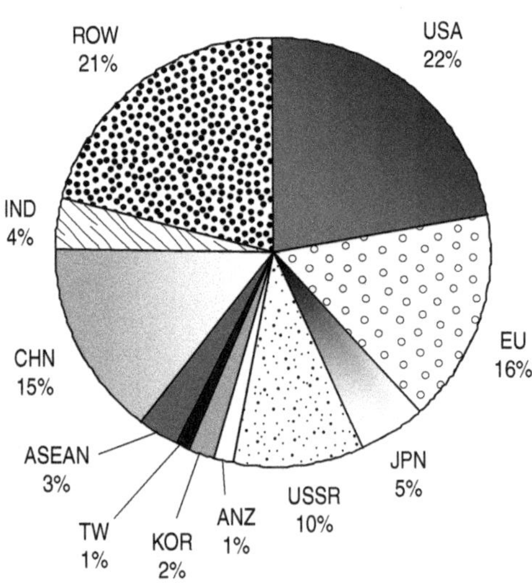

Note: Primary energy comprises commercially traded fuels only—excluded, therefore, are fuels such as wood, peat and animal waste.
Source: British Petroleum Global Limited (BP), 2006. BP Statistical Review of World Energy, 2006, British Petroleum Global Limited, London.

Second, developing economies—particularly the newly industrialised economies in East Asia—have shown a rapidly increasing trend of energy demand. In the period 1965–2005, the annual growth rate of energy demand in South Korea was 9.3 per cent, in Taiwan 7.2 per cent, among ASEAN members 7.3 per cent and in China 5.5 per cent—well above the world average annual growth rate of energy demand (2.5 per cent) during the same period (Figure 12.5). These rates were much higher than those in Japan (3.2 per cent), Australia and New Zealand (3 per cent), the European Union (1.5 per cent), the United States (1.4 per cent) and Russia (1.2 per cent).

Third, the newly increased demand from developing and newly industrialised economies focuses mainly on fossil fuels such as crude oil and coal. During the period 1965–2005, the annual growth rate of demand for crude oil in South Korea was 11.6 per cent, Taiwan 7.6 per cent, ASEAN members 5.8 per cent and China 8.8 per cent. The annual growth rate of demand for coal was 6.2 per cent in South Korea, 6.6 per cent in Taiwan, 16.7 per cent among ASEAN members

Figure 12.4 **World primary energy consumption structure, by product, 1965–2005** (million tonnes of oil equivalent)

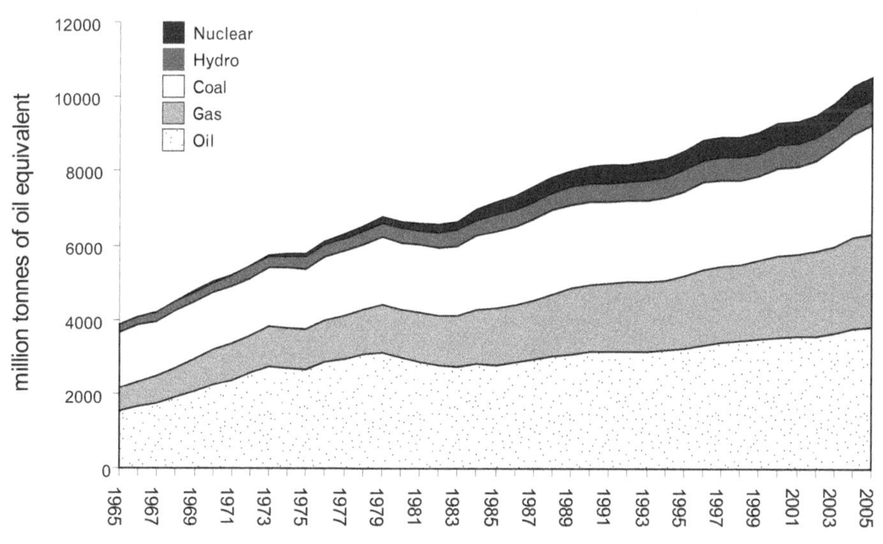

Note: Primary energy comprises commercially traded fuels only—excluded, therefore, are fuels such as wood, peat and animal waste.
Source: British Petroleum Global Limited (BP), 2006. *BP Statistical Review of World Energy*, 2006, British Petroleum Global Limited, London.

and 4.8 per cent in China. These rates were much higher than the global average growth rates for crude oil (2.3 per cent) and coal (1.7 per cent).

These trends provide evidence that the centre of gravity of global energy demand has been shifting from Organisation for Economic Co-operation and Development (OECD) countries—which were traditionally large consumers of fossil fuels—to East Asian developing economies. The developing economies in East Asia have had higher rates of economic and population growth than OECD countries. Underlying forces behind such a shift towards high energy intensity in these economies include rapid urbanisation, high investment shares of output and high and increasing export orientation. The same forces that worked for Japan, Korea and Taiwan in the past are now working for China; the only difference is the increasing absolute and relative size of the Chinese economy, which will magnify the impact on world markets beyond the high levels experienced in the recent past. For this reason, the strong growth in demand for energy in China is likely to continue through its period of rapid industrial transformation, which will be associated with strong economic growth, in the next two decades (Garnaut and Song 2006).

Due to the lack of domestic energy supplies and being in the catch-up phase of industrialisation, many economies in East Asia have had lower price and income elasticities for energy products than those in industrialised countries. As a result, they have become increasingly dependent on imports of energy from overseas, underlying changes in world energy prices. In fact, East Asian industrialisation was closely associated with two world oil price rises. One was in the 1970s—which occurred with rapid economic growth first in Japan, and then in Korea and Taiwan—and the other is the current one, to which China's growing economy has contributed (Figure 12.6). Another factor causing the price rise is that energy suppliers have been concentrating increasingly on certain countries or country groups such as Russia and the major Middle Eastern producers.

Compared with the price for oil, the surge in the price of natural gas has been more recent (Figure 12.7), reflecting the tendency of industrialised and developing economies to move towards cleaner energy options. World prices for coal were coming down from their peak in the 1970s, but started picking up again in this current resource boom (Figure 12.8). This trend is likely to continue, especially considering the fact that China—for the first time in recent decades—became a net importer of coal during the first quarter of 2007.

With the above trend of world energy demand identified, we can now have a close look at the changes of energy demand over time in China in order to explain its role in determining the changes in world energy demand and trade.

Figure 12.5 **World primary energy consumption structure, by country, 1965–2005** (million tonnes of oil equivalent)

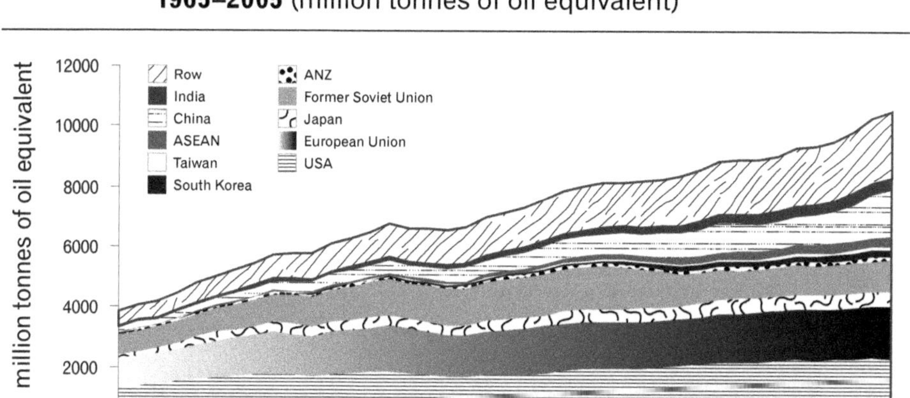

Note: Primary energy comprises commercially traded fuels only—excluded, therefore, are fuels such as wood, peat and animal waste.

Source: British Petroleum Global Limited (BP), 2006. *BP Statistical Review of World Energy*, 2006, British Petroleum Global Limited, London.

Figure 12.6 **World real price of crude oil, 1965–2007** (US$ per barrel)

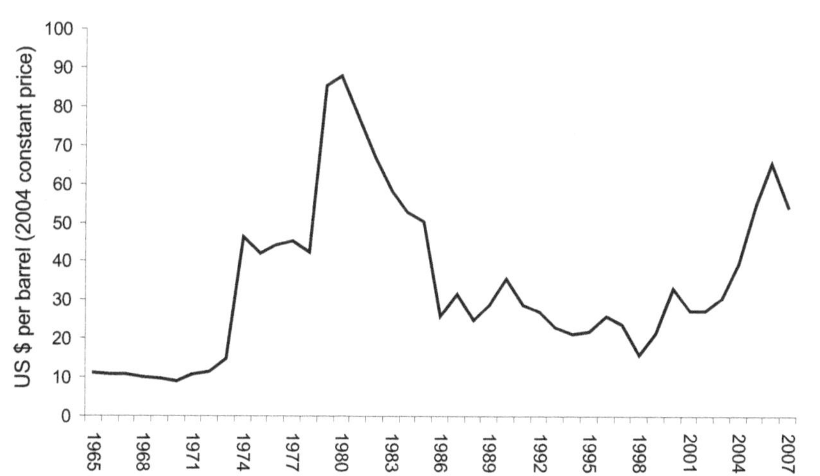

Note: The nominal price for the period 1965–83 is the US average and the nominal price for the period 1984–2007 is Brent dated.

Sources: British Petroleum Global Limited (BP), various issues. *BP Statistical Review of World Energy*, 1965–2005, British Petroleum Global Limited, London; International Monetary Fund (IMF), 2007. *International Financial Statistics*, 2006–07, International Monetary Fund, Washington, DC.

China's primary energy demand, supply and trade

With an annual gross domestic product (GDP) growth rate of about 10 per cent, on average, China's total primary energy consumption increased by 36.3 per cent in the past decade, reaching 1.6 billion tonnes of oil equivalent in 2005. China has now become the second largest energy consumer in the world. The share of China's primary energy consumption in the world increased from 4.7 per cent in 1965 to 14.7 per cent in 2005. China's share of the increase in world primary energy consumption increased from 4.4 per cent in the period 1965–70 to 12.6 per cent during the period 2000–05. In the past few years, the growth rate of primary energy consumption in China has accelerated (Figure 12.9),[2] prompting the Chinese government to set a target for improving energy efficiency by 20 per cent in the period 2006–10.

China's increasing demand for energy can be discussed by looking at the consumption pattern of different kinds of energy products. For example, its demand for coal has been driven by the need for electricity generation and industrial production, and China's rich endowment of coal means the product accounted for 70 per cent of total energy consumption growth during the period 1995–2005 (Figure 12.10).

Figure 12.7 **International real price of natural gas, 1985–2007**
(US$ per '000 cubic metres, 2004 constant prices)

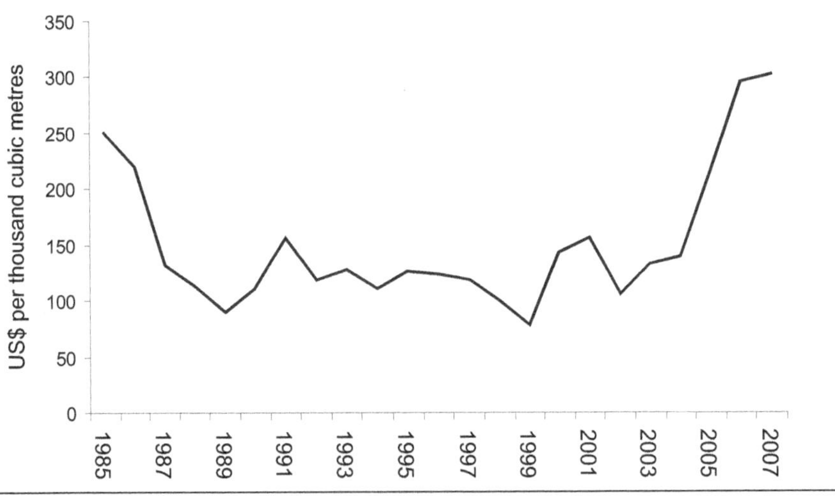

Note: The spot price of natural gas is the border price of Russian natural gas in Germany.
Source: International Monetary Fund (IMF), 2007. *International Financial Statistics, 2006–07*, International Monetary Fund, Washington, DC.

Figure 12.8 **Real prices of internationally traded thermal coal, 1967–2007** (US$ per metric tonne)

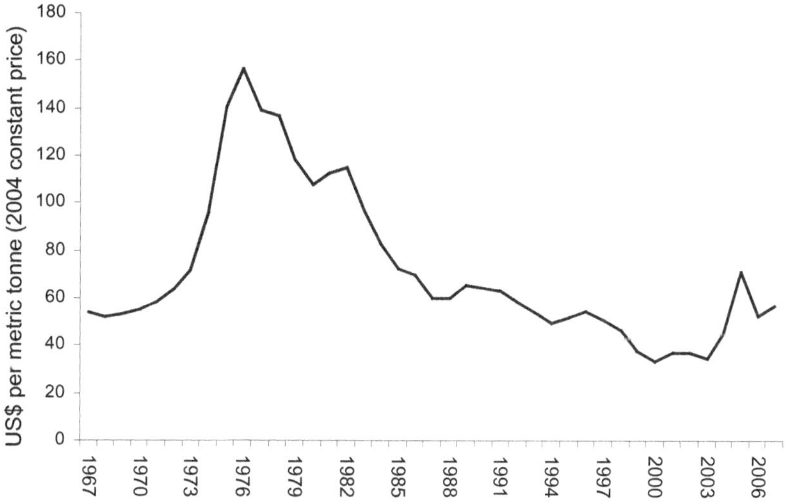

US$ per metric tonne (2004 constant price)
180
160
140
120
100
80
60
40
20
0
1967 1970 1973 1976 1979 1982 1985 1988 1991 1994 1997 2000 2003 2006

Note: The spot price of coal is the free-on-board (f.o.b.) price of Australian thermal coal—1,200 btu/pound, less than 1 per cent sulphur, 14 per cent ash—at Newcastle/Port Kembla.
Source: International Monetary Fund (IMF), 2007. *International Financial Statistics, 2006–07,* International Monetary Fund, Washington, DC.

Figure 12.9 **China's primary energy consumption structure, by product, 1965–2005** (million tonnes of oil equivalent)

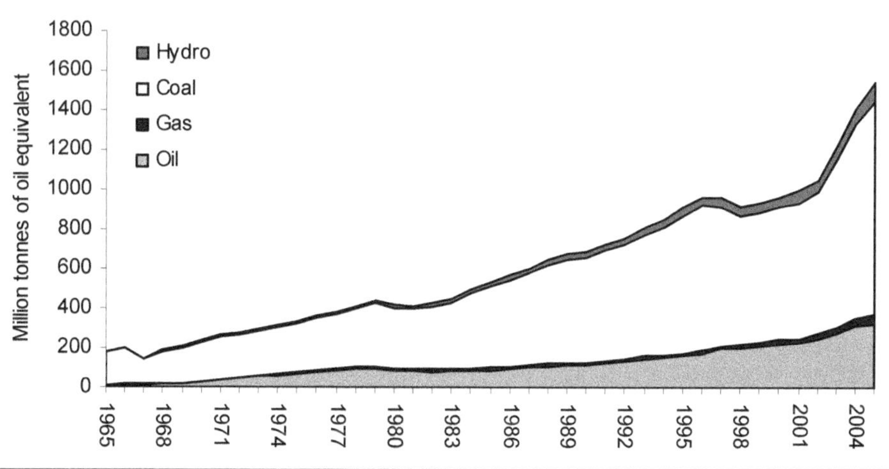

Source: British Petroleum Global Limited (BP), 2006. *Statistical Review of World Energy*, 2006, British Petroleum Global Limited, London.

China's demand for oil is a result largely of the rapid increase in vehicle ownership and industrial development, with oil accounting for 17.7 per cent of the total energy consumption growth in the same period. Other energy products—such as natural gas, hydropower, nuclear power and so on—account for the remaining 11.7 per cent. In 2005, the consumption of major energy products over the total primary energy consumption reached 21.1 per cent for crude oil, 69.6 per cent for coal, 5.8 per cent for natural gas, 2.7 per cent for hydropower and 0.8 per cent for nuclear power.

To meet its ever increasing demand for energy consumption, China has been intensifying production of all types of energy by increasing the total amount of investment in energy production. Figure 12.11 shows the share of investment in energy sectors over the total GDP in China during the period 1992–2004, in comparison with the world average shares during the same period.

The average ratio of investment in energy sectors to total GDP in China during the period 1992–2004 was 0.25 per cent—more than four times that of the world average, which was only 0.06 per cent during the same period. The highest ratio of investment in energy sectors in China reached a peak of 0.6 per cent in 1997. Although the East Asian financial crisis in 1997 had broken this trend by about 2000 and slowed the pace of investment in energy sectors, a new wave of investment in energy production in China seemed to accelerate after 2002.

As a consequence of the large-scale investment in energy, the production of various types of energy products in China increased significantly. Figure 12.12 shows the changes of the production of some major energy products in China during the past decade or so. With increased output from Western and offshore fields, crude oil production increased from 162 million tonnes of oil equivalent in 2000 to 181 million tonnes of oil equivalent in 2005. Coal production increased from 656 million tonnes of oil equivalent in 2000 to 1,107 million tonnes of oil equivalent in 2005. Natural gas production increased from 24.5 million tonnes of oil equivalent in 2000 to 45 million tonnes of oil equivalent in 2005, with an annual growth rate of more than 10 per cent—much higher than the average growth rate of 8.7 per cent during the previous three decades. With the Three Gorges Dam hydropower project completed—and other electricity-related construction in Guangdong and Guangxi Provinces—electricity generation has also increased, from 1,368 million tonnes of oil equivalent in 2000 to 2,474 million tonnes of oil equivalent in 2005. This trend of increasing capacity of electricity generation is continuing, with 60 gigawatts, or 2.5 per cent of established capacity, added annually.

Despite the rapid increase of energy production in China, the gaps between domestic supply and demand have been increasing, especially for crude oil

Figure 12.10 **Share of primary energy consumption growth, by product, 2000–2005** (per cent)

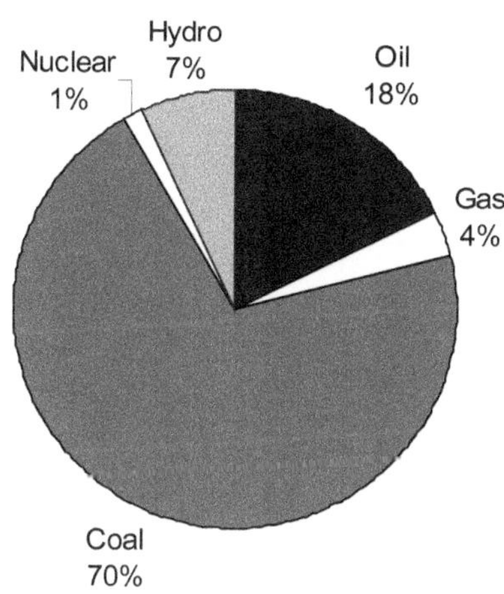

Source: Authors' calculations with data from British Petroleum Global Limited (BP), 2006. *Statistical Review of World Energy,* 2006, British Petroleum Global Limited, London.

Figure 12.11 **Comparison of investment shares in primary energy sectors between China and the world average, 1992–2004** (per cent)

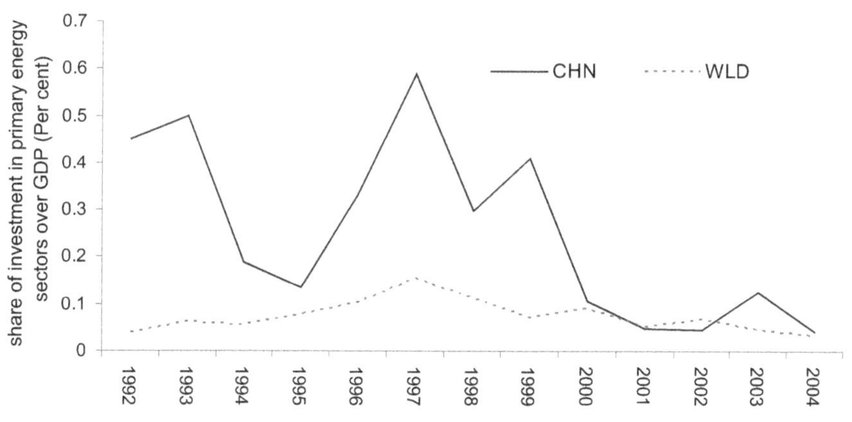

Source: World Bank, 2006. *World Development Indicators Online Database*, World Bank Group, Washington, DC.

and its products. These gaps will have to be met by imports. Between 1971 and 2003, China was a net energy exporting country. The situation has changed, however, since 1997, when the share of net imports of energy products of total energy consumption increased considerably—providing clear evidence that there has been an increasingly tight balance between energy demand and supply in China.

Figure 12.13 shows the net imports of crude oil, natural gas and coal, measured by the difference between their production and consumption during the past four decades. Since 1993, China has been a net importing country for crude oil and its related products and the average annual growth rate of net imports was 44 per cent, which was higher than that in any other country in the world in the same period. Although production of natural gas has exceeded its consumption in China since 1993, this gap has decreased significantly, with increased domestic demand after 2000. Coal is relatively more abundant than either crude oil or natural gas in China. With a significant increase in production of coal, it has almost met demands since 2000; however, owing to the substitution effect between coal and crude oil caused by rising oil prices in the world market, increases in demand for coal turned China into a net importer of coal by early 2007.

China is, therefore, becoming a new global centre of energy consumption—on par with the United States. Over time, a further increase in Chinese energy imports from the global market could add much more pressure to energy supplies and, consequently, prices—especially for fossil fuels—in China and the world. Thus, finding solutions to meet China's energy needs is not only important for China to sustain its long-term economic growth, it is critical to maintain market stability for energy products, which affects the global economy. These solutions are specified in China's eleventh Five-Year Plan on energy development, issued by the National Development and Reform Commission (NDRC) in April 2007. For these strategies to work effectively, it is useful to explore further how rising energy intensity in China at this phase of industrialisation has been determined.

China's economic growth and demand for energy

Economic growth impacts on the demand for energy in the following fashion. First, when economic growth increases GDP per capita in a country, the increased consumption per capita can generate additional demand for energy. For example, a rich country could consume more energy-intensive goods—such as appliances for cooling and heating, family automobiles, air transportation and so on—than less developed countries. The growth

Figure 12.12 **Production of crude oil, coal, natural gas and electricity in China, 1965–2005** (million tonnes of oil equivalent)

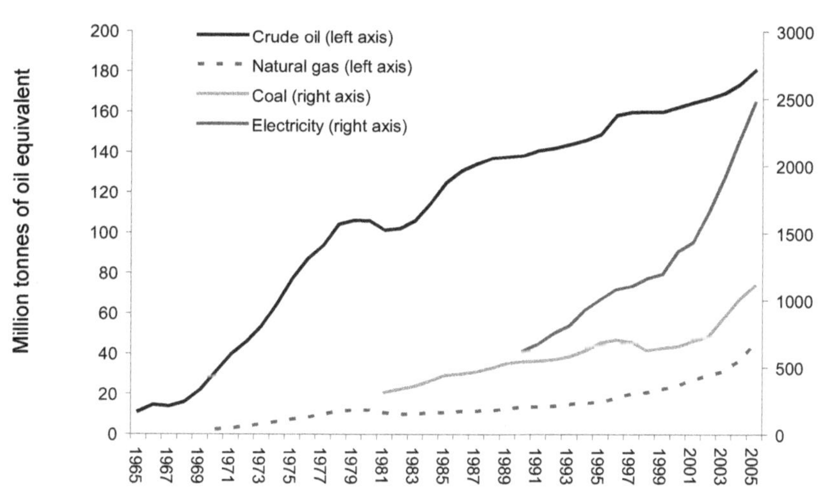

Source: British Petroleum Global Limited (BP), 2006. *Statistical Review of World Energy*, British Petroleum Global Limited, London.

Figure 12.13 **China's net imports of crude oil and coal, 1965–2005** (10,000 metric tonnes)

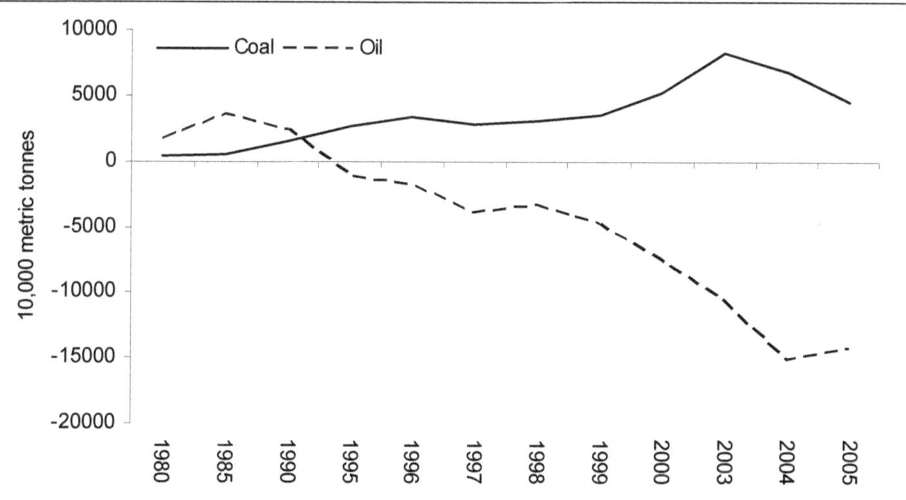

Note: Net imports are measured by the difference between consumption and production.
Source: British Petroleum Global Limited (BP), 2006. *Statistical Review of World Energy*, British Petroleum Global Limited, London.

pattern of this type of energy demand induced by economic growth is usually continuing and stable over time.

Second, when economic growth makes a country cross certain economic development stages, the adjustment in production technique and consumption pattern can lead to structural changes in energy demand. For example, when a country grows from a farming society into an industrialised society, it is expected that capital and energy-intensive industrial production will substitute for primary products or labour-intensive production and thereby generate a large demand for energy. This type of energy demand induced by economic structural changes usually takes place at an accelerated pace over certain periods of economic development. The two effects combined determine the level and scale of energy demand resulting from economic growth (or growth of GDP per capita) when population growth is controlled.

In linking changing patterns of energy demand to economic growth, most previous studies used the cross-country differences of consumption elasticity for energy (Fiebig et al. 1987; Churchill 1994; Brenton 1997; Garcia-Cerrutti 2000; Bernstein and Griffin 2005). The results obtained, however, vary and are hardly consistent. For example, Dahl (1992) argued that energy demand was price inelastic and slightly income elastic, but found no clear evidence that the developing world's energy demand was less price or more income elastic than for the industrial world. Churchill (1994) and Brenton (1997), using some cross-country estimations, found that the income elasticities of demand for energy products were higher in poorer countries than in wealthy countries. Such inconsistency in the previous studies leads us to think that this could be due to the different stages of economic development rather than country-specific characteristics that determine the changing pattern of energy consumption. To test this, we use the seven-country data for the period 1965–2005 to examine the impact of different economic development stages on primary energy consumption by using a demand function as specified below.

$$\ln C_{it}=\beta_0+\beta_1 \ln Y_{it}+\beta_2 \ln P_{it}+\beta_3 D_1+\beta_4 D_2+\beta_5 D_3+\beta_6 D_4+\beta_7 D_5+\beta_8 D_6 u_i+\varepsilon_{it} \quad (1)$$

where C_{it} stands for primary energy consumption (tonnes of oil equivalent), Y_{it} is GDP per capita with constant price (the 2000 US dollar price) and P_{it} is the real price of primary energy (the real price of crude oil). D_1 - D_2 denote different economic development stages, measured by GDP per capita following the method from Chenery et al. (1986). That is, we define that the primary industrialisation stage, D_1, equals one if GDP per capita is between US$1,138 and US$2,275 (with the 2000 constant price); the medium industrialisation stage, D_2, equals one if GDP per capita is between US$2,275 and US$4,550 (with the 2000 constant price); the advanced industrialisation stage, D_3, equals one if GDP per capita is between US$4,550 and US$9,100 (with the 2000 constant price); the primary developed economic stage, D_4, equals one if GDP per capita is between US$9,100 and US$17,063 (with the 2000 constant price); the advanced developed economic stage, D_5, equals one if GDP per capita is between US$17,063 and US$27,300 (with the 2000 constant price); and the post-development economic stage, D_6, equals one if GDP per capita is more than US$27,300 (with the 2000 constant price).

Using the regression estimation results, Figure 12.14 plots the predicted relationships between energy consumption intensity (consumption of the primary energy per capita) and GDP per capita (in the 2000 constant US dollar price). It is shown that when GDP per capita in a country rises from US$2,500 to US$10,000 (in particular, from US$3,000 to US$5,000), there will be significant increases in energy consumption per capita. Beyond the US$5,000 level of per capita income, energy consumption intensity will continue to rise, but at a slower pace. After a country reaches per capita income of US$10,000, increases in energy consumption intensity become slower still.

This result is consistent with the changes of energy consumption intensities in East Asia during the period 1965–2005 (Figure 12.15). For example, Japan experienced a dramatic increase in per capita energy consumption in the 1960s, while South Korea and Taiwan experienced a similar increase in the 1980s. ASEAN countries demonstrated a similar trend in the 1990s and China entered a phase of rapidly increasing energy intensity after 2000. Interestingly, most of these significant changes in energy consumption intensity took place when the countries' GDP per capita was within the range of US$3,000 to US$5,000 (in the 2000 constant price)—except Japan. This could suggest that different stages of economic development generate structural changes, which underlie the changes in countries' energy intensities. This finding helps us to judge how China's energy intensity will relate to the level of its per capita income, and to predict the future trajectory that China is likely to follow in increasing its energy intensity.

With per capita GDP of US$1,444 (in the 2000 constant price) in 2005, China entered a stage of development or industrialisation in which there would be a dramatic increase in its energy intensity in production. Following the estimates, we can predict that energy consumption will continue to accelerate at least until China reaches a per capita income level of US$5,000. Figure 12.16 compares energy consumption intensity in China with the world average of energy intensity during the period 1971–2005. The figure shows that a rapid increase in energy consumption intensity in China started to take place after 2000, driving Chinese energy consumption per capita above the one-tonne level.

Figure 12.14 **Estimated average primary energy consumption per capita across different stages of economic development** (per capita, tonnes of oil equivalent)

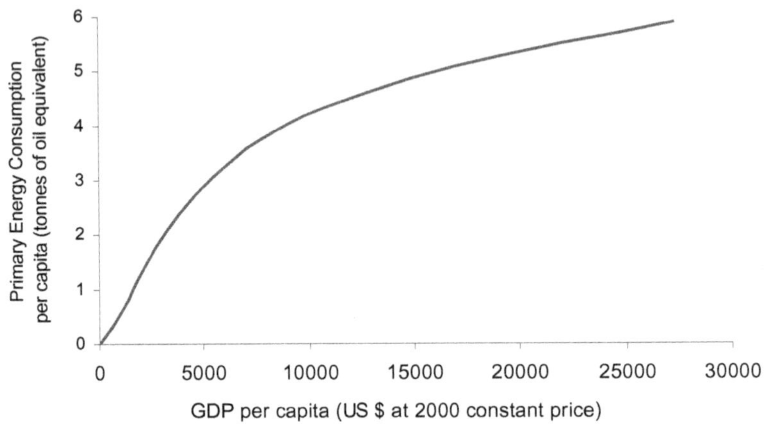

Sources: Authors' calculations using data from British Petroleum Global Limited (BP), 2006. *Statistical Review of World Energy*, British Petroleum Global Limited, London; Penn World Tables: Table 6.1.

Figure 12.15 **Primary energy consumption intensity in East Asia, 1965–2005** (per capita, tonnes of oil equivalent)

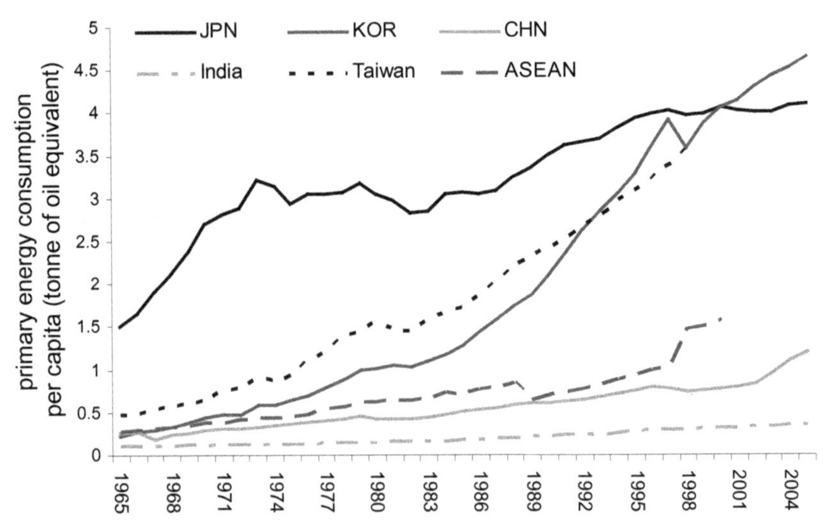

Sources: Authors' calculations using the data from British Petroleum Global Limited (BP), 2006. *Statistical Review of World Energy*, British Petroleum Global Limited, London; World Bank, 2006. *World Development Indicators Online Database*, World Bank Group, Washington, DC.

Moreover, a structural change analysis of energy consumption intensity, with the control of real income and price over time, can also be reflected using the accumulated CUSUM index (which ranges from zero to one).[3] The index is a set of procedures that can be used for testing for structural changes in the regression parameters. In applying this approach, emphasis is placed on graphical methods. A simple way of interpreting such a graph is to see whether the calculated indexes (the CUSUMS sequence) can cross the lines of given levels of significance. Such indexes are plotted in Figure 12.17, which shows that there is a breaking point at the turn of the new century, which indicates that China has entered a new phase of industrialisation in which structural changes with respect to its pattern of energy consumption intensity have been occurring. This breaking point in the changes in China's primary energy consumption is close to the time when its per capita income surpassed the mark of US$1,000—a clear signal that China has entered the new phase of industrialisation associated with increasing energy intensity.

Given the estimate of the International Energy Agency (IEA) of an annual growth rate in China of 6.4 per cent during the next 20 years, China's real GDP per capita could reach US$2,686 in 2015 and US$4,996 in 2025.[4] This essentially means—from what we have just described regarding the stages-of-development

Figure 12.16 **Comparison of primary energy consumption intensity between China and the world, 1971–2005**

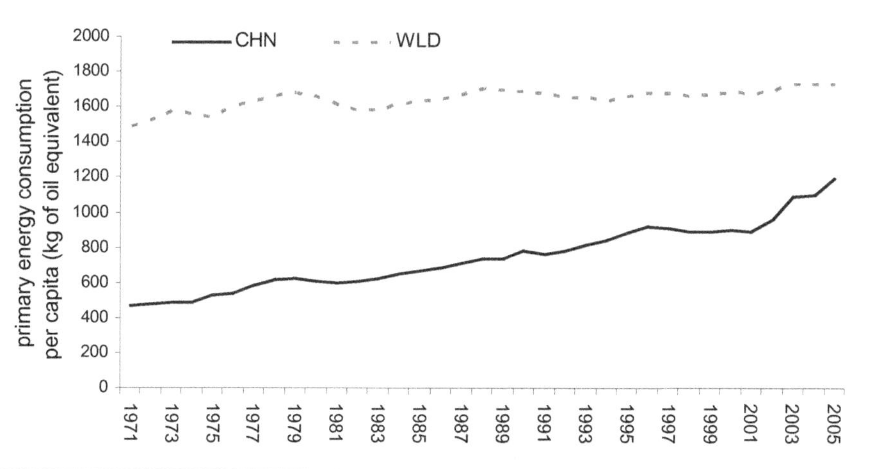

Sources: Authors' calculations using the data from British Petroleum Global Limited (BP), 2006. *Statistical Review of World Energy,* British Petroleum Global Limited, London; World Bank, 2006. *World Development Indicators Online Database*, World Bank Group, Washington, DC.

argument—that China's energy intensity will continue to rise at an accelerated pace in the next 15 to 20 years. This is largely because China has just entered a phase of industrialisation in which its industrial activities will concentrate mainly on those heavy industries that now consume about 54 per cent of China's total energy consumption—up from 39 per cent only five years ago (Rosen and Houser 2007). These conclusions would be even stronger if the IEA were to apply a higher, more realistic estimate of China's future growth rate.

Furthermore, with the rapid increase in per capita income, consumers' energy consumption has been increasing too, which has been boosted by household consumption such as for cooling and heating appliances and private vehicles and transportation. According to Rosen and Houser (2007), however, the commercial and transportation sectors won't surpass industry as energy demand drivers until a country reaches US$5,000 per capita GDP. By this criterion, the industrial sectors will continue to be the key drivers for energy

Figure 12.17 **Structural change of China's primary energy consumption (CUSUM index), 1968–2005**

Sources: Authors' calculations using the data from British Petroleum Global Limited (BP), 2006. *Statistical Review of World Energy*, British Petroleum Global Limited, London; World Bank, 2006. *World Development Indicators Online Database*, World Bank Group, Washington, DC.

consumption at least for the next 10–15 years. In that time frame, it is likely that the world will witness Chinese energy consumption per capita double—or more than triple if we think in terms of more realistic Chinese growth rates.

The environmental impact of the rising energy intensity in China will be enormous because the relatively high energy consumption intensities are associated closely with increases in greenhouse gas emissions. Such a prospect could be altered, of course, by improvements in technology, efficiency and the implementation of environmental policies and regulations that moderate growth in greenhouse gas emissions. One factor that makes it difficult for China to tackle its worsening environmental problems, however, is the composition of its energy consumption and production, which are dominated by coal. For example, according to China's eleventh Five-Year Plan on energy development (NDRC 2007), production of coal will continue to take the largest share (74.7 per cent) of China's total primary energy production by 2010, followed by oil (11.3 per cent), hydropower (7.5 per cent), natural gas (5 per cent) and nuclear power (1 per cent). By then, the share of coal production is forecast to drop only marginally, by 1.8 percentage points.

As a result, the IEA predicts that China will—from now until 2030—account for 40 per cent of the growth of global annual carbon dioxide emissions. These may turn out to be underestimates—bear in mind that this is based on estimates of Chinese economic growth that are only two thirds of those discussed in Chapter 1 as being relevant to the Platinum Age of economic growth.

The inefficient use of energy in China has worsened even further supply constraints and placed added pressure on the environment. China has made great progress in improving its energy efficiency, but there is considerable room for it to do more compared with the levels of energy efficiency in more advanced countries (Figure 12.18).

Given the rising energy demand and constraints on energy supply, China has made energy security the top priority of its energy policy goals. The eleventh Five-Year Plan delineates measures for the enhancement of energy security, with a strong emphasis on increasing investment in energy production and improving the efficiency of energy use.

To achieve the targets, a number of measures could be implemented (Bradley and Yang 2006). First, energy industries could by modernised by closing small and inefficient coal-mines and power plants and refineries with backward technology, while at the same time intensifying investment in the energy-production sector. Second, efficient technologies could be introduced into the process of energy consumption—from production and transportation to consumption. Small and inefficient iron and steel production plants could be closed. Third, sources of international energy supply could be diversified

Figure 12.18 **Primary energy consumption efficiency across countries, 1965–2005** (tonnes of oil equivalent per US$)

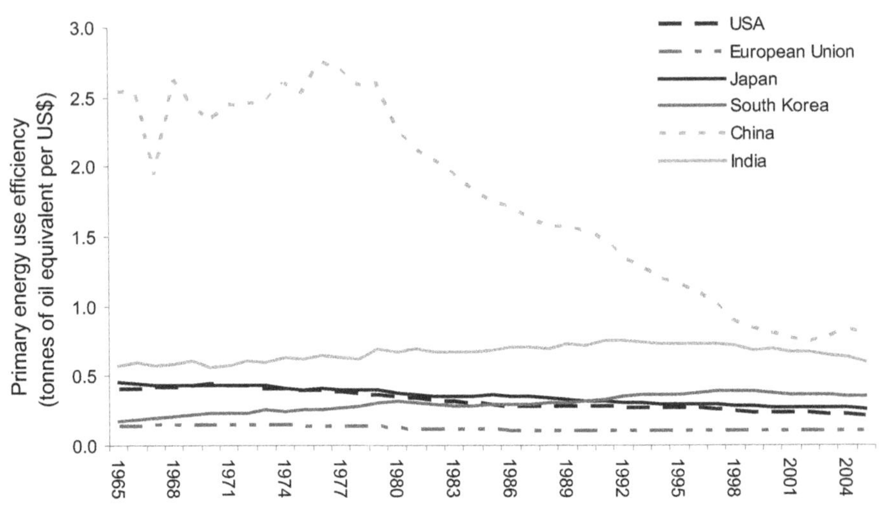

Source: World Bank, 2006. *World Development Indicators Online Database*, World Bank Group, Washington, DC.

Table 12.1 **Future growth of China's economy, energy consumption and CO2 emissions, 2000–2020 and 2020–2050** (per cent)

	2000–2020	2020–2050
Annual growth rate of GDP (per cent)	7.2	4.8
Annual growth rate of energy consumption (per cent)	4.3	1.7
Elasticities of energy consumption[a]	0.59	0.35
Annual decreasing rate of energy intensity of GDP (per cent)	2.8	3.0
Annual growth rate of CO2 emissions (per cent)	3.5	0.7
Annual decreasing rate of CO2 emissions intensity of GDP (per cent)	3.4	3.8

[a] Elasticities of energy consumption were calculated by dividing annual growth rate of energy consumption by annual growth rate of GDP.

Source: China, 2007. *National Assessment Report on Climate Change*, prepared by the Ministry of Science and Technology, China Meteorological Administration, and the Chinese Academy of Sciences, Scientific Publisher, Beijing:Table 22.3.

through multilateral and bilateral trade treaties. Fourth, current energy consumption could be diverted further from dirty, non-renewable fossil fuels to clean, sustainable energy—such as hydropower and nuclear power. Fifth, the energy price system could be reformed to enhance more efficient use of energy. Finally, new laws and regulations could be enacted to regulate exploration, production and consumption of energy, and their impact on the environment could be mitigated by designing and implementing an efficient, effective and fair pollution trading regime.

The adoption of these measures could pave the way for China to achieve its long-term objectives of economic growth, energy consumption and CO2 emissions (Table 12.1). According to this projection, China could reduce its emissions intensity of GDP by 42 per cent over the period 2006–20.

Conclusions

China, together with other East Asian economies and India, will increasingly become the new centre of global primary energy consumption and a major source of environmental pollution in the next 20 years. Previous studies on energy seem to have underestimated the potential impact of China's economic growth on the balance of energy supply and demand. In particular, previous studies tended to neglect the incremental energy demand from China resulting from the shift from a lower economic development stage to a more advanced stage of industrialisation as well as understating likely economic growth rates. Increasing investment in energy production and improvements in energy efficiency could help to alleviate the pressure of balancing energy supply and demand in the short term. Seeking new sources of energy through technological innovations and international economic and technological cooperation would, however, be an important long-term solution to the dilemma of maintaining the sustainability of economic growth while protecting the environment.

Notes

1 China is considering seriously such a strategy as it overtook the United States in carbon dioxide emissions by 8 per cent in 2006 according to a report released by the Netherlands Environmental Assessment Agency on 19 June 2007.

2 China's energy demand elasticity—which is the ratio of energy demand growth to GDP growth—increased from less than 0.5 between 1978 and 2000 to 1.5 between 2001 and 2006 (Rosen and Houser 2007).

3 See Brown et al. (1975) and Maskus (1983) for the technical details for applying this approach, and see Johnston (1984) for the statistical tests and interpretation of these indexes.

4 These are rather conservative estimates compared with most forecasts of 7–8 per cent annual growth rates in the Chinese economy during the next decade or so (see, for example, Maddison 2006).

References

Bernstein, M.A. and Griffin, J., 2005. Regional differences in the price elasticity of demand for energy, Technical Report TR-292-NREL, Rand Corporation, Santa Monica.

Bradley, R. and Yang, M., 2006. *Raising the profile of energy efficiency in China—case study of standby power efficiency*, Organisation for Economic Co-operation and Development/International Energy Agency Working Paper, No. 2006/01, Paris.

Brenton, P., 1997. 'Estimates of the demand for energy using cross-country consumption data', *Applied Economics*, 29:851–9.

British Petroleum Global Limited (BP), various issues. *BP Statistical Review of World Energy*, 1965–2005, British Petroleum Global Limited, London.

——, 2006. *BP Statistical Review of World Energy*, 2006, British Petroleum Global Limited, London.

Brown, R., Durbin, J. and Evans, J., 1975. 'Techniques for testing the constancy of regression relationships over time', *Journal of the Royal Statistical Society*, Series B37:149–92.

Chenery, H., Robinson, S. and Syrquin, M., 1986. *Industrialisation and Growth: a comparative study*, published for the World Bank by Oxford University Press, Oxford.

China, 2007. *National Assessment Report on Climate Change*, prepared by the Ministry of Science and Technology, China Meteorological Administration, and the Chinese Academy of Sciences, Scientific Publisher, Beijing.

Churchill, A.A., 1994. 'Energy demand and supply in the developing world, 1990–2020: three decades of explosive growth', *Proceedings of the World Bank Annual Conference on Development Economics 1993, Supplement to World Bank Economic Review*:441–58.

Dahl, C., 1992. *Energy and energy product demand elasticities for the developing world: a survey of the econometric evidence*, Working Paper 92-14, Department of Mineral Economics, Colorado School of Mines.

Fiebig, D.G., Seale, J. and Theil, H., 1987. 'The demand for energy: evidence from a cross-country demand system', *Energy Economics*, 9:149–53.

Fridley, D., Sinton, J. and Lewis, J., 2003. 'Working out the kinks: understanding the fall and rise of energy use in China', *Oxford Energy Forum*, No.AC03-76SF00098.

Garcia-Cerrutti, L.M., 2000. 'Estimating elasticities of residential energy demand from panel county data using dynamic random variables models with heteroskedastic and correlated error terms', *Resource and Energy Economics*, 22(4):355–66

Garnaut, R. and Huang, Y., 2005. 'The risks of investment-led growth', in R. Garnaut and L. Song (eds), *The China Boom and its Discontents*, Asia Pacific Press, The Australian National University, Canberra:1–18.

Garnaut, R. and Song, L., 2006. 'China's resources demand at the turning point', in R. Garnaut and L. Song (eds), *The Turning Point in China's Economic Development*, Asia Pacific Press, The Australian National University, Canberra:276–93.

International Energy Agency (IEA), 2006. *World Energy Outlook*, Organisation for Economic Co-operation and Development/International Energy Agency, Paris.

International Monetary Fund (IMF), 2007. *International Financial Statistics*, 2006–07, International Monetary Fund, Washington, DC.

Johnston, J., 1984. *Econometric Methods*, Third edition, McGraw-Hill Book Company, New York.

Maddison, A., 2006. 'Asia in the world economy 1500–2030 AD', *Asian–Pacific Economic Literature*, 20(2):1–37.

Maskus, K.E., 1983. 'Evidence of shifts in the determinants of the structure of US manufacturing foreign trade', *Review of Economics and Statistics*, 65:415–24.

National Development and Reform Commission (NDRC), 2007. *Eleventh Five-Year Plan on Energy Development*, April, Beijing.

Netherlands Environmental Assessment Agency, 2007. 'China now no. 1 in CO2 emissions; USA in second position', Press Release, 19 June, The Netherlands Environmental Assessment Agency, Wageningen. Available from http://www.mnp.nl/en/service/pressreleases/2007

Penn World Tables. Centre for International Comparisons, University of Pennsylvania. Available from http://pwt.econ.upenn.edu

Rosen, D.H. and Houser, T., 2007. *China Energy: a guide for the perplexed*, Peterson Institute for International Economics, Washington, DC.

Scandklef, K., 2004. *Energy in China: coping with increasing demand*, Working Paper, No. SE-17290, FOI Swedish Defence Research Agency, Stockholm.

Smil, V., 1998, 'China's energy and resource uses: continuity and change', *The China Quarterly*, 31(3):935–51.

World Bank, 2006. *World Development Indicators Online Database*, World Bank Group, Washington, DC.

Acknowledgments

Funding for the research described in this chapter is from the Australian Research Council Linkage Project Grant No LP0775133.

13

Crouching bull, hidden bear

The Chinese equities markets in fat years and lean years

Ted Rule

When I last visited the Chinese stock exchanges two years ago, they were in dire straits (Rule 2005). The market indices had been in decline since 2001. In May 2005, the Shanghai Index stood at 1,060—less than half of its 2001 peak of 2,245. During 2005, the Shenzhen and Shanghai exchanges were two of the three worst performing exchanges in the world, with year-on-year declines of 11.7 per cent and 8.3 per cent respectively. Only the Tehran Stock Exchange performed worse (World Federation of Exchanges 2007a). In terms of market capitalisation, the once great Shanghai Exchange had slumped to nineteenth in the world, similar in size to Singapore but significantly smaller than the Mumbai and National Stock Exchanges of India (World Federation of Exchanges 2007a). Key price–earnings ratios had declined from their peak of 37.7X in 2001 to 16.3X in 2005 (World Federation of Exchanges 2007a). As Chinese companies made up an ever-greater proportion of the Hong Kong board, such declines in price–earnings ratios started to influence the less volatile Hong Kong ratios. Hong Kong price–earnings ratios fell from a high of 19X in 2003 to 15.6X in 2005 (World Federation of Exchanges 2007a).

Even though the Chinese economy continued to be the fastest growing major economy in the world and the world's largest recipient of foreign direct investment (FDI), the role of the Shanghai and Shenzhen markets in mobilising new capital declined drastically. This was due partly to a ban on new initial public offerings (IPOs). But it seems doubtful whether market conditions were conducive to successful IPOs even if they had been permitted. At US$3.6 billion raised, Shanghai ranked twenty-fourth among world exchanges in terms of capital raised. This was a little more than Tel Aviv, less than Oslo, Athens or Tehran and significantly less than the Indian exchanges, which raised US$19 billion between them. Shenzhen raised a mere US$351 million in new capital in 2005 and not a single cent was raised in secondary issues. Only Colombo, Budapest and Ljubljana exchanges performed worse. Turnover in Shanghai and Shenzhen declined by 26 per cent and 20.6 per cent respectively in the already disappointing 2004 figures (World Federation of Exchanges 2007b).

This was not a happy picture. Indeed, the mood around regulators and other government bodies associated with the markets was growing increasingly frantic. Too many ordinary people had lost too much money speculating on stocks and the spectre of social unrest loomed. In May 2005, there was a series of meetings around the country to discuss measures to stimulate the markets. It was hoped that these measures would return a northerly aspect to the figures and, hopefully, a smile to the faces of the tens of millions of retail investors. Measures proposed even included an extraordinary suggestion that the government should establish a fund to stimulate the market.[1]

Hong Kong gathers strength

Meanwhile, outside the closed shop of the two domestic markets, life went on as normal. The economy was growing at 10 per cent per annum, there was an enormous demand for expansion and other capital and it was being met from the markets. Hong Kong, however, was the market supplying this demand. In 2005, the previous mould of international capital raising was broken and Hong Kong started to come into its own as China's capital gateway to the world and one of the world's leading exchanges.

In 2005, three of the five largest IPOs in the world were of Chinese companies on the Hong Kong exchange (Table 13.1).

Despite the weakness in the Chinese domestic markets and the slump in IPO and secondary raising activity, China dominated Asian IPO activity in 2005. More than half of the US$41 billion raised in Asian IPOs was raised by Chinese companies. This was almost four times the amount raised by Japanese companies and 10 times the amount raised by Indian companies (Table 13.2).

Partly as a result of all this Chinese activity, Hong Kong became the fourth largest capital-raising exchange in the world after New York, London and Toronto (Toronto was boosted by the boom in minerals raisings resulting from Chinese demand for resources). Professionals commented, 'This marks a new era, not just for China but for the global capital markets in general. By listing in Hong Kong and selling tranches of shares to qualified investors in the US and Europe, Chinese companies have sidestepped traditional assumptions that the only way for large corporations to gain access to global capital pools was to complete a full US listing' (Ernst and Young 2006a).

Thus the problem did not lie with the Chinese economy. The economy was fine. It did not mean that there was a limited demand for capital, nor did it mean that foreign suppliers of capital were not interested in Chinese paper. The enormous success of Hong Kong-based Chinese IPOs at the nadir of the domestic markets gave the lie to that proposition. The problem lay within the Shanghai and Shenzhen markets themselves.

The long decline

It is appropriate at this juncture to restate the reasons I enumerated in my previous paper (Rule 2005) for the decline of the domestic markets. Essentially, there were three reasons.

- The markets had been overpriced and were due for a serious correction. At the peak in 2001, Shanghai average price–earnings ratios were 37.7X and Shenzhen's were averaging 39.8X—the same ratio as applied in Tokyo in 1990 close to the peak of the Japanese bubble.[2] This overpricing was ascribed variously to market immaturity and lack of a large institutional sector.
- There was too much money chasing too little product. This was because of a regulatory system that rationed IPO slots and took listing decisions out of the hands of underwriters and others who took the actual IPO risk. A 2000 decision partly resolved this problem by giving more weight in deciding who should go to IPO to the people who took the underwriting risk. This put further downward pressure on prices.
- The market was seriously spooked by a 2001 decision to experiment

Table 13.1 **Leading international IPOs, 2005**

	Domicile	Industry	Proceeds (US$ billion)	Primary exchange
China Construction Bank	China	Banks	9.2	Hong Kong
Electricité de France	France	Power	8.2	Euronext
Gaz de France	France	Power	4.2	Euronext
China Shenhua Energy	China	Mining	3.3	Hong Kong
Bank of Communications	China	Banks	2.2	Hong Kong

Source: Ernst and Young, 2006a. *Accelerating Growth—Global IPO Trends 2006*, Ernst and Young.

Table 13.2 **IPO activity in Asia, 2005** (capital raised by nationality of firm)

Domicile	Total capital raised (US$ million)	Number of IPOs
China	24,263	114
Japan	6,231	157
South Korea	2,903	83
India	2,283	53
Malaysia	1,406	83
Kazakhstan	1,362	2
Thailand	721	37
Singapore	505	33
Other	1,524	69
Total	41,199	631

Source: Ernst and Young, 2006a. *Accelerating Growth—Global IPO Trends 2006*, Ernst and Young.

with selling down state-owned shares. The two-thirds of Chinese-listed company shares owned by the state in one form or another were non-tradable and would never come to market. On 12 June 2001, a modest proposal was implemented that would see a limited sell-down of state shares. Under the proposal, new IPOs of state-owned enterprises would sell down a block of 10 per cent of existing state shares with the proceeds going to the Social Security Fund. No existing listed company was affected. This scared the market and marked the beginning of the decline. The market was afraid of enormous amounts of state paper flooding the board and leading to a collapse in value.

In April 2005, the China Securities Regulatory Commission (CSRC) announced the 'experimental' conversion of the non-tradable shares of three listed companies to tradability, and in June a further 42 companies joined the 'experiment'. This marked the nadir of the domestic markets.

This, possibly coincidentally, marked the bottom of the Chinese bear market. Four years of decline were replaced by a boom, which continues today. The markets remain spritely and extremely volatile, subject to violent movements on whim, rumour and occasional manipulation. Although the domestic markets are back, Hong Kong has strengthened its position as the 'big brother' of the Chinese equities market.

But there are signs of a growing maturity. Lots of ordinary people were hurt badly during the bear market and are no longer so eager to believe in their own invincibility or to rely on their own judgement. This has led to the growth of a fledgling institutional sector—especially in the area of mutual funds—a concept that Chinese retail investors have adopted with characteristic gusto. And, for a brief moment in March 2007, even mighty Wall Street trembled momentarily in response to sentiment on the east bank of the Whangpoo River and on the Shanghai Bund.[3]

Before looking at the boom, however, let us examine some of the factors that helped put a bottom on the bear market. These were the resolution for the time being of the non-tradable share issue, growth of mutual funds and the introduction of sophisticated hedging instruments to help manage risk.

Administrative measures

The key administrative measure adopted to revive the Chinese share markets was the reform of the state shareholding system. This is usually referred to as the non-tradable share reform. This reform did not mean the complete privatisation of state-held shares, although this is what was feared most by shareholders. Not even all state shares were held directly by the state. Many 'state' shares were held by incorporated bodies, which, as registered businesses, had 'legal-person' status. This artificially created some of the benefits of share ownership, even though the ultimate owner was still the state. Directly held state shares were also held at different levels of government, and were 'owned' and managed by different levels of State Assets Supervision and Management Commissions. Centrally held shares were managed by the Central Commission, provincially held shares were managed by the Provincial Commissions and so on. Some owners of non-tradable shares were private individuals and even foreigners. The Chinese Companies Law locked up the shares of sponsor organisations.

When the non-tradable share issue first came to public notice in 2001, the occasion that brought it to the fore was a proposal to prop up the State Pension Fund and the State Social Security Fund by a small sell-down of state shares and the allocation of 10 per cent of the state's holdings in future IPOs to those funds. Using state share holdings to capitalise the Social Security Funds remains a subject of active debate today (*The People's Daily* 2006a), however, the objective of the reform was never mass privatisation and a sudden dumping of state shares on the market.

The objective of the non-tradable share reform was the further extension of the benefits of the shareholding system to state-owned listed companies. Because their shares were non-tradable, state-owned companies were unable to enjoy two of the benefits of the shareholding system: they could not cash out their holdings and apply the proceeds to other purposes, and they were immune from takeover pressure. This reduced the influence of minority opinion on business decisions. Some state-owned companies had quite varied registers of legal-person owners and state owners at different levels. Since these shares were non-tradable, however, the legal-person owners were unable to cash out in the event of poor share performance or a takeover offer. This meant that sometimes quite small controlling interests could afford to ignore the interests of large minority shareholders. Share price performance was clearly an issue for listed companies that wished to maintain access to the capital markets, but there was never that sinking realisation that the market might decide that its interests were better served by having a different person looking after its investment.

Chairman Shang Fulin and his colleagues at the CSRC undertook the delicate task of introducing an essential reform, which the market was very afraid of. The delicacy of the task was compounded by its timing. The market had been declining for four years and the index was at less than half of its peak.

Fear and greed

Fear

Chairman Shang is an interesting character. He has never been considered one of the intellectual or policy powerhouses of the Chinese financial system, but he was often the man whom Zhu Rongji called on to fix unfixable problems in the financial system. His first navigation of shark-infested waters was in 1994 when he resolved the issue of triangular debt between state-owned enterprises—an issue that had threatened to paralyse the whole payments system. In 2000, he was made Governor of the Agricultural Bank, which was still the weakest of the state-owned banks. There he made and carried through several of the most difficult decisions, including closing 3,000 branches and laying off 50,000 staff.

Shang understood that in dealing with shareholders it was necessary to deal simultaneously with the conflicting emotions of fear and greed. On 27 June 2005, Shang addressed the issue of fear. He announced that the aim of the reform was not to sell out all non-tradable shares on the market but to eliminate the trading right differential. 'Making all shares tradable doesn't mean selling out all shares,' he commented (ChinaPaper Online 2007). Any sales of state shares would have to be approved by the State Assets Supervision and Management Commission. There would be guidelines specifying the amount of shares that should remain in state hands at any time and also lock-ups. He was commenting on the 'Notice regarding the issue of experimenting with reforms to the split-share structure of listed companies' (CSRC 2004). Under this notice, the method of making shares tradable was to be decided by the company itself. The method had to be approved by not only a full EGM, but two-thirds of attending tradable shareholders. Flotation of the shares on the market was forbidden in the first year of reform and limited to 5 per cent of outstanding shares in the second year.

A further decision also expanded the pool of capital available for buying shares held by the public. It was decided that state-owned enterprises could expand their holdings in companies by buying shares held by the public. This put the public and the state on an equal footing and gave the public a potentially large buyer. The basic rationale appears to have been to allow controlling shareholders to buy in the market, thus holding up market prices in case small shareholders began dumping stock after the reforms.

The issue of foreign shareholders holding non-tradable shares in listed companies was also addressed. On 7 November, it was announced jointly by the CSRC and the Ministry of Commerce that foreign strategic investors would be able to enter Chinese companies by buying previously untradable 'A' shares from state and other sources. 'A' shares had previously been available to foreigners only via Qualified Foreign Institutional Investors (QFIIs). This was subject to various lock-up arrangements but potentially significantly widened and deepened the market (Ministry of Commerce 2007). Foreign stakes of more than 25 per cent would attract normal Sino–foreign joint-venture privileges.

Greed

This successfully addressed the fear issue. The issue of greed was addressed by simply throwing large amounts of money at public shareholders. Each reforming company was to compensate tradable shareholders for potential losses that might be incurred in the reform process. Each company was to make its own decisions on the quantum and form of compensation, subject to approval by the CSRC. Compensation took the form of cash, bonus shares and other measures. Many of these compensation schemes were extremely generous to minority shareholders, especially in the early stages. A couple of examples demonstrate this. One of the first companies to float its non-tradable shares, Sany Heavy Industries, offered three free shares plus 8 yuan in cash for every state share sold (*South China Morning Post* 2001). Jiangxi Changli Automobile Spring offered 3.5 shares for every state share floated; Zhuhai Huafa Industrial offered three shares for every state share floated; and Aeolus Tyre Company Limited offered holders of its non-tradable shares 4.2 shares for every 10 owned (Forbes.com 2007a). Generally speaking, between two and five shares' compensation was offered for each state share floated.

Warrants were offered for the first time as part of this compensation package. They were warmly welcomed by investors and quickly became an integral part of the market mix. Indeed, market wisdom was that when a company completed its reform, share prices immediately went up.

It is hard to look at the skill with which these very fundamental reforms were carried out without some feeling of admiration. Far from causing a market collapse, the reforms sparked off the boom that continues today. After the first three experimental conversions in April 2005, there came 42 firms in June 2005. Many of these were newly listed firms from the Shenzhen small and medium enterprise (SME) board. The logic appears to have been that many of them already had substantial private participation and they would thus require less change in their structures.

Then the reform started in earnest. Each week, two or three companies would announce their reform plans. By late November 2006, Qi Bin, the research director of the CSRC, could report that 90 per cent of listed firms had resolved their non-tradable share issues. This was spread across 1,161 companies representing 96 per cent of the market capital of the Shanghai and Shenzhen listed companies. One hundred and thirty companies had still not complied with the CSRC's requirements but most of these had either 'huge losses' or had their shares used as collateral or frozen by the courts. Qi encouraged them to use mergers and acquisitions to solve their problems. After all, bringing the pressure of the threat of takeover to bear on majority shareholders had been one of the original objectives of the reform (*The People's Daily* 2006c).

At the same time, the CSRC felt strong enough to start attacking some of the abuses that the previous system had found difficult to control. At a meeting in Changsha in October 2006, the CSRC announced that it would prosecute controlling shareholders of listed companies who had applied listed company funds to their own use. This had been made a criminal offence only in June 2006, reportedly after personal intervention by Premier Wen Jiabao. Between then and the end of September 2006, 309 companies had recovered 20.4 billion yuan from controlling shareholders and 15 executives had been arrested or prosecuted for misappropriation of funds (*The People's Daily* 2006b). The CSRC also felt comfortable enough to reopen the issue that had originally been the occasion for the decline of the market in 2001, namely the possibility of transferring state-owned shares to the pension and social security funds. At the end of September 2006, it was reported that the government was once again studying the possibility of transferring 10 per cent of state shares in listed companies to the National Pension Fund and the National Social Security Fund.

New trading products

As the markets progressed through 2006, it quickly became clear that a new style of Chinese market was starting to emerge from the chaotic slump of the previous five years. The exuberance and volatility remained but there was a new sophistication. This could be seen most clearly in the emergence of new trading products and in the growth of investment institutions, particularly retail mutual funds.

Warrants became a fundamental part of the tradable share reform and spread from there to the general market. A warrant is an instrument that gives the holder an option to buy or sell a share at a fixed price—often at a discount to market price—within a given period. There is no obligation to exercise the option, which simply falls away if not exercised. It is used mostly as a hedging instrument, but it can rise and fall rapidly in price depending on whether the exercise price is higher or lower than the current market price of the underlying share. Because of this volatility, it is a popular investment with the less risk-averse end of the investor spectrum. This end of the spectrum is well represented in the Chinese markets.

The tradable share reform concentrated its approach to compensation originally on issuing cash and new shares to tradable shareholders as compensation for a potential fall in share price. The fact that share prices did not fall after the first couple of reform experiments, however, coupled with a mid 2005 decision to allow the creation of covered warrants, opened a new avenue of compensation. Soon the issue of warrants by reforming companies became the normal path to compensate existing shareholders. As the market reversed its decline, the gearing effect of warrants in a bull market suddenly became apparent to even the most amateur investors. From a trickle in mid 2005, Shanghai boomed to become the world's third largest issuer and trader of covered warrants in 2006, after the Deutsche Börse and Hong Kong (World Federation of Exchanges 2007c).

It was a similar story with mutual funds. It had long been an ambition of the intellectuals behind the Chinese markets—particularly former reform commission chairman Liu Hongru—to avoid the casino-like behaviour associated with retail investing and to support the development of institutions. History teaches us, however, that institutions that invest on behalf of individuals grow up only when individuals feel that they are unable to get the full benefits of their investments by themselves, and turn to professionals.

This is what has happened in China. Ordinary investors had watched the value of their holdings dwindle by half in the period 2000–05 and were suddenly prepared to put their business in professional hands. Foreign participation was a key stimulus for the development of mutual funds. Bloomberg reported that the arrival in Shanghai of Franklin Templeton in 2003 was one of the first foreign-invested fund management businesses (International Herald Tribune 2006). It was followed rapidly by international firms such as ING's Asia Pacific Investment Management Unit, Deutsche Bank, Credit Suisse, Société Générale and Australia's Colonial First State. During 2006, mutual funds raised an astonishing 387 billion yuan for investment in the share markets (International Herald Tribune 2006). The peak of the mutual fund madness seemed to come on 7 December 2007, when Beijing-based Harvest Fund Management—19.9 per cent owned by Deutsche Bank—raised 40 billion yuan in a single day (Forbes.com 2007b). This prompted the CSRC to put a 10 billion yuan per day limit on fund raising in the hope of controlling funds rushing into the market. The top performer for 2006 was reported to be Invesco's Great Wall Domestic Demand Fund, which returned 182 per cent for the year (International Herald Tribune 2006). Interestingly, although it is difficult to confirm from published data, the general view among the investing community is that Shenzhen is a major beneficiary of this development, with some informants estimating that up to 40 per cent of funds are managed out of this southern city.

Thus, from the ashes of the bear market a new market was born. It was still recognisably Chinese, speculative and retail based, but it had a new sophistication, new products and new institutions.

The boom

The measures that the CSRC took to reform and stimulate the markets were extremely successful. The four-year bear market had turned around into 2006's greatest boom and the CSRC was inclined to take the credit for this.

On 26 April 2007, the Shanghai Index stood at 3,783. This was a 283 per cent increase from its lowest point of just under 1,000 in early June 2005 (China Exchanges Web 2007). At the end of March 2007, the Shanghai Index had grown by 161.2 per cent from March 2006 and the Shenzhen Index had increased by 55.3 per cent in the same period. These were the two highest increases in the world. Only Lima Stock Exchange had grown faster (World Federation of Exchanges 2007d). At the end of 2006, the Shanghai market cap had grown by 220.8 per cent from the end of 2005—the highest increase in the world—to US$917,507 billion, which made it the fourteenth largest market in the world as measured by market cap. In the same period, the Shenzhen market cap had grown by 97.1 per cent—the third highest increase in the world for the period—to US$227,947 billion. Together, at US$1,145,454 billion, they constituted the twelfth largest market in the world in terms of market cap, ahead of the

Australian Stock Exchange. When Hong Kong's market cap is added into the mix, at US$1,714,953 billion, they constitute the sixth largest market in the world (World Federation of Exchanges 2007e).

The frantic activity of the first quarter of 2007 further emphasised the coming role of the Chinese markets. By the end of March 2007, Shanghai's market cap had increased by a massive 314 per cent on the same period in 2006, to US$1,297,387 billion, which made it by itself the tenth largest market in the world. In the same period, Shenzhen's market cap grew by 182 per cent. Shanghai and Shenzhen together, at US$1,656,275 billion, were the ninth largest market in the world, and with Hong Kong, at US$3,390,392 billion, the sixth largest in the world (World Federation of Exchanges 2007f).

Market turnover figures are the indicators that best give a feeling for the wild and unrestrained nature of the activity on the Chinese markets during the boom. Looking at the numbers for the end of 2006, an increase in market turnover of 209.4 per cent in Shanghai and 174 per cent in Shenzhen on the same period in 2005 seems impressive. Shanghai is still only fifteenth in the world and Shenzhen only nineteenth (World Federation of Exchanges 2007g), but trading volume for January to March 2007 in Shanghai was an almost unbelievable 640.2 per cent higher than in the same period in 2006, and Shenzhen was up 529.4 per cent for the same period. It seemed that everybody was beginning to get that feeling of omnipotence and infallibility that drives human behaviour during serious booms. At US$652 billion, Shanghai by itself had the seventh highest trading volume in the world. Shenzhen, at US$339 billion, was tenth in the world, with a higher trading volume than Hong Kong (US$327 billion) (World Federation of Exchanges 2007h). Together, Shanghai and Shenzhen, in US dollar terms, represented the fifth largest market in the world during this period.

We should not take these boom-time figures as indicators of the long or medium term future of the domestic markets. The figures are extremely volatile and, in the medium term, almost certainly unsustainable. Current price–earnings ratios are in the high 30s—already back to close parity with Tokyo's at the peak of its bubble—and a correction, probably a serious one, is not very far away. This correction, when it comes, will probably once again push the Chinese markets back into the second league of international markets for a period.

If we are looking to the longer term, however, the most interesting figures for the period 2006–07 are those for funds raised. Here we see yet more evidence of a strong underlying demand by very large companies for access to world capital markets for very large sums of money. The recapitalisation of the Chinese banks gave Hong Kong the world's largest ever IPO (the International

Commercial Bank of China IPO of October 2006) during the period under review. It drew the attention of international capital providers to the Chinese markets seriously for the first time. This was evidenced when, for the first time since the 1930s, volatility on the Shanghai market was cited by observers as the cause of a serious hiccup on Wall Street. The Chinese markets could be due for some serious pain, but they aren't about to go away.

The boom in capital raising and the dominant role of Hong Kong

The 2005 mega-listings of Chinese banks were the precursors of the revolution in international fund raising, which the world witnessed with a mixture of bemusement and—on the part of New York—mild panic during 2006. The domestic exchanges were players in terms of cash raised but they continued to suffer from the suspicion in the international markets that they weren't quite kosher and that their regulatory standards were not up to scratch. And even if international investors had wanted to play in the domestic markets—there was plenty of evidence that they were too scared to do so—currency and other regulatory considerations meant that their ability to do so was severely circumscribed. Once again, the great beneficiary was Hong Kong.

Hong Kong was the primary market for international offerings by major Chinese banks during 2006. The requirement of Chinese banks for capital to bring them into conformity with the Basel rules was enormous and, in the judgement of their boards, could be satisfied only by access to international markets. There was also a consideration of prestige. International institutional investors brought respectability. The threat of greater scrutiny by the world market was also thought to be a disincentive to the dodgy practices—legal and illegal—that had characterised the performances of Chinese banks to date. This was their third refinancing in a decade and nobody was keen to dip into the state coffers for a fourth round.

Thus in 2006, three massive Chinese bank IPOs were launched from Hong Kong. On 1 June 2007, the Bank of China listed on the Hong Kong exchange, raising US$11.1 billion. On 22 September, Shenzhen-based China Merchants Bank listed, raising US$2.7 billion. On 27 October, the International Commercial Bank of China (ICBC) listed, after raising a massive US$21.9 billion in a simultaneous Hong Kong–Shanghai listing. The Hong Kong H-share listing raised US$16 billion while the Shanghai A-share listing raised US$5 billion (ICBC 2007). This was the largest ever IPO, eclipsing NTT DoCoMo's US$18.4 billion listing in 1998 (CBC News 2007). The Shanghai A-share listing alone ranked as the world's fourth largest IPO of the year (Ernst and Young 2006b).

This pushed Hong Kong to the position of the world's second largest stock exchange in terms of capital raising, eclipsing even Wall Street. In 2006, London raised US$55.8 billion, Hong Kong raised US$43 billion, while New York raised US$37.1 billion (World Federation of Exchanges). Of Hong Kong's US$43 billion, US$37.5 billion was raised in IPOs of H-share or red-chip companies (Hong Kong Exchanges and Clearing Limited 2007).

One country, two systems: Hong Kong Exchange's dependence on Chinese business

I have commented previously on just how dependent the Hong Kong Exchange has become on Chinese business and how much it has become the world gateway for China's capital raising, but it is worthwhile revisiting how this tendency has progressed in the two years since I last addressed this issue.

In 2006, 'H' shares and red chips accounted for 47.68 per cent of Hong Kong's total market capitalisation (28.13 per cent in 2004; 26.88 per cent in 2000) and 56.39 per cent of total market turnover (45.58 per cent in 2004; 29.34 per cent in 2000). At 14 out of 38, the number of Chinese constituents of the Hang Seng Index remained fairly stable. A couple of Chinese companies—such as Denway Motors and Lenovo—had been deleted from the index, however, the addition of the heavyweight Chinese banks meant that the weighting of Chinese companies in the index increased significantly. Against this it should be noted that the free-float factor assigned to H-share companies by Hang Seng Services was relatively low. The Bank of China's free-float factor is as low as 30 per cent, and the Construction Bank's is a mere 15 per cent (HSI Services Limited 2007). Nonetheless, these are massive enterprises and, when China sneezes, the Hong Kong Stock Exchange gets a severe flu.

A new scale of deal comes to Hong Kong: can the deals keep flowing?

The flotation of the big banks was obviously the key factor in Hong Kong's rise to near domination of the world's capital-raising markets. But how sustainable is Hong Kong's new prominence in international equity markets in the near to medium term?

The entry of China into the Hong Kong market has fundamentally changed the scale of deals in that market and brought Hong Kong a new respectability in world markets. An interesting manifestation of this is the total disappearance of the small British merchant banks such as Wardleys, Standard Chartered Asia and Schroeders, which dominated the market in the 1980s and early 1990s, and their replacement with Wall Street heavyweights such as Goldman Sachs.[4]

Since the early 1990s, China has consistently supplied the Hong Kong market with a stream of deals that were much bigger than anything Hong Kong had seen before.

The banks are the latest indications of this trend. The large size of the bank deals is a response to the specific set of circumstances mentioned above. Are there any other large enterprises waiting in the wings to keep up the stream of deals to allow Hong Kong to maintain this prime position? In the long term, unquestionably; in the short to medium term, possibly. The best potential source of similar deals in the short to medium term lies in the terms of the tradable share reform. Implicit in this reform is the notion of mergers and acquisitions as a method of consolidation of shaky state enterprises and ultimately their privatisation. Privatisation is a fraught word in Chinese politics, but the action already taken in the banking sector recognises that minority shareholders are not simply cash cows to be milked at will but real participants in the decision-making processes of the enterprises. The search on the part of the listing banks for strategic partners makes this clear. So on-market mergers and acquisitions appear to be the coming trend in the domestic markets and particularly in state-owned companies. This is the area where we should look for the future mega-deal flow source for Hong Kong.

If we accept this proposition, the next question is which sector of the Chinese economy is poised to take advantage of this new set of opportunities? In my estimation, the next area for consolidation, financial strengthening and listing for international capital is the iron and steel sector. China is now the world's largest steel maker—producing 419 million tonnes in 2006, or more than one-third of total world production—but its steel companies are small and scattered. In the past couple of years, Chinese economic policymakers have looked with increasing concern at the consolidation of the world steel industry and the on-market merger and acquisition activities of Arcelor and Mittal. They recognise the urgent necessity for consolidation in the Chinese steel industry but have difficulty finding a base company for this consolidation. Local governments are too protective of the vested interests of their own local steel makers to allow this to happen easily. One possible solution being discussed actively in Beijing at the moment is the extension of the tradable share reform to the steel industry, the invitation of strategic partners, the raising of capital on world markets and consolidation through classic on-market mergers and acquisitions.[5] If this comes to pass, as now seems increasingly possible, Hong Kong is sure to have a major role and there are many other state-controlled industries lining up for similar reforms. These deals will probably not be as large as the banks, but they will be very large by any other standards.

So at this stage, Chinese deal flows do not seem to be a problem for the Hong Kong Stock Exchange. The real challenge to Hong Kong's pre-eminent position as China's world capital-raising gateway will come when the renminbi becomes freely tradable and foreign investors are able to put their money directly into Chinese enterprises. At that stage, all three Chinese exchanges suddenly become potential market leaders. It is invidious to make predictions at this stage as to which one will ultimately prevail. Hong Kong supporters point to Hong Kong's reputation as a well-regulated market that international capital can trust, and certainly there is plenty of evidence that that assertion is true. It is equally true, however, that the regulation of domestic markets has improved steadily and impressively in the past seven years to a stage where it is recognisable as being of international standard. Equally, capital is notoriously fickle. Institutional investors often make sheep look like animals of independent judgement and, if there's a buck to be made and all your colleagues are telling you to go to Shanghai ahead of Hong Kong, anything can happen—and surprisingly quickly.

Irrational exuberance? The valuation of the banks

The current boom could well be the source of future problems for Hong Kong. I am not in the business of predicting prices or market levels; I simply make the point that every boom is followed eventually by a bust, in which markets typically lose between 75 and 90 per cent of their boom value. The Japanese boom and bust of the 1980s and 1990s was eerily compliant with this old market saw.[6]

The current Chinese boom shows a lot of similarities with the Japanese boom of the 1980s. Price–equity ratios are hovering about the 40s—just where Japan was when things started to go south. A particularly worrying parallel is the emergence of Chinese banks among the world's largest by market cap. In the late 1980s, any list of the world's largest banks by market cap was dominated by Japanese banks, to the extent that there appeared to be little competition. A subsequent near-collapse of the Japanese banking system demonstrated that this status reflected the enormous amount of cash swishing around in the Japanese economy, not the underlying financial strength of the banks.

Now we see the phenomenon of the ICBC becoming the world's third largest bank by market cap, after Citibank and Bank of America, but ahead of HSBC. Between its listing in October 2006 and early March 2007, the ICBC's share price rose by 43 per cent (Reuters 2007). The ICBC and the other listed Chinese banks were trading at between 2.5 and 2.7 times book value—a significant premium to international banks, which typically trade at approximately 2.1 times book value (*The People's Daily* 2006d).

It is instructive to compare the quality of the ICBC's loan book with that of its now smaller rival HSBC. At first blush, the ICBC's loan book doesn't look too bad. During 2006, the ICBC saw its non-performing loan ratio decrease to 3.79 per cent for the year, from 4.69 per cent in 2005; however, this was after two major recapitalisations. The corresponding figure for 2004 was 21.16 per cent (*The People's Daily* 2006d). For the September quarter 2006, HSBC declared its non-performing loans to be 6.54 per cent of total assets (Lace Financial 2007). This is a poor figure coming on the heels of HSBC North America's problems with sub-prime loans and, on the face of it, would appear to be significantly worse than the ICBC's figure. The difference is that HSBC has a long track record of fixing problems caused by occasional poor credit decisions and the market usually prices it accordingly. The ICBC, in contrast, has a long record of recapitalisations and dilution of shareholder value. Perhaps it would be more reasonable to compare HSBC's 6.54 per cent with the ICBC's 2004 figure of 21.16 per cent. On this basis, investors' valuations of the ICBC would seem to reflect what Alan Greenspan, referring to another boom, called 'irrational exuberance'.

A coming bear market? Political implications?

Several other measures suggest that the domestic markets seem poised for a severe correction at best. Charting is an inexact science but it often has good predictive effects at the end of bull markets and the beginning of bear markets. Several chartists have pointed out similarities between the Shanghai chart and the NASDAQ chart shortly before the 'Tech wreck' of 2000. This involves a series of retests at the second standard deviation with Shanghai's April–July 2006 retests corresponding with NASDAQ's of June–April 1999 and Shanghai's of November 2006 – January 2007, corresponding with NASDAQ's of August–October 2007. The current (May 2007) Shanghai retest of the second deviation appears to correspond with NASDAQ's final retest of 2000, before it went into deep decline.

Who knows? So far, the market's random walk continues, but if a serious correction comes, the fact that even the institutions have a retail bent in China means that there will be political consequences. Many commentators believe that under Hu Jintao, the Left has taken advantage of his seeming vacillation on his own political stance to further its position. Certainly, in recent months the trickle of articles from sources such as the Chinese Academy of Social Sciences attacking 'neo-liberalism' in economic policy has become a torrent. Particularly during the refinancing of the banks and their subsequent listing, there was a raft of articles, sometimes in leftist publications such as *Utopia* but often in trade publications such as *Zhengzhuan Shichang Zhoukan*, arguing that the banks were being sold off too cheaply.[7] Whether this trend will have sufficient momentum in a securities-crash scenario to push the influence of the Left back into economic policymaking—where it has been weak for more than a decade and a half—is a contentious question. Certainly, the flagship of reform, *Caijing* magazine, felt it necessary on 28 January 2006 to publish a stinging article supporting the achievements of reform and exhorting policymakers not to turn from this path.[8]

In such an eventuality what does the Left have to replace the stock exchanges, other than a set of failed financing mechanisms? Whatever the shortcomings of the exchanges, it is clear that no one wants to go back to the methods of a planned economy. Too many people are involved, too many people make a living out of the exchanges and, at the end of the day, they solve an intractable problem: how to get capital for China's development. To replace this mechanism would require a revolution with unpredictable consequences, which is precisely what New China, with its emphasis on 'harmony', is not about to have.

Notes

1 Notes of discussion between the author and participants in the meeting. The precedents quoted for such action were Alexander Hamilton's support of the market in the panic of 1792 and US President Ronald Reagan's supposed intervention in the market (actually a loosening of liquidity by the Federal Reserve) after the crash of 1987.

2 World Federation of Exchanges 2007a. Note, however, that Japanese price–earnings ratios reached even more absurd levels during the mid 1990s when, it was rumoured, the Japanese government used Postal Savings Bank funds to support the market and avoid a feared melt-down in the banking system. The average price–earnings ratio in Tokyo in 1994 was 79.5X and in 1995 86.5X.

3 This sudden decline of nearly 10 per cent in one day took place just after the Chinese New Year holiday. Many investors were either away on holidays or hurting after the disbursements of the holiday period. It was possibly just a coincidence, but in a market as heavily retail weighted as the Chinese domestic market, such considerations matter.

4 Author's discussions with the Hong Kong Stock Exchange, May 2007.

5 Discussions between the author and economic ministries and commissions, Beijing, June 2006.

6 Note, of course, that the Japanese bust was distorted by the Japanese government's use of the Postal Savings Bank deposits to prop up the market at just above the level where it was estimated that a drop in value of the shareholdings of the banks threatened the integrity of the banking system.

7 For examples of the leftist criticisms of neo-liberalism, see *Guangming Daily* (2004) and *Securities Market Weekly* (2006).

8 Puping (2006). There is speculation that Huang Puping is the pseudonym of the intellectual father of *Caijing* and one of the early sponsors of the stock exchanges, Wang Boming.

References

CBC News, 2007. Available from http://www.cbc.ca/money/story/2006/10/27/icbcsharestrade.html (accessed 25 April 2007).

China Exchanges Web, 2007. Available from http://www.hkex.com.hk/csm/homepage.asp?LangCode=en (accessed 29 April 2007).

ChinaPaper Online, 2007. Available from http://www.chinapaperonline.com/en/content.asp?id=1094 (accessed 29 March 2007).

China Securities Regulatory Commission (CSRC), 2004. 'Notice regarding the issue of experimenting with reforms to the split-share structure of listed companies', issued 29 April 2004, China Securities Regulatory Commission, Beijing. Available from http://www.sse.com.cn/cs/zhs/xxfw/flgz/temp/temp20050520.htm

Ernst and Young, 2006a. *Accelerating Growth—Global IPO Trends 2006*, Ernst and Young.

——, 2006b. *IPO Year-End Update Charts*, Ernst and Young. Available from http://www.ey.com/global/download.nsf/Finland/2006_Year_end_IPO/$file/year-end%202006%20global%20IPO%20deck.pdf (accessed 26 April 2007).

Forbes.com, 2007a. Available from http://www.forbes.com/markets/feeds/afx/2005/07/07/afx2127128.html (accessed 2 April 2007).

——, 2007b. *China's harvest fund raises 40 bln* yuan *from one-day offer*, Report, Forbes.com. Available from http://www.forbes.com/business/feeds/afx/2006/12/07/afx3238401.html (accessed 22 May 2007).

HSI Services Limited, 2007. Available from http://www.hsi.com.hk/ (accessed 22 May 2007).

Hong Kong Exchanges and Clearing Limited, 2007. Available from http://www.hkex.com.hk/data/chidimen/CD_FR.htm (accessed 30 April 2007).

International Commercial Bank of China (ICBC), 2007. Available from http://www.icbc.com.cn/detail.jsp?column=%B9%A4%D0%D0%BF%EC%D1%B6&infoid=1161938465100&infotype=CMS.STD (accessed 25 April 2007).

International Herald Tribune, 2006. 'Funds jockey for China foothold', *International Herald Tribune*, 5 January 2006.

Lace Financial, 2007. Available from http://www.lacefinancial.com/documents/HSBCNorthAmerica.pdf (accessed 22 May 2007).

Ministry of Commerce, 2007. *Foreign investors to be allowed to buy A shares*, Ministry of Commerce, Beijing. Available from http://english.mofcom.gov.cn/aarticle/newsrelease/significantnews/200511/20051100730600.html (accessed 30 March 2007).

Puping, H., 2006. 'We must be resolute in reform', *Caijing*, 28 January 2006.

Reuters, 2007. Reuters, 3 April 2007. Available from http://www.reuters.com/article/bankingfinancial-SP/idUSHKG23960820070403 (accessed 5 May 2007).

Rule, T., 2005. 'How are the markets performing?', in R. Garnaut and L. Song (eds), *The China Boom and its Discontents*, Asia Pacific Press, The Australian National University, Canberra:174–95.

Securities Market Weekly, 2006. 'Who is promoting a cheap sell off of China's banks?', *Securities Market Weekly*, 26 December.

South China Morning Post, 2001. *South China Morning Post*, 24 October 2001.

The People's Daily, 2006a. *The People's Daily*, 28 August.

——, 2006b. *The People's Daily*, 13 October.

——, 2006c. *The People's Daily*, 24 November.

——, 2006d. *The People's Daily*, 27 December.

World Federation of Exchanges, 2007a. Available from http://www.world-exchanges.org/publications/Ts6%20PER%2C%20Dividend%20Yield.XLS (accessed 21 March 2007).

——, 2007b. Equity 1.3 Value of Share Trading. Available from http://www.world-exchanges.org/publications/EQU1305.xls (accessed 25 March 2007).

——, 2007c. Available from http://www.world-exchanges.org/publications/EQU1606.xls (accessed 22 May 2007).

——, 2007d. Available from http://www.world-exchanges.org/WFE/home.asp?menu=385&document=3647 (accessed 1 April 2007).

——, 2007e. Available from http://www.world-exchanges.org/WFE/home.asp?menu=374&document=4065 (accessed 1 April 2007).

——, 2007f. Available from http://www.world-exchanges.org/WFE/home.asp?menu=396&document=4126 (accessed 1 April 2007).

——, 2007g. Available from http://www.world-exchanges.org/WFE/home.asp?menu=374&document=3960 (accessed 1 April 2007).

——, 2007h. Available from http://www.world-exchanges.org/WFE/home.asp?menu=396&document=4128 (accessed 1 April 2007).

Guangming Daily 2004. 'Maintain vigilance against the trend towards neo-liberal thought', 9 November.

14

How effective are China's capital controls?

Guonan Ma and Robert N. McCauley

Competing interpretations of the interaction of domestic monetary policy and the foreign exchange rate in China often arise from different assumptions regarding the effectiveness of capital controls. At one end of the spectrum is the view that capital controls merely alter the form of capital flows without altering their magnitude. In this view, the heavily managed renminbi exchange rate implies that China imports its monetary policy and lacks control over local short-term interest rates. At the other end is the view that capital controls are still binding enough to allow the Chinese government to set short-term interest rates, despite the limited flexibility of the exchange rate. The contrasts between these views sharpen in the context of growing cross-border flows under the current and capital accounts in the past 10 years as well as the accelerated foreign reserve accumulation since 2005.

Different views on the *status quo* also inform the interpretation of outcomes for future liberalisation of capital flows. Again, at one extreme, this would unevenly lower transaction costs and thereby alter the mix of cross-border capital flows, but without necessarily affecting their total volume. In this interpretation, capital account liberalisation might be of interest to specialists in international finance, but not to those who follow the Chinese macroeconomy. At the other extreme, capital account liberalisation would influence the scale and composition of capital flows and ultimately force a choice between exchange rate management and an independent monetary policy.

This chapter examines price evidence to determine how effective China's capital controls have been in the past and how effective they remain. We focus on the analysis of price evidence because it provides the most telling evidence on the question (for a discussion of the flow evidence, see Ma and McCauley forthcoming). Our basic conclusion is that sustained interest rate differentials mean that Chinese capital controls have continued to bind. These observed differentials cannot, in our view, be accounted for plausibly by liquidity or credit factors. Even the narrowing of these differentials since the unpegging of the renminbi in July 2005 leaves them at substantial levels. If capital controls still bite, future liberalisation is likely to proceed incrementally in order to accommodate a shifting balance of exchange rate and financial and monetary stability objectives.

We define monetary autonomy narrowly in terms of the government's ability to set short-term domestic interest rates. Such a definition could be appropriate to many industrial countries where monetary policy has confined itself to setting a short-term interest rate. In fact, China's monetary policy employs a wide variety of other instruments, including administrative controls of deposit and minimum lending rates as well as quantitative measures such as reserve requirements, lending quotas, window guidance and restrictions on investment. Such measures could give China's monetary policy room to manoeuvre even if its short-term interest rates were tightly constrained by the exchange rate policy. Thus, a finding that short-term interest rates are not tightly constrained implies *a fortiori* monetary independence in the broader sense, which is more relevant in the case of China.

Growing cross-border flows in China

China's capital control regime has two important features. First, capital controls tended to be tighter for cross-border flows thought to be more volatile than for more stable flows. Second, the regulatory regime over time has shifted from one biased against outflows towards one managing two-way cross-border capital flows in a more balanced fashion. Related to the latter is the tendency for policymakers to systemically 'lean against the wind' in the sense that control measures on outflows are strengthened to resist depreciation pressures on the exchange rate and vice versa. While such a discriminatory control regime could complicate any analysis, more stringent control measures over short-term flows to resist prevailing market pressures would highlight short-term interest rates as a useful measure of the efficacy of capital controls.

One factor conditioning the efficacy of capital controls is the size of external flows. Despite continued capital controls, the past two decades have witnessed a rapid rise in China's cross-border flows on the current and capital accounts. As a share of gross domestic product (GDP), China's gross cross-border flows more than quintupled to more than 120 per cent in 2005, from less than 20 per cent in 1982 (Figure 14.1), with a noticeable acceleration in the 1990s. Also, notwithstanding the remarkable expansion of the gross current account flows, China's capital account flows have been gaining relative importance.[1] In 2005, gross capital account flows represented one-third of China's total gross cross-border flows, compared with just 13 per cent in 1982 and 25 per cent in 1990.[2]

The backdrop of growing cross-border flows suggests that the Chinese economy has become increasingly open and integrated into the global economy and is thus more prone to influences from global markets than before. In particular, larger external flows point to more opportunities to avoid and evade capital controls. This in turn raises questions about the efficacy of capital controls, with implications for monetary autonomy, financial stability and future capital account liberalisation.

Figure 14.1 **China's gross cross-border flows,[a] 1982, 1990 and 2005** (per cent of GDP)

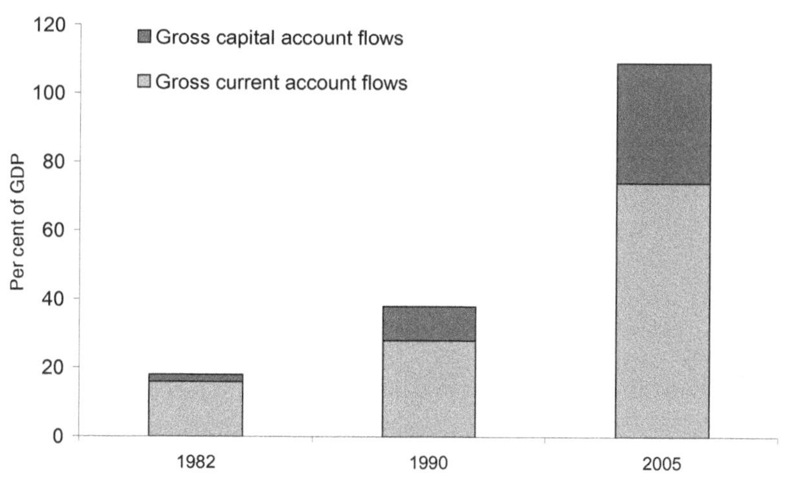

[a] Defined as the sum of debit and credit flows on China's balance of payments, excluding net errors and omissions.

Source: CEIC Data Company.

Growing trade and financial openness, however, does not support an immediate conclusion about the efficacy of capital controls. In particular, even large and highly responsive cross-border flows could limit without gutting capital controls, just as small and stable flows need not imply effective controls. A more direct and stringent test of capital control effectiveness is whether substantial cross-border arbitrage opportunities persist for a considerable period. Such a test—based not on flows but on onshore and offshore prices—can also indicate how the effectiveness has varied over time. When price and flow measures are consistent with each other, one can arrive at an easy conclusion regarding capital mobility; but when they point in different directions, price evidence should be given more weight. In a departure from the existing literature, we examine only the price measures in gauging the capital mobility.

Price test of capital mobility: onshore and offshore renminbi yields

The combination of onshore renminbi interest rates, offshore US dollar rates and non-deliverable forward (NDF) exchange rates is analysed next, to test for capital mobility between China and the offshore financial markets. The null hypothesis is that there are no substantial differences between renminbi interest rates onshore, on the one hand, and those implied by the offshore NDFs in conjunction with US dollar Libor, on the other.[3] The methodology of estimating such onshore–offshore renminbi yield gaps is based on Ma et al. (2004), as detailed in the Appendix. The idea is that large and persistent onshore–offshore yield gaps suggest significant cross-border market segmentation and thus binding capital controls; but occasional small gaps do not necessarily imply ineffectiveness of capital controls. We interpret the evidence as supporting the alternative hypothesis of there being an economically substantial gap between onshore and offshore renminbi yields. Acceptance of this hypothesis favours the view that capital controls in China have so far remained substantially binding.

Measuring onshore and offshore renminbi yield differentials

Especially in the case of relatively less-developed money and foreign exchange markets, instruments must be chosen carefully to perform this test. Care must be exercised in the dimensions of maturity, liquidity and credit. Ideally, one wants to compare instruments of identical maturity, enjoying the same liquidity, which are issued by the same private parties, usually banks. An appropriate comparison would be between the yields on large US dollar certificates of deposit in New York versus yields on US dollar deposits posted in London by the top-rated banks that report to the British Bankers Association (BBA). Such a comparison often is based on the three-month maturity that is representative of domestic and offshore yields. The banks involved in the comparison are quite similar in their double-A credit standing.

Liquidity considerations. In the case of China, the challenge has in practice come from getting a reasonable match between a representative renminbi money market yield, on the one hand, and the NDF rate, on the other. In particular, the interbank renminbi money market trades with greatest liquidity at very short maturities—overnight to seven days—while the NDF market trades with greatest liquidity at longer tenors of three months to one year.

This chapter improves on the previous estimates of onshore–offshore renminbi yield gaps in the dimension of liquidity (Ma et al. 2004). The latter traded off the above considerations and chose to compare the three-month China interbank offered rate (CHIBOR) yield to the three-month NDF.[4] This comparison stretched to a relatively long and illiquid maturity in the domestic money market, on one hand, and took a relatively short maturity in the offshore market, on the other. Here, we update these earlier measures as well as complement the earlier analysis with a new comparison based on a different pair of instruments. In particular, we also compare the weekly auction rates for PBC one-year bills available since 2004 with the one-year NDF. This choice compares liquid instruments in both markets, although it introduces possible credit differences between the sovereign bill and the bank NDF or deposit (see below).

Liquidity across the two markets matches well at the one-year tenor. The PBC issued 1.2 trillion renminbi (about US$150 billion) of its one-year bills in 2005 out of a total bill issuance of 2.8 trillion renminbi, for an average weekly issuance of about US$3 billion equivalent.[5] From January to March 2006, issuance ranged between 40 and 120 billion renminbi a week. In the NDF market, the one-year maturity is reportedly the most traded maturity (Ma et al. 2004; Debelle et al. 2006).

The less liquid the instruments that are used for arbitrage of onshore and offshore yields, the less telling are observed small yield differences. One can think of an arbitrage tunnel inside of which further arbitrage transactions are not profitable, given bid-ask spreads and any tendency for flows of orders to move the market. The upshot is that a finding that capital controls are ineffective could well be consistent with observed yield gaps of, say, 25 basis points or less.

Credit considerations. With regard to credit, comparing sovereign and bank yields on onshore and offshore instruments, respectively, is problematic in principle, but in practice it does not skew the comparison substantially. Credit default swaps suggest that the credit standing of China attracts an insurance payment of only a handful of basis points more than that of the major international banks that form the US dollar Libor panel (see Table A14.2). Since offshore renminbi rates were lower than the onshore PBC bill yield in the period 2004–06, the mixing of sovereign and bank credit does widen the estimated yield gap for this period, thus favouring the finding that capital controls are effective. But as we will see below, the scale of the estimated yield differences of 100 to 400 basis points dwarfs the five basis point credit difference.

With our earlier comparison of CHIBOR and offshore yields, credit differences tended to reduce the absolute value of the observed yield differentials over much of the sample period. From 1999 to 2001, highly rated banks dealing offshore under international law paid higher (implied) yields than did domestic Chinese banks dealing onshore. Taking into account the credit difference would only have widened the gap.

An example of cross-border arbitrage on renminbi interest rates. Before examining the data, it might be useful to consider a particular example of an arbitrage transaction at the one-year tenor by a multinational firm with a profitable operation in China. Since September 2003, the offshore speculative demand to be long in renminbi has given the treasurer of such a firm a strong incentive to, in effect, hold renminbi onshore and sell them forward offshore (that is, lending renminbi onshore and borrowing them offshore). One way of constructing such a position is for the affiliate in China not to convert renminbi into dollars in order to remit a dividend to its parent outside China. Instead, the funds are retained in renminbi and invested in the Chinese money market. The yield on the one-year deposit is proxied by the PBC bill rate (one can think of a bank taking the funds in trust and investing in the PBC bill). Thus, renminbi funds have been lent onshore.

Simultaneously, the affiliate borrows dollars at one-year Libor, replacing the cash flow of the unpaid dividend from China, and sells renminbi one year forward against US dollars, say, to a hedge fund. This combination of dollar borrowing and forward position amounts to borrowing renminbi offshore and converting the proceeds into dollars, and the rate of interest paid is (by construction) the relatively low NDF-implied renminbi yield. At the year's end, the renminbi invested onshore can be sold for dollars at the then-prevailing spot exchange rate, which is also used to determine any profit or loss on the NDF, leaving the firm with the arbitrage gain between the interest rate in the Chinese money market and the lower offshore yield. Thus, by lagging a current dollar payment—namely, the profit repatriation—the firm has in effect acquired a long renminbi position and locked in a gain by selling it offshore.

One of the useful features of this example is that it shows that arbitrage between the onshore money market and the offshore forward market is not limited to banks. Of course, not all foreign firms operating in China are profitable; some have entered joint ventures that constrain such arbitrage and not all would be willing to increase their balance sheet in China. Nevertheless, such corporate opportunities are telling because otherwise a failure to equalise interest rates could be taken to be merely a symptom of the inefficiency of Chinese banks. Instead, the profit opportunities present themselves to global companies, which can be presumed to bring to China efficient treasury operations and indeed the benefit of having operated within and around capital controls in other economies.

Onshore–offshore renminbi yield differentials based on three-month CHIBOR

Our earlier analysis compared a domestic interest rate—the so-called three-month CHIBOR—with the offshore renminbi rate implied by three-month NDFs and dollar Libor. We found economically very significant differences. Figure 14.2 compares the three-month yield gap for the renminbi with Asian peers for the periods 1999–2001 and 2002–04. The absolute value of the gap between renminbi yields onshore and offshore averaged 250–300 basis points in the five years to early 2004. This placed China in the middle of our sample and indeed is very wide compared with the onshore–offshore differential of 50–100 basis points for the Korean won in the same period, and a gap of 20–30 basis points observed for the Japanese yen before capital controls were lifted in the early 1980s (Otani and Tiwari 1981). The narrowing of the differentials in 2002–04 was in fact less evident in the case of China than for most of the other Asian currencies.

An updated estimate of the yield gap for 1999–2006 reveals an even bigger average gap of 310 basis points in absolute value and also suggests several distinct phases of market conditions (Figure 14.3). In general, if controls bind, one would expect offshore rates to be above onshore rates when market participants are positioning for renminbi weakness and the net direction of flows of funds is outward. Conversely, offshore rates would fall below onshore rates when positioning favours renminbi strength and funds are seeking to enter China.

In the period from the East Asian financial crisis through until early 2001, the weight of offshore positioning was in the direction of a weakening renminbi, resulting in higher yields offshore. Then followed a period of smaller differences during 2001–02, which saw offshore rates below those onshore, but with a gap of less than 150 basis points. This period featured more balanced positioning on the renminbi. With the intensification of public pressure from

Figure 14.2 **Average absolute onshore–offshore yield spreads, 1999–2001 and 2002–2004** (in basis points)

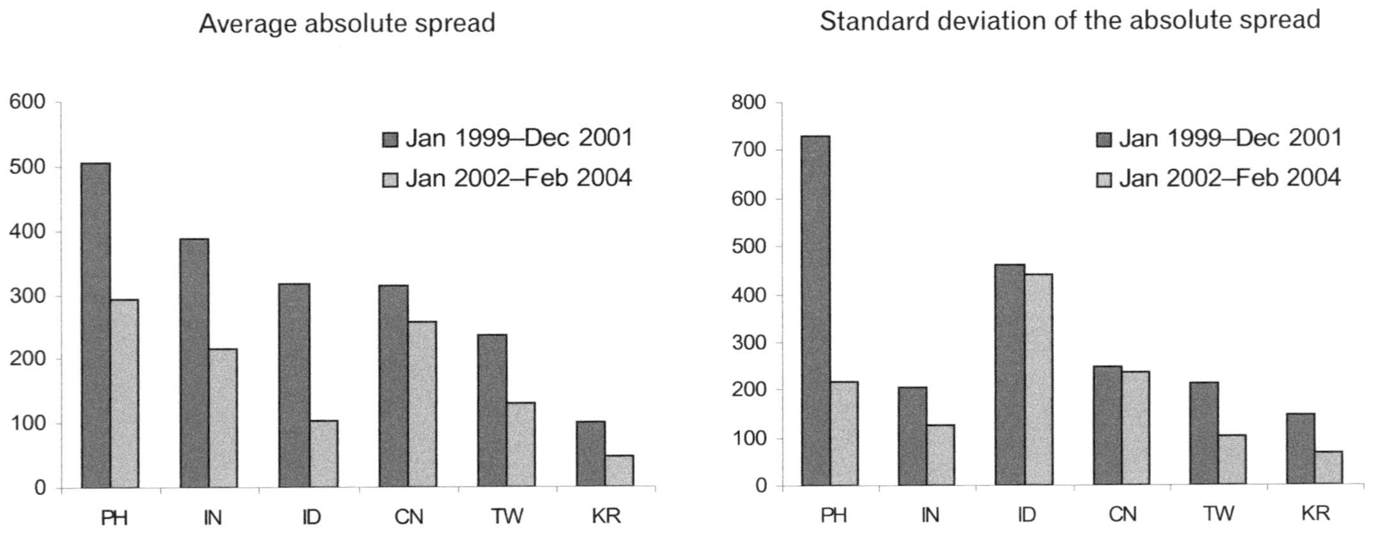

Notes: PH Philippines, IN India, ID Indonesia, CN China, TW Taiwan (China), KR Korea.
Source: Ma, G., Ho, C. and McCauley, R.N., 2004. 'The markets for non-deliverable forwards in Asian currencies', BIS Quarterly Review, June:81–94.

trading partners on China's exchange rate policy in September 2003, however, offshore yields dropped substantially below their onshore counterparts. The weight of offshore positioning was in the direction of a strengthening renminbi. As Chinese companies converted dollar holdings or borrowings into renminbi, reserve growth accelerated, far exceeding the pace that could be explained by the current account surplus and direct investment inflows. The average yield gap widened to more than 360 basis points from January 2003 to April 2006. The gap reached a peak of 800 basis points in mid 2005, when the implied offshore yield fell well below zero.[6] Since the July 2005 policy change, however, the yield gap has narrowed markedly—to less than 200 basis points.

The principal message based on our previous and more updated estimates of three-month tenor of the CHIBOR and renminbi NDF is that the onshore–offshore gap in the renminbi yields has been persistently substantial in absolute terms and its sign has been consistent with prevailing market pressures. In other words, hitherto, China's capital controls have prevented sufficient cross-border arbitrage to equalise onshore and offshore short-term yields.

Figure 14.3 **The onshore less offshore renminbi yields, based on three-month CHIBOR, 1998–2006** (in basis points)

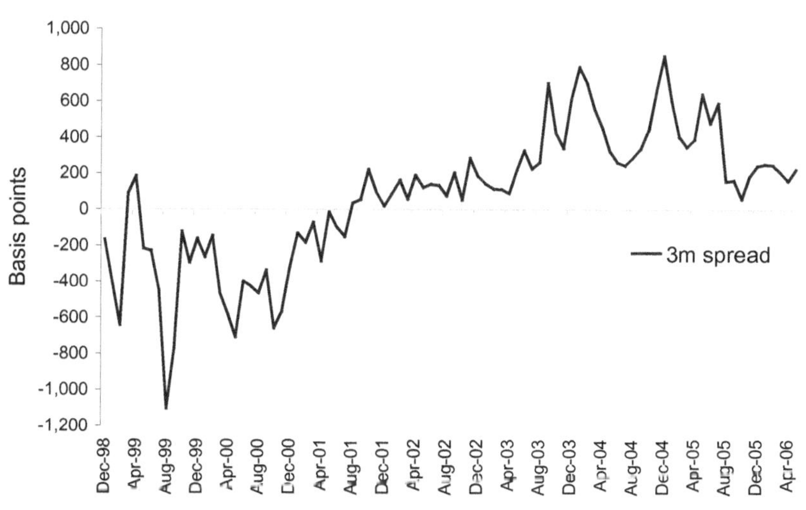

Note: Onshore less offshore yield.
Sources: Bloomberg; PBC; authors' own estimates.

Onshore–offshore renminbi yield differentials based on PBC bills

The above finding that offshore renminbi yields have traded consistently below those onshore in the past two years is confirmed by another test based on a newly available and more liquid benchmark money-market yield in renminbi in China. As noted above, the introduction of a weekly auction of PBC bills in early 2004 has provided an alternative basis for comparison of domestic renminbi money-market yields with the renminbi yields implied by the NDFs traded offshore. This more telling and updated test—covering the two and half years between April 2004 and November 2006—produces a much smoother estimate of the yield gap, consistent with better liquidity in both markets (Figure 14.4).

This more refined and updated test based on trading in liquid market segments offers further evidence of binding controls. From April 2004 to April 2007, the one-year PBC bill yielded, on average, 250 basis points more than the yield implied by the offshore NDF. This gap of 250 basis points compares with an average of 320 basis points based on the three-month CHIBOR. Both suggest two distinct phases in the yield gaps since April 2004. Before the July 2005 policy move, the gap was wider and more volatile, reacting to policy comments and market rumours. The average spread for this first phase was about 400 basis points on both estimates. After the July 2005 policy shift, the yield gap shrank to 100–200 basis points for three-month CHIBOR and the one-year PBC bill auction yields and stayed there until the gaps widened again into 2007.

Onshore–offshore yield gaps since the July 2005 policy change

How should this convergence of offshore to onshore renminbi yields in 2005–06 be interpreted? It is remarkable that the onshore–offshore interest differential narrowed sharply in the wake of the July 2005 policy change and remained quite narrow until the end of 2006. Those observers with a prior conviction that capital controls lost effectiveness in the presence of growing cross-border flows might read the reduction of the onshore–offshore renminbi interest rate differential as demonstrating their convictions. This possible interpretation is simple. We offer a more nuanced interpretation that allows scope for policy and temporary opportunities to evade controls.

Regarding policy, we see the initial narrowing of the onshore and offshore renminbi yield differential as a chosen outcome of policy rather than as a forced outcome of the weight of money. In the approach to the depegging, the Chinese authorities doubtless appreciated the risk of a market reaction to any managed exit strategy. In these circumstances, prudence might suggest a policy of not relying too heavily on capital controls, even if these were judged generally effective. As it happened, rising US interest rates offered the option

Figure 14.4 **Onshore less offshore NDF-implied yields, 2004–2007** (in basis points)

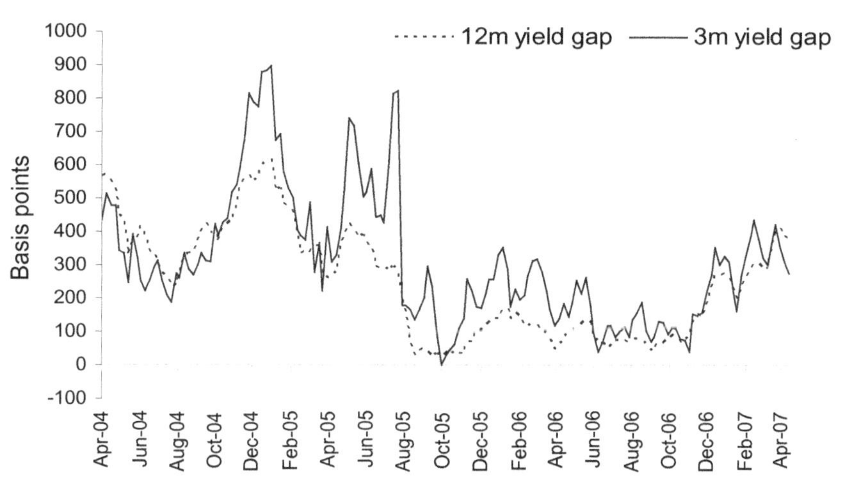

Note: weekly data; 12-month (three-month) NDF, one-year PBC bill yield (three-month CHIBOR) and 12-month (three-month) Libor.
Sources: People's Bank of China; Bloomberg; Bank for International Settlements estimates.

of what might be termed an opportunistic policy of uncovered interest parity. Thus, in the months before and after July 2005, Chinese authorities widened the renminbi–dollar interest gap by reducing the one-year PBC bill rate through policy rate cuts against the backdrop of rising US policy rates. This opened up a 3–4 per cent gap between US dollar and renminbi yields.

Then after July 2005, the Chinese authorities shaped expectations of a 3–4 per cent annual appreciation through statements and the actual pace of the spot crawl. Indeed, market expectations seemed to have been remarkably well contained during the transition (Ma and McCauley forthcoming). The consistency of such exchange rate expectations and the dollar–renminbi interest rate differential served to keep onshore and offshore renminbi rates not too far out of line. Our interpretation suggests that the PBC *de facto* behaved as though interest rate parity were an operating target in setting interest rates and the speed of the crawl, thereby possibly lowering the risks inherent in the regime transition. This approach reduced reliance on the considerable capital controls still in place, albeit to some extent at the cost of relying more on the non-interest rate instruments of monetary policy.

There were also temporary opportunities to evade the capital controls that arose because of the lag between market development and the articulation of capital controls. In particular, the development in 2006 of an onshore forward market might have added a new channel for inflows that helped to narrow the onshore–offshore differential. An onshore renminbi forward market was first introduced in late 2005.[7] This onshore forward market allowed some players with a presence in both the onshore and offshore markets to engage in arbitrage. In particular, such players could buy renminbi forward in the onshore market (at relatively high implied interest rates) and simultaneously sell renminbi forward in the offshore market (at relatively low implied interest rates). Much like borrowing renminbi offshore and placing renminbi onshore, such transactions would tend to raise the offshore interest rates towards domestic interest rate levels, bringing the onshore and offshore forward curves closer to each other than otherwise. Such transactions were apparently made possible by a lacuna in the onshore prudential regulation of net foreign currency positions for banks, which set limits on net spot but not forward positions. In effect, the development of the onshore forward market created a temporary channel for arbitrage, though not one wide enough to raise offshore rates to domestic levels.

Our nuanced interpretation is supported by development since early 2007, when the onshore–offshore renminbi yield gaps started widening again to more than 300 basis points, putting capital controls to a stronger test. In our view, this latest widening has less to do with the resurgent efficacy of capital controls than with a partial reversal of the above factors. In response to the inflows related to arbitrage between the offshore and emerging onshore forward markets, Chinese authorities have, since the third quarter of 2006, tightened the rules. Measures taken have included an explicit prohibition of onshore institutions from participating in the offshore NDF market, an inclusion of forward positions in the new prudential regulations of net bank foreign currency positions and a sharp reduction in the *de facto* ceiling on Chinese residents bringing dollars onshore.[8] Moreover, since mid 2006, the accelerated pace of spot appreciation and the larger recorded trade surpluses have conditioned market expectations of future appreciation, forcing the implied offshore yields to return to zero or even into negative territory. Since the one-year PBC bill yield rebounded from a low of 1.5 per cent about mid 2005 to 2.8 per cent by late 2006, the onshore–offshore yield gap widened further.

In total, the wide differences between onshore and offshore renminbi interest rates point to the efficacy of capital controls. Most recently, the Chinese authorities guided domestic interest rates and expectations of appreciation into broad consistency with rising US dollar interest rates to reduce the risks inherent in the initial exchange rate regime shift. The resulting one percentage point gap between onshore and offshore renminbi yields might have been desired in order to lessen the policy burden on capital controls, which have been binding but not watertight. The experience with the onshore forwards in 2005–06, however, suggests that maintaining effective capital controls gets harder with the development of financial markets and further deregulation of cross-border transactions. The wider yield gaps since early 2007 nevertheless point to a regime of still-binding capital control in China.

Price measures: tests of uncovered interest parity

The failure of the onshore and offshore renminbi yields to equalise through cross-border arbitrage indicates that capital controls bite. This in turn points to a degree of monetary independence in China. This section addresses this question directly by first assessing the relationship between short-term yields in China and the United States and then by comparing the renminbi–dollar short-term interest rate gap with those of the Hong Kong dollar–US dollar and euro–US dollar pairs.

Interest rate differentials in a period of *de facto* fixed exchange rates

China and the United States went through very distinct interest rate cycles between 1996 and 2006, despite the *de facto* dollar peg of the Chinese renminbi until July 2005. Figure 14.5 reveals sizeable and sustained, albeit varying, differentials between short-term renminbi yields in China and the US dollar yields in the United States and the United Kingdom. Yield differentials, whether measured in terms of policy rates or short-term money market rates, have generally been 100 basis points or more in absolute value. In sum, experience between the tightening of the peg to the dollar in 1997 and its loosening in mid 2005 suggested that Chinese monetary authorities could still set a somewhat independent domestic policy (even in the face of capital flows responsive to the resulting yield gap, as shown below).

Cheung et al. (2003) fit autoregressive models to the short-term interest rate differential between China and the United States and find that

> ...the lagged uncovered interest differential variables are positively significant and indicative of strong persistence...If monies are free to move across markets, arbitrage can generate profits based on the pattern of persistent deviation and help restore the parity. However, this kind of arbitrage activity is quite difficult, especially in the short run, given the prevailing capital controls in the PRC (Cheung et al. 2003:11).

Another finding of Cheung et al. (2003) has been read by Eichengreen (2004) as indicating that the capital controls have become less effective over time.

In particular, Cheung et al. (2003) report a statistically significant downward trend in the interest rate differential in the sample period from January 1996 to May 2002.[9] Eichengreen's interpretation is weakened, however, since the result depends on data from the early to mid 1990s. Recall that China experienced a bout of moderately high inflation—reaching 20 per cent—in 1994–95, triggering a draconian tightening by the authorities. The one-month Chinese interbank rate remained at double-digit levels in 1995–97 and remained at 6–8 per cent throughout 1998. Only after the East Asian financial crisis had delivered sharp deflationary shocks to the Chinese economy through its appreciation of the effective exchange rate of the renminbi did Chinese policymakers cut interest rates repeatedly.

We test the following three hypotheses: that the US dollar–renminbi interest rate differential (in absolute terms) is significantly different from zero; that the differential has shown a declining trend; that the average differential or its trend changed during the sample period. Our tests are based on the three measures of interest rates in Figure 14.6 for July 1997 and July 2005 and allow for possible datum breaks within this sample period. Table 14.1 reports the test results, confirming the view that China's capital controls remain effective.

Figure 14.5 **Domestic renminbi yields less US dollar yields, 1997–2005** (in basis points)

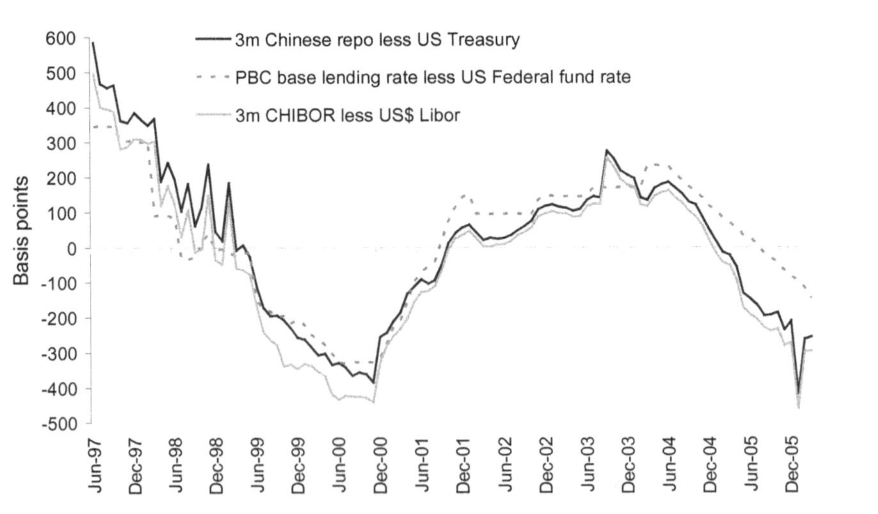

Source: CEIC Data Company.

First, for the whole sample period from 1997 to 2005, or for subsamples, the absolute values of the dollar–renminbi nominal interest rate differentials differ significantly from zero for all three interest rate measures. Secondly, though it appears from the entire sample period that the differential was trending downwards, the hypothesis of a declining trend in the dollar–renminbi interest rate differentials is rejected within the subsamples.

Finally, when the data are allowed to determine the most likely shift point, the tests reject the null hypothesis of no break. In particular, induction identifies a break in the neighbourhood of mid 2001—roughly the mid point of the sample period. Given this break, the absolute sizes of the interest rate differentials between the renminbi and the US dollar are narrower for the second half of the sample than for the first half, but remain substantial statistically. As noted, however, there is little evidence of a declining trend within the subsamples, and indeed we find the wrong sign for the estimated trend coefficients in all cases.

The econometric evidence in Table 14.1 confirms the hypothesis of significant renminbi–US dollar interest rate differentials. This is a strong statement that, on average, China's capital controls have been effective in maintaining a wedge between interest rates on the US dollar and renminbi, despite the *de facto* dollar peg of the renminbi. Our statistical tests do not support the hypothesis of a declining trend in the interest rate differentials, once a break in the sample is allowed. In particular, during 2001–05, when China deepened its participation in the global economy considerably and controls were generally relaxed, the estimated trend convergence of short-term interest rates has the wrong sign in all of the cases. If closer financial integration forces interest rate convergence given exchange rate stability, it is hard to account for the lack of convergence in more recent years.

Thus, the distinct interest rate cycles in China and the United States support the idea that China's capital controls have bound sufficiently to provide policymakers some degree of short-term monetary autonomy under a *de facto* dollar peg.[10] We interpret the observed convergence of policy rates in the 1990s as owing more to inflation convergence than to weaker capital controls. Rather than happenstance, the inflation and interest rate convergence in 1996–2000 can be seen as reflecting the dollar peg's provision of a useful medium-term monetary anchor through prices for traded goods.[11] What matters for the present analysis, however, is that, in the context of low inflation in both countries, capital controls have permitted Chinese interest rates to diverge from those of the Federal Reserve, notwithstanding the exchange rate linkage.

Relative monetary independence

It might be argued that the yield differentials just considered are not wide enough to indicate monetary independence. This objection suggests the usefulness of some benchmarks. How do the differentials between the domestic renminbi yields and US dollar yields compare with those between the Hong Kong dollar and US dollar yields as well as those between the euro and US dollar yields? As a small open economy, Hong Kong has a dollar-based currency board system and no capital controls whatsoever. The euro area, on the other, is a large economy, but one with a flexible exchange rate and an open capital account. The latter is a much more stringent test than a benchmark based on the US dollar–Hong Kong dollar pair. Any similarity in dollar and euro yields cannot

Table 14.1 **Renminbi–US dollar interest rate differential**

Y = differential between the PBC lending rate and US Federal fund rate

(1)	$Y = 194.5 - 0.73\ T$	Adj-R^2 = 0.033; DW = 0.119
	(4.10)** (–1.05)	
(2)	$Y = 152.8\ D_1 + 106.5\ D_2 + 1.57\ T_1 + 0.79\ T_2$	Adj-R^2 = 0.11; DW = 0.145
	(1.89)* (4.28)** (0.65) (0.66)	Wald Tests: F(2, 93) = 2.06

Y = differential between three-month Chinese repo and three-month US T-bill

(1)	$Y = 266.0 - 1.87\ T$	Adj-R^2 = 0.155; DW = 0.153
	(5.4)** (–2.82)**	
(2)	$Y = 186.3\ D_1 + 47.9\ D_2 + 2.69\ T_1 + 1.88\ T_2$	Adj-R^2 = 0.413; DW = 0.287
	(2.39)** (1.86)* (1.1) (1.89)*	Wald Tests: F(2, 132) = 9.48

Y = differential between three-month CHIBOR and Libor

(1)	$Y = 272.0 - 2.02\ T$	Adj-R^2 = 0.218; DW = 0.258
	(5.83)** (–2.96)**	
(2)	$Y = 274.6\ D_1 + 64.0\ D_2 - 1.35\ T_1 + 1.64\ T_2$	Adj-R^2 = 0.334; DW = 0.327
	(3.75)** (2.87)** (–0.6) (1.65)*	Wald Tests: F(2, 132) = 7.19

Notes: All dependent variables are expressed in absolute value. T = linear trend; T_1 (T_2) = linear trend for the first (second) period; D_1 (D_2) = dummy variable for the first (second) period. Newey-West estimation on the monthly data for July 1997 and July 2005: according to the log likelihood ratios, the most likely breaking points vary but concentrate around May, June and July 2001, so we impose a common break point at June 2001. The Wald Test statistics are for the joint null hypothesis of equal intercepts and slopes. Numbers in parentheses are t-statistics: ** indicates 5 per cent significance; * indicates 10 per cent significance.

Source: Authors' calculations.

reflect the exchange rate policy of the euro area (unlike, say, any similarity in US dollar and Hong Kong dollar yields).

The Hong Kong dollar–US dollar benchmark highlights the efficacy of capital controls in China, since Hong Kong has complete capital mobility but China has maintained substantial controls, yet both linked their currencies tightly to the US dollar. As expected, the Hong Kong dollar–US dollar yield pairs exhibit much narrower and more stable differentials and much higher correlations than do the CHIBOR–Libor pairs at one-week and three-month maturities (Table 14.2). In particular, the Hibor–Libor correlations are close to unity, compared with less than one-third for the CHIBOR–Libor pairs. This is a classic case of a small open economy choosing a fixed change rate and giving up its monetary autonomy, regardless of the respective business cycles. Hence the Hong Kong dollar–US dollar benchmark is highly advantageous to our argument that China's capital controls have substantially hindered cross-border arbitrage. One drawback of using the Hong Kong dollar–US dollar benchmark, however, is that it can only suggest that China's interest rate setting has more room to manoeuvre than an economy with very little such room.

A more stringent test based on the euro–US dollar benchmark—where there is a strong presumption of autonomy in interest rate setting—still supports our arguments. It is more stringent because, even with other things being equal, the sheer size of the euro area or of China would secure itself greater autonomy relative to Hong Kong. The euro–US dollar yield pairs have narrower and more stable differentials than do the renminbi–US dollar pairs (Table 14.3).

Table 14.2 **Interbank rate differentials: renminbi–US dollar and Hong Kong dollar–US dollar** (bps)

	One-week		Three-month	
	CHIBOR–Libor	Hibor–Libor	CHIBOR–Libor	Hibor–Libor
Average of absolute difference	160.5	54.1	166.6	47.0
Maximum of differential	173.4	71.2	213.2	99.7
Minimum of differential	–429.6	–222.8	–439.0	–213.0
Standard deviation	181.4	54.8	194.9	58.9
Correlation coefficient	0.32	0.97	0.21	0.97

Note: The interbank market offer rates are CHIBOR for the renminbi, Libor for the US dollar and Hibor for the Hong Kong dollar. Monthly data from January 1999 to March 2006.
Source: CEIC Data Company.

Table 14.3 **Interbank rate differentials: renminbi–US dollar and euro–US dollar** (bps)

	One-week		Three-month	
	CHIBOR–Libor	Euribor–Libor	CHIBOR–Libor	Euribor–Libor
Average of absolute difference	160.47	143.45	166.64	144.56
Maximum of differential	173.36	190.04	213.16	166.81
Minimum of differential	–429.58	–281.50	–439.01	–284.07
Standard deviation	181.39	156.60	194.88	157.37
Correlation coefficient	0.32	0.58	0.21	0.60

Note: The interbank market offer rates are CHIBOR for the renminbi, Libor for the US dollar and Euribor for the euro; monthly data from January 1999 to March 2006.
Source: CEIC Data Company.

More tellingly, for the period under consideration, Euribor and Libor exhibit greater positive co-movements than do the CHIBOR and Libor. These results hold as well across split samples. Thus, the evidence from interbank market yields suggests that China—with a fixed exchange rate and continued capital controls—does not import its interest rate policy from the United States to any greater extent than the euro area. This observation is consistent with the view that capital controls in China remain binding.

Conclusion

The analysis in this chapter finds that China's capital controls remain substantially binding. They prevent the equalisation of onshore renminbi yields and those implied by offshore NDFs. We also find that the observed convergence of short-term interest rates between China and the United States was more characteristic of the mid to late 1990s than of the years since. With its remaining capital controls, China's short-term interest rate setting seems less imported from the United States than either that of Hong Kong (as a small open economy with a hard dollar peg) or that of the euro area (as a large economy with a flexible exchange rate).

The partial convergence of onshore and offshore renminbi yields during mid 2005 and late 2006 is interpreted as reflecting the authorities' choice to act as though they were bound by interest rate parity. That is, in the transition from the pegged regime, the Chinese authorities found it convenient to take the burden off the capital controls by signalling a rate of appreciation against the dollar that was broadly consistent with the US dollar–renminbi interest rate differential. We also recognise an element of unintended and temporary relaxation of capital controls resulting from financial market development getting ahead of the controls. The latest onshore–offshore gaps have, however, widened and remain large; and it appears that the authorities are again testing the effectiveness of capital controls.

Over time, financial market development and further lessening of controls should pave the way for phased integration of China into the global market, and will diminish the importance of the remaining controls. Nevertheless, our findings of binding capital controls in China could also help shed light on how policymakers in China will pace the country's continuing capital account liberalisation. Our analysis suggests that the choices regarding liberalisation will affect more than the form of inflows.

Notes

1 Lane and Milesi-Ferrantti (2006) find that China's stock of international assets and liabilities has barely kept pace with the global stock, in contrast with China's growing share of global GDP and international trade. They compare asset/liability stocks with GDP flows, while we compare two types of international flows. On our measure, China's financial integration is outpacing its trade integration.

2 Gross capital account flows are likely underestimated relative to gross current account flows because some capital flows take the form of current account transactions in order to avoid official restrictions (see below). Also, most reported bank-related gross flows represent changes between two dates and do not capture any intervening gross flows.

3 For related literature on capital mobility and controls, see Frankel (1992) and Otani and Tiwari (1981). Capital controls are also discussed in the contexts of liberalisation sequence (Frankel 2004; Prasad et al. 2005) and financial contagion (Kawai and Takagi 2001). An overview of the Asian NDF markets can be found in Ma et al. (2004) and Debelle et al. (2006). The key inter-bank interest rates used in this chapter are London inter-bank offer rate (Libor) for the US dollar, the Chinese inter-bank offer rate (CHIBOR) for the renminbi and Hong Kong inter-bank offer rate (Hibor) for the Hong Kong dollar.

4 The PBC introduced a new set of benchmark interbank money market reference rates, Shanghai Interbank Offered Rates (SHIBOR), in January 2007.

5 *China Money*, No. 2, 2006:76.

6 Negative nominal interest rates implied by the pricing of forward exchange rates are not prima facie evidence of an inefficient market. It might be recalled that, during the period of zero yen interest rates, fractionally negative interest rates in yen were implied by yen–dollar swaps. What kept the negative interest rate only fractionally negative was foreign banks parking the yen funds in non-interest-bearing current accounts at the Bank of Japan. The analogy is imperfect because the negative interest rate in yen available to foreign banks reflected the credit standing of the Japanese banks and their need to raise dollars. But the analogy is

useful in that it highlights the fact that in the Chinese case controls prevented non-residents from obtaining interest-bearing or even non-interest-bearing long positions in the renminbi onshore, so some were willing to pay interest on long forward positions offshore.

7 In the onshore forward and swap market, the forward rates have been priced primarily by differentials between onshore interest rates and US dollar interest rates and made available mainly for hedging for real underlying transactions.

8 A Chinese individual now can bring onshore only a maximum of US$50,000 per annum under the current account, down from a previous *de facto* ceiling of US$300,000.

9 The authors caution: '[t]here is a subtlety involved in using parity conditions to evaluate the level of integration. When a parity condition is rejected, then...diminutions of deviations may be due either to greater economic integration, greater convergence of economic policies, or both' (p.6). We incline to policy convergence.

10 Indeed, Granger causality tests suggest that of the three interest rate pairs shown in Figure 14.6, none of the causality runs from the US rate to the Chinese rate. Indeed, the null hypothesis that the three-month Chinese repo yield does not cause the three-month US Treasury bill yield cannot be rejected. This runs counter to the general view that the United States is a global interest rate setter and China a follower.

11 Robert Mundell and Ron McKinnon have long stressed the importance of the renminbi's *de facto* dollar peg as a credible nominal anchor. It remains, however, an empirical question as to how much of the inflation convergence should be attributed to this anchor as opposed to strong-arm Chinese macro controls. The US Federal Reserve tightened aggressively from 1994 to mid 1995 when the renminbi was first stabilised against the US dollar. In the next three years, the Federal Reserve eased somewhat while former Chinese Premier Zhu Rongji took forceful measures to control domestic inflation until the East Asian financial crisis delivered strong deflationary shocks to the Chinese economy.

References

Cheung, Y-W., Chinn, M.D and Fujii, E., 2003. *The Chinese economies in global context: the integration process and its determinants*, Working Paper No.10047, October, National Bureau of Economic Research, Cambridge, MA.

Debelle, G., Gyntelberg, J. and Plumb, M., 2006. 'Forward currency markets in Asia: lessons from the Australian experience', *BIS Quarterly Review*, September:53–64.

Eichengreen, B., 2004. Chinese currency controversies, Paper presented at the Asian Economic Panel of Hong Kong, April.

Frankel, J., 1992. 'Measuring international capital mobility: a review', *American Economic Review*, 82(2):197–202.

——, 2004. On the renminbi: the choice between adjustment under a fixed exchange rate and adjustment under a flexible rate, Paper presented at the High-Level Seminar on Foreign Exchange System, Dalian, 26–27 May.

Kawai, M. and Takagi, S., 2001. Rethinking capital controls (unpublished).

Lane, P. and Milesi-Ferrantti, G.M., 2006. *The external wealth of nations Mark II: revised and extended estimates of foreign assets and liabilities, 1970–2004*, Working Paper, No. 06/69, International Monetary Fund, Washington, DC.

Ma, G., Ho, C. and McCauley, R.N., 2004. 'The markets for non-deliverable forwards in Asian currencies', *BIS Quarterly Review*, June:81–94.

Ma, G. and McCauley, R. (forthcoming). *Are China's capital controls still binding?*, BIS Working Papers, Bank for International Settlements, Basel.

Otani, I. and Tiwari, S., 1981. *Capital controls and interest rate parity: the Japanese experience 1978–81*, Staff Papers, December, International Monetary Fund, Washington, DC:793–815.

Prasad, E., Rumbaugh, T. and Wang, Q., 2005. *Putting the cart before the horse? Capital account liberalization and exchange rate flexibility in China*, Policy Discussion Paper, PDP/05/01, International Monetary Fund, Washington, DC.

Prasad, E. and Wei, S.J., 2005. *The Chinese approach to capital inflows: patterns and possible explanations*, Working Papers, No. 05/07, International Monetary Fund, Washington, DC.

Acknowledgments

The authors wish to thank participants of the conference China and Emerging Asia: reorganising the global economy, 11–12 May 2006, Seoul; the New Monetary and Exchange-Rate Arrangements for East Asia conference, 22–27 May 2006, at the Bellagio; and a Bank for International Settlements seminar for their comments. Special thanks go to Claudio Borio, George M. von Furstenberg and Yu Yongding. The views expressed are the authors' and not necessarily those of the Bank for International Settlements.

Appendix

The spread between onshore yields and NDF-implied offshore yields

In the absence of capital controls, the forward exchange rate of the home currency is linked by arbitrage to its spot rate and the interest rate differential between the home currency and the dollar through the covered interest parity condition (Ma et al. 2004).

$$F = S(1+r)/(1+r^{\$})$$

where 'F' is the forward rate, 'S' the spot rate, 'r' the interest rate on the home currency and $r^{\$}$ the dollar interest rate. When there are no cross-border restrictions, borrowing and lending ensure that the above holds.

When capital controls bind, however, non-residents might not have full access to onshore credit or placements, giving rise to NDFs.

$$NDF = S(1+i)/(1+r^{\$})$$

where 'i' is the NDF-implied yield on the home currency offshore. Note that by definition, 'i' is not constrained by the zero lower bound and could be substantially negative. To the extent that the arbitrage between the onshore money market and offshore NDF market is effectively constrained by capital controls, the NDF-implied offshore interest rate, 'i', can differ considerably from the interest rate prevailing in the onshore money market, 'r'. A large and persistent onshore–offshore spread (r – i) indicates the presence of effective cross-border restrictions. The sign of the yield gap could also reveal prevailing market conditions: a positive sign implies appreciation pressures on the home currency in the presence of capital controls and vice versa.

While a persistently big onshore–offshore yield gap indicates market segmentation, a temporarily narrower gap will not necessarily suggest less effective capital controls. One possibility is that market conditions are such that appreciation or depreciation pressures on the currency are largely absent so that the estimated yield gap is relatively small.

Another, in principle equivalent, approach is to estimate the implied onshore yield on the home currency using the onshore deliverable forwards and then to compare it with the NDF-implied offshore yield. Alternatively, one could compare the onshore deliverable forwards directly with their NDF counterparts to derive a forward premium spread. The merits of these different approaches depend in part on data availability and market liquidity. In China's case, these alternative measures could become more useful over time, as the relevant onshore markets develop and data become more available.

Table A14.1 **Credit default swap rates for People's Republic of China and British Bankers Association's Libor panel banks** (at the one-year maturity in 2004–2006, in basis points)

Issuer	Low	High	Average
People's Republic of China	5.4	27.6	11.2
US dollar Libor panel members:			
Bank of America	2.7	24.6	6.8
Barclays	5.0	9.0	6.9
Citibank	1.9	15.5	4.7
HBOS	1.8	9.0	4.5
HSBC	2.2	9.8	4.2
JP Morgan Chase	1.3	23.0	4.9
Lloyds	1.9	6.5	3.4
BMTU	6.8	63.0	19.0
Norinchukin	5.8	20.0	9.4
Rabobank	3.4	11.9	5.9
Royal Bank of Scotland	2.7	6.2	4.0
Royal Bank of Canada	2.0	11.4	5.1
UBS	1.9	7.3	3.5
WEST LB	2.8	22.8	6.9
Average across banks	3.0	17.1	6.4

Source: Markit (available online at http://www.markit.com/marketing/index.php).

15

Reforming China's exchange arrangements

Monetary and financial sovereignty, sequencing and the foreign exchange market

Huw McKay

China's choice of foreign exchange regime has been a topic of busy debate for more than a decade (Goldstein 2004; Eichengreen 2004; Frankel 2004; Prasad et al. 2005; McKinnon 2006; and McKay 2003, among many others). This discussion has been entwined logically with the question of capital account reform (Prasad et al. 2005; McKay 2005a) and the degree of monetary sovereignty China enjoys under its evolving international financial arrangements (Ma and McCauley forthcoming; Cheung et al. 2003; Ma et al. 2004; He Dong et al. 2005; McKay 2005b). A less populated field applies current, historical and projected regime parameters to the development of, and prospects for, the Chinese financial system and the foreign exchange market itself (McKay 2006; Ho et al. 2005).

The decision to reform the parameters of China's exchange arrangements has always been about more than rapprochement with the United States in the matter of financial suzerainty. There is no attempt in this chapter to address the international externalities generated by the combination of China's policy choices and those made simultaneously by other current account surplus economies and the United States. China's policy deliberations are viewed as a predominantly internal matter, which involve the balancing of a number of competing endogenous priorities and mismatched incentives.

This chapter details the state of play in Chinese foreign exchange markets and sketches a potential development path that envisages respectable growth in trading activity over a multi-year horizon. This outcome is contingent on a gradual phased reduction in outward capital controls and a more rapid (but still managed) pace of currency appreciation. Issues surrounding this assumption form a significant portion of the body of this chapter.

The basic conclusion is that foreign exchange turnover—which is currently exceptionally low in absolute and relative terms—will expand with increasing symmetry in the capital control regime and increased volatility in the US dollar–renminbi exchange rate. The anticipated increase in onshore liquidity, and in renminbi trading generally, should be seen as a benign development for the regional and global foreign exchange market. It is natural to anticipate that some of the gross increase in onshore trading will be diverted from other centres. Yet with aggregate turnover so low at present, and given that this low level of liquidity is an outgrowth of administrative design rather than market forces, it is natural to predict that a shift towards a more liberal constellation of exchange arrangements will provide a continuing net fillip for global foreign exchange market liquidity.

Historical background and the state of play

China unified onshore currency trading in 1994, with the establishment of the Shanghai-based China Foreign Exchange Trading System (CFETS). Before the inauguration of this trading platform and clearing system, trading took place in upwards of 100 independent centres. Initially only US dollar–renminbi and Hong Kong dollar–renminbi were traded. Japanese yen–renminbi was added to the system in 1995 and euro–renminbi in 2002. In May 2005, eight non-renminbi crosses were also made available: US dollar–Japanese yen, euro–US dollar, US dollar–Swiss franc, US dollar–British pound, US dollar–Hong Kong dollar, Australian dollar–US dollar, euro–Japanese yen and US dollar–Canadian dollar. Forward trading was added to the platform in August 2005, two months after the revaluation of the renminbi against the US dollar.

Turnover data from the early years of CFETS' operation show that little growth occurred between 1994 and 1998. The triennial foreign exchange survey for 1998 by the Bank for International Settlements (BIS 1999a) estimated that foreign exchange turnover in mainland China averaged US$211 million a day, one-tenth of 1 per cent of the global total.[1] The interim survey in 2001 implied relative stasis (BIS 2002), but turnover for 2004 (BIS 2005) showed resounding growth. In April 2004, onshore turnover had risen to US$614 million a day, equivalent to three-tenths of 1 per cent of the global total. It is important to note that the BIS data could exclude a number of transactions involving the non-bank sector, and interbank clearing activity that occurs outside of the CFETS platform (Ho et al. 2005). So it is likely that renminbi turnover is underestimated to a degree. Adding in an estimate of non-reported onshore trades, plus all other recorded trades involving the renminbi, irrespective of location, including the non-deliverable forward market,[2] raises the total to US$3.6 billion. That would be equivalent to 1.5 per cent of global foreign exchange turnover.

By counter-currency, in the December quarter of 2004, the US dollar was involved in 53.2 per cent of CFETS trades, the Japanese yen in 38.7 per cent, the Hong Kong dollar in 8.1 per cent and the euro in a negligible portion (CFETS data from the CEIC China database). A factor that will impact on foreign exchange market development will be the evolution of the invoicing practices of China's trading firms. At present, the US dollar is by far the dominant invoice currency for Chinese trade transactions, however, that might not always be the case. As Chinese exporters move up the value chain, it is possible that they will pursue an 'invoicing-to-market' currency denomination strategy. This trend has been observed among the G7 countries and in Korea (Yun 2005). This would bias turnover away from the US dollar and towards other international currencies such as the euro and the Japanese yen. If and when the renminbi becomes internationalised, it could become the invoice currency for many Chinese imports. That would bring those firms which export to China into the renminbi markets, offering depth and an injection of foreign exchange risk management experience.

The BIS data for April 2004 show a dominance of spot transactions relative to forwards or swaps in the traditional market space, and a relatively low level of overall activity in the renminbi. Spot transactions accounted for about 55 per cent of all renminbi trades, compared with 47 per cent for the Indian rupee, 21 per cent for the Hong Kong dollar, 49 per cent for the Korean won, 37 per cent for the Indonesian rupiah, 30 per cent for the Singaporean dollar and 38 per cent for the Thai baht. In the derivatives market, renminbi turnover is extremely low. Cross-currency swaps reportedly averaged just US$4 million a day, and options just US$136 million—far below the levels prevailing in the markets of the new industrialised economies.[3] Relative volume and market structure are summarised in Figures 15.1 and 15.2. These figures indicate that not only is the Chinese foreign exchange market rather shallow, it is far from sophisticated. The fact that the CFETS platform accommodated forwards trading only from August 2005 underscores this point.

Analysis

It is useful to scale the turnover data to help define the relative depth of the Chinese foreign exchange market. Three figures have been prepared with this in mind, representing the relationship between foreign exchange turnover and income, scale and real demand proxies, respectively. Figure 15.3 plots foreign exchange turnover against a measure of relative living standards: gross domestic product (GDP) per capita at purchasing power parity (PPP) exchange

Figure 15.1 **Asian foreign exchange turnover, by transaction type, 2004** (US$ billion)

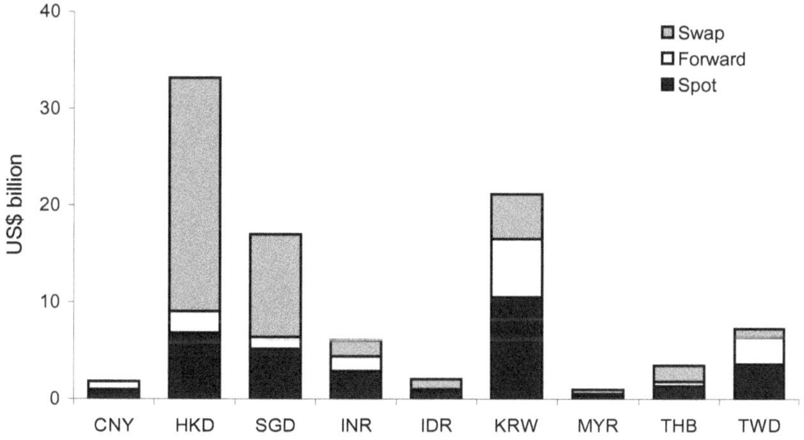

Notes: CNY Chinese renminbi, HKD Hong Kong dollar, SGD Singaporean dollar, INR Indian rupee, IDR Indonesian rupiah, KRW Korean won, MYR Malaysian ringgit, THB Thai baht, TWD Taiwan dollar.
Source: Bank for International Settlements (BIS), 2005. *Triennial Central Bank Survey of Foreign Exchange and Derivatives Market Activity in April 2004*, Bank for International Settlements, Basel.

Figure 15.2 **Shares of foreign exchange turnover, by transaction type, 2004**

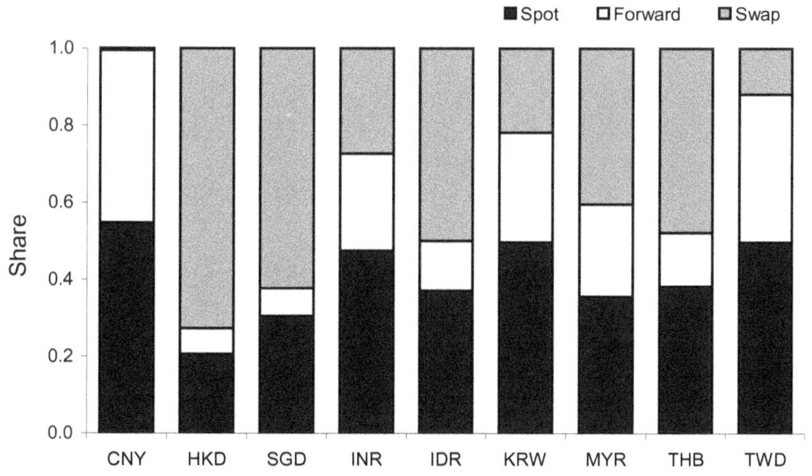

Notes: CNY Chinese renminbi, HKD Hong Kong dollar, SGD Singaporean dollar, INR Indian rupee, IDR Indonesian rupiah, KRW Korean won, MYR Malaysian ringgit, THB Thai baht, TWD Taiwan dollar.
Source: Bank for International Settlements (BIS), 2005. *Triennial Central Bank Survey of Foreign Exchange and Derivatives Market Activity in April 2004*, Bank for International Settlements, Basel.

rates as a percentage of the US level. Figure 15.4 plots foreign exchange turnover against a scale measure (share of world GDP at PPP exchange rates). Figure 15.5 plots foreign exchange turnover as a ratio to gross trade flows, which are an approximation of the real underlying demand for foreign exchange.

The last two measures show that China is a clear outlier, exhibiting sharply lower turnover than might be expected given the economy's overall size and the scale of its trading activity. The first relationship, however, implies that China's low foreign exchange turnover figures are a state of nature that might be deduced from its low relative living standard.

The correct way to balance these apparently contradictory results is to argue that, as a low-income country China should not be expected to exhibit highly open exchange arrangements at this point in time; but given that China's foreign exchange markets are even less liquid than its East Asian peers, the current constellation of exchange arrangements is less liberal than it might be at this stage of economic development.

China's lowly ranking in the foreign exchange turnover stakes has implications for the debate on the effectiveness of the capital control regime. To stylise somewhat, China's capital controls are relatively porous with regards to inward flows, but relatively binding on outward flows. This view rejects the claim that China's controls are ineffective at the aggregate level, eroding monetary sovereignty.[4] If outward controls are binding—as they certainly appear to be (Ma and McCauley forthcoming)—onshore parties will experience an unrequited (latent) demand for foreign exchange transactions. Yet binding controls prevent these demands from being requited. Ergo, Chinese foreign exchange liquidity will be lower than in markets where similar outflows are not restricted, all other things being equal.

Note that this hypothetical reasoning says nothing about the exchange rate itself, which is the price at which actual transactions take place. The discussion is for the moment interested solely in turnover rather than the demand–supply balance. The proposition being established is that turnover is low not because the demand for foreign exchange is low, but because the market is distorted (suppressed) by regulation. The distortion serves to penalise turnover by disallowing transactions that might otherwise take place. Remove the restrictions and liquidity will rise.

Future development

Any effort to sketch a development path for China's foreign exchange markets must incorporate a view on the evolution of the regulatory environment for capital flows. It must also encompass a view on the future course of the

Figure 15.3 **Foreign exchange market depth and income level**

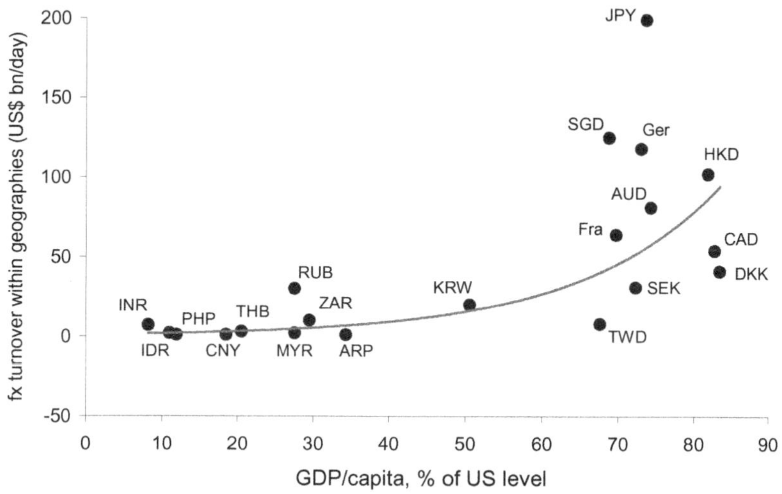

Sources: Turnover data from Bank for International Settlements (BIS), 2005. *Triennial Central Bank Survey of Foreign Exchange and Derivatives Market Activity in April 2004*, Bank for International Settlements, Basel. GDP per capita and PPP weights from International Monetary Fund WEO Database. Available from http://www.imf.org/external/pubs/ft/weo/2007/01/data/index.aspx

Figure 15.4 **Foreign exchange market depth and scale**

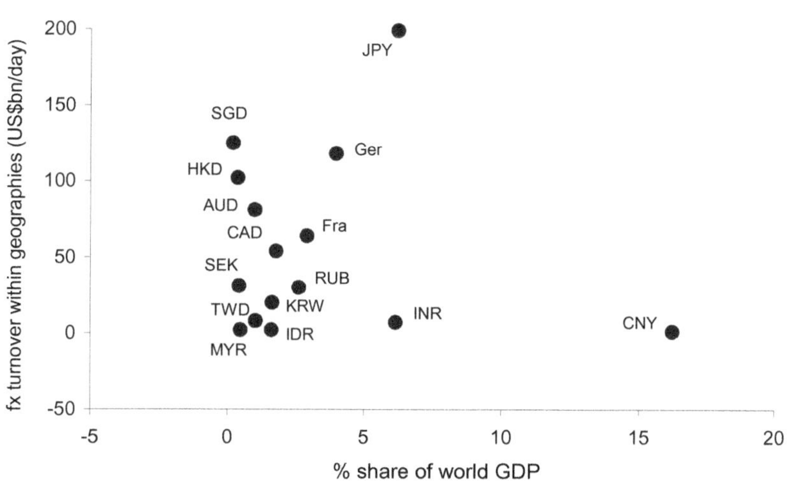

Sources: Turnover data from Bank for International Settlements (BIS), 2005. *Triennial Central Bank Survey of Foreign Exchange and Derivatives Market Activity in April 2004*, Bank for International Settlements, Basel. Share of world GDP and PPP weights from International Monetary Fund WEO Database. Available from http://www.imf.org/external/pubs/ft/weo/2007/01/data/index.aspx

Figure 15.5 **Foreign exchange turnover and real demand, 2004** (ratio*)

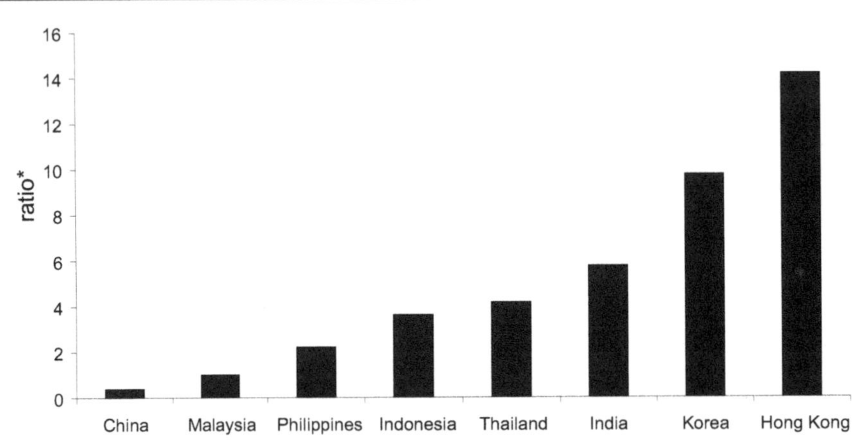

[a] Annualised foreign exchange turnover scaled by gross merchandise and services trade for 2004 calendar year, converted at market exchange rates.
Sources: Turnover data from Bank for International Settlements (BIS), 2005. *Triennial Central Bank Survey of Foreign Exchange and Derivatives Market Activity in April 2004*, Bank for International Settlements, Basel. Ratios are author's calculations using trade data from the World Development Indicators database. Available from https://publications.worldbank.org/WDI/

exchange rate regime itself. These issues cut deep into the umbrella theme of macroeconomic policy design for the next decade.

The choice of an exchange rate regime and the basic regulatory approach to cross-border capital flow is inseparable from the broader issue of monetary policy design. Theory is unequivocal on the point that the combination of a fixed exchange rate with an open capital account and an independent monetary policy is incompatible. Yet China and a number of developing economies arguably attempt to run a monetary policy that is in effect a bastardised form of this 'unholy trinity'.[5] The virtue of each arm of monetary policy is compromised while the authorities search for a pragmatic constellation that is not obviously damaging but always feels like second best, or worse (Corden 2002; Tarapore 2006).

Figure 15.6 shows two arms of the trinity—the degree of exchange rate flexibility and the degree of capital account openness—in concert with per capita GDP. The large equilateral triangle represents the United States, with its wealth, its open capital account and its flexible exchange rate. The middle-sized triangle represents the average economy in East Asia (excluding Japan). The smallest triangle is China.

Note the illiberal overall policy regime in Asia, and China's low absolute scores on capital account openness and foreign exchange flexibility. There is also information content in the skew of these two triangles. In Asia generally, the skew is moderately towards a more flexible currency and away from an open capital account. This reflects in part the failure of intermediate regimes in Korea, Thailand and Indonesia during the East Asian financial crisis, dragging policymakers reluctantly down the more flexible path. At this time, policymakers across Asia reacted by strengthening capital controls, exercising *ex post* financial sovereignty after the collapse of the *ex ante* exchange rate regime. Open capital accounts in Singapore and Hong Kong boost the average on the bottom left axis substantially.

In China, the skew goes the other way. The policy mix in China is a clear illustration of the 'cherry-picking' approach to regime design. The higher score on capital openness comes from China's willingness to indulge inflows, particularly of direct investment. The lower score on exchange rate flexibility derives from the heavily managed exchange rate regime and the low turnover created jointly by the lack of volatility and the depressing impact of capital controls.

Figure 15.6 **The triangular dynamics of regime parameters**

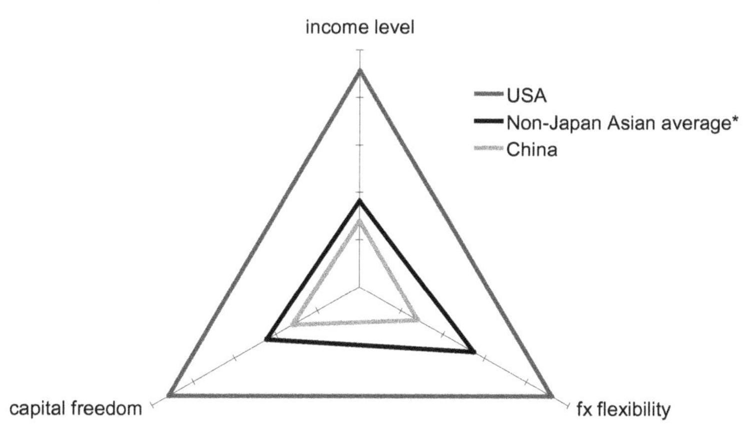

Note: * Non-Japan Asian average computed from author's estimate of foreign exchange flexibility and capital openness in the newly industrialised economies (as defined in Note 3) plus Malaysia, Thailand, the Philippines, Indonesia and India.
Sources: Author's estimates for foreign exchange flexibility and capital openness. Income levels from International Monetary Fund WEO Database. Available from http://www.imf.org/external/pubs/ft/weo/2007/01/data/index.aspx

The loophole in the unholy trinity conditions that China exploits is that you can have your cake (an inflexible exchange rate and domestic monetary sovereignty) and eat it too (capital inflow of the desired kind), if you are willing and able to intervene in the foreign exchange market and sterilise capital inflows sufficiently to neuter the impact on domestic monetary conditions. In other words, the People's Bank of China must be willing to accrue foreign exchange reserves equivalent to the sum of the current account balance and the capital and financial accounts. It must also withdraw the liquidity that its foreign exchange intervention generates. In a macro regime sense, Figure 15.7 shows the ever-increasing intervention/sterilisation imperative if China's exploitation of the loophole is to be prevented from leaking into domestic liquidity conditions.

By March 2007, China's foreign reserves had risen to a total of US$1,202 billion. In the six months to March, reserves accumulated at an average monthly pace in excess of US$50 billion. In addition to mopping up liquidity through bond

Figure 15.7 **Loophole strategy drives big foreign exchange reserve accretion**

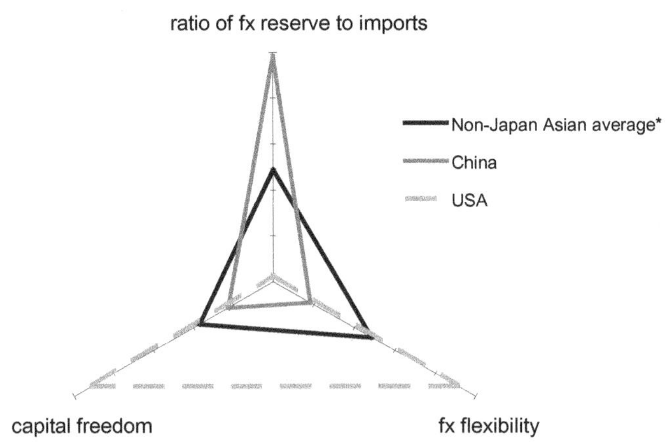

Note: * Non-Japan Asian average computed from author's estimate of foreign exchange flexibility and capital openness in the newly industrialised economies (as defined in Note 3) plus Malaysia, Thailand, the Philippines, Indonesia and India.
Sources: Author's estimates for foreign exchange flexibility and capital openness. Foreign exchange reserves and import levels from the CEIC Data Company. Where necessary, imports were converted to US dollars using exchange rates from the Reserve Bank of Australia *F Tables* (available from http://www.rba.gov.au/Statistics/Bulletin/index.html).

issuance—an activity that was sufficient for sterilisation purposes from 2003 to the first half of 2006—the authorities began using other tools as well. Through progressive policy shifts, the proportion of bank deposits held compulsorily at the central bank (the required reserve ratio) increased from 6 per cent in 2003 to 11 per cent in April 2007. Further increases in the required reserve ratio are just a matter of time.

The effectiveness of the administrative sterilisation effort in the early stages of the boom in capital inflow is assessed in He Dong et al. (2005) and McKay (2005b). Both papers argue that China's sterilisation activity was sufficient to successfully insulate domestic credit conditions from capital inflow. In other words, monetary sovereignty was maintained. Admittedly, the datum samples in each paper do not extend to the second half of 2006, when the sterilisation burden was rising dramatically in line with the spectacular increase in the monthly trade surplus from August. Further, as interest rates are not fully market determined, it is difficult to deduce a clear signal from the onshore money markets in this regard. Thirdly, McKay (2005b) found tentative evidence that foreign exchange reserve growth leaked into the grey lending market in a limited fashion. The statistical relation was judged to be of insufficient strength to be of macroeconomic significance, but that could easily change if the degree of intervention required to stabilise the currency were to rise steeply.

China has not yet reached a point where its sterilisation operation is becoming a major macroeconomic or logistical problem. Other Asian economies—such as Korea, Taiwan and Malaysia—have directed a far greater effort to sterilisation at times in the past 10 years, consistent with their higher trade-to-GDP ratios relative to China. Issuance of sterilisation instruments in these three economies peaked at 431 per cent, 228 per cent and 132 per cent of base money, respectively, during the current US dollar downturn. In China, central bank bond issuance rose to about 125 per cent of base money in mid 2006. Huge inflows in the March quarter of 2007 pushed issuance above 140 per cent of base money. Hikes in the required reserve ratio began to be instituted from mid 2006, reducing the burden somewhat (see Figures 15.8 and 15.9).

Given the superordinate long-term policy goal of achieving a consumer-oriented economic structure, it seems natural that in future the authorities will compromise less and less in terms of their control over domestic credit conditions. Further, while the present methods of intervention and sterilisation can continue for some indeterminate time, it is clearly a finite method. The resources chewed up by the sterilisation effort (labour and capital, funds kept as reserves and therefore not employed elsewhere) have an opportunity cost that at some point will exceed the perceived benefits. Consumerism also implies a

Figure 15.8 **Sterilisation effort is the price of sovereignty**

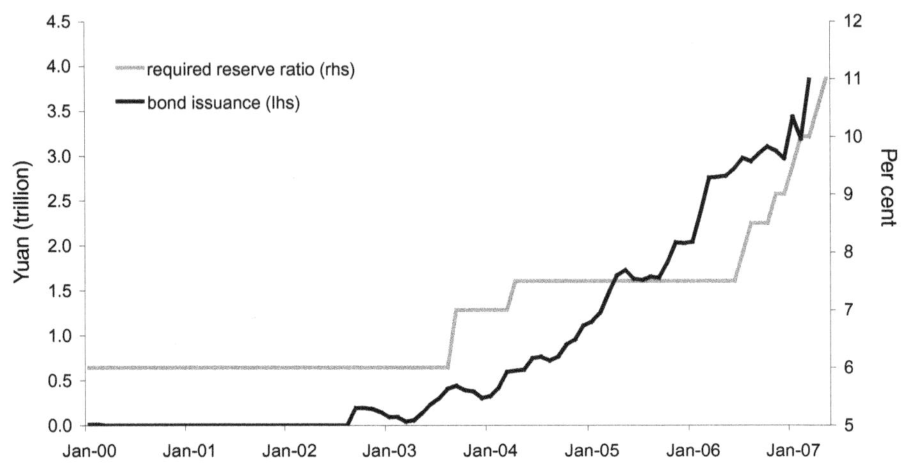

Source: CEIC Data Company.

Figure 15.9 **Reserve ratio hikes take the pressure off bond issuance**

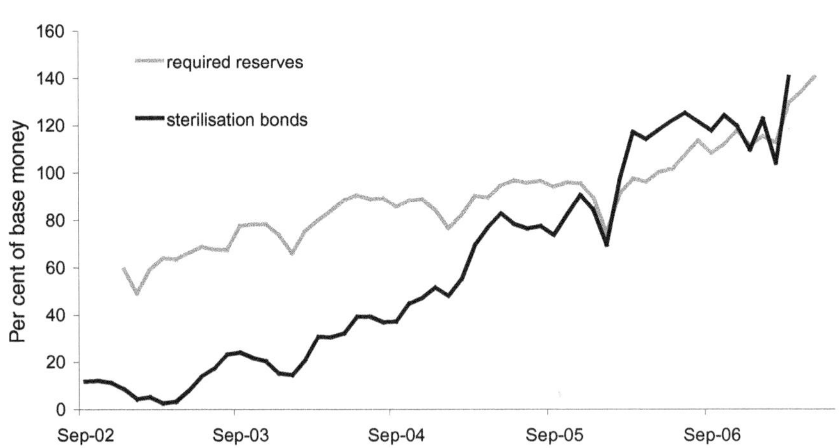

Note: The last datum point in the required reserves ratio to base money was calculated before the 29 April 2007 announcement of a rate hike.
Sources: CEIC Data Company.; author's calculations.

reduced focus on exchange rate stability and external competitiveness issues in the future. That in turn would ease the pressure to maintain capital controls. In short, the parameter loophole that China is currently exploiting will at some point decline in popularity with policymakers.

The present mix of parameters is consistent with the export-driven development model that has served China well. The maturation and exhaustion of this strategy will signal a new approach to monetary policy and international financial arrangements.

If the authorities did have it in mind to move away from the current constellation of regime parameters, preparatory activity and policy changes would be observed following a sequence similar to that outlined below. Under benign internal and external economic conditions, the normative path from a fixed to a floating exchange rate is reasonably well defined. The following catalogue of tasks will get the job done in a decade or so. The benchmark work in the 'sequencing' field is McKinnon (1993).

1. Establish convertibility on the current account and unify onshore trading of the currency.
2. Work towards establishing an alternative anchor for monetary policy. This step also incorporates progressive liberalisation of interest rate determination. Inflation targeting is one possible alternative model/anchor, successful application of which requires central bank independence, the unification of monetary and foreign exchange policy[6] and the establishment of inflation-fighting 'credibility' with the market.[7]
3. Establish an onshore forward market to provide domestic institutions with the tools to hedge the risks associated with increased exchange rate flexibility.
4. Widen the allowable trading band around the existing peg to give domestic institutions a chance to 'train' themselves to deal with exchange rate volatility under protected conditions. Progressively decrease the market-making role of the monetary authority as the interbank market matures.
5. Work to alleviate any existing asymmetries in capital account regulations to avert a bias in capital flows that will create skewed risks regarding movement in the exchange rate. Design a strategy for ensuring fuller capital account convertibility in the future (more on this theme below). This could include the highlighting of concomitants, although they should be couched in such a way as to not materially reduce policy flexibility in the future.

6. Progressively increase the allowable degree of exchange rate volatility as competency improves and the market deepens organically.
7. When the allowable degree of volatility approaches a level where it is essentially redundant, quietly move to a free-floating, market-determined exchange rate.

In China, we have seen activity in many of these areas, notably a widening of the allowable trading band against the US dollar to +/– 0.5 per cent on 18 May (Figure 15.10). Yet with the exception of the initial step of current account convertibility—which was completed in the mid 1990s—conditions remain fluid. The central bank has been working on the greater application of market-based counter-cyclical tools, yet they continue to be mixed with administrative controls. The intended benchmark for market-based interest rate determination—the newly instituted Shanghai interbank offered rates (SHIBOR, in multiple tenors)—was unveiled on 4 January 2007 (*China Money* 2007). Deposit and lending rates are still constrained by floors and ceilings. The interbank money markets are immature and relatively illiquid. The direction of reform is clear, but there are obvious hurdles still to surmount in this area. Song (2005) provides a useful analysis of developments in interest rate liberalisation and offers a compelling efficiency argument for deregulation.

Figure 15.10 **Flexibility has increased, appreciation pace gradual, 2005–2007**

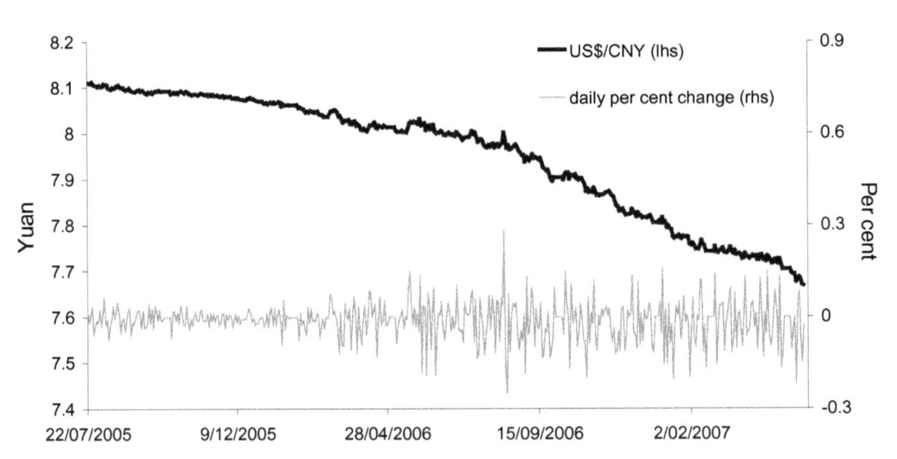

Sources: Bloomberg; author's calculations.

The relative immaturity of the onshore forward foreign exchange market has already been detailed. It was established in August 2005, so it is a very young market. Spot transactions still dominate overall turnover. It is not credible to say to the private sector that 'the currency is going to be more flexible, do something about it', in the knowledge that a liquid onshore forward market is not readily available to firms wishing to hedge the newly created risk.

One way that the authorities are seeking to boost liquidity is by imposing private turnover targets on the major players in the onshore market. This tactic has, however, not been a great success. Interviews with market participants show that these targets are often met through dummy trades that are position neutral, and are therefore not adding real liquidity to the market.[8] Players with the credit worthiness to access onshore and offshore markets tend to transact in the deeper and more sophisticated of the two, which undoubtedly is offshore. In short, the market participants who could do the most to deepen the onshore market are choosing to conduct a minimum of transactions there.

The authorities are simultaneously working hard to simulate two-way risk within the newly minted +/– 0.5 per cent band without deviating from a 3–5 per cent annualised rate of nominal appreciation against the US dollar. The announced daily fixing rate sometimes looks incongruous in the larger context of broader foreign exchange market movements, but sometimes it must be so to train firms to expect the unexpected, thereby encouraging them to protect themselves accordingly. Once again, this activity is preparatory for a more flexible future, but not a bold new world starting tomorrow.

Once again, the incentives of the bureaucratic architects of the market are in conflict with those of potential participants. The bureaucrats would like firms to begin transacting in forwards now to build competency and familiarity under the benign conditions of weak volatility exhibited by the current regime. But firms are not transacting, because conditions have been too benign. To be blunt, firms will not bear hedging costs unless they are scared by what they have observed on the exchange rate appreciation front. But scaring firms with sharp renminbi gains would remove the protective conditions the authorities have been cultivating so carefully. It is the latter that is most likely to give, as the non-hedgers hold the rational ground.

US dollar–renminbi moves since the revaluation in 2005 have clearly not been sufficiently frightening to spur hedging activity. The new allowable daily volatility of +/– 0.5 per cent, announced in the lead-up to the 2007 Strategic Economic Dialogue with the United States, was instituted despite the old band of +/– 0.3 per cent not being consistently tested. The lack of volatility has generated complacency rather than panic. It seems likely that hedging activity,

Figure 15.11 **Outward direct investment[a] still the poor cousin, 2002–2006** (US$ billion)

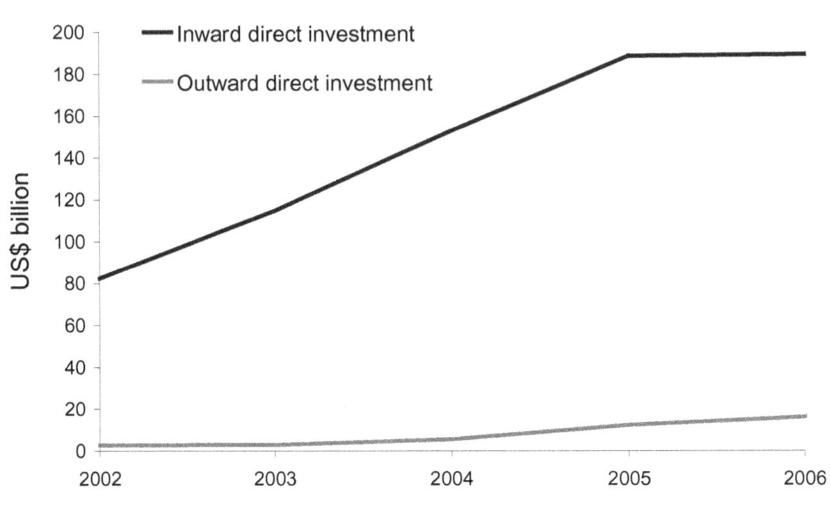

[a] Both series exclude investment in financial firms.
Sources: CEIC Data Company; 2006 data for inward investment are author's estimate.

and forward turnover, will remain low until the trading band is widened (or tested with more frequency) and more aggressive appreciation is delivered.

The fifth item in the catalogue is another major sticking point. As stated many times already, Chinese capital controls are of the cherry-picking variety. Foreign direct investment (FDI) attraction is a stated policy goal, and a performance metric for provincial governments. Newly instated Qualified Foreign Institutional Investor (QFII) inward-bound investment quotas will add to overall inflow. More than 50 QFII applications have been approved since May 2003, with combined quotas in excess of US$8 billion (State Administration of Foreign Exchange n.d.). Further, the FDI exemption potentially allows not only genuine investment but capital flow of a less permanent nature (Ma and McCauley forthcoming). Consequently, the capital account is quite porous in the inward direction. In addition, China's immense trade surplus (US$177 billion in 2006 and likely to easily exceed US$200 billion in 2007 after recording a US$46 billion outcome in the seasonally unfavourable March quarter) generates a large and expanding inward flow. On the other hand, domestic savings are fenced in, with outflows limited to official reserve asset management, a meagre amount of debt repayments and currently modest Qualified Domestic Institutional Investor (QDII) outward-bound investment flows. A burgeoning demand for outward foreign direct investment, particularly in the strategic areas of energy, food and metals, is yet to make much of a splash. Figure 15.11 highlights the imbalance between inward and outward direct investment flows.

The asymmetry inherent in this structure leads to an appreciation bias for the renminbi. If funds come in, without a corresponding flow in the opposite direction, an excess supply of foreign currency is generated, putting appreciation pressure on the local unit. In effect, China runs a twin external surplus on its current and capital accounts. The asymmetry could be corrected either by waiving controls on outflow or penalising inflow. The momentum of reform clearly favours the former option.

Projecting reforms designed to liberalise capital outflow is not as easy as it might at first seem. The difficulty comes due to the fact that liberalising outflow means the potential release of captive domestic savings. China's financial asset

Figure 15.12 **The financial asset stock in selected countries**

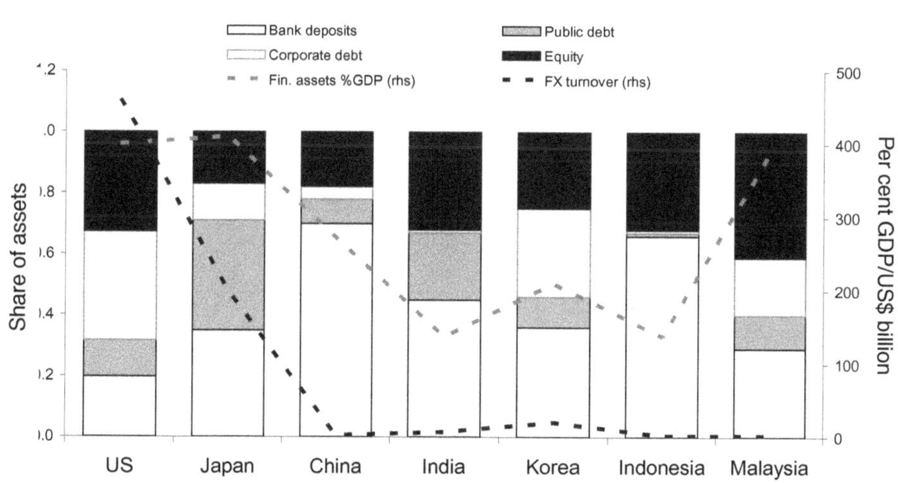

Sources: Turnover data from Bank for International Settlements, 2005. *Triennial Central Bank Survey of Foreign Exchange and Derivatives Market Activity in April 2004*, Bank for International Settlements, Basel. Financial stock data sourced from McKinsey Global Institute global financial stock database, cited in Farrell, D., Lund, S. and Morin, F., 2006. 'The promise and perils of China's banking system', *The McKinsey Quarterly*, July (available from http://www.mckinseyquarterly.com).

stock features an unusually high share of bank deposits (Figure 15.12). This has not come about by chance. Keeping a high level of household savings in deposits is a form of subsidy for the banks. Bank balance sheets have been weak since the sharp inflationary boom of the mid 1990s turned sour (Lardy 1998; Bank for International Settlements 1999b; Huang 2001; Ma and Fung 2002; Ma 2006; McKay 2005c).

China's bank profits rely to a large extent on an artificially wide margin between deposit and lending rates. This margin is created by official controls on 'floor' lending rates and 'ceiling' deposit rates. If, however, the pool of domestic savings were to shrink due to heightened capital egress, these cosy arrangements would have to end. The local banks would require the flexibility to offer more attractive terms to maintain depositors. Two per cent of China's population controls close to 60 per cent of deposits (Farrell et al. 2006). This wealthy population segment can safely be described as sophisticated investors. They will no doubt seek to diversify their cash holdings in terms of asset class, geography and currency denomination once the opportunity to do so arises. That said, the weak take-up of QDII products may indicate that the recent strength of the A share market and the threat of the currency eroding offshore gains may indicate that at present there is a rational incentive to be over-weight domestic assets.

If the banks had robust balance sheets, this would not be a great threat. As things are, legacy non-performing loans (NPLs) have not been fully carved out, creating an inherent vulnerability. The administration knows that these loans—and those sitting unsold on asset management company balance sheets—are basically contingent fiscal liabilities. That being the case, it is not in the government's interest to expose the banks to a material loss of deposits at this time, particularly in the light of the World Trade Organization-inspired increase in competition from foreign banks in domestic currency business since December 2006.

The recent initial public offerings of major state banks were attractive for many reasons, not the least of which was to get strategic foreign investors to provide capital injections that paid a huge premium over book value without ceding controlling interests. These new shareholders are part of the NPL bail out story, as are the existing shareholders (Ministry of Finance, Huijin) and bank customers. But the main loser is likely to be the taxpayer (Ma 2006).

Figure 15.13 represents a story similar to the catalogue of normative reform steps outlined above. The difference is that with knowledge of the vulnerability of Chinese banks, the assumption of benign internal conditions must be overturned. Indeed, when the banking equation is considered, the arguments on international financial reform become somewhat circular.

Figure 15.13 **The circularity of the flexibility argument**

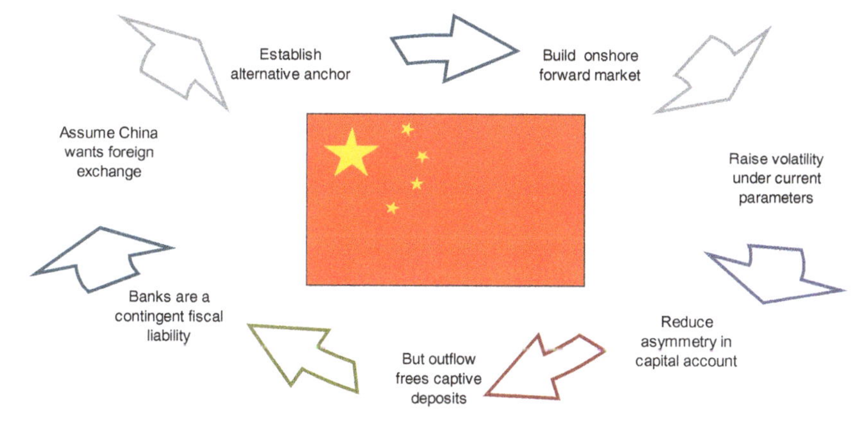

Figure 15.14 **Banking sector strength and foreign exchange volatility**

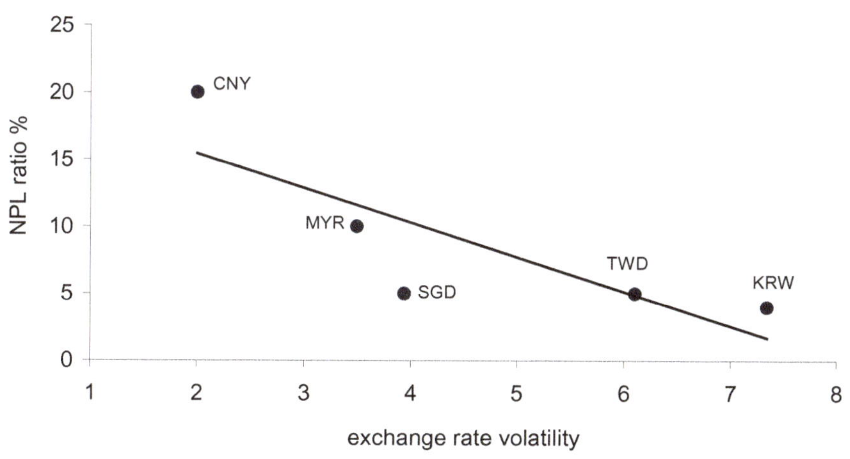

Sources: Standard and Poor's rating agency for NPL estimates (subscription only newsletter); Westpac Strategy for foreign exchange volatility estimates. In many cases the Standard and Poor's estimate will be many multiples of the official estimate. Standard and Poor's is used to ensure consistent methodology across the sample.

The major sticking point is the need to reduce asymmetry in the capital account to reduce the existing one-way bias on the exchange rate. That means allowing significant outflows and that in turn means freeing bank deposits to find a new home. That is obviously anathema. Yet if the capital account is left asymmetric, appreciation pressure will remain undimmed due to a continuation of the excess of inflows. Figure 15.14 shows the relationship between foreign exchange volatility and financial system strength in selected Asian countries. The countries in the sample have been chosen for their demonstrated capacity to manage volatility in their exchange rate. Ergo we can style observed volatility levels as a policy choice. The negative relationship between bank balance sheets and sanctioned volatility is strong and consistent with the core of the argument.

A strategy for gradual capital account liberalisation

From the Chinese administration's point of view, the path of least resistance seems clear: try to muddle through on the reform front until the banking system grows out of its NPL problem. Yet a bolder administration can do more than muddle through. Here we revisit point five in our catalogue, where the concept of a road-map for fuller capital account openness was introduced. India has formalised this concept with the publication of a report from a working committee of the Reserve Bank of India on fuller capital account convertibility (Tarapore 2006).

Capital outflows can be liberalised in a selective fashion that makes it difficult for household savings to move offshore but enables firms and institutional investors to do so more freely. A heightened degree of outward foreign direct investment is the obvious first point of call.

Outward direct investment is permitted only after an examination of the source of the foreign exchange funds for the venture is undertaken and the relevant ministries have been informed and have authorised the transaction. Strategic activities such as export promotion, resource development and scientific research and development are already given preferential treatment (International Monetary Fund 2006). Yet outward direct investment flows have been weak (see Figure 15.11).

One reason for the lack of direct investment outflow could be that Chinese manufacturing firms have little desire to build production capacity offshore, when they can produce much more competitively at home. Further, advanced-country tariff rates are not presently restrictive, so there is little reason to set up behind these barriers. Another factor could be that due to the legacy firm structure, the conglomerate/network structures that encouraged upstream vertical integration by Japanese corporate groups during that economy's industrialisation drive are less evident in China.[9] In the particular case of resources, including energy, it is only since 2003 that prices have become onerous. Large importers of commodities and energy faced a benign price and supply environment through much of the 1990s. Therefore, direct control of resources was not a major issue. That has clearly changed.

It would seem natural that in the current environment the Chinese administration would heighten its focus on acquiring suitable offshore assets in the resources arena. That would be very easy to formalise in the policy rhetoric, as nothing in particular has to be done to the letter of the law to boost outward direct investment. The authorities can play a firmer signalling role though, perhaps via bilateral trade arrangements with resource-rich jurisdictions that could allow preferential treatment for Chinese entities in the direct investment field.[10]

Stronger outflows of direct investment would also provide a vehicle through which other funds could find their way offshore. Just as hot money reportedly currently makes its way into China under the guise of 'real demand' flows, well-connected domestic investors could use the same clandestine methods to get their money out.

On the portfolio side, as discussed above, domestic investors can apply to move funds offshore for specific purposes. By requiring approval for everything, the authorities hope to minimise the sort of outflows that might be problematic given the backdrop of bank balance sheet vulnerability. It is not difficult to foresee a modest increase in outward portfolio flow through the QDII channel. It is more difficult to see the sort of reforms that would enable Chinese household savers to directly send their funds offshore.

In sum, China's strategy regarding capital egress is likely to focus on outward direct investment in the first instance, and portfolio flows at a more distant date.

Capital account deregulation is an immense and complex task, particularly so when an élite bureaucracy has bound up the gamut of international financial arrangements with red tape. Examples abound across East and South Asia in this regard. It should be noted that Japan took some 30 years to unwind its once pervasive capital account regulations. That seems like a long time, particularly when much of the work was done against the backdrop of apparently healthy bank balance sheets in the 1980s. The reforms were not due to outside pressure; they were a response to internal demand (McKay 2004).

In India, it is now 16 years since the initial liberalising reforms of then Finance Minister Dr Manmohan Singh. The issue had been moot for a decade before now Prime Minister Singh put it back on the agenda last year (Tarapore 2006).

The lesson from these countries is that capital account deregulation proceeds at an unpredictable pace, with flurries of energy interspersed with long periods of inactivity. Contrary to foreign exchange regime choice, which can be thrust on a country by market forces (McKay 2003; Bubula and Ötker-Robe 2003), capital control is a discretionary legislative matter: sovereignty is always maintained. That implies firmly that capital account (de)regulation can be conducted voluntarily at times of domestic need and can stand aloof to external or market pressures.

How long might China take to achieve symmetry in its capital flow regime against the present backdrop of a strikingly weak financial system? That is beyond the scope of this work. What is important to note is that, for the moment, a proactive approach to boosting outward direct investment and a prudent approach to increasing portfolio flows by the corporate and professional investment communities is probably in China's best interests. Equally importantly, any reform should be designed to keep household savings captive for a while longer.

Summary and conclusions

China's foreign exchange market is characterised by a low level of turnover and a lack of sophistication. Low absolute and relative levels of liquidity are an outgrowth of the risk-averse umbrella policy regime. The current regime restricts capital outflow and exchange rate flexibility. A material increase in turnover in the onshore market awaits a more liberal policy setting on both counts.

Prospects for deregulation are sound but not completely overwhelming. The weakness of the banking system intrudes rather rudely on the normative arguments for exchange rate flexibility and accompanying de-restriction of the capital account. Indeed, the line that China is ready to accommodate greater exchange rate flexibility and a substantially more open capital account appears circular when the banking issue looms into view. Yet a selective easing of restrictions on outflow by corporations and professional investors would help alleviate a portion of the existing asymmetries, without unduly threatening captive bank deposits.

Greater outflows are needed to reduce the strong one-way bias for the exchange rate and to stem the rapid accumulation of foreign exchange reserves. In turn, this would reduce the required sterilisation effort. China's loophole approach towards its core policy parameters is clearly a finite one. At some future point, the sum of the sterilisation effort and the opportunity cost of reserve holding will exceed the perceived stability benefits in the minds of policymakers.

Once China commits fully to the pursuit of a consumer-driven economic structure, the current mix of policy parameters will be discarded rationally. The present mix of parameters is consistent with the export-driven development model that has characterised the economy in the reform era. The maturation and exhaustion of this strategy will signal a new approach to monetary policy and international financial arrangements. The emphasis will shift from an external anchor—the fixed exchange rate—to levers controlling internal liquidity.

On the exchange rate regime itself, the appreciation trajectory of the renminbi since the revaluation has been managed so tightly that firms have chosen to eschew hedging activity. Turnover is likely to be relatively suppressed until the imperative to hedge rises. The very gradual appreciation of the renminbi observed so far has not been sufficient to convince firms that the costs of hedging are less than those of not doing so. Given this reality, the administration could decide that greater appreciation and associated volatility are a necessary evil on the way to building a developed foreign exchange market.

Notes

1 The data presented here are for turnover by country, not by currency. They are taken from Table E-4 of the triennial BIS surveys (1996, 1999a, 2002, 2005).

2 'Non-deliverable forwards', or NDFs, are a cash-settled forward contract on a non-capital account convertible (that is, 'non-deliverable' offshore) currency. The notional principal amount, the outright foreign exchange rate and maturity (fixing date) are all agreed at inception. On maturity there is no exchange of principal. A cash differential, in US dollars, is paid or received depending on the relativity between the fixing rate and the original contract. For an overview of the Asian NDF market, see Debelle et al. (2006) and Ma et al. (2004). For logistics of NDFs relative to deliverable forwards, see Westpac Institutional Bank (2006).

3 New industrialised economies as defined by the International Monetary Fund: Republic of Korea, Taiwan Province of China, Hong Kong Special Administrative Region of China and Singapore.

4 This debate is played out in Cheung et al. (2003); Eichengreen (2004); Ma et al. (2004); and Ma and McCauley (forthcoming).

5 The 'unholy trinity' of an open capital account, a fixed exchange rate and an independent monetary policy is a logical finding from the open-economy macroeconomics developed in the early 1960s by Mundell (1960, 1963) and Fleming (1962). Their ideas on the exchange rate were synthesised and augmented by Dornbusch (1976). It can be found in contemporary texts as the 'Mundell–Fleming–Dornbusch' model: for example, in Obstfeld and Rogoff (1996).

6 The Bank of Korea is an inflation targeter, but the Ministry of Finance and Economy still controls foreign exchange policy. It is not an impossible separation of powers, but is likely a sub-optimal one.

7 The literature on inflation targeting is immense. For a useful survey, see Lowe (1997). For a discussion of the applicability of inflation targeting for Asia, see Debelle (2001).

8 Interview subjects came from local Chinese banks and foreign banks with a high-profile presence in the onshore and offshore markets.

9 This is a huge topic and far beyond the reaches of this work. For a comparative study of firm structures across Asia, see Tipton (2007).

10 Bilateral free trade agreements currently under discussion with Chile and Australia could eventually meet this criterion.

References

Bank for International Settlements (BIS), 1996. *Triennial Central Bank Survey of Foreign Exchange and Derivatives Market Activity 1995*, Bank for International Settlements, Basel. Available from http://www.bis.org/triennial.htm

——, 1999a. *Triennial Central Bank Survey of Foreign Exchange and Derivatives Market Activity 1998*, Bank for International Settlements, Basel. Available from http://www.bis.org/triennial.htm

——, 1999b. *Strengthening the banking system in China: issues and experiences*, Policy Paper No. 7, October, Bank for International Settlements, Basel.

——, 2002. *Triennial Central Bank Survey of Foreign Exchange and Derivatives Market Activity 2001*, Bank for International Settlements, Basel. Available from http://www.bis.org/triennial.htm

——, 2005. *Triennial Central Bank Survey of Foreign Exchange and Derivatives Market Activity in April 2004*, Bank for International Settlements, Basel. Available from http://www.bis.org/triennial.htm

Bubula, A. and Ötker-Robe, I., 2003. *Are pegged and intermediate exchange regimes more crisis prone?*, Working Paper 03/223, International Monetary Fund, Washington, DC.

CEIC Data Company (various years). China Database, ISI Emerging Markets, New York. Available as a subscription-based service from http://ceicdata.com.

Cheung, Y.-W., Chinn, M.D. and Fujii, E., 2003. *The Chinese economies in global context: the integration process and its determinants*, Working Paper No. 10047, October, National Bureau of Economic Research, Cambridge, MA.

China Money, 2007. *China Money*, 63, January.

Corden, W.M., 2002. *Too Sensational: on the choice of foreign exchange regimes*, MIT Press, Cambridge, MA.

Debelle, G., 2001. 'The case for inflation targeting in East Asian countries', in D. Gruen and J. Simon (eds), *Future Directions for Monetary Policies in East Asia*, Reserve Bank of Australia, Sydney.

Debelle, G., Gyntelberg, J. and Plumb, M., 2006. 'Forward currency markets in Asia: lessons from the Australian experience', *BIS Quarterly Review*, September:53–64.

Dornbusch, R., 1976. 'Exchange rate expectations and monetary policy', *Journal of International Economics*, 6(August):231–44.

Eichengreen, B., 2004. Chinese currency controversies, Paper presented at the Asian Economic Panel of Hong Kong, April.

Farrell, D., Lund, S. and Morin, F., 2006. 'The promise and perils of China's banking system', *The McKinsey Quarterly*, July. Available from http://www.mckinseyquarterly.com

Farrell, D., Lund, S. and Peri, L., 2006. 'India's financial system: more market, less government', *The McKinsey Quarterly*, August. Available from http://www.mckinseyquarterly.com

Fleming, M., 1962. *Domestic financial policies under fixed and under floating exchange rates*, Staff Papers 9, November, International Monetary Fund, Washington, DC:369–79.

Frankel, J., 2004. On the renminbi: the choice between adjustment under a fixed exchange rate and adjustment under a flexible rate, paper prepared for a High-Level Seminar on Foreign Exchange System, Dalian, May.

Goldstein, M., 2004. *Adjusting China's exchange rate policies*, Discussion Paper of the Institute for International Economics, presented at the International Monetary Fund seminar on China's foreign exchange rate system, Dalian, 26–27 May.

He, D., Chu, C., Shu, C. and Wong, A., 2005. *Monetary management in mainland China in the face of large capital inflows*, HKMA Research Memorandum 07/2005, Hong Kong Monetary Authority, Hong Kong.

Ho, C., Ma, G. and McCauley, R.N., 2005. 'Trading Asian currencies', *BIS Quarterly Review*, March:49–59.

Huang, Y., 2001. *China's Last Steps Across the River: enterprise and banking reforms*, Asia Pacific Press, The Australian National University, Canberra.

International Monetary Fund, 2006. *Annual Report on Exchange Arrangements and Exchange Restrictions*, International Monetary Fund, Washington, DC.

——. International Monetary Fund WEO Database. Available from http://www.imf.org/external/pubs/ft/weo/2007/01/data/index.aspx

Lardy, N., 1998. *China's Unfinished Economic Revolution*, Brookings Institution Press, Washington, DC.

Lowe, P. (ed.), 1997. *Monetary Policy and Inflation Targeting*, Reserve Bank of Australia, Sydney:65–87.

Ma, G. and Fung, B.S.C., 2002. *China's asset management corporations*, BIS Working Paper, August, Bank for International Settlements, Basel.

Ma, G. and McCauley, R.N., (forthcoming). *Do China's capital controls still bind?*, BIS Working Paper, Bank for International Settlements, Basel.

Ma, G., 2006. 'Who foots China's bank restructuring bill?', in R. Garnaut and L. Song (eds), *The Turning Point in China's Economic Development*, Asia Pacific Press, The Australian National University, Canberra:103–27.

Ma, G., Ho, C. and McCauley, R.N., 2004. 'The markets for non-deliverable forwards in Asian currencies', *BIS Quarterly Review*, September:81–94.

McKay, H., 2003. 'A timeline for Chinese exchange rate liberalisation', *Westpac Economic Research Bulletin*, October. Available on request from economics@westpac.com.au.

——, 2004. 'Capital account and fx reform: Japanese experience and Chinese prospects', *Westpac Economic Research Bulletin*, September. Available on request from economics@westpac.com.au.

——, 2005a. 'What about the capital account?', *Asian Times*. Available from http://www.atimes.com/atimes/China/GG26Ad02.html

——, 2005b. 'Capital inflow, the PBoC, sterilisation and the money supply', *Westpac Economic Research Bulletin*, October. Available on request from economics@westpac.com.au.

——, 2005c. 'China's banks: non-performing loans, systemic risk and WTO', *Westpac Economic Research Bulletin*, March. Available on request from economics@westpac.com.au.

——, 2006. 'Asian foreign exchange turnover: why so low?', *Westpac Economic Research Bulletin*, November. Available on request from economics@westpac.com.au

McKinnon, R., 1993. *The Order of Economic Liberalization*, Second Edition, Johns Hopkins University Press, Baltimore.

——, 2006. *Why China should keep its exchange rate pegged to the dollar: a historical perspective from Japan*, Stanford Working Paper, October, Standfor University, Stanford. Available from http://www.stanford.edu/~mckinnon/papers/International%20Finance%20China%20peg.pdf

Mundell, R.A., 1960. 'The monetary dynamics of international adjustment under fixed and flexible exchange rates', *Quarterly Journal of Economics*, 74:227–57.

——, 1963. 'Capital mobility and stabilization policy under fixed and flexible exchange rates, *Canadian Journal of Economics and Political Science*, 29:475–85.

Obstfeld, M. and Rogoff, K., 1996. *Foundations of International Macroeconomics*, MIT Press, Cambridge, MA.

Prasad, E., Rumbaugh, T. and Wang, Q., 2005. *Putting the cart before the horse? Capital account liberalization and exchange rate flexibility in China*, IMF Policy Discussion Paper, PDP/05/01, International Monetary Fund, Washington, DC.

Reserve Bank of Australia. *F Tables*. Available from http://www.rba.gov.au/Statistics/Bulletin/index.html

Song, L., 2005. 'Interest rate liberalization in China and the implications for non-state banking', in Y. Huang, T. Saich and E. Steinfeld (eds), *Financial Sector Reform in China*, Harvard University Asia Centre, Cambridge, MA.

State Administration of Foreign Exchange n.d. Available online at http://www.safe.gov.cn/model_safe_en/glxx_en/glxx_detail_en.jsp?id=3&ID=30500000000000000,3

Tarapore, S.S., 2006. *Report of the Committee on Fuller Capital Account Convertibility*, Reserve Bank of India, Mumbai.

Tipton, B., 2007. *The Asian Firms: history, institutions and management*, Edward Elgar, London.

Westpac Institutional Bank, 2006. *Westpac Asian FX Guide: a guide to trading, speculating and hedging in Asian currencies*, May, Westpac Institutional Bank. Available on request from economics@westpac.com.au.

World Bank, various years. *World Development Indicators*, World Bank, Washington, DC. Available online from https://publications.worldbank.org/WDI

Yun, S.H., 2005. 'An essay on invoicing currency practices for Korean exports', *Bank of Korea Economic Papers*, 8(1):75–100.

16

China's real exchange rate

Jane Golley and Rod Tyers

There is increasing international pressure for the Chinese authorities to allow the currency to float more freely. It has been argued that the appreciation of the renminbi since 2005 is just the beginning of a necessary upward trend, given the belief that the currency is currently undervalued, by margins ranging from 'small' to as high as 50 per cent (Frankel 2004; Wang 2004; Goldstein 2004; Coudert and Couharde 2005). Expectations that China's underlying real exchange rate will appreciate in the future are based commonly on the Balassa (1964)-Samuelson (1964) hypothesis. This implies a positive relationship between economic growth and the real exchange rate, driven by productivity catch-up in developing economies' tradable sectors and, in association, rising prices in their non-traded sectors. Yet, while the Balassa-Samuelson characterisation of the growth process is a useful abstraction, it is suspect on several fronts, not least of which is its omission of productivity gains in the non-tradable sector, which tend to be depreciating.[1] Moreover, at its core it relies on the law of one price for tradable goods. Departures from this assumption are now widely recognised, under which circumstance there are numerous other drivers of China's economic growth that affect the real exchange rate (Tyers et al. 2006). These include labour force expansion, skill acquisition, changes in the saving rate and trade and financial reforms, many of which are also depreciating. Thus, the net effect of China's rapid economic growth on its real exchange rate depends on the sources of that growth and the consequent pattern of endowment changes and sectoral distributions of productivity growth and tradability.

This chapter explores the interactions between sources of growth and the real exchange rate and considers the Balassa-Samuelson hypothesis in the context of recent and future sources of Chinese economic growth, offering a variety of reasons why China's behaviour need not be consistent with the hypothesis. China's macroeconomic policy regime and its continuing reforms to the financial sector, both of which have profound implications for the trend of its real exchange rate, are discussed. The issues arising in these sections are assessed using a simulation model of the global economy in which a full demographic sub-model is incorporated. The inclusion of demography captures the impending decline in China's overall labour force and the rise in its skill intensity. Baseline and comparator simulations are constructed to examine the sensitivity of real exchange rate paths to changes in the labour supply (achieved via changes to fertility policy that encourage larger families), alternative labour productivity and skill upgrading scenarios, and financial sector reform.

Balassa-Samuelson: theory and reality

If the nominal exchange rate, E, is defined as the number of units of foreign exchange obtained for a unit of the domestic currency, the real exchange rate, e^R, can be defined correspondingly as the rate of exchange between the home product bundle and corresponding bundles produced abroad. It follows that the bilateral real exchange rate for a focus (home) country with foreign trading partner i can be approximated as the common currency ratio of the gross domestic product (GDP) prices (deflators) of the two countries, $P^Y\left(p^N, p^T\right)$ and $P_i^Y\left(p_i^N, p_i^T\right)/E_i$, where p^T and p^N are indices over all the focus country's non-traded and traded goods and services, respectively.[2]

$$e_i^R = \frac{P^Y\left(p^N, p^T\right)}{P_i^Y\left(p_i^N, p_i^T\right)/E_i} = E_i \frac{P^Y\left(p^N, p^T\right)}{P_i^Y\left(p_i^N, p_i^T\right)} \quad (1)$$

This is the fundamental relationship between the real and nominal exchange rates. Consider the case in which prices at home and abroad are measured in a common currency, the share of non-traded products in GDP, θ, is the same at home and abroad, prices are aggregated appropriately using a Cobb-Douglas index and the law of one price applies to all traded goods. The latter implies that trade is costless and undistorted, so that $p^T = p_i^T$. Under these conditions, the real exchange rate becomes

$$e_R = \frac{\left(p^N\right)^\theta \left(p^T\right)^{1-\theta}}{\left(p_i^N\right)^\theta \left(p_i^T\right)^{1-\theta}} = \left(\frac{p^N}{p_i^N}\right)^\theta \quad (2)$$

From this, the key role of non-traded goods prices is clear. When prices are measured in a common currency, or relative to a common numeraire, it is the ratio of the home and foreign non-traded goods prices that matters in determining the real exchange rate.

Consider a Ricardian exchange in which output per worker is $A^T = ab$, $A^N = ac$, $A_i^T = ab_i$ and $A_i^N = ac_i$. Here, a is common to both sectors and regions, b is a component of productivity that is biased towards the traded sector and c is a component biased towards the non-traded sector. The parameters b and c are different between countries. The relationships between the wage rate and product prices in the traded and non-traded sectors respectively are

$$P^T = P_i^T = \frac{W_i}{A_i^T} = \frac{W}{A^T}\text{, so that } \frac{W}{W_i} = \frac{A^T}{A_i^T} \tag{3}$$

and

$$P^N = \frac{W}{A^N}, \quad P_i^N = \frac{W_i}{A_i^N} \tag{4}$$

We then have that

$$\frac{P^N}{P_i^N} = \frac{A^T / A^N}{A_i^T / A_i^N} = \frac{b}{b_i} \Big/ \frac{c}{c_i} \text{ and } e_i^R = \left(\frac{b}{b_i} \Big/ \frac{c}{c_i} \right)^{\theta} \tag{5}$$

By the Balassa-Samuelson hypothesis, if the focus country has higher tradable productivity growth, $b > b_i$, and assuming that $c = c_i$, its real exchange rate must be appreciating. The hypothesis then implies that, if developing economies are poorer because their tradable labour productivity is lower, then comparatively rapid growth should cause real appreciations.

The key assumptions of the hypothesis are, however, suspect.

Tradable productivity gap

During some periods and in some developing economies, productivity growth has been observed to be higher in the non-tradable sector,[3] leading to $c > c_i$ and tending to depreciate the real exchange rate. Modern transport, financial, health and education services offer considerable potential for productivity catch-up. Whatever the relative performance of China's services sector in the past, recent evidence suggests substantial potential for catch-up and accelerated productivity growth in the future (see Ma 2006).

The law of one price for tradable goods

Failures of the law of one price have been observed for tradable goods in specific instances.[4] Goods and services are not homogeneous across countries but are differentiated at minimum by country of origin.[5] Supply and/or demand side factors that raise the volume of tradable production move the home country down the global demand curves for its product varieties, reducing its supply prices and resulting in deterioration in the terms of trade and a depreciation of its real exchange rate. Factor endowment growth and changes in policy that lead to substitution in demand for home products depreciate real exchange rates and the magnitudes of their effects depend crucially on the degree of substitutability between the differentiated products.

Labour arbitrage In most developing economies, the marginal product of industrial labour exceeds that of rural labour due to the more rapid accumulation of industrial capital. There is, therefore, a Harris-Todaro gulf between the wages in the expanding and contracting sectors. If labour mobility between the rural and industrial sectors is inferior to that between the rural and service sectors (particularly the construction sector), then industrial productivity growth does not necessarily drive up service wages or service costs.[6]

Closed capital account

The assumption that the real exchange rate depends only on interactions among countries associated with trade in merchandise is clearly violated in many of today's developing economies, and particularly in China. Its violation, in concert with failures of the law of one price for traded goods, means that any influx of payments (in the form of a foreign direct investment or portfolio capital flow) raises aggregate demand. Since traded goods are supplied more elastically via imports than are non-traded goods—which depend on home resources—such an influx must raise relative non-traded prices and therefore appreciate the real exchange rate. Conversely, effluxes will cause depreciation.

Not surprisingly then, empirical evidence in support of the Balassa-Samuelson hypothesis is mixed. Choudhri and Khan (2004), for example, find favourable evidence using a small sample of developing economies that does not include mainland China, Taiwan or Hong Kong. Bergin et al. (2006) find a positive association between price levels and real per capita income that is strong only in large samples of countries. Miyajima (2005) uses a sample of 15 Organisation for Economic Co-operation and Development (OECD) countries between 1970 and 2000 to establish that the hypothesis does not always hold during growth surges, which on numerous occasions were led by productivity growth in non-traded sectors. The East Asian evidence since 1980 also appears mixed. Figure 16.1 plots bilateral real exchange rates against the United States for mainland China and some of its neighbours, demonstrating that there is no clear pattern.

To examine the productivity-gap component of the hypothesis for China, we estimate simple Solow residuals for the economy as a whole and for three sectors: 'Food', 'Industry' and 'Services', adjusting the officially published urban employment data for underestimation, as discussed in Cai and Wang (2006).[7] The average annual changes in the Solow residuals for each sector are given in Table 16.1. These show strong productivity performance by the Chinese economy since the mid 1980s, with a slow-down in the 1998–2001 period associated with the East Asian financial crisis. Consistent with the analyses of Lu (2006) and Fogel (2006), productivity growth appears to have been strongest in the industrial sector and weakest in the service sector.[8] Yet,

Figure 16.1 **Asian real exchange rates against the United States, 1980–2006[a]**

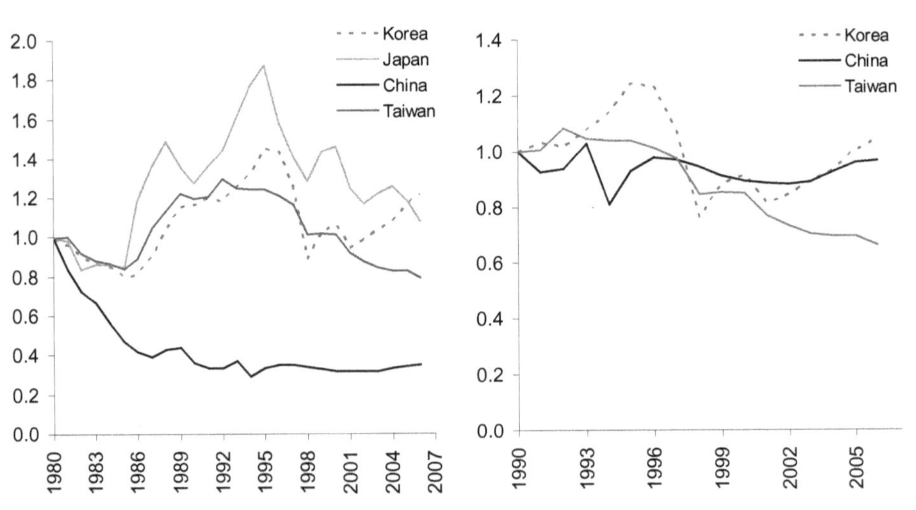

[a] These are indices of nominal bilateral rates deflated according to $e_R = E \cdot P_Y / P_Y^{US}$, where E is the nominal exchange rate in US dollars per unit of local currency; P_Y is the local GDP price; and P_Y^{US} is the corresponding US GDP price. The left graph sets 1980=1.00 while, to show the trends in the later years, that on the right sets 1990=1.00.

Sources: For Korea, Japan and mainland China the data are from International Monetary Fund (IMF) 2007a. *International Financial Statistics*, the International Monetary Fund, Washington, DC. For Taiwan they are from the websites of the Central Bank of China (Taiwan) and the Directorate-General of Budget, Accounting and Statistics, Executive Yuan.

particularly in recent years, the differences are not large. This has limited the extent of service price inflation, which, while evident in Figure 16.2 since 1995, is not overwhelming.

Taking a different approach, Rodrik (2006) measures the productivity associated with China's exports and shows it to be significantly higher than what would normally be expected for a country at China's income level. He also shows that this has been an important determinant of China's growth during the period 1992–2003. Relevant to the discussion here, he asks whether the Chinese economy will run out of steam once the convergence in export productivity nears completion, or whether it will be able to 'discover' new products on world markets and enable export-led growth to continue. While such speculation suggests future real appreciations based on productivity growth in the tradable sector, considerable future growth could stem from productivity catch-up in the service sector—a depreciating force. The fact that recent productivity growth in manufacturing has been associated with foreign direct investment (FDI) and that service FDI has begun to grow only recently, suggests that services productivity will be a major contributor in the future. Clearly, the sectoral distribution of productivity gains is critical in determining the real exchange rate.

In turn, productivity differences across sectors will be affected by levels of education and training. Fogel (2006) predicts that investment in human capital has the potential to serve as China's key engine of economic growth for the next two decades, a point that is well recognised by China's leaders (as emphasised in the eleventh Five-Year Plan). He qualifies the impact of enhancing the quality of labour through education on the growth rate of per capita income and shows that increasing secondary and tertiary enrolment ratios has a sizeable impact on the growth of labour productivity and the per capita GDP growth rate.[9] To the extent that services are skill intensive (as they are according to past data), this will boost performance in the service sector—again, tending to depreciate China's real exchange rate. Of course, to the extent that structural changes lead to rapid upgrading in the skill intensity of tradables in the process of economic growth in China, as it has in other countries, this relationship will operate in reverse.

Allowing for failures of the law of one price for tradable goods, there are numerous other forces tending to depreciate the real exchange rate in the long term. During the past two decades one such force has been China's 'demographic dividend', stemming from the high proportion of working-aged people in the total population. This, according to Cai and Wang (2005), accounted for about one-quarter of per capita GDP growth between 1980 and 2003.[10] It has played a critical role in keeping wages and hence the real exchange rate low, thereby enabling the rapid expansion of labour-intensive manufactured exports. In the

Table 16.1 **Estimated Chinese total factor productivity growth, by sector, 1986–2005** (per cent per annum)

	Whole economy	Food	Industry	Services
1986–89	3.5	1.4	3.8	3.8
1990–94	5.0	1.6	7.7	2.3
1995–97	5.7	5.5	3.7	3.2
1998–2001	4.1	-0.2	8.9	-0.5
2002–2005	6.0	5.4	6.3	4.6

Source: Tyers, R., Golley, J., Bu, Y. and Bain, I., 2006. *China's economic growth and its real exchange rate*, Working Papers in Economics and Econometrics, No. 476, The Australian National University, Canberra.

Figure 16.2 **Chinese sectoral price indices, 1979–2005**[a]

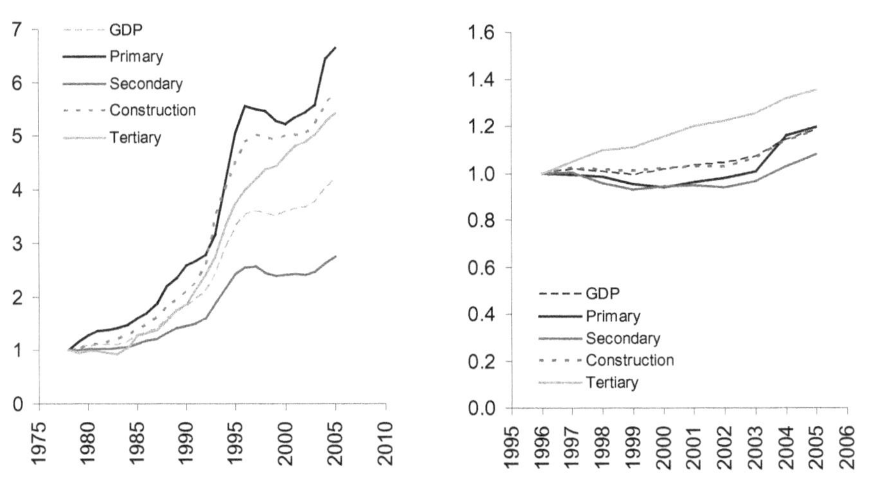

[a] These are sectoral price indices for 'primary industry', which is mainly agriculture; 'secondary industry', which is primarily manufacturing and construction; and 'tertiary industry', which is other services. The left graph sets 1978=1.00 while, to show the trends in the later years, that on the right sets 1996=1.00.
Source: The price indices are implied by volume and value data from National Bureau of Statistics, 2007. *China Statistical Abstract 2006*, China Statistical Press, Beijing.

future, however, the ageing of the population and the consequent decline in the labour supply will have the opposite effect, placing upward pressure on real wages and the real exchange rate.[11] Alternative population policies, such as the relaxation of the One Child Policy, clearly stand to affect economic growth via the labour supply, and therefore on the real exchange rate as well.

The Balassa-Samuelson assumption that productivity gains translate into higher wages (Equations 3–5) is underpinned by the assumption of full employment and labour-market arbitrage. While Miyajima (2005) finds that this assumption is satisfied for his OECD sample, it is far from clear that it has also held for China in the past. Cai and Wang (2006) show that, during the period 1995–2002, average annual manufacturing wage growth was 11.6 per cent in China—below their estimate of productivity growth (12.2 per cent), a point that is also supported by Fan (2006). And if, as noted above, rural labour is more mobile into some services than into manufacturing, the wage cost effect on services might have been yet smaller. Thus, labour mobility into the non-rural sectors could have offset the appreciating forces in recent decades.

Yet there is evidence that this is about to change. The emergence of a shortage of rural migrant workers in the past few years signals a transition to a more limited labour surplus (Cai and Wang 2006).[12] In combination with the demographic transition towards a declining proportion of the population of working age, it is likely that wage growth will keep pace with productivity growth in the future. Moreover, continuing World Trade Organization (WTO) commitments could deliver further productivity gains in traded sectors—especially in agriculture—as domestic markets are increasingly expected to compete internationally or perish. If these trade-related productivity gains dominate China's pattern of growth then, in combination with tightening labour markets, Balassa-Samuelson appreciations could start to materialise.

The nominal exchange rate regime and capital controls

The exchange rate reforms launched by the Chinese authorities in July 2005 were intended to at least demonstrate a departure from the *de facto* fixed US dollar peg, nominally allowing the currency to fluctuate by up to 0.3 per cent a day. These reforms have, however, had a limited impact so far, yielding a cumulative bilateral appreciation of about 6 per cent by May 2007. These are long term not recent forces. Notwithstanding China's high rate of inward FDI, the past decade has seen net outflows on its combined financial and capital accounts (hereafter referred to simply as 'the capital account') and associated current account surpluses. These net outflows represent an excess of domestic savings over investment.

To see this, note that the equality of net flows on the capital account to the investment–saving gap follows from the standard aggregate expenditure and disposal identities.[13] Defining net inflows as positive, the result can be written as

$$KA = S_{NF} - \Delta R = I - S_D \quad (6)$$

where I is investment, S_{NF} (net foreign saving) is net private inflow on the financial account and ΔR is the annual addition to official foreign reserves. In the presence of capital controls, S_{NF} is roughly equal to inward FDI. Both sides of the equation are negative in the case of China, indicating net outflows. These net outflows have expanded since the mid 1990s, particularly since 2004 (Figure 16.3). Extraordinarily, even though investment accounts for 45 per cent of China's GDP, more than half of its GDP is saved.

Figure 16.3 **China's investment–saving and external balances, 1985–2010** (percentage of GDP)[a]

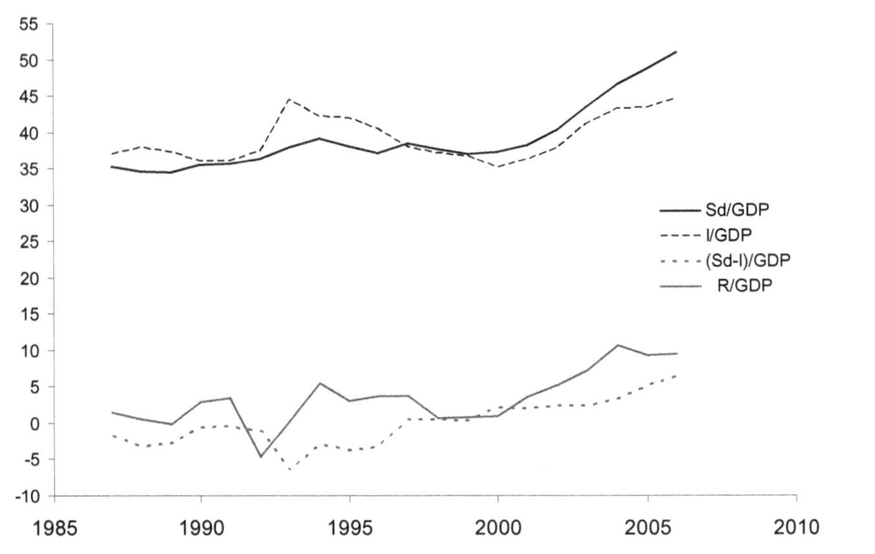

[a] Since errors and omissions are large, we have adjusted the least accurately measured items in each sub-account (usually net factor income and net private flows on the financial account) to ensure balance.

Sources: International Monetary Fund, 2007a. *International Financial Statistics,* International Monetary Fund, Washington, DC; International Monetary Fund, 2007b. *World Economic Outlook Database*, International Monetary Fund, Washington, DC. Some 2006 figures are from the Economist Intelligence Unit as derived from National Bureau of Statistics (2007).

It would therefore appear that a key to the puzzle as to why China's real exchange rate has not appreciated in the Balassa-Samuelson manner is its very high total saving rate. Some external commentators bemoan the dearth of consumption and advocate its stimulus (Bernanke 2006). Expressing a widely held view outside China, Lardy (2006:85) argues that: 'As the world's second largest surplus country, China must allow its currency to appreciate against the dollar and it must take steps to allow a transition to a growth path driven more by domestic consumption than by further increases in its external surplus.' Since the gross outflows on its capital account take the form of reserve accumulation, China, in combination with other Asian economies that are also raising reserves, has been accused of 'monetary mercantilism' (Aizenman and Lee 2006). It is implied that reserve accumulation is chosen freely in order to keep the real exchange rate low. That this is unfair criticism is evident from the identities. By definition, from Equation 6 we have that

$$\Delta R = S_D - I + S_{NF} \tag{7}$$

This indicates that, as long as total domestic savings exceed investment and capital controls prevent the matching of inward FDI by private outflows, ΔR must be positive. The magnitudes in Equation 7 are also indicated in Figure 16.3. The monetary mercantilist critique of the rate of reserve accumulation would therefore be better directed at the high saving rate and the capital controls.

Prasad et al. (2005) posit that, with persistent external political pressure for real exchange rate appreciation, it would be better to let this happen by allowing the nominal exchange rate to appreciate rather than through domestic inflation, and they describe in detail how greater exchange rate flexibility would pave the way for capital account liberalisation. This raises two issues. First, are there non-mercantilist reasons why China has resisted the pressure to make the renminbi significantly more flexible, even while its financial sector is being reformed? And, second, what would be the effects of the reforms (combined with the removal of capital controls) on the real exchange rate and the renminbi?

Consider whether it is reasonable to expect increased exchange rate flexibility before the uptake of the reforms essential to financial and capital account liberalisation. The reason why the People's Bank of China (PBC) sterilises US dollar inflows net of import costs is because, short of these reforms, there is no private market on which those large volumes of US dollars can be exchanged for renminbi. Hitherto, China's banking system has lacked derivative markets for currency and debt instruments to do the necessary hedging and it is not sufficiently distant from decades of soft budget constraints associated with the channelling of government subsidies to state-owned enterprises through accumulated debt. This has necessitated the placing of the PBC's US dollar receipts abroad. And, to avoid excess liquidity, these placements have been sterilised. However, holdings of domestic credit have been insufficient to sterilise this flow on the asset side of the balance sheet, so 'sterilisation bonds' have been issued on the debit side (Table 16.2). Just as the reserves have come to dominate the asset side of the balance sheet, sterilisation bonds have assumed significance on the debit side. In effect, the PBC has acted as a conduit for domestic savers who might otherwise acquire foreign assets but are restricted from doing so by capital controls. The current pressure from abroad to revalue therefore places the PBC in a difficult position. Since the PBC's assets are primarily in US dollars and its liabilities are in renminbi, too prompt an appreciation of the renminbi would result in substantial losses that would need to be covered in renminbi from the government budget. This suggests that a larger role for the nominal exchange rate must await the fruits of continuing financial reforms and capital market deepening.[14]

Second, when capital controls are eventually relaxed and the renminbi becomes fully convertible, it is not guaranteed that an appreciation will result. While the majority of recent scholarly research finds the renminbi to be undervalued, a number of studies do not.[15] Prasad et al. (2005) point to the potential for depreciation after the gradual liberalisation of the capital account,

Table 16.2 **The balance sheet of the People's Bank of China, ca. 2006**

Assets	Liabilities
Domestic credit, DC Central bank claims on depository and other financial corporations and on the central government 20 per cent of GDP	**The monetary base, M_B** Currency and bank reserves 37 per cent of GDP
Official foreign reserves, R 41 per cent of GDP	**Sterilisation bonds, SB** Debt to the Chinese public 14 per cent of GDP
	Other liabilities, OL Includes government ownership 10 per cent of GDP

Source: People's Bank of China, 2006. *Balance Sheet of Monetary Authority*, People's Bank of China, Beijing.

which could lead to net outflows as domestic investors seek to diversify their portfolios. Moreover, there is already substantial evidence of informal private outflows from China (Prasad and Wei 2005), which would be expected to expand if legalised, placing further downward pressure on the real exchange rate.[16] In addition, the recent surge in speculative inflows in anticipation of appreciation is likely to be temporary and could easily be reversed.[17]

The eventual establishment of a complete and stable private market for the renminbi will have two effects. First, a more flexible exchange rate will allow the PBC to follow the practice of central banks abroad and focus on the control of inflation. This means that the forces underlying real exchange rate dynamics will also determine the path of the nominal exchange rate. Second, the accumulation of official foreign reserves can abate, to be replaced by private outflows. Yet, at least in the short term, whether this will cause an appreciation (nominal or real) depends on whether the PBC's reserves are the equivalent of the private sector's desired foreign holdings. If the net effect of the capital controls (with reserve accumulation replacing private outflows) is to have restricted the scale of China's collective foreign holdings, depending on the PBC's response, liberalisation will raise outflows and, at least temporarily, depreciate the real exchange rate. If, on the other hand, the reserves are larger than the foreign holdings that would otherwise be chosen by the private market, liberalisation would result in net inflows and a real appreciation.[18]

A further determinant of the direction of any change in external flows is perceived risk. The two key determinants of investment are the anticipated rate of return on installed capital, net of depreciation, on which the investment volume depends positively, and the real cost of funds (the real borrowing rate), on which it depends negatively. Although these might be expected to converge on common values in a steady state, this is rare in practice. In developing economies, there are interest premiums that drive both above the corresponding levels in the industrialised world. Indicative of this premium for the case of China is the spread between its domestic bond yields and those of US Treasury bonds, which has held at about 40 per cent during the past decade. These 'interest premiums' have two components: a risk-free component, due in China's case to the financial market segmentation that will be relaxed with liberalisation, and a risk premium that compensates investors for exchange rate risk, information asymmetries and perceived risks of expropriation. Changes in the stability of the Chinese economy or of its politics will greatly influence this risk component, casting further uncertainty over the short-term path of financial flows.[19]

Modelling the determinants of China's real exchange rate

Here we examine quantitatively the relationship between shocks associated with China's economic growth and its real exchange rate. To do this effectively, a numerical model is required that is global in scope and that incorporates the generalisations of the Balassa-Samuelson assumptions discussed above. Recall that these included a means to allow productivity growth in non-tradable as well as tradable sectors, departures from the law of one price for tradable goods, a more sophisticated representation of the labour market and an open capital account. With these generalisations, almost all shocks to the economy have implications for the real exchange rate.

We use a model that offers these generalisations. Adapted from Tyers and Shi (2007a, 2007b), it is a multi-region, multi-product dynamic simulation model of the world economy.[20] In the version used, the world is subdivided into 14 regions (Table 16.3). Industries are aggregated into three sectors: food (including processed foods), industry (mining and manufacturing) and services (including construction)—the latter being little traded in comparison with the other two. Failures of the law of one price are represented by product differentiation, so that consumers substitute imperfectly between products from different regions. As in other dynamic models of the global economy, the endogenous component of simulated economic growth is physical capital accumulation. Technical change is introduced in the form of exogenous productivity growth that is sector and factor specific, allowing the analysis of productivity performance that differs between tradable and non-tradable sectors. Consistent with the results indicated in Table 16.1, baseline productivity in the food sector is assumed to grow more rapidly than that in the other sectors in China. This allows continued shedding of labour to those sectors.[21] In general, baseline productivity growth rates in services are modelled as lower than in the tradable goods sectors in all regions.

All regional capital accounts are open and investors have adaptive expectations about real regional net rates of return on installed capital. In each region, the level of investment is determined by a comparison of expected net rates of return on domestic installed capital with borrowing rates yielded by a global trust, to which each region's saving contributes, adjusted by calibrated region-specific interest premiums. Lagged adjustment processes ensure, however, that financial capital is not fully mobile internationally in the short term, but that the paths of domestic and global interest rates become parallel, separated only by exogenous premiums in the long term. In representing China, however, one caveat is that no explicit control is imposed on the outflow of private financial capital. General financial reform is represented by a diminution of the interest premium and this causes an unambiguous influx of financial capital to China.

To augment the model's characterisation of changes in labour supply and quality, it encompasses demographic and economic change. It tracks populations in four age groups, two genders and two skill categories: a total of 16 population groups in each of the 14 regions. The skill subdivision is between production labour (unskilled) and professional labour (skilled).[22] Each age–gender–skill group is represented as a homogeneous sub-population with a group-specific birth and death rate, labour force participation rate and rates of immigration and emigration. By thus capturing the effects of China's low fertility, the model projects the reversal of its labour supply trend, as indicated in Figure 16.4. The implication of this for the real exchange rate is that a labour

Table 16.3 **Regional composition in the global model**

Region	**Composition of aggregates**
Australia	
North America	Canada, Mexico, United States
Western Europe	European Union, including Switzerland and Scandinavia but excluding the Czech Republic, Hungary and Poland
Central Europe and the former Soviet Union	Central Europe, including the Czech Republic, Hungary and Poland
Japan	
China	Includes Hong Kong and Taiwan
Indonesia	
Other East Asia	Republic of Korea, Malaysia, the Philippines, Singapore, Thailand and Vietnam
India	
Other South Asia	Bangladesh, Bhutan, Maldives, Nepal, Pakistan and Sri Lanka
South America	Argentina, Bolivia, Brazil, Chile, Colombia, Ecuador, Peru, Venezuela and Uruguay
Middle East and North Africa	Includes Morocco through to the Islamic Republic of Iran
Sub-Saharan Africa	The rest of Africa
Rest of world	Includes the rest of Central America, the rest of Indo-China, the small island states of the Pacific, Atlantic and Indian Oceans and the Mediterranean Sea, Myanmar and Mongolia, New Zealand and the former Yugoslavia

Source: GTAP Global Database, Version 5.

force that is growing faster than those of trading partner countries—other things being equal—lowers costs and depreciates the real exchange rate. A relative decline in the labour supply would be expected to have the reverse effect.

For the Balassa-Samuelson hypothesis, the key is the difference between the performances of traded and non-traded sectors. To the extent that their labour intensities differ, labour supply trends make a difference. As it turns out, however, trends in skill composition are more important. These depend on the rate at which each region's education and social development institutions transform unskilled (production-worker) families into skilled (professional-worker) families. Each year a particular proportion of the population in each production-worker age–gender group is transferred to professional status. The initial values of these proportions depend on the regions' levels of development, the associated capacities of their education systems and the relative sizes of

Figure 16.4 **China's projected population and labour force, 1995–2035[a]**

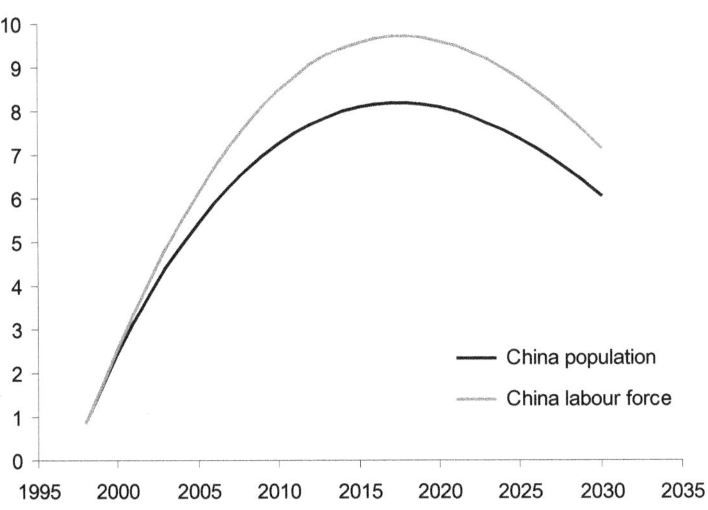

[a] These are cumulative percentage departures from the base year 1997, drawn from the baseline simulation in which China's fertility is projected to decline from 1.9 to 1.5.
Source: Base line simulation of the model described in the text. For a more detailed description of the demographic aspects of this simulation, see Golley, J. and Tyers, R., 2006. 'China's growth to 2030: demographic change and the labour supply constraint', in R. Garnaut and L. Song (eds), *The Turning Point in China's Economic Development*, Asia Pacific Press, The Australian National University, Canberra:203–26 (version in Chinese forthcoming in *Chinese Labor Economics*).

their production and professional labour forces. Rates of transformation change through time with real per capita income and the level of the skilled wage premium. China's skill share is projected to rise through time while that in North America remains static. The contrast is due to North America's higher initial skill share, its high rate of unskilled immigration and its higher fertility rate.

The 16 age-gender-skill groups differ in their shares of regional disposable income, consumption preferences, saving rates and labour supply behaviour. While the consumption–savings choice differs for each group, it is dependent for all on group-specific real per capita disposable income and the real lending rate. Governments are assumed to balance their budgets while saving and borrowing are undertaken by the private sector. The baseline scenario is a 'business-as-usual' projection of the global economy until 2030. In part because of its comparatively young population and hence its continuing rapid labour force growth, India attracts substantial new investment and is projected to take over from China as the world's most rapidly expanding region. Comparatively rapid population growth, however, detracts from India's long-term real per capita income performance. By this criterion, China is the strongest performing region through the three decades.

Growth shocks and China's real exchange rate

Our focus is on shocks that enhance the rate of GDP growth, for which we draw on simulations carried out by Tyers et al. (2006). These include once-and-for-all productivity increases, skill transformation rate increases, birth-rate increases, interest premium decreases and tariff decreases (increases in openness). In each case, we run a new simulation in which the determinant in question is shocked once and for all, as of 2005. We then extract the elasticity of China's real exchange rate to each shock, tracking the values through time to 2030. We focus on the bilateral real exchange rate, measured as in Equation 1, against the region 'North America', since this best parallels China's nominal exchange rate policy and the renminbi valuation debate.

Productivity growth increase

We first shock total factor productivity separately in each sector. The elasticity is the percentage departure of the projected real exchange rate for each percentage per annum increase in total factor productivity. The overall rate of economic growth proves to be quite sensitive to such productivity shocks since the larger these are for a particular region, the larger is that region's marginal product of capital. The region therefore enjoys higher levels of investment and hence a double boost to its growth rate. Productivity growth in both tradable sectors yields real appreciations but 'industry' is by far the greater contributor to China's trade and therefore the most significant for the real exchange rate (Figure 16.5). The appreciating effects of tradable productivity increases are consistent with the Balassa-Samuelson hypothesis and are, as expected, due to wage growth and relative service price inflation. They are bolstered in the short term by increased investment and hence greater net inflows on the capital account. In the long term, however, the enlargement of the capital stock reduces costs and hence offsets the real exchange rate gains. Also, as expected from the dominance of non-traded sector prices in Equation 2, faster service productivity growth depreciates the real exchange rate—modestly in the early years but to a dominant extent in the long term, when it is reinforced by associated capital accumulation.

If productivity is boosted equi-proportionally in all sectors, the net effect is a small real appreciation in the short term and a substantial real depreciation in the long term. The Balassa-Samuelson effect is dominant in the short term

Figure 16.5 **Elasticities of the projected real exchange rate to the rate of total factor productivity growth in each sector, 1995–2035[a]**

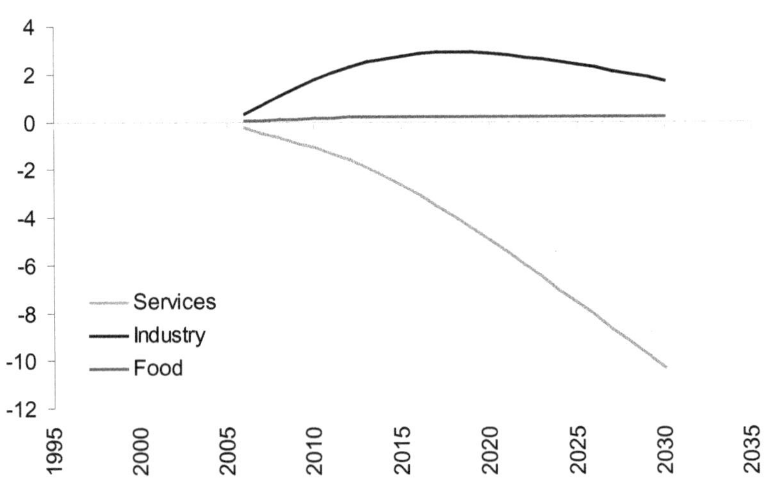

[a] This is the percentage departure of the projected real exchange rate for each percentage per annum increase in total factor productivity in each of the three sectors after 2005.

Source: Tyers, R., Golley, J., Bu, Y. and Bain, I., 2006. *China's economic growth and its real exchange rate*, Working Papers in Economics and Econometrics, No. 476, The Australian National University, Canberra.

but is overwhelmed by services productivity in the long term. The short-term net appreciation is bolstered by the associated rise in capital returns and hence the attraction of increased investment from abroad. Beyond a decade, as costs are reduced by the across-the-board rise in productivity, combined with the associated capital expansion, the elasticity turns negative and very quickly expands in that direction. The particular strength of changes in service productivity is notable, suggesting that the forecasting of real exchange rates depends importantly on this difficult-to-measure behaviour. Indeed, if our productivity estimates in Table 16.1 are correct, recent differences between China's productivity performance in the tradable and service sectors are not large. This suggests that, if China's future growth is driven increasingly by services productivity improvements, its real exchange rate could continue on a depreciating trend.

Skill acquisition rate increase

When the skill acquisition rate is increased in developing regions such as China, where the unskilled (or production) worker population is larger than its skilled (or professional) counterpart, the proportional boost to skilled workers is larger than the proportional loss of unskilled workers. The result is greater output and, other things being equal, a real depreciation. This tendency is enhanced, however, by the fact that the services sector is comparatively skill intensive, so that the shock causes a relatively large boost to service output and hence a relatively large fall in the service price. The result is a strong responsiveness of GDP growth to skill acquisition and a relatively large real depreciation. The elasticities in this case are percentage departures of the growth rate and real exchange rate for each percentage of the population in production-worker families that is transformed each year. Defined this way, skill transformation places downward pressure on the real exchange rate of a magnitude similar to total factor productivity in services (Figure 16.6).

Birth rate increase

The birth rate affects the real exchange rate by raising the population (initially) and the labour force (subsequently). The initial effect is to raise aggregate demand but not to contribute to supply since income is redistributed to the non-saving and non-working young. Net inflows on the capital account rise and the real exchange rate appreciates. In the long term, when the increased birth rate yields a larger workforce, the supply effects predominate. Wage costs are lower and the real exchange rate declines. It is somewhat surprising that the

Figure 16.6 **Elasticities of the projected real exchange rate to the fertility rate and the skill acquisition rate, 2000–2035[a]**

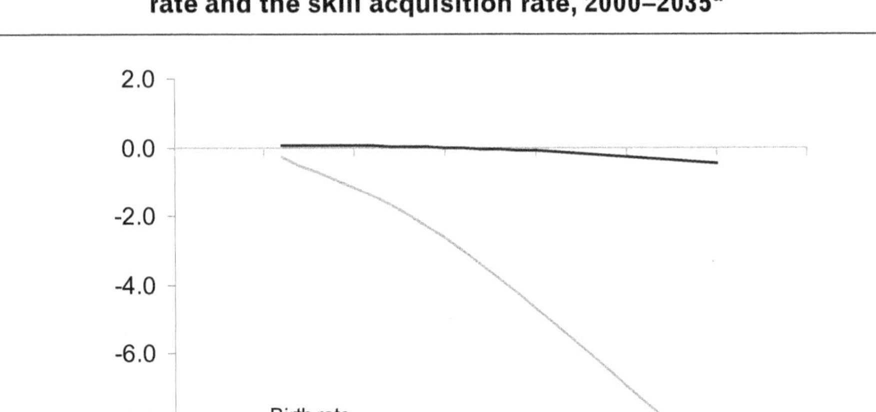

[a] This is the percentage departure of the projected real exchange rate for each percentage point change in the total fertility rate and for each additional percentage of the population of production-worker families that is transformed annually to professional status.
Source: Tyers, R., Golley, J., Bu, Y. and Bain, I., 2006. *China's economic growth and its real exchange rate*, Working Papers in Economics and Econometrics, No. 476, The Australian National University, Canberra.

elasticity of the real exchange rate to the birth rate is so small (Figure 16.7). The results suggest that China's birth rate, and hence its low fertility, will be only a modest contributor to the future of its real exchange rate.

Interest premium decline

In the short term, the decline in China's interest premium results in net capital inflows, which raises investment and therefore increases aggregate demand and the real exchange rate. A positive demand-driven effect is therefore expected in the first instance. In the long term, however, when the effect of the investment on the capital stock is realised, the supply side dominates. More abundant and hence cheaper capital reduces production costs, yielding a real depreciation. The elasticity-to-premium decline is large and positive in the short term, with the lag to the switch in sign at least 15 years (Figure 16.7).

This simulation helps to explain the lack of appreciation of the real exchange rate to date. It says that an expansion of net inflow on the financial and capital accounts of the balance of payments causes a real appreciation in the short-medium run. Since there has in fact been an expansion in net outflows on these accounts (Figure 16.3), the effect has been to apply downward pressure on China's real exchange rate. While domestic savings continue to dominate investment, this substantial depreciating effect is likely to continue offsetting the short-term (Balassa-Samuelson) appreciating effect of productivity changes (Figure 16.5).

Figure 16.7 **Elasticities of the projected real exchange rate to trade openness (penetration rate), the savings rate and interest premium decline, 2000–2035[a]**

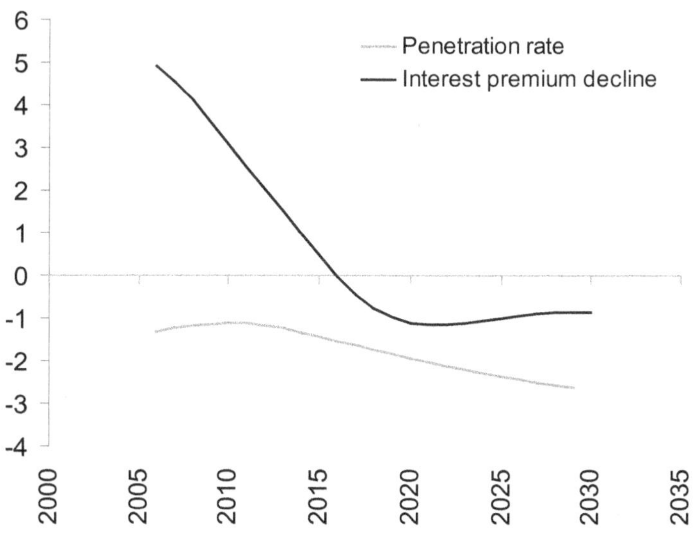

[a] This is the percentage departure of the projected real exchange rate for each 1) percentage increase in the overall import penetration ratio, 2) percentage point increase in the concurrent average savings rate (all group savings rates are shifted by equal proportions), and 3) percentage point reduction in the domestic interest rate due to a reduced premium, starting in 2005.

Source: Tyers, R., Golley, J., Bu, Y. and Bain, I., 2006. *China's economic growth and its real exchange rate*, Working Papers in Economics and Econometrics, No. 476, The Australian National University, Canberra.

Trade liberalisation

Trade liberalisation switches demand away from home-produced goods and services towards imported varieties. For a single region, the supply of goods and services from the much larger foreign market is more elastic than that of home varieties, constrained as they are by local factor supplies and technology. The effect of the demand switch, then, is to reduce the relative prices of the home varieties and hence to depreciate the real exchange rate. The elasticity of openness is constructed by dividing the percentage change in the real exchange rate by the percentage point change in the overall import penetration ratio (the ratio of the value of imports to the total value of domestic consumption). The shock on which it is based is a phased removal of all China's merchandise trade barriers over five years.[23] The elasticity has the expected negative sign, and its magnitude grows through time (Figure 16.7). The decline occurs because of the concentration of China's merchandise protection in capital-intensive industries. Although the effects on GDP are positive, lower home-product prices in these industries reduce average home capital returns and hence reduce investment and capital growth, enlarging the negative elasticity through time.

Conclusion

While the Balassa-Samuelson hypothesis is borne out for China—in that productivity has apparently grown faster in the tradable than in the non-tradable sectors and there has been relative service price inflation—the effect of this on the real exchange rate has been counteracted by other forces. It is likely that the strongest of these forces is the rise of China's total savings relative to its investment and the associated expansion of net outflows on its capital account. Other depreciating forces that are likely to have contributed include the demographic dividend and the associated elasticity of labour supply, trade reform, skill acquisition and services productivity growth. Much attention is paid in the literature to China's monetary policy and, in particular, to the PBC's accumulation of foreign exchange reserves. In our view, however, the PBC's monetary stance—embodying as it does the objective of exchange rate stability—is necessitated by financial immaturity. In particular, while China's savings exceed its investment, the reserves and capital controls merely alter the public–private composition of external flows but need not significantly affect their magnitudes. Indeed, it is possible that the future removal of China's capital controls could see accelerated outflows as Chinese institutions seek to enlarge their private holdings of foreign assets. Depending on the PBC's response, the short-term effect of this could be further downward pressure on the real exchange rate.

Figure 16.8 **Elasticities of the projected real exchange rate to its key determinants, 2000–2035**[a]

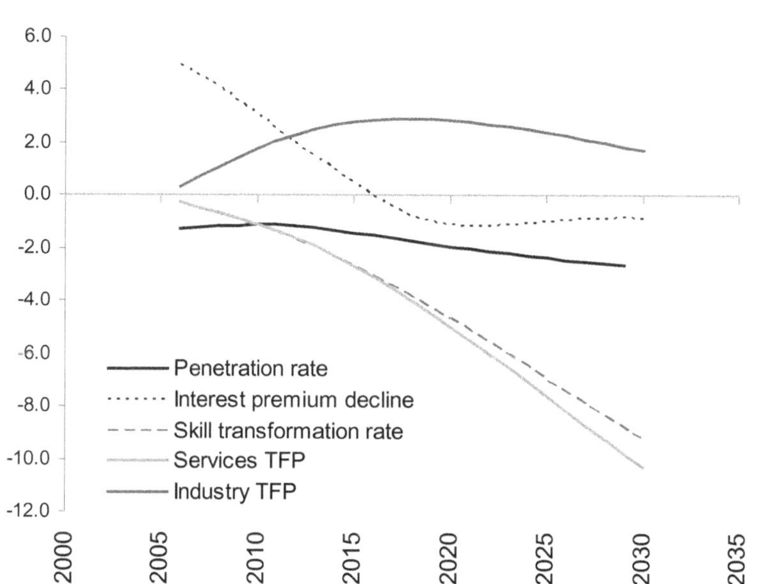

[a] This is the percentage departure of the projected real exchange rate for each percentage increase in the overall import penetration ratio, *M/C*, caused by tariff reductions that began in 2005.

Source: Tyers, R., Golley, J., Bu, Y. and Bain, I., 2006. *China's economic growth and its real exchange rate*, Working Papers in Economics and Econometrics, No. 476, The Australian National University, Canberra.

To examine the effects of the full variety of growth-related shocks on the real exchange rate in the future, we turned to a dynamic model of the global economy. A baseline business-as-usual simulation is constructed to 2030, wherein China's growth rate slows due to ageing and slower labour force growth. The principal determinants of China's economic growth are then shocked separately and their independent effects on the real exchange rate observed over time. Sectoral total factor productivity is raised, the rate of skill acquisition by the workforce is increased, the fertility policy is relaxed, financial reform reduces China's interest premium, and trade reforms further open the economy. In each case, an elasticity of the real exchange rate to the original shock is charted (Figure 16.8).

The results suggest that, while population policy affects the real exchange rate in the directions expected, demographic change is not a strong determinant, at least within the three decades examined. In the short term, the key determinant is net financial capital influx, which appreciates the real exchange rate, or efflux, which depreciates it. In the medium term, scope does emerge for Balassa-Samuelson real appreciation, if services lag sufficiently behind industrial productivity. In the long term, however, if services remain relatively skill intensive on average, their performance will be bolstered by both direct productivity improvements and skill acquisition, and the sensitivity of the real exchange rate to these effects is very large. Since Chinese productivity growth has been higher than that of its trading partners for more than a decade, and considerable scope remains for productivity catch-up in services, these long-term forces might bear down on the real exchange rate in future. If, instead, service sector productivity growth continues to be comparatively weak, real appreciations could also occur. It is difficult to ignore the fact, however, that the majority of the growth-related shocks examined—including overall (and particularly services) productivity growth, professional training and further trade reform—cause the real exchange rate to depreciate in the long term.

Fundamentally, whichever productivity pattern dominates, the future path of the real exchange rate will depend most on the continuation of shocks to aggregate demand due to net flows on the capital account and hence on the future path of China's domestic savings relative to its investment. It is difficult to imagine increases in its savings rate beyond those already recorded. Eventually, it must fall. When it does, net flows on the capital account are likely to be reversed, resulting in an appreciating force. The long-term outcome will then depend on the extent to which this force is offset by continued skill acquisition and services productivity growth.

Notes

1 Miyajima (2005) notes the prominence of services productivity in the growth experience of many Organisation for Economic Co-operation and Development (OECD) countries.

2 Here we imagine that, rather than the continuum of tradability that is observed across goods and services, traded and non-traded goods are separated starkly as T, N.

3 For example, the Cold War infrastructure investments in Korea and Taiwan reduced service costs at early stages in their periods of rapid expansion.

4 See, for example, Bergin et al. (2006); Crucini et al. (2005); and Drine and Rault (2005).

5 This is a standard assumption in the most widely used numerical models of open economies and global trade (see, for example, Dixon et al. 1982; McKibbin and Sachs 1991; Hertel 1997; and Dixon and Rimmer 2002).

6 Evidence for this is offered by Chang and Tyers (2003).

7 The 'Food' sector is defined as Primary Industry plus Food Processing; 'Industry' as Secondary Industry minus Construction and Food Processing; while 'Services' is defined as Tertiary Industry plus Construction. See Tyers et al. (2006) for further details.

8 Moreover, it must be borne in mind that services output volumes and prices are measured more poorly than those in merchandise sectors in all countries. These comparative measures therefore carry large error margins. Lu (2006) estimates labour productivity in China's manufacturing and service sectors between 1978 and 2004. He describes the evolution of China's manufacturing labour productivity after 1978 as a two-stage process: during the first stage (1978–90) it was only 1.9 per cent per annum, compared with a per capita GDP growth rate of 7.5 per cent; while during the second stage (1991–2004) it increased dramatically, averaging 13.1 per cent—significantly higher than the official per capita GDP growth rate of 8.2 per cent. Labour productivity in the service sector averaged 4.3 per cent per annum for the entire period. Fogel 2006 disaggregates per capita income growth between 1978 and 2002 and shows that 69 per cent of growth was due to increases in labour productivity, which grew most rapidly in industry (6.2 per cent per annum), nearly as high in agriculture (5.7 per cent) and lowest, but still substantial, in services (4.5 per cent).

9 For example, he calculates that if the tertiary enrolment ratio rose from six to 25 in the next 20 years (putting China where the Western European nations were in 1980), the growth rate of labour productivity would rise by 4.4 per cent between 2000 and 2020, and that this would account for more than 60 per cent of the per capita GDP growth target set in 2002. With the tertiary ratio increasing from 12.5 per cent to 19 per cent between 2000 and 2004, if anything, his estimates could be too conservative.

10 See Bloom and Williamson (1998) for a generic discussion of the demographic dividend in developing economies.

11 Golley and Tyers (2006) confirm this, finding that the non-working aged dependency ratio could rise to 43 per cent.

12 They note that by 2003, there was a shortage of migrant workers in the Pearl River Delta region, a phenomenon that has since spread to the Yangtze River Delta region and even to some central provinces, such as Jiangxi, Anhui and Henan, which are usually the source of migrants, not the destination.

13 The right hand side of this identity stems from the combination of aggregate expenditure on GDP, $Y = C + I + G + X + M$; the fact that GNP is $Y_N = Y + N$, where N is net factor income from abroad; the GNP disposal identity, $Y_N = C + T + S$, and the balance of payments, $BoP = 0 = KA + CA$, where the current account is $CA = X - M + N$.

14 In the meantime, the approach being taken by the Chinese government to control 'external imbalances' focuses on the rate of economic expansion. Growth is constrained by control over land releases and liquidity, the latter through limits on base money growth, aided by sterilisation bonds, as Figure 16.4 indicates. Other policies serving this purpose include reductions in export facilitation (in the rate of reimbursement of some export taxes) and, at least in prospect, the reduction of import tariffs on some luxury products. Financial reforms are proceeding quickly, however, so that some increased exchange rate flexibility is being offered by the People's Bank of China, as suggested by the extension of the daily renminbi–US dollar rate fluctuation bounds from 0.3 per cent to 0.5 per cent as of late May.

15 Frankel 2004 finds that the renminbi was undervalued by 36 per cent in 2000; Goldstein 2004, who claims it was undervalued by 15–30 per cent in 2004; and Coudert and Couharde 2005, who find the undervaluation to be larger. See Dunaway and Li 2005 for a survey, including one that finds overvaluation (Wang 2004, 2005). Tyers et al. (forthcoming) use a structural model to find evidence of undervaluation in the mid to late 1990s but offer no clear finding for 2004.

16 Further evidence of large sums of capital flight out of China is offered by Sicular (1998) and Gunter (2004).

17 According to Fan (2006), speculative inflows were as high as US$105 billion in 2004 (see also Prasad and Wei 2005).

18 In separate work by the authors, the foreign asset share of China's collective portfolio is estimated to be lower than average for countries of its size and development level, its substantial reserves notwithstanding. This suggests the former outcome is the more likely one.

19 Tyers and Golley (2006) use measures of China's investment premium to explore the implications of financial reform. Their modelling approach underlies the results presented in the remainder of the chapter.

20 The model has its origins in *GTAP-Dynamic*, the standard version of which is a derivative of its comparative static progenitor, *GTAP* (Hertel 1997). Its dynamics are described in Ianchovichina and McDougall (2000).

21 Wang and Ding (2006) recently estimated that there were 40 million surplus workers in China's agricultural sector. While underemployment is not explicit in our model, the assumption of high labour productivity growth in agriculture implies that agriculture is capable of shedding labour more quickly than other sectors. This essentially mimics the surplus labour problem, which is thereby accounted for implicitly.

22 The subdivision between production workers and professionals and para-professionals accords with the International Labour Organization's occupation-based classification and is consistent with the labour division adopted in the GTAP Database. See Liu et al. (1998).

23 The elasticity is insensitive to the scale of the liberalisation though not to the composition of China's protection. For the levels of protection embodied in the database for 1997, see Dimaranan and McDougall (2002).

References

Aizenman, J. and Lee, J., 2006. *Financial versus monetary mercantilism: long run view of large international reserves hoarding*, Working Paper WP/06/280, International Monetary Fund, Washington, DC.

Balassa, B., 1964. 'The purchasing power parity doctrine: a reappraisal', *Journal of Political Economy*, 72(6):584–96.

Bergin, P.R., Glick, R. and Taylor, A.M., 2006. 'Productivity, tradability and the long run price puzzle', *Journal of Monetary Economics*, 53(8):2,041–66.

Bernanke, B., 2006. Speech to the Chinese Academy of Social Sciences, Beijing, 15 December.

Bloom, D.E. and Williamson, J.G., 1998. 'Demographic transitions and economic miracles in emerging Asia', *World Bank Economic Review*, 12(3):419–55.

Cai, F. and Wang, D., 2005. 'Demographic transition: implications for growth', in R. Garnaut and L. Song (eds), *The China Boom and its Discontents*, Asia Pacific Press, The Australian National University, Canberra:34–52.

——, 2006. 'Employment growth, labour scarcity and the nature of China's trade expansion', in R. Garnaut and L. Song (eds), *The Turning Point in China's Economic Development*, Asia Pacific Press, The Australian National University, Canberra:143–71.

Chang, J. and Tyers, R., 2003. 'Trade reform, macroeconomic policy and sectoral labour movement in China', in R. Garnaut and L. Song (eds), *China:*

new engine of world growth, Asia Pacific Press, The Australian National University, Canberra:231–75.

Choudhri, E.U. and Khan, M.S., 2004. *Real exchange rates in developing countries: are Balassa-Samuelson effects present?*, Working Paper, No.WP/04/188, International Monetary Fund, Washington, DC.

Coudert, V. and Couharde, C., 2005. *Real equilibrium exchange rate in China*, Working Paper, No.2005-01, CEPII, Paris.

Crucini, M.J., Telmer, C.I. and Zachariadis, M., 2005. 'Understanding European real exchange rates', *American Economic Review*, 95(3):724–38.

Dimaranan, B.V. and McDougall, R.A., 2002. *Global Trade, Assistance and Production: the GTAP 5 data base*, May, Center for Global Trade Analysis, Purdue University, Lafayette.

Dixon, P.B., Parmenter, B.R., Sutton, J. and Vincent, D.P., 1982. *ORANI, a Multi-Sectoral Model of the Australian Economy*, North Holland, Amsterdam.

Dixon, P.B. and Rimmer, M.T., 2002. *Dynamic General Equilibrium Modelling for Forecasting and Policy: a practical guide and documentation of Monash*, North Holland, Amsterdam.

Drine, I. and Rault, C., 2005. 'Can the Balassa-Samuelson theory explain long run real exchange rate movements in OECD countries?', *Applied Financial Economics*, 15(8):519–30.

Dunaway, S. and Li, X., 2005. *Estimating China's 'equilibrium' real exchange rate*, Policy Discussion Paper 05/202, International Monetary Fund, Washington, DC.

Fan, G., 2006. 'Global imbalance, China and the international currency system', in R. Garnaut and L. Song (eds), *The Turning Point in China's Economic Development*, Asia Pacific Press, The Australian National University, Canberra.

Fogel, R., 2006. *Why is China likely to achieve its growth objectives?*, Working Paper W12122, National Bureau of Economic Research, Cambridge, MA.

Frankel, J., 2004. *On the* renminbi*: the choice between adjustment under a fixed exchange rate and adjustment under a flexible rate*, Working Paper 11274, National Bureau of Economic Research, Cambridge, MA.

Golley, J. and Tyers, R., 2006. 'China's growth to 2030: demographic change and the labour supply constraint', in R. Garnaut and L. Song (eds), *The Turning Point in China's Economic Development*, Asia Pacific Press, Canberra; version in Chinese forthcoming in Chinese Labor Economics.

Goldstein, M., 2004. Adjusting China's foreign exchange rate, Revised version of a paper delivered at the International Monetary Fund's seminar on China's Foreign Exchange Rate System, Dalian, 26–27 May. Available from www.iie.com (accessed September 2006).

Gunter, F., 2004. 'Capital flight from China: 1984–2001', *China Economic Review*, 15:63–85.

Hertel, T.W. (ed.), 1997. *Global Trade Analysis Using the GTAP Model*, Cambridge University Press, New York.

Ianchovichina, E. and McDougall, R., 2000. *Theoretical structure of Dynamic GTAP*, GTAP Technical Paper, No. 17, Purdue University, Lafayette.

International Monetary Fund (IMF), 2007a. *International Financial Statistics*, International Monetary Fund, Washington, DC.

——, 2007b. *World Economic Outlook Database*, International Monetary Fund, Washington, DC.

Lardy, N., 2006. 'China's interaction with the global economy', in R. Garnaut and L. Song (eds), *The Turning Point in China's Economic Development*, Asia Pacific Press, The Australian National University, Canberra.

Liu, J., Van Leeuwen, N., Vo, T.T., Tyers, R. and Hertel, T.W., 1998. *Disaggregating labor payments by skill level in GTAP*, Technical Paper, No. 11, Center for Global Trade Analysis, Department of Agricultural Economics, Purdue University, Lafayette.

Lu, F., 2006. *China's productivity growth, an international comparison*, China Center for Economic Research Working Paper C200604, Peking University, Beijing (in Chinese).

Ma, Y., 2006. *A comparative study of the competitiveness of the domestic and foreign-invested service industries in China*, Centre for Public Policy Studies Working Paper, No. 176, Lingnan University, Hong Kong, December.

McKibbin, W.J. and Sachs, J., 1991. *Global Linkages: macroeconomic independence and cooperation in the world economy*, Brookings Institution, Washington, DC.

Miyajima, K., 2005. *Real exchange rates in growing economies: how strong is the role of the nontradables sector*, Working Paper 05/233, International Monetary Fund, Washington, DC.

National Bureau of Statistics, 2006. *China Statistical Abstract* 2006, China Statistical Press, Beijing.

People's Bank of China, 2006. *Balance Sheet of Monetary Authority*, People's Bank of China, Beijing.

Prasad, E., Rumbaugh, T. and Wang, Q., 2005. *Putting the cart before the horse: capital account liberalization and the exchange rate in China*, Policy Discussion Paper 05/01, International Monetary Fund, Washington, DC.

Prasad, E. and Wei, S.J., 2005. *The Chinese approach to capital inflows: patterns and possible explanations*, Working Paper WP/05/79, International Monetary Fund, Washington, DC.

Rodrik, D., 2006. *What's so special about Chinese exports?*, Working Paper, No. 11947, National Bureau of Economic Research, Cambridge, MA.

Samuelson, P., 1964. 'Theoretical notes on trade problems', *Review of Economics and Statistics*, 46(2):145–54.

Sicular, T., 1998. 'Capital flight and foreign investment: two tales from China and Russia', *The World Economy*, 21(5):589–602.

Tyers, R. and Golley, J., 2006. *China's growth to 2030: the roles of demographic change and investment premia*, Working Papers in Economics and Econometrics, No. 461, The Australian National University, Canberra.

Tyers, R., Golley, J., Bu, Y. and Bain, I., 2006. *China's economic growth and its real exchange rate*, Working Papers in Economics and Econometrics, No. 476, The Australian National University, Canberra.

Tyers, R. and Shi, Q., 2007a. 'Global demographic change, policy responses and their economic implications', *The World Economy*, 30(4):537–66.

——, 2007b. *Global demographic change, labour force growth and economic performance*, Working Papers in Economics and Econometrics, No. 462, The Australian National University, Canberra.

Tyers, R., Bu, Y. and Bain, I., (forthcoming). 'China's equilibrium exchange rate: a counterfactual analysis', *Pacific Economic Review*, October.

Wang, J. and Ding, S., 2006. 'A re-estimation of China's agricultural surplus labour—the demonstration and modification of three prevalent methods', *Frontiers of Economics in China*, 1(2):171–81.

Wang, T., 2004. 'Exchange rate dynamics', in E. Prasad (ed.), *China's Growth and Integration into the World Economy: prospects and challenges*, International Monetary Fund Occasional Paper 232, Washington, DC.

——, 2005. 'Sources of real exchange rate fluctuations in China', *Journal of Comparative Economics*, 33(4):753–71.

Acknowledgments

Funding for the research described in this chapter is from the Australian Research Council Discovery Grant No.DP0557889. Thanks are due to Bu Yongxiang, Huang Yiping and Chris Milner for useful discussions on the topic; to Christopher Kent and participants in an April 2007 Reserve Bank of Australia seminar for valuable comments; to Terrie Walmsley for technical assistance with the GTAP Database; Wang Xiaolu for help with China's national accounts; and to Iain Bain and Hsu Pingkun for research assistance.

17

An externally dependent economy and real estate bubbles

Lijian Sun and Shengxing Zhang

The two prominent phenomena in the world economy in recent years have been excessive monetary liquidity and asset price bubbles (Bank for International Settlements 2004; United Nations 2006; OECD 2006). In the past, Western industrialised countries experienced different kinds of bubbles, for example: information technology (IT) stock bubbles from 1996 to 1999; bond price bubbles from 2000 to 2002; and real estate bubbles from 2002 until now. Although each bubble had specific characteristics (Hunter et al. 2005),[1] the latest research shows that excessive monetary liquidity is an indispensable factor in explaining recent price bubbles in capital markets—for example, stock, bond and real estate markets (Issing 2002; Gouteron and Szpiro 2005).

The co-movement of excessive monetary liquidity and asset price bubbles began to attract economists' attention as early as 1929 with the start of the Great Depression. At that time, economists agreed that a lending boom would stimulate bubbles in capital markets (White 1990). Specifically, for the case of the Japanese bubble economy in the late 1980s, many Japanese scholars also pointed out that the Japanese government's expanded monetary policy during yen appreciation resulted in stock and real estate bubbles. Some have described the Japanese economy as suffering from depression because of the bursting of the bubble (Okina and Shiratsuka 2005). On the other hand, many other researchers explain that tight monetary policy can induce the collapse of financial markets (Friedman and Schwartz 1982; Bernanke 2001; Posen 2006). Much recent empirical research, however, reveals that there is no direct causal link between a central bank's monetary policy and asset price bubbles

(Bordo and Jeanne 2002; Mishkin and White 2002; Detken and Smets 2004). In this sense, monetary policies are neither the cause of nor the cure for asset price bubbles.

Nevertheless, monetary liquidity has now become obviously excessive all over the world, so the key point is to uncover the main cause of this phenomenon and its relationship with asset bubbles. In recent years, many scholars have explained the mechanism of excessive liquidity. Ortalo-Magne and Rady (2006) argued that the impact of business cycles on personal income induced changes in monetary liquidity, which in turn influenced housing demand, causing surges in real estate prices. Additionally, a lack of investment channels would force investment to concentrate in well-behaved markets so that speculative bubbles in these markets became increasingly pervasive (Ventura 2004; Caballero and Krishnamurthy 2005). Other scholars found that in bank-based countries, real estate bubbles and collapses were common, which was an outcome of the myopic behaviour of banks: when the economy was booming, banks increased lending for real estate purchases when prices were rising, and cut lending when real estate prices were falling. Thus, the myopic behaviour of banks intensifies price fluctuation (Herring and Wachter 2005).

Excessive monetary liquidity in China is fierce and the growth rates of M1 and M2 are much greater than that of gross domestic product (GDP) (People's Bank of China 2006). Yuan and Fan (2003) and the research group of the China Real Estate Chamber of Commerce (2006)[2] report that excessive monetary liquidity indeed leads to real estate bubbles, although it does not bring about high inflation in commodity markets, as the central bank worried it would. Sun (2006) indicates that the mechanism of real estate bubbles in China is significantly different from that in Western industrialised countries. Therefore, the objective of this chapter is to explore the reasons for excessive monetary liquidity in China and its impact on real estate prices.

From examination of the fundamental macroeconomic indices, and the overlapping generation (OLG) model explaining the high saving ratio of the younger generation (Tirole 1985), and using empirical analysis of provincial panel data, we make three contributions. First, we examine the logic behind real estate bubbles in China. We focus on the way that excessive monetary liquidity—as the root of real estate bubbles—results from the increasingly externally dependent economic structure. Second, we test the view that excessive monetary liquidity does not stimulate private consumption because residents are less confident of maintaining their incomes. On the contrary, it increases the burden on the banking system by encouraging excessive private savings as a result of inefficient capital markets. Third, we look at how real estate bubbles are a result of private precautionary savings. While each agent, including banks and individuals, tries to invest in assets with safe and high returns, the aggregate result is over-investment in these assets. The risk of a 'credit crunch' thus increases and social welfare is impaired.

Admittedly, some scholars have also investigated the influence of surpluses in the balance of payments on asset prices in emerging markets. For instance, Park and Park (1995) take the example of financial liberalisation in South Korea—which led to foreign capital inflows in the 1990s—and applied the Keynesian general equilibrium model to explain how the appreciation of nominal exchange rates accompanied by capital inflows influenced the relative price of tradable and non-tradable goods. They found that although the real interest rate was very high because of tight monetary policies, optimistic expectations towards the real estate market offset the effort to restrict the money supply, in the end leading to real estate bubbles.

The common point in these articles is that a real estate bubble results from huge capital inflows, which alter the nominal exchange rate and the domestic price level, distorting the real exchange rate. In the case of the Chinese economy, however, we argue that even if the nominal exchange rate does not change and the capital account remains strictly regulated, real estate bubbles can occur, as long as foreign reserves driven by exports keep growing and the financial system is underdeveloped. Collyns and Senhadji (2002) found in the empirical analysis of the East Asian financial crisis that foreign investors' over-optimism and the fragile financial system caused bubbles in stock markets and real estate markets. This research is also a reflection of the opening of the capital account in a vulnerable financial system. Still, the above research on the fragility of financial systems cannot explain why bubbles occur only in real estate markets without the opening of the capital account in countries such as China (Ogawa and Sun 2001), while our paper validates the relationship between excessive monetary liquidity and real estate bubbles in China's economy, based on our theoretical model about private saving and investment behaviour and related empirical analysis.

Real estate bubbles are complex that scholars have not yet achieved agreement on their causes, features and influences (Hunter et al. 2005).[3] Accordingly, there are conflicting policy suggestions (Meltzer 2003; Trichet 2005; Roubini 2006). In this chapter, we are not so ambitious as to explore a complete set of related economic indices or an integrated one affecting real estate bubbles. In this sense, monetary liquidity is just one of many important factors causing real estate bubbles and our research is complementary to other research in this field. The index of excessive monetary liquidity, however, emphasises the effect of imbalances in the economic structure on real estate bubbles, which has not been studied systematically before. On the other hand, many factors revealed by previous research explaining bubbles are related to excessive monetary liquidity, such as money illusion (Brunnermeier and Juilliard 2006), incomplete information (Morris and Shin 2002; Favara and Song 2006), inelastic house supply (Gyourko et al. 2006), buyer optimism (Herring and Wachter 2005; Case et al. 2003) and incomplete financial markets (Stein 1995; Ortalo-Magne and Rady 2006).

To fully reflect the influence of structural excessive monetary liquidity on real estate bubbles, we make several improvements on the existing literature. First, we find that excessive monetary liquidity results from twin surpluses (the capital account and the current account) in the balance of payments under the rigid exchange rate system, rather than from expanding monetary policies, which is derived from fundamental principles of open macroeconomics and related macroeconomic indices commonly accepted by scholars (Calvo et al. 1993; Agénor and Montiel 1999). Second, excessive consumer savings will lead to over-investment in bubble assets in an incomplete financial market where bubbles are expected, according to the OLG model for private savings and investment behaviour (Caballero and Krishnamurthy 2005). Third, we select bank deposits as the index for excessive monetary liquidity rather than bank loans (used by previous researchers), based on the phenomenon that savings accompanied by the growth of foreign reserve increase rapidly and banks over-invest in real estate assets. Last but not least, we create an index for liquidity spillover effects to identify the influence of liquidity differences on real estate bubbles across provinces.

Our research shows that in the case of real estate bubbles in contemporary China, the savings index is statistically more significant than the loan index, which manifests the structural excessive monetary liquidity to be an indispensable reason behind real estate bubbles. Therefore, our suggestion of a radical approach to appeasing the surge of real estate bubbles in China is to solve the structural imbalance in the Chinese economy—specifically, the conflict between the expansion of trade and the fragility of financial systems.

The externally dependent economy and excessive monetary liquidity

China's rapidly growing economy has the following features: extensive fixed investment (I) grows rapidly; domestic demand led by individual consumption (C) remains mild; while at the same time, residential disposable incomes keep increasing and private savings (S) in banks grow proportionally[4] (Figure 17.1 and

Figure 17.1 **Growth rate of residents' savings, 1995–2006**

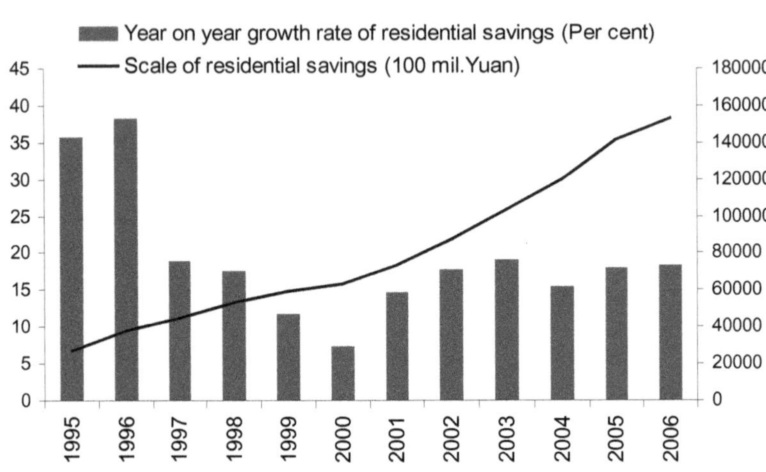

Source: China Wind Database.

People's Bank of China 2006). That is, investment in China is surplus compared with domestic consumption but insufficient compared with domestic savings since S-I>0. Third, though net exports (EX-IM) are increasing substantially, the scale is still limited. China's gross exports account for more than 60 per cent of GDP, which is much larger than the figure the United States and Japan (the ratio of net exports to GDP is a commonly used index for the external dependence of an economy). Most exports are of manufactured products, a high proportion of which are from foreign-owned enterprises (Figure 2). The increase in exports is accompanied by the importation of high value-added intermediate goods (IM).[5] The last characteristic is that the Chinese government's fiscal policy tends to be conservative (T>G).

From a basic principle of open macroeconomics, the combination of superfluous domestic savings and conservative fiscal policy will lead to a trade surplus.

$$(S-I)+(T-G)\equiv(EX-IM) \quad (1)$$

In fact, with the persistently fast-growing Chinese economy and the increasingly externally dependent economic structure accompanying that growth (dependent on exports and foreign direct investment), the twin surpluses in the balance of payments are inevitable. Therefore, with a stable exchange rate,[6] a lasting surplus in the current account (CA), led by a trade surplus (EX-IM), and the capital account (KA). led by foreign direct investment (FDI), trigger increases in foreign reserves, recently in China, to historical heights (see Equation 2 and Figure 17.2).

$$CA + KA \equiv RE \tag{2}$$

Excessive liquidity (uncontrollable increase in monetary supply, M) resulting from the expanding foreign reserve will restrain the 'miracle' of lasting rapid economic growth in an externally dependent economic structure. In order to maintain the price competitiveness of domestic enterprises, the central bank has to implement contractive monetary policies[7] (we define a contractive monetary policy as forcibly lowering domestic credit, DC, to stabilise monetary supply, M)[8] (see Figure 17.3).[9]

Figure 17.2 **Twin surplus of balance of payments, 1990–2005**

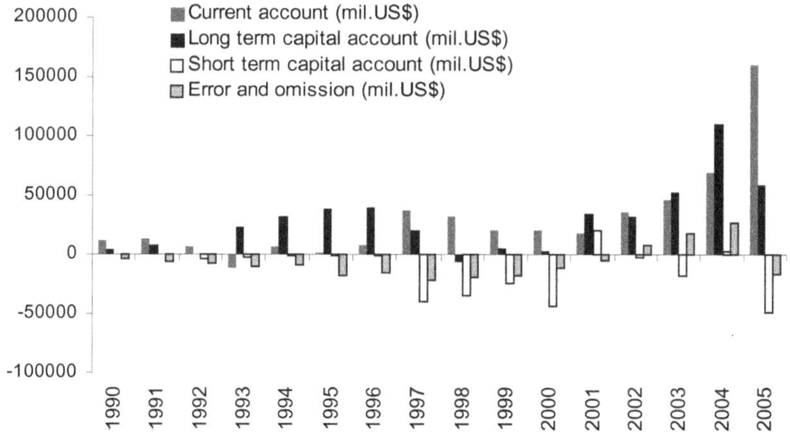

Current account (mil.US$)
Long term capital account (mil.US$)
Short term capital account (mil.US$)
Error and omission (mil.US$)
200000
150000
100000
50000
0
-50000
-100000
1990 1991 1992 1993 1994 1995 1996 1997 1998 1999 2000 2001 2002 2003 2004 2005

Source: China Wind Database.

Figure 17.3 **Comparison of growth rates of M1, M2 and bank loans, 2001–2006** (per cent)

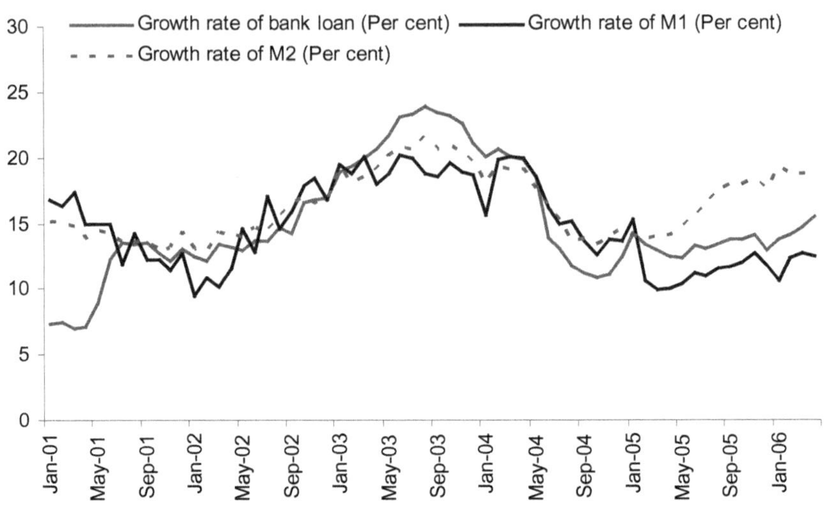

Source: China Wind Database.

Figure 17.4 **Growth rate of real estate prices, 1999–2005** (per cent)

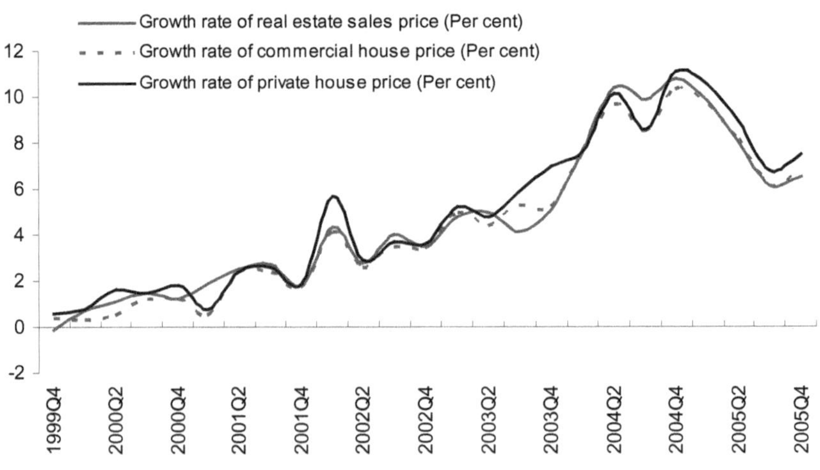

Source: China Wind Database.

Specifically, we employ the equation of the central bank's balance sheet to show the mechanism of money supply

$$M \equiv DC + RE \tag{3}$$

Although the combination of tight monetary policy, persistently growing fixed investment and the over-saving behaviour of consumers effectively relieve the pressure of inflation in the commodity market, the fragile banking system is facing the challenge of excessive monetary liquidity (Figure 17.3). For instance, confined by the macro control policy and institutional restrictions, banks cannot freely expand loans to enterprises and adjust deposit and credit interest rates. Hence, the boosting of deposits (see Figure 17.1 and M2 in Figure 17.3) worsens the imbalance on commercial banks' balance sheets.

Once banks try to balance their balance sheets, they have to pursue high-return assets[10] such as real estate loans. On the demand side, Chinese consumers have to suppress current consumption and save most of their increasing income in banks in order to invest in safe and increasingly valuable assets[11] for future health insurance, pensions, educational expenditure and unemployment insurance. The expanding supply and demand of liquidity can boost real estate prices (see Figure 17.4).[12]

It is the externally dependent economic structure (export dependent and FDI dependent) that brings excessive monetary liquidity (private savings or M2), rather than relaxed monetary policy (the inflation of M1 or DC), as in industrialised countries. Will excessive monetary liquidity from externally dependent economic structures cause real estate bubbles, as the relaxed monetary policy does in industrialised countries? What is the mechanism for and features of it? We will answer these questions through formal theoretical models in the next section.

A simple OLG model

We use an OLG model[13] to analyse the inherent connection between the externally dependent economy and real estate bubbles. We note the coexistence of a lack of social security, lagged development of financial systems and fast growth of private savings in China. Muth (1961), Brock (1975) and Gaber (1990) set up the rational bubble mechanism. The pioneering paper of Tirole (1985) introduced the rational bubble mechanism into the OLG model to study asset price bubbles, which shows that in a dynamically inefficient economy with excessive capital accumulation, rational bubbles would reduce the excessive capital accumulation and thus realise Pareto's improvement.[14] The model of

Caballero and Krishnamurthy (2005), however, and our paper suggest that in an externally dependent (dynamically inefficient) economy, the rational bubble could lower social welfare[15] by a credit crunch in the banking system when bubbles burst, although it could stimulate enterprises to expand their production when the real estate market booms. While Caballero and Krishnamurthy (2005) focus on economies dependent on foreign debt, we focus on economies depending on exports and FDI growth, which is the case in China. So, we believe that our model can better explain the story behind excessive monetary liquidity and real estate bubbles in the Chinese economy.

Model set up

First, we assume an externally dependent economy of two overlapping generations. Specifically, the young generation born at the beginning of period 't' works in foreign enterprises that are export oriented and grow at a constant rate 'g'. For precautionary incentives mentioned above, the young generation saves all its income, F_t, in the form of foreign savings or investment in the real estate market (the only two instruments with safe and high returns) in order to get high and smoothed income. The total assets of the old generation in period t+1 amounts to $F_{t+1,t}$ (measured by foreign currency), which the old generation uses either to produce as entrepreneurs or to fund entrepreneurs' production as bankers.[16] For simplification, income from the old generation's career will cover the consumption of the whole society. In addition, the fixed asset K_t owned by the old generation will be bequeathed to the young generation.

Obviously, income difference between the young generation in period 't' and period t+1 is determined by the growth rate of exports, since the young all work in export-oriented enterprises:

$$F_{t+1} = (1+g)F_t \tag{4}$$

If the young generation invests δ part of their income in the real estate market and the annual return of real estate investment is $\tilde{r}^b$ (a stochastic variable), then the total foreign assets[17] of the old generation in period t+1, accumulated from period 't', when they are young, is

$$\tilde{F}_{t+1,t} = F_t[\delta(1+\tilde{r}^b)+(1-\delta)(1+r^*)] \tag{5}$$

Furthermore, the old-generation entrepreneurs collateralise their fixed assets, K_t, to borrow banks' fixed assets for manufacturing and use their foreign assets (marked as $\tilde{F}_{t+1,t}$) to import raw materials from abroad. The rates should be above one, denoted as R and $\tilde{r}_{t+1}^{BL}$ respectively. All funds are utilised to manufacture domestic non-durable products, which in turn brings a return of 'R' per unit of investment. ('R' is determined exogenously by productivity.) Therefore, the *ex post* trade surplus at period 't' is equal to the exports of the young generation minus the imports of the old generation,

$$F_{t+1} - F_{t+1,t} = [(g - r^*) - \delta(r^b - r^*)]\, F_t \tag{6}$$

Namely, the trade surplus increases with the growth rate of exports, while it decreases with the investment scale and return in the real estate market.

With the equilibrium of the credit market, banks' maximum lending should be equal to entrepreneurs' maximum borrowings,

$$\tilde{F}_{t+1,t} = \frac{\rho R}{\tilde{r}_{t+1}^{BL}} K_t \tag{7}$$

in which ρ is the valuation coefficient for the collateralised fixed assets given by banks (ρ is a positive number, usually smaller than one, since banks will not lend as much as the collateralised value). Entrepreneurial value is determined by production technology, return on investment and capital cost, so the return is

$$RK_t + R\tilde{F}_{t+1,t} + (R - \tilde{r}_{t+1}^{BL}) \frac{\rho R}{\tilde{r}_{t+1}^{BL}} K_t \tag{8}$$

Banks' profits are from rent of their real estate and interest from lending so they will receive at the end of period t+1

$$RK_t + \tilde{F}_{t+1,t} \tilde{r}_{t+1}^{BL} \tag{9}$$

Since the probability for the young generation to become bankers or entrepreneurs is fifty-fifty, the young will choose their house investment ratio to maximise their expected incomes in the future,

$$\max_{0 \le \delta \le 1} E_t \left\{ RK_t + \tilde{F}_{t+1,t} \frac{R + \tilde{r}_{t+1}}{2} + \frac{R - \tilde{r}_{t+1}}{2} \times \frac{\rho R}{\tilde{r}_{t+1}} K_t \right\} \tag{10}$$

Second, regarding the mechanism of bubbles in the real estate market, we assume that the intrinsic value of real estate is zero. This simplification focuses our attention on the 'bubble side' of the real estate market. Since the intrinsic value of real estate is stable when bubbles emerge in the market, we believe this simplification to be reasonable. When the young generation in period 't' believes that the purchased real estate can be sold to the next generation at a higher price, speculation will prevail and the self-fulfilling rational bubble will come into existence. In this setting, the growth rate of real estate prices is determined by the growth rate of the young generation's earnings and exports. More specifically, $r^b = g$, in which r^b represents the growth rate of real estate prices.

In this model, we see that the 'structural' twin surpluses of the balance of payments (see Equations 1, 2) bring about excessive liquidity, which in turn forms bubbles in the real estate market. The young will sell their assets in advance altogether[18] only when external shock forces bubbles to expand too rapidly ($r^b > g$). So people begin to consider that income growth cannot sustain the bubbles and the bubble bursts because of their selling action. If the probability of a bubble burst is π, then the expected return of real estate investment ($\hat{r}^b$) is

$$1 + \hat{r}^b = (1 - \pi)(1 + g) \qquad (11)$$

Since we focus on consumers' motivation for real estate investment and the corresponding real estate bubble, we assume the expected return of real estate investment to be always greater than foreign savings,

$$\hat{r}^b - r^* = (1 - \pi)(g - r^*) - \pi(1 + r^*) > 0 \qquad (12)$$

In addition, the movement of real estate prices could influence the loan supply and demand in the credit market (see Equations 5, 7), which in turn influences banks' lending rates. Therefore, during the bubble economy, the lending scale is $F^B_{t+1,t} = [1 + r^* + \delta(g - r^*)]F_t$ and the loan rate is $\tilde{r}^{BL}_{t+1} = r^B_{t+1}$; when the bubble has burst, the lending scale will be $F^C_{t+1,t} = (1 + r^*)(1 - \delta)F_t$, with the lending rate assumed to be $\tilde{r}^{BL}_{t+1} = r^C_{t+1}$.[19]

The optimal portfolio allocation of the young generation

The first order condition of the optimisation problem (Equation 10) is

$$(1 - \pi)\frac{g - r^*}{1 + r^*}(R + r^B_{t+1}) - \pi(R + r^C_{t+1}) = 0 \qquad (13)$$

The optimal allocation parameter, δ, does not appear in the first order condition. The economic meaning is that as long as the lending rates (r^B_{t+1} and r^C_{t+1}) under the condition of a sustained bubble and bubble collapse are determined in advance by the young generation, they can always maximise their expected income and they are indifferent about the portfolio allocation, since the potential loss (return = -1) of the bubble collapse (the probability is π) is always offset by the potential gain (g-r^*) of the bubble sustaining (the probability is 1-π). Here, $(R+r_{t+1}^{B})$ is the normal return of banks in a bubble-sustaining period and $(R+r_{t+1}^{C})$ in a bubble-burst period.

On the other hand, we need to make sure that the credit market is clear. Utilising the equilibrium of the credit market (Equation 7), we can get the equilibrium lending rate when bubbles are sustained

$$r_{t+1}^{B} = \max\left\{1,\ \frac{\rho R}{1+r^{*}+\delta(g-r^{*})}\right\} \tag{14}$$

For simplification, we let $F_t = K_t$, and assume that $\rho R < 1$.[20] Obviously, $r_{t+1}^{B} = 1$ means that the savings in the young generation are so abundant that supply of loans of the old generation forces the lending rate to the bottom line.

Likewise, the lending rate when bubbles burst is

$$r_{t+1}^{C} = \max\left\{1,\ \min\left[\frac{\rho R}{(1+r^{*})(1-\delta)},\ R\right]\right\} \tag{15}$$

The equation means that when bubbles burst, the savings of the young generation contract, as does the lending of the old generation. Therefore, the lending rate rises. Of course, the lending rate should be no smaller than one and no greater than the return of production 'R'.

Using the first order condition (Equation 13), together with $r_{t+1}^{B} = 1$ (and Equation 15), we can get the *ex ante* optimal portfolio allocation (δ*).[21]

According to the individual optimal portfolio allocation, we can confirm the conclusion of existing references in the introduction that bubbles do stimulate real investment. The increase of real investment does not, however, necessarily justify the allocation. In the next section, we will judge the appropriateness of the optimal allocation, δ*, according to its influence on social welfare.

Evaluation of social welfare and over-investment in the real estate market

Since the asset value of the young generation is elevated in a bubble economy, the values of the entrepreneurs' capital and the banks' loan scale both increase. The total social output is

$$Q^{B} = \frac{R+1}{2}F_t[1+r^{*}+\delta(g-r^{*})] + \frac{1}{2}(R-1)\rho RK_t + RK_t \tag{16}$$

There would, however, be two possibilities when bubbles burst. The first is that without credit crunch, featured by $r_{t+1}^{C}=1$, the total social output is

$$Q^{C,S}=\frac{R+1}{2}F_t(1+r^*)(1-\delta)+\frac{1}{2}(R-1)\,\rho RK_t+RK_t \tag{17}$$

The second is that with credit crunch, featured by $r_{t+1}^{C}>1$, the total social output is

$$Q^{C,L}=RF_t(1+r^*)(1-\delta)+RK_t \tag{18}$$

Comparing the three equations on aggregate output, we find that bubbles have two effects. One is to stimulate production (Equation 16); the other is to restrain production (Equations 17 and 18). Therefore, the government will maximise the expected social output taking both effects into account. Notice that the objective function of social welfare is different from that of individual expected income:

$$\max_{0\le\delta\le1}\pi Q^{C}+(1-\pi)Q^{B}$$

here $Q^{C}=Q^{C,S}$ or $Q^{C}=Q^{C,L}$. Then we could obtain

$$F_t\left(\frac{R+1}{2}\right)[(1-\pi)(g-r^*)-\pi(1+r^*)]>0,\ \textit{where}\ r_{t+1}^{C}=1 \tag{19}$$

or

$$(1-\pi)(R+1)\frac{g-r^*}{1+r^*}-2\pi R<0,\ \textit{where}\ r_{t+1}^{C}>1 \tag{20}$$

The first order conditions do not hold and we get the corner solution. For the first inequality, the model has assumed that the expected return of bubble assets is greater than the foreign deposit rate. To the other inequality, since this is when the loss of social output reaches its maximum, the inequality is still acceptable. Besides, bank credit rates are rigid in the two extreme points, which indicates that the increase of real estate investment ratios does not affect the lending rate in the two extreme points, but the real estate investment ratio has a positive monotonic correlation with the credit rate in the middle area. If we denote δ^{S} and δ^{L} as the critical values for the conditions of 'middle term=1'[22] and 'middle term=R' respectively, we can conclude (see Equations 19 and 20) that the government's optimal preference investment ratio, δ^{G}, is always δ^{S} in both conditions. As well, δ^G is always lower than the individual optimal ratio, δ^*. This means that individual investment in the real estate market is speculative and, from the perspective of social welfare, individual rational investment in real estate markets is excessive.

$$\delta^G = \delta^S < \delta^* \tag{21}$$

In short, the model demonstrates that with an incomplete financial market, the excessive monetary liquidity brought about by export increases will be transformed into individual motivation to invest in the real estate market, resulting in rational or speculative bubbles. From the viewpoint of social welfare, the investment is excessive. Following the stylised fact and the OLG model, quantitative analysis will be given below.

Data, variable selection and empirical modelling

This section intends to answer quantitatively two important questions. Is excessive monetary liquidity is the main contributor to real estate bubbles in China? Is there speculative investment in the real estate market?

We adopt panel data analysis based on the regional data from 28 provinces[23] in China rather than the time-series analysis using macroeconomic data. This is because excessive monetary liquidity is a new phenomenon that has emerged only in recent years.[24] Therefore, the time-series analysis cannot identify the bubble for lack of sufficient data (Kalra et al. 2000).

The cross-provincial panel data in this chapter are from February 2004 to December 2005. Even if year-on-year adjustment is conducted to ensure the consistency of empirical analysis with the theoretical model, and to relieve the problem of the time-series characteristic, each variable still has as many as 308 observations. We further study the ripple effect (Cameron et al. 2006), that is, to introduce the spillover liquidity variable in order to discuss the influence of cross-provincial liquidity differences on local real estate prices. It is an important criterion of speculative investment (the second issue to be tested) uncovered by the stylised fact and the theoretical model of whether the ripple effect is statistically significant.[25]

Since we want to examine the real estate bubble resulting from the externally dependent economy, we use the difference between the growth rate of real estate prices in China minus the short-term US bond rate as the dependent variable in our empirical model, according to the theoretical model (see Equation 12). As real estate prices are not obtainable directly, we calculate the prices from the division of the sales revenue and the sale price of commercial houses.

When selecting independent variables, we choose the growth rate of savings,[26] rather that of bank loans or monetary supply, because we want to emphasise the role of monetary liquidity. In fact, banks are regulated with respect to the ratio of deposits to loans during the sample period; the scale of loans is therefore determined by that of savings. And the down payments of individuals and the autonomous lending of enterprises, while not included in credit variables, are reflected in savings. So, the growth rate of savings can better illustrate real estate bubbles.

The spillover effect variables are measured by the difference between the growth rate of local savings and aggregate savings. This index can examine whether capital will flow from capital-rich areas to capital-deficient areas. Such capital flow will promote real estate bubbles in capital-deficient areas. With cross-provincial capital flows, the growth rate of real estate prices all over China could tend to converge. As for other independent variables that need to be controlled, we choose variables according to the survey on empirical works about real estate bubbles (Cameron et al. 2006) and the availability of Chinese data. Specifically, these variables are the growth rate of residential income, enterprise profits, losses of loss-making enterprises and land prices.[27] Residential income and enterprise profits can reflect fundamentals of the economy, but can also control the influence of cross-provincial differences of economic development on real estate prices. The inclusion of the variable of losses of loss-making enterprises follows a new argument that enterprises with low productivity and profitability tend to speculate in the real estate market (Ventura 2004). Construction cost is also a fundamental factor that cannot be omitted. But since the regional data for this variable are not accessible, we use land price as its index. Land prices were found in the same way as the real estate price.

Therefore, the panel data model we employ is

$$\begin{aligned}&[\text{the rate of change in real estate price after adjustment}]_{it} = \\ &\alpha + \beta 1[\text{growth rate of personal savings}]_{it} + \beta 2[\text{growth rate of corporate savings}]_{it} \\ &+ \beta 3[\text{residential overflow savings}]_{it} + \beta 4[\text{entrepreneurial overflow savings}]_{it} \\ &+ \beta 5[\text{growth rate of personal income}]_{it} + \beta 6[\text{growth rate of corporate profits}]_{it} \\ &+ \beta 7[\text{growth rate of corporate losses}]_{it} + \beta 8[\text{growth rate of land prices}]_{it} + \varepsilon_{it}.\end{aligned}$$ [28]

For each variable in the model, we examine its characteristics, from which we can intuit the influence of excessive monetary liquidity on real estate bubbles (not tabulated).

Most of the monthly data in this chapter are from the China Wind Database and data about provincial savings are from *Statistics Monthly,* published by the People's Bank of China. All variables are adjusted to eliminate seasonal effects (the year-on-year growth rate) as well as inflation (adjusted by the consumer price index). The US interest rate is adjusted by the US Consumer Price Index.[29]

Results of empirical analysis

Table 17.1 shows the estimation of the empirical model of panel data discussed above. Models 1 and 2 are analysed in order to test the robustness of the general Model 3, especially for the significance of the indices for excessive monetary liquidity. In Model 1, we consider only the impact of the scale of savings on real estate prices. Model 2 further examines the spillover effect of excessive monetary liquidity.

Obviously, whether in the general model or the simplified models, the growth of local savings (monetary liquidity) also has a positive influence on the real estate price. In the sample period we selected, the monetary liquidity of local enterprises has a larger influence on the real estate price. Interestingly, after controlling the liquidity indices, although the sign of the estimated parameters of the growth rates of residential income, land prices and enterprise profits are consistent with the general economic principles, none are statistically significant. For the growth rate of losses of loss-making enterprises, the parameter is also insignificant and even the sign of the parameter is incorrect.[30] Therefore, the excessive monetary liquidity is probably the dominant factor supporting real estate bubbles. This result answers the first question raised at the beginning of the previous section.

As for the spillover effect indices, only the enterprise savings spillover variable has a significant effect on real estate prices, while the residential savings spillover variable does not contribute to the bubbles.[31] This result confirms the speculative behaviour of enterprises in the real estate market since we believe the cross-regional capital flows are, to a large extent, speculative. Thus, we have answered the second question.

The constant is significant, which shows that those important variables we put into the constant do have influence over real estate bubbles. Since we use growth rates for all the variables in the regression, the determinant coefficient (R square) is relatively low.

In order to ensure the precision of the panel data analysis method, we apply the Breusch-Pagan LM Test and the Hausman Test to the sample (see Table

Table 17.1 **Estimation of random effect[a, b]**

Dependent variable: housing price adjusted	Model 1	Model 2	Model 3
Explanatory variable (all in annual growth rate)			
Residential savings	0.487***	1.284***	1.263***
	(0.174)	(0.348)	(0.368)
Enterprise savings	1.709***	2.075***	2.179***
	(0.212)	(0.493)	(0.501)
Residential savings spillover effect		0.307	0.226
		(0.542)	(0.554)
Enterprise savings spillover effect		1.727***	1.839***
		(0.518)	(0.525)
Residential income			0.048
			(0.110)
Land price			0.023
			(0.017)
Enterprise profit			0.003
			(0.043)
Losses of loss-making enterprises			-0.015
			(0.031)
Constant	-0.137***	-0.274***	-0.285***
	(0.034)	(0.050)	(0.051)
R-squared overall	0.1588	0.1884	0.2049
Number of observables	308	308	308
Rho (fraction of variance due to u_i)	0.539	0.548	0.561

Notes: * p<0.10 ** p<0.05 *** p<0.01
[a] Stata is employed to perform the panel data analysis. The number in parentheses '()' represents the standard error of the estimation.
[b] Since in Breusch-Pagan's LM Test, Chi-sq(27) = 90.23988, P-value = 9.7e-09; heteroskedasticity in group OLS regression is phenomenal so that it is necessary to use panel data models. Furthermore, in the Hausman Test, Chi-sq(8) = 2.06, P-value = 0.9790, which means that the null hypothesis of no correlation between the fixed term and independent variables cannot be rejected. Therefore, we use random-effect models in our estimations.
Source: Authors' calculations.

17.1). From the random effect model employed, we can see that the regional characteristics of real estate price growth is not fixed, which could be a result of the overflow effect of monetary liquidity.

Conclusions

First, we argue that an externally dependent economy with structural imbalances characterised by twin surpluses can, for example, bring about excessive monetary liquidity under a rigid exchange rate system. Excessive liquidity of this kind is distinctly different from that of the standard case in which excessive liquidity is the result of a kind of loose monetary policy aimed at combating economic slowing or depression.

Second, we extend C–K's saving-investment model to uncover that excessive monetary liquidity can incur rational bubbles in real estate markets in an economy such as China's, where its financial market has not been well established. Under these circumstances, people tend to speculate in the real estate market out of the precautionary savings motivations of smoothing their income. This mechanism is not covered in the current literature about Chinese real estate bubbles (Wang 2005; Yi 2005). The existing studies of the influence of excessive monetary liquidity on real estate prices have not paid enough attention to the relevant effect of the externally dependent economic structure on real estate bubbles.

Third, we select savings and spillover variables of savings to test the mechanism of real estate bubbles introduced by basic macroeconomic principles and the OLG model. Through panel data analysis of 28 provinces, we found that the current real estate bubble in China is caused mainly by the externally dependent economic structure, which results in excessive monetary liquidity. Enterprise savings and their spillover effect play more important roles than their residential counterparts.

Based on the above results, our policy suggestion to solve the problem of excessive monetary liquidity is that, in the short term, the government should intensify fiscal and monetary restraint on speculative real estate investment (for example, to increase the capital adequacy ratio of the banks and raise taxes on real estate investments). This will modify individuals' rational expectations of the surge of real estate prices: in the long term, the government should change the current rigid exchange rate system, develop Chinese financial markets, improve the social security system and adjust the dependence of growth on expansion of net exports.[32]

Notes

1 There has been much research on the issue of real estate bubbles recently. Some excellent surveys are included in Hunter et al. (2005). Most focuses on the following aspects: the causes and measurement of real estate bubbles, their impact on the real economy and government supervision and regulation of real estate investment. Some excellent surveys are included in Hunter et al. 2005.

2 Investigations of housing reform and relative questions on the late 1990s could take Zhou 2003 and Sato 2006 as references. It is obvious that the abundance of individuals involved in real estate speculation nowadays is a consequence of government-distributed affordable housing in the early reform period.

3 Kindleberger (1987) defined asset bubbles this way: '[a] sharp rise in price of an asset or a range of assets in a continuous process, with the initial rise generating expectations of further rises and attracting new buyers—generally speculators interested in profits from trading rather than in its use or earning capacity. The rise is then followed by a reversal of expectations and a sharp decline in price, often resulting in severe financial crisis—in short, the bubble bursts.'

4 Recently, enterprise savings have been increasing gradually, because profits are declining and the renminbi is expected to appreciate.

5 Though the contribution of net exports to GDP is low, processing-trade enterprises absorb numerous low-paid workers and exports help relieve the deflationary pressure from the growth of production capacity.

6 If the price-adjusting monetary policy is effective, exchange rate adjustment can inhibit excessive monetary liquidity better than the contractive monetary policy in the current situation of the twin surpluses. Due to the fragility of the Chinese financial system, however, and the externally dependent economy, the central bank cannot actively employ price-adjusting policies (Mckinnon 2005 and Frankel 2004).

7 The inflation pressure triggered by excessive monetary liquidity could intensify polarisation between the rich and the poor.

8 The central bank also actively applied the sterilised monetary policy in the foreign exchange market from 2003 to 2005, although the intervention was weak compared with the surges of capital inflows. The government's burden will, however, become large if sterilisation is used for a long time.

9 M1 stands for cash and demand deposit, M2 includes saving deposit and M1. Figure 17.3 shows clearly the central bank's sterilised monetary intervention.

10 In circumstances of interest rate regulation, banks have no right to lower the savings interest rate. Even if banks can, most people could also put excessive liquidity into the banking system for real estate investment with safe and higher returns.

11 In this paper, assets with safe and higher returns refer to assets with rational bubbles. Currently in China, bubbles occur most easily in those assets well supported by government policies and by optimistic expectations in the market. As long as the market believes the boom is sustainable, safe and higher returns will persist. Real estate bubbles in contemporary China illustrate the mechanism.

12 From Figure 17.4, the price decline from 2005 is due to stricter regulation by the government on the entrance of foreign capital into the real estate market. Therefore, some foreign hot

money left this market, which is consistent with the phenomenon of hot money flight from China as displayed in Figure 17.2, which shows negative net short-term capital inflow. This positive correlation between monetary liquidity and real estate prices is in accordance with our theory and empirical results.

13 Blanchard and Fischer (1989) covered various theoretical mechanisms of OLG models using three chapters in Lectures on Macroeconomics. Ljungqvist and Sargent (2004) explain the application of OLG in the second edition of the famous Recursive Macroeconomics Theory. There are also some classical papers on OLG models. For instance, we can categorise OLG models according to asset attributes into the following types: the OLG model with money (Samuelson 1958); with corporate bonds (Diamond 1965); with corporate bonds and bubble assets (Tirole 1985); with equity and corporate bonds (Abel et al. 1989); with government bonds (Barro 1973); and with pension funds (Diamond and Mirrlees 1978).

14 Blanchard and Watson 1982, Weil 1987 and Ventura 2004 also value bubbles positively.

15 King and Ferguson 1993, Saint-Paul 1992 and Grossman and Yanagawa 1993, while studying economic growth, point out that bubbles can also occur in a dynamically efficient economy, which could lower the investment ratio in real capital, and technology advancement slows down accordingly. Thus, economic growth is hampered and social welfare declines.

16 Such a set up is to emphasise 'investment' instead of 'consumption'. Adding consumption behaviour into the model, such as done by Tirole (1985), will not change the result of our paper.

17 We assume that the fixed exchange rate is one for simplicity and domestic currency is convertible through the current account.

18 The fall of real estate prices in 2005 in China cannot be interpreted as a burst of bubbles; it was just a temporary effect of macro control policies (currently, $r^b < g$).

19 Although the lending rate is rigid, credit rationing is popular in China. In this sense, the latent lending rate is changing.

20 Lacking efficient credit risk management, banks in emerging markets would greatly discount collateral assets.

21 There are two extreme situations. If $r_{t+1}^C = 1$, according to Equation 12,

$$(1-\pi)\frac{g-r^*}{1+r^*}(R+1)-\pi(R+1)>0$$

The optimal investment ratio should be *=1, that is, to put their whole income in the real estate market. On the contrary, if $r_{t+1}^C = R$ and when

$$(1-\delta)(g-r^*)-\delta(1+r^*)\frac{2R}{1+R}<0$$

dumping all real estate assets would be the optimal choice—in other words, $\delta^*=0$. The credit market, however, is not clear in these two situations, so these two solutions do not hold.

22 The middle term equals

$$r_{t+1}^C = \frac{\rho R}{(1+r^*)(1-\delta)}$$

23 The following provinces and cities are included: Beijing, Tianjin, Hebei, Shanxi, Neimengu, Liaoning, Jilin, Heilongjiang, Shanghai, Jiangsu, Zhejiang, Anhui, Fujian, Jiangxi, Shandong, Henan, Hubei, Hunan, Guangdong, Guangxi, Hainan, Chongqing, Sichuan, Guizhou, Yunnan, Shanxi, Gansu and Ningxia.

24 The reform of housing markets in China started less than 10 years ago. Time-series data of real estate prices are very limited.

25 Since data about the asset allocation variable in the theoretical model are unavailable, we use the spillover variable as the proxy for the portfolio allocation to see if there is speculative behaviour.

26 Data on the renminbi counterpart of foreign reserves are not accessible as required by our theoretical model.

27 There are some other import-control variables, such as demographic structure, the population growth rate, bank mortgage rates, the stock of real estate and the portfolio allocation to securities. Monthly provincial data of these variables are not available, so we put them into the constant because we assume that these variables are relatively stable in the short term.

28 $\varepsilon_{it} = k_i + u_{it}$: i represents the cross-sectional information, t represents time, k is the fixed effect. The Hausman Test will be conducted to determine which of the two effects—fixed and random—is relevant for our panel data analysis (Hsiao 2003).

29 We abandon the data from Qinghai, Xinjiang and Xizang because of its incompleteness. For two missing observations of the land price and residential income, we use smoothing modification.

30 The reason for insignificance of residential income is that people can easily access the speculative real estate market by borrowing to cover the down payment. Similar mechanisms can explain the insignificance of enterprise profits and losses of loss-making enterprises. Even if land prices can affect real estate prices, a transaction cannot be reached without enough liquidity. Therefore, land prices are not significant after controlling monetary liquidity.

31 Such contrasts could be because individual cross-provincial investment is much more inconvenient and costly than enterprise investment, because enterprises can borrow and lend from each other freely and thus enjoy indirectly the high return of real estate investment in other areas.

32 As long as people's worries about future income persist, surplus savings will not disappear even if the renminbi appreciates and residents' disposable incomes increase.

References

Abel, A.B., Mankiw, M.G., Summers, L.H. and Zeckhauser, R.J., 1989. 'Assessing dynamic efficiency: theory and evidence', *Review of Economic Studies*, 56:1–20.

Agénor, P.R. and Montiel, P.J., 1999. *Development Macroeconomics*, Second Edition, Princeton University Press, Princeton, NJ.

Allen, F. and Gale, D., 2000. *Asset price bubbles and monetary policy*, Center for Financial Institutions Working Papers 01-26, Wharton School Center for Financial Institutions, University of Pennsylvania, Philadelphia.

Bank for International Settlements (BIS), 2004. 'What drives housing price dynamics: cross-country evidence', *BIS Quarterly Review*, March.

Barro, R.J., 1973. 'The control of politicians: an economic model', *Public Choice*, 14:19–41.

Bernanke, B., 2000. 'Japanese monetary policy: a case of self-induced paralysis?', in R. Mikitani and A. Posen (eds), *Japan's Financial Crisis and Its Parallels to US Experience*, Institute for International Economics, Washington, DC.

Bernanke, B. and Gertler, M., 2001. 'Should central banks respond to movements in asset prices?', *American Economic Review*, May:253–57.

Blanchard, O.J. and Fischer, S., 1989. *Lectures on Macroeconomics*, MIT Press, Cambridge, MA.

Blanchard, O. and Watson, M., 1982. 'Bubbles, rational expectations, and financial markets', in P. Wachtel (ed.), *Crisis in Economic and Financial Structure*, Lexington Books, Lexington, UK.

Bordo, M.D. and Jeanne, O., 2002. *Boom-busts in asset prices, economic instability and monetary policy*, CEPR Discussion Paper 3398, Centre for Economic Policy Research, London.

Brock, W.A., 1975. 'A simple perfect foresight monetary model', *Journal of Monetary Economics*, 1:133–50.

Brunnermeier, M. and Julliard, C., 2006. Money illusion and house prices, Princeton and London School of Economics (unpublished).

Caballero, R.J. and Krishnamurthy, A., 2005. *Bubbles and capital flow volatility: causes and risk management*, Working Papers, No. 11618, National Bureau of Economic Research, Cambridge, MA.

Calvo, G.A., Leiderman, L. and Reinhart, C.M., 1993. *Capital flows to Latin America: the role of external factors*, Staff Papers 40(1), International Monetary Fund, Washington, DC.

Cameron, G., Muellbauer, J. and Murphy, A., 2006. *Was there a British house price bubble? Evidence from a regional panel*, CEPR Discussion Paper, No. 5619, Centre for Economic Policy Research, London.

Case, K.E., Quigley, J.M. and Shiller, R.J., 2003. 'Home-buyers, housing and the macroeconomy', in A. Richards and T. Robinson (eds), *Asset Prices and Monetary Policy*, Reserve Bank of Australia, Canberra.

China Real Estate Chamber of Commerce, 2006. 'Macro financial risk analysis of China's real estate', *Economics of Trade and Finance*, 5.

Collyns, C. and Senhadji, A., 2002. *Lending booms, real estate bubbles and the Asian crisis*, Working Paper WP/02/20, January, International Monetary Fund, Washington, DC.

Detken, C. and Smets, F., 2004. *Asset price booms and monetary policy*, ECB Working Paper, No. 364, May, European Central Bank, Frankfurt.

Diamond, P., 1965. 'National debt in a neoclassical growth model', *American Economic Review*, 55:1,126–50.

Diamond, P. and Mirrlees, J., 1978. 'A model of social insurance with variable retirement', *Journal of Public Economics*, 10:295–326.

Duca, J.V., 2005. *Mutual funds and the evolving long-run effects of stock wealth on US consumption*, Working Papers 05-11, Federal Reserve Bank of Dallas.

Favara, G. and Song, Z., 2006. Imperfect information and housing price dynamics, University of Lausanne (unpublished).

Frankel, J., 2004. 'On the yuan: the choice between adjustment under a fixed exchange rate and adjustment under a flexible rate', Paper presented to IMF Seminar on the Foreign Exchange System, Dalian, 26–27 May.

Friedman, M. and Schwartz, A.J., 1982. *Monetary Trends in the United States and the United Kingdom*, University of Chicago Press, Chicago.

Gaber, P., 1990. 'Famous first bubbles', *Journal of Economic Perspectives*, 4(2):35–54.

Gouteron, S. and Szpiro, D., 2005. Excess monetary and asset prices (unpublished).

Grossman, G. and Yanagawa, N., 1993. 'Asset bubbles and endogenous growth', *Journal of Monetary Economics*, 31:3–19.

Gyourko, J., Mayer, C. and Sinai, T., 2006. *Superstar cities*, Working Paper, No. 12355, National Bureau of Economic Research, Cambridge, MA.

Herring, R. and Wachter, S., 2005. 'Bubbles in real estate markets', in W.B. Hunter, G.G. Kaufman and M. Pormerleano (eds), *Asset Price Bubbles: the implications for monetary, regulatory and international policies*, MIT Press, Cambridge, MA.

Hsiao, C., 2003. *Analysis of Panel Data*, Cambridge University Press, Cambridge, MA.

Hunter, W.C., Kaufman, G.G. and Pomerleano, M. (eds), 2005. *Asset Price Bubbles: the implications for monetary, regulatory and international policies*, MIT Press, Cambridge, MA.

Issing, O., 2002. 'Monetary policy in a world of uncertainty', *Economie Internationale*, Issue 4Q, Center for Economic Policy Research, London.

Kalra, S., Mihaljck, D. and Doenwald, C., 2000. *Property prices and speculative bubbles: evidence from HK SAR*, IMF Working Paper, January, International Monetary Fund, Washington, DC.

Kaufman, G.G., Hunter, W.C. and Pomerleano, M. (eds), 2003. *Asset Price Bubbles: the implications for monetary, regulatory and international policies*, MIT Press, Cambridge, MA.

Kindleberger, C., 1987. 'Bubbles', in J. Eatwell, M. Milgate and P. Newman (eds), *The New Palgrave: A Dictionary of Economics*, Stockton Press, New York:281.

King, I. and Ferguson, D., 1993. 'Dynamic inefficiency, endogenous growth and ponzi games', *Journal of Monetary Economics*, 32:79–104.

Ljungqvist, L. and Sargent, T.J., 2000. *Recursive Macroeconomic Theory*, MIT Press, Cambridge, MA.

McKinnon, R.I., 2005. *Exchange Rates under the East Asian Dollar Standard*, MIT Press, Cambridge, MA.

Meltzer, A.H., 2003. *A History of the Federal Reserve*, Vol.I, University of Chicago Press, Chicago.

Mishkin, F.S. and White, E.N., 2003. 'US stock market crashes and their aftermath: implications for monetary policy', in W.B. Hunter, G.G. Kaufman and M. Pormerleano (eds), *Asset Price Bubbles: The implications for monetary, regulatory and international policies*, MIT Press, Cambridge, MA.

Morris, S. and Shin, H.S., 2002. 'The social value of public information', *American Economic Review*, 92:1,521–34.

Muth, J.F., 1961. 'Rational expectations and the theory of price movements', *Econometrica*, 29:315–55.

Obstfeld, M. and Rogoff, K., 1996. *Foundations of International Macroeconomics*, MIT Press, Cambridge, MA.

Ogawa, E. and Sun, L., 2001. 'How were capital inflows stimulated under the dollar peg system?', in T. Ito and A.O. Kruger (eds), *Regional and Global Capital Flows: macroeconomic causes and consequences*, University of Chicago Press, Chicago.

Okina, K. and Shiratsuka, S., 2005. 'Japan's experience with asset price bubbles: is it a case for inflation targeting?', in W.C. Hunter, G.G. Kaufman and M. Pomerleano (eds), 2005. *Asset Price Bubbles: the implications for monetary, regulatory and international policies*, MIT Press, Cambridge, MA.

Organisation for Economic Co-operation and Development (OECD), 2006. *House price developments: the role of fundamentals*, Economics Department Working Papers, No. 475, Organisation for Economic Co-operation and Development, Paris.

Ortalo-Magne, F. and Rady, S., 2006. 'Housing market dynamics, on the contributions of income shocks and credit constraints', *Review of Economic Studies*, 73:459–85.

Park, Y.C. and Park, W.A., 1995. 'Capital movements, real asset speculation, and macroeconomic adjustment in Korea', in S. Edwards (ed.), *Capital Controls, Exchange Rates and Monetary Policy in the World Economy*, Cambridge University Press, Cambridge.

People's Bank of China, 2006. *China Monetary Policy Report, Quarter Four*, People's Bank of China, Beijing.

Posen, A.S., 2006. *Why central banks should not burst bubbles*, Working Paper WP06-10, Institute for International Economics, Washington, DC.

Roubini, N., 2006. 'Why central banks should burst bubbles', *International Finance*, 9(1):87–107.

Saint-Paul, G., 1992. 'Fiscal policy in an endogenous output growth model', *Quarterly Journal of Economics*, 106:1,243–59.

Samuelson, P.A., 1976. 'Economics of forestry in an evolving society', *Economic Inquiry*, 12:466–92.

Stein, J.C., 1995. 'Prices and trading volume in the housing market: a model with down payment constraints', *Quarterly Journal of Economics*, 110(2):379–405.

Sun, L., 2006. *Troubles from China's double identity as a trading power and a financially marginal country*, Symposium of the Fifth WTO and China Academic Annual Meeting, 2006:10.

Tirole, J., 1985. 'Asset bubbles and overlapping generations', *Econometrica*, 53:1,499–528.

Trichet, J.C., 2005. 'Asset price bubbles and their implications for monetary policy and financial stability', in W.B. Hunter, G.G. Kaufman and M. Pormerleano (eds), *Asset Price Bubbles: the implications for monetary, regulatory and international policies*, MIT Press, Cambridge, MA.

United Nations (UN), 2006. *Trade and Development Report 2006*, United Nations Conference on Trade and Development, New York.

Ventura, J., 2004. *Bubbles and capital flows*, Meeting Papers 102, Society for Economic Dynamics, Storrs.

Wang, L., 2005. 'Law institutions shouldn't alleviate social credit and trade response', *Chinese Real Estate Finance*, No.5.

Weil, P., 1987. 'Confidence and the real value of money in an over-lapping generations economy', *Quarterly Journal of Economics*, 102:1–22.

White, E.N., 1990. 'When the ticker ran late: the stock market boom and crash of 1929', in E. White (ed.), *Crashes and Panics: the lessons from history*, Dow-Jones Irwin, Homewood.

Yi, X., 2005. 'Dependence and influence of real estate on domestic financial sector', *Modern Commercial Banks*, No.4.

Yuan, Z. and Fan, X., 2003. 'Analysis of rational bubbles in real estate markets', *Economics Studies*, No. 3.

Acknowledgments

We are grateful to R. Caballero and A. Krishnamurthy, from whose papers we got many useful hints for our theoretical analysis. We are grateful to Yu Yongding, Gao Haihong, Huang Haizhou, Xu Mingqi, Hua Ming and other participants in the ninth conference of the China Society of World Economics for their excellent comments on our empirical analysis. We also would like to thank Eiji Ogawa and other participants in the seminar in Hitotsubashi University (Japan) for their useful advice on this paper.

18

Economic opening and domestic market integration

Min Chen, Qihan Gui, Ming Lu and Zhao Chen

Does economic opening lead to international as well as domestic market integration? The objective of this chapter is to examine whether China's policy of opening promotes domestic economic integration. Do the growing external links work against the local protectionism and market segmentation? Particularly since the beginning of the Chinese economic reformation, regional protectionism and segmentation have blocked a unified national market, brought about inefficiency in inter-regional resource allocation, distorted the market mechanism and disturbed the price signal. Ultimately, they weaken macroeconomic policies. Therefore, it is necessary to understand the causes of domestic market segmentation and to find the ways of dealing with them.

This chapter examines the determinants of segmentation of the Chinese inter-regional goods market on the basis of provincial panel data, focusing on the impact of economic opening—a fundamental component of Chinese economic reform, driving privatisation and deregulation. The correlation between international and domestic integration is explored, and the analysis predicts a continuing trend of domestic market integration in China.

There has been academic contention over whether there has been a tendency towards inter-provincial integration or segmentation in post-reform China. The process through which it happens still requires theoretical and empirical analysis. Empirical research in this field is recent (Poncet 2005; Bai et al. 2004). There can be further development in measuring market segmentation, the selection and definition of independent variables, and increased sophistication in regression analysis. This chapter makes three contributions. First, in order to measure China's inter-provincial segmentation, we use Chinese provincial retail price index (RPI) data instead of industrial concentration or trade flow data. Second, we focus on the effect of economic opening on market segmentation. In addition, our approach captures the effects of employment pressure, government consumption, inter-regional technology differentials and geography. Third, the methodology improves on previous papers by attempting to eliminate endogenous bias, including simultaneity bias and omitted-variables bias.

Literature review

What has influenced Chinese domestic market integration? Bai et al. (2004) and Poncet (2005) reached some pertinent conclusions in their empirical research.

Bai et al. (2004) estimated the overall level of geographic concentration of China's industries and factors influencing changes. He used the Hoover coefficient as the dependent variable, and examined the impacts of local protectionism, scale of economy and externalities on industrial concentration. The data supported the hypothesis that industries with a higher tax-plus-profit ratio in the past and those with a higher share of state-owned enterprises tended to have a higher degree of local protectionism, and therefore a lower level of industrial concentration. There is significant negative correlation between the output share of state-owned enterprises and local industrial concentration (Hoover coefficient), so he concluded that local protectionism could lead to market segmentation.

Poncet (2004) applied a gravity model (Head and Mayer 2000) for estimation of the domestic border effect in inter-provincial and intra-provincial trade flows for 1992 and 1997. She used an index representing the degree of domestic market segmentation. She then examined the relationship between endogenous protection and the border effect on trade. She also argued that local protectionist policy was an outcome of demand (by private agents and interest groups) and supply (politicians and government), which eventually caused increased domestic segmentation. Hence, her independent variables include fiscal expenditure, public consumption (the supply factors) and the unemployment rate (the demand factor). The regression results showed that an increase in the unemployment rate and government intervention enhanced market segmentation.

This literature is pioneering in this area, but needs further development.

First, the effect of economic opening has not been given adequate emphasis.[1] The fact is, in China, economic reform virtually coincided with the new openness to international trade. The open economy could change the integration of the domestic market profoundly, by affecting inter-regional trade flows, the behaviour of local governments, the strategies of enterprises and people's thoughts. For example, some variables in Bai et al. (2004) and Poncet (2005), such as the share of state-owned enterprises and public consumption, are influenced by economic opening.[2] Furthermore, opening led to a decreasing government role in the economy. Therefore, simply putting economic opening into unobserved residuals could generate an omitted-variables bias in estimates.[3]

Second, the measurements used represented poorly the magnitude of domestic market integration. Bai et al. (2004) investigated the coefficient of industrial concentration as a substitute for integration. However, there is no necessarily positive correlation between industrial concentration and market integration. This needs to be analysed more closely.

Similarly, the 'border effect' derived from trade flows (Poncet 2005) needs more analysis. It is hard to distinguish other economic effects, such as resource endowment or scale economics from those of integration on trade flows. For example, little difference between resource endowments or scale of economy makes the border effect noisy. Additionally, if the products of two areas are highly substitutable, a small rise in trade costs could lead to a large reduction in inter-regional trade volume (Parsley and Wei 2001a). Therefore, these two measurements have their limitations.

Third, the two studies emphasised local protectionism, but this is extremely difficult to evaluate. Bai et al. (2004) argued that local governments benefitted from inter-regional trade barriers, so they tended to protect industries with higher past tax-plus-profit ratios and with a higher share of state-owned enterprises. Therefore, the two ratios represented the degree of local protectionism. This is doubtful, however, because local governments have incentives to protect some lower tax-plus-profit enterprises (Lin and Liu 2004).[4] Poncet (2004) claimed that local protectionism pursued a dual objective: fiscal revenue maximisation, and social stability and economic equity. She looked at the demand and supply of local protectionism, which comes from employment (unemployment rate), fiscal autonomy (fiscal expenditure) and intervention power (public consumption). Yet none of these variables equates directly to local protectionism. The unemployment rate is particularly controversial. On one hand, much of the literature debates whether China's unemployment statistics badly underestimated the real situation (Lu 2002; Wang et al. 2004; Cai et al. 2004; Xue and Wei 2004). On the other hand, provincial governments engaged in maintaining existing employment in state-owned industries, which is a latent unemployed group, rather than helping the unemployed to find new jobs.

By comparison, this chapter has three innovations. First, we use the Chinese provincial RPI to abstract the measure of China's provincial market segmentation. Second, we investigate the effects of economic opening, employment pressure, government consumption, inter-regional technology differentials and geographic distance on market segmentation. Existing studies have provided several explanations of how economic opening impacts on domestic integration. Poncet (2002, 2003b) pointed out that international trade substituted for national trade, thus economic opening fragmented the domestic market. Li et al. (2003) set up a model demonstrating that when tariffs were sufficiently low, opening made the domestic market more competitive and improved market integration. We provide new evidence on the relationship between them. Third, we eliminate simultaneity bias by putting in lagged policy variables. As for economic opening, we also use instrument variables to reduce simultaneity bias and omitted-variable bias.

In addition, our segmentation index is developed from a convincing theoretical foundation (Parsley and Wei 1996, 2000a, 2001b). It presents new evidence of an integrated Chinese domestic goods market, consistent with the findings of Naughton (1999), Xu (2002) and Bai et al. (2004), but differs from those of Young (2000) and Poncet (2002, 2003b).

The heated debate about market segmentation in China began with Young (2000), who found that provincial economic structures were increasingly similar after examining the structure of gross domestic product (GDP) and manufacturing output, per capita output of main products and some price data. The explanation was that inter-regional competition and local protection led to fragmentation of the domestic market and distortion of regional production away from local comparative advantage. Relying on the evidence that Chinese provinces were more involved in international trade with a decrease in domestic trade flow, Poncet (2002, 2003b) concluded that China's provincial borders increasingly segmented the whole country. Numerous analyses, however, took a sceptical view of such claims. The prevalent criticism was that Young's (2000) indices were too simple to capture the tendency of domestic segmentation. As we have already discussed, the measure derived from trade flow (Poncet 2002, 2003b) was noisy because many factors, such as resource endowment and scale of economy, could change the trade flow. Still a small cost of trade could lead to a large reduction in trade volume if the substitution effect was strong (Parsley and Wei 2001a).

Naughton (1999) compared the commodity composition of inter-provincial trade between 1987 and 1992. He revealed that the increase of trade volume was caused mainly by the rise in intra-industry trade within manufacturing (final goods), rather than the trade of intermediate inputs. This coincides with the observed competition among producers in different regions. Xu (2002) decomposed provincial sectoral real value-added growth into common national effects, industry-specific effects and province-specific effects by an error-components model. The empirical analysis for the period from 1991 to 1998 showed that with significant co-movements in the long term, even province-specific factors still accounted for 35 per cent of the variance of short-term real output growth. His results suggested that the provincial economy was integrated incompletely under the reforms. Finally, the findings of Bai et al. (2004) also supported an increase in Chinese market integration: in the period from 1985 to 1997, the concentration of Chinese industries fell initially, and then increased significantly. As we pointed out, however, industrial concentration is not equivalent to market integration.

These debates have relied on indirect measures from production structure, trade flow, prices and industry concentration. In fact, the previous literature has used 'relative prices' to abstract direct indices of integration in two ways. Fan and Wei (2006) first applied the Augmented Dickey-Fuller (ADF) test to time series of each category of Chinese goods, then used the MW Test (Maddala and Wu 1999) on unbalanced panel data as a whole. According to the parameters of the model, they estimated the half-life for price convergence, which offered strong evidence of price convergence and market integration in China. Such a finding sits well with the view that China's transition to a market economy has been quite successful during the past two decades. Nevertheless, their analysis illuminated only the status of competition in the domestic market and not the course of convergence, so it cannot be extended to further research on causes of integration.

Here, we follow Parsley and Wei's model (1996, 2001a, 2001b) to observe the variance of relative price, $Var(P_i/P_j)$. Small $Var(P_i/P_j)$ implies that the relative price is falling. We can take the relative price as a dynamic index of market integration. The details will be demonstrated in a later section.

The determinants of China's domestic integration

Numerous publications have argued that Chinese market integration is affected by the behaviour of local governments. After decentralisation and taxation system reform, local governments had the chance to obtain rents from local firms' profits, so they had an incentive to reinforce regional segmentation. Hence, we group the potential determinants into three categories. The first is economic opening, the key of this chapter. The second includes factors related to government behaviour. The last covers other factors that need to be controlled.

To the best of our knowledge, economic opening has multiple impacts on market integration, some of which are positive, and others negative. First of all, in a relatively closed economy marked by low-level opening and a high tariff rate, local governments can implement segmentation policies to protect their industries. In this sense, a decrease in inter-provincial trade intensity is accompanied by rapid international trade opening (Poncet 2002, 2003b, 2005). As the economy opens further and tariff rates fall, however, the cost of local protection and segmentation augments this because of competition, and eventually international trade liberalisation restrains local protectionism (Li et al. 2003). Second, by influencing the external situation that local governments face, economic opening accelerates integration indirectly. For example, when the economy opens further, more foreign investments enter and the behaviour of individuals is transformed in diversified enterprises. As a result, the power of non-state enterprises increases and the economic intervention of the government fades.

Meanwhile, much foreign capital is invested in joint ventures. Jointly operated industrial groups need to cooperate with local governments. Furthermore, opening has an irreversible effect on people's thinking, such as their understanding of government: the public pushes local governments to remedy their welfare functions and to facilitate domestic integration. Therefore, there might be a non-linear correlation between economic opening and domestic integration. In this story, when opening is in its initial stages, it could strengthen market segmentation, but further opening could enhance domestic market integration. Finally, opening promotes domestic integration. The evidence for this will be shown in the next sections.

There are also some issues concerning local governments. Briefly, Chinese local governments have dual objectives: to optimise their benefits and to maximise the utilities of residents. For the first goal, they tend to implement segmentation policies for increased fiscal revenue. For the second one, they engage in maintaining employment and developing strategic industries. Therefore, we pay attention to the following determinants in our empirical model.

- Economic intervention of local government. In a planned economy, the fiscal system is highly centralised. Since 1978, fiscal decentralisation of revenue, taxation, control of enterprises, investment and financing has strengthened the capability of official intervention. Under this system, policymakers gain benefits from the local economy, so they have an incentive to participate in economic activities directly. Our hypothesis is that provinces with a larger share of fiscal revenue relative to the size of the economy are more willing than others to segment inter-regional markets to protect their industries.

- Economic nationalisation. In a transitional economy such as China's, maintaining employment is always a primary government objective. China's employment pressure comes directly from local state-owned industries. Historically, the pre-reform employment system disguised large urban unemployment in the state-owned sector. In the 1990s, a shortage of capital brought about increasing deficiency of non-labour investment. There were more and more redundant workers in state-owned enterprise as a result of intense goods market competition, shrinking demand, wage rises in non-state-owned counterparts and the constraint of reducing the number of employees (Dong and Putterman 2002). So, we take the state-owned employment share as the weight of the nationalised economy, which shows the employment pressure and therefore the pressure of domestic segmentation. The noteworthy point is that there are some alternative explanations for the correlation between economic nationalisation and domestic segmentation, such as state-owned capital being commanded by local governments (Ping 2004), or local governments benefitting from state-owned enterprises (Bai et al. 2004).
- The inter-regional technology differential. Lu et al. (2004) argued that the fiscal target and employment goal was not the only explanation for duplicative industries and inter-regional economic segmentation. If high-tech industries have increasing returns, less-developed regions will not specialise according to static comparative advantage but will raise their bargaining position by inter-regional segmentation and by developing 'strategic' industries. Thus, they could gain a higher bargaining position in the future and even catch up with the rich regions. Therefore, we expect that the less-developed regions prefer a segmented economy and protect local strategic industries.

Last but not least, two factors must be controlled for in the empirical models.

- Geographic distance. In general, long distances mean high transportation costs, then more transaction costs. Even if governments are neutral, the commodity flow is still restricted by geographic space. We think distance might 'create' market segmentation.
- The stage of marketisation reform. China's marketisation could be divided into two stages. Before 1994, the process was relatively sluggish. In 1993, the third session of the fourteenth Congress of the Communist Party

of China enacted a decision to establish a socialist market economy. Taxation system reform, unification of exchange rates, financial system reform, state-owned enterprise reform and some other reforms began the next year. Therefore, 1994 was the starting point of the new phase of China's marketisation reform. From then on, the evolution of domestic goods market integration might be different from the pattern demonstrated in the period before 1994.[5] We hypothesise that the post 1994 reforms saw an increased level of market integration.

The measure of market segmentation for Chinese domestic goods

How to find a credible measure of integration or segmentation is the most difficult part of empirical studies. Given the drawbacks of the existing approaches—production, trade flow and the specialisation index—we construct the panel data of the inter-regional segmentation index using regional RPI of consumer goods by the method of Parsley and Wei (2001a, 2001b).

Datum and index computing

The logic of measuring market segmentation by relative prices is based on the iceberg model (Samuelson 1954), which amends the original Law of One Price (LOP) theory. Generally, there are certain kinds of transportation costs, such as freight costs, that are consumed during transactions like an iceberg melting. Only a fraction of the goods' value survives. This implies that perfect arbitrage requires only the relative price fluctuating within a range but not being constant. Suppose Pi is the price of a product in location 'i', and Pj is its price in location 'j'. The proportional transaction cost (wastage occurring as commodities are traded between two regions) is 'c' (0<c<1). The necessary condition for the existence of arbitrage is Pi(1-c)>Pj or Pj(1-c)>Pi, in which trade occurs. Otherwise, the relative price of product Pi/Pj falls into a non-arbitrage range [1-c, 1/(1-c)]. Here, the transaction cost in a broad sense includes all sorts of factors that wear down the value of goods in the process of trade, such as physical geography or institutional arrangements. Under this principal, a reduction of freight costs or a decrease in institutional trade barriers reduce transaction costs and improve market integration; correspondingly, the range of fluctuation of the relative price shrinks.

Our primary data are retail price indices of commodities by region obtained from the *China Statistical Yearbook* for various years. We calculated 17 years (1985 – 2001) with 61 pairs of conjoint provinces' relative price variances, $\mathrm{Var}(P_i^t/P_j^t)$. The total number of observations is 1,037 (17×61). Because $\mathrm{Var}(P_i^t/P_j^t)$ data are time series for every conjoint province pair, we can observe their movements by region. The evolution of time series reflects the tendency of goods market integration. Additionally, Parsley and Wei's (2001b) approach has another virtue. By synthesising the price information of various goods, we get the estimate of goods market segmentation.

Our study starts with relative price variances of conjoint province pairs, because these kinds of data can be synthesised to provincial segmentation indices (see the next section). In the real story of national trade, the provincial trade policy is generally consistent between neighbouring and other provinces, so when domestic integration increases, the trend might be shown first in conjoint province pairs. Such common sense is, however, difficult to prove.

We focus on the absolute value of the relative price $|\Delta Q^k_{ijt}|$, where $\Delta Q^k_{ijt} = \mathrm{Ln}(P^k_{it}/P^k_{jt}) - \mathrm{Ln}(P^k_{it-1}/P^k_{jt-1})$ [6] is the first-order difference of percentage price difference of identical product 'k' in two conjoint provinces, 'i' and 'j', at time 't'. We construct this form of relative price index from the retail price indices of commodities by region according to Equation 1; it demonstrates how indices P^k_{it}/P^k_{it-1} and P^k_{jt}/P^k_{jt-1} transform to ΔQ^k_{ijt},

$$\Delta Q^k_{ijt} = \ln(P^k_{it}/P^k_{jt}) - \ln(P^k_{it-1}/P^k_{jt-1}) = \ln(P^k_{it}/P^k_{it-1}) - \ln(P^k_{jt}/P^k_{jt-1}) \qquad (1)$$

Further, when a market is segmented, it is the extreme case that the iceberg cost, 'c', reaches a maximum; eventually Q^k_{ijt} will converge along with ΔQ^k_{ijt}. In this respect, Q^k_{ijt} is equivalent to ΔQ^k_{ijt} in describing the process of segmentation. The problem is, for any province pair or time period, ΔQ^k_{ijt} could be positive or negative. In fact, in the same year and with the same province pair, taking the price of 'i' or 'j' province as numerator, our results are opposites: that is, $\Delta Q^k_{ijt} = -\Delta Q^k_{jit}$. That is to say, the order of provinces affects the value of $\mathrm{Var}(\Delta Q_{ijt})$. The absolute value avoids this kind of inconsistency. Looking back at the iceberg model, the logarithm of the non-arbitrage interval, [1-c,1/(1-c)], is symmetrical, $[\mathrm{Ln}(1\text{-c}), -\mathrm{Ln}(1\text{-c})]$. It implies that the opposite number of ΔQ^k reveals the same extent of relative price fluctuation, but arbitrage happens in the reverse direction with different signs of ΔQ^k.

The method of relative price analysis requires a three-dimensional database (t×m×k), where the indices 't', 'm' and 'k' represent time, province and goods respectively. Our primary data are the retail price indices of commodities by region, three-dimensional panel data (17×28×9) covering 17 years from 1985 to 2001, 28 provinces, municipalities or autonomous regions and nine commodities. Our filtration rules of goods are as follows.

- 1985 is the starting year, because there were no RPI statistics by region before 1985, and 1985 was the first year of the price reform after the third session of the twelfth Congress of the Communist Party of China. From then on, prices were decided mainly by the market.

- Three provinces—Hainan, Chongqing and Tibet—are excluded due to incomplete data.[7]
- The old commodity categories listed only before 1985 are excluded.

Therefore, the data in this chapter include nine types of goods with continuous records: grain; fresh vegetables; beverages, tobacco and liquor; garments, shoes and hats; traditional Chinese and Western medicines; newspapers and magazines; stationery and sports goods; daily use articles; and fuel. 4) There was a commodity reclassification after 1987 with minor adjustments, so in order to get as much data as possible, we fill in the data for beverages, tobacco and liquor; garments, shoes and hats; traditional Chinese and Western medicines; newspapers and magazines; stationery and sports goods in 1985 and 1986 with data for tea, tobacco and liquor; clothes; medicines and medical equipment; newspapers and magazines; stationery and entertainment goods, respectively.

According to the computation above, we get the vectors of the differential in the relative price index, $\left|\Delta Q_{ijt}^{k}\right|$, containing 9,333 (9×61×17) observations without missing data. It is still a little far from the segmentation index. We need to calculate the cross-sectional variance with respect to goods. Under our assumption, a higher variance means a wider arbitrage interval and implies more serious segmentation.[8] With the purpose of abstracting regional effects, we must remove the goods-specific effects first. For instance, in a certain period, the grain market experiences significant price fluctuation within two locations, 'i' and 'j'. The cause could be divided into two parts: one is related to the nature of the grain market (for example, the price of grain changes markedly, since grain yields are easily influenced by natural conditions); the second is independent of the characteristics of goods, but determined by market conditions between locations 'i' and 'j', or some random factors. For instance, location 'i' is hit by a natural calamity, so the grain price jumps, or the local government of 'i' strengthens trade barriers. If we calculate the variance without filtering the goods-specific effects from $\left|\Delta Q_{ijt}^{k}\right|$, the result could overrate the real value caused by inter-regional trade barriers. We use de-mean to remove the goods-specific effect: let $\left|\Delta Q_{ijt}^{k}\right| = a^k + \varepsilon_{ijt}^{k}$ (Parsley and Wei 2001a, 2001b), where a^k is a kind of fixed effect of goods, 'k', and ε_{ijt}^{k} represents the regional specific effects between locations 'i' and 'j'. In fact, $a^k = \overline{\left|\Delta Q_t^k\right|}$, the mean of $\overline{\left|\Delta Q_t^k\right|}$, for 61 province pairs at time 't' and for goods 'k'. Then de-mean yields $\left|\Delta Q_{ijt}^{k}\right| - \overline{\left|\Delta Q_t^k\right|} = (a^k - \overline{a^k}) + (\varepsilon_{ijt}^{k} - \overline{\varepsilon_{ijt}^{k}})$. Let $q_{ijt}^{k} = \varepsilon_{ijt}^{k} - \overline{\varepsilon_{ijt}^{k}} = \left|\Delta Q_{ijt}^{k}\right| - \overline{\left|\Delta Q_t^k\right|}$.[9] Finally, our segmentation index is the variance of q_{ijt}^{k}, defined as Var(q_{ijt}^{k}). As the preceding shows, q_{ijt}^{k} is related only to regionally specific effects and other random effects and we have a total of 1,037 (61×17) observations.

The integration of the Chinese domestic goods market

Based on our segmentation index, we can summarise the integration evolution process of each region and the whole country. In the first place, we compute the average segmentation level for regions by year. The result is a time series containing 17 years' data. We can detect an oscillatory path in the period 1985–2001 in Figure 18.1. The aggregate segmentation index first rises and eventually falls, which demonstrates that China's goods market is integrating gradually. This is the opposite finding to Young (2000) and Poncet (2002).

The purpose of this chapter is to verify that economic opening and other variables will affect domestic market integration via the behaviour of local governments. Thus we need to transform the data by 61 province pairs to data by province. For example, the segmentation index of Shanghai is the mean of the inter-regional index of Shanghai–Jiangsu and Shanghai–Zhejiang. Other regional segmentation indices are created following the same logic, so we get 476 (28×17) observations. They present the movement of goods market segmentation of 28 regions in 17 years. Authentically, the provincial

Figure 18.1 **Domestic goods market segmentation, 1985–2001**

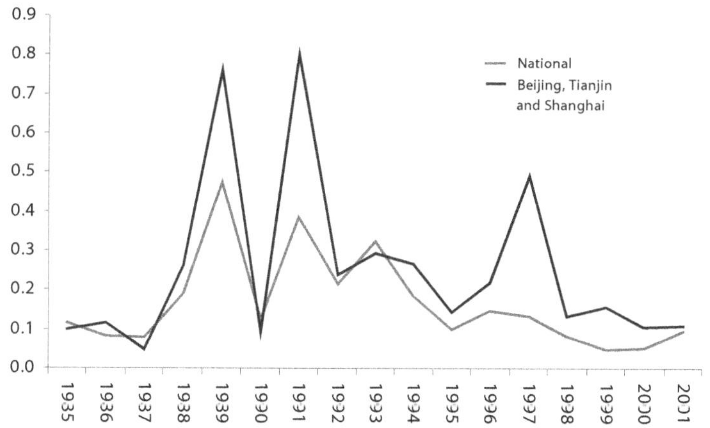

Source: Authors' calculations.

segmentation index captures the magnitude of integration between this province and all its neighbours. Figure 18.2 depicts the individual region's segmentation indices. There is a great diversity of movements, some of which are insignificant in certain regions such as Sichuan (23) and Guizhou (24), but as a whole, the trends coincide with that of the whole country: most regions' goods markets are converging to a certain level of integration.

Finally, we calculate the average index for years by region. There is great diversity across different areas (Table 18.1). A noticeable point is the three municipalities of Beijing, Tianjin and Shanghai—rank first, second and fourth respectively. Some municipalities enjoy special policies, have a better economy and a smaller area, so local government interventions work better. Hence, their market integration is relatively slower than others. Focusing on the rankings between 1985 and 2001, another point of view is that the ranks of most regions change dramatically.

Data and estimation

Now we turn to the theoretical frame and determinants discussed in section three. We begin our formal investigation with the basic model

$$\text{Segm}_{it} = c + \Sigma\beta_k X_{kit\text{-}1} + \gamma_1 \text{Area} + \gamma_2 \text{Dummy94} + \alpha_i + \varepsilon_{it} \qquad (2)$$

Let Segm_{it} be the segmentation index of region 'i' at time 't'. As we mentioned, it is a dimensionless variable, so our final dependent variables are 100 times the original ones; this treatment helps us get larger estimated parameters. The improvement of integration occurs with the smaller Segm value. So, variables with negative parameters promote integration; those with positive parameters impede integration.

The right hand side of Equation 2 lists our independent variables. The primary data in period 1985–98 were obtained from *Comprehensive Statistical Data and Materials in 50 Years of New China* (National Bureau of Statistics 1999); the remaining data for 1999–2001 were obtained from *China Statistical Yearbooks*. Our sample covers 28 regions. The data for Sichuan Province do not include Chongqing.[10] The statistics for Hainan, Tibet and Chongqing were incomplete for 1985–2001, so were not included in our sample.

'X' is the vector of policy variables influencing local government decisions. These variables are endogenous due to simultaneity bias, for which we use the one-year lag of Xs to treat. The entries of X include

- *Trade*—the share of total international trade in GDP—or the dependency ratio of international trade[11]—denotes the degree of economic opening.

Figure 18.2 **Market segmentation index by region, 1985–2001**

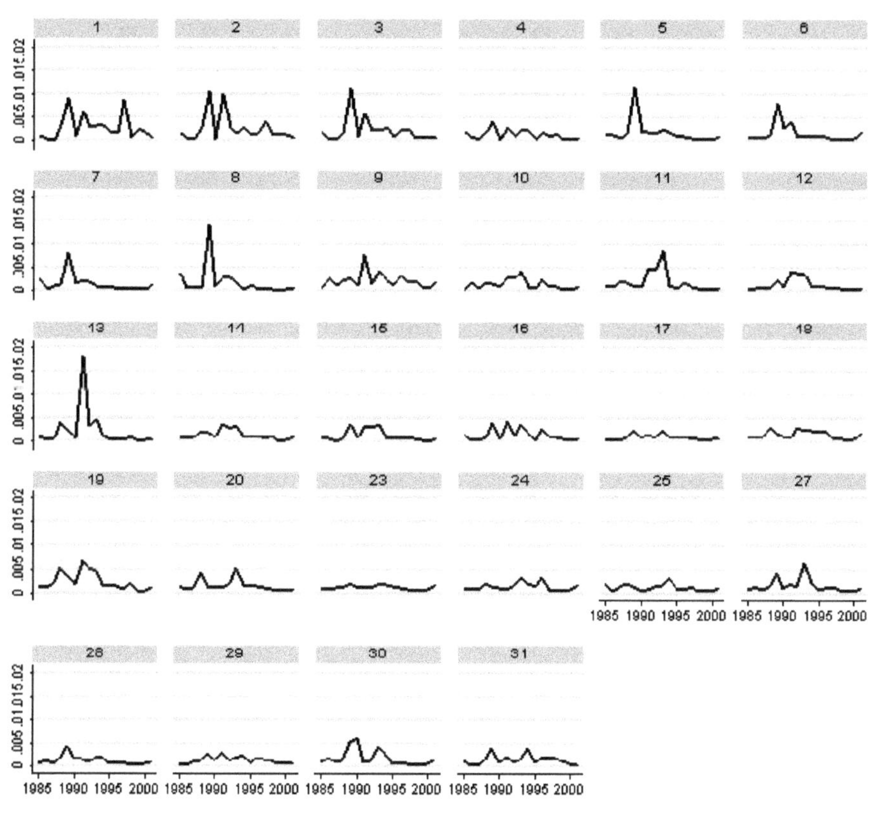

1 Beijing
2 Tianjin
3 Hebei
4 Shanxi
5 Inner Mongolia
6 Liaoning
7 Jilin
8 Heilongjiang
9 Shanghai
10 Jiangsu
11 Zhejiang
12 Anhui
13 Fujian
14 Jiangxi
15 Shandong
16 Henan
17 Hubei
18 Hunan
19 Guangdong
20 Guangxi
21 Hainan
23 Sichuan
24 Guizhou
25 Yunnan
27 Shaanxi
28 Gansu
29 Qinhai
30 Ningxia
31 Xinjiang

Note: The trade/GDP ratio with one year lag is used as an explanatory variable in the regression. To make the figure readable, the original data multiplied by 100 are reported.
Source: Authors' calculations.

Table 18.1 **Ranking of segmentation index by region**

Province	Means over 17 years	Rank	1985	Rank	2001	Rank
Beijing	0.273	1	0.099	14	0.057	22
Tianjin	0.260	2	0.152	7	0.078	14
Fujian	0.240	3	0.102	13	0.051	25
Shanghai	0.233	4	0.05	26	0.195	1
Guangdong	0.233	5	0.135	9	0.091	11
Hebei	0.217	6	0.164	6	0.046	27
Zhejiang	0.197	7	0.092	16	0.074	17
Heilongjiang	0.194	8	0.393	1	0.068	20
Inner Mongolia	0.175	9	0.117	10	0.108	8
Ningxia	0.166	10	0.074	21	0.141	6
Hunan	0.166	11	0.087	17	0.191	2
Shaanxi	0.164	12	0.076	19	0.104	10
Henan	0.157	13	0.182	4	0.072	19
Liaoning	0.153	14	0.081	18	0.169	4
Guangxi	0.152	15	0.142	8	0.074	16
Jiangxi	0.148	16	0.113	11	0.089	12
Jiangsu	0.147	17	0.038	27	0.087	13
Xinjiang	0.143	18	0.092	15	0.033	28
Jilin	0.142	19	0.244	2	0.124	7
Anhui	0.141	20	0.035	28	0.055	23
Guizhou	0.137	21	0.108	12	0.185	3
Shanxi	0.134	22	0.174	5	0.049	26
Shandong	0.131	23	0.075	20	0.052	24
Qinhai	0.124	24	0.063	23	0.064	21
Yunnan	0.115	25	0.206	3	0.105	9
Gansu	0.113	26	0.056	25	0.074	18
Sichuan	0.109	27	0.067	22	0.169	5
Hubei	0.106	28	0.059	24	0.076	15

Source: Authors' ranking.

Considering that the effect is in non-linear form, we construct the quadratic term of opening (*Tradesq*) in our model. Figure 18.3 presents the upward trend of the dependency ratio on international trade from 1985 to 2001. It is consistent with increasing economic opening. The prominent case is Guangzhou Province: in terms of the level and the rate of change, this province exceeds that of other regions. As we deduced in section three, there could be a non-linear effect of economic opening, so that the coefficient of the linear term could be positive, and that of the quadratic term could be negative.

- *Govcons*—the ratio of government consumption to GDP is the proxy of the fiscal objectives of local governments—an important motive for local protection—so we expect to detect a positive correlation between this variable and the segmentation. In empirical studies, an alternative of government interference is the ratio of provincial government expenditure to GDP.[12] We tried it in our regression and the result was consistent but less significant, so we report only the estimates with *Govcons*.
- *SOE*—the share of state-owned employees in total employees. As we mentioned in section three, this is an indicator for employment pressure and public authority in the local economy. The coefficient could be positive.
- *Techdiff*—the ratio of GDP per worker per region with that of its neighbours, which is a proxy of technology difference. The GDP per worker of neighbouring regions is the simple arithmetic mean of that of all conjoint regions, which assigns each neighbour the same weighting coefficients. Lu et al. (2004) presented a theoretical framework to prove that the less-developed regions had a motive to set segmentation, but better-developed regions pursued market integration. In this logic, the coefficient of *Techdiff* could be negative.

We also included two important control variables in our regression model

- *Area*—the average size of a region and its neighbours. We use this variable to indicate roughly the average physical size of local and conjoint provinces. *Area* = local size + (total area of neighbours ÷ the number of neighbours). Because most provinces have several neighbours, a simple straight-line distance cannot capture the nature of geographic distance. The anticipated sign of this variable is positive.[13]
- *Dummy94*—the dummy variable of time—let them be one after 1994, otherwise they equal zero. After the implementation of a series of reforms in 1994, integration could be strengthened significantly. Therefore, this variable could be negatively related with the segmentation index.

Figure 18.3 **The ratio of dependence on international trade by region, 1985–2001**

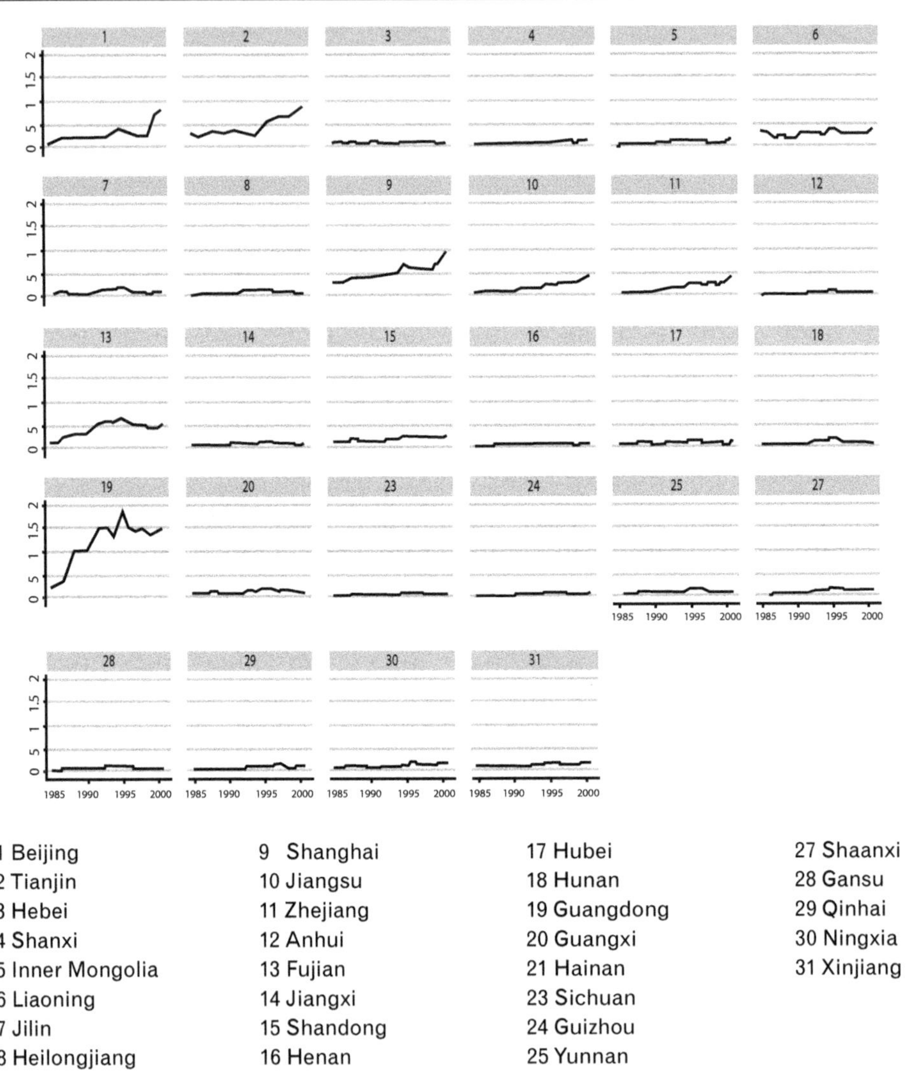

Note: The trade/GDP ratio with one year lag is used as an explanatory variable in the regression.
Source: Authors' calculations.

In our model, α_i is the unobservable provincial fixed effect, which is constant over time and specific to the province, 'i', and ε_{it} is the disturbance. Since the unobservable term α_i could be correlated with some independent variables, the OLS estimates are biased. One of the general ways to reduce the bias caused by omitted variables represented by the constant α_i is the method of de-mean imposed on all variables before regressions, which is the fixed effects (FE) approach. If α_i is uncorrelated with the other regressors, the random effects (RE) model is more efficient and we can test the fixed and random effects regressions by the Hausman Test to decide which of the two alternatives is better. If two coefficient estimators differ systematically, α_i is correlated with one of the explanatory variables and only the FE treatment is consistent. Otherwise, the fact that the individual effect α_i is uncorrelated with the other regressors cannot be rejected, and the efficient estimators of the RE model are better.

That α_i is constant over time is, however, a very strong assumption. Unobserved time-varying factors can cause estimators to be inconsistent, so instrument variable estimation is helpful. The results could also be tested with the Hausman Test. If the estimate of the instrument variable model is significantly different from that of the OLS estimation, the hypothesis that some of the regressors are endogenous cannot be rejected, the instrument variable estimation is consistent and the original OLS estimation is more efficient.

Results are reported in Table 18.2. The regression (1) begins with explanatory variables *Trade*, *Govcons*, *SOE*, *Area* and *Dummy94*. The Hausman Test rejects the RE estimation, so we cannot estimate the effect of physical distance (*Area*). In this model, *Govcons* and *SOE* strengthen segmentation, and the estimate of *Dummy94* shows that, after 1994, the accelerated marketisation reform caused segmentation to abate. Our results show, the coefficient of economic opening is positive, suggesting trade opening raises segmentation. For the sake of examining the effect of economic opening more precisely, we add *Tradesq* in regression (2) to capture a potential non-linear effect. The Hausman Test rejects the RE approach. Compared with (1), coefficient estimates of *Govcons* and *SOE* change slightly with this specification, but with the significant positive estimate of *Trade* and negative estimate of the quadratic term, *Tradesq*, model (2) is more compatible with our theoretical framework. The effect of opening is non-linear. At its initial stage, opening strengthens market segmentation, but further opening enhances domestic market integration. Numerically, the critical point is Trade = 1.272. Before this point, economic opening increases segmentation; after this, it increases integration. The value 1.272 falls into the observable interval; the data for Guangdong Province exceeded this level after 1991.

In the next step, *Techdiff* is added in model (3). The estimate of *Techdiff* is insignificant, but the sign is negative as the theory predicts. The negative coefficient means that lagged regions have a smaller index of *Techdiff*, and more serious market segmentation, while the better-developed regions with higher *Techdiff* have smaller segmentation magnitude. The insignificant estimate is reasonable here. Firstly, the technology difference theory works better in high-tech industries with increasing turns (Lu et al. 2004), but our explanatory variables are set up from price indices of ordinary consumer goods. Secondly, the technological difference has a long-term effect, so our one-year lagged model cannot capture this characteristic. Thirdly, like the effect of opening, the technological difference could influence segmentation in a non-linear form, but our model has only a linear term of technology.

Looking back at the results so far, we extend the study on the critical value of the inversed-U shape of the effects of economic opening. In regression (2), the point is *Trade* = 1.272, but in regression (3), the point is *Trade* = 1.043. Although these two values are within our sample, only Guangdong has exceeded that level of economic opening. We worry that the non-linear effects of opening are due only to the outliers in our sample. So the next step is to drop all observations in Guangdong from our sample, and repeat the regression (3); we get the result in column (4). The basic finding is similar, but the critical value drops to *Trade* = 0.7273, a value within our new sample. Now, we can draw the convincing conclusion that a non-linear relationship exists between economic opening and market segmentation.

Finally, considering the extraordinarily high values of the segmentation indices in the three municipalities, we drop them, and repeat the estimation. Table 18.2, column (5) reports the random effect estimates, the coefficients of regressors meet our expectation and most of them are statistically significant, except *Techdiff*.

The estimates in Table 18.2 might be biased if omitted variables contain time-varying ones. In that case, the FE and the RE are inconsistent. Table 18.3 presents the test results of instrument variable estimations. Our goal is to find the unbiased estimator of economic opening, so we implement three instrument variables.

- The pre-reform opening index in 1978, denoted as *trade78*. It is the international trade share in GDP in 1978 and represents the historical influence.
- The minimum railway distance from the capital of a region to the main Chinese ports of Hong Kong or Shanghai (denoted as *port*).[14] This instrument variable represents the geographic effect and is the valid

Table 18.2 **Market segmentation and its determinants**

Dependant variable	Segmentation				
		All regions		Guangdong excluded	Beijing, Tianjin and Shanghai excluded
	(1)	(2)	(3)	(4)	(5)
Independent variables	FE	FE	RE	RE	FE
Trade	0.2621***	0.7180***	0.5653***	0.6944***	0.7831***
	(0.0864)	(0.2073)	(0.1216)	(0.1707)	(0.2216)
Tradesq	n.a.	−0.2821**	−0.2711***	−0.4773**	−0.3067**
		(0.1167)	(0.0769)	(0.2422)	(0.1200)
Govcons	1.0059***	0.9019**	0.3449	0.3405	0.9589**
	(0.3835)	(0.3838)	(0.2648)	(0.2694)	(0.3733)
Soe	0.9279***	1.0085***	0.7199***	0.6481***	0.9876***
	(0.2174)	(0.2187)	(0.1960)	(0.2227)	(0.2235)
Techdiff	n.a.	n.a.	−0.0104	−0.0075	−0.0430
			(0.0192)	(0.0212)	(0.1060)
Area	(dropped)	(dropped)	−2.4197	−2.1790	(dropped)
			(2.0891)	(2.1210)	
Dummy94	−0.0831***	−0.0957***	−0.0969***	−0.1012***	−0.1028***
	(0.0221)	(0.0226)	(0.0209)	(0.0219)	(0.2252)
Constant	−0.8533***	−0.9692***	−0.5702***	−0.5125**	−0.9187***
	(0.2350)	(0.2386)	(0.2039)	(0.2234)	(0.2494)
Within R^2	0.1441	0.1554	0.1463	0.1351	0.1812
F-value	18.35	16.01	n.a.	n.a.	14.24
Wald chi2	n.a.	n.a.	90.68	78.82	n.a.
Hausman Test					
P-value	15.12	9.72	9.76	10.20	14.64
	0.0045	0.0835	0.1352	0.1158	0.0232
No. of observations	468	468	468	451	417
No. of regions	28	28	28	27	25

Notes: standard errors in parentheses; ***, **, * denote significance at 1 per cent, 5 per cent, 10 per cent level; the null hypothesis of the Hausman Test has no systematic difference between FE and RE models.
Sources: Authors' calculations.

Table 18.3 **Market segmentation and its determinants (instrumental variable estimation)**

Dependant variables	Segmentation			
	All regions		Guangdong excluded	Beijing, Tianjin and Shanghai excluded
	(6)	(7)	(8)	(9)
Independent variables	IV-FE	IV-RE	IV-RE	IV-FE
Trade	3.1001***	0.7202	0.5060*	3.0345***
	(0.9308)	(0.6589)	(0.2629)	(0.9454)
Tradesq	–1.5240***	–0.4635	–0.3350	–1.6581***
	(0.5826)	(0.5879)	(0.4245)	(0.6054)
Govcons	0.3820	0.3113	0.3623	0.5508
	(0.4838)	(0.2996)	(0.2763)	(0.4604)
Soe	1.7757***	0.5382*	0.5487*	1.2645***
	(0.3898)	(0.2795)	(0.2989)	(0.3160)
Techdiff	n.a.	–0.0138	–0.0030	–0.2533
		(0.0383)	(0.0282)	(0.1702)
Area	(dropped)	–1.6967	–3.0731	(dropped)
		(3.9994)	(2.2910)	
Dummy94	–0.1551***	–0.1089***	–0.1010***	–0.1616***
	(0.0358)	(0.0304)	(0.0236)	(0.0352)
Constant	–1.9349***	–0.3974	–0.4038	–1.1359***
	(0.4459)	(0.2717)	(0.2860)	(0.3761)
Within R^2	.	0.1236	0.1316	.
Between R^2	0.5373	0.4085	0.4409	0.3016
IV	portrate	trad78rate	trad78rate	portrate
Hausman Test				
P-value	8.29	1.17	1.34	6.11
	0.1410	0.9916	0.9874	0.4111

Notes: Standard errors in parentheses; ***, **, * denote significance at 1 per cent, 5 per cent, 10 per cent level; the null hypothesis of the Hausman Test is that there is no systematic difference between IV estimation and original models; the within R^2 of (6) and (9) are too small, so Stata does not report them.
Sources: Authors' calculations.

instrument variable for economic opening in Wei and Wu (2001). We compare the distances only to Hong Kong or Shanghai because they are two biggest ports in China, located in the Pearl River Delta and the Yangtse River Delta, respectively, and their throughputs are far beyond those of other ports.

- The exchange rate (denoted as *rate*) determines the international relative price directly and affects the volume of international trade of each province accordingly, but it does not influence integration directly, so it is a valid instrumental variable.

Exchange rate and international trade interplay mutually, so we use the lagged *rate* as the IV of opening. In our regression model, opening is a one-year lagged trade variable, so the *rate* IV in estimation is the two-year lagged exchange rate. The problem is, in Table 18.2, columns (2) and (5) are all FE models; IVs constant over time are eliminated in the de-mean process. So we set up two interaction terms, the interaction of *trade78* and *rate* (*trade78rate*), and the interaction of *port* and *rate* (*portrate*). These two instruments are composed of time-varying exchange rate and time-fixed regional specific or historical effects. The justification for using the interaction terms as instruments is that the effects of the instruments on economic opening depend on each other. In more concrete terms, the effects of history and geography on opening will be greater if the price of international trade is more advantageous, and the exchange rate will have more significant effects on opening in regions with better geographic and historical conditions. We have used both instrumental variables in the model alternately. All results of the Hausman Test do not reject the null hypothesis of no systematic difference between IV and the original models. Table 18.3 reports the corresponding IV models of columns (2)–(5) in Table 18.2, and the models with alternative IVs that we do not report here also reject the endogeneity of opening, so the estimates in Table 18.2 are convincing.

Conclusions

Many studies on the Chinese domestic market have provided evidence in support of the general trends of market integration as a result of economic transformation. The existence of domestic market segmentation, however, and the negative effects of local protectionism can hardly be rejected (Zhen and Li 2003; Poncet 2003a). For this reason, examining the determinants of domestic market integration is still an important issue facing researchers as well as decision makers in China.

Our empirical results answer two questions. First, has the domestic goods market become more integrated since the reforms? The segmentation index constructed by Chinese RPI data shows a different tendency from that found by Young's (2000) and Poncet's (2002) findings. The main finding is that the trend of market integration is persistent and increases over time, although such a trend also experiences serious short-term aberrations, and until now the progress in market integration has varied across different provinces.

Second, did more integrated international trade substitute inter-provincial trade and intensify domestic market segmentation, as stated by Poncet (2002, 2003b)? We investigated the incidence of trade opening, which has been a primary policy focus in Chinese economic reform. Our study captures a non-linear correlation, meaning that the opening policy could worsen the extent of market segmentation in its initial stage of development, but further opening enhances and strengthens the process and the extent of domestic market integration. Such findings endorse the view that moving towards an open economy is fundamentally conducive to the objective of building an integrated market system in China.

We also analysed the influence of geography, pressure for employment, government consumption and technology differentials. Evidence reveals that employment pressure and government consumption worsen market segmentation.

In conclusion, economic opening benefits domestic market integration. However, most provinces still have a long way to go to be integrated more into the national market system. Meanwhile, institutional reforms, such as those aimed at constraining local government intervention and continual privatisation, will help to further enhance the process of market integration in China.

Notes

1 Poncet 2004 argued that the volume of intra-provincial trade flow was not influenced by the parallel evolution of international trade. But her former paper (2003b) stated that Chinese provinces' greater involvement in international trade went hand-in-hand with a decrease in domestic trade flow intensity between 1987 and 1997.

2 In our data, economic opening has a negative correlation with the share of state-owned enterprises and public consumption.

3 Moreover, these two papers partially overlooked the simultaneity bias. In most studies of this field, however, the variables of government policy are usually correlated with market integration to different degrees; the simple way to mitigate this kind of bias is to use the lagged explanatory variables. The treatment of these two papers was incomplete. Bai (2004) considered only the lagged tax-plus-profit ratio and Poncet 2004 considered only the lagged rate of unemployment and the share of the public sector in total consumption.

4 Theoretically, a higher tax-plus-profit ratio could be the result of, rather than the motive for, local protectionism, so Bai (2004) used lagged tax-plus-profit ratios to mitigate this type of endogeneity bias.

5 Some of the literature chooses 1992, when Deng Xiaoping toured southern China, as the start point of the new stage of reform. Considering the execution time of policies, however, we think 1994 is the better division standard.

6 There are three forms of relative price in empirical studies of the iceberg model. The other two forms are the direct price ratio between two places, P_{it}^{k}/P_{jt}^{k}, and the logarithm of price ratio, $Q_{ijt}^{k} = \mathrm{Ln}(P_{it}^{k}/P_{jt}^{k})$. The main improvement in the second form is that the estimator of the independent variable is independent of the unit of measurement. Furthermore, a logarithm can mitigate the disturbance of heteroskedasticity and skewing (Wooldridge 2003). Details of the relative price forms are introduced by Parsley and Wei (1996, 2001a, 2001b).

7 The earliest data for Hainan, Chongqing and Tibet began in 1988, 1997 and 1999 respectively. Before 1987, statistics for Guangdong covered Hainan. Before 1997, data for Sichuan included Chongqing.

8 A formal discussion is presented in Parsley and Wei (2001a and 2001b).

9 Alternatively, Parsley and Wei (2001a and 2001b) used OLS regressions to remove fixed effects of $|\Delta Q_{ijt}^{k}|$. The model was $|\Delta Q_{ijt}^{k}| = \beta\overline{|\Delta Q_{t}^{k}|} + \varepsilon$ and the residual was $q_{ijt}^{k} = |\Delta Q_{ijt}^{k}| - \hat{\beta}\overline{|\Delta Q_{t}^{k}|}$, which is an inexplicable term of $\overline{|\Delta Q_{t}^{k}|}$. We can get the same result through these two approaches.

10 In *Comprehensive Statistical Data and Materials in 50 Years of New China*, all data for Sichuan peel off those for Chongqing, so Sichuan's explanatory variables do not contain the portion for Chongqing. The dependent variable of Sichuan, however, comes from the RPI that covered Chongqing before 1996. We suppose the RPI of one area will not change much if peeling off only a portion of it. For more sample numbers, we keep these 11 components.

11 The data for imports and exports are the values in renminbi transferred by middle prices for the renminbi–US dollar. The exchange rates were obtained from *China Statistical Yearbooks*.

12 In the literature on economic growth, the government expenditure to GDP ratio—with expenditure for education and national defence subtracted—is used commonly as the proxy of government interference. But Chinese local governments have no statistics on national defence, and there is no separate category for education—only total numbers of expenditure for culture, education, research and health—so we subtracted the share of expenditure for culture, education, research and health from total government expenditure.

13 The study of Head et al. 2002 measured the distance by $0.376\sqrt{\mathrm{Area}}$, where 'Area' denoted the numerical value of area. The calculation strategy was based on the assumption of a uniform distribution of consumers. We also used this index in regressions, and the conclusions were the same as the ones we report.

14 Shenzhen is one of the largest ports in China, but it is close to Hong Kong, so the distances from provincial capitals to Hong Kong are also the distances to Shenzhen. These data were collected from the *China Electronic Map for Transportation and Travel* (Beijing Tuling Software Ltd). We acknowledge Yu Jin's help for data collecting.

References

Bai, C.E., Du, Y., Tao, Z. and Tong, S.Y., 2004. 'Local protectionism and regional specialization: evidence from China's industries', *Journal of International Economics*, 63(2):397–417.

Cai, F., Wu, Y., Giles, J. and Park, A., 2004. 'How does economic integration affect urban employment and welfare' (in Chinese), *China Labor Economics*, Chinese Labor and Social Security Publishing House, 1(1):1–32.

Dong, X. and Putterman, L., 2002. 'Investigating the rise of labour redundancy in China's state industry' (in Chinese), *China Economic Quarterly*, 1(2):397–418.

Fan, C.S. and Wei, X., 2006. 'The law of one price: evidence from the transitional economy of China', *The Review of Economics and Statistics*, MIT Press, 88(4):682–97.

Head, K. and Mayer, T., 2000. 'Non-Europe: the magnitude and causes of market fragmentation in the EU', *Weltwirtschaftliches Archiv*, 136(2000):284–314.

Li, J., Qiu, L.D. and Sun, Q., 2003. 'Interregional protection: implications of fiscal decentralization and trade liberalization', *China Economics Review*, 14:227–45.

Lin, Y. and Liu, P., 2004. *Local protection and market segmentation: the angle from development strategy*, (in Chinese), Working Paper, No. C2004015, China Center for Economic Research, Peking University, Beijing.

Lu, M., Chen, Z. and Yan, J., 2004. 'Increasing returns, development strategy and regional economic segmentation', *Studies in Regional Development*, 36(1):275–306.

Lu, M., 2002. *Labor Economics: a perspective of the modern economic system* (in Chinese), Fudan University Press, Shanghai.

Maddala, G.S. and Wu, S., 1999. 'Comparative study of unit root tests with panel data and a new simple test', *Oxford Bulletin of Economics and Statistics*, 61:631–52.

Naughton, B., 1999. How much can regional integration do to unify China's markets?, Paper presented at the Conference for Research on Economic Development and Policy Research, Stanford University, Palo Alto.

National Bureau of Statistics, 1999. *Comprehensive Statistical Data and Materials on 50 Years of New China*, China Statistics Press, Beijing.

Parsley, D.C. and Wei, S.J., 1996. 'Convergence to the law of one price without trade barriers or currency fluctuations', *Quarterly Journal of Economics*, 111:1,211–36.

——, 2001a. 'Explaining the border effect: the role of exchange rate variability, shipping cost, and geography', *Journal of International Economics*, 55(1):87–105.

——, 2001b. *Limiting currency volatility to stimulate goods market integration: a price based approach*, NBER Working Paper 8468, National Bureau of Economic Research, Cambridge, MA.

Ping, X., 2004. 'The motivation and effect of government protection—an empirical analysis', (in Chinese), *Finance and Trade Economics*, 5:3–10.

Poncet, S., 2002. 'Is China disintegrating? The magnitude of Chinese provinces' domestic and international integration' (in Chinese), *World Economic Papers*, 1:3–17.

——, 2003a. 'Domestic market fragmentation and economic growth in China', paper presented at the 43rd European Congress of the Regional Science Association, Jyvsky, Finland, 27–30 August.

——, 2003b. 'Measuring Chinese domestic and international integration', *China Economic Review*, 14(1):1–21.

——, 2005. 'A fragmented China: measure and determinants of Chinese domestic market disintegration', *Review of International Economics*, 13(3):409–30.

Samuelson, P., 1954. 'Theoretical notes on trade problems', *Review of Economics and Statistics*, 46:145–64.

Wang, D., Wu, Y. and Cai, F., 2004. 'Migration, unemployment and urban labor market segmentation' (in Chinese), *World Economic Papers*, 1:37–52.

Wei, S. and Wu, Y., 2001. *Globalization and inequality: evidence from within China*, NBER Working Paper 8611, National Bureau for Economic Research, Cambridge, MA.

Wooldridge, J.M., 2003. *Introductory Econometrics, A Modern Approach*, South-Western, Thomson Learning, Mason, OH.

Xu, X., 2002. 'Have the Chinese provinces become integrated under reform?', *China Economic Review*, 13:116–33.

Xue, J. and Wei, Q., 2004. 'Urban unemployment and poverty in China' (in Chinese), *China Labor Economics*, Chinese Labor and Social Security Publishing House, 1(1):58–71.

Young, A., 2000. 'The razor's edge: distortions and incremental reform in the People's Republic of China', *Quarterly Journal of Economics*, CXV:1,091–135.

Zhen, Y. and Li, C., 2003. 'The efficiency loss in China's regional segmentation' (in Chinese), *Chinese Social Science*, 1:64–72.

Acknowledgments

Financial support came from the National Natural Sciences Fund (70403004), the MOE Project of Key Research Institute of Humanities and Social Sciences in Universities, and the MOE Project Granted for the Authors of Distinguished PhDs. These are greatly appreciated. The authors also thank the 985 Project of the School of Economics and the China Center for Economic Studies, Fudan University, for providing the provincial panel data.

19

Stepping stones to market integration

The role of economic and technological development zones

Wei Zhang

China's National People's Congress passed the Enterprise Income Tax Law of the People's Republic of China in March 2007. This new law unified enterprise income tax rates applied to domestic and foreign-invested firms. The passage of the new law is part of the Chinese government's efforts to provide a level playing field for business competition between domestic and foreign-invested firms. This legislation is also a significant step towards China fulfilling its World Trade Organization (WTO) obligations. After a short transitional period, the changes in tax rates and taxing practice will end most of the privileges enjoyed by foreign-invested enterprises located in various special economic zones (SEZs) in China. This attracts broad attention to the role and the future of China's SEZs.

Setting up SEZs has been a popular policy tool for developing and industrialised countries to implement their trade, industry and regional policies. An SEZ is an area that has economic laws and management systems different from those in the rest of the country. The main goals of developing such a zone are to attract inward foreign direct investment (FDI), expand exports, increase the fiscal income of foreign exchange, spur local employment and promote development of technology. Special policy incentives provided to achieve such goals usually include provision of better infrastructure, preferential tax treatments, privileged trading terms and less bureaucratic administrative procedures.

SEZs have various forms. The World Export Processing Zones Association categorises different zones according to their various size, industry and performance specifics (WEPZA 2007). For example, there are some large SEZs in the world that cover or are integrated within an entire city, or even a whole region; there are also some relatively small export processing zones with an area less than 1,000 hectares. There are some industrial parks specialised in certain industries, and some high-tech parks attracting and supporting firms that possess or develop high or new technologies.

The various forms of SEZs have developed very rapidly in the past few decades. According to Crittle and Akinci (2004), the number of SEZs in the world increased from 80 to 3,000 from the late 1970s to the early 2000s; the number of countries that hosted SEZs increased from about 30 to more than 120. The value of export goods produced in such zones increased from US$6 billion to US$600 billion, and the number of people employed within the zones increased from one million to 50 million.

Since China started its economic reforms in 1978, it has become the country that holds the largest number of various forms of SEZs in the world. The first SEZ in China was approved in 1979. By the end of 2006, there were 1,568 SEZs across the country. The total planning area of SEZs was 9,949 square kilometres (State Commission of Development and Reform, Ministry of Land and Natural Resources, and Ministry of Construction 2006).

During the same period, the Chinese economy also witnessed the fastest growth, compared with its own history and compared with the rest of the world.

The phenomenal surge in the number of SEZs, coinciding with rapid economic growth, has invited broad attention from scholars and policymakers. The role of SEZs has always been highly contentious, globally and in China (Aggarwal 2006). Very often, creation of SEZs has been described as one of the most powerful engines driving China's economic growth. On the other hand, the pro-SEZ policies of the Chinese government have also drawn much criticism, especially because of their negative impacts, such as the misuse of arable land, distortion of the domestic market, expansion of regional disparities and unfair trade competition in the international market (Carttier 2001; Weil 1996; Gopalakrishnan 2007).

There are many different forms of SEZs in China. They can be divided into two main categories: '*Jingji Tequ*' (special economic zones: in order to distinguish this specific form from the general term of SEZ, it is specified in this chapter as China's Special Economic Zones, hereafter CSEZs); and '*Kaifaqu*' (Economic Development Zones, EDZs). Within the category of the EDZs, there are *Jingji Jishu Kaifaqu* (Economic and Technological Development Zones, ETDZs), *Gaoxin Jishu Kaifaqu* (High and New Technology Development Zones, HTDZs), *Baoshuiqu* (Free Tariff/Trade Zones, FTZs), *Chukou Jiagongqu*

(Export Processing Zones, EPZs), *Bianjing Jingji Hezuoqu* (Bordered Economic Cooperative Zones, BECZs), and others.

This chapter attempts to explain the historical and special policy treatments of SEZs in China, to evaluate their role in promoting national economic reform and development and to analyse the challenges they are facing in the WTO era. While the paper presents the general development of various forms of SEZs, it will focus more on ETDZs—in particular, national-level ETDZs. This is due not only to the lack of research on ETDZs in China compared with the abundant research literature on CSEZs, but because ETDZs have hugely outnumbered SEZs and now spread to every province, municipality and autonomous region. This broad geographical coverage and resulting close relationships between ETDZs and their surrounding areas enables them to play a very effective role in introducing new management ideas, internationally recognised business practices and competitive technological innovations to the rest of the country.

Other forms of EDZs are either small pieces of land located within ETDZs—such as EPZs and HTDZs—or zones that enjoy similar preferential policies to those of ETDZs, although they are located in separate locations, such as TDZs and BECZs.

Creation and development of ETDZs

ETDZs were an extension of successful experiments with CSEZs. In July 1979, as part of a national reform plan, the central government decided to establish four CSEZs in southern Chan State: Shenzhen, Zhuhai and Shantou in Guangdong Province, and Huli (expanded to the whole island of Xiamen in 1984) in Fujian Province.[1]

With privileges such as a much higher degree of autonomy and a series of favourable treatments in taxation, international trade and other aspects, the four CSEZs quickly stood out from their surrounding areas and from the rest of the country in economic growth, increases in employment, surges in FDI and expansion of exports. In less than four years, almost all of the CSEZs doubled their GDP (Table 19.1). The development of Shenzhen was particularly stunning. By the end of 1983, Shenzhen's GDP reached 1.3 billion yuan—about five times the figure for 1979—and inward FDI reached HK$2.98 billion. Industrial output reached 1.66 times the total output during the whole period from 1949 to 1978; and fiscal revenue was 10.9 times that of 1978 (Zhao and Chen 1984:82).

Encouraged by the success of the four CSEZs, the central government decided to further open 14 cities in the coastal area while continuing support for the four experimental CSEZs.[2] Among 10 new policy initiatives in promoting economic reform and development in the coastal areas, establishing the ETDZs has been regarded as the most effective.

Expectations for the newly established ETDZs were initially very high. The central government required the first group of ETDZs to function as 'four windows'; that is, a window of advanced technology, a window of excellent management, a window of new knowledge and a window for the open-door policy. These high expectations reflected the great ambitions of then leaders

Table 19.1 **GDP of five SEZs and national total, 1980–2005** (RMB million)

	Shenzhen	Zhuhai	Shantou	Xiamen	Hainan	National total	Share (per cent)
1980	270	261	1,079	640	1,933	454,562	0.92
1981	496	318	1,262	741	2,223	488,946	1.03
1982	826	353	1,416	867	2,886	533,045	1.19
1983	1,312	406	1,340	944	3,112	598,555	1.19
1984	2,342	678	1,740	1,229	3,718	724,375	1.34
1985	3,902	981	2,404	1,836	4,326	904,074	1.49
1986	4,164	1,110	2,836	2,119	4,803	1,027,438	1.46
1987	5,590	1,590	3,865	2,549	5,760	1,205,062	1.61
1988	8,698	2,507	5,714	3,598	7,713	1,503,682	1.88
1989	11,566	3,081	6,547	4,792	9,140	1,700,092	2.07
1990	17,167	4,143	7,245	5,709	10,249	1,871,832	2.38
1991	23,666	6,237	8,958	7,200	12,051	2,182,620	2.66
1992	31,732	10,320	10,910	9,767	18,171	2,693,728	3.00
1993	44,929	13,400	14,862	13,232	25,810	3,526,002	3.18
1994	61,519	15,720	19,719	18,704	33,090	4,810,846	3.09
1995	79,570	18,506	26,203	25,055	36,417	5,981,053	3.11
1996	95,004	20,732	31,366	30,635	38,950	7,014,249	3.09
1997	113,001	23,520	37,352	31,780	40,990	7,765,313	3.18
1998	128,902	26,350	42,318	41,806	43,890	8,302,428	3.41
1999	143,602	28,660	45,459	45,829	47,120	8,818,895	3.52
2000	166,547	33,026	47,698	50,187	51,850	9,800,045	3.56
2001	195,465	36,833	48,438	53,192	55,220	10,806,822	3.60
2002	223,941	40,903	48,978	56,135	58,557	11,909,569	3.60
2003	289,541	47,671	51,976	62,173	65,169	13,517,398	3.82
2004	342,280	55,167	54,768	68,375	72,016	15,958,675	3.71
2005	400,468	63,495	57,397	74,788	79,150	18,395,610	3.67

Sources: Data of five SEZs before 2000 are from Wang, G., 2004. *Research on Sustainable Development of China's Five Special Economic Zones* (in Chinese), Jingjiguanli Chubanshe, Beijing. After 2000, the data are from the local statistical yearbooks in each year; national data are from National Bureau of Statistics, 2006. *China Statistical Yearbook*, China Statistical Press, Beijing.

of the reforms to narrow the gaps in technology and economic development between China and the newly industrialised states in East Asia. Particularly, they expected ETDZs to play a key role in introducing high technologies, which was the goal they thought the four CSEZs had failed to achieve.

Expectations, however, appeared unrealistic. The new ETDZs were not able to achieve these requirements due to the rigid administrative system of the local governments, lack of knowledge of internal business practices, poor infrastructure and other factors. In 1989, the central government modified the guiding principle from four windows to 'three foci': focusing on industrial development, utilisation of FDI and exports. The key change of the principles was to relax the requirement for introduction of high and new technologies and attracting more foreign investment.

The central government granted the ETDZs most of the preferential polices and administrative autonomy that the four CSEZs had enjoyed (State Council of the PRC 1984). Those special policies included preferential tax rates on foreign-invested firms located in ETDZs, a high degree of administrative autonomy from the local government and a more flexible management system for foreign trade, land development and banking services.

Preferential tax treatment for foreign-invested enterprises located in ETDZs

The income tax rate for foreign-invested enterprises located in ETDZs was 15 per cent, while it was 24 per cent in the provinces of Guangdong and Fujian, and 30 per cent in the rest of the country. For the foreign-invested enterprises with terms of operation of more than 10 years, starting from the first year of profit making, their income tax for the first two years would be exempted and that for the next three years would be only 7.5 per cent. If the foreign partner of a foreign-invested enterprise reinvested its profit directly into a business in the ETDZ with a term of operation of more than five years, it could apply for a refund of 40 per cent of the income tax paid. If the foreign investor used its profit to launch or expand an export-oriented or technologically advanced enterprise with a term of operation of more than five years, its income tax paid would be fully refunded.

Higher degree of administrative autonomy for the ETDZs

The ETDZs were granted power to approve foreign investment, manage international trade and make local regulations. Originally, any foreign investment in China had to be approved by the central government. Under that system, the process of approval was not transparent and the waiting period was very long. After the decentralisation of economic management in the early 1980s, provincial governments were granted power to approve foreign-invested projects of less than US$5 million. The ETDZs, however, were granted much higher administrative autonomy than most provinces. For example, ETDZs in Shanghai and Tianjin were granted power to approve foreign-invested projects up to US$30 million. The governments of provinces and cities that hosted ETDZs also gave some administrative powers to the ETDZs in order to accelerate the procedure of approving foreign-invested firms.

Other preferential policies

Such policies include lower interest rates for banking loans, no import duty for investment goods, office equipment and other products used within the ETDZs. Before China unified exchange rates in 1994, the ETDZs were also granted a certain quota of foreign exchange at the official exchange rate, which allowed them to import some consumer goods to make profits to raise capital for construction of infrastructure. Before 1996, the central government also rebated all the tax revenue collected from the firms located in the ETDZs.

These policy incentives have stimulated provincial and local governments' enthusiasm for setting up ETDZs in their areas. In addition to those preferential policies given by the central government, many provincial and local governments promised financial and other support for the ETDZs. This includes selling land for development at lower than market prices, offering full rebates of local tax and providing special treatment in services including electricity and water supply and telecommunications.

The first ETDZ, Dalian Economic and Technological Development Zone (Dalian ETDZ), was approved by the central government in August 1984. Since then, thousands of ETDZs have been established across the country. The development of the ETDZs in China can be divided into three stages: 1984 to 1988, 1992 to 1996, and 2000 to 2004.

The period from 1984 to 1988 was the infant stage of the ETDZs' development. Only 14 ETDZs were approved by the State Council during this period and all were concentrated in nine coastal provinces (see Table 19.2).

Most of the first group of ETDZs was built in remote areas far from the main cities due to concerns about 'the impacts of capitalism'. This made the investment environment extremely harsh. Poor infrastructure, lack of investment capital, restrictions on original management systems and a shortfall of talent were the main constraints on development at this stage.

Table 19.2 **Establishment of economic and technological development zones** (ETDZs), 1984–2002

Period	Number	Approved ETDZs	Province [a]
1984–88	14	Dalian, Qinhuangdao, Tianjin, Yantai, Qingdao, Lianyungang, Nantong, Minhang, Hongqiao, Caohejing, Ningbo, Fuzhou, Guangzhou, Zhanjiang	Shanghai, Tianjin, Liaoning, Hebei, Shandong, Jiangsu, Zhejiang, Fujian, Guangdong (9 provinces)
1992–93	18	Yingkou, Changchun, Shenyang, Harbin, Weihai, Kunshan, Hangzhou, Xiaoshan, Wenzhou, Hongqiao, Dongshan, Guangzhou Nansha, Huizhou Dayawan, Wuhu, Wuhan, Chongqing, Beijing, Urumchi	Beijing, Chongqing, Heilongjiang, Jilin, Hubei, Xinjiang, Hainan (7 provinces)
2000–02	17	Hefei, Zhengzhou, Xi'an, Changsha, Chengdu, Kunming, Guinyang, Nanchang, Shihezi, Xining, Huhhot, Taiyuan, Nanning, Yinchuan, Lanzhou, Lasa	Inner-Mongolia, Shanxi, Anhui, Jiangxi, Henan, Hunan, Sichuan, Yunnan, Guizhou, Shaanxi, Qinghai, Ningxia, Gansu, Tibet (14 provinces)

[a] Provinces that were allowed to build ETDZs for the first time.
Source: Department of Foreign Investment Management in Ministry of Commerce, 2007. *National Level Economic and Technological Development Zones Main Economic Indices*, Beijing.

The efforts of the newly approved ETDZs in this period focused mainly on infrastructure construction, making connections with potential overseas investors and reforming management systems. These efforts laid a sound foundation for future development, but the inflow of foreign investment and other economic development were very limited in this period. The ETDZs experienced severe stagnation, particularly in the period from 1989 to 1991, because of political retrogression and resulting adverse changes in the international environment. By the end of 1991, the main economic indicators of the first group of ETDZs were not impressive at all (Table 19.3).

The second stage of ETDZs' development—regarded as the 'golden period'—was from 1992 to 1996. A large number of new ETDZs and other forms of EDZs were approved, including 18 ETDZs approved by the State Council (Table 19.2). During this period, the first group of 14 ETDZs were really taking off. Table 19.3

Figure 19.1 **Distribution of state-level ETDZs in China**

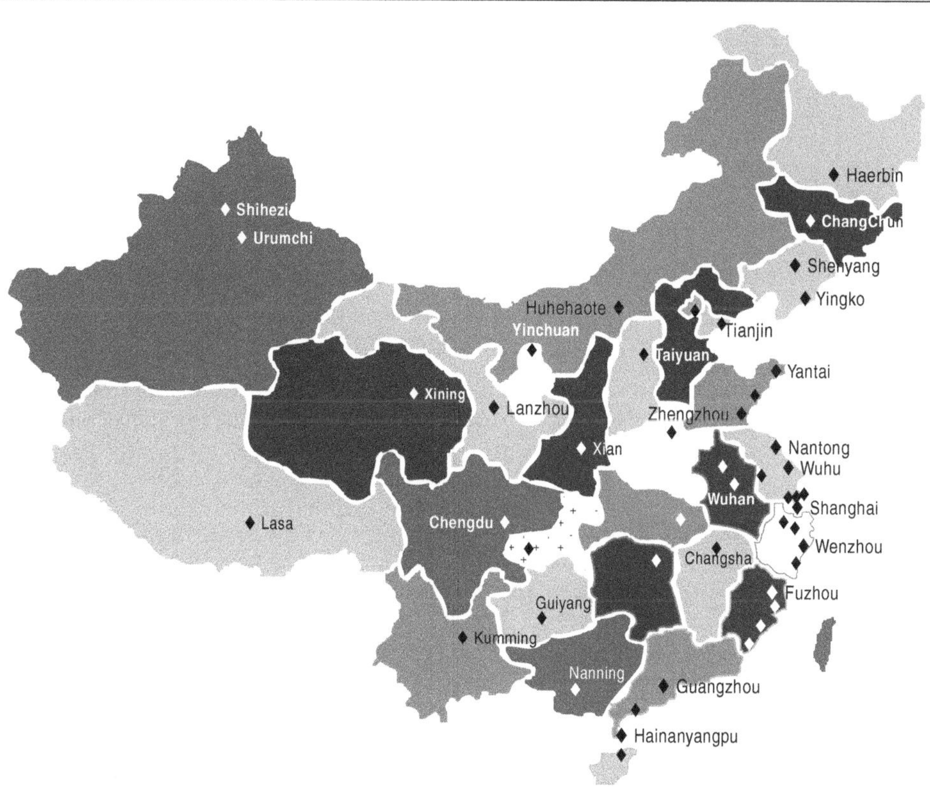

Table 19.3 **Economic indicators of the first group of 14 ETDZs, 1991, 1996 and 2005**

	GDP (RMB million)	Industrial output (RMB million)	Import (US$ million)	Export (US$ million)	Realised FDI (US$ million)	Tax revenue (RMB million)
1991	5,611.5	14,594.0	1,094.4	1,140.0	1,377.0	790.0
1996	72,590.0	188,786.0	6,127.0	6,419.0	3,832.0	10,145.0
2005	356,285.4	916,384.2	44,231.1	45,308.1	4,662.6	55,134.3

Source: Department of Foreign Investment Management in Ministry of Commerce, 2007. *National Level Economic and Technological Development Zones Main Economic Indices*, Beijing.

shows that the main economic indicators of the first group of ETDZs improved dramatically. In 1996, their GDP was 12.9 times that in 1991. Industrial output increased 12.9 times, imports and exports 5.6 times, foreign investment 2.8 times and tax revenue 12.8 times. Many multinational corporations started to enter the ETDZs, including Motorola, West Pacific Petrochemical, P&G and Samsung.

The third development period of the ETDZs was from 2000 to 2002. The ETDZs had spread quickly to all areas of the country, but the rapid increase in this period followed a very different pattern compared with the previous two periods in terms of geographic distribution. Newly established ETDZs were located mainly in the central and western areas, in contrast with the previous geographical concentration in coastal areas. Table 19.2 shows that all of the newly established national-level ETDZs were located in the western and central areas (Figure 19.1). As a result, by the end of this period, every province, municipality and autonomous region had at least one national-level ETDZ. This new trend was in accord with the government's regional policy of developing the western area.

By the end of 2002, the number of various kinds of ETDZs in the whole country had soared to 6,866; and the planning area for various ETDZs reached 38,600 square kilometres. In July 2003, the State Council decided to stop approving new ETDZs and started a nation-wide clean-up and rectification of existing ETDZs. Up to the end of 2006, the number of ETDZs was reduced to 1,568, and the planning area was reduced to 9,949 square kilometres (Zhu 2007). Among the surviving EDZs, 222 were approved directly by the State Council as national-level EDZs. They include 49 ETDZs, 53 HTDZs, 15 TFZs, 58 EPZs, 14 BECZs and 33 other zones, such as special tourist zones and special logistical zones.

Impacts of ETDZs on China's economic reform and development

The purpose of establishing SEZs or ETDZs is to promote economic growth, create employment opportunities, attract FDI and expand international trade. Suffice to say, ETDZs have played a significant role in China's economic reform and economic growth.

A driving force for economic growth

Many local governments have regarded ETDZs as an effective means of fostering a new point of economic growth within their area. That is part of the reason why the number of ETDZs had proliferated to more than 6,000 by the end of 2002. The major economic indicators of 54 national-level ETDZs (hereafter NETDZs) demonstrate the significant contribution of the zones to

China's national economic growth.[3] The economic size of the 54 NETDZs is estimated to account for about 73 per cent of all EDZs and about 86 per cent of all 222 NEDZs.[4]

Continuously higher GDP growth rates in the NETDZs compared with the national total in the past two decades means constant increases of their GDP share in the national total. This trend implies a direct contribution of the ETDZs to the country's economic growth.

Tables 19.4 and 19.5 show that the share of the 54 NETDZs in the national total of GDP reached 4.5 per cent and 4.8 per cent in 2005 and 2006, respectively. Their growth rates were 24.14 per cent and 24 per cent respectively—14.2 and 13.3 percentage points higher than the national level. The contribution of the NETDZs to the net growth of GDP was 9.7 and 9.69 per cent respectively. The GDP produced in the first group of 14 NETDZs accounted for about 43.4 per cent of that of the total NETDZs, and their share in the national total GDP was 1.95 per cent (Table 19.6).

In addition to the contribution from the NETDZs, the five CSEZs have made a significant contribution to national economic growth. Their share in total national GDP increased from less than 1 per cent in 1980 to 3.7 per cent in 2005 (Table 19.7).

People could argue that the higher GDP growth in the NETDZs and the CSEZs might not be due to a creation effect but a diversion effect. Some people question whether the high GDP growth of the NETDZs and the CSEZs has been realised at the expense of a slowing of GDP growth in other areas. I do not have a complete data set to answer this question fully. However, based on the data in Tables 4 and 5, without the contribution from the ETDZs in 2005 and 2006, the national growth rates would still be very high: 8.9 and 9.7 per cent respectively—only about one percentage point lower in each year than they were.

Investigation of the economic structure in the NETDZs also seems to support the creation argument. Tables 4 and 5 show a clear international orientation of the NETDZs' economies. The expanding speed of international trade was much faster than the growth rates of GDP—a significant sign of market creation rather than resource diversion. The growth rates of exports were about 36 and 31 per cent in 2005 and 2006 respectively. Imports witnessed similar rapid growth. The two tables also show that the shares of the NETDZs' international trade and FDI in the national total were three to four times their share of GDP in the national total. Their contribution rate to total exports and FDI in the country was as high as 17 and 62 per cent respectively in 2006.

Table 19.4 **Economic indicators of 54 NETDZs, 2005**

	GDP (RMB billion)	IVA (RMB billion)	Tax revenue (RMB billion)	Exports (US$ billion)	Imports (US$ billion)	FDI (US$ billion)
54 ETDZs	819.5	598.1	121.9	225.2	111.4	13.0
Growth (per cent)	24.1	23.2	30.7	35.5	29.7	–4.3
National	18,232.1	7,619.0	3,086.6	762.0	660.1	60.3
Share of total	9.9	16.4	20.0	28.4	17.6	-0.5
Share of 54 ETDZs	4.5	7.8	3.9	15.8	16.9	21.6
Contribution to total growth (per cent)	9.7	10.5	5.6	22.0	25.8	

Source: Department of Foreign Investment Management in Ministry of Commerce, 2006. *Development Report of National Development Zones, 2006*, Beijing.

Table 19.5 **Economic indicators of 54 NETDZs, 2006**

	GDP (RMB billion)	IVA (RMB billion)	Tax revenue (RMB billion)	Exports (US$ billion)	Imports (US$ billion)	FDI (US$ billion)
54 ETDZs	1013.7	741.4	157.0	149.2	133.9	14.7
Growth (per cent)	24.0	24.5	28.8	31.1	20.1	13.0
National	20940.7		3763.7	969.1	791.6	63.0
Share of total	10.7		21.9	27.2	20.0	4.5
Share of 54 ETDZs	4.8		4.2	15.4	16.9	23.3
Contribution (per cent)	9.7		5.2	17.1	17.0	62.3

Source: Department of Foreign Investment Management in Ministry of Commerce: 2006 Major Economic indices of NETDZ (2007).

Table 19.6 **Main economic indicators of the first group of 14 ETDZs, 2005**

	Ratified	GDP (RMB million)	Industrial output (RMB million)	Exports (US$ million)	Imports (US$ million)	Realised FDI (US$ million)	Tax revenue (RMB million)
Dalian	Sep. 1984	45,011.2	96,200.0	5,010.0	5,020.0	350.0	5,031.2
Qinhuangdao	Oct. 1984	9,204.9	23,599.2	583.0	913.1	166.7	907.5
Yantai	Oct. 1984	28,004.0	64,022.6	2,411.3	3,214.5	294.6	3,347.8
Qingdao	Oct. 1984	37,226.9	80,849.0	2,778.4	2,808.1	741.7	4,543.2
Ningbo	Nov. 1984	23,526.6	66,300.0	2,506.4	2,980.0	420.0	3,826.1
Zhanjiang	Nov. 1984	4,313.6	10,417.9	381.8	199.2	9.4	515.4
Tianjin	Dec. 1984	64,229.4	230,519.2	13,970.7	11,467.5	1,284.9	13,324.5
Lianyungang	Dec. 1984	6,553.7	17,662.6	276.6	710.9	122.4	1,093.4
Nantong	Dec. 1984	8,282.1	24,178.7	1,177.2	803.5	351.0	1,376.5
Guangzhou	Dec. 1984	65,294.1	160,823.9	6,251.2	7,540.5	681.1	14,635.0
Fuzhou	Nov. 1985	13,534.9	27,138.5	893.3	1,357.8	70.2	1,239.0
Minhang	Aug. 1986	10,876.6	31,075.9	755.9	679.3	75.7	2,845.8
Hongqiao	Aug. 1986	7,251.1				19.7	484.8
Caohejing	June 1988	32,976.4	83,596.7	8,312.3	6,536.7	75.3	1,963.9
Subtotal		356,285.4	916,384.2	45,308.1	44,231.1	4,662.6	55,134.3
National total		18,308,480.0	25,161,950.0	761,950.0	659,950.0	63,805.0	2,877,854.0
Share in national total (per cent)		1.95	3.64	5.95	6.70	7.31	1.92

Source: Department of Foreign Investment Management in Ministry of Commerce: 2006 Major Economic indices of SETDZ (2007).

A positive factor for improving economic quality

The NETDZs have not only made great contributions to national economic growth, they have played a positive role in improving the quality of the national economy.

There is no absolute measurement for economic quality. If we use the absolute level of technology contained in production or products as a measurement, compared with industrialised economies, most developing economies would be regarded as low-quality economies. If, however, we take a dynamic perspective and regard the economic quality as a constantly changing variable, it should not be difficult to measure a process of improvement in economic quality.

A simple way to measure the economic quality of a country is to look at the changes in its international competitiveness, especially its export share in the world total, except for natural resource-intensive commodities. Based on this measurement, the share of China's exports in the world total was less than 0.9 per cent in 1980 (World Bank 2005); it increased to 7.3 per cent by 2005 (WTO 2005). BECZs have played a strong role in strengthening China's international competitiveness and expanding China's share in total world trade.

We can also look at changes in the economic structure, especially changes in the share of high-tech industries in the whole economy. China's State Commission of Science and Technology promulgated the *High-Tech Products Catalogue* in 1991, based on international standards, particularly the definition made by the Organisation for Economic Co-operation and Development (OECD). The catalogue has since been updated every few years (State Commission of Science and Technology 1991). The current catalogue covers mainly information technology, software, aerospace, optical, mechanical and electrical integration, bio-medicine and medical equipment, new materials, new energy and highly efficient energy savings, environmental protection, oceans and space, nuclear application technology and modern agriculture.

According to this definition of high-tech products or high-tech industries, the NETDZs have played an active role in improving China's economic quality by increasing the number of high-tech enterprises in China and expanding the shares of high-tech products in production and exports.

By the end of 2005, the number of high-tech enterprises in the NETDZs reached 3,205—an increase of 6.7 per cent on a year-on-year basis. In the meantime, employees in high-tech enterprises totalled 830,800, accounting for 20 per cent of all employees in the 54 NETDZs.

In 2005, the high-tech enterprises realised industrial output of 1,086.1 billion yuan, an increase of 31.9 per cent from the previous year, accounting for 46.5

per cent of the total. Sales revenue of high-tech products reached 1,088.8 billion yuan, an increase of 24.5 per cent, accounting for 47.1 per cent of the total sales revenue of industrial products in the zones. Exports of high-tech products in the zones reached US$77.4 billion, an increase of 49.5 per cent, accounting for 68 per cent of total exports in the zones (Table 19.8).

The surge of high-tech enterprises and their production, sales and exports of high-tech products in the NETDZs has been driven by the investment of many large multinationals. Among them, the top 500 businesses increased their investment in the ETDZs rapidly in recent years. In 2003, the top 500 had invested in 915 enterprises. This number increased to 1,308 by the end of 2005, an increase of 393 in two years—more than 20 per cent of the average annual growth rate.

Table 19.7 **Average annual changes in GDP share of five CSEZs in the national total, 1980–2005**

Period	Share (per cent)	Anuual increase in share (percentage point)
1980	0.9	
1981–85	1.5	0.1
1986–90	2.4	0.2
1991–95	3.1	0.2
1996–2000	3.6	0.1
2001–05	3.7	0.02

Source: Author's calculations based on Table 19.1.

Table 19.8 **High-tech enterprises in 54 NETDZs, 2005**

	High-tech	Change (per cent)	Share (per cent)
Enterprises	3,205.0	6.6	..
Employment ('000 persons)	830.8	..	20.0
Industrial output (RMB billion)	1,086.1	31.9	46.5
Industrial sales (RMB billion)	1,088.8	24.5	47.1
Exports (US$ billion)	77.4	49.5	68.0

Source: Calculations based on Department of Foreign Investment Management in Ministry of Commerce, 2006. *Development Report of National Development Zones*, 2006, Beijing.

Since the share of NETDZs in the national economy has become significant and is still growing, improvements in industrial quality in the NETDZs have been an important part of improvements in the national economy. In addition, through the industrial linkages with enterprises located outside the NETDZs, high-tech enterprises in the NETDZs help with the general improvement of quality in the national economy through a spillover of technologies, international standard management and marketing practices, as well as other business activities.

An effective catalyst for national economic reform

Developing NETDZs has been a major component of China's open-door policy. As is well known, such policies have been aimed not only at the development of China's external sectors—including foreign trade and investment—they have functioned very well as a pioneering experiment for many of China's domestic reform policies.

Many new policies were first experimented with in the CSEZs or the NETDZs before being adopted as national policies and implemented elsewhere, such as simplifying government approval procedures for foreign investment, decentralising the control of trade rights from the central to local governments, liberalising the labour market and personnel management systems, establishing socially pooled pension systems and other insurance schemes. These policies were all implemented first in the CSEZs and the NETDZs.

For example, in the early 1980s, to gain government approval to open a joint venture or a foreign-owned enterprise in China, potential foreign investors had to visit more than 50 government agents, from the local to the provincial government, and finally to the central government in Beijing. This procedure took more than a year—in many cases even longer. It was time-consuming and financially costly, making most foreign-invested projects, especially small business projects, impossible.

When the central government approved the first group of NETDZs in the coastal areas, it decided to decentralise the approval power to the governments of the provinces where the NETDZs were located. Most of the provincial governments further passed on the power to the NETDZs in order to improve foreign investment management efficiency. The decentralisation enabled the NETDZs to cut red tape and streamline the approval process. These policy measures became a key attraction for overseas businesspeople to invest in the NETDZs. They also facilitated a surge in foreign investment in the 1990s.

Using a special zone to experiment with some reform measures was not always necessary (Madani 1999). The obstacles to implementing many reform policies at the national level in transitional countries are mainly to do with political unwillingness, not economic logic.

In the case of China, the society as whole might have benefitted more if some reform policies could have been implemented directly at the national level—such as cutting red tape in government business administration, reforming the labour market and encouraging private business. Reformist leaders did not want to restrict such policy experiments to the CSEZs and the ETDZs. Instead, the experiment usually came about as a result of political compromise.

Government agencies at the central and local levels did not want to give up their powers and risk losing opportunities for rent seeking. They found political allies among conservative leaders. At the same time, although the reformist leaders were willing to adopt much more flexible economic management systems, they could not afford to lose political support from the bureaucratic system and therefore risk their political control of the country. So they chose the second best: that is, to let the bureaucrats continue to exert administrative power over national economic activities for a certain period. At the same time, they could experiment with new policies in limited areas.

This became a process of creation of demand for the reform policies. The basic political logic was that the success of the new policies experimented with in the CSEZs and the NETDZs caused fierce competition among regions to attract foreign investment and to develop local economies. Therefore, it created new demand in other areas for the popularisation of such policies; it also changed public views and gained political support.

The CSEZs and the NETDZs gained huge advantages in economic competition because of the implementation of many bold reform policies, while most other areas in the country were still being restrained by the old system. Their success reduced political obstacles to implement those policies nation-wide.

Limitation of the ETDZs and new challenges in the WTO era

China has experienced profound changes in the past three decades. These changes occurred not only in its macroeconomic management system, economic strength and structure, but in its economic and political relations with the rest of the world. In a changed environment, the CSEZs and the ETDZs have started to show some inherent limitations.

Although their role in promoting national economic growth will continue for a certain period, the growth rate of the marginal contribution to the national economy will slow. This trend has already appeared in the CSEZs' performances in recent years. The GDP share of the five CSEZs in the national total increased rapidly from the early 1980s to the early 1990s, but the growth rate of the GDP share started to slow from the middle 1990s (Figure 19.2).

One explanation for this trend is that with improved investment environments nation-wide, the competition to attract investment has become increasingly fierce. Particularly since many economic reform policies have already spread to the whole country, the original institutional advantages the CSEZs and NETDZs enjoyed will disappear.

It seems unlikely that the CSEZs and the ETDZs will continue to benefit from future reform experiments. China has maximised the benefits it could have received from a piecemeal reform strategy. The Chinese government has tried hard to identify and solve problems with easy solutions and the least amount of risk. Now it has to face uphill battles. Future reforms will focus on the financial sector, social insurance, income disparities and other important economic and social issues. They will have to be dealt with in a more systematic method and experiments in limited areas will simply not work.

In addition to the above-mentioned factors, rapid increases in land and labour costs in coastal areas will limit further growth of ETDZs. All the CSEZs and most of the ETDZs are located in coastal areas, where population intensity is high. Therefore, land supply is limited. Rapid increases in land prices will directly increase investment costs. At the same time, land prices will also push

Figure 19.2 **GDP share of five SEZs in the national total, 1980–2005** (per cent)

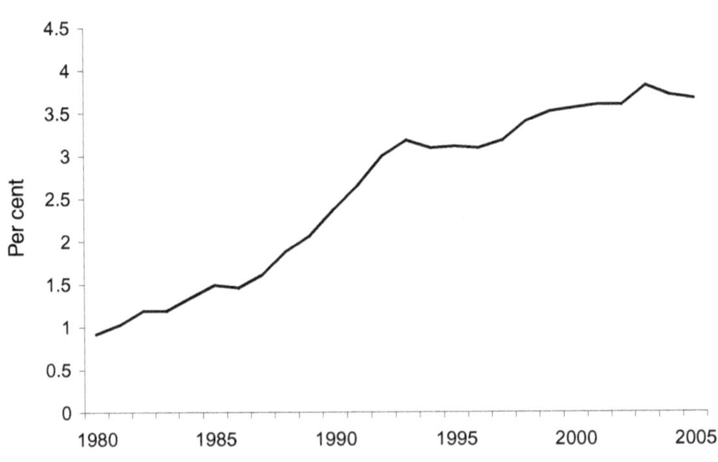

Source: Author's calculations based on Table 19.1.

housing costs up further, which will flow on to living and labour costs.

China has been a member of the WTO since December 2001. Its WTO obligations have some important direct policy implications for the CSEZs and the ETDZs. With all the agreements China signed when it was admitted into the WTO, two are particularly relevant to SEZs: the Agreement on Subsidies and Countervailing Measures (SCM), and the Trade Related Investment Measures (TRIMS) Agreement.

According to the SCM agreement, if three elements are satisfied at the same time, any investment incentives provided by the government should be regarded as subsidies. The three elements are a financial contribution by a government or any public bodies; a benefit is conferred; a subsidy specific to an enterprise or industry or group of enterprises or industries.

The SCM agreement also specifies a definition of financial contributions. It states that any of the following actions equate to a financial contribution

- a direct transfer of funds such as grants, loans and equity infusion, and potential direct transfers of funds or liabilities such as loan guarantees
- if revenue otherwise due to government is forgone or not collected, that is, fiscal incentives such as tax credits
- the government provides goods or services other than general infrastructure, or purchases goods
- the government carries out one of the above functions through a private body that would normally be vested in the government.

All subsidies under the SCM agreement are categorised into two types: prohibited subsidies and actionable subsidies. Export subsidy is one of two types of prohibited subsidies.

According to the definitions in the SCM agreement, many of the existing preferential treatments for foreign-invested enterprises in the ETDZs should be deemed as subsidies, and are thus inconsistent with China's WTO obligations. For example, the CSEZs and the ETDZs provide several forms of incentives, such as lower enterprise income tax rates, exemption from income tax for a certain period, further reduction of income tax for export-oriented enterprises, provision of basic services at a price lower than market prices, and so on.

China's alleged export subsidy has always been one of the main trade disputes between China and the United States, the European Union and its other main trade partners. Some of the disputed products are produced in the CSEZs and the ETDZs.

Being aware of the inconsistency between its preferential polices granted to various forms of SEZs and its commitment to its WTO obligations, the Chinese government has been gradually changing some policies. Passing the new enterprise income tax law is a significant step towards eliminating the *de facto* subsidies to foreign-invested firms located in CSEZs and ETDZs.

Although facing some limitations and challenges, the ETDZs will have to change their role in the national economy in future. Suffice to say, after more than two decades of development, many ETDZs—in particular, NETDZs—have built up a relatively modern infrastructure and a sound industrial foundation. Some of them have formed an industrial cluster with the characteristics of 'geographic concentrations of interconnected companies, specialized suppliers, service providers, and associated institutions in a particular field' (Porter 1998). As industrial centres in the regions, they will be able to receive benefits from the economy of scale and become self-sustaining and self-enhancing, according to Krugman's theory of geography and trade (1991).

Conclusion

Since 1979, in order to promote economic growth and develop international economic relations, the Chinese government has set up various forms of SEZs. It started with four SEZs in southern China in 1979, then 14 economic and technological development zones in the coastal areas in 1984. In the 1990s and early 2000s, the economic and technological zones and other forms of SEZs flourished across the country. Now there are 1,568 economic and technological development zones with a total planning area of 9,949 square kilometres.

With special preferential treatments in taxation and other financial incentives, as well as a higher degree of administrative autonomy, the various forms of SEZs—in particular, 54 national-level ETDZs—have witnessed rapid increases in FDI, international trade and industrial production. They have played a significant role in promoting national economic growth, improving overall economic quality and pioneering economic reform.

There appear to be some limitations that will restrain China's SEZs from continuing to grow and expand their share in the national economy with the speed they experienced in the past two decades. This is mainly because the institutional gap between these SEZs and the rest of the country has gradually narrowed and will soon disappear. As a result, they will not continue to benefit from preferential treatment. Realisation of China's WTO obligations will further speed up this process.

After two decades of development, however, some SEZs and ETDZs have established an advantageous status as regional industrial centres. This status will enable them to continue to receive the benefits of the economy of scale and to realise self-enhancement in future development.

Notes

1 The central government approved the fifth SEZ, Hainan, in April 1988.

2 The 14 coastal cities are Shanghai, Tianjin, Dalian, Qinhuangdao, Qingdao, Yantai, Lianyungang, Nantong, Ningbo, Wenzhou, Fuzhou, Guangzhou, Zhanjiang and Beihai.

3 In China's official document, 54 ETDZs include 49 ETDZs listed in Table 19.2 and another five EDZs, which enjoy the same preferential policies as the 49 state-level ETDZs: Suzhou Industrial Park, Hainan Yangpu ETDZ, Shanghai Jinqiao Export Processing Zone, Ningbo Daxie ETDZ and Xiamen Haicang Investment Zone (Department of Foreign Investment Management in Ministry of Commerce 2006).

4 A complete data set for all 1,568 EDZs, or even for 222 state-level EDZs, is unavailable. A short time data set for 54 state-level ETDZs is, however, relatively reliable. I have based my analysis of the ETDZs on the data of 54 state-level ETDZs.

References

Aggarwal, A., 2006. 'Special economic zones: revisiting the policy debate', *Economic and Political Weekly*, 4 November:4,533–6.

Carttier, C., 2001. 'Zone fever, the arable land debate and real estate speculation: China's evolving land use regime and its geographical contradictions', *Journal of Contemporary China*, 10(28):445–69.

Crittle, J. and Akinci, G., 2004. *Do the benefits of special economic zones outweigh their costs?*, Archived Discussion, July, World Bank, Washington, DC. Available from http://rru.worldbank.org/Discussions/Topics/Topic40.aspx (accessed 25 April 2007).

Department of Foreign Investment Management in Ministry of Commerce, 2006. *Development Report of National Development Zones, 2006*, Beijing.

——, 2007. *National Level Economic and Technological Development Zones Main Economic Indices*, Beijing.

Gopalakrishnan, S., 2007. 'Negative aspects of special economic zones in China', *Economic and Political Weekly*, 28 April:1,492–4.

Jayanthakumaran, K., 2003. 'Benefit–cost appraisals of export processing zones: a survey of the literature', *Development Policy Review*, 21(1):51–65.

Krugman, P., 1991. *Geography and Trade*, The MIT Press, Cambridge, MA.

Madani, D., 1999. *A review of the role and impact of export processing zones*, World Bank Policy Research Working Paper, No. 2238, World Bank, Washington, DC.

National Bureau of Statistics, 2006. *China Statistical Yearbook*, China Statistical Press, Beijing.

Porter, M.E., 1998. *On Competition*, Harvard University Business School Press, Cambridge, MA.

State Commission of Development and Reform, Ministry of Land and Natural Resources, and Ministry of Construction, 2006. *Contents of National Development Zone Auditing Notice* (in Chinese), Beijing.

State Commission of Science and Technology, 1991. *High-Tech Products Catalogue* (in Chinese), State Commission of Science and Technology Beijing.

State Council of the PRC, 1984. *The Minutes of the Conference of Some Coastal Cities* (in Chinese), Beijing.

Wang, G., 2004. *Research on Sustainable Development of China's Five Special Economic Zones* (in Chinese), Jingjiguanli Chubanshe, Beijing.

Weil, R., 1996. *Red Cat, White Cat: China and the contradictions of market socialism*, Monthly Review Press, New York.

World Bank, 2005. *World Development Indicators*, World Bank, Washington, DC.

World Export Processing Zones Association (WEPZA), 2007. *WEPZA Table of Zone Countries*, Evergreen, CO. Available from http://www.wepza.org (accessed 16 April 2007).

World Trade Organization (WTO), 2005. *World Trade in 2005—Overview*:Tables 1–5, World Trade Organization, Washington, DC.

Zhao, Y. and Chen, Z., 1984. *Economies of the Special Economic Zones in China* (in Chinese), Kexue Puju Chubanshe Guangzhou Fenshe, Guangzhou.

Zhu, J., 2007. '*Quanguo Qingli Gelei Kaifaqu Chujian Chengxiao* (Initial achievement has been made in putting various development zones in order)', *Renmin Ribao*, 23 April, Beijing:1.

20

The implications of China's economic transformation for modern economics

Justin Yifu Lin

China started its transition from a planned economy to a market economy at the end of 1978. In the past 28 years, China's average annual gross domestic product (GDP) growth rate was 9.7 per cent and the trade growth rate averaged 17.2 per cent. China's GDP, measured by the official exchange rate, now ranks fourth and, by purchasing power parity, second in the world. China's trade volume is currently the third largest in the world and its foreign reserves, which exceed US$1.2 trillion, are the largest.

In the first 12 years of reform, from 1978 to 1990, China's GDP grew by 9 per cent annually and its trade volume at 15.4 per cent. During this period, urban per capita income grew 5.9 per cent annually, while that of rural areas grew at a spectacular rate of 9.9 per cent (National Bureau of Statistics 2002:17, 94, 148). Living standards in China increased significantly and disparities between urban and rural areas decreased.

In the late 1980s and early 1990s, however, the reform process was poorly understood by the economics profession and many economists had little confidence in China's transformation.[1] Most economists believed that a market economy should be based on private property rights—a feature that the Chinese economy apparently lacked at that time. China's state-owned enterprises were not privatised; a dual-track resource allocation system was prevalent, with state planning still playing an important role alongside markets in resource allocation. These pessimistic economists thought that although China's economic transition was blessed with beneficial initial conditions,[2] the dual-track system would soon lead to efficiency loss, rent seeking and institutionalised state opportunism (Balcerowicz 1994; Woo 1993; Sachs and Woo 1994, 1997; Qian and Xu 1993). Some economists even claimed that, despite its initial success, China's dual-track approach to economic transition would eventually lead the economy to a disastrous collapse (Murphy et al. 1992; Sachs et al. 2000).

At that time, most economists were optimistic about the transition in the former Soviet Union and Eastern Europe due to the fact that those countries were following policy recommendations based on the basic principles of existing modern economics—that is, neoclassical economics.[3] The most representative of these policies was the 'shock therapy' implemented in Poland, the Czech Republic and Russia. Such an approach had three primary components: price liberalisation, rapid privatisation and macroeconomic stabilisation through elimination of fiscal deficits (Lipton and Sachs 1990; Blanchard et al. 1991; Boycko et al. 1995). These components are considered to be the basis of an efficient economic system in neoclassical economics.

Economists recommending shock therapy also knew the transition from one economic system to another took time and that it was costly to cast aside vested interests. Nevertheless, they predicted optimistically that the economies would grow after six months or a year, after an initial downturn resulting from implementation of the shock therapy (Brada and King 1991; Kornai 1990; Lipton and Sachs 1990; Wiles 1995). According to their arguments, the former Soviet Union and Eastern Europe would soon out-perform China, even though the first two had instituted their reforms much later than China. China's progress would be limited by inconsistencies in its economic system exacerbated by incomplete, dual-track reforms.

As described, however, China's average annual GDP and trade continued to grow at high rates—10.3 per cent and 15.2 per cent, respectively, in 1991–2000—the former at higher rates than in the early reform period. Inflation, as measured by the retail price index, was 5.5 per cent per annum in the same period (NBS 2006). In the same 10 years, the countries that implemented shock therapy experienced serious inflation and economic decline. Russia's inflation rate reached 163 per cent per annum, while Ukraine's reached 244 per cent per annum in 1991–2000. The cumulative output decline in countries in central and southeastern Europe and the Baltic states reached 22.6 per cent; in countries of the Commonwealth of Independent States, output fell 50.5 per cent. In 2000, Russia's GDP was only 64 per cent of what it had been in 1990, while in Poland—the best performing economy in the former Soviet Union and Eastern Europe—GDP increased only 44 per cent, compared with 1990.

Meanwhile, the Gini coefficient of income per capita—a measurement of income disparity—increased from 0.23 in 1987–90 to 0.33 in 1996–98 in countries of central and southeastern Europe and the Baltic states, and from 0.28 to 0.46 in countries of the Commonwealth of Independent States (World Bank 2002). Overall, the countries that implemented shock therapy experienced great difficulties in their reforms—in contrast with the optimistic expectations of most economists. Poland's economic record is the best among the countries of the former Soviet Union and Eastern Europe, however, it did not implement shock therapy completely. Although prices in Poland were liberalised, most of its large state-owned enterprises have yet to be privatised (World Bank 1996; Dabrowski 2001).

In the 1990s, the Chinese economy did suffer myriad problems, as predicted by those economists who favoured shock therapy. For example, the state-owned enterprise reforms initiated in the early 1980s have yet to be completed. Interregional and urban–rural disparities increased after the decline in the 1980s. The financial system remains weak. As noted above, however, China's GDP and trade continued to grow. Moreover, living standards improved rapidly, especially in urban areas. Economic development in China not only promoted the welfare of the Chinese people, it contributed greatly to the world economy. During the East Asian financial crisis in 1997–98, the Chinese currency (the renminbi) did not depreciate, which played an important role in the quick recovery of the East Asian economies from the crisis.

China's economic transformation did not follow the standard policy prescriptions based on existing modern economics, and performed outstandingly. Those countries that followed the standard policy recommendations in their transitions performed poorly. This dramatic contrast indicates that there is an inherent limitation in established modern economics—represented by neoclassical economics—in analysing the problems in economic transitions. This chapter suggests directions for improvement of neoclassical economics.

Neoclassical economics, the viability assumption and the formation of a planned economy

Theories are used to explain and predict real-world phenomena. If they fail to do so, the theories must have some fundamental flaws and should be revised or abandoned (Friedman 1953). Existing neoclassical economic theories have performed reasonably well in explaining what happens in the economies of industrialised countries, but they have been less successful in explaining what happens in transitional economies and developing countries.

Neoclassical economics has a well-known assumption of rationality: given the choices available to a decision maker, he or she will choose what is considered to be the best option. There is, however, another assumption—the 'viability' assumption—that is incorporated implicitly by neoclassical economists in their analyses. The term 'viability' is defined with respect to the expected profit of a firm in an open, competitive market. If a normally managed company is expected to earn a socially acceptable normal profit in an open, competitive market, it is viable. For a non-viable company, its establishment or continuing operation is possible only if it receives external subsidies or protection.[4]

By implicitly assuming that all firms are viable in their analyses, economists will conclude that a firm that does not earn acceptable profits in an open, competitive market must lack normally efficient management. They infer that problems must stem from corporate governance, incentive mechanisms, property rights arrangements or other market intervention that impede the firm's management. Problems in corporate governance, property rights arrangements and so on did exist in socialist economies. Therefore, under the influence of existing neoclassical economic theories, it was believed that the success of state-owned enterprise reforms and the transition to a market economy depended on the elimination of those factors that impeded a company's normal management. Shock therapy is based on this theoretical foundation.

Since the inception of neoclassical economics, economists in industrialised countries have conducted most theoretical explorations. Their research, however, focuses mainly on issues relating to industrialised countries. It is reasonable for them to assume that firms are viable, since—except for those in a few sectors—governments in industrialised countries rarely provide subsidies and other types of support directly to companies. If a company with normal management is not expected to earn acceptable profits in the market, it will not be set up in the first place. If a non-viable firm is established due to misleading information or mistakes in judgment, investors will withdraw their investments and close down the firm. Consequently, firms that can survive in an open, competitive economy must be viable: that is, they are expected to earn acceptable profits under normal management. It is therefore appropriate to have an implicit viability assumption in neoclassical economics for analysing phenomena in industrialised countries.

As argued by Lin (2003), however, many firms in transitional economies and developing countries are not viable—that is, they cannot earn acceptable profits in an open, competitive market even though their management is normally efficient. The non-viability of these firms arises from the fact that the sector in which they operate, the products they produce and the technology they use in production are inconsistent with the economy's comparative advantage as determined by the factor endowment structure—namely, the relative abundance of labour, capital and natural resources.

Figure 20.1 illustrates the idea of viability in an open, competitive market that produces only one product with two factors: capital and labour. Curve 'I' is an isoquant. Each point on the isoquant represents a specific technology or combination of capital and labour required to produce a given amount of product.[5] The technology represented by 'A' is more labour intensive than that represented by 'B'. In an open, competitive economy, the least-cost technology is the best. If 'C' is the isocost line in the economy, the adoption of technology 'A' costs the least, while the adoption of any other technology will make the firm incur losses in an open, competitive market. For example, if a firm adopts the technology represented by 'B', it is expected to incur a loss equivalent to the distance from 'C' to C_1. Market competition will make firms that adopt technologies other than 'A' non-viable. Therefore, in an open, competitive market with given relative prices of labour and capital, the viability of a firm depends on its choice of technology. Only the firm that chooses the least-cost technology is viable.

Whether the economy's isocost line corresponds with 'C' or 'D' depends on the economy's endowment structure. When labour is relatively abundant and capital is relatively scarce, the isocost line will have the flatter slope of 'C' rather than 'D'. When capital becomes relatively abundant and labour relatively scarce, the isocost line will change to something like Line D in Figure 20.1. Therefore, the viability of a firm in an open, competitive market depends on whether its choice of technology is consistent with the comparative advantage of the economy's endowment structure.

This conclusion can be extended to multi-product and multi-industry cases. That is, in an open, competitive market, whether a firm is viable depends on whether or not its industry, product and technology choices are consistent with the comparative advantages determined by the economy's endowment structure.[6] If a firm's choices are not consistent with this condition, it cannot earn acceptable profit in an open, competitive market even under normal management and its survival requires government subsidies and/or protection.

A good example that illustrates the viability concept is the agricultural sector in Japan. The majority of farms in the Japanese agricultural sector are small and owned by individual owners/operators. There are, consequently, no problems of property rights and corporate governance.[7] Japan is, however, a country endowed with only limited arable land and it has no comparative advantages in land-intensive agricultural products such as grain. It is also a high-wage country with no comparative advantages in labour-intensive agricultural products such as vegetables and fruit. Although Japan's agricultural sector is famous for its delicate, intensive cultivation, the survival of Japanese farms relies on high

Figure 20.1 **Relative price of production factors and technique choice**

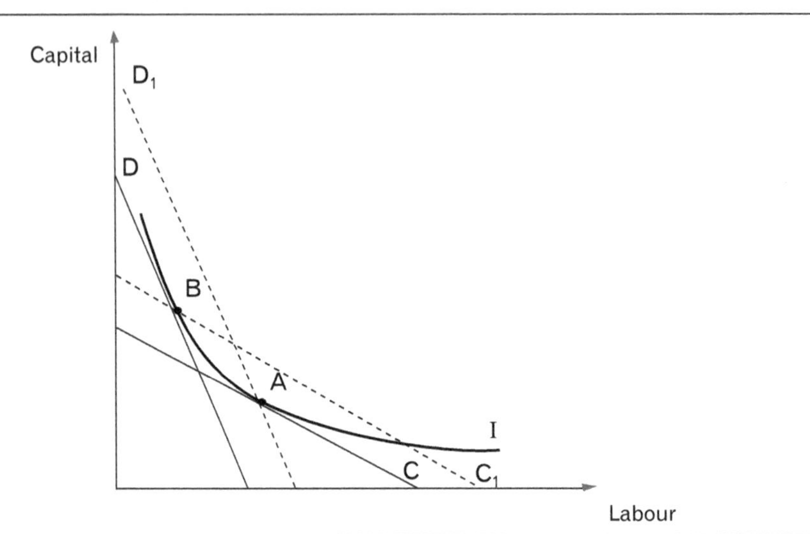

levels of government fiscal subsidies and tariff protections, without which most Japanese farms could not survive.[8]

Many state-owned enterprises in transitional economies face the same viability problems as Japanese farms, due to the fact that these enterprises—especially large state-owned enterprises—are established by governments with the aim of competing with industrialised countries in capital and technology-intensive sectors, even though their economies are still low income and capital scarce. These strategies clash with the comparative advantages of the countries' particular economies.

In fact, the traditional centrally planned systems in socialist economies were formed endogenously to support and protect these non-viable heavy industrial firms that were not consistent with the economy's comparative advantages.[9] Socialist countries—including Russia and China—were capital scarce, backward, agrarian economies before they adopted a centrally planned system. In a capital-scarce, agrarian, low-income country, the establishment of a firm in a capital-intensive heavy industry must overcome numerous difficulties. First, construction of the firm takes a long time. Second, the key equipment and technologies necessary for the firm must be imported. Third, the initial investment is dauntingly large. At the same time, in a low-income agrarian country, the economic surplus from each period of agricultural production is very small and scattered widely and thinly across numerous small rural farms. As a result, such an economy has three distinct characteristics.

First, capital is relatively scarce due to the lack of economic surplus, making market-determined interest rates extremely high. Second, exportable goods are limited in variety and quantity. Consequently, foreign exchange is scarce and market-determined exchange rates are high. Third, the mobilisation of resources for a project that requires large, lump-sum investment is difficult due to the fact that the economic surplus is limited and scattered widely across the economy. The conflicts between the three characteristics of a low-income, agrarian country and the three characteristics of investing in capital-intensive heavy industries in the country require the government to adopt special institutional arrangements to make such investment feasible.

Specifically, to make long-gestation investment projects feasible in China, Russia and other socialist countries, governments artificially depressed interest rates; to lower the costs of imported equipment and technologies, governments distorted exchange rates by artificially overvaluing the domestic currency; and to mobilise enough surplus for the large, lump-sum investment projects, governments gave the firms monopolies in their output markets and artificially depressed prices of all kinds of inputs—including wages—so that the firm could accumulate enough surplus for its own investment. As wage rates were suppressed, governments were required to provide workers with low-price living necessities. The distortions in interest rates, foreign exchange rates, wage rates, inputs and the price of necessities resulted in shortages of capital, foreign exchange, raw materials and necessities. To ensure that these scarce resources would be allocated to firms in the priority sectors, planning and administrative allocation of resources according to the state plans were required. This was the logic for the emergence of a traditional, centrally planned system in socialist economies.

Furthermore, if the firms were in private hands, the state could not ensure that the surpluses mobilised through these distortions would be invested in heavy industries according to the state's plans. Therefore, the firms were nationalised so that the state could directly control the rights to invest the surplus. In addition, even though the firms were owned by the state, the state could not overcome the problems of information asymmetry and incentive incompatibility. If company managers had discretionary powers, moral hazards would ensue, resulting in a reduction of the surplus available for investment. To prevent the erosion of the surplus, the government deprived managers of any autonomy in input, output and market decisions and in personnel appointments, wage settings and other managerial discretions (Lin and Tan 1999).

In fact, the various institutional arrangements—such as distortions in interest rates, foreign exchange rates, prices of raw materials, wage rates and commodity prices, the replacement of the market mechanism with plan allocation, and the deprivation of managerial autonomy—are all endogenous to the fact that the firms in the government's priority sectors are not viable in an open, competitive market (Lin et al. 2003). In the jargon of neoclassical economics, these arrangements are 'second best'. They are required for the maximum mobilisation of surpluses in different sectors for investment in the priority sectors. With such arrangements, a backward agrarian country such as China could develop nuclear bombs and launch satellites within a short time. The resource allocation, however, was poor, due to investments being made in non-viable firms. The incentives for workers and managers were low due to the manager's lack of autonomy and the disconnection between performance and reward. As a result, the whole economy was inefficient.[10] Moreover, without the government's intervention, an economy will import the goods produced in industries in which the economy does not have comparative advantages and export goods in industries in which the economy has comparative advantages.

Under the comparative advantage-defying (CAD) strategy, however, imports will become smaller due to efforts to produce goods that industries are supposed to import, and exports will become smaller due to the fact that resources are diverted from industries in which the economy has comparative advantages to industries in which it does not have comparative advantages. Therefore, the trade-dependent ratio—measured by the total value of exports and imports as a share of GDP—under the CAD strategy will be much smaller than in a country that follows the comparative advantage-following (CAF) strategy. The case of China is a good example. The trade-dependent ratio in 1978 was 9.75 per cent. After China made the transition from the old strategy, the ratio increased to 64.1 per cent in 2005.

Most distortions in the socialist planned economies were formed endogenously by the government for the purpose of facilitating the development of non-viable firms in sectors that were not consistent with the economy's comparative advantages. Since many existing firms were not viable, it is not surprising that existing neoclassical economic theories—with their implicit viability assumption—cannot provide adequate solutions for problems in socialist and transitional economies. If the problem of non-viability is not eliminated, and if the government is unwilling or unable to let the non-viable firms go bankrupt, eliminating distortions and reforming institutional arrangements according to the existing neoclassical economic theories are likely to turn the arrangements from second best to third best. Therefore, the reforms, at best, will not achieve the intended effects and, at worst, will exacerbate the situation.

Neoclassical economics and policies of economic transition

The model of the world we have in our minds will shape our understanding of the real world (North 2002). Existing neoclassical economic theories—formulated in industrialised market economies—have proved that ineffective corporate governance, deficient property rights arrangements and government intervention in resource allocation are harmful to economic efficiency. Economists trained in neoclassical economics tend to think that existing neoclassical economic theories are appropriate models for the analysis of problems in transitional economies when they observe familiar problems in corporate governance, property rights and government intervention. They fail to see the endogeneity of these problems to the non-viability of firms in the government's development strategy. Invited by governments in the former Soviet Union and Eastern Europe to design their transition policies, neoclassical economists reached a remarkable consensus about the need to eliminate the distortions and government intervention immediately (Summers 1994:252–3).[11]

The most prevalent reform policy advice according to neoclassical economic theories is the 'Washington consensus', which calls for strengthening fiscal discipline, increasing public investment in areas with 'public goods' characteristics to improve income distribution, enlarging the tax base, unifying exchange rates, liberalising trade, removing foreign direct investment (FDI) barriers, privatising state-owned enterprises, lifting regulations on market entry and protecting private property rights (Williamson 1997). The shock therapy proposed by economists for the transitional economies in the former Soviet Union and Eastern Europe was based on this Washington consensus (Kolodko 2001). Therefore, we can understand why, in the 1990s, economists with neoclassical training were more optimistic about reforms in the former Soviet Union and Eastern Europe, which implemented shock therapies, than about the piecemeal, gradual, dual-track reform approach being taken in China.

Neoclassical economic theories not only have an impact on economists working on issues related to industrialised market economies, they influence economists working on issues related to other economies. For example, in the famous debate on socialism in the 1930s, economists such as Oscar Lange, who believed that the socialist planned economy could achieve the same allocation efficiency by simulating markets, and Friedrich Hayek, who believed that the socialist economy was doomed to fail due to informational problems, took the viability of firms in a socialist economy as an implicit assumption in their analyses.

Neoclassical economic theories also influence economists living in socialist countries when they analyse the problems of their own economies. Janos Kornai of Hungary is one of the most eminent economists specialising in socialist economies. One of his most important contributions is the concept of the 'soft-budget constraint' (Kornai 1986). In many socialist countries, state-owned enterprises suffering from poor performance can ask for preferential treatment and subsidies, while private firms in market economies have no choice but to go bankrupt. Kornai proposed that the soft-budget constraint was the main reason for a lack of incentives to improve efficiency and for the prevalence of moral hazards in state-owned enterprises. He attributes the existence of the soft-budget constraint to the paternalism of socialist governments towards state-owned enterprises. Therefore, he argued that reform in property rights and the severance of firm–state connections must be carried out in order to eliminate the soft-budget constraint and to promote company efficiency.

In Kornai's theoretical framework, state-owned enterprises are implicitly assumed to be viable. However, the soft-budget constraint in socialist economies emerges essentially from the viability problem of state-owned enterprises. In an open, competitive market, these firms would not be able to attract investment in the first place and, if they had investment due to misjudgment or other reasons, investors would not continue to support their operations once the misjudgments were clarified. To establish these non-viable firms, socialist governments must protect and subsidise them. Because of incentive incompatibility, the managers of state-owned enterprises have incentives to attribute their losses to insufficient government support or protection, even though the losses arise from incompetent operations and poor managerial discretion. Because of information asymmetry, governments cannot know what levels of protection and subsidy are adequate. Therefore, governments cannot resist the companies' requests for more support and the companies' budget constraints become soft (Lin and Tan 1999). Therefore, the soft-budget constraint of state-owned enterprises results essentially from the problem of non-viability rather than from the paternalism of socialist governments. Similarly, even in non-socialist countries, the soft-budget constraint will exist in non-viable firms if the government is responsible for the establishment of those firms. The large *chaebols* in Korea are illustrative of this fact.

If the viability problem is the root of the soft-budget constraint, we can predict that if the viability problem is not solved, the soft-budget constraint will not be eliminated, even though the socialist government is overthrown and all firms are privatised. In fact, that is what happened in the former Soviet Union and Eastern Europe. In these countries, democratically elected governments replaced socialist governments and shock therapy and privatisation were implemented, but the soft-budget constraint still existed and in many cases incentives for privatised company managers to bargain for more support and protection became significantly higher than the incentives for state-owned enterprise managers.[12] According to the World Bank's studies, after full-scale privatisation in the former Soviet Union and Eastern Europe, the subsidies that firms received from governments did not decrease—in some cases, they even increased (World Bank 1996, 2002).[13] At the same time, taxation capacities were weakened significantly after shock therapy. This, combined with high subsidies to companies, led to extremely high inflation in these countries.

It is not only that the shock therapy formulated according to neoclassical economic theories did not work in the former Soviet Union and Eastern Europe, many reform measures based on such theories or on the experiences of industrialised economies created problems in China.[14] The reform of state-owned enterprises is an example.[15] At the beginning of the reforms in the early 1980s, it was believed that the root of the problems with state-owned enterprises was the lack of autonomy of managers, with disconnection between performance and rewards. Therefore, decentralisation reforms were initiated to increase managerial autonomy and to allow state-owned enterprises to retain a certain share of their profits to be used at their own discretion. These measures were effective in pilot experiments, but were ineffective when they were implemented nation-wide. Empirical studies found that the reform increased state-owned enterprises' productivity but their profitability declined (Lin et al. 2001).

Many scholars thought the discrepancy arose from the arrangement of property rights because the firms were owned by the state but were operated by managers, who were not the owners and did not have incentives to increase returns to the equity owner—the state. Based on this diagnosis, the reform measures, starting in the late 1980s, promoted modern corporate governance in state-owned enterprises with the establishment of boards of directors and supervision boards to delineate clearly the owners' rights. A publicly listed company was considered to have the best corporate governance and property rights arrangements, since the value of the firm would be evaluated before it went public and, after being listed, equity would be held by the state and non-state investors. In addition to monitoring by the board of directors, non-state shareholders would have incentives to monitor the company's management and operations since they would care about the returns on their investment.

Nevertheless, in reality, after a few years, the financial performance of the majority of listed companies did not differ from those of non-listed companies (Lin 1999). In the beginning, the poor performance of listed companies was attributed to the fact that only small, individual investors owned the non-state stocks and these investors had little incentive to monitor the managers because the returns for their efforts would be negligible. These small shareholders were thought to be interested in the short-term price changes in stocks, which made stock-markets highly speculative, with high turnover rates and short holding periods.

In industrialised countries, institutional investors play an important role in equity markets. An institutional investor has the capacity to hold a substantial portion of a listed company's shares and thus has greater incentive to monitor the invested company's management than does an individual investor. In addition, an institutional investor can hire professionals to analyse the listed companies' reports and operations. If an institutional investor decides to hold the shares of a company, that investor is likely to hold the shares for a long time.

Chinese researchers thought that the introduction of institutional investors would stabilise China's stock-markets, so investment funds were introduced in 1998; however, speculation in the stock-markets did not stop. Making things worse, many investment funds not only speculated in the stock-market, they manipulated stock prices. How could this happen? The reason lies in the problem of the non-viability of these listed companies. Without the ability to earn acceptable profits in an open, competitive market, these companies cannot afford to distribute dividends to shareholders, which means that small individual shareholders as well as institutional investors can profit only through speculation on stock prices. With large amounts of money at their command and a small portion of stocks in circulation for each listed company,[16] institutional investors resorted to manipulation of stock prices to make profits (Lin 2001, 2004).

In conclusion, for firms to survive in the markets of industrialised countries, they must be viable. Therefore, viability is an acceptable implicit assumption in neoclassical economic theories for explaining phenomena in industrialised countries. Policy reforms based on neoclassical economic theories or the experiences of industrialised countries have failed to achieve their intended goals in transitional economies because most firms in transitional economies are not viable.

The prevalence of the viability problem and the expansion of the neoclassical framework

Companies' viability problems and the resulting institutional arrangements not only appear in transitional economies, they are widespread in developing countries. On seeing the decisive role of industrialisation in promoting the economic and political powers of industrialised countries, many leaders of developing countries that achieved independence after World War II attempted to develop advanced industrial sectors comparable with those in industrialised countries against their own comparative advantages (Chenery 1961; Krueger 1992).[17] They did so by intervening in factor prices, the financial system, international trade and investment—without realising that the industrial structures of industrialised countries were determined endogenously by their own particular factor-endowment structures. Through such efforts, developing countries were able to establish companies in advanced sectors. Those companies were not, however, viable in an open, competitive market, and government intervention on prices, resource allocation and market competition were required to ensure their survival. Such intervention led inevitably to the prevalence of rent seeking and crony capitalism, which resulted in unequal distribution of income, low efficiency and social and economic instability (Krueger 1974; Lin 2003).[18]

This phenomenon also existed in some newly industrialised economies. Korea's situation serves as a good illustration. Taiwan has higher per capita income than Korea, but the *chaebols* in Korea are more technologically advanced and capital intensive than comparable firms in Taiwan.[19] During the East Asian financial crisis in 1998, Taiwan's foreign exchange rate devalued by only 15 per cent and it was the only economy that achieved positive growth in East Asia—except for Mainland China, which was insulated from the crisis by its currency inconvertibility and control of capital accounts. Taiwan grew by 4.5 per cent in 1997 and 5.7 per cent in 1998, which was remarkable considering the terrible external environment at that time. Taiwanese firms manifested themselves as being competitive and viable. The Korean economy collapsed during the East Asian financial crisis and Korea had to borrow heavily from the International Monetary Fund (IMF). After the elimination of state protection and subsidies to large firms—in accordance with the conditions of the IMF's rescue package—20 out of 30 Korean *chaebols* went bankrupt, which showed that these firms were not viable and could not survive without government protection.

In market economies, the protective measures provided to non-viable firms are similar to those in socialist economies: depression of interest rates, administrative allocation of bank loans to provide cheap funds to non-viable firms and establishment of various import barriers to prevent competition from industrialised countries. The protected firms are in sectors that clash with the economy's comparative advantages and produce little economic surplus. The firms, consistent with the economy's comparative advantages, face discrimination and eventually experience difficulties. As a result, the funds that could be mobilised for development purposes dry up. If external borrowing is not allowed—as was the case in India, Pakistan and most socialist countries—economies stagnate. If external borrowing by firms or governments is permitted—as in Latin America, Korea, Thailand and Indonesia before the East Asian financial crisis—debt crises ensue (Krueger 1992).

When debt crises occur, countries have to seek rescue packages from the IMF under existing international financial arrangements. Such packages usually come with conditions, requiring a series of reforms and structural adjustments in the recipient countries. The concept of such conditions is itself based on the Washington consensus, which requires that macro-policy distortions be corrected, that governments cease intervention in banks and companies and that corporate governance be improved. The Washington Consensus—reflecting the basic principles of neoclassical economic theories—implicitly assumes that firms are viable. Therefore, the conditions aim to eliminate protection and subsidies without any attempt to solve the companies' viability problems. If non-viable firms constitute only a small share of the economy—as is the case in Bolivia—shock therapy is possible and growth can resume quickly when increases in efficiency offset the shock of bankruptcy suffered by non-viable companies in the wake of Washington consensus measures. If, however, non-viable firms constitute a large share of the economy—as is the case in transitional economies—shock therapy would lead to an 'L' curve rather than a 'J' curve in the pattern of GDP growth after implementing the therapy (Lin 1998).[20]

Since the existence of non-viable firms is a common reality in socialist, transitional and developing economies, it is inappropriate to assume implicitly that companies are viable in the analysis of the economic problems in these economies and to formulate reform policies based on such assumptions and analyses. Problems of viability should be taken into consideration in analysing economic development and transition.

On reflection, neoclassical economics has been enriched through a process of abandoning unrealistic and implicit assumptions. The basic framework of neoclassical economics was laid down in Alfred Marshall's *Principles of Economics* in 1890. Among others, Marshall's framework had several implicit assumptions, including perfect information, zero transaction costs and the viability of firms in an open, competitive market.

Economic theories are instruments to help people explain what has been observed and to predict what will happen. According to Friedman (1953), the acceptability of a theory depends not on whether the assumptions of the theory are realistic, but on whether the implications drawn from the theory are consistent with empirical observations. Marshall's framework is very powerful in explaining and predicting a number of economic phenomena in market economies. For example, when the prices of certain products increase, purchases of those products will generally decline. The assumptions in Marshall's framework, however, also limit its explanatory power on certain issues. For example, under the assumption of perfect information and zero transaction costs, there will be only one price for a product in a competitive market, allowing little room for price differentiation.

One of the main contributions by George Stigler at the University of Chicago was to abandon the implicit assumption of perfect information and to introduce the concept of incomplete information into economics, with the added considerations of the value of information and the cost of information collection and processing. His contribution makes information an important variable in modern economic analysis. Other economists—such as Joseph Stiglitz, George Akerlof and Michael Spence—further emphasised that not only is information incomplete, it is often distributed asymmetrically among producers, consumers, principles and agents. Furthermore, according to Marshall's framework, resource allocation by markets is the most efficient option. Knowing this, it is difficult to explain why there are firms operating in accordance with non-market allocation mechanisms. Ronald Coarse contributed to neoclassical economics by abandoning the zero transaction cost assumption and initiating research on contracts, property rights and non-market institutions.

Economic theories are like maps. A map is not the real world; it is a convenient tool to help us understand the surrounding environment and what will be seen in different directions. Maps, by nature, must be simplified, but if some important landmarks are ignored or incorrect, the maps will mislead us. When we discover mistakes in a map, and similarly in a theory, corrections must be made. Due to the prevalence of viability problems in socialist economies, transitional economies and developing countries, the implicit assumption of viability should be relaxed in analysing the economic problems and designing policies to solve problems in these economies. Transition and reform policies should be designed according to the understanding that many firms are not viable. The success of transition and reform depends on the creation of conditions that make non-viable firms viable, in lieu of following shock therapy and Washington consensus reforms unconditionally.

In addition, the objective pursued in national development must be reformulated. Traditionally, political leaders, economists and the social élite in developing countries aimed to develop advanced technologies and industries similar to those of the most industrialised countries within the shortest time. The structures of industry and technology that are consistent with an economy's comparative advantages are, however, determined endogenously by the economy's existing factor endowment structure. Ignoring the existing differences between its own endowment structure and that of industrialised countries, the government in a developing country often tries hard with good intentions to develop the same industries and technologies as those in industrialised countries. In effect, the government's efforts make companies in the priority sectors non-viable because they lack the ability to survive in open, competitive markets. Therefore, the government has to subsidise and protect these companies through price distortions, intervention in resource allocation, and so on. Rent seeking, the soft budget constraint, macroeconomic instability, income disparities, stagnation and crises are the consequences of the government's development attempts in spite of the initial good intentions.

Based on the concept of viability, the objective of national economic development should be to upgrade the economy's endowment structure. With such upgrading, companies in open, competitive markets will upgrade their industrial, product and technological levels accordingly in order to ensure their competitiveness in the market (Lin 2003). Since the endowment of land (and natural resources) in a country can be treated as given, the upgrading of the endowment structure means an increase in the amount of capital to each worker. Capital comes from the accumulation of economic surplus. To upgrade the endowment structure rapidly, a maximum economic surplus should be produced in each period, and a large proportion of this surplus should be saved for capital accumulation. If a country develops its industries, technologies and products along the lines of its existing comparative advantages, its economy will be most productive, produce the maximum possible surpluses, create the highest possible returns to capital and have the highest incentive to save. Consequently, the upgrading of the factor endowment structure in the economy will proceed at its maximum speed. Companies' decisions will be based on product prices and production costs, but not on the factor endowment structure in the economy. Therefore, the government should maintain openness and sufficient competition in the market so that the price structure will reflect the relative abundance of the factor endowment structure.[21]

Viability and economic transition

Companies in heavy industries prioritised by the government in traditional centrally planned economies are not viable in open, competitive markets. The objective of the transition from a traditional centrally planned economy is to establish an open, competitive market economy. In the process of transition, however, the viability problem of those firms in the sectors inconsistent with the economy's comparative advantages turns from implicit to explicit. Whether the transition will be stable and successful depends very much on how the viability problem is solved.

Non-viable firms cannot survive in open, competitive markets without government subsidies or protection. The shock therapy adopted in the former Soviet Union and Eastern Europe attempted to eliminate all distortions and government intervention simultaneously, or in a short period. If implemented forcefully, shock therapy inevitably led to large-scale bankruptcy and unemployment, thus prompting economic collapse and social instability. Such results are, understandably, not acceptable to a functioning government. Consequently, many governments in the former Soviet Union and Eastern Europe had to find ways to provide protection or subsidies continuously to a large number of non-viable firms, resulting in the embarrassing situation of shock without therapy (Galbraith 2002).

China has adopted a gradual, piecemeal, dual-track approach since its transition started in 1979: on one hand, the Chinese government has relaxed its strict control of resource allocation and has allowed new entries to sectors in which the economy has comparative advantages; on the other hand, the government has continued to provide protection and support to firms in traditional sectors to buffer them against the threat of bankruptcy, while taking measures to reform them. The first track enhanced the efficiency of resource allocation, created a new stream of resources and resulted in rapid economic growth and trade expansion. The second track prevented the collapse of the economy during the transition process. This dual-track approach has maintained social and economic stability, achieved dynamic growth and ensured the transition has been a Pareto or Kaldor improvement (Lin et al. 1996).

China's transition towards a market economy depends, however, on a final solution to the viability problem of firms in traditional sectors. Since the viability problem is not yet solved, the Chinese government has been required to continue its intervention in markets in order to protect or subsidise non-viable firms—and such intervention comes with consequences. For example, along with China's rapid economic growth in the transition process, the share of non-performing loans in the four big state-owned commercial banks has increased sharply, corruption is widespread and regional income disparities are widening. To a large extent, these problems arise from the fact that state-owned enterprises still depend on government subsidies and protection to survive. After 1983, the form of Chinese government support to state-owned enterprises changed from direct fiscal appropriation to offering low-interest loans from the four state banks. Until now, more than 70 per cent of loans from the four state banks went to state-owned enterprises, but due to their poor performance, many state-owned enterprises have been unable to repay the loans. Therefore, the banks have accumulated large amounts of non-performing loans.

The government also limits the market entry of private interests into certain sectors to give state-owned enterprises in those sectors a monopoly position. Therefore, rent seeking to obtain preferential loans or market-entry licences is prevalent among state-owned and non-state-owned enterprises, adding to widespread corruption. In addition to subsidising state-owned enterprises, the government artificially depressed the prices of agricultural products and minerals under the traditional planning system. Such price distortion has continued since the reforms as a means to subsidise the non-viable state-owned enterprises.

The comparative advantages of eastern China lie in manufacturing industries; those of central China lie in agriculture; and those of western China lie in minerals and natural resources. Since the reforms began, the eastern region has made huge progress in the development of manufacturing industries by taking advantage of the superior geographical and market conditions and has increased substantially imports of low-priced agricultural and mineral products from the central and western regions. In essence, the relatively poor central and western regions have been subsidising the development of the relatively rich eastern, industrial region. Regional disparities are widening as a result. If the viability problem of state-owned enterprises is solved, there will be no reason to continue subsidisation and protection through low-interest loans, monopolistic practices and the depression of prices for agricultural and raw materials. The remaining distortions and government intervention can then be eliminated (Lin et al. 2001).[22]

The viability problem of state-owned enterprises can be solved according to four different strategies, depending on the nature of the state-owned enterprises' outputs (Lin et al. 2001). The first group includes mainly the defence-related state-owned enterprises, whose production—which is capital and technology intensive—runs against China's comparative advantages, but whose outputs are essential for national security. For this group of state-owned enterprises, direct fiscal appropriation is necessary for their survival and the government should directly monitor their production and operation. It is reasonable to expect that there are only a few state-owned enterprises in this category.

The second group also requires intensive capital and technological inputs for their production, but their outputs are not sensitive to national security and they have large domestic markets. Examples of this category are the telecommunications and automobile industries. For this category, the government can adopt a 'market-for-capital' approach to gain access to capital from international markets and remove the adverse impact of the domestic endowment structure on these firms' viability. There are two ways to achieve this goal: one is to encourage state-owned enterprises to go public on international equity markets; the second is to set up joint ventures with foreign companies and gain direct access to foreign technologies and capital. China Mobile, China Telecom and China Petroleum have followed the first approach and many automobile makers in China have followed the joint-venture approach.

The third category of state-owned enterprises has limited domestic markets for their products and thus this group cannot adopt the market-for-capital approach. The way for them to solve the viability issue is to make use of their engineering and managerial capacities and to shift their production to labour-intensive products, which have large domestic markets and are also consistent with China's comparative advantages. The most famous example of a firm following this approach is the colour-television maker Changhong. This firm used to produce old-style military radar. After switching to the production of colour televisions, the firm has dominated the Chinese market and is very competitive in the international market. Most state-owned enterprises have advantages in engineering and managerial personnel. If they are given the opportunity to shift their production lines to labour-intensive products, many of them can become viable. The fourth group consists of non-viable firms that lack engineering capacity and are thus unable to shift their production to new markets. These state-owned enterprises should be allowed to go bankrupt.

After the viability problem of the existing firms is solved, whether or not a firm can earn acceptable profits in an open, competitive market becomes the responsibility of the firm's managers. The performance of a firm will depend on the corporate governance, incentive mechanisms and other factors—as identified in neoclassical economics. The government will no longer be responsible for a firm's performance. Only then can the reform of institutions that are inherited from the traditional centrally planned system, with the functions of subsidising and protecting state-owned enterprises, be carried out thoroughly and the transition from a planned economy to a market economy be completed.

Conclusion

In this chapter, I have shown that modern neoclassical economics did not play a direct role in helping China's formulation of successful transition policies to a market economy and that those countries that followed transition policies based on modern neoclassical economics performed poorly in the process. The reason for the failure of neoclassical economics to provide useful policy guidance for transition is because its current framework, beginning with Marshall, implicitly assumes that a company existing in the market is viable: that is, the company is expected to earn a socially acceptable profit in an open, competitive market as long as it is under normal management. With this implicit assumption, the focus of economic research has been on the problems of corporate governance, the competitive environment, the arrangement of property rights and other factors that can obstruct a firm's normal management.

Many firms in transitional economies and developing countries are, however, not viable because, due to their governments' ambitious development strategies, they are in sectors that are inconsistent with their economies' comparative advantages. In an open, competitive market, these firms, even under normally efficient management, will not be able to earn acceptable profits. To set up these firms and to maintain their continuous operation, governments provide them with protection and subsidies through price distortion, limitations on market competition, administrative allocation of all kinds of resources, and so on. The results of such intervention are inadequate competition, lack of effective corporate governance, rent seeking, disparities in income distribution, inefficient resource allocation and, quite possibly, economic crisis.

Under the rubric of existing neoclassical economic theories, when designing policies for economic transition or crisis management, economists and government officials are likely to focus on strengthening property rights, improving corporate governance, removing government intervention in resource allocation, and so on, to improve the efficiency of the market. They are not aware of the fact that such market-impeding distortions and interventions are, in fact, endogenous to a company's viability problem. When a majority of the companies in an economy are non-viable, the implementation of these reform and transitional policies sometimes leads to an awkward situation of shock without therapy, as in the former Soviet Union and Eastern Europe, and the lost decades in other developing countries (Easterly 2001; Lin and Liu 2004).

Since many existing companies in socialist centrally planned economies, transitional economies and developing countries are not viable, it is necessary to relax the implicit viability assumption in neoclassical economics when applying the neoclassical approach to study the problems in those economies. The explicit consideration of the viability problem will enrich neoclassical economics and help to define the economic functions of governments in developing countries, preventing them from adopting CAD development strategies to set up non-viable firms and enabling them to achieve convergence with industrialised nations in an expedient manner (Lin 2003).

Notes

1 There were also economists who held China's reform in high regard. They include Jefferson and Rawski 1995; McKinnon 1994; McMillan and Naughton 1992; Naughton 1995; Singh 1991; Harrold 1992; Perkins 1992; and Murrell 1991, 1992.

2 The initial conditions that have been regarded as beneficial to China's transition include high proportions of cheap rural labour, low social security subsidies, a large population of overseas Chinese and a relatively decentralised economy, which helped to achieve some short-term progress.

3 The critique in this chapter is on the existing economic theories, which assume implicitly that the existing firms in a market are viable, rather than on the neoclassical economic approach, which assumes that a decision maker is rational: that is, he or she will make a choice considered to be the best among his or her available choices. I owe this clarification to Gary Becker.

4 The term viability was introduced formally in Lin and Tan 1999. The most comprehensive analysis of this concept can be found in Lin 2003.

5 The curve can be considered as the envelope of all different kinds of technologies that can be used to produce the product.

6 For detailed discussions of a firm's viability issues in a multi-good and multi-sector context, see Lin 2003. The term viability refers only to whether a firm's choices of technology and product are consistent with comparative advantage determined by the economy's endowment structure. It is noteworthy that a viable firm might not be profitable if its management is poor.

7 The problem of corporate governance is due to the separation of ownership and control that leads to incentive incompatibility and information asymmetry between owners and managers. If the same person is owner and manager of a firm, there will be no problems of incentive incompatibility, information asymmetry and moral hazard.

8 The price of rice in Japan is about eight times that in the international market. Japan's deflation has lasted for more than a decade, since 1991. The formation of the Free Trade Area of the Association of South East Asian Nations (ASEAN) Plus Three—including Japan, Korea and China—stands to increase Japan's exports and FDI and will help Japan get out of its current deflation. China proposed the ASEAN Plus Three Free Trade Area in 2001, but Japan's response was hesitant due to its need to protect its agricultural sector.

9 On the logic of the formation of a traditional planning system in socialist countries, see Lin et al. 2003.

10 For efficiency indicators for China before the transition, see Lin et al. 2003:Chapter 3. For a detailed study of efficiency in the former Soviet Union, see Desai 1990.

11 Certainly, there were exceptions. For example, Murrell 1991 questioned the power of the neoclassical paradigm to explain the differences in the economic performance of market and centrally planned economies and the appropriateness of using neoclassical economics to underpin the reform of centrally planned economies.

12 Before the introduction of shock therapy, firms were state owned and managers were civil servants of the state. The subsidies they received from the government could not fall into their own pockets without the managers facing the possibility of corruption charges. After privatisation, however, government subsidies could be channelled into the legal incomes of managers. Thus, the incentive to push for subsidies and preferential treatment increased and the problem of the soft-budget constraint became all the more serious.

13 According to empirical research, some firms increased their efficiency after privatisation, but others did not (Lavigne 1995:175; Djankov and Murrell 2002). In my judgment, the key lies in whether or not the firm was viable before privatisation. If it was, then efficiency would increase after privatisation; if it was not, such firms would experience a decrease in efficiency. After

seeing that privatisation did not help solve the soft-budget constraint or improve efficiency, many economists realised the importance of improving corporate finance and market competition. As former Chief Economist of the European Bank and Vice-President and Chief Economist of the World Bank, Nicolas Stern, commented, '[G]ood corporate governance of public firms and sound competition policy are at least as essential for recovery as privatization and liberalization' (Stern 1996:8). Poland's former First Deputy Premier and Minister of Finance, Grzegorz Kolodko (2000:Ch.4), holds the same opinion. The fact that many shareholding companies in China did not show significant differences in their financial indicators from non-listed companies after five years of being listed shows, however, that if the problem of viability goes unresolved, good corporate governance and sufficient market competition will not come about unless bankruptcy is permitted (Lin and Tan 1999; Lin et al. 2003).

14 Since 1978, when China initiated its reforms, the two most significant changes—summarised by Deng Xiaoping as the two 'unexpected results'—were the success of the household responsibility system (Lin 1992) and the remarkable growth of township and village firms (Lin and Yang 2001). These reforms were not designed by reformers *ex ante*, but adopted by peasants spontaneously in practice.

15 Regarding academic debates and policy measures on state-owned enterprise reform, see Lin et al. 2001.

16 In China, about only 25 per cent of the total stock of a listed company was issued to non-state investors and could be traded in the stock-markets. The other 75 per cent was still owned by the state and could not be traded in the stock-market. Among the 1,200 or so listed companies, only a few have distributed dividends to stockholders (Lin 1999).

17 The view of former Indian Prime Minister Jawaharlal Nehru is most representative of this. In 1938, before India's independence, he was the President of India's State Planning Commission. He wrote: '[I]n the context of the modern world, no country can be politically and economically independent, even within the framework of international interdependence, unless it is highly industrialized and has developed its power resources to the utmost. Nor can it achieve or maintain high standards of living and liquidate poverty without the aid of modern technology in almost every sphere of life' (Nehru 1946:413, quoted in Srinivasan 1994:155–6).

18 Such tendencies characterise India and Latin America. On India, see Swamy 1994. On Latin America, see Cardoso and Helwege 1992.

19 Take the information technology (IT) sector as an example. Taiwanese firms, such as TSMC, mainly do original equipment manufacture (OEM), while Korea's Samsung and Hyundai Electronics carry out independent research and development and product innovation. For a comparative study of IT development strategies in Taiwan and Korea, see Lin 2000. Furthermore, in the automobile industry, Korea produces complete cars, while Taiwan is renowned only for parts production.

20 The difference in the shares of non-viable firms in the economy might explain why the shock therapy recommended by Sachs succeeded in Bolivia but not in the former Soviet Union and Eastern European economies. Bolivia is a poor, small economy and the resources that the government could mobilise to subsidise the non-viable firms were small. Therefore, the share of non-viable firms in the economy must also be relatively small. Stiglitz 1998 also questioned the universal applicability of the Washington consensus, but did not consider the possible impact of non-viable firms in developing and transitional economies and their limitations on policy choices.

21 In a developing country, the government can also use an industrial policy to assist firms' upgrading of technology, product and industry in responding to change in the economy's endowment structure by providing relevant information, coordinating required investments and compensating for externalities of innovation. The industry promoted by the industrial

policy should, however, be consistent with the comparative advantages of the new endowment structure and, as such, the firms are viable in an open, competitive market (Lin 2003).

22 Besides the viability problem, state-owned enterprises in China have a problem of social burdens. Before the economic transition, the investment in heavy industry provided limited employment opportunities. The government was responsible for urban employment and usually assigned several workers to a job, resulting in labour redundancy in state-owned enterprises. The workers also received low wages, which were enough only for covering current consumption. Before the transition, state-owned enterprises remitted all their revenue to the government, and the government used fiscal appropriation to cover state-owned enterprises' wages, the pensions of retired workers and other expenditure. Therefore, the labour redundancy and pension expenditure were not burdens on the state-owned enterprises. After the reforms, state-owned enterprises started to be responsible for their workers' wages and retirement pensions. The newly established town and village enterprises, joint ventures and other non-state firms are in sectors that are consistent with China's comparative advantage and they do not have the problem of labour redundancy and unfunded pensions for retired workers. I call the issue arising from the viability problem of the state-owned enterprises the 'strategic burden' and the additional cost arising from labour redundancy and pension expenditure the state-owned enterprises' 'social burden'. Together, they constitute the state-owned enterprises' 'policy burdens'. As long as these policy burdens exist, the government is responsible for the firms' losses and the soft-budget constraint cannot be eliminated (Lin and Tan 1999). There is a consensus in China about the necessity for and the way to eliminate social burdens. Therefore, the remaining issue is how to solve the strategic burden.

References

Balcerowicz, L., 1994. 'Common fallacies in the debate on the transition to a market economy', *Economic Policy*, 9:16–50.

Blanchard, O., Dornbusch, R., Krugman, P., Layard, R. and Summers, L., 1991. *Reform in Eastern Europe*, MIT Press, Cambridge, MA.

Boycko, M., Shleifer, A. and Vishny, R., 1995. *Privatizing Russia*, MIT Press, Cambridge, MA.

Brada, J.C. and King, A.E., 1991. *Sequencing measures for the transformation of socialist economies to capitalism: is there a J-curve for economic reform?*, Research Paper Series, No.13, Socialist Economies Reform Unit, World Bank, Washington, DC.

Cardoso, E. and Helwege, A., 1992. *Latin America's Economy: diversity, trends and conflicts*, MIT Press, Cambridge, MA.

Chen, K., Wang, H., Zheng, Y., Jefferson, G. and Rawski, T., 1998. 'Productivity change in Chinese industry: 1953–1985', *Journal of Comparative Economics*, 12:570–91.

Chenery, H.B., 1961. 'Comparative advantage and development policy', *American Economic Review*, 51:18–51.

Dabrowski, M., 2001. 'Ten years of Polish economic transition, 1989–1999', in M.I. Blejer and M. Skreb (eds), *Transition: the first decade*, MIT Press, Cambridge, MA:121–52.

Desai, P., 1990. *The Soviet Economy: problems and prospects*, Reprint edition, Blackwell, New York.

Djankov, S. and Murrell, P., 2002. *Firm restructuring in transition: a quantitative survey*, Discussion Paper Series, No.3319, National Bureau of Economic Research, Cambridge, MA.

Easterly, W., 2001. 'The lost decades: developing countries' stagnation in spite of policy reform 1980–1998', *Journal of Economic Growth*, 6:135–57.

Friedman, M., 1953. 'The methodology of positive economics', in *Essays in Positive Economics*, University of Chicago Press, Chicago.

Galbraith, J.K., 2002. 'Shock without therapy', *The American Prospect* (online), 13.

Gregory, P. and Stuart, R., 2001. *Russian and Soviet Economic Performance and Structure*, Seventh edition, Addison Wesley, New York.

Harrold, P., 1992. *China's reform experience to date*, World Bank Discussion Paper 180, World Bank, Washington, DC.

Hayek, F.A. (ed.), 1935. *Collectivist Economic Planning*, Routledge and Kegan Paul, London.

Jefferson, G. and Rawski, T., 1995. 'How industrial reform worked in China: the role of innovation, competition, and property rights', *Proceedings of the World Bank Annual Conference on Development Economics 1994*, World Bank, Washington, DC:129–56.

Kolodko, G.W., 2000. *From Shock to Therapy: the political economy of post-socialist transformation*, Unu/Wider Studies in Development Economics, Helsinki.

——, 2001. 'Postcommunist transition and post-Washington consensus: the lessons for policy reforms', in M.I. Blejer and M. Skreb (eds), *Transition: the first decade*, MIT Press, Cambridge, MA:45–83.

Kornai, J., 1986. 'The soft budget constraint', *Kyklos*, 39:3–30.

——, 1990. *The Road to a Free Economy*, Norton, New York.

Krueger, A.O., 1974. 'The political economy of the rent-seeking society', *American Economic Review*, 64:291–303.

——, 1992. *Economic Policy Reform in Developing Countries*, Basil Blackwell, Oxford.

Lange, O., 1937. 'On the economic theory of socialism', *Review of Economic Studies*, 4:53–71, 123–42.

Lavigne, M., 1995. *The Economics of Transition: from socialist economy to market economy*, St Martin's Press, New York.

Lin, J.Y., 1992. 'Rural reforms and agricultural growth in China', *American Economic Review*, 82:34–51.

——, 1998. 'Transition to a market-oriented economy: China versus Eastern Europe and Russia', in Y. Hayami and M. Aoki (eds), *The Institutional Foundations of East Asian Economic Development*, St Martin's Press in association with the International Economic Association, New York:215–47.

——, 2000. 'IT development and the principle of comparative advantage', *World Economy and China*, 8(4):3–9.

——, 2001. 'Four problems of China's stock market', *CCER Briefing* (in Chinese), 7.

——, 2003. 'Development strategy, viability and economic convergence', *Economic Development and Cultural Change*, 53:277–308.

——, 2004. 'Viability and the development of China's capital markets', *China and World Economy*, 12(6):3–10.

——, 2005. 'Viability, economic transition, and reflection on neoclassical economics', *Kyklos*, 58(2):239–64.

Lin, J.Y. and Liu, M., 2004. 'Development strategy, transition and challenges of development in lagging regions', in F. Bourguignon and B. Pleskovic (eds), *Annual World Bank Conference on Development Economics 2004: accelerating development (Bangalore conference proceedings)*, World Bank, Washington, DC.

Lin, J.Y. and Tan, G., 1999. 'Policy burdens, accountability, and the soft budget constraint', *American Economic Review: papers and proceedings*, 89:426–31.

Lin, J.Y. and Yao, Y., 2001. 'Chinese rural industrialization in the context of the East Asian miracle', in J.E. Stigilitz and S. Yusuf (eds), *Rethinking the East Asian Miracle*, Oxford University Press, Oxford and New York:143–95.

Lin, J.Y., Cai, F. and Li, Z., 1996. 'The lessons of China's transition to a market economy', *Cato Journal*, 16:201–31.

——, 1999. 'Competition, policy burdens, and the state-owned enterprise reform', *American Economic Review: papers and proceedings*, 88:422–7.

——, 2001. *China's State-Owned Firm Reform*, Chinese University of Hong Kong Press, Hong Kong.

——, 2003. *China's Miracle: development strategy and economic reform*, Revised edition, Chinese University Press, Hong Kong.

Lin, J.Y., 1999. 'The third institutional innovation in the security market and the state-owned firm reform', *Jingji Yanjiu (Economic Research)*, 10:46–52.

Lin, J.Y. et al., 1994. 'The impacts of hybrid rice on input demand and productivity: an econometric analysis", *Agricultural Economics*, 10:153–64.

Lipton, D. and Sachs, J., 1990. 'Privatization in Eastern Europe: the case of Poland', *Brookings Papers on Economic Activities*, 2:293–341.

McKinnon, R.I., 1994. 'Gradual versus rapid liberalization in socialist economies: financial policies and macroeconomic stability in China and Russia compared', *Proceedings of the World Bank Annual Conference on Development Economics 1993*, World Bank, Washington, DC:63–94.

McMillan, J. and Naughton, B., 1992. 'How to reform a planned economy: lessons from China', *Oxford Review of Economic Policy*, 8:130–43.

Murphy, K.M., Shleifer, A. and Vishny, R.W., 1989a. 'Income distribution, market size, and industrialization', *Quarterly Journal of Economics*, 104:537–64.

——, 1989b. 'Industrialization and big push', *Journal of Political Economy*, 97:1,003–26.

——, 1992. 'The transition to a market economy: pitfalls of partial reform', *Quarterly Journal of Economics*, 107:889–906.

Murrell, P., 1991. 'Can neoclassical economics underpin the reform of centrally planned economies?', *Journal of Economic Perspectives*, 5:59–76.

——, 1992. 'Evolutionary and radical approaches to economic reform', *Economic Planning*, 25:79–95.

——, 1995. 'The transition according to Cambridge, MA', *Journal of Economic Literature*, 33:164–78.

National Bureau of Statistics (NBS), 2002. *China Statistical Abstracts, 2002*, China Statistical Press, Beijing.

——, 2006. *China Statistical Abstracts, 2006*, China Statistical Press, Beijing.

Naughton, B., 1995. *Growing Out of the Plan: Chinese economic reform 1978–1993*, Cambridge University Press, New York.

Nehru, J., 1946. *The Discovery of India*, John Day Company, New York.

North, D.C., 2002. 'The process of economic change', *China Economic Quarterly*, 1:797–802.

Perkins, D.H., 1988. 'Reforming China's economic system', *Journal of Economic Literature*, 26:601–45.

——, 1992. *China's gradual approach to market reforms*, UNCTAD Discussion Paper No. 52, Geneva.

Qian, Y. and Xu, C., 1993. 'Why China's economic reforms differ: the M-form hierarchy and entry/expansion of the non-state sector', *The Economics of Transition*, 1:135–70.

Rawski, T., 1995. 'Implications of China's reform experience', *China Quarterly*, 144:1,150–73.

Sachs, J.D. and Lipton, D., 1990. 'Poland's economic reform', *Foreign Affairs*, 69:47–66.

Sachs, J.D. and Woo, W.T., 1994. 'Structural factors in the economic reforms of China, Eastern Europe and the Former Soviet Union', *Economic Policy*, 18:101–45.

——, 1997. *Understanding China's economic performance*, NBER Working Papers 5935, National Bureau of Economic Research, Cambridge, MA.

Sachs, J.D., Woo, W.T. and Yang, X., 2000. 'Economic reforms and constitutional transition', *Annals of Economics and Finance*, 1:435–91.

Singh, I.J., 1991. *China and Central and Eastern Europe: is there a professional schizophrenia on socialist reform*, Research Paper Series, 17, Socialist Economies Reform Unit, World Bank, Washington, DC.

Srinivasan, T.N., 1994. *Agriculture and Trade in China and India: policies and performance since 1950*, ICS Press, San Francisco.

Stern, N., 1996. 'The transition in Eastern Europe and the former Soviet Union: some strategic lessons from the experience of 25 countries over 6 years', OECD/CCET Colloqium, Paris, 29–30 May.

Stiglitz, J., 1998. More instruments and broader goals: moving toward the post-Washington consensus, WIDER Annual Lecture 2, United States University World Institute for Development Economics Research, Helsinki.

——, 1999. 'Whither reform? Ten years of the transition', Annual World Bank Conference on Development Economics, World Bank, Washington, DC, 28–30 April.

Summers, L., 1994. 'Comment', in O.J. Blanchard, K.A. Froot and J. Sachs (eds), *The Transition in Eastern Europe*, Vol. 1, Chicago University Press, Chicago:252–53.

Swamy, D.S., 1994. *The Political Economy of Industrialization: from self-reliance to globalization*, Sage Publications, New Delhi.

Wiles, P., 1995. 'Capitalist triumphalism in the Eastern European transition', in H.-J. Chang and P. Nolan (eds), *The Transformation of the Communist Economies*, Macmillan Press, London:46–77.

Williamson, J., 1997. 'The Washington consensus revisited', in L. Emmerij (ed.), *Economic and Social Development into the XXI Century*, Inter-American Development Bank, Washington, DC.

Woo, W.T., 1993. 'The art of reforming centrally planned economies: comparing China, Poland and Russia', Paper presented at the Conference of the Tradition of Centrally Planned Economies in Pacific Asia, Asia Foundation in San Francisco, San Francisco.

World Bank, 1996. *World Development Report: from plan to market*, Oxford University Press, Oxford.

——, 2002. *Transition: the first ten years, analysis and lessons for Eastern Europe and the Former Soviet Union*, World Bank, Washington, DC.

Acknowledgment

This chapter draws heavily on Lin (2005).

Index

www.ingramcontent.com/pod-product-compliance
Lightning Source LLC
LaVergne TN
LVHW052349100826
845147LV00013B/796

* 9 7 8 0 7 3 1 5 3 8 1 3 3 *